The Journals of

ANDRÉ GIDE

ANDRÉ GIDE

The Journals of

ANDRÉ GIDE

TRANSLATED FROM THE FRENCH AND

ANNOTATED BY

Justin O'Brien

VOLUME II: 1914-1927

1 9 4 8

Alfred A. Knopf : New York

THIS IS A BORZOI BOOK,
PUBLISHED BY ALFRED A. KNOPF, INC.

CONTENTS

Journal 1914   PAGE   3

The Turkish Journey   6

Journal 1914 (CONTINUED)   21

Journal 1915   98

Journal 1916   116

Numquid et tu . . . ?   169

Detached Pages   187

Journal 1917   191

Journal 1918   222

Detached Pages   236

Journal 1919   253

Journal 1920   255

Journal 1921   261

Detached Pages   282

Journal 1922   295

Journal 1923   318

Detached Pages   341

Journal 1924   346

Journal 1925   367

Detached Pages   371

Journal 1926   379

Journal 1927   391

Detached Pages   425

Glossary of Persons   429

The Works of André Gide   459

Index
Index to Gide's Works   follow page 462

The Journals of

ANDRÉ GIDE

VOLUME II: 1914–1927

1914

Yesterday I had left Auteuil early in the morning to stop at the *Mercure,* at the Theater, and at the Review.[1] I planned to lunch with Paul A. Laurens and, not having found him in his studio, was walking up and down in front of 126 boulevard Montparnasse. Instead of Paul, Léon Blum came along. To avoid an invitation to lunch with M., I thought it expedient to invite him at once. I was not shaved; after a sleepless night, or rather one in which I was constantly awakened by the sick cat, I had got up with a bad headache. I felt ugly, dull, and stupid, and since Blum has the precise kind of mind that congeals mine at a distance and whose lucid brilliance keeps mine muscle-bound as it were and reduced to impotence, I said nothing during the whole meal that was not inane.

As I reflect tonight on Blum's character — in which I cannot fail to recognize nobility, generosity, and chivalry, even though when applied to him these words must be considerably distorted from their usual meaning — it seems to me that his apparent resolve always to show a preference for the Jew and to be interested always in him, that predisposition to recognize talent and even genius in him, comes first of all from the fact that a Jew is particularly sensitive to Jewish virtues. It comes above all from the fact that Blum considers the Jewish race as superior, as called upon to dominate after having been long dominated, and thinks it his duty to work toward its triumph with all his strength.

Perhaps he glimpses the possible dominance of that race. Perhaps he glimpses in the coming to power of that race the solution of many social and political problems. A time will come, he thinks, that will be the age of the Jew; and right now it is important to recognize and establish his superiority in all categories, in all domains, in all the divisions of art, of knowledge, and of industry. He has a marvelously organized, organizing, clear, and classifying intelligence, which ten years later would be capable of finding each idea exactly in the place where his reasoning had put it, just as you find an object again in a cupboard.

---

[1] Almost since its beginning in 1890, André Gide had been a contributor to the literary review *Le Mercure de France,* and from 1896 until 1911 the publishing house of the same name had been the principal publisher of his books. The theater is the Théâtre du Vieux-Colombier, founded by Jacques Copeau in 1913 as an offshoot of the *Nouvelle Revue Française,* the monthly literary periodical established by Gide and a group of writers in 1909, to which he refers here as the Review.

Although he is sensitive to poetry, he has the most antipoetic brain that
I know. I believe also that in spite of his value he overestimates himself
somewhat. His weakness lies in letting this be seen. He likes to give
himself importance; he wants to be the first to have recognized the
value of this or that one; speaking of little Franck, he says: "I must
have sent him to you some time ago"; and speaking of Claudel: "That
was the time when Schwob and I were among the very few to admire
him." He also says: "T. has only to mention my name to the fencing-
master X., who will give him some help." He always talks to you as a
protector. At a dress rehearsal, when he meets you by chance in a
theater lobby, he puts his arm around your waist, neck, or shoulders
and, even if you have not seen him in a year, makes everyone think
that he saw you yesterday and that he is the most intimate friend you
have in the world.

But why should I speak here of shortcomings? It is enough for me
that the virtues of the Jewish race are not French virtues; and even if
the French were less intelligent, less long-suffering, less virtuous in all
regards than Jews, it is still true that what they have to say can be said
only by them, and that the contribution of Jewish qualities to literature (where nothing matters but what is personal) is less likely to provide new elements (that is, an enrichment) than it is to interrupt the
slow explanation of a race and to falsify seriously, intolerably even, its
meaning.

It is absurd, it is even dangerous to attempt to deny the good points
of Jewish literature; but it is important to recognize that there is today
in France a Jewish literature that is not French literature, that has its
own virtues, its own meanings, and its own tendencies. What a wonderful job could be done and what a service could be rendered both
to the Jews and to the French by anyone who would write a history of
Jewish literature — a history that would not have to go back far in
time, moreover, and with which I can see no disadvantage to fusing
the history of Jewish literature of other countries, for it is always one
and the same thing. This would clarify our ideas somewhat and would
perhaps check certain hatreds that result from false classifications.

There is still much more to be said on the subject. One would have
to explain why, how, and as a result of what economic and social reasons the Jews have been silent until the present. Why Jewish literature
hardly goes back more than twenty years, or at most fifty. Why during
these last fifty years its development has followed a triumphant progress. Had they suddenly become more intelligent? No, but before that
they did not have the right to speak; perhaps they did not even have
the desire to, for it is worth noting that of all those who now speak,
there is not one who does so through an imperious need to speak — I
mean whose eventual aim is the word and the work, and not *the effect*

of that word, its material or moral result. They speak with greater ease than we because they have fewer scruples. They speak louder than we because they have not our reasons for speaking often in an undertone, for respecting certain things.

I do not deny, indeed, the great worth of certain Jewish works, for example the plays of Porto-Riche. But how much more naturally I should admire them if they did not come to us in translation! For what does it matter to me that the literature of my country should be enriched if it is so at the expense of its significance. It would be far better, whenever the Frenchman comes to lack sufficient strength, for him to disappear rather than to let an uncouth person play his part in his stead and in his name.

28 March

I tear from this notebook page after ill-begot page. I no longer enjoy writing in it, any more than I enjoy observing myself live, and my pen is not sufficiently alert or I have not enough time to speak of others.

I note here merely this as points of reference: a short stay in Florence (from 3 to 17 March), spent in going over with Fabulet his translation of Whitman. The young Raverat couple came to join me there; the four of us found lodgings at 22 Lung' Arno Acciaioli, at the house of the good Mme P. I occupied as before the large middle parlor, where she had set up a makeshift bed, so narrow that I slept very badly in it. The only things that I saw again (with the young Raverat couple) were Castagno's *Last Supper* and Angelico's *Crucifixion*.

It was in Florence that I received Claudel's comminatory letter which was set off by page 478 of the *Caves*.[2] Would to God that I should not be outdistanced by events! Is it very wise to go off on a trip as I am planning to do with Mme Mayrisch and Ghéon, while nothing is ready yet either of my *Corydon* or of the rest? . . .

But all life long and constantly I have experienced everywhere that fear of having too little time and the feeling that the earth will suddenly disappear under my feet.

---

[2] The passage about the priest of Covigliajo, at the beginning of the fifth book, appeared on page 478 of the *Nouvelle Revue Française* for March 1914. Despite Claudel's protest, no change was made when the novel appeared in book-form.

THE TURKISH JOURNEY

For Em.

April (1914)

For you I tear from my travel diary and copy out as a postscript to the insufficient letters I sent you these even more insufficient leaves. I was planning to complete and to perfect them; I cannot do so. While traveling, one notes down from day to day in the hope of recomposing these stories at leisure and of carefully retracing the landscapes on one's return. Then one notices that all the art put into this work only manages to dilute the original emotion, of which the most naïve expression will always be the best. Consequently I transcribe these notes just as they are, without sweetening their tartness. Alas! the days which were most completely filled with the liveliest emotions are also those of which nothing remains in this notebook, those when I had time only for living.

April

When you look at the aridity of the soil in the immense vacant space between Adrianople and Chatalja, you are less surprised that the Turks never defended it more bitterly. For miles and miles there is not a single house, not a single soul. The train follows the circuitous way suggested by the meanderings of a little stream, and these continual curves force it to go very slowly. Not a tunnel, not a bridge, not even an embankment. M. Loucheur, who is traveling with us, explains that Baron Hirsch, who was in charge of the undertaking, was paid by the kilometer. He must have made a fortune!

Nomadic dogs run from a distance toward the train; from the dining-car people throw out the remains of their meal in paper bags that the dogs tear open.

Among the clumps of blossomless iris and of reeds on the edge of a ditch half filled with gray water — tortoises, families of tortoises, hordes of tortoises, stuck against the mud, flat and mud-colored; they look like bedbugs.

Delight at seeing storks again. Here are even a few camels. Here and there flaming clumps of wild peonies, which our neighbor, a rich Armenian woman from Brusa, insists on calling poppies.

My companion enters into conversation with a young Turk, the son of a pasha, who is on his way back from Lausanne, where he was "learning painting." It is seven months since he left his family for the first time; he is returning home with a volume of Zola under his arm, *Nana,* which he says he likes very much, as much as he likes "the books of Madame Gyp." He declares himself to be a fervent member of the "Young Turk" movement, and he believes in the future of Turkey; but this is enough to keep me from believing in it.

1 May

Constantinople justifies all my prejudices and joins Venice in my personal hell. As soon as you admire some bit of architecture, the surface of a mosque, you learn (and you suspected it already) that it is Albanian or Persian. Everything was brought here, as to Venice, even more than to Venice, by sheer force or by money. Nothing sprang from the soil itself; nothing indigenous underlies the thick froth made by the friction and clash of so many races, histories, beliefs, and civilizations.

The Turkish costume is the ugliest you can imagine; and the race, to tell the truth, deserves it.

Oh Golden Horn, Bosporus, shore of Scutari, cypresses of Eyoub! I am unable to lend my heart to the most beautiful landscape in the world if I cannot love the people that inhabit it.

2 May

The joy of leaving Constantinople, the praises of which I shall have to leave to others. Laughing sea in which the dolphins rejoice. Charm of the Asiatic shores; great trees near by under which the herds seek out shade.

Brusa, Saturday

Garden of the Mosque of Murad I, where I have sat down, not on the edge of that trickling basin in the center of the balcony terrace, but far on the left of the terrace, on the marble lip of another smaller basin, sheltered by a painted wooden kiosk. A simple round opening in the deep and cool heart of the basin pushes the water upward so that it rises and falls in a silent blossoming of the spring, over which I lean for some time. In the bottom of the basin likewise, over on the side, a similar mouth sucks the water out. In this marble dish where the water tarries for a moment, tiny leeches move about.

Against the white wall of the mosque stirs the shadow of a plane tree. As in Siena, yet in an entirely different spirit, a simple arch almost without relief rises above and joins two younger arches. In the recesses of the relief lie the nests of a whole race of swallows. At my feet the green Sahel of Brusa, filled with luminous peace. It is calm. The air is indescribably limpid and the sky is clear like my thought.

Oh, to begin all over again with nothing to carry over from the past! To thrill to that exquisite sensation of one's cells, into which emotion filters like milk. . . . Brusa, with its dense gardens, pink with purity, indolent pink in the shade of the plane trees, can it be that I

did not know you in my youth? Already? Am I living in a memory?
Is it really I sitting here in the little courtyard of this mosque, I breath-
ing and loving you? Or am I merely dreaming of loving you? . . . If
I really existed, would that swallow have flown so close to me?

Brusa, Sunday

As soon as I love a country, I wish to live there. But here I should
never make any friends. My solitude feels sympathy only for the trees,
only for the sound of the running waters, only for the shades woven
by the trellises above the market streets. The people are ugly; they are
the froth left by various civilizations.

Five little Jews accompany us today from the Green Mosque to the
bazaar and to the hotel. Each one of them seems of a different race
and you could guess only two of them to be Jews. They are Jews from
Spain, like all of them in Brusa. They go to the French school and
speak our language with a disconcerting flow of words. They ask our
companion: "Is it true, madame, that in France every dog has a
master?" and again: "In France it is true, isn't it, that the water is no
good and that you have to drink wine?" Each one of them plans to
reach Paris in two years after a first examination, and to pursue his
studies at the École Juive Orientale in Auteuil, in order to become
eventually a *Monsieur*.

Tuesday

The first day I bought nothing but a little porcelain bowl, antique,
which one would have thought had come from a more distant Orient.
It is not any larger than the hollow of my hand. Bluish designs cover
a background of crackled yellowish white.

Nothing is more disappointing at first than this bazaar where we
went on the first day for a disillusioned walk. Above the stereotyped
shops the uniformly gaudy silk streamers drove us away. But the second day we entered the shops themselves. . . .

This second day I bought three dressing-gowns; one green and another amaranth-purple; each of them flecked with gold threads. The
green one has lavender glints; it is suitable for days of meditation and
study. The purple one has silver glints; I need it to write a drama. The
third is flame-colored; I shall wear it on days of doubt to stir up my
inspiration.

These gowns forced me to buy Oriental shirts with broad, button-
less sleeves, then Turkish slippers with concave soles in which one's
foot feels strange.

As I was returning from the bazaar, I saw that morning, in the narrow street that rises in the distance toward the mountain, two donkeys
loaded with snow. It had been gathered on Olympus; a woolen cloth

half wrapped around it held it up and kept it from the penetrating contact of the ropes; it looked like a block of marble on each side of the donkey.

A little above the town I discovered a delightful place of rest; the grass is fresh for stretching out in; a curtain of high poplars casts a light shadow. Before me the town spreads out; at my feet the torrent which crosses the town and which I was just now following upward going deep into this last gullying of Olympus, arid and ugly, but which held the promise higher up, and perceived from a great distance, of a flock of goats that a shepherd was probably driving to pasture. Ah! how many hours I have lost in this way on the slopes of the Apennines or of the Aurès, following the sheep or the goats along with the herdsmen, a herdsman myself, listening to the song of their rustic flute murmuring to my heart: *Utinam ex vobis unus. . . .*[3]

Brusa, the Green Mosque

Place of rest, of brightness, and of equilibrium. Sacred azure; unruffled azure; perfect intellectual health. . . .

An exquisite God inhabits you, O Mosque. He it is who recommends and permits the spiritual suspension, in the middle of and breaking the pointed arch, of that flat stone at the very point where the two curves should meet, that they may relax at that secret active spot, that they may have respite and rest at that place of coincidence and love. O subtle smile! Activity in well-defined liberty! How easy you take it, O my intellectual finesse!

I meditated at length in this holy place and eventually understood that it is the god of criticism that awaits our devotions here, and that he invites us to purification.

Brusa, Wednesday

Last night a strange, incomprehensible noise wakened us. Waking from the deepest sleep, I first thought it was my neighbors getting ready to leave at about six o'clock; but, looking at my watch, I saw that it was only three a.m. No, the sound came from outside; people were running and shouting, and behind those distinct shouts one could make out a constant clamor made up of many cries and lamentations; then dull detonations and other sharper ones, shots that were particularly disturbing because they came simultaneously from different parts of the town. For a moment I thought it was a riot, a massacre (you are always ready to expect such a thing in this country), a St. Bartholomew of Armenians, Greeks, or Jews . . . or of foreigners. I ran to my

---

[3] "Would that I had been one of you. . . ." Virgil: *Bucolics,* X, 35.

window: a vast, uneven, red glow tragically lighted up the higher trees; the shots were the fire-alarm.

The fire seemed very close; I dressed in haste. A distillery and wine-shop were burning about a hundred yards from the hotel. When I got there the fire was at its height; the crowd was rushing about in an indescribable disorder, with shouts and screams intended either to express fright or to urge on those who were running with water in miserable, half-broken tin cans. Other houses were close by, most of them wooden, and the memory of the recent fires in Istanbul still haunts every mind. . . . For a half-hour I enjoyed a rare sight; then the pumps arrived; not just one or two but almost at the same time eight or ten, answering the call of the shots, from all the fire-stations in the town. And since water is very abundant here, the fire was soon circumscribed and then checked. Dawn was just appearing when I went back to sleep.

On the way toward Nicæa, 9 May

I should have felt less regret on leaving Brusa a few days ago; that little town has a charm, a very mysteriously captivating beauty. At first I was too eagerly seeking to recapture my memories of Algeria, and I was disappointed not to find there any native music or white garments and nothing but hideous faces. But how shall I now ever be able to forget that evening walk, yesterday, at the hour of the muezzins and going on into the night, through those alleyways broken by garden-cemeteries; and finally that view over the whole town bathing, floating in a blue smoke pierced by the high minarets. . . .

We left Brusa at five o'clock. The weather was overcast; rather thick fog veiled the distance like that curtain of gray netting which is dropped in fairy-plays to change the backdrop. The trees on the edge of the road seemed even more enormous as a result. Underneath those huge trees rising momentarily out of the fog, tight rows of cultivated mulberry bushes cover the immediate environs of Brusa. Farther on, one finds fields, then rather vast empty spaces. Eventually the road rises slowly and the plowed fields become rarer. The Greeks and the Armenians cultivate these fields, almost never the Turks. Hence without immigration the land would be almost utterly wasted. At least this is what our dragoman tells us, a Jew from Buenos Aires who speaks every language except Hebrew, is a subject of the Sultan and an Italian by birth despite his German name, so hard to pronounce that he has had to take a pseudonym: Nicholas.

Nicholas wears the garb of a globe-trotter: knickerbockers and polished leather leggings. His fez has a coiflike lining; he often takes it off to mop his round, shaved head, for he sweats easily. He shaves his head on the advice of a doctor friend: in Cairo his eyes used to pain

him because of the flies and the sand; this doctor then told him to
shave his head and to wash his eyes in lemon juice every morning.
Ever since that day he is always shaved and his eyes have never given
him any more trouble.

He struts and swaggers, is familiar with the local authorities, ob-
sequious with foreigners, lofty toward inferiors on the strength of all
the money of the tourists he is with. Whatever you question him about,
he always has a ready answer and goes on replying long after you have
ceased to question him.

As the slope gets steeper, we get out of the carriage. Nicholas ac-
costs the people along the way. First we meet a shepherd, then a wood-
chopper bending under a load of wood who smiles as he sees us pass.
Nicholas pointing his finger at the man's face:

"Look at his teeth! And he never washes them. Charming young
man! Very extra-special! They are all like that here. I have never seen
such a place. Just see how happy they are to see foreigners. That is
really interesting. That alone is worth the trip," etc. . . .

My emotion at finding in the mountain the bushy daphne of Cuverville, and in blossom. The flora does not seem very foreign here: I find
the cistus of the Esterel mingled with the Norman dog-rose. But every
plant here seems more robust and fuller, its whole foliage spread out
evenly. Very likely these plants owe their perfect health to the great
abundance of birds, which rid them of insects.

How many birds! Each tree is peopled with them, and the fog is
filled with their melancholy songs. The Turks protect them religiously.
At Brusa, on the market-place, two old featherless hawks and four
wounded storks walk about calmly. You see storks everywhere; they
continue to amuse me as on the first day and make up somewhat for
the absence of camels.

At about nine o'clock the fog rose, then opened up after we had
gone around the mountain so that we could see behind us the whole
snowy range of Olympus.

Heavy rains have washed out the road. To be sure, it is paved in
spots, in the manner of the old royal roads; but the stones of that day
are so large, so uneven, and so badly set that the best thing is to leave
the road and cut your own path beside it. The repairing of a part of
this road has been entrusted to a Frenchman whom we met just now.
He was on horseback and escorted us for a time; then he left us at
the limit of his concession with a warning that the road would soon
"get bad."

At first it followed the edge of a vast swampy space, once cultivated, it seems, but in the middle of which four years ago springs

burst unexpectedly forth covering the cultivation with a dead water that would not run off, where reeds have now replaced the grain and frogs the sparrows. From one edge of the horizon to the other the frogs make a frightful racket, and we wonder if the falcons flying over the edge of the swamp live on them, for it doesn't seem as if there was anything else for them to hunt. At times, however, a marsh-hen or a teal flies up. Probably a wilder game lives in the middle of the swamp; pelicans, it is said; and I obstinately search with my eyes in the thick rushes and reeds whose dry shafts and wilted tufts of last year suspend a sort of ruddy cloud above the fresh green spikes.

At Yenisehir, however, we find a better road; but we have lost so much time that we shall not reach Nicæa until after dark.

Oh, how beautiful the light was when, after having gone through the pass, I discovered the other slope! . . . I had let my companions go back to the carriages and had continued upward on foot, taking a short cut and hastening my step, eager to reach the pass before them and to tarry there a moment. But it constantly withdrew into the distance, as it happens in the mountains, where what seems the last height hides another more distant one from which you discover a new peak. It was the hour when the homing flocks people the slopes of the mountain and I had been walking for some time in the growing darkness filled with the singing of the birds before they go to sleep.

On the other slope everything was golden. The sun was setting beyond the Lake of Nicæa, toward which we were going to descend and which was sparkling in a single horizontal ray. We could make out, half hidden by the foliage, the little village of Isnik, rattling around loose within the walls of the ancient fortified city. Urged on by the hour, our brakeless carriages rushed down as if falling, scorning the bends in the road, taking dangerous shortcuts. I fail to understand what upsets carriages since ours were not upset. . . . At the foot of the mountain the horses stopped to catch their breath; a spring was near by and I think they were watered also. We had set out ahead. The air was strangely warm; clouds of dayflies were dancing in the golden light of the setting sun. To our right, although the sky was already dark, not a star was to be seen; and we were amazed that Venus could already shine so strong, alone, above the glow in the sky. As we were about to enter through Hadrian's gate, the moon began to appear above the shoulder of the mount, the full moon, enormous, sudden, and surprising as a god. And since my first arrival at Touggourt, I don't think I ever enjoyed a stranger emotion than this entry by night into the little village of Isnik, ashamed, musty, rotted with poverty and fever, huddling in its solemn ruins and its too large past.

After a hasty meal made up of the supplies we had brought with us from Brusa, we went out again into the night. The moonlight was soft and splendid. Slushy holes in the road right outside the inn: the ground seems rotten. In front of the door a child stands motionless, leaning against the wall; his face is half eaten away by an ulcer. We start out guided by chance. At the end of a street full of holes a vacant space opens out; before us broad pale flowers, of which we cannot see the stems, rock back and forth as if floating; it is a field of poppies. Not far off an owl moans on the ruin of a mosque; the bird flies away at our approach. . . . We go back toward the mysterious sleeping town. Not a single fire; not a single sound; everything seems dead.

10 May

By carriage to Mekedje; then by railway to Eskishehir. Immense, unattractive plain, on which the light holds full sway. At times a great herd of those black buffaloes that we had already admired at Constantinople; and storks. My eye never tires of the inexhaustible charm of space.

12 May

At five a.m. we left Eskishehir, where we spent the day yesterday. The train enters the mysterious pass that we had noticed to the southwest of the town. Narrow valley between mountains of crumbling red soil; not very high mountains, and everywhere of the same height, as if they had been measured, which finish off in a sort of table: without any vegetation whatever. Strange nobility of that valley under the wonderfully clear sky.

Soon the hills on each side of the river become even lower; the top of the hills is silvered; a few pines fleck their slopes. Eventually we enter a sort of plain strewn with odd rocky efflorescences. From time to time a village, each one flanked by a cemetery planted with upright stones.

Soon the landscape changes again. The soil loses its redness. A narrow stream between steep little banks meanders among the wide undulations of the ground. Vast cultivated fields stretch out to the foot of those odd rocky formations which now and then burst through the earth in fits and starts like gray, baroque citadels, green-spotted with lichen and clothed, in the flat spots, with short grass. The earth is cultivated, but where are the cultivators? As far as one can see, and for some time now, not a single creature, not a single village, not even an isolated tent.

Afyonkarahisar

"The black castle of Opium."[4] Empire of the bleak and the ferocious. Around the town great fields of grain, but not a trace of the
fields of poppies that Joanne speaks of and which, he claims, are so
beautiful in May.[5]

Our train is bringing home a great number of soldiers. Those we
found in the train when we got on at Eskishehir are coming from Constantinople; they fought in the Balkan war and are just now getting
out of hospitals and prisons. Those who get on at Afyonkarahisar are
returning by way of Smyrna from the Yemen after having put down an
Arab uprising. They themselves are terribly low. Most of them are
sordid and in tatters; some of them seem to be dying. Nicholas calls
us to point out one who has only one legging and nothing but a shoe
on his other foot and who is clothed in rags. His torn duck trousers
keep falling down on his bare leg. His thinness is hideous and his
weakness such that he had to be lifted into the train. On the station
platform at Afyon, to begin with, he remained seated on a duffel-bag;
a comrade was stooping over him and was probably answering him by
shaking his head; the look in his eyes reminded me of that of a camel
I once saw abandoned along the trail leading from M'Reyer to Touggourt, which for a moment raised his head to watch our carriage pass
and then let it fall back once and for all; eventually he accepts a little
water or something else that the other soldier gives him to drink and
by way of thanks he attempts a smile, a frightful grimace uncovering
all his teeth.

"Madame has noticed how he is dressed," said Nicholas. "They are
all like that in the Turkish army. I've never seen anything like it!"

At a little station after Aksehir we saw him get out. He seemed not
to be quite sure that he ought to get out there. Was it really his town?
It looked as if he didn't recognize it. No one recognized him. As he
passed, he saluted an officer who did not return his salute. A great
number of people had come from the village, some kilometers away.
The train stopped for some time and we saw all these people go gaily
away in carriages, taking with them those who had just come. We expected to see him get into one of the carriages. But he didn't, and
when no one remained in the vicinity of the station, we saw him — as
our train was drawing out — take a few steps along the road, then
stand still, upright and alone under the blazing sun.

---

[4] *Afyon* means "opium" and *karahisar* means "black castle," as André
Gide learned from the *Itinéraire descriptif de l'orient* by Adolphe Joanne
(1861).

[5] The famous *Guides Joanne* were made in the nineteenth century by
the French geographer Adolphe Joanne.

The track rises rather rapidly to the heights, from which one can see the vast plain stretching toward the north as far as Ankara. The sun sets as we are going through the pass leading into the other plain, that of Konya, which goes all the way to the Taurus. It is already filled with shadow. When we reach Konya night has fallen.

Konya

Mme M. de S. is the only woman here, just as we are the only tourists. The people dining near us are here *on business*. They belong to all possible nationalities, but you have only to look at them to see that they haven't come here for nothing.

The hotel is beside the station, and the station is far from the town; a little streetcar leads to it through the dullest of suburbs. . . . But before speaking of Konya, I must say how worked up my imagination had been about this town. This is partly because I still thought (and it is hard for me not to think so even now) that the farther one goes, the stranger the country becomes. It is not very long now that the railway has made it possible to get to Konya almost with ease. Before setting out, I had seen a photograph of wonderful remains of Seljoukian monuments that I was to find here. According to them I had built up a whole town, as sumptuous and Oriental as one could wish. Finally I knew that it was the city of the dervishes, something like a Turkish Kairouan. . . .

And right after dinner, intellectually hungry for marvels and ready for every form of amazement, Ghéon and I set out; we didn't know that the town was so far off, and the solitude around the hotel surprised us. A few lights along a broad avenue came from ordinary cafés and characterless booths; then a vacant space full of darkness. Yet a few hundred yards away a much brighter glow attracted us; some casino, we thought; no, it was the headlights of an auto, belonging, as we learned the next day, to Enver Bey, who goes from town to town to check up on the military strength Turkey still possesses. Despite all his promises not to go to war again within five years, this trip was not reassuring, and, since we have been in Anatolia, we have heard the most disturbing rumors.

We came back this first evening very discomfited by our nocturnal exploration. The next day, having got up before five o'clock, I took the first car to town.

I am forced eventually to confess that Konya is by far the most hybrid, most vulgar, and ugliest thing I have seen since being in Turkey, just as I am forced to confess that the entire country and the race as a whole outdo in infirmity and informity any fears or hopes one could have. Did I have to come here to realize how pure and special everything I saw in Africa was? Here everything is soiled, warped,

tarnished, adulterated. To be sure, Konya is becoming a bit more
ordinary every year, especially since the Bagdad railway has reached
it, especially since a police ruling has ordered, for reasons of health,
that all the flat-roofed houses be torn down and replaced by a new
model with tile roof. But, I fancy, one would have to go back, not
twenty or fifty years, but rather several centuries to find some authentic
and special flavor in Konya. To add to its lack of charm (I should
rather say: to its discredit in my mind), Konya, through its position
in relation to the neighboring mountain and the plain, irresistibly re-
calls Biskra. But how much less beautiful these mountains are, in both
color and shape, than the mountains of Hamar Khadou; how much
less beautiful these trees than the palm trees, and than the Arabs these
Turks.

In all this vast country we have covered we have hardly seen a
single costume or face that it was a pleasure to look at, and even then
it always turned out to be some *tzigane* or Kurd or Albanian brought
here by some adventure or other. As for the others, whether Turks or
Jews, whether Armenians or Greeks or even Bulgarians, all these be-
fezzed creatures struck me as uniformly ugly. And of all those races
with such different vocations that are jumbled together in a thick
rabble in each province of Turkey, not one of them can arouse my
sympathy unless I learn that it is being oppressed.

The general appearance of the town predisposes me even against
the few fragments of the thirteenth-century Konya that remain intact.
Not with the result of making me consider them less admirable, perhaps, but with that of convincing me even more that they are not
natural products of the country. The exquisite art of these ceramics
and sculptures, like everything clean, solid, and beautiful that one finds
in Turkey, comes from somewhere else.

I take great delight in meeting on a public square our dragoman,
who claims to know Konya so well. It is not yet six a.m. I greatly
suspect him of coming here for the first time: he is learning his part
in haste before we get up.

Enver Bey is leaving Konya this morning at eleven. A special train
is to take him off. We are present at his departure. We have no trouble
getting onto the railway platform, where many local, business, and railway representatives are already gathered. One of them is wearing a
top hat; the others are wearing the fez; they all look like croupiers. In
a little waiting-room that opens onto the platform Enver Bey is awaiting the hour set for departure; he is surrounded by his Germano-
Turkish general staff; through the open door one can see them seated
around a table; others, officers of lower rank and newspaper reporters,

are standing at a respectful distance; on the right of Enver Bey can
be made out the German general Liman von Sanders.

In front of us parade in turn the boy scouts, or something similar,
in pale-blue, canary-yellow, and cabbage-green jerseys; the smallest
are in front; the last ones are carrying Occidental musical instruments;
they are marching on parade, all of them already ugly as Turks; then
athletic clubs or rifle clubs, the future strength of the country, grotesque and hideous but already prepared to be killed for "the cause."
Enver Bey will go away happy.

He is now receiving the delegation of dervishes. As they get out of
the two landaus that brought them, they are recognizable by the coffee
bombe they are wearing as headdress; some of them are rather dignified, even noble in appearance, and would not be out of place in the
ceremony of the *Bourgeois Gentilhomme*.[6] I am even willing to admit
that some of them have wonderful faces. They come and bow before
this new minister and probably declare their devotion. Their chief will
escort Enver Bey to Afyon along with the generals and journalists.

The various delegations line up along the station platform. The
hour has struck. Enver gets into his compartment; he is well propor-
tioned and has poise; you feel that his attention never deviates from
the path ahead. Liman follows him, very tall, a bit too pink, a bit too
fat, his hair graying, but still a handsome man; then behind them the
crowd of dignitaries hurries along. . . . I feel as if I am watching a
news-release on the screen.

The car is now filled. Enver Bey reappears at the window and begins waving his hand with dignified restraint while the train gets
slowly under way to the sound of the rose polka executed by the
brasses with a ridiculous profusion of squawks.

This afternoon we go to the Mosque of the Dervishes. A closed
garden surrounds it; opposite the entrance to the mosque a succession
of little rooms, probably inhabited by the dervishes, open onto the
garden, which they surround. Other larger and more handsome halls
are reserved for dignitaries. With exquisite courtesy one of the latter
invites us, in the name of the leader of the dervishes, to sit down for
a moment. We go into a sort of kiosk, opening wide onto the garden
on two sides, at the end of the building containing the dervishes'
lodgings.

No furniture; nothing but these lateral benches on which we sit

----

[6] Molière's *Would-Be Gentleman* contains a rollicking ballet in which
some mock Turks in native costume confer upon M. Jourdain the honor of
"Mamamouchi."

down. Oh, how gladly I should take off my shoes and squat on these
mats in the Oriental manner as I used to do in the Green Mosque!
. . . We are served coffee. With our dragoman interpreting, I express
our regret not to be at Konya on the proper day to see one of their
bimonthly ceremonies. Even more than their monotonous whirling
dance, which we were able to see at Brusa, I regret missing their music. I should like to know how old that music is and whether or not
it is the same in all the convents of the dervishes. What are their instruments? . . . To answer my insistent questions, one of the dervishes
goes and gets two long bamboo flutes with the mouthpiece on the end
and a rather voluminous notebook in which they have recently tran-
scribed according to the Occidental system of notation the complete
repertory of their tunes. I wonder if the outline of their subtle melodic
arabesques has not suffered considerably from that noting down and
if they did not often have to mar the melody to fix it to our scale.
Are they henceforth going to play and sing according to this transcrip-
tion?

At my request they very kindly begin to blow their pipes; but one
of the flutes is too dry and comes to life slowly; the other, with which
it was playing in unison, gets out of breath; and this complimentary
concert, very ordinary moreover, soon ends.

We go back out into the garden. It is filled with the perfume of
flowers and the discreet laughter of a fountain. Returning to the
mosque, we pass close to the rooms of the other dervishes; each one is
like a bay opening onto the garden, the broad cell of a honeycomb
filled with shadow and meditation. In several of these alcoves we see
gatherings of dervishes seated in the Persian fashion as in a miniature.

These dervishes are surely very holy men, but so little austerity
enters into the great calm of this spot, this fountain is so unlikely to
recommend prayer, that one would not be very much surprised if the
miniaturist had indulged a fancy and added a few dancing-girls here
and there.

In the mosque a large, bright room is devoted to the whirling practices of these gentlemen. Right next to it a no less large but much
darker hall is sanctified by the tombs of famous marabouts. Hideous
modern rugs cover the ground. From the ceiling hang an unbelievable
number of lanterns and lamps of all kinds, all shockingly new and in
the worst taste. If by chance I look closely at a copper hanging lamp
that seems to be Byzantine in form, I see at once that it is modern,
very ordinary in workmanship, and garishly bright. The dervish who is
guiding us explains that the real lamp has gone to America and that
this is just a copy, which the college of dervishes accepted in its place.
He says this as the most natural thing in the world, without the slightest embarrassment, and ready I fancy to accept some new exchange of

this type — if only there remained in this venerable spot anything whatever that deserved to be coveted.

From Konya to Ushak

At the station of S. a large number of conscripts, absentees, or deserters are piled into the third-class cars of our train. Mothers are sobbing on the platform. They themselves affect a devil-may-care attitude and the car is soon filled with laughter and gay songs. Most of them are still wearing their varied local garb, warm and lively in color and forming of these gaudy splashes from one end to the other of the car an amusing and rich harmony.

At the station before Aksehir two Russian muzhiks get on; their dress and appearance are strangely surprising here. A thick beard covers the lower part of each one's face and a felt hat is pulled down over his eyes. Large blouses cover them, falling outside their brown breeches almost to their muddy boots. They are much taller and heavier than all these Turks, but the expression of their eyes is shy, almost childish, and so very kind that when it turns toward you, you feel like opening your heart to them. The dragoman tells us that they are fishermen from the fish-filled Aksehir-Gheul, the pond we have just skirted. The carriage that was taking them to the train was attacked and the driver, who is now being lifted into the car, was shot in the face. He seems to be on the point of dying. Ghéon and I approach him, making our way through the verminous crowd filling up the passageway. He has sunk down on the floor with his head leaning against the bench and bent forward as if to vomit; blood is flowing rather freely from his mouth or nose, one can't tell which, for his handkerchief, serving as a bandage, hides the lower part of his face. The Turks in the car hardly glance at him, though he is himself a Turk.

At the station of Aksehir he is taken out inert, unconscious, perhaps dead, bathing with blood the shoulder of the porter who is carrying him away.

After Afyonkarahisar we leave the line by which we came and head off toward the western shore. Soon the landscape seems to become more civilized; that is, the undulations of the land are less sweeping and the soil more frequently cultivated.

. . . .

I no longer enjoy these notes and soon give up my notebook altogether. I did not return to it either at Ephesus or at Smyrna, where we tarried a few days more; after that I felt drawn toward Greece with all the very strength of my aversion toward Turkey. If I begin to write again when I get there, I shall use another notebook.

It is better to come from Turkey rather than from France or Italy to admire as one should the miracle that was Greece — to have been "the weary, way-worn wanderer . . . on desperate seas long wont to roam" of Poe's *To Helen* who feels brought "home to the glory that was Greece." [7]

The very educative value that I derive from this trip is in proportion to my disgust for the country. I am glad not to like it more. When I feel the need of the desert air, of wild and strong perfumes, I shall go seek them again in the Sahara. In that woebegone Anatolia humanity is not so much undeveloped as it is definitely deteriorated.

Should I have gone farther? To the Euphrates? To Bagdad? No, and now I don't want to. The obsession of that country, that painful curiosity that had so long tormented me, is now conquered. What a relaxation it is to have enlarged on the map the space one no longer wants to go and see! For too long I believed (out of love of exoticism, out of fear of chauvinistic self-satisfaction, and perhaps out of modesty), for too long I thought that there was more than one civilization, more than one culture that could rightfully claim our love and deserve our enthusiasm. . . . Now I know that our Occidental (I was about to say French) civilization is not only the most beautiful; I believe, I know that it is the *only one* — yes, the very civilization of Greece, of which we are the only heirs.

"Brought me home to the glory that was Greece." On the ship taking us to the Piræus I already repeat these lines from Poe. My heart is filled with peace, with laughter and serenity. Fearing the noisy admiration of my companion, I take out of my bag a little English book and hide my emotion behind an inattentive reading. Why go to any effort? There is nothing intense about my joy. I am so little surprised to be here. Everything seems to me so familiar. I seem so natural to myself here. My infatuation fills this known landscape; I recognize everything; I am "at home": this is Greece.

On the Adriatic, 29 May

Voluptuous calm of the flesh, as much at rest as this unruffled sea. Perfect equilibrium of the mind. The free flight of my thoughts is supple, even, bold, and voluptuous, like the flight of these gulls through the dazzling blue.

Between Verona and Milan, 30 May

How much can the geographic position of countries influence the pleasure we take in them — to make us, according to our mood, con-

---

[7] Gide quotes the poem in Mallarmé's French translation.

sider the distant one more beautiful, or on the other hand the nearer one! . . . Just because they are easier of access, am I going to like any the less these charming approaches to Lago Maggiore, where the water in excess seems unwilling to yield to the earth? Overflowing, it oozed and sparkled through the grass; the sky was loaded with humidity, and as we went through the shower, above this springtime in tears, above the intoxication of the foliage, from one end to the other of my sky the rainbow stretched.

* * *

11 June

Repeat to myself every morning that the most important remains to be said, and that it is high time.

The synovial sheaths in my right wrist have again become inflamed; most likely the cold and humidity we have had since my return are the cause; but even more so piano-practice, which I have exaggerated of late and which has considerably distracted me from work. I had been so long cut off from music! And I feel, I now know so well how to work. I have gone back to Chopin's *Études* (second book) and his Scherzos, Schumann's Allegro, Beethoven's Variations in E flat and in C major—and the first book of Albéniz's *Iberia*.

Probably it is fortunate that the pains and ankylosis of the wrist have stopped me. One must get oneself to give the best moment in the day to what most deserves it. The piano should come along only to rest me from work. The best hour is the first; the hard thing is to protect it.

Just as I finish writing these lines, a big package sent by the N.R.F. is brought from the station.[8] It contains the other volumes of Albéniz, the Symphonies of Beethoven (Liszt), Fauré's Impromptus, the Transcriptions of Bach (J. Herscher), and the complete work of Chopin in the big Ricordi edition.

I cling to my work-table.

12 June

It is beautiful weather. I should be completely happy if my heart were not full of Ghéon's sorrow. I have written to Jean Schlumberger to alleviate it if he can in a note.

Wrote to Mme Mayrisch and to Élie Allégret about Mme d'Etche-

[8] The *N.R.F.* (familiar abbreviation for *Nouvelle Revue Française*) is the literary review founded by André Gide and a group of writers in 1909, to which was added soon after a publishing house under the same name, directed by Gaston Gallimard.

vère, and to Gallimard about Mme Mayrisch; and thus my whole morning was taken up with correspondence, as it often happens. Yet I had got up early, hoping to have finished before breakfast; but the mail brought me new work.

The Insel Verlag sends me a *"Probekapitel"* by M. Bassermann, the new translator, which I must go over.

I have got to the point where I can play decently the first two pieces of *Iberia,* which are devilishly difficult: but I cannot practice seriously as long as my wrist remains so stiff and painful.

Read two chapters of *Wuthering Heights* with uninterrupted pleasure.[9]

13 June

This morning's mail brings me from Ruyters a huge pile of newspaper clippings. The wise thing to do would be not to read any of them. Yet at times certain misjudgments are instructive; in general, I notice that they are due less to imperfections in my work than to oddities in my way of life.

The important thing is to keep on; the stupidity of certain criticisms will appear automatically. I must confess, however, that almost nothing in my writings up to the present lets it be clearly seen *where I am heading.* I think it is better for this not to be discovered until later on.

The sky is again completely overcast. This is probably also why I slept badly.

14 June

Yesterday, late in the afternoon, not succeeding in concentrating on those travel notes which I get no pleasure from ruminating on, I again went down into the valley. Seated on a bank reading *Wuthering Heights* aloud. The Dumont children saw me from a distance and ran to huddle, as they always do, against me. I find nothing to say to them and try to imagine that they do not come solely for the penny that I give each one of them when I leave. Their faces would be pretty if they were less marked by poverty; their little hands look like old men's; even the skin of their necks is creased like the skin of a hawk's neck; a great many nits in the girl's hair and the youngest boy's. They are wearing absurd rags more or less held together by strings. And yet they are always smiling, but with a smile that seems sadder every year — or else am I simply a little more touched by their poverty from year to year?

While they were sitting so close to me, their father passed on a bicycle and stopped when he saw me. He asked me "if Madame Gille

---

[9] The novel by Emily Brontë (1847).

liked honey," and announced that his wife would bring us a pot of it on Monday.[10]

The sky darkened; I left them, but, while the storm was gathering, I continued for a while in the valley, reading aloud the last meeting of Catherine and Heathcliff without restraining my sobs. The sky became so threatening that I had almost to run to get home before the rain, but when I got up to the avenue I stopped to watch the storm rise. Despite the threatening sky the people from the farm went down to the valley to milk the cows. And moreover the storm soon passed over, disappeared as by magic after a little shower.

I am practicing simultaneously three or four compositions by Albéniz and practicing nothing but them; the difficulties are of so special a nature that a sort of general acclimatization is necessary before tackling each one of them in detail. Besides, I have never mastered anything without learning it by heart at the same time, and the strangeness of these harmonies seems a challenge to the memory. I have already succeeded, however, in getting a few pages into my head. May they remain there!

This morning, at work at six thirty, I got fairly well ahead with my notes; but the mail brought me absurd bits of newspaper gossip to which I had to reply, for they question my friendship for Claudel. All this because of the epigraph for the third book of the *Caves*, which I had used with his approval and later suppressed at his request.[11] Had to write likewise to Fontainas and Rivière, etc.

In the morning, a special-delivery brought the two volumes of the big edition of the *Caves*, which should have appeared more than a month ago. The portraits by Paul Laurens in the front of the first volume had been held up by the customs, etc. The book looks attractive; but I have no sooner opened it than I discover still further misprints.

15 June

Yesterday finished the morning most unpleasantly with the memory of M. E., to which I returned or which returned to me several times

---

[10] "Gille" is apparently a peculiarly local pronunciation of *Gide* in the part of Normandy in which Cuverville lies.

[11] When the novel appeared in the *Nouvelle Revue Française*, prior to publication in book-form, the third book bore the following lines from Claudel's *Tidings Brought to Mary* as an epigraph: "Pierre de Craon — But of which king are you speaking, and of which pope? For there are two of them and it is not known which is the right one." Claudel was probably referring to the Babylonian captivity, but the lines are equally applicable to the situation in Gide's fiction.

during the day. Last night my nerves were on edge and I was barely able to sleep a few hours.

Today the weather is clear and the air balmy. I feel all right again.

It is almost seven o'clock. I expect the Copeaus at any moment; I think I shall be less distracted than stimulated by their presence. The rewriting of my Turkish notes progresses with absurd slowness; yet I keep at it and shall get them as far as the arrival in Greece; but I cannot look upon them as anything but a training and preparation for a more important and more serious work. At times, when I think of the importance of what I have to say, of my *Christianisme contre le Christ,* of *Corydon,* and even of my book on Chopin, of my novel, or merely of my *Traité des Dioscures,* I tell myself that I am mad to delay and to temporize in this way.[12] If I were to die right now I should leave only a one-eyed image of myself, or an eyeless one.

16 June

Copeau is as much touched as I by Ghéon's withdrawal. Schlumberger's letter, which I receive this morning, irritates me somewhat by treating the affair lightly. However unjustified Ghéon's vexation may be, it is none the less real, and I feel his sorrow to be even greater than his vexation.

We took a rather long walk this morning. Copeau talks to me of Rivière and the emotional crisis he is experiencing; "Naturally I came out on top," he told him. "I always come out on top of my crises. . . ." The poor fellow!

17 June

This morning I tried to practice the piano, but my awareness of our guests' presence inhibits me; in vain I struggle against that absurd, unjustified embarrassment which I have always known; but no good; it is not merely a muscular paralysis; it is an inhibition of all my faculties. Furthermore, I experience it only in the presence of certain persons; but I can't recall ever having conquered it.

I am losing all patience over these Turkish notes; they did not deserve that I should spend more than four days on them and it will soon be ten days that I have been at them. In addition I cannot make

---

[12] No such work as *Christianity against Christ* or *Treatise on the Dioscuri* was ever published. *Corydon* first appeared, anonymously and without place or publisher's name, in 1911 as *C.R.D.N.;* a second, enlarged edition appeared in 1920 with the same anonymity. *Notes on Chopin,* not written until 1931, first appeared in the *Revue musicale* for December 1931. The "novel" is of course *The Counterfeiters.* Fragments of the *Treatise on the Dioscuri* appeared in 1919 as *Considerations on Greek Mythology.*

up my mind to write something insignificant any less well than something important; there is a certain weakness in this.

This evening, after dinner, Copeau read us the first act of *La Maison natale*.[13]

18 June

At last, a radiant day! I feel well despite my lapses of yesterday and the bad night that followed. Copeau set out for Étretat on a bicycle; spent an hour practicing the Étude in A flat to see if I couldn't get over that embarrassment I spoke of yesterday; my fingers remain trembling and paralyzed to the very end. Shall I keep at it any longer? I am wasting strength and time on it.

Mathilde Roberty sends us an article from the *Journal de Genève* declaring that there are only two theaters in Paris that matter: the Vieux-Colombier and the Comédie-Française, then pulling to pieces the showing of *Macbeth* at the latter and extolling *Twelfth Night* at the former.[14] This triumphant success almost embarrasses me, so accustomed was I to predict a lack of success for real worth and to put off beyond the grave the recognition of *our* virtues.

Copeau again declares to me his intention of establishing in the article he is writing the close relationship between the Review and the Theatre and of claiming the same praise for the former.

Copeau makes up his mind to read me the long letter he has just received from Rivière, which justifies my worries and shows how well founded were my fears. Copeau, who suffers as much as I do from Ghéon's sorrow and is unwilling to allow Jean Schlumberger or Jacques Rivière to treat it lightly, reads me at the same time the harsh, indignant letter he is writing in reply to Rivière. This letter will doubtless upset its recipient; yet I cannot but approve it. And none of this misunderstanding would have taken place if Rivière had gone to talk the matter over with Copeau as I begged him to do.

The sadness I feel about this (for I like Rivière very much too) keeps me awake a part of the night. Before going to bed I had read the manuscript (sent to Copeau) of a very good play by Villeroy,

---

[13] *The Family Home,* Jacques Copeau's first full-length play, was first presented by him at the Vieux-Colombier in 1923 and published in the same year.

[14] The Théâtre du Vieux-Colombier founded by Jacques Copeau and his friends of the *N.R.F.*, which did more than any other theater to revive French drama in our time, gave its first performance on 22 October 1913 with Thomas Heywood's *A Woman Killed with Kindness* and Molière's *Amour médecin*. *Twelfth Night* was produced at the end of the first season on 22 May 1914 and ran for thirteen performances.

which I strongly urge him to accept and which would be very amusing to play.[15]

Copeau urges me to translate *As You Like It*. I am rather taken with the idea.

This morning the mail brings a new issue of *Les Marges* containing the drop of poison intended for us, as in each of its issues without exception.[16] I should be interested if someday someone amused himself by collecting them.

19 June

Yesterday Cuverville went to sleep in a cloud, which this morning is still chilling the surrounding country. Perhaps this numbing climate is partly responsible for the contraction, the strangling of almost all my books, which we discussed with Copeau last evening. I had to finish almost every one of them in Cuverville, contracted and striving to recapture or maintain a fervor that in a dry climate (in Florence, for example) came easily and naturally. I am inclined to believe that, with a little help from the climate, my production would have been easier and, hence, more abundant.

To say nothing of the physiological equilibrium that is so difficult and dangerous to find here.

20 June

While I was reading on the bench, not far from me one of our cats began to play with a shrewmouse. I approached quietly and for a long time observed the play. Once more I wondered at the extraordinary *precautions* the cat takes *not to harm* its captive. How carefully he kept his claws folded and with what delicacy he occasionally seized it in his mouth! All along, the shrewmouse continued to be more afraid of me than of the cat; and several times, even, the mouse sought refuge between the cat's paws when I made a movement toward it. After ten minutes of play the cat got a little bored, gave its prey more liberty, and then, as a cat often does, let it get away. The shrewmouse went away altogether whole and without the least scratch.

[15] This may well be *La Traverse* (*The Short Cut*) by Auguste Villeroy, which Copeau first played in New York in 1918.

[16] *Les Marges*, a literary review, was founded and entirely written by Eugène Montfort between 1903 and 1908. When André Gide founded the *Nouvelle Revue Française* in November 1908, Montfort was one of the editors, but as a result of a quarrel over the first issue he was dropped from the board and a new first number appeared without him in February 1909. He revived *Les Marges* in January 1909 as a regular review, accepting contributions by others, and in this form it ran until suspended during the war. It regularly attacked the *N.R.F.* and all its writers.

21 June

Having slept perfectly last night, I set to work this morning at five o'clock; but getting under way badly and shivering with cold and humidity, I hardly did anything worth while.

Read the first scene of *Love's Labour's Lost* (in English); I should have continued were it not that my edition of Shakespeare is in too fine type and tired my eyes. Then I busied myself with my Turkish notes, which are now almost completed. I am impatient to get to something more important.

The desire to write a comedy torments me every day and almost every hour of the day. I should like Copeau to give me a subject as Pushkin gave Gogol the subject of *The Government Inspector*. I believe that a good subject would grow marvelously in my head, but I cannot find this subject *within me* as I do for my other books. The subject of a drama must either be given by someone else or at least come from the outside, be *suggested*.

Dramatic art must no more seek to create the illusion of reality than does painting; it should work through its own special means and aim toward effects that belong to it alone.

Just as a painting is a space to set in motion, a play is a space of time to animate.

22 June

I found in the driveway yesterday morning a little starling that had fallen from the nest but was almost ready to fly. While I am writing now, he is right here beside me on the table, or more exactly between the fingers of my left hand, which are holding this notebook in place; that is the spot he most likes. He folds up his legs, puffs up like a little ball; you can tell he is comfortable. I had tried to put him into a cage, but he beat against it; I had to leave him free in the room, where he soils everything. Every ten minutes he lets fall anywhere and everywhere a little liquid, corrosive dropping. I give him bread soaked in milk to eat, mixed with the yolk of a hard-boiled egg; or little earthworms, which he is very fond of. He just flew from the table to my shoulder as soon as he saw me come in. After he has sat for some time on my hand, I feel an odd little itch moving over the back of my hand; this is tiny parasites moving from him to me. Another dropping.

23 June

Finally finished those lamentable Turkish notes. I am ashamed to produce such ordinary stuff. My ideas become numbed and shrunken here to such a degree that, some days, nothing I have in my head seems worth the trouble. . . .

I have regained my self-control in regard to the piano and played yesterday — with Agnès Copeau listening — almost as well as I can ever play when I don't practice more.

My starling amuses me as much as he bothers me; besides the fact that I never get tired of observing him, he is never satisfied unless he is perched on my shoulder, where I should be glad to leave him if he did not soil me. I picked him up about twenty times to put him back on the table and finally I got tired; I went to get a rag and wrapped the upper part of my body in it, but now he is no longer interested in perching on me.

He throws himself so hungrily on the earthworms that I haven't time to chop them up; he snaps them up all at once, then a moment later strangles and gurgles as if he were stifling once and for all. He follows me when I walk up and down in the hall, trotting along behind me, and when I stop climbs fluttering up my leg.

To air out the linen-room I leave two windows open, but with the shutters closed, and this darkens the room rather lugubriously. To divert my starling I risked taking him down onto the lawn at tea-time, when only the Moune, Miquette, and Toby were with us. The last-named was so excited that he trembled all over; Em. ran in fright to get the lead and tie him up. As for the Moune and Miquette, they are so obedient that I had no fear about them; the bird even approached and hopped around Miquette, who, probably finding her position humiliating, turned her head aside and pretended not to see him. I left the starling out about ten minutes; then I took him back into the linen-room, without holding him, freely perched on my finger.

24 June

I have had to give up the linen-room, which my bird makes uninhabitable; every hour I go up to feed him. He had dunked himself in the plate of milk I had left; I tried to wash him; the water I brought in a saucer seemed to delight him so that I immediately went to get him a deeper receptacle in which he can take a bath; and he did so at once. Afterward he seemed a little chilled, and since with the fog this morning I feared that he might have trouble getting warm, I kept him for a long time in the palm of my hand.

About midday, while the cats were in front of the house, I took him down under the copper beech; but probably intoxicated by the little wind that was blowing, he suddenly left my finger and fluttered straight into the hedge of Portuguese laurels edging the flower path. I was very much afraid not to be able to catch him again; fortunately I had brought with me a can of worms; I held one out to him, and while he tried to snatch it, he let himself be caught.

As soon as he was in the grass he set off ahead of me and, since he was no longer hungry, it did no good to hold out my worm . . . I thought I had lost him. I felt painfully disappointed.

I hope so fervently that in a few days, when he can fly and get out the linen-room window, which I shall leave open, I hope so fervently that he will get into the habit of coming back to peck the worms that I shall always keep in readiness for him on the table.

I finished my Turkish notes last night; read them to Copeau as we both sat on the road embankment near Dumont's house.

I am now going over my translations of Whitman.[17]

25 June

The tub I gave my bird is much too narrow; he can just barely get into it, but once in it, he cannot shake himself and beat his wings; wherefore, after he has moistened his feet, his beak, and the end of his tail, he gets out and, standing right beside the basin and parallel to it, he stoops down, squats, and flaps his wings exactly as if he were in the water. But none the less he is not deceived; then he gets angry, beats his beak against the edges of the basin, goes in and out of it several times, and eventually sprinkles himself more or less all over.

But I fear not to be able to keep him; he has a sort of diarrhea that I don't know how to remedy; it is frothy and yellowish and terribly frequent; furthermore, it smells horribly; it's hard for me to remain in the room. Yet he is very lively; but now he refuses earthworms . . .

27

I thought this was only the 26th of June. I am not aware of having let a day pass without writing in this notebook. Most likely I would give up writing in it altogether if I did not jot down something every day.

It was very beautiful all day today. I got up rather early and took my bird for a walk in the vegetable garden before the cats had come out of the attic. The little fellow probably recognized a starling's cry in the air, for suddenly he, who is usually altogether mute, began to chirp and call urgently. For a moment I hoped that the other one would reply. I had taken a chair down with me and for a long time I waited. At about eight o'clock I took the bird back up to the linen-room. I went back to him after tea; he seemed so sad and the room seemed so dark after the dazzling light outside that I decided to put him back in the large cage, where I had originally put him the first

---

[17] The translations of eight selections from Whitman were published in 1918 in the volume of *Œuvres choisies* together with translations by Jules Laforgue, Louis Fabulet, Valery Larbaud, Jean Schlumberger, and Francis Vielé-Griffin.

day. He squatted down in the sunlight and hardly stirred all morning. I busied myself getting him some worms and seeds, then arranging a tub, into which he rushed at once; then he returned to his original place. He does not try to get away when I approach and seems to like me to stroke the top of his head as one does to a cat; he stretches out his neck and stands up as high as he can.

I spent the whole morning taking care of him, except for an hour of practicing.

Last night I had read *The Post-Office,* of which Macmillan had sent me the proofs.[18] This morning I write them my intention of translating it. Copeau, who has just read it too, is very inclined to put it on at the Vieux-Colombier.

Sent back to Kippenberg the *"Probekapitel"* of the *Caves* translated by Bassermann after writing in the corrections suggested by Mme Mayrisch.

Went over my translation of Walt Whitman. I am working absurdly little, shamefully little.

Two days from now I shall go to Paris with Copeau and take part in the meeting of the *N.R.F.* board. On my return here, no longer distracted by anything, I hope, I shall have a month of hard work ahead of me.

28 June

This evening before dinner I gave my starling his liberty. In the morning I had taken him out in the hothouse garden, but he stayed perched on the branch of a plum tree; I thought he would be too easy a prey for my cat and took him back into his cage; but later in the day he began to fly so well that I thought I could let him go.

I carried him beyond the gate leading to the tennis court. This time, as soon as I opened my hand, he flew off, almost above my head, and settled on the branch of an apple tree, where he remained. I had to leave him to go to dinner; after dinner he was still there and I imagine that is where he spent the night.

Cleaned up my translations of Whitman, with which I am satisfied.

In my relations with Copeau I suffer almost constantly from the realization that he knows my limits too well, and I am constantly aware of his awareness of them. I remember my sorrow as a child when for the first time I reached the end of the forest of La Roque and realized that I should never again get lost in it.

---

[18] A play by Rabindranath Tagore, first published in English in 1914. André Gide's translation did not appear until 1922 under the more appropriate title of *Amal et la lettre du roi* (*Amal and the King's Letter*).

It is strange, moreover, it is disconcerting how my entire being is determined according to the opinion someone else has of it.

29 June

This afternoon Copeau asked me to help him in his translation of Whitman — that is, to act as his secretary.

We had sat down on the bench behind the house that is sheltered by a hazel tree; then soon, leaving the bench, we stretched out on the lawn beside the path. We were about to leave our work and go in for tea when there came toward us, hopping through the grass in great haste, my little starling. By himself he came right up close to my hand and made no effort to get away when I tried to catch him. In my hand he didn't struggle at all; he seemed perfectly happy to be there. I ran into the kitchen to ask for some bread and milk and, for fear of the cats, I carried the bird into the aviary. He ate quite willingly but without throwing himself on the food with such eagerness that it seemed that mere hunger brought him back. I could have shouted with joy. I prepared his mush with a hard-boiled egg, changed the water in his tub, and stayed for some time with him. Very sorry to have to leave tomorrow. As soon as I get back from Paris I shall give him his liberty.

30 June

I find in Paris both Souday's article and Lucien Maury's article on *Les Caves*. The latter article interests me because it could not have been written — or not just as it is — if I had kept the preface I had almost finished writing; among other things, I ended the preface thus:

"Whether tales or satirical farces, I have written up to now nothing but ironic — or, if you wish, critical — works, of which this is probably the last."

There is a certain amusement and even some advantage in letting the critics make a mistake at first. But how could I be surprised that they didn't immediately see in my *Porte étroite* a critical work? Now, in *Les Caves*, Lucien Maury thinks he sees an affirmation of nihilism.

How beautiful were the vast fields of grain under the broiling sun today! How ugly were the men in the train!

1 July

Throughout this stormy day I have dragged around a humiliating headache.

This morning, however, I went to Orsay, thinking that my unexpected visit would please Ghéon more than our encounter tomorrow at the board meeting, where we should be unable to talk to each other. It was terribly hot in the train. Walking through a torrid zone, Ghéon

and I went to sit in the large park of Orsay, which is about to be sub-
divided. We sat down on a wooden bench near a little lake in which
swans were floating majestically. One of them, a huge swan with
heavy, downy plumage, probably the most beautiful swan I have ever
seen, came out of the water to smooth his feathers right near us on the
path. My memory of Ghéon's tales will be joined to the memory of that
swan; Ghéon told me of the end of his trip in Greece and his crossing
of Italy. I am quite willing to live often by proxy through Ghéon.

Lunched at Orsay with Ghéon and his uncle, whom I accompanied
to Paris. In our compartment was Croué, who, like me, was going to the
Vieux-Colombier. Slept a half-hour in Copeau's dressing-room (thanks
to Ruyters's Vouvray I hardly closed my eyes last night). Took my
headache to the Van Rysselberghes' without finding them in, then onto
the boulevards, where I have dinner.

Why do I note all this? Simply for fear of breaking the thread.

After dinner my headache disappeared. I went to see poor old La
Pérouse. At eight o'clock he hadn't yet come home. It so happened
that it was his wife's birthday and she received me surrounded by
flowers. I had already been there some time when the poor old fellow
arrived and complained interminably, going over and over his imaginary fears. The window was open onto the street, and the room
was lighted only by the street-lamp. Old La Pérouse was facing the
window, and the complicated shadow of the balcony grill sketched
arabesques over his cheeks. Because of that I could not make out the
condition of that poor face I have loved so much and so deeply
venerated. He kept me a long time, later, on the threshold, in the
darkness, then finally took me in his arms and kissed me once more as
if he were never to see me again.

He is deeply touched by his granddaughter's departure for America. She is to spend two months in Chicago, at the house of some of
her grandfather's pupils, quite devoted and "thoroughly reliable," as
Mme de La Pérouse asserts. But "a young girl must not leave her
mother," the poor old man never tires of repeating; and it is impossible
to drive this axiom out of his head.

I thought I would then go to Marcel Drouin's, but as I passed by
the Place de l'Étoile, the lights from the Neuilly Fair attracted me. I
took the métro to the Porte Maillot and then walked back some distance without meeting anything that was not dull and insipid. . . .[19]
No, it was not my fault, for my headache had left me altogether and
I should have been easily satisfied.

---

[19] The Porte Maillot can be seen from the Étoile, down the slope of the
avenue de la Grande Armée; there the annual Neuilly Fair is held in the
open air.

3 July

Back to Cuverville.

Not able to note anything yesterday; was not alone for a moment. In the morning I saw Marcel, then the Théos, at whose house I lunched.

Then in an auto to the office of the Review, where were gathered Copeau, Schlumberger, Gallimard, Tronche, Rivière, Drouin, and Ghéon. Our meeting lasted until almost six.

Having set out with little Jean T. by the 1.09 train, I get here in time for dinner, worn out and exasperated by the length of the trip. I am writing as in a dream.

I have brought back for my starling a fine big cage with wooden bars. He certainly recognized me, for he hastened toward me to come and have his head scratched — whereas Em. tells me that he was frantic every time she entered the aviary.

4 July

This morning, departure of Mme Copeau and the three children, who are returning to Le Limon.

There is no question about the starling's recognizing me. I took him down into the garden; he doesn't attempt to get away, although he can fly perfectly. He is even a little too tame; when he is on the ground and I push him away with my foot, he attacks my shoe, just like the penguins of the Scott expedition. For fear of the cats, I put him back in the cage after a very short time. Mius insists that it would be good to pierce with a pin a certain little white capsule, above his tail, which is full of pus and bothers him. He claims to have performed the same operation on his turtledove and that the parents do it for their children until they are old enough to do it for themselves, since, according to him, it has to be done every four days.

I reread this morning my Turkish notes that I had promised to the Review. I envy J.-É. Blanche, who covers a dozen pages every evening. I have ceased to like things that are slowly written. This notebook, like all the other "journals" I have kept, is intended to teach me to write rapidly. I repeat to myself the remark from *Armance:* "I spoke much better as soon as I began each sentence without knowing how I should end it." [20] One would have to accept a certain incorrectness in the choice of words and some errors in syntax. Above all, I must not yield to that cadence which measures my sentences and often decides as to the choice of words. And first of all my mind should not be numbed as it almost always is at Cuverville.

---

[20] *Armance* is a novel by Stendhal.

Sunday

There are just the three of us here: I mean Em., Jean T., and I. Nothing could be more different from the Copeau children than Jean T. I think he is intelligent; even very intelligent; but he utters only stupidities, shouting in a loud voice without rhyme or reason, all day long, not so much through natural expansiveness and a need of using up his energy as through a desire to attract attention and get others to notice him. He never makes a gesture without first announcing it, and he makes the gesture only for the sake of being admired while he is doing it. He is constantly changing from one game to another; it seems that he is not amused by any of them, but aims to be seen having a good time. Yet all of that child's shortcomings seem to be acquired and I believe they are merely superficial. S. T. thinks she is raising her children properly because she is constantly concerned with them; left to himself, this child would be quite different and his nature, which is good, would appear; but right now even his joy and laughter are falsified. Em. too listens attentively to everything he has to say. The worst is that his habit of saying everything that occurs to him, without ever being made fun of, makes him almost incapable of reflection. I should be surprised if this did not mark him with unfortunate intellectual tendencies. Meanwhile, not a single one of those charming remarks which were so frequent not long ago. — Yet this child who is so disobedient and so unbearable with his parents is goodness itself while he is here.

6 July

I receive Griffin's latest volume, *Voix d'Ionie*. No matter what affectionate attention I give it, the volume puts my mind and nerves on edge, even if it does occasionally somewhat satisfy my heart. The extraordinary misconception of the quality of words and of the demands of syntax. ". . . before the ploughshare of which I broke open the dry sand."—"Mentor placed your wailing and slender grace." Etc.[21]

Unsatisfactory work; I am giving too much to my piano-practice; and, with the excuse of freeing myself, I always put off the most important things beyond the insignificant little chores. I read a manuscript by Combette: *L'Isolement* (which I like very much); I begin to translate *The Post-Office*; I write letters; time flies — and everything important that I have to say remains to be said. Everything I have written up to now was simply to get ready for it. I have only prepared

---

[21] ". . . *devant le soc dont j'éventrais le sable aride*" and "*Mentor déposa ta grâce vagissante et exiguë*" are lines from *Voices from Ionia* by the American-born poet Vielé-Griffin.

the ground. All my work up to now has been merely negative; I have given a false impression of my heart and mind.

7 July

The difficulty lies in letting one subject get ahead of all the others; as always, the lightest is the most agile and gets out ahead. I am concerned this morning with the *Traité des Dioscures*. But, even here, the tangle of my ideas is such that each of them in turn seems to me capable of serving as an opening, as the crux of the argument, or as a closing. Probably I shall be satisfied to note them down on separate sheets, without seeking to give them any order. Furthermore I have found in my papers brought from Paris a certain quantity of materials intended to be used in the construction; I shall leave all this in a fragmentary state.

My cat is expecting her kittens at any moment; she is prowling restlessly from room to room throughout the house. Her basket is prepared in the attic; but that is not enough for her; what she wants is to have her whole family gathered around her and she is constantly coming down to collect her other children. One of them is frantically nursing her. How can she already have milk?

8 July

For the last three days I have been trying to help Jean T. to study, or at least to keep his mind busy and force him to reflect. This child, who did not seem stupid however, has a most disconcerting intellectual versatility. (I can't find a word better suited to describe his inattention and lack of logic.) I should like to teach him to differentiate masculine and feminine, but he gets this all mixed up with the notion of "opposites," and after three half-hours of effort (a half-hour every morning) he tells me that the opposite of *blanc* is *blanche* or that the feminine of *grand* is *petit*. I go about it in every possible manner and bring as much patience to the task as I should for a dog or for my bird, and even more, but I cannot succeed in arousing any common sense in this young mind.

This evening he has just given me a real exhibit of illogic and lack of co-ordination of ideas. I had gone into my starling's aviary, for I let him out every evening after the cats are locked up, and he comes back every morning by himself. Some children had amused themselves by frightening him from behind the aviary, so that I had some trouble in retaming him. Jean T. had come to the door, had stayed awhile watching me, then, since I feared that he too might frighten the bird, I had told him to go away. When a little later, the bird now being calmed, I want to go out with him, I discover that Jean, as he went away, had closed the door of the aviary from the outside. I had untold difficulty manipulating the bolt; since it had rained, the wood had swollen and did not help my efforts; I had to invent a sort of hook with a wire from the cage, etc. It is not for all this that I am relating this little story but rather for the questioning of Jean that ensued.

"Did you know that you closed the door as you left?"

"Yes! How did you get out?"

"Oh, you wanted to lock me in, then?"

"No. When I was there, you signaled; I thought you wanted to get out."

"But you saw that I hadn't gone out."

"Of course I saw that you hadn't gone out."

"Then you knew that you were locking me in."

"Oh no, I didn't know that I was locking you in."

"Yet you knew that I couldn't open the door from the inside."

"Of course. How did you get out?" Etc.

During dinner Em. again questioned him with the same result. And most certainly the child didn't intend to play a trick on me; he was simply unable to realize intellectually that closing the bolt kept me from getting out of the aviary. There was nothing but thoughtlessness in all this; but the amazing thing is that his thoughtlessness continues and that he seems unable to notice it.

Likewise when Em. reads him a story, he laughs in the wrong places and interrupts to ask if the pail is in the moon or the moon in the pail, or else the fox. Everything is disjointed in him.

* * *

Cuverville, 8 July

It does no good to take hold of myself; I get nothing out of myself — or so little!

This morning an hour at the piano.

A half-hour teaching Jean T.

An hour of translating Tagore.[22]

A half-hour of letter-writing.

In the afternoon — two hours at the piano.

Read some Combette.

Wrote various recollections.

My head is heavy and I feel devoid of value, vigor, and virtue.

9 July

This notebook inspires me much less than the other one; it's absurd and I am ashamed to confess it, but the format, quality and color of

---

[22] *The Post-Office.*

the paper hamper or favor my thought to an extraordinary degree; I should have liked to continue this journal in notebooks of the same format as the first one.

I cling to work as much as I can, but am worth nothing and am horribly tormented.

A carrier-pigeon lighted just a short while ago on one of the hall windows. You could see the little ring on his leg holding the correspondence.

The maids told me that I had only to try to catch him and then to put an ad in a Rouen or Havre newspaper that I was holding him for whoever would come to claim him. But the pigeon flew away when I went to open the window, lighting first on the edge of the roof and then disappearing. I have bitterly reproached myself for not having waited until night to approach him; I should then have caught him easily. Where did he come from? What message was he bearing? Perhaps in code. . . . For some time I have been able to think of nothing else.

Toward evening I went down in the direction of the valley, taking advantage of the fine weather. Went as far as the Dumonts'. Only three of the children came toward me; the one I was most attached to began work yesterday on a farm and I don't know when I shall see him again. The other brother, who sat beside me on the embankment, has his hair infested with nits.

I am writing this almost without seeing what I am writing, seated after dinner on the bench in front of the house. Such a restlessness throughout my whole body that I cannot read, or work, or sleep.

10 July

I nevertheless took it upon myself to practice the piano last night, and this morning, after a half-sleepless night, I don't feel so very bad. Wonderful weather. This morning: piano; helped Jean T. to study; then went out into the avenue to write a few lines on Greek mythology.

Little Jean T. answered considerably better and I think that everything bad in him can be reduced to an extraordinary lack of attention.

Every morning I wonder all over again at the sweetness of my starling, which, released the night before and having spent the night out, comes to wait for me on the lawn and flies up when I appear with his mush of egg and bread in a saucer. First he perches on my arm, then, after pecking once, flies up again; then I put the saucer in the cage, which he enters by himself in a moment. Then I carry him up to the aviary.

Better regime, better health, better work.

11 July

Almost sleepless night.

It has been extraordinarily hot. I have been able to do almost nothing but read *Wuthering Heights,* which I almost finished this evening.

12 July

I receive this morning, forwarded by Tronche, the issue of *L'Éclair* (22 June) in which Henri Massis thinks it necessary to sound the alarm about the *Caves.*

It has been of great help to me; for even if the accusations he directs against me are false, at least I must admit that I behaved in such a way as to provoke them.

After all, what Massis and the others reproach me with is having made a mistake in their first judgments of me.

In the judgment they formulate today they are making an even greater mistake and will be less inclined to forgive me it. I believe my books would have been judged quite differently if I had been able to publish them all at once, just as they grew up in my mind.

"Publish one's complete works all together for the first time" — I remember how this remark dazzled me when I read it in Flaubert's *Correspondance.* But that would not have been *natural.*

And how could I have agreed to reject the enlightenment I get from the reaction of my books on the public?

I write to Beaunier:

"Consequently I am calling out all my patience" (a letter from him, the day before yesterday, tells me that his article on the *Caves* which was to appear in the *Revue des deux mondes* for June will not be out until September); "you did well to write me, for already I was on the point of thinking: he is giving it up.

"But, if you will permit, I am going to take advantage of this delay to bring to your attention the preface I had written for the *Caves* and then deleted from the proofs.

"In it I told the reader that *Les Caves du Vatican* had been in my mind for more than fifteen years just as I had been big with *La Porte étroite* for more than fifteen years and scarcely less *L'Immoraliste,* the first to come out.

"All these subjects developed parallelly, concurrently — and if I wrote one book before another it is because the subject seemed to me more 'at hand' as the English say.[23] If I had been able to, I should have written them *together.* I could not have written *L'Immoraliste* if I had not known that I was one day to write also *La Porte étroite,* and I needed to have written both of them to be able to allow myself the *Caves.*

---

[23] The expression *at hand* appears in English.

"Just as I also need to have written the *Caves* in order to write . . . the rest.

"Why do I call this book a *Sotie* or satirical farce? Why *tales* the three preceding ones? In order to bring out quite clearly that they are not *novels*. And I ended my preface thus: Satirical farces or tales, I have up to now written nothing but *ironic* — or, if you prefer, critical — books — of which this is doubtless the last.

"Then I suppressed this preface, thinking that the reader had no concern with such confidences. But perhaps the critic . . . and that is why I am rewriting all this for you. But after all you are quite free not to pay any attention to it and you can go on as if you didn't know it if this upsets your article.

"Most sincerely yours. . . ."

Braffy, 13 July

This morning as early as six o'clock I was able to get my starling back into the cage, for he flew toward me as soon as he saw me coming.

It was cold and the whole landscape was covered with fog. This evening the sky is indescribably brilliant. I took a rather long walk with Jean Schlumberger in the woods.

Talked with him at length, after dinner, walking back and forth on the road between the entrance gate and the house. Too tired this evening to note down anything whatever.

14 July

The secret of almost all my weaknesses is that frightful modesty of which I cannot cure myself.

I can never persuade myself that I have a right to anything.

They took me for a rebel (Claudel and Jammes) because I was unable to get — or unwilling to force — myself to that cowardly submission which would have assured my comfort. That is perhaps the most Protestant trait I have in me: my horror of comfort.

Havre, 15 July

I took Jean Schlumberger to the nine-thirty boat that was to take him back to Trouville. I am returning to Cuverville by the eleven-o'clock train. We prowled endlessly last night, and as we were finally returning home at twelve thirty, I let Jean continue chasing and went on chasing on my own. He did not come in until half past two. I had been in bed for more than an hour.

Set in the middle of certain sordid little streets there were modest orchestras made up of an ophicleide and a cornet perched on a tem-

porary stage, and these provided the music for a few couples dancing
on the pavement. Hordes of very small children wandered around
among the harlots. On the square and all along the quay a fair,
shooting-stands, merry-go-rounds, etc. . . . In a sort of sentry-box
with a front panel of glass can be seen the bust of an "astrologer" who
tells fortunes. He is seated in profile in front of an enormous book in
Latin (I was unable to make out just what the book was — but only
that it was in Latin); he is wearing spectacles and looks exactly like
Léautaud. When someone comes to consult him (I didn't see anyone
but young girls going up to him), he raises to his mouth the end of a
loudspeaker, or rather a speaking-tube, which goes through a hole in
the glass and the other end of which the client puts to her ear. She
smiles almost in spite of herself and blushes a great deal; then, cling-
ing to the arm of a girl friend, runs away in a hurry and is lost in the
crowd.

In front of a sort of large square circus in which some "strong men"
are exhibiting themselves, a poor dwarf with an oily face is moaning.
Her eight-year-old son has not been home in two days. She describes
his appearance: "He was wearing a little red and green jersey. . . ."
"With yellow and blue," shouts a wag in the group surrounding her.
She protests, stamping on the ground: "No, sir, he wasn't wearing any
yellow! It's just a lie; he wasn't wearing any yellow." Most surely the
woman is drunk, but what she says is perhaps none the less true. I go
up to her: "And you have no idea where your child went?" "Why, yes,
sir; he is in there" (she points at the canvas tent). "He says he wants
to be a clown. Isn't that terrible? . . ." The crowd's jeers keep her
from finishing. Jean and I go into the tent, but we look in vain for a
child answering the mother's description.

In front of the terrace of the big Café Tortoni, as we were on our
way home, a miserable juggler was amusing the seated customers by
thrusting ever bigger and bigger objects into his mouth; first his lips
surrounded a goblet; he put it in head-first so that it made the sound
of an exhaust-valve when he took it out; then it was the bottom of a
bottle, which stretched hideously the whole lower part of his face;
around it his lip was reduced to a thin pink thread that seemed on the
point of breaking; it was so ugly, so painful-looking, that everyone
thought it deserved a reward, and his receipts were large.

16 July

Corrected my proofs for the Review; after all, not too disappointed
with that *Turkish Journey.* I hope anyway that it is insignificant enough
not to cause too much howling; I need a breathing-space.

Fine subject for a novel: the girl who is about to marry, against
her parents' will, someone whose past is subject to criticism. Little by

little she succeeds in getting them to accept her husband. But while the family is discovering more and more virtues in this husband, she begins to understand that she was wrong about him. Out of pride she hides her sorrows and mortifications and finds herself all the more alone because her family now takes her husband's side against her and because of her original cleverness in setting her husband off to advantage.[24]

K. arrived at nightfall.

17 July

Talked a little to K.; asked him if he was sure that he was not aiming beneath the target in getting ready to enter the École de Commerce.[25]

Wrote to Copeau, who is surprised that there is not more said about the *Caves:* "How could I be amazed that it doesn't ring a bell? I didn't push any button."

18

This morning the new issue of *Les Marges* reaches me. Not satisfied to strangle me in an ample article signed Le Cardonnel, it also quotes, in the section devoted to reviews, the most unkind passages from Massis's article and ridicules Souday's meager praises.

The two quotations that Le Cardonnel makes from the *Caves* are shot with obvious errors which make an amorphous thing of my text: "the vague stream of the town" for "the vague sound," etc.[26]

I try not to let myself be too much poisoned by such examples of meanness. I expect help and support solely from *the unknown.*

This evening, moreover, I feel well and strong enough — despite an entirely sleepless night following on a too long tennis game that I couldn't refuse to play with K. (the poor fellow has no distractions here) — and I convince myself that the situation created for me by these combined hatreds is unique and decidedly the one I should have longed for.

But no wincing!

I left my bird outside almost all day. He comes when I call; he rises from a bush, first flies around me, then goes off in the distance, and finally returns to perch on my shoulder or arm. He does not fly

---

[24] This is very close to the subject of André Gide's *École des femmes* (*The School for Wives*), which appeared originally in 1929.

[25] Business School.

[26] This error in copying has substituted *"le vague ruisseau"* for *"la vague rumeur."*

away when I walk, and I go for a walk with him in the garden. At about tea-time the cats noticed him on the grass and, if I hadn't rushed to him, it would have been all over with him. He let me take him back to the aviary without leaving my shoulder, where he had again perched.

19 July

This morning my poor starling let himself be torn to pieces by the cats. They threw themselves on that poor defenseless little thing that didn't know fear; I was at the piano, but suddenly I recognized his call. At the same moment Em., who saw the scene from the steps, ran to them with a little fish in the hope of making them let go. The bird had eventually escaped only to fall exhausted a little farther away. He was still stirring; I took him in my hand; I did not immediately lose all hope of reviving him, for at first nothing but an insignificant wound could be seen, or so it seemed to me; I tried to get him to drink a little water, but he couldn't swallow it and soon dropped back dead.[27]

20 July

The night before last I took it upon myself to talk to K. It was after dinner and we were walking side by side on the flower path. "Though I am quite willing to believe," I said to him, "that F. is following the right path for him by going to the École de Commerce, I am not equally sure in your case. I should like to be more assured (I kept repeating my words, painfully trying to finish my sentences), more assured that in a few years you won't suddenly become aware that you left the best parts of yourself unused." At that point he started suddenly. I thought he was going to protest, but, since he said nothing, I took his arm and went on: "I like F. very much and what I am about to say doesn't imply any scorn for him. But I have always felt that you had in you more gifts than he and that you were destined for something . . ." (I did not dare say: "better" — and on the contrary I added: "Oh! I'm not establishing any hierarchy here, but I know how easily you are . . ." And again I was seized with shyness and didn't dare say: "influenced") . . . "I mean: how easily you catch the tone of the group in which you happen to be. And I should like precisely to be more assured that it is not the influence of that milieu, of those friendships that is causing you now to head also toward . . ."

He did not let me finish, but protested that after studying the offerings he clearly understood that the Business School was what fitted

---

[27] The patience and "velvet paw" that the cat uses with earthbound animals, which I have often observed, is never in evidence when he is dealing with flying creatures that could get away from him. [Note supplied by the author in the French edition. Such notes will hereafter be indicated by an A. in brackets.]

him best and that, besides, I was wrong if I thought that its intellectual
or social level was inferior.

There was great assurance in the tone of his voice, in his manner.
And when he heard me speak of him as of an easily influenced nature,
I felt a movement of protest throughout his whole body; but he dominated it at once as if he were saying to himself: "What's the use of
trying to change his opinion of me? What need have I that he should
understand me? . . ." And suddenly I understood, I clearly felt on the
contrary his strength in resistance and revolt and that everything I was
saying about him was based on my recollection of his affectionate
childhood and that, since puberty, he had become another person.

(I had already observed with Gérard a similar transmutation.)

He seemed to say: "I can get along without your affection and approval; I'll make my way alone."

I am noting all this elsewhere, for it seemed to me that we were
acting out one of the chapters of my novel.

His father thought up the idea of sticking him in the science group
because the child's natural bent would have inclined him, it seemed,
toward the humanities — so that T. feared that he might succeed too
easily and get accustomed to putting forth very little effort. But, as
his father now recognizes, this did not give him a taste for the sciences
and yet it took away his taste for the humanities.

I didn't think it was possible to miss a bird so much. When I would
go out, I would look for him; even without seeing him, I would feel
him in the foliage. I used to like to feel that little winged thing on my
shoulder or see him flutter around me, then suddenly fly off toward a
very high branch and finally return.

Most certainly he used to recognize me, for he never showed the
same confidence toward others. And that very last morning I had tried
in vain to get him to light on Em.'s arm; he would let her approach,
but would fly away at the last moment seized with fear.

My bed has been set up in an upstairs room (the one Copeau occupied next to the linen-room), where I slept much better. I had great
need of this after these last few almost sleepless nights.

21 July

That odd habit I have always had of putting to work, to begin with
and by preference, the laziest parts of myself.

This morning I had to go and fetch Toby, who ran away yesterday
to the Dumonts', attracted by their bitch. He allowed himself to be
brought home without resisting; I didn't even have to attach his leash.

Miquette went along with me, like a legitimate wife going to get her
husband at a prostitute's. I should like to know whether or not bitches
are capable of jealousy. I doubt it. I fancy that, even among birds,
jealousy belongs only to the male.

Jean Schlumberger told me, in this connection, of the extraordinary
scene witnessed by Roger Martin du Gard and his wife. They are very
proud of the pigeons they are raising and keep a close eye on them.
This year the broods succeeded wonderfully; but the male pigeons
soon began to be jealous of the little ones; they pursued the females
and tried to keep them from approaching the nests. Then, one morning, changing tactics, they all at once hurled themselves on the little
ones, both male and female, and raped them with such brutality that
all the little ones, bashed in, died of it. Not one of them escaped.

No matter how unbelievable this may seem, it is sworn to be true,
and Martin du Gard is not a man to invent anything of this sort.

22 July

Bassermann, my translator, arrived by the six-o'clock train. Went
to meet him at Criquetot; frightful weather: sky so dark and overcast
that we had to light the lamp for dinner.

Bassermann is an enormous youth of twenty-four or twenty-five,
clean-shaven and with sharp features, but not as you look at him in
profile. He looks like a portrait by Lhote. He speaks French perfectly.

Too tired to write anything this evening.

23

Rather exhausting cycle from Bénouville to Étretat along the edge
of the sea with Bassermann, Marcel, and K. I fear that I shan't close
my eyes all night long, especially after the rather brilliant conversation
this evening.

Offranville, 25 July

I stupidly left at Cuverville, in the excitement of leaving, the little
notebook just like this one, only four days old, but in which I had
written last night, or this very morning, some rather somber reflections
about K. Will the fate we associate with fiction arrange it so that he
reads them? I am almost inclined to wish so, if only this would lead to
some protest, some salutary reaction on his part.[28]

But since I don't want to help fate too much, I write to Em. to get
hold of the notebook and send it to me at J.-É. Blanche's.

I am writing these lines in the train taking me to Offranville,
whence I plan to set out tomorrow for London.

---

[28] In *Les Faux-Monnayeurs* the novelist Édouard arranges to warn his
nephew Georges by leaving some notes for him to read.

I had hardly arrived at the Blanches' when a fire started in the nearest farm building; it was only a big old shed, fortunately with no harvest in it; the whole thing went up in flames, thatched roof, beams, and stud-work. A huge pile of logs joined this building to another, which serves as a garage for the auto and lodging for the chauffeur. We began by moving everything in great haste, for the wind was blowing the flames in that direction and the logs were so vulnerable that we wondered whether or not we could get them out of the way quickly enough. Happily the wind changed direction, thus helping the inadequate work of the pumps.

Since Austria's ultimatum to Serbia, which yesterday morning's papers published, everyone is so nervous that when they heard the fire-alarm many people took it for the call to arms.

This morning the refusal of the delay requested by Russia increases the general nervousness; this is the only subject of conversation and J.-É. Blanche has given way to the blackest misgivings. We read aloud the leading article of *L'Écho de Paris*, then the leader in Clemenceau's paper, *L'Homme libre*, in the drawing-room, where Mme Blanche and her two sisters have gathered this evening. I sat down at the piano to change our train of thoughts and played a few compositions, or parts of compositions, by Albéniz, reading the music — then by heart the first part of Chopin's Sonata in B minor, the first Ballade, the B-minor Scherzo, the first Prelude, and the one in E-flat major. All this horribly played, except for the first Prelude.

I felt as if someone else's hands were attached to the ends of my arms; nevertheless I forced myself to play; I wonder at having been able to finish the Ballade. I should have liked J.-É. Blanche to hear it at Cuverville on certain days when I play it *properly*. Nothing is farther from what I achieved this evening. I was sweating over it.

The ladies, however, had the kindness to declare themselves "charmed."

27 July

A certain easing of the strain this morning. People are relieved and at the same time disappointed to hear that Serbia is giving in. The wind has fallen too; a thick fine rain has followed the squall; I should leave, but J.-É. Blanche suggests going this afternoon to see Walter Sickert and J. T. R., whom he described to me rather curiously yesterday. We spent long hours yesterday reading and patching up his manuscript. This morning I completely rewrote three pages of it, changing hardly anything, moreover, except the word-order and arrangement of the sentences, which were tied together any which way. The extraordinary weaknesses of his style enlighten me as to those of his

painting: he never embraces his object; his good points always spring
from *impatience:* he is easily satisfied. As soon as he has made four
slight changes on a page as he copied it, he thinks he has "worked over
it considerably," and since he paints even more easily than he writes,
he is amazed not to get ahead faster. He asks me: "When you were
writing *La Porte étroite,* did you make many corrections?"

Three titled and rich ladies came this afternoon; one of them
(Countess de C.?) I liked; great traveler with a free and easy manner
. . . but it was the other one who especially talked with me, embark-
ing on the subject of *La Porte étroite,* which she had "read almost ten
years ago, but which was an event in her life." [29] She leads me to a
corner where we are alone and at each compliment she pays me, I feel
like sticking out my tongue at her or shouting: Shit! "You so delicately
depicted spiritual solitude. It's an entirely different thing from *Mensonges* or *La Dame devant le miroir;* [30] you have discovered a new
psychological law that no one had ever stated before. The wall! Monsieur! The horrible wall! And we ourselves built it. . . ."

I: "And without windows! Madame, without windows!"

SHE: "No possibility of communication. When you sense it between
two others you would like to knock it down."

I: "But the others would be angry at you for doing so," etc. . . .

And it goes on and on. . . . It was time to write the *Caves.*

28 July

The auto took me to Dieppe, where I expected to get on board at
noon. Already I had sent a telegram to Valery Larbaud announcing
my arrival at Newhaven in the thought that he could come from Hastings to meet me. A half-hour later I sent him another telegram saying
that I was delaying my departure. Meanwhile we had gone to the
newspaper office, where the latest developments are posted (Mme
Blanche and her sister came to Dieppe with me), and had met Xavier
Léon, who puts the finishing touch on our anxiety. Impossible to go
away with this terrible worry. I shall probably return to Cuverville
tomorrow. My bags were already on the quay beside the steamer; they
were loaded back on the auto. Mme Blanche went to get a little money
at the Dieppe branch of the Crédit Lyonnais. Xavier Léon plans to
return to Paris tomorrow. The hotel busses are loaded with the trunks
of departing guests. Everyone expects the worst.

---

[29] The tale had first been published five years before, in 1909.

[30] *Mensonges* (*Lies*), short stories by Paul Bourget, had first appeared
in 1897; the other title is doubtless an error for *La Danse devant le miroir*
(*The Dance before the Mirror*), a psychological play by François de Curel,
first presented in January 1914.

Yesterday, from rising to bedtime, we talked of nothing else. One cannot get one's mind off *it*. In addition to the papers, Mme Mühlfeld's telephone calls twice a day keep us informed. "The situation couldn't be more serious," she said at about eight o'clock (out of consideration for the Blanches, the postmistress kept the line open). Although she didn't want to name anyone, it seemed that she must have had her information directly from Philippe Berthelot, whose role at the Ministry of Foreign Affairs, during the absence of the ministers, is most important. Moreover, Poincaré and Viviani are returning today. I read with the greatest satisfaction Barrès's letter calling for a general rallying of strength. Despite everything there is some comfort in seeing private interests, dissensions, and discords disappear before the common danger; in France emulation quickly becomes a sort of fury urging every citizen to heroic self-sacrifice.

I suffered somewhat yesterday at not having a chance to talk with anyone but Jews: the Xavier Léons, Mme Langweil, Stern. They think themselves obliged (with the exception of Stern) to go everyone else one better in a chauvinism that doesn't always strike me as quite genuine: "Wasn't Bernstein wonderful!" exclaimed Mme Xavier Léon; "we read his testimony through three times aloud." As for Mme Langweil, she announces that her son-in-law, "if the storm breaks, will come from Florence to Paris immediately to volunteer" — and this seems rather difficult to us since he is an Italian subject. . . . Moreover, I enjoyed the conversation I had with Xavier Léon, whom I had met only the day before and whom I liked very much. Quite surprised to discover that he is only a year older than I; he already looks like an old man. He told me of his desire, in case of war, to organize an information service to correspond with families and keep them informed about the wounded. This would have the advantage of utilizing those who were rejected for military service. I gave him my address, asking him to call upon me as soon as he needed me.

And, all morning long, I imagined myself having to announce to Juliette the death of her son. Into what horrors shall we soon have to plunge!

Yet the approach of the tragic in whatever domain galvanizes me. Poor Blanche, on the other hand, confesses to me that the news undoes him and that, during the morning, he had to go "to the end of the corridor" five times. He has what he calls the jitters. He claims that, to avoid it, one would have to be blind; then he tirelessly exaggerates the innumerable and nameless calamities he sees lying in wait for him.

And besides, for over two years already he has felt the storm approaching and has refused to invest whatever his portraits bring in. Lazare Weiler told him: "Monsieur Blanche, do you want a piece of

advice? — don't buy anything. Keep your money. Stocks, founders'
shares, even bonds . . . in a little while they will all be nothing but
paper; take my word for it." (The result is that in Paris and London
and Brussels he now holds rather considerable liquid assets, which he
is going to try to bring home, at least in part.)

He is very much concerned to know where he should live in case
of war. At Offranville he fears isolation, but in Paris he fears riots;
Lépine warned him one day: "If the bourgeois only knew how badly
equipped we are to defend them in case of an uprising, they wouldn't
sleep calmly a single night!" Etc. . . .

30 July

What is the value of the notes I have taken down the last few days?
I don't know. If I begin to reread myself, I am lost. I shall want to
make corrections, and if there are many changes to make, I shall drop
this notebook right there. The best thing is to keep on, then.

Back at Cuverville since yesterday. Arrived by the same train as
Valentine and the two little girls. Toward evening a telegram from K.
tells us that he was flunked in the oral, which means that his written
examination was barely satisfactory. T. does not even try to hide his
resentment. (But of all those who surround a child, the parents are the
most blind.)

In face of the impossibility of remedying this now (whereas a little
earlier it would have been much easier), T.'s irritation only increases.
He is likewise obliged to recognize that he was not very well inspired
when he put K. into the science group; but no one mentions this.

The long conversation I manage to have with him after dinner concerns the plans to be made for next year. I know that he doesn't approve of my idea of sending K. to England next year, and I grant him
that I should approve any other project that would take K. out of his
lamentable environment. He thinks it would be enough to put him
into another school. I am not sure of it.

The papers have no very sensational news this morning. Georges,
who has just got back from Havre, tells us of the endless queues and
the policemen to keep order outside the banks, where everyone has
gone to get money. In the restaurants, before serving, the waiters warn
the customers that banknotes will not be accepted.

31 July

We are getting ready to enter a long tunnel full of blood and
darkness. . . .

In reply to a letter from Copeau I telegraph to Le Limon that we
are expecting his wife and children at Cuverville. Georges has received orders for the requisition of wagons and horses. Only three are

listed for the commune and two of them have broken their knees since the last census; the third belongs to K., whose four sons are to be taken and who protests: "And what do you expect me to do my work with, with my sons already gone? Listen, M'sieur Gille [sic], I don't mind them taking my horse, but they'll have to pay me for it." On the other hand, in the afternoon Georges receives a visit from Y. who, blushing and stammering, has come to confess that his situation is illegal; his horse should have been declared, but at the time of the last census "it wasn't quite old enough." Georges makes him read the decree mentioning the fine of from 250 to 1,000 francs that he will incur, and this puts the finishing touch on the poor fellow's anguish. The fact that he has two sons in the service will be taken into account, I fancy; but his horse will probably be taken anyway, without making him pay the fine.

The savings-banks refuse to give more than fifty francs at a time, and the regular banks release only a portion of the sum requested.

We are expecting J. and K. this evening.

It is very threatening weather; a gray film floats between sky and earth. The day before yesterday was divinely fair; one of those skies under which you can only imagine happiness.

Good conversations with T. With him I still am full of embarrassment and fear, but it seemed to me that I irritated him somewhat less.

In the conversation he has with K. this evening, T. is much too concerned to keep his son's friendship. He talks to him not as a father but as a comrade. This comes partly from his need of convincing himself that he is still young, younger than he appears. . . .

I answered rather brutally yesterday when Em. interrupted me in my reading; this grieved me all evening long.

I have had a heavy heart for the last few days, and especially this evening.

1 August

J. returned yesterday evening with K., more happy-go-lucky, more a creature of whims, more thoughtless than ever. I like her this way, and her illogical remarks enliven every meal with delight. Just when everyone else is gathering together the little money that he can, she buys a rather expensive dinner service that no one needs at the moment.

If L. does not send us the money I am asking for, I shall have to leave Cuverville with an absurdly insufficient sum in our drawer. Cuverville is the only house to which the poor of the district, from several miles around, will come to be fed; at least eight women and eight children will be there and the only men Mius and K., after T. and I have left.

A day of painful waiting. Why don't we mobilize? Every moment we delay is that much more advantage for Germany. Perhaps we owe it to the Socialist Party to let ourselves be attacked. This morning's paper tells about the absurd assassination of Jaurès.

Under pretense of gathering some apricots, I went to talk with Mius. I spoke of my departure and of my worry at having to leave so many women and children here almost without protection. He then told me of his intention not to leave the house in September.

"No, no, I'll not go away like that; you needn't worry, sir. I'll pay the three hundred francs' penalty if need be. But I'll not go away." He says this in the same grumbling, obstinate tone in which he used to say that he didn't want to do the buying at the market. But we both had tears in our eyes as we shook hands.

At about three o'clock the alarm-bell began to toll. Nevertheless J. insisted at first, in order not to miss a chance to contradict, that it was tolling for a funeral as it had been all morning. I ran to find Mius in the garden and to warn him; and as I returned, having met no one but Edmond, I saw Em. on the flower path, who, with drawn features, said to us, barely restraining her sobs: "Yes, it's the alarm; Hérouard has just come from Criquetot; the order to mobilize has been posted."

The children had set out for Étretat by bicycle. Feeling a need to keep busy, I wanted to go to Criquetot to mail two letters and to get the registered envelope that I knew had arrived. The bell was silent now; after the great alarm throughout the whole countryside, there was nothing but an oppressive silence. A fine rain was falling intermittently.

In the fields a few fellows all ready to leave were going on with their plowing; on the road I met our farmer, Louis Freger, called up on the third day, and his mother, who is going to see her two children go away. I was unable to do anything but shake their hands without a word.

At Criquetot people are gathered in front of the notice that has just been posted. Someone is heard to say: "It appears that this time they will ask us for thirty million."

"We are just beginning the season of false rumors," I shouted.

"I read that in *Le Matin*," the fellow retorted.

At the post office I go in for a chat with the postmistress, who has just lost her father. The envelope she gives me contains but a part of the sum I had asked for; L. (at least one of his clerks) has enclosed a letter apologizing for not being able to send more.

On the way back I meet no one. Anticipating the mobilization, the baker's, shoemaker's, and saddler's apprentices were already sent off today at five o'clock. In the place of my heart I feel nothing but a wet rag in my breast; the thought of the war stands like a frightful rod between my eyes, and all my thoughts stumble against it.

In the evening after dinner, during which we were unable to speak of anything else, K. comes to smoke a cigarette with T. and me in the office. I tell him that in a few days his father and I are going to have to go, leaving him the only man in the house with his mother, his aunts, and the younger children; and I speak to him of his role in the house in case of a possible attack — not so much from the enemy as from brigands come from the towns to ravage the countryside.

This child, whom but a short while ago we feared to be indifferent to events, listens attentively to me. His handsome face is in the shadow; he is hiding in his left hand the rolled-up handkerchief with which he occasionally mops his cheeks.

2 August

I am writing in the train carrying me to Paris, the last one, it is said, to be left open to civilians. I was tormented at the thought of being cut off at Cuverville. . . . T. is with me.

In Paris we shall make out somehow and shall look for something to do. Before leaving Em. this morning, I knelt down beside her (something I hadn't done since . . .) and asked her to recite the Lord's Prayer. I did this for her sake and my pride yielded to love without difficulty; moreover, my whole heart participated in her prayer.

K. was indeed very moved to see us leave. Mius accompanied us; he wanted to go get news of his daughter at Yvetot. I had his ticket, which I stupidly let the collector take at the entrance, for they are not admitting third-class travelers for local stops.

Crowd on the platform, both serious and vibrant. A workman shouts as he goes by: "All aboard for Berlin! And what fun we'll have there!" People smiled but did not applaud.

In Paris only an hour late. Our train was filled to overflowing. We lost time letting all the others get out ahead of us so that it was impossible for us to find an auto or even a mere carriage. But the suburban line took us to Passy; from there an auto took us to rue Decamps. I left my bag at Uncle Charles's and started out again almost at once. My uncle struck me as having aged very much; his clothes were worn thin and his gaiters split; he looked like Marmeladov.[31] How I like him this way!

---

[31] Marmeladov is a disreputable retired functionary in tatters whom Raskolnikov meets in a bar at the beginning of Dostoyevsky's *Crime and Punishment*.

When I left him I hurried to rue du Dragon. Poor Copeau must have got under way too late and now he is going mad with the responsibility of his mother, mother-in-law, wife, and children. How tormenting not to know where to find him in order to help him! He left no word with the concierge. . . . I hurry to the office of the Review; fortunately Tronche is still there, for he is not called up until tomorrow. He is with Mme Suarès and a young man whom I must have met once somewhere or other. All are leaving or have already left. . . . The air is full of a loathsome anguish. Fantastic appearance of Paris, its streets empty of vehicles and full of strange people, calm but hypertense also; some are waiting with their trunks on the sidewalk; a few noisy fellows at the entrance to cafés are bawling the *Marseillaise*. Occasionally an auto loaded down with luggage passes at great speed.

Agnès Copeau, the three children, the mother-in-law, and the governess must have left for Cuverville. I am tormented by the thought of them.

3 August

I had to get back to rue Decamps on foot last night; stopped at Arthur Fontaine's, but he was not there. The métro is still running, but with a warning that no connections are guaranteed, so that I get out at the Gare Montparnasse. The whole appearance of Paris has changed so much that I get mixed up and lose my way behind the École Militaire. I get home exhausted. Cannot close my eyes all night long; I *sense* that everyone is awake; every ten minutes an auto dashes through the rue Decamps at high speed and honks at the corner.

Saw Gérard this morning; he is leaving tomorrow for Évreux, then for Châlons. Pierre Espinas is going to try to reach Les Sources in the auto he would like to leave there for my aunt's use. Together they drive me to the rue du Dragon, where I find Copeau still in bed. Yesterday he took his whole family to the Gare Saint-Lazare. I am impatient to know whether they got as far as Cuverville. Why did he get under way so late? Just one more who thinks that "things are going to be fixed up"! . . .

Copeau and I go to the office of the Review. On the way we encounter Jouvet, whom we take along with us. Conversation with Tronche, whom we are to meet here again at five o'clock to divide up what remains in the safe, according to each one's needs.

Then Copeau and I set out to find Arthur Fontaine, who was not at avenue de Saxe, not at the Ministry of Public Works, not at rue de Varenne. We get lost and go much farther than necessary. At last I leave Copeau to try to find Jean Schlumberger at the Red Cross, where I have been told that he heads a section. The head office is at 21 rue

François Ier. Extraordinary activity; ladies of all social classes, but chiefly of the highest, are noting down the offers of volunteers. I do not find Jean Schlumberger, but am seized by Sert and Mme Edwards, who, here as everywhere else, immediately takes an important part. On her own authority, backed by the insigne of the Red Cross, she has gone from hotel to hotel in her auto to requisition a large number of sheets and towels, which she is now bringing to the organization. She is bringing something even better: a whole hotel, the Hôtel du Rhin, which, yielding even more to the fear of being sacked because of its name than to a burst of generosity, has turned over to the Red Cross all its rooms, bedding, linen, etc. It is said that another hotel, still larger (the Ritz, I believe), will do the same. It is merely a matter of getting the Ministry of War to approve.

If I do not find any possibility through Arthur Fontaine, I shall sign up with the Red Cross, where Ghéon has already offered himself as a doctor.

Meanwhile I let myself be taken by Mme Edwards to the dispensary, where Sert and I unload the four heavy bundles of sheets. Then to the Foreign Office, where we talk first to Philippe Berthelot and then to someone else more specifically concerned with such things. Most likely the Red Cross flag will fly tonight over the Hôtel du Rhin.

I lunch at Mme Edwards's on soft-boiled eggs and a slice of pressed beef. Then go to Copeau's to take a nap, in order not to give in too rapidly.

On returning to the rue du Dragon, I witness the sacking of a Maggi dairy store. I get there a bit late; the shop is already empty; two big fellows, with a sort of tacit approval on the part of the police, are just finishing breaking the shop windows with a kind of wooden rake. One of them has climbed onto the show-case; he is holding up a big, brown, earthenware coffee-pot, which he exhibits to the crowd and then throws onto the sidewalk, where it crashes noisily. There is much applause.

This morning some guttersnipes took advantage of the lack of police to take apart a little automatic scale and rob it of its deposit of coppers.

We are almost without news. This, however, which seems monstrous, astounding, unbelievable: Herr von Schoen is still in Paris! [32]

4 August

Herr von Schoen has left. Yesterday he announced his decision.

"Very well, sir," Viviani said to him (Marcel, who reported this yesterday, has it from Dumas, the professor, who himself had got it

---

[32] Von Schoen was the German Ambassador.

from a high-placed person). "Very well, sir. A special car will be put at your disposal."

"But — I must tell you —" replied von Schoen, "there are ninety of us."

Copeau meets Werth on the sidewalk. . . .

"I've just arrived by chance. But what do I hear! It's barbarism! The Middle Ages. What is the good of all we have done!"

Péguy said to Paul Laurens: "Some people are extraordinary. They are surprised not to find people and things in their usual places. They fancy they can superimpose a state of war on a state of peace; and then they are amazed that the two don't coincide, that all the flaps don't fit into all the little slots."

While I am writing this (at rue Decamps, where I spent the night), Gérard is packing up; he leaves in an hour (it is now seven a.m.). Yesterday we saw off Tronche, who was wonderfully vibrant and martial. With what emotion we embraced him! — first at the Review, where Copeau, Ghéon, Mme Lemarié, Mme Gallimard, and I were. André Salmon, who is going to sign up in some service or other, came along too (he is charming, but so frail in appearance!) and Tronche's friend, who was already with him yesterday. Copeau, Ghéon, and I went to see Laurens; then we met Tronche again opposite the Gare Montparnasse, where we said farewell.

Then went to dine at the Café de Flore, where Suzanne Bing, Marcel, and Jean Schlumberger came to join us.

After dinner Ghéon goes back to Copeau's and, since Marcel has his bicycle, I return home alone on foot, in the rain, with plenty of leisure to meditate on the events of the day.

The enthusiasm, calm, and determination of the mass of the people are wonderful. If England goes along with us, the chances are definitely on our side, but will England go along with us? Parliament has proposed a vote of more than a billion in military subsidies.

5 August

Yesterday, invasion of Belgium. Schoen has left.

Spent the morning in Auteuil. Met Pierre de Lanux as I was leaving my uncle's. He informs me of his engagement. He goes with me to rue du Ranelagh, where I invite myself to lunch. At the Allégrets', where they are fourteen, their supplies are low; with André Allégret I go to the villa, where we break the pantry lock and put into a napkin and a net bag all the macaroni, rice, noodles, sugar, vermicelli, etc., that we can carry. Plus a bottle of punch that I am going to take to André Ruyters. All the rest we take to the Allégrets'.

By a miracle, poor old Catherine is there; she almost bursts into tears on seeing me and tells me that her eldest son has been sent to the Belgian frontier. I give her some sugar and macaroni, but at the last moment forget to leave her some money. I shall have to return and make up for that today.

Lunch with Marcel and Ghéon at Ruyters's.

We stop by my uncle's to pick up my bag; Ghéon and I are with an unknown man who permits us to share the auto he has just stopped. We check my bag at the Red Cross dispensary, where we find Mme Edwards. I let Ghéon go on the boulevards and go to leave my bag at Jean Schlumberger's.

Dinner with Copeau at the Café de Flore.

He is somewhat annoyed with his day. Having entered the Invalides at nine a.m., he did not get any instructions until the morning was almost over. And what instructions! He was given two francs fifty for his day and then told to go and get lunch. In the afternoon he found himself in a large room with a few human outcasts and nothing to do. . . .

But things will improve. For the moment every effort is bent toward the east, and the supplying of Paris consequently suffers somewhat. Food supplies have arrived by rail, all right, but there is no way of transporting them to the Central Markets since all the trucks have been requisitioned.

The understanding, order, calm, and determination of all is really remarkable.

After dinner, call on Blum.

I am ashamed to note down so dryly my use of these throbbing hours overflowing with life, but a bad night has left me with a heavy mind; these notes will interest me later on and will serve as landmarks.

Spent the morning looking for the cleaning-woman, rue du Cherche-Midi. Then spent a quarter of an hour at the *Mercure*, where they are rising to the occasion as best they can, but how old, faded, skeptical, and drab everything seems there to anyone coming from the *N.R.F.*!

5 August

Germany declares war on Belgium, and England on Germany.

6 August

The idea of a possible collapse of Germany gains strength little by little; one struggles against it, but one does not convince oneself that it is impossible. The wonderful behavior of the government, of everyone, and of all France, as well as of all the neighboring nations, leaves room for every hope.

One foresees the beginning of a new era: the United States of Europe bound by a treaty limiting their armaments; Germany subjugated or dissolved; Trieste given back to the Italians, Schleswig to Denmark; and especially Alsace to France. Everyone talks of this remaking of the map as of the forthcoming issue of a serial.

7 August

Went yesterday morning to the Théos'; lunched in a *bistro* near the rue François Ier, where I worked all afternoon making out lists of stretcher-bearers.

Dinner at Arthur Fontaine's with Copeau.

This morning at the Red Cross. I have a sore throat and a headache.

Went to rue Laugier, where I hope to rest. No one there. Went away again in the driving rain.

Went home to take an *antigrippine* tablet, absolutely done in and ready for the ash-can. It is better to write nothing.

No news from Cuverville.

I made myself some tea and snoozed for an hour. Altogether revived, I slowly go back through the Luxembourg to the corner where I hope to find Copeau.

Several gates to the garden are closed. Children are playing. A group of little girls are following and hooting at a poor creature whose features are worn as if he had been dipped in boiling water or vitriol. He is wearing short trousers; from the back he looks like a twelve-year-old schoolboy, but seen from the front he is forty years old. The children run up and touch him, laugh and shout: "How old are you?" He smiles without answering.

My indignant scolding breaks up the group.

Yesterday, on the way to Fontaine's, I saw two urchins under twelve given rough treatment. "Stop them! Stop them!" a workman shouted. A passer-by knocked down the elder one with a resounding slap. The little one, terrified, went on running with all his might. . . . He was brought back to the other one, whose cheek was red and already swollen.

He was protesting wildly and in cowardly fashion:

"I didn't do anything. It was the other fellow."

"I have been watching them for a quarter of an hour," the workman said.

"But what did they do?"

"They broke the glass on a fire-alarm and tried to steal the handle."

Around them, a compact gathering. The two children don't look at all like *apaches;* most likely the children of shopkeepers; they are puny. I watch the little one tremble. There is no one in the crowd who is

not definitely *against them*. Besides, I feel too that they should be
taken to the police station and given a scare.

Copeau comes toward me as I am crossing the boulevard Saint-
Germain. He holds out to me an excellent letter from his wife that he
has just received. At last!

I go with him as far as the Opéra. Almost in a whisper he tells me
what he believes to have from a rather reliable source: "The French
are said to have entered Mulhouse. . . ."

Yet Liége is still holding out.

Walk on the boulevard after dinner. Encounter Valery Larbaud.
On each traffic-island a little bouquet of cops keeping an eye on the
purged sidewalks.

8 August

Ghéon is leaving tomorrow for Nouvion-en-Thiérache.

Day spent at the Red Cross, like the day before, registering those
who come to volunteer and classifying the cards.

Lunch at the Théos' with Marcel Drouin and the Schlumbergers.

9 August

Battle of Altkirch.

The French enter Mulhouse.

Obstinate resistance of Liége.

The Germans withdraw.

Monday, 10 August

This morning, at last, a long, exquisite, and comforting letter from
Em. Everything seems to be going all right at Cuverville.

Édouard put in an appearance the Sunday before last, before joining up.

"For forty-four years now they have seen nothing but our rear.
Now we are going to show them our face and they will remember it!"

The evening of the 8th, dinner with Valery Larbaud, then evening
at Suarès's where we find Copeau and Pierre de Lanux.

As Larbaud and I were going up the rue de Rennes, we are ac-
costed in the darkness by a tall woman wearing an old, brownish
traveling-cloak and carrying under her arm a bundle wrapped in newspaper. Her face was covered with a veil. Her voice, like her whole
body, trembled. She said to us: "*Sprechen Sie Deutsch?*" and when I
replied: "*Ein wenig,*" she told us, without tears but in a desperate tone
of voice, that she hadn't eaten in two days, that they would not let

her return to her hotel, where she hadn't been able to pay for her room, and that she had been wandering in the streets since morning, dead tired.

We told her first that she had only to go to the police station.

"I already went there this morning," she replied in German; "I couldn't register."

"Come back there with us."

She protested that she was too tired; we saw that what she wanted was a little money that would allow her to spend one more night in her room. She lived rue du Dragon, almost opposite Copeau's apartment. We accompanied her that far and went in to make arrangements with the hotel proprietor. She owed only five francs, which we paid; and since she was paying by the week, she could have stayed on Monday; but we urged her to go and hand herself over tomorrow. She was a seamstress, who had been in this place for three months and seemed quite respectable. . . .

We have great fun, at Suarès's, over the German bluffs: stopped by one of the Liége forts and giving up hope of overcoming it, they wrote a note to the military governor couched in about these terms: "If you refuse to surrender, we shall be obliged most reluctantly to send against you one of our zeppelins, which will drop picric acid on you." That must be said with the tone of Père Ubu.[33]

Yesterday evening I was returning to Auteuil after my duty at the Red Cross; I was about to stop at Uncle Charles Gide's. An auto in front of the door: it was Jeanne Espinas, who had just arrived with her three children and the maid. Having left Boulogne at six a.m., she had traveled without mishap; she had merely had to get out as they were crossing a bridge.

I had lunched with Ghéon and Copeau; Ghéon was leaving soon after for Nouvion. Dullin came for a moment to the Café de Flore, where we were. He has just arrived from Spain, where, he tells us, the wildest rumors, originating in dispatches from Berlin, are circulating: "Poincaré assassinated. Paris in the hands of the insurrection. France invaded by the German army." It wasn't until he had crossed the frontier that he realized the truth.

Jeanne Espinas, during her whole trip in the auto, was struck by the "gala" appearance of the country.

[33] The hero of Alfred Jarry's coarse farce *King Ubu*, which was first played in 1896, is a boastful grotesque of the conqueror and ruler.

Visit to the Allégrets, and to Gilbert, the pharmacist (I was worried whether he had enough money).

Dinner at the Ruyterses' with the Schlumbergers. André Ruyters, in a ferocious mood, declares himself ready to kill anything German he meets, women and children as well as soldiers. Before dinner he told me that my conversation the first day had shocked him considerably, for he can't understand how anyone can talk of anything but the war. This made me most uncomfortable and I immediately ceased to be natural in his presence. I was aware that he was judging everything I said, and consequently I couldn't say anything sensible.

We are told this evening at the Red Cross (where I worked all day) that it has been decided not to accept any ambulance men or male stretcher-bearers — so that everything that has been done during the past week is useless.

11 August

The papers announce in veiled terms the French withdrawal at Mulhouse. The day before yesterday it seemed that Mulhouse had been reconquered; it was merely a bold and limited advance, which will doubtless cost the life of many a family in the town.

This evening the papers explain this withdrawal; there seems to be nothing alarming about it. But there are hints about a forthcoming battle that will be formidable.

Spent the whole day at the Red Cross, except for an hour spent at Ruyters', since he is leaving for Évreux at noon.

Lunched at the Théos'.

Too tired this evening to note anything interesting.

We are living in expectation.

12, 13, 14

Seen nothing, done nothing, heard nothing. One buys eight papers a day. First *Le Matin* and *L'Écho* — then *Le Figaro* for Ghéon, who telegraphed for it to be sent to him at Nouvion; then the *Daily Mail;* then *Paris-Midi;* then *L'Information,* the evening *Matin, La Liberté,* and *Le Temps* — and although each sheet repeats the preceding one in the same terms, one rereads the least bit of news, constantly hoping to know a bit more.

Spent the evening before last with Élie Allégret after having dinner with Marcel. This good Élie, to whom I had expressed my desire to find something to do, has found a place for me: I am going to be commissioned by the Mairie of the XVIth Arrondissement to register all the boys between twelve and eighteen who come and to think up ways of keeping them busy . . . ! I told him that I didn't think I was quite the right man for the job.

In the meantime I am continuing my work at the Red Cross — but there is so little to do that, since yesterday, I am going there only in the morning.

Jean Schlumberger and I have left the rue d'Assas for the rue Laugier, where the Théos are putting us up with the most charming hospitality. I arrived as fatigued as if I had come from the front; this is also why I hadn't written anything in this notebook for several days.

14 August

Twelfth day since the mobilization.

The terrible battle that has been announced and expected for the last week has not yet taken place.

"I believe that my heart will not be strong enough for the great joy or the great trial," Em. writes me.

I reproach myself for every thought that is unrelated to this anguished waiting; but nothing is less natural to me than anything that upsets my intellectual equilibrium. Were it not for *opinion*, I feel that even under the enemy five I should enjoy an ode of Horace. Ruyters is misled by this and was shocked because the other evening, at our first meeting since the war, I was able to talk of *something else* and to take with me as I left a package of clippings I had noticed on the table. Was it not much more significant that I picked up the package so absentmindedly that I carried away with it a group of letters addressed to Ruyters, as I noticed only much later? In the same way I shocked Ghéon by reading *Wuthering Heights* as our ship was approaching the Piræus.

I did not go this afternoon, any more than yesterday afternoon, to the Red Cross, where I merely make a pretense of being useful. There is no instance in which privilege takes on an uglier taste. But hypocrisy is even uglier, and the deceit is absurd that one is tempted to practice on oneself for fear of falling behind the others.

The weather is wonderful; the sky is full of an excess of warmth and beauty. The nights are calm and one feels like saying: pacific. One thinks of the camps, of sleep in the open, and of all those for whom this beautiful night is the last.

15 August

Now a new rubber stamp is being created, a new conventional psychology of the patriot, without which it is impossible to be respectable. The tone used by the journalists to speak of Germany is nauseating. They are all getting on the band-wagon. Each one is afraid of being late, of seeming a less "good Frenchman" than the others.

Théo went this morning to see Mme Griffith, who was caught by the events in Weimar, where she had gone to see her children; she has just got back to Paris after a most exciting twelve-day trip. Théo finds her still in bed and gets from her an amazing story. No one she saw in Germany would believe in war, and since the railways were cluttered with soldiers, everyone spoke of "army maneuvers." As she was approaching the Alsatian border, she saw regiments of Bosnians. In general (she insists) the privates, almost all the privates, were weeping; the officers and non-commissioned officers were strutting.

She was going to Cologne, but when she reached Frankfurt, seeing that the situation was getting worse, she cut off toward Metz with the idea of reaching Paris.

At Metz she was told that she could go no farther and she was headed off toward Basel, then toward Geneva — after several false starts. At Basel she sought out the British consul at once, who received her very badly and refused summarily to see some other English-women who were traveling with her. It appeared to her quite clear that this consul, a representative of England, must be a German. "Use-less to try to reach Paris," she was told. "You will never get there. Paris is in the midst of a revolution" (is "on fire," others said). "Just return to Germany; that is where you will be best off." She did not meet anybody in Switzerland who did not believe in these false reports. The Swiss papers, she says, in an effort at impartiality are satisfied to pub-lish, opposite the reports from the Wolff agency, those of the Havas service, thus leaving the public free to choose and to believe the most likely news: an insurrection in Paris or all France marching like a single man. You can well imagine that people are not going to believe the latter — any more than the resistance of Liége and the confusion of that army which we have so long been accustomed to look upon as formidable, invincible, etc.

It was only after she got into France that she became aware of the truth. In the Dijon station she saw some closed, stationary railway cars; unarmed soldiers were sitting on the steps. She had been told so much about a conquered France that she was surprised not to find these soldiers in German uniform. "The German soldiers are inside," she was told. They were cars filled with prisoners.

As soon as she got back to Paris, she went to the British Embassy to complain of the attitude of British consuls in Switzerland: every-thing seems to indicate that they are interested only in playing Ger-many's game. What she related seemed so serious and so important that the secretary who received her asked her to please make out a report; she did this as soon as she got home.

Dullin, who has just returned from Spain, relates exactly the same thing. It was only after he had crossed the border that he allowed him-self to be convinced that perhaps Poincaré had not been assassinated and that perhaps the Louvre was not on fire. . . .

Théo and I went to get foreign newspapers on the boulevards. During the past two days Belgian papers have been coming in again. But not a single Swiss newspaper has crossed the border since the declaration of war; and this explains in return why Switzerland has no news except what Germany pours into it.

Again spent my morning at the Red Cross doing nothing but discouraging those who offer their services. It is probably my last session there. Nothing is so silly as this work that I now know can lead to nothing. The hospitals are well organized and refuse the teams we offer them. These unemployed teams break up. Many offered their services in the hope of being fed. What are all these people without money and without work going to do now? . . .

Yesterday near the Parc Monceau I saw two little boys of about six and eleven. Both were in tatters, shirtless, and sockless, their faces gaunt and unwashed, yet they were smiling. The elder was carrying on his arm a large square basket in which a few wilted flowers were lying on a bed of pine branches; he was holding in his hand a sort of bouquet, or rather broom, and he was chewing and spitting out the petals; the flowers were so dirty and wilted that I was unable to recognize them.

"Your bouquet is not very pretty, my boy," I said. "Who is likely to buy it from you?"

Whereupon with a rapid gesture he gathered together in his basket a handful of carnations that were not too faded. "Look, sir; these are fresh. They're yours for fifty centimes."

He was aiming less to move me than to amuse me, ready to laugh and make a joke of it himself. And as he walked away with his little brother, I saw each of them light a cigarette.

Jean Schlumberger lunched with his mother today. She has just returned from Val-Richer and confirms with certainty the rumor that the French have been in Colmar for the last four or five days. Certainly the government is holding this piece of news in reserve; it is good to have a little joy in readiness.

The sky clouded over during the night, and in the early morning a big storm broke east of Paris.

The first rolling of the thunder at about four o'clock seemed enough like the explosion of bombs to make one think a flight of zeppelins had raided Paris. And in my half-sleep I imagined for some time that Paris was being bombarded and that it was even the end of the world. From my lack of emotion I realized that I was ready for anything and everything; but it was only a dream. Yet can I know how I might react when faced with real danger? Of what simple stuff are they made, the people who can guarantee their reactions at any hour of the day or night! How many soldiers anxiously wait for the event that will prove whether or not they are brave? And he who doesn't react as *he would like to* — whose will alone is brave! . . .

The despair of the man who thinks he is a coward because he yielded to a momentary weakness — when he hoped he was courageous (*Lord Jim*).[34]

Copeau came to dinner at the rue Laugier; I walked part of the way home with him and told him of my visit to poor old La Pérouse. Yes, yesterday afternoon I thought I could do nothing better than call on him. Mme de La Pérouse opened the door and immediately button-holed me, bursting forth in recriminations against her husband, who, she claims, does whatever he can to be disagreeable to her and has now thought up the idea of letting himself die of hunger. For several days, ever since the declaration of war, I believe, he has been refusing almost all nourishment. After a few affected courtesies, she got up to "announce" me. And since she warned me that "Monsieur de La Pé-rouse" was in bed, I spoke of going into his bedroom.

"Oh! sir, you could hardly get in; Monsieur de La Pérouse is so finicky that no one is allowed to clean up his room. . . ."

But when she returns she announces to me that M. de La Pérouse is expecting me.

The room I now enter for the first time is rather dark because of the only half-open shutters. The open, uncurtained window looks out on a court, and the position of the shutters keeps people across the way from seeing into the room.

Old La Pérouse is not in bed. Up against the bed he lies deep in a mahogany armchair covered in worn red velvet that reveals the stuffing. I sit down in another armchair just like it. He hardly makes a gesture when I come in; he lets me grasp his inert left hand; he is leaning on the right against a square table, and his elbow is resting on two little cushions in the shape of a tea-cozy; on a lower level of the same table two metal bowls are lying one in the other. I hold his hand in mine and put my arm behind him without saying a word. He doesn't say anything either. I observe his face, mottled with red and yellow, deathly pale in spots, which seems made of such a strange material that if one scratched the skin anything but blood would run from the scratch. I look at the room's odd disorder: on the right a pile of hat-boxes rising almost to the ceiling; then a bureau, one half of which is covered with a pile of unbound books; on the other half, a bottle of cider standing in a saucepan, a dirty glass, a small hot-plate, and sev-

---

[34] Joseph Conrad's novel.

eral spirit-lamps, one of which is burning imperceptibly. On the left, in front of the fireplace,.a low table holds a collection of mysterious pots, all of the same size and each with a cover on it. In the middle of the room another table with toilet articles on it and, under the table, a garbage-can filled with old shoes.

Eventually the poor old man raises his head a bit and murmurs: "I am very weak."

I try then to persuade him to accept a little nourishment. Finally he confesses that, in addition to a lack of appetite, he has decided not to eat any more, to end it all. Then turning toward me: "Be good; give me a drink. Just a little cider." And with a flabby hand he points at the bottle.

I refuse to give him more than a quarter of a glass.

"Ah! I could drink the sea itself!" he sighs.

However, while talking, I lead him gradually to the idea of accepting a gruel that Mme de La Pérouse is going to prepare for him. And while the soup is heating, he returns to old complaints: particularly his wife's jealousy toward all those who show esteem and affection for him:

"She has all the faults," he says; then, correcting himself, he adds: *"all the petty ones."*

For the first time I inquire about his reasons for marrying Mme de La Pérouse. As one could well imagine, those reasons were altogether sentimental: he loved her. And going back into the past, he tells me about his brother, that brother he loved most tenderly and passionately and who died at the age of seventeen. La Pérouse himself was hardly more than twenty-one at the time. A few months later he got married. In a little trunk to which he kept the key, he had locked up his brother's letters, which he did not *dare* read for several years. Then one day (most likely after his first conjugal disappointments) he locked himself in a room where he knew he would not be disturbed, opened the little trunk, and reread that correspondence. From that day on, he got into the habit of seeking consolation and support in that reading; these were hours when he could be almost sure of not being watched by his wife. But he soon became convinced that she was spying on him and suspected his little trunk; for some time she had already been rummaging in his drawers among his other papers. The day finally came when, opening his trunk, La Pérouse found his brother's letters in disorder. "It was," he told me, "just as if someone had put them back in a hurry, someone who had been surprised while reading them and hadn't had time to put them in order." He had no words with Mme de La Pérouse, but he burned those papers at once.

Next he tells me of his excessive shyness, which so often made people misjudge him. This is why he could never express his gratitude

to Mme de Rothschild, who, on many occasions, had obliged him most
charmingly. Eager to speak with her, he accepted an invitation to a
dance, arrived among the first, could not screw up his courage to approach her at the rare moments when he saw her alone, stayed until
the end, and, since the only person he knew at the dance constantly
dragged him off to the buffet, he must have looked like the kind of
person who comes to stuff himself. This stuck in his mind as a burning
remorse.

He talks with extreme slowness, without turning toward me, his
eyes staring into space; occasionally I hear an odd sound in his mouth
as if he were chewing his teeth. But then he becomes lively; once more
I succeed in reassuring him, in consoling him; probably the soup he
ate ("with pleasure," as he confesses) is doing him good; now, surprised at it himself, he asks me to help him get up; he looks for his
hat; he wants to go out. We go downstairs together and, after I have
said good-by to him in the street, I feel his eyes following me for a
long time and, when I turn around again, he waves to me. . . .

17 August

Japan's declaration of war on Germany.

Yesterday, very bad morning — perhaps due entirely to the fact that
I had gone to bed very late the night before, ashamed as I was to have
put my day to such poor use and eager, before going to bed, to read
some more (Chuquet's book on 1870).

After luncheon there came a lady friend of the Théos who had just
returned from Bayreuth by way of Brussels; her story is most moving.
She was present at the last performance; everything took place in the
greatest calm; the mobilization (or the declaration of war?) had just
been posted. On leaving the theater, in evening gown, she went to the
station and asked when there was a train that would take her in the
direction of Luxembourg. On the basis of the information she was
given, she hurried home to pack and left at five a.m.

After untold difficulties she reached Belgium. She told us of the
wonderful calm in Brussels but also of the hatred the Germans have
aroused. No one there took the wise precaution that caused the Paris
gunsmiths' shops to be closed; hence they were immediately pillaged
so that many civilians are ready for any foolhardiness. All the German
hotels and shops were sacked so that only their walls remain. The region around Liége is completely devastated.

At four o'clock I went to call on Paul Desjardins. He listens to
everything that is said to him with a courteous and smiling "Oh!
really?" which implies all possible reservations. It goes without saying
that he already knew everything that he pretended to learn from me

and had already analyzed it critically. He is preparing, with the approval of Viviani, a bulletin to be printed in more than a hundred thousand copies (he told me the exact figure) containing many stories, eyewitness accounts, letters from soldiers, etc., followed by commentaries and the "moral" of these facts.

At five o'clock I go to the house of Belot, the professor of philosophy, whom I do not yet know; I was invited by Élie Allégret to meet, at rue du Ranelagh, where he lives, various professors, philosophers, etc., who are worried about the idle situation in which the state of war leaves boys between the ages of twelve and eighteen. Tristan Bernard is there, Élie Allégret, my Uncle Charles, Marcel Drouin, Buisson (?). . . . In all there are fourteen of us. Tristan Bernard speaks in a low, soft voice that people listen to all the more attentively since it is hard to hear; I am sitting beside him and occasionally he puts his hand on my arm or shoulder; he says "my friend Gide" when he speaks of me; I shouldn't like this from another, but in his gesture and tone of voice there is more simple good-heartedness than indiscreet familiarity, and something ironic and good in his smile. He suggests keeping these young boys busy with physical exercises that will tire them out, military training, football, and walking in the stadium which the editor of *L'Auto* is quite willing to put at their disposal. . . . It is agreed that it would be good to complement these exercises by a sort of short speech, a commentary on the events, an exhortation, etc. . . .

I was commissioned to see Arthur Fontaine (which I did this morning) and to ask him if we could not get some factory to reopen and take on these boys. Couldn't it be possible, someone else suggested, to convince some small manufacturers, cabinet-makers, shoemakers, locksmiths, etc. . . . to take the responsibility of training two, three, or four willing lads? (Fontaine noted down this suggestion, which he will point out in a report he is writing.)

Then, when we leave, Tristan Bernard walks along with me and tells me of the situation of the young boulevard pimps, called on to *take the place of* their elders and intoxicated by their sudden importance.

At five o'clock, at the Mairie of the VIIth Arrondissement, thirty-five people gathered around the mayor volunteer to pass on news of individual soldiers to their families. It is a matter of being in the information bureau once or twice a week at definite hours when worried parents can come for information; the lists that will be provided will have only the briefest indication: wounded, seriously wounded, prissoner, no news. It is also a matter of calling directly on the families, to "break the news to them," in case of death.

18 August

Still nothing. The papers vie with each other in exaggerating the importance of petty details: the capture of the first flag, for instance. Yesterday we saw it on exhibit in the inner court of the Ministry; a large crowd shouldered in to see, but there was no demonstration since no one would have known whether it was better to applaud or to boo. The Baravian flag was extremely beautiful — purplish red, quartered with white, against which stood out in the middle the black eagle. It was silk and seemed to be fluttering, quivering, like a living thing.

Seizure of an Austrian warship. The Germans held in check at various points along the border; but when you see the various places where they are said to be repulsed, you deduce that they had advanced a bit farther than the papers had at first dared to report. We are told that Altkirch has been *taken back*, which implies that we must have yielded it for a time. I learned yesterday from Fontaine that the French had entered Colmar the same day as Mulhouse, coming down through one of the passes, but that they had left again almost at once.

A card from Ghéon, quite disappointed: the little hospital that he is supposed to direct is merely a vacation-spot, since no wounded are sent there.

Will the same event that is to reveal their courage to so many others be for us simply a training in sloth and inertia? Here we are forced to egotism, and this is what we are struggling against in vain.

19

Yesterday by way of the Bois de Boulogne I went to the Villa, where I was to get a suit, then to Belot's house, where we had made an appointment. I noticed in fact, at various places along the old fortifications in the direction of the Bois, gatherings of young fellows in the ditches. They had dragged together some metal chairs taken from somewhere or other and, seated in a circle, were playing cards.

It would probably not have been wise to approach and, besides, I had no wish to do so; I remained therefore on the little path along the edge of the ditch and soon I went back to the main path.

The outskirts of the Bois struck me as much less spoiled than usual, probably as a result of the interruption of the races.

The meeting at Belot's was not useless and I think that it will succeed in organizing work, or at least a distraction, for these idle youths. But I had nothing to do with this assembly and I shall not go to the next one.

Began again to practice the piano — without any pleasure, moreover.

The wounded that have been transported to Vichy all repeat that the Germans shoot the wounded and the stretcher-bearers. The newspapers are full of horrible tales.

20

Yet one must let oneself be convinced that the front line is not the only place where one can be of service; the important thing is that each man should be at his post.

Every evening, under the gas flame in the Théos' little dining-room, all four of us gathered around the oak table, the Théos, Jean Schlumberger, and I, plunge into the evening papers. For the fourth or fifth time we dig the marrow out of the same stories, the same news-reports that, since the day before, we have read in *Le Matin*, in *L'Information*, in *Le Figaro*, in *L'Écho*, in the evening issue of *Le Matin* — and in English in the *Daily Mail*, where for a moment they took on a sort of new life. And if the papers are exhausted before the curfew, I have Chuquet (*1870*), *Le Désastre* by Margueritte, and Zola's *La Débâcle*.[35] Last night, fed up, irritated by this militarization of my mind, I took out of Elisabeth's library *Sesame and Lilies*, of which I read almost the whole preface (new edition);[36] I felt as if I were plunging into a lake of clear water in which all the dust and burning of too long a walk on a dry road were being washed off.

Doubtless for those who are mobilized the wearing of the uniform authorizes a greater freedom of thought. But those of us who cannot put on the uniform mobilize our minds.

I stopped rue du Louvre to find out just what was the "Ligue de la Pensée Nouvelle";[37] a poster had given hope that we might be able to turn over to this organization the unemployed orderlies registered with the Red Cross. They make home-visits to seek out invalid families to receive free care from doctors attached to the league. On the third floor, courtyard side, of a large building in the rue du Louvre, the man who received me spoke French with a pure Germanic accent that might have called itself Alsatian, that might even have been Alsatian . . . but everything about the appearance of the place filled me with suspicion. He took my name, gave me a card, and I think that our relations will not go any further.

Jean Cocteau had arranged to meet me in an "English tearoom" on

[35] Both *The Disaster* and *The Collapse* are fictional accounts of the defeat of 1870. Chuquet's book on *The War of 1870–1* appeared in 1895.

[36] A collection of lectures by John Ruskin on the primacy of art and literature. Marcel Proust had recently translated this work, but André Gide quotes the title in English.

[37] The New-Thought League.

the corner of the rue de Ponthieu and the avenue d'Antin. I had no
pleasure in seeing him again, despite his extreme kindness; but he is
incapable of seriousness, and all his thoughts, his witticisms, his sensations, all the extraordinary brilliance of his customary conversation
shocked me like a luxury article displayed in a period of famine and
mourning. He is dressed almost like a soldier, and the fillip of the
present events has made him look healthier. He is relinquishing nothing, but simply giving a martial twist to his usual liveliness. When
speaking of the slaughter of Mulhouse he uses amusing adjectives and
mimicry; he imitates the bugle call and the whistling of the shrapnel.
Then, changing subjects since he sees that he is not amusing me, he
claims to be sad; he wants to be sad with the same kind of sadness
as you, and suddenly he adopts your mood and explains it to you.
Then he talks of Blanche, mimics Mme R., and talks of the lady at
the Red Cross who shouted on the stairway: "I was promised fifty
wounded men for this morning; I want my fifty wounded men." Meanwhile he is crushing a piece of plum cake in his plate and nibbling it;
his voice rises suddenly and has odd twists; he laughs, leans forward,
bends toward you and touches you.The odd thing is that I think he
would make a good soldier. He asserts that he would and that he
would be brave too. He has the carefree attitude of the street-urchin;
it is in his company that I feel the most awkward, the most heavy, the
most gloomy.

21

Yesterday at Élie Allégret's and then at M. P.'s about the free meals.
M. P. is stuffed with civic virtues. He is in charge of a soup kitchen in
the XVIth Arrondissement, which makes him take a dim view of the
similar work done by the Mairie. If his virtue ceases to be exceptional,
it is going to turn sour and poison him; you can already feel that this
is beginning.

In the late afternoon I returned to Élie Allégret's to report the
results of my visit.

Copeau arrives at the rue Laugier just as we were about to go up
to bed and delays our curfew an hour. He seems younger, more Diderot than ever, eagerly embracing every new project. He talks of re-
opening the Vieux-Colombier for theatrical presentations and recitals
improvised for the occasion, and he would like to organize them at
once. He also talks of going abroad since he is doing nothing in Paris;
he would like to become more involved; he would like to write for the
newspapers, the articles he reads — even those by Barrès — striking him
as very ordinary and unsatisfactory; he thinks he could do better; and
I can easily believe it, at least for the first ones he wrote. . . .

There begin to be seen walking the streets, hugging the walls, odd lucifugous creatures such as the tide uncovers when the water withdraws.

Yesterday a sort of Colonel Chabert,[38] stiff-jointed and almost voiceless, who nevertheless did his best to sing in order to attract the charity of passers-by. People didn't hear him at all and no one stopped. He was holding a little boy by the hand and another smaller one was following. Both of them ugly, gaunt, and looking as if they had forever forgotten how to smile. I asked for their name and address and this morning I went to rue Bolivar, near the Buttes-Chaumont, to see their poverty at closer hand. The two little boys were not there; on the first floor of a low house I found the old man of the other day beside an enormous, whining, panting woman who told me her story. Twice married, she has given birth to seventeen children, of which ten — all tubercular — are still alive. The two eldest sons are in the services. The municipality supports them in an almost satisfactory fashion, after all. I expected to find an even worse poverty in these sorry quarters; that is also because it was very beautiful weather.

Read Yeats's preface to W. Blake as I was walking.

23

Special editions of the papers appear at all hours of the day, keeping up the public's fever. The poorest people buy them; newsboys run through the streets, and the thick bundles of papers under their arms are soon sold out. Everyone hopes constantly and wants to know a little bit more; but nothing comes from the theater of war except what the Ministry agrees to pass; and since solely the official communiqués are authorized, all the papers say exactly the same thing. We promise ourselves to resist their appeal and to boycott the extras.

The day before yesterday at seven a.m. I went to the Gare Saint-Lazare with Jean Schlumberger, who was taking Jouvet's wife to Braffy for her accouchement.

In the afternoon I went to the Invalides to see again the Bavarian flag we have taken. A large crowd was gathered in the lower passage leading from one chapel to the other. The flag was exhibited above the door that opens into the big inner court; it seems to me much less beautiful than the other day and already stiffened in death; this comes also from the fact that the staff was almost horizontal so that the cloth fell without a fold; not a breath of wind stirred it either; even its color seemed to me less striking.

---

[38] The hero of Balzac's story by the same name returns to life and civilization after having been buried alive during the Napoleonic Wars.

25

I have again let a day escape. Yesterday, Monday, I went to pick up Copeau at the Invalides and asked him to come and lunch at the rue Laugier, to which I brought a melon. He is pulling himself together, and his energy (I should say rather his excess of life) galvanizes all those who come in contact with him.

The evening before last Pierre de Lanux came to dinner. He is leaving for Venice and whatever points he can reach on the Austrian coast as a correspondent of the *Figaro*. All evening Jean Schlumberger and I blow up the plan of getting ourselves sent to Italy too as war correspondents. But, having slept on it, we agree in realizing that the services we could render in this way would be vague and that our personal inclination would come off pretty well in the matter.

I continue my reading of Blake with amazement. Begun *Tess of the D'Urbervilles*, which I have already read (but not carefully) in French.[39]

My vaccination is taking in a ferocious way and giving me a fever. Last night I thought for some time of the military tale I was planning, which will doubtless take its place in, and perhaps even serve as conclusion to, my novel. I must note it down. I have always regretted not having set down every project at the very moment when it was assuming form and bursting forth in my mind.

The day of the 25th was most gloomy. From the height of what mad hope we fell! The papers had done their job so well that everyone began to imagine that our army had only to appear to put the entire German army to rout. And because we had fallen back on those positions which a week before had seemed so good, already people predicted the imminent siege of Paris. Everyone was seeking a word of encouragement and hope, for they were not completely crushed — more exactly, everyone was awakening from a dream — and people looked almost with stupor at the picture postcards representing "famine in Berlin": a big Prusco, seated in front of a toilet and fishing up, with a long fork plunged through the seat, suspicious sausages that he swallowed at once; or another German green with fear at the sight of a bayonet; others fleeing — in which, as never before, the silliness, filth, and hideousness of vulgar stupidity were revealed in the most compromising and shameful manner.

26 August

The French, who were playing fair, were indignant at the fact that in war the Germans did not observe the rules of the game.

As for the latter, it seemed as if they were aiming to discredit war

---

[39] The novel by Thomas Hardy (1891).

forever; and as if to prove that war was an evil thing — if it is true that
in war the aim is to conquer — they won by the worst means.

On the 25th and 26th began to rush into Paris the people fleeing
burning villages. An old man arrived almost mad (Mme Ruyters's
uncle) who spread terror among those around him. "We are not up to
it!" he kept repeating. "We are not up to it! Those people respect
nothing." On foot he had covered a long way, crawling, hiding, crossing the lines, seeing villages and farms burning all around him. Taken
by surprise a few kilometers away from the village of which he was
mayor, he had been unable to get back to his post, separated from his
family and duty by a sudden barrage of fire.

Those who came from Valenciennes were camped in the Cirque
d'Été; some children were taken in at rue Vaneau. Mme Edwards asserted that many of these children had their hands cut off, that she
had seen them. Others had their eyes put out and others terrible
wounds.

This could never be verified.

Mme Théo met yesterday, in front of a butcher-shop, a poor woman
so bedraggled that at first she thought of giving her some coins; then,
hesitating a moment, she thought that the best thing would be to in-
troduce her to the charitable organization in which she had just registered and of which she had already noticed the competent manage-
ment. She first asked her then if she belonged to this arrondissement.

"Oh, madame," the other replied with that drawl which Mme Théo
recognized at once, 'I am from . . ." (here the name of a village that
I did not recognize).

She had come with two little children, of whom a kind lady had
immediately offered to take charge; she was lodged at the Cirque
d'Été with so many others.

"I imagine you are satisfied with us," she added (and indeed we
get all our comfort today from the example of the Belgians' noble
courage). Mme Théo then told her that she too was a Belgian and
happened to have been born in the same village.

"Ah, the Russians! If you think you can count on them! Their officers are as rotten as their functionaries! Would you believe that they
sold their own horses' hay to Austrian officers!"

Meanwhile little Joseph Retinger had managed to return from Poland after a thousand adventures, one of the most sinister of which
was his incarceration upon arriving in Paris.

Mme Edwards was speaking most passionately of the Polish cause.

What guarantees does the Russian declaration offer them? It is not even signed by the Czar, but only by Grand-Duke Nicholas (?). Of the three Polands, the Russian one was always the worst off and the Austrian one the best. (Joseph Retinger is an Austrian Pole.) "And the very country that took from our people all freedom of religion and thought, that wanted to suppress even our language, now comes to promise us freedom with no guarantee!" Retinger was taken to see Philippe Berthelot, but what could the latter say to him? Mme Edwards is indignant that he did not commit himself. People would have liked France to ratify the Russian gesture, but France feared future diplomatic difficulties and refused to take a stand.

Later on it was asserted that Joffre had wanted an immediate offensive, but that Messimy had obstinately refused.

Meanwhile Messimy, overworked and almost terrified by his unforeseen responsibilities, was not up to his task. A governmental crisis at such a moment would probably have been dangerous and, whatever party he belonged to, no Frenchman who was chiefly concerned with the interests of his country would have wished for such a thing. But it was probably not impossible to double or triple this Ministry; a sort of higher council formed of Delcassé, Millerand, and Briand would take Messimy's place; that could be done very simply without shaking the other ministries at all. It is for this that Clemenceau was preparing public opinion in his clever article of the 26th, which so angered Marcel: "This is the last time that I shall buy *L'Homme libre,*" he exclaimed in such a furious tone of voice that it forced one to withdraw into silence.

See the reshuffling of the Ministry on the very next day.

(Why not Clemenceau? He had been sounded out, it was said, but had declined the offer.)

The article in question took note of what was later called the "*Times* incident," which *Le Temps* pointed out that very evening. Yet Marcel shrugged his shoulders and, getting even more angry, declared that this wasn't important at all and that it was perfidious to turn it into an argument against the government.[40]

---

[40] In its issue of 27 August 1914 *Le Temps* ran an article on page one entitled "L'incident du *Times*." A correspondent of the London *Times* had written to Clemenceau to call his attention to the fact that beginning on 23 August the *Times* had been forbidden entrance into France. Clemenceau replied that Viviani had told him he was going to intervene with Messimy; the next day the *Times* was admitted, after which it was again forbidden.

Absurd and criminal headlines in *Le Matin:* "The Russians only five stages away from Berlin"; "The Allies' vice is closing"; etc. . . .

Then the next morning (the 27th) we learned that the Ministry had been reconstituted! It was called the *Ministry of National Defense.*

On the 28th, lunch at Arthur Fontaine's with Copeau and Tannery. I bring along Joseph Retinger. The way in which the servant observes him while serving. Fontaine, abnormally sweet and smiling, drinks an infusion during the meal and takes little tablets. Intermittently he presses his left hand against his stomach. I don't dare ask for news of his sons. Speaking of Charleroi, he says: "Had it been a victory, Italy would have come in."

Tannery is in Delcassé's office with the job of intercepting the German wireless messages to neutral countries, which pass through France; he says:

"I have been able to build up very considerable files in this way. It seems that until now Germany has not suspected anything; she has continued to correspond or at least to believe that she was corresponding. I have a folder for Spain, another for Portugal . . . I even have one for France. And this is what has allowed us to pick up a certain number of spies, most surely."

It is certain that the Germans do not see the same aspect of the war as we do. We are seeing the horrible side.

The conversation in the train, before the declaration of war, of the "lost" uhlans constantly crossing the border and asking to be put on the right road. The country rotten with spies is warned that the border is not protected at that point. The Germans enter as if they were at home and, for three weeks, settle into the village, which is successively retaken by the French, then by the Germans, and finally once again by the French until the Germans get hold of it again. When they left it for the first time, they said to the inhabitants: "We shall return!" and when they came back they put everything to fire and sword. They set fire to the four corners of buildings (they had a special detachment for this); then, taking their stand in front of the doors, shot down whoever tried to get out. According to one's taste, one chose between burning to death and being shot.

"At the moment of fleeing, all bundles ready, the mother cannot find her older boy; this over-inquisitive little fellow (thirteen years old) had gone back *to see.*

Clemenceau adds that a Prime Minister should be able to do something more effective than merely to express a wish.

"At that age they see everything. Nothing escaped him, sir. And in addition, too brave; he and his comrades used to go up to the German soldiers and shout at them: 'You won't get Verdun; you are too stupid!'

"Our neighbor's little girl was raped. Her mother didn't want to say so, out of pride, but the doctor established the fact. One of them wanted to have a good time; he came toward me laughing and offered me money. Finally I complained to his commanding officer. He laughed in turn and said: 'German soldiers are not capable of such things.' But the other kept on insisting; then one of his companions defended me and drove him out; they are not all bad. For example, those from Silesia are decent. But the cuirassiers (?) are brutes."

They see the manager of the flour-mill step up and take command of the battalion entering the village. "Ah, sir, we can understand that Germans should come and hand us over. But most of the spies were French. The country was lousy with spies."

With her two children she covered thirty kilometers on foot to flee the burning village.

Her neighbor, pregnant, maltreated, gave birth in a ditch.

T. felt his stomach, heart, and knees give way; it was an extraordinary relaxing of his whole being; he had no more thought, no more warmth, no more breath; at moments a frightful dizziness seized him as if the blood were fleeing his head and heart at the same time. He was sweating.

Back in his town. He was almost amazed to find everything still in place. His imagination jumped ahead so that he would have considered it almost natural that the avenue of trees surrounding the house had been already razed for some "defense necessity" or other.

He was surprised by the calm of certain people; at first he admired it until he realized that this calm was due to an utter lack of imagination.

The dog that *might be* in the way:
The target one destroys; that one doesn't know where to hide; that one drowns in the cess-pit.

Characters:
He who deceives himself with fine words, who feels that he is not believed and is annoyed by it, but little by little becomes aware that people were right not to believe him.

At the moment of danger he is not there; it isn't exactly that he wanted not to be there; without thinking he just happened to favor the little circumstance that would let him out. He did not cling to his post.

On the other hand, those on whom you didn't count and who do their duty wonderfully. You suffer for having spoken ill and thought ill of them.

At certain hours everything that seemed as if it were to our advantage turned against us. The "dash" of our troops — who are constantly overstepping the line of artillery protection so that our own soldiers are killed by our projectiles.[41] The fury of our black troops and their excessive fierceness, which drags all their officers to death after them because there is no way of getting them to let go and to re-form their units.

At first he is pleased to hear that all the wounded men arrive with rather slight wounds; then he learns that this is merely because of the lack of stretcher-bearers, so that all those whose wounds prevent them from escaping themselves remain on the field of battle.

29 August

At Havre a very odd dispatch was posted; most likely an official communiqué; one could read, written with a brush on sheets pasted to the window, and the whole population gathered to read:

"OUR POSITION REMAINS THE SAME ALONG THE WHOLE FRONT, FROM THE SOMME TO THE VOSGES."

X. took cognizance of this dispatch in the main hall of the Bourse, where he had gone to get his mail. I recognized him among those who were examining a map attached to the wall and sprinkled with little flags. I heard someone say: "I have the explanation: it's a misprint, a misreading; the dispatch read: 'of the crest of the Vosges.'[42] Besides, this is the text given in the window of *Havre-Éclair* (the other information-center)." We rushed there. On the dispatch could be read nothing but "from the Somme to the Vosges," exactly as in the window of *Petit Havrais*.

T. predicts that three months from now, both on the east and on the west of Germany, everyone will be back on his own frontiers, exhausted.

31 August

Poor Uncle Yung, reading the papers with pencil in hand according to his habit, makes violent pencil-thrusts at the accounts of German atrocities. He would like such things never to have taken place.

---

[41] On 4 September Joffre gave special instructions about this. [A.]

[42] This reading involves substituting *du sommet des Vosges* for *de la Somme aux Vosges*.

V.'s two old aunts at Étretat:

"Clémence, during the month that we have been here you have terrified me, you have driven me crazy."

"That is because you recognize that everything I predict comes true."

The other one would like to leave, but cannot resign herself to leaving her friend, who cannot resign herself to leaving her eleven trunks.

Difficulty of making Jeanne decide to leave. "They won't come this way. If they do come, it will not be for a long time. If they come, they won't do any harm." Etc. Terrible spirit of contradiction and opposition, added to one's inability — so horrible are the things that are told — to admit that these horrible things can *happen to us.*

2 September

The Copeaus and the Gilberts make up their minds to leave Cuverville.

Yesterday's train, completely filled with wounded, did not take any civilians.

Each one has a right to only sixty pounds of excess weight.

The ups and downs.

Conversation with the school-teacher. He explains his strategy all over again: the impossibility of conquering the country otherwise than by following the rivers. (Suddenly comforted.)

Strange sound that is heard at night. Extraordinary serenity of the night. The slight rustling of the branches can be heard. They go down to the garden fence and stay there for some time, without a single thought, as if overwhelmed by the beauty of the moonlight; not far from them in the grass, a group of little heifers all lying down except one that seems to be keeping an eye on the herd; the sound of their tranquil chewing can be heard. But beyond these great peaceful voices, despite them, one's ear picks out other sounds.

At Étretat, X. (I, in other words) accepts an invitation to lunch with the proprietress of the Hôtel Hauville, whose sister he had met in the train from Havre to Criquetot. They are starting out by auto this very day for Nice, planning to make several stops on the way. They would have liked to flee the day before, but the chauffeur was drunk. The sister advises against resistance; country estates are their first objective, etc. . . . She has just come from there and knows what she is talking about. He feels his courage ebbing.

Then he sees a flock of poor children arrive from Paris — a hundred and fifty motherless children whose fathers are in the services. These kids are worn out, for the innumerable stops the train made kept them eighteen hours on the way. But he tells himself that, nevertheless, these innocents would not be allowed to come here if anyone foresaw a slaughter. The two or three hundred who have been here for a month don't prove anything, but as for sending more! . . . and these considerations reassure him.

But then the next day's mail brings his brother, the mayor, a sheet to fill out with the list of all the requisitioned people capable of furnishing lodgings for the troops. . . . Are they expected, then?

He can see the town only in relation to this problem.

He was moved to silly pity in the presence of innocent, weak creatures; a group of little girls drew tears from him.

Active courage and passive courage. Different to the point of opposition.

And as soon as his mind was not overstrained, he relapsed into a dull torpor from which he felt that even the sound of the near-by cannon could not wake him.

He reflected that, after all, those men whose courage he admired were manifesting their complete worth at such times. This was their sole opportunity to reveal themselves, and for them nothing lay beyond the great shadow from which this call roused them. Each of them was only one among many. If he felt himself to be inferior to them in this, it was because he was an *individual*.

At first some one had thought up the slogan: "If we hold out we'll win." Then, later on: "The German army absorbed by France."

3 September

The bombs that the Taubes dropped on Paris that day harmed no one; but the stray bullets that were shot at them killed and wounded several people when they fell.

4 September

As soon as it was called "a *localized* invasion," events began to look better.

No defeat, no victory will change the good and bad points of these two nations. Even though German commerce may be stifled, French commerce will be unable to take its place; even without a rival it would have yielded all along the line.

The Belgian lady was annoyed by those five thousand francs promised to the first soldier to bring back an enemy flag. "To win a flag they would be willing to lose a battle. Oh, the others are well aware of that! It's just like the Mulhouse business. Any other nation would have avoided such a thing. Three quarters of the mistakes made in France are due to love of the dramatic remark or gesture or sentiment. Oh, don't get the idea that such motives mean anything to them! They are practical and you are romantic. Ah, you certainly deserve Rostand! The white plume, champagne, whatever suits that incurable triviality which makes you joke under a rain of bullets and never admit that the others are prepared. Besides, you count too much on chance. Self-confidence is a good thing, but especially when it is justified."

Élise, Georges's maid, opens the door to me and tells me that Georges is out. But she buttonholes me; she needs someone to talk to her; she tells me so:

"Sir, you know Monsieur Georges. He doesn't talk very much. You always have to question him; and even then he doesn't always answer. He gives me the newspaper. I don't know how to read writing, but I can read printing. No matter how much people try to reassure me, I still know that things are not going so well. Madame Gilbert and Madame Drouin, when they used to go by, would talk to us a bit. I need to see someone from the big house. What am I going to become now that they've left! And besides, no one can make me believe that they left without there's danger; I'm not so dumb as all that."

In an order of the day entitled "Note for All the Armies" that General Galliéni ordered to be read three times on three successive days to all the officers and men in the fortified area of Paris, the commander-in-chief begins by pointing out the reasons for the heavy losses of certain army corps: "Every time the infantry has been given the signal to attack from too great a distance, before the artillery has made its action felt, the infantry has encountered machine-gun fire and taken losses that could have been avoided."

Sunday, 6 September

The *Petit Havre* informs us this morning, quite incidentally, that the Germans have been occupying Amiens since last Tuesday.

The papers have been talking for the last two days, according to the *Daily News* (?), of a "formidable factor" that, when it is known, "will astonish Europe." I can imagine uneducated people reading that and wondering how a "factor" can become "formidable"! [43]

---

[43] In French the common meaning of *facteur* is "postman."

7 September

I do not recall ever having seen in this region such a long succession of uniformly beautiful days. One's heart is overwhelmed by the sky's serenity.

8 September

All you could get from him was an aphorism like this: "It is a rule of nature that the common should triumph over the exquisite."

His *despair* derived above all from the fact that he knew that the German armaments were in no wise factitious or sham but just as natural to that race and to that country as a shell and claws are to a crustacean. Between this and that there were deep and essential relationships. With us the army remained an instrument; with them it is an organ; so that, without much exaggeration, it could be said that, for that organ, war was the necessary function.

The attitude of the Germans toward their own wounded. It seems certain that they finish them off on the field of battle.

Everyone repeats the story of that hospital where French and German wounded were gathered together in the same ward. The village fell into the hands of the Germans and was then retaken; at the moment of their evacuation they killed the six wounded Germans and left the four Frenchmen alive. Explain it if you can.

Likewise, in the naval battle near Heligoland they were seen to shoot at the German sailors that an English lifeboat was about to rescue.

And finally it is told that, having to cross a river over which the bridges had been cut, they did not hesitate to upset in the river three of their ambulances still full of wounded that they didn't bother to take out. Then they crossed the river on the ambulance-tops.

12 September

X. crosses the Seine to gather together and bring back the people who had fled in the panic of the first of the month.

Havre, which twelve days earlier was full of English, seems dull. The weather, perfect during the last two weeks, is beginning to change.

Between Criquetot and Havre only one train, which leaves Criquetot at ten fifty and just gives people a chance to catch the one-o'clock boat for Honfleur. At about three o'clock a train for Pont-l'Évêque, where he orders a carriage for Braffy. He gets there in time to spend the night.

The next morning X. listens to the tales of soldiers sent from Lisieux to finish their convalescence. They are living near the farm of Braffy in a building in which three large rooms have been turned over to them.

One serves as a mess and the other two as dormitories. There are fifteen of them. None of them is badly wounded. Their tales seem borrowed from the newspapers.

Describing the terrifying effects of the new explosives and the surprise of seeing soldiers dead though still standing and apparently without wounds, an Algerian concluded: "It's sad because they are standing; but it's funny because they are dead."

X. is amazed not to hear any more personal note. (He would have had to spend more time with them.) Most of them have come from Charleroi or thereabouts. It seems certain that the artillery failed in its job of protecting the infantry. One of them thinks that he owes his life to the fact that he was picked up and thrown forward by the shell, of which a fragment hit him, while the shell itself exploded in the ground. Another, a barber from Beauvais and a bit too much of a talker, pursued a German for some distance in a sunken road; the German was running rather fast, but stumbled over a stone and fell; it was then that he drove his bayonet into the German's back. It went in so far that he had to step on the body to get it out.

Another had on his conscience, if you could believe him, the slaughter of fifteen Germans he had surprised dead drunk or asleep in a barn.

Each one of them insists that the enemy shells do not all explode; only one out of two, they say, and even then they don't have any serious effect. "Cheap stuff," they say.

They say that the cases of sunstroke, during long marches in the sun, were very frequent. "Everyone was in a hurry to find a bit of shade before he dropped." Some of them fell suddenly in the ranks; an unbelievable number were left in the ditches.

Édouard completely *sunk* when his offer of self-sacrifice was not accepted. He should have been taken at his word.

The sky's whole radiant poise yields to the terrific pressure of the clouds. The night of the 12th to the 13th was filled with the horrible voices of the storm. In anguish, X. wondered *against* whom the tempest was raging.

16 September

The impossibility of keeping oneself in a state of tension (which is after all artificial) as soon as nothing in the *immediate surroundings* motivates it. X. goes back to reading, to playing Bach, and even to preferring the fugues with a joyful rhythm from the *Well-Tempered Clavichord,* which he can forbid himself only with great reluctance.

Meanwhile, in the old house where he had remained alone with his wife, the clan begins to gather. Jeanne was still tarrying in Étretat, where she had gone against her will since her mania for contradicting common sense and the facts kept producing optimism. She declared: "They will never come this way," in the same tone that she assured us that the Russians were going to cut off the Austrians headed toward Belgium.

But since, after all, the Germans hadn't come, the discussion became retrospective and X. was reduced to asserting that they could have come. This was enough to dispute about endlessly.

Forced to take part again in the family worship. His discomfort. His horror of the gesture that might exceed his feeling.

His embarrassment when commissioned to choose the verses to read; he understands why ministers so often turn to the texts of St. Paul, which are less specific, more suitable for any emergency, than those from the Gospels. He also looks for a Psalm and a chapter from the Prophets, but everything strikes him as too "improvised for the occasion."

This pushes him farther in that direction than he would like to go.

My dear André (Ruyters): — Of all my recent companions of whom I think insistently every day, it seems that you are one of the least favored. To go off to the wars and then end up at a rear echelon in front of a cook-stove or a wash-tub is not very exciting. I know also that you were seriously upset the first few days as a result of the change of diet; I know too that your discomfort did not last.

I should most likely have written you earlier, but I have very little liking for general reflections about the events and I find nothing new or special to tell you. You probably know that I returned to Cuverville as soon as conditions began to appear not too favorable and a dreadful cloud temporarily darkened our outlook. Copeau became somewhat alarmed at the thought that his wife and children were in a spot that might seem dangerous; it was my mission to send them across the water. At the same time I emptied Cuverville of my nephews, nieces, and sisters-in-law, who were then pleasantly but unwisely filling the place; and I remained alone with my wife and K. (who was to get back to Havre by bicycle at the first serious alarm), Em. and I with our minds made up to remain to the last like my brother-in-law Georges, mayor of Cuverville, as you know. On the day of my return here the "official communiqué" proclaimed the Germans' onslaught on "the Somme" — the lack of preciseness had the effect of spreading panic throughout the Caux district. Étretat, Fécamp, even Criquetot were literally emptied of everyone who could afford flight. The spectacle was rather disgusting and its repercussion on the poverty-stricken and on those detained by their functions was most painful. On the other hand, I was able to notice the comfort they took from my wife's calmness and courage. My return likewise contributed toward reassuring them, for they thought: "Since Monsieur Gille is coming back, there can't be any danger!" Fortunately they couldn't read my heart! I lived through ten days of frightful anguish, expecting the worst from one hour to the next — and perhaps not entirely without reason. . . . And when the "communiqués" gave us reason to believe that the flood no longer threatened Normandy, they showed it to be so close to Paris that our anguish merely changed form. . . .

How easily life takes shape again, closing up its gaps! Too easy healing of wounds. Surrender to that paltry comfort which is the great enemy of real happiness.

The position of X., who stays behind while those who insisted on the necessity of staying all go.

The converse position of the L.'s at Yport — whom F. urges to leave, even fixing an appointment with them at such and such a station — then abandons after making up his mind to stay till the last moment, as if he lacked the courage of his cowardice.

18 September

This morning, before eight o'clock, a telegram brought by the postmistress's great-nephew: "Charles Péguy fell before the enemy Argonne." Théo sent it to me.

23 September

Since 26 August I have ceased keeping the journal I had resumed on the . . . and had kept regularly since then. It seemed to me inappropriate, in the face of such serious events, to continue my notes in such a subjective tone. I opened a new notebook (larger in format, yellow with a red back), in which I noted down, with no reference to myself, everything that I thought could furnish material for my novel. At first this was a help, for I noted down things that I never could have in journal form. But this new method is no help as soon as outside events cease to overshadow my personal life. I haven't written anything for the last eight or ten days, and this silence corresponds to a new sagging of my will, of my virtue, over which this journal must again lead me to triumph.

A telegram from Jacques Raverat called me to Havre, whence I brought him back to Cuverville. For several days the weather had been frightful. I had brought back from Trouville Valentine Gilbert and my two nieces. Jeanne Drouin returned from Étretat. Mme Copeau asked to remain at Braffy until after Mme Jouvet's delivery: moreover Jean Schlumberger deemed it unwise to let her return here too soon with train-connections so unsure.

K. brought back from Havre, where he had gone four days before, three young Lafauries (twins and their cousin Maurice), the last one very funny, somewhat of a buffoon without meaning to be but always aware of his comic side; his eyes laughing and rather sly, his mouth greedy, his nose bulbous, and his hands extraordinarily short, thick, and inexpressive. He amuses me very much and even does more than amuse me.

24 September

The three young Lafauries left yesterday. The evening before last I read them Turgenyev's *The Dog* with success, though the twins remained on the defensive. Jacques Raverat has prolonged his stay twenty-four hours; yesterday we took a long walk with K. in the wooded valley of Fongueusemare. I am not reconciled to seeing that youngster remain ignorant of so many provinces of pleasure; poetry, thought, music, and painting seem to him forbidden realms as they were for Gérard and for so many others of that generation.

The invasion of the barbarian.

Last night read some Courteline and Duvernois to the children.

25

Yesterday Jacques Raverat left. We had read together Milton's wonderful *Ode on the Nativity* and several of Shakespeare's *Sonnets*. Talked endlessly of ethics and religion. He believes in the devil; he even told me that he believed in the devil before believing in God. I told him that what kept me from believing in the devil was that I wasn't quite sure of hating him. Certainly there will be someone in my novel who believes in the devil. These conversations will prove to have been of rather great advantage to both of us. He tells me that he is leaving full of new vigor for work.

Ride to Étretat in the afternoon in a carriage. I regret not having learned until too late that one could visit the wounded (from one to three on Thursdays and Sundays).

This morning Marcel arrived unexpectedly just while I was in the act of writing him.

26

Went to take a bottle of wine and a box of biscuits to poor old Mme Freger (née Urémie Débris!). I had left her, about a fortnight ago, in her bed without much hope of ever getting out of it. The only traces her illness has left are great pains in her head and a rather violent inflammation of the left eye, which she keeps covered with a black band. She finishes "her round of chores," then leads me to her house and there, as I was about to leave her, for the first time gives free rein to her feelings of gratitude and affection, which draw tears to my eyes. She takes my arm familiarly; she herself weeps as she speaks of Em., and this sudden effusion is all the more impressive since it can express itself only through words as thick, crude, and heavy as slabs of stone. She is astonished that Mius could leave us and will be even more surprised if he doesn't soon return.

On the way back I go down the Groseilliers road as far as Dumont's house to ask for news of the child that Valentine had gone to take care of the day before yesterday. I find the door closed.

Rather long chat with the D. woman, who arranged for me to catch up with her on the lower road and who walks along with me. She questions me almost at once about the war and how long it will last. Her remarks, like those of everyone else I have talked with in the township, are not stupid. All of them probably have the same second-hand opinion, but not only are altogether remarkably well informed about what is going on, alas, in our own country, but even speak of the Russians, the Japanese, even the Serbs not too incompetently. I was already surprised, the day before yesterday at Étretat, by the way the fishermen's children spoke of the bombardment of the Reims Cathedral; certainly their indignation reflected their elders', which came from that expressed by the papers; yet one nevertheless felt it to be sincere and of the desired quality. Certainly the D. woman felt too that there was something irreparable about it that no war indemnities could ever make up for.

Every day I get a bit more enjoyment from teaching Françoise; almost as much as from practising myself — and this is saying a great deal.

27

Oh yes, when S. arrived, I felt a rush of joy into my heart, for despite everything my old friendship for him is not dead and would like nothing better than to revive. But after a very few minutes everything in his words, his posture, and his gestures convinces me all over again of his indifference and coldness toward me. The best he can be with me is "full of attentions." Politeness long ago took the place of friendship in him.

Oh, how willingly I should forget all my past griefs and even those which, despite my bad memory, remain the most painful, if only every new day, every hour, spent with him did not bring me new proofs of his coldness! He never forgets it except to get angry with me.

He wrote me: "Misunderstandings are much more often due to things left unsaid than to things that have been said." But how could I talk to him when he rises up against everything I say or else receives it with a sly, indulgent assent that does not involve his real self at all?

Not a single one of S.'s remarks that have hurt me is intentional or said with the intention of hurting me, and that is the cruelest thing about them; I feel them to be absolutely spontaneous, sprung from his depths. Probably he would not remember them; he is hardly aware that he has said them; they are sincere without his knowing it.

28

Instead of constantly yielding to S., I have made up my mind to stand up to him, and it has worked rather well. If this had gone on a little longer nothing would have been possible between us but puns. I couldn't say anything that he did not question or greet with an indulgent and distant "Oh, yes" as for a child or crazy person. But my patience was really exhausted, and if I balked I did so at first in spite of myself. Furthermore, I take great care not to put forth any statement without proof and evidence to back me up. This is a good regime for my mind, only too inclined to vagueness.

It seems, moreover, that S. is grateful to me for getting angry and that he is less rebuffed than when he encounters no resistance.

Dreadful night. Over-tense nerves; body as jumpy as when I am at my worst. I was unable to get any sleep at all until three a.m.

Yet I do not feel too tired this morning, but *susceptible* and my self-respect exposed.

Nevertheless rather good work (or at least English reading and Françoise's piano lesson. I am learning Dukas's Variations by heart all over again); but a frightful anguish weighs constantly on all my thoughts; I cannot forget for a moment that yonder a dreadful indecisive struggle has been going on for a fortnight now. . . .

Friday, 2 October

Sixtieth day since the mobilization.

The days pass in a monotonous expectation. At moments I long to be in Paris. But, once there, wouldn't I regret having left Cuverville?

Wednesday, the whole household having gone out for a walk, I remained alone with Em. stringing beans on the bench in front of the house. The sky was marvelously pure. We hardly exchanged a word or two from time to time, for we could talk of nothing but *that*; and yet the great silence around us and in us filled us with happiness despite ourselves. . . . Then I joined Valentine and the children in the woods above the valley and we did not come back until after dark.

Thursday the break took us to Étretat. I rather hated to leave Em., alone in the house with Odile. The sky was just as radiant as the day before, but the air was already cold. I was on the seat with little Jacques.

At Étretat I left the others and went down to the lower edge of the Great Gate by way of the rocks that the sea had uncovered. As I was returning I met Valentine, who was taking Françoise and Jacques to wade in the puddles. The two children were barefoot. Jacques declared that he was not having a good time at all and that he would rather have stayed with his mother. Valentine tried in vain to convince him that it is great fun to walk barefoot on the seaweed. Obviously the rocks hurt him a bit, but above all he was terribly afraid of all the mysterious animals he imagined in the puddles and nothing could get him to dip his toes into them. With his shoes back on he was somewhat more courageous and soon I got him to risk a few little adventures in climbing. There is nothing more engaging than a child who doesn't yet know himself and who thinks himself a coward because his mother has constantly warned him against all the kinds of harm that could happen to him. I rather made fun of his fears and, wherever there was no danger, let him get along by himself. At first the fear of nasty creatures kept him from putting his hands on the rocks; but he was sensitive to my kidding and soon made a point of honor of being bold.

Today (Friday) the weather is overcast. The air is soft. Still the papers have no news.

Jacques, who, despite what he heard his mother say yesterday evening, was well aware that he had been wrong, came this morning, quite on his own, to ask Valentine's forgiveness for having been so bad with her. Then, eager to show me that he is not such a coward as he seemed, he began to climb almost to the top of a little tree in my presence, and, I declare, with a certain agility! He would never have done this if I had encouraged him yesterday in his fears.

In the evening continued my reading of *Arthur Gordon Pym* to the children.[44]

3 October

We learned of our successes in the valley of the Marne. Then there was a sort of apparent calm; for a fortnight we had almost no other news than this: the battle is going on; along the whole front the struggle is bitter; the front line has hardly undergone any change.

---

[44] *The Narrative of Arthur Gordon Pym of Nantucket* by Edgar Allan Poe.

4 October

Still nothing. The horrible struggle continues. Never ceasing to think of it, one would like to contribute to the outcome.

Began a letter to Ruyters; but on the third page my memory of his last conversation interrupts me. His unjust accusation, however slight it may be, and without decreasing my friendship at all, keeps me from being frank and open with him; and as soon as I cease to be natural I am nothing at all.

Letter from Jeanny Valéry; I write at length to Paul (twelve pages).

Took Miquette to Fellow, Valentine's dog now being boarded by Georges. For more than a half-hour the poor animal exhausted himself in useless attempts; he is no better than Toby.

Finished *Tess of the D'Urbervilles,* which I had begun in Paris; this means that I spent a little more than a month on it. I admire this book more than I like it and cannot understand how anyone can prefer it to *Jude the Obscure.*[45]

Went to the house of Dumont, whose little child died the day before yesterday. Was able to see only the sister-in-law and the three youngest, who came to sit beside me on the embankment on the edge of the woods.

5 October

Every day I make Françoise practice two hours; I should like to teach her to practice alone. The chief difficulties (I was about to say the only ones) I find in her are due to bad habits picked up some time ago; particularly the habit of never giving its full value to each note, so that it yields only to the following note. She plays in strict time, but does not hold the notes she strikes. Because of this, I make her practice the first of Handel's *Little Fugues,* which calls for the perfect linking of each note to the following one and the holding of the white and full notes through the black ones.

Took Miquette back to Fellow; the bitch is just as willing as can be and even tries to help, but he insists on being out of line despite all I do to help him. Since, eventually, I left him to himself and he got nowhere, he came to get me, pulling and pushing me toward the bitch, again begging for my help.

I wish it were forbidden for anyone to make statements about sex who had not had experience in breeding and observing animals. Perhaps they would finally come to understand that many difficulties, deviations, and irregularities that they insist on calling abnormal and "against nature" are no less *natural* than others.

---

[45] Both novels are by Thomas Hardy.

7 October

Horrible nights. Headaches as frequent as during my childhood, and, in so far as I can remember, of exactly the same nature. Since about the age of eighteen they had not come back.

Two letters, one from Jacques Copeau, the other from Mme Copeau, both telling us that there has been no news from Rivière since 24 August.[46]

8 October

All day yesterday I had a headache, which subsided only toward evening. Was able to read nevertheless a few pages of Browning (of *Pauline* and of *Pippa Passes*), finding more interest and pleasure in them than in any other English poet. If only this liking and admiration were a bit older, I should give Browning the first place in my heart and mind.

Yesterday epic discussion about the automobiles now on our roads and about the way of stopping them to make sure that their occupants' papers are satisfactory. Marcel and Jeanne claim that the police use a whistle and in so far as possible avoid showing themselves, etc. — a most useless discussion since it concerns a precise and frequently renewed fact, which would consequently be easy to verify. But on both sides we get excited, Marcel backing up Jeanne and I backing Valentine, while Em., frightened by the noise, withdraws as she always does in such cases. With Marcel and Jeanne conversations always assume the aspect of a battle in which everyone's honor is involved in maintaining the position he has taken. I say "everyone" since after a short while — and no matter how little desire you may have to triumph over someone you cannot look upon as an adversary — you are forced into this type of dialogue and end up by becoming involved.

Beautiful weather. This morning I feel well, despite (or perhaps because of) a wakeful night. Marcel has again become almost pleasant, obviously somewhat embarrassed at having let himself be carried away the night before. We returned to the subjects of discussion but without any irritation and on the contrary with a longing for agreement that puts me at ease at once, agreeing that, without the two ladies, the conversation would never have degenerated.

I am writing these lines in the little second-floor room that I have been occupying since my return here; Hérouard's large green courtyard is full of joyous light. Some children are knocking the apples down with poles and I take delight in hearing the rain of fruit, which the women pick up in the short grass.

---

[46] Jacques Rivière was taken prisoner on 24 August at the Battle of Eton and did not return to France until 1918.

Françoise, Nicole, and Jacques set out to meet the Copeaus, who are coming on the three-o'clock train. This is my next-to-last day spent here in peace; while, on the other side of France, the country is plunged into mourning, devastation, and horror. A letter from Édouard, which Georges brings us this morning, recounts his absurd and lamentable odyssey from Pont-l'Évêque to Tarbes, then to Versailles, then to Pont-l'Évêque again, encountering everywhere nothing but disorder and negligence.

We have frightful faults that defeat did not correct and victory will not correct. Those we mourn today paid for them with their lives.

10 October

The remark of the lady who was experiencing difficulties, at the station: "And besides, you know, I am beginning to have enough of your war!"

Left Cuverville the 10th. Arrived at about nine p.m. at the Théos', rue Laugier, where I find Copeau and Ghéon, who have been there for a month, and Jean Schlumberger, who, coming for two days, arrives at the same time as I.

My letters to Em. have taken the place of this journal.

At the Criquetot station, as I am getting my ticket for Paris, the station-master in a bantering tone: "Well! It seems there's no more danger in the capital!" At once I flared up: "Well I declare! So you think we all act according to our fear? I came here because there was danger here; and I am leaving because there is no further danger here!" Then, as Marcel was passing close to us, I call him in, glad of this opportunity to show him the general opinion: "Come over here, old man, and listen to the station-master: according to him, I took refuge here to get away from danger. . . ." But already the fat station-master, red in the face, backs down.

Luce Ruyters writes to her mother: "I am so bored that I am working for the poor." A remark that I think her father would like.

Almost complete insomnia every night.

•   *16 October*

It seems to me, also, that massacre hasn't the same meaning for a nation with a declining birth-rate as for a very prolific nation. The German who decimates a village knows that he can repopulate it; over-population invites to massacre; they have to "clear the way" ahead of them.

The will not to be melancholy. Copeau: "I should like to beat any-one who weeps." On the other hand those who want to take upon themselves all sorrow: P. A. Laurens, who locks himself in his studio between his brother's portrait of Péguy and his anguish about that brother of whom they have no news!

Ghéon and he joke *as if they were in the front-line trenches.* X. thought that, when one is safe oneself and with all one's family safe, it is a bit too easy to laugh and almost unseemly.

23 October

At Évreux.

Beginning this morning, telegrams have to be countersigned again, but at the police station where they are initialed you don't have to show your papers

Night of 29 October

Frightful last twitches. All I have left is just enough intelligence to be aware that I am going crazy.

10 November

At Cuverville for two days. Rest. During the last week, moreover, I have somewhat resumed my assurance. My horrible fatigue came, I think, from being exposed to sympathy all day long. At the Foyer Franco-Belge,[47] not a moment alone in which to assume one's own personality and relax. I felt myself *absorbed* by others. Busy morning and afternoon caring for those refugees whom we lodge, clothe, and feed and for whom we seek work, I would return at lunch and at night to Ghéon's vibrant gaiety and to the excessive energy of my friends and hosts.

15 November

An American came just the other day to the Foyer Franco-Belge to inform us that he would give our institution a large sum of money if we could succeed in putting him into direct contact with a child who had been mutilated by the Germans.

Richepin, in an indignant article, spoke of *four thousand* children who supposedly had had their right hands cut off. That assertion without any proof had irked Romain Rolland (see his letter) and doubtless a number of Swiss people also.

However, Mme Edwards, at the end of August (check the date), had told me of the arrival at rue Vaneau of a procession of children, all boys from the same village and all similarly amputated.

---

[47] Franco-Belgian Center.

The day before yesterday I went to her, pointing out the great interest we would have in definite proof of such monstrosities. She told me then that she had not seen the children herself, that she knows they were coming from the Cirque de Paris, where they had first been sent. She invites me to come back and lunch with her on the following day (yesterday), promising me — until I find better proof — photographs of those mutilations.

Yesterday she had not been able to get the photographs, but she was expecting Cocteau right after lunch, who was to bring them. Cocteau came after lunch without the photos, which he promised me for tomorrow evening. Meanwhile he led me to the clinic on rue de la Chaise, where we could speak with a Red Cross nurse who had taken care of those children. The lady was not there yet and, expected at the Foyer, I had to leave Cocteau before learning anything.

Ghéon also tells me that two amputated children, one fifteen and the other seventeen years old, were being cared for at Orsay right now. He is to bring me further information.

Not one of these statements could be proved.

He who feels that he will not be up to it. Would like to disappear. If only people would pay no more attention to him.

On such and such a date, the soldier who puts forth a tremendous effort (related at length) so that the event in which he played a part is enlarged and magnified — and who then reads, in that day's "Communiqué": "from X. to Y. *nothing worth noting.*"

In the métro Mme Théo encounters a young English officer. He, so fresh and bursting with health, is sitting opposite her. . . . Not a single word exchanged during the whole trip, but as he is about to get out, suddenly he leans toward her and says very quickly in an undertone:

"I want to be wounded in a hurry so that you can take care of me."

"Oh! I hope you will not," Mme Théo immediately exclaims.[48]

That inner flame that burns in her has not yet purified all her features.

The soldier who takes upon himself his comrades' adventures — and to whom, after all, nothing has ever happened. He has more to tell than anyone else.

(At Cuverville.) Then it was discovered that the E. girl was pregnant. She confessed that she had let the butcher-boy have his way with her the night before he left for the front.

---

[48] Her speech is in English in the original.

The chapter of the refugees. Their arrival at the little house. Their hope of something else, something more. Their disappointment. They deserved better. The first evening they take out the papers and cards on which are written the addresses of the people who received them. Both of them close to the lantern. Their will not to give in to their mounting distress.

"They were requisitioned horses," Houssonloge, the wounded man from Liége whom we are lodging, tells us. "Mine, as soon as we had started out, gets excited and — But I must first tell you that at that moment we were not far from my village and that my family knew it. When the Germans began shooting, just then I see two women coming toward us; they were running. As my lieutenant's orderly, I had his binoculars on me; I look at the two women and recognize my wife and my mother. They were running toward us, among the bullets; they were bringing us food. They were already very close to us when I hear the command: 'To the left — gallop.' It was just then that my horse runs away and takes me within range of the bullets, right toward the enemy lines. I tell myself: 'Old man, if you are not killed now, that's because you're never going to die. . . .' Because, whether on our side or on theirs, no one takes isolated prisoners; you just shoot them right away.

"To begin with, they put me in a big box-car with thirty others and a sentry to guard us. Must tell you that this took place right near the Dutch border. I say to myself: 'Old man, you're not so dumb as not to know how to get out of this. . . .' Because on the other side of the car, opposite the sentry, there was a little round window covered with bars, through which, if there hadn't been bars, you could have slipped out. And as I was noticing that the grill could be unscrewed, I see a woman passing; she is bringing me civilian clothes, which she pushes through the window, from which I had meanwhile removed the bars. There were enough for several; but I say to the others: 'I am the one who had the idea; it's only right to begin with me.' But naturally I take the least possible clothes for me and leave everything I can for the others. I stick my head through the opening; when my shoulders got through, the rest of my body had to follow. I fell on my head on the other side of the car, and then, lying on the ground, I waited because I had a pal who had said he would follow me. I waited exactly two minutes, and then I said: 'If he prefers to stay, there's no reason why I should wait any longer.' Then I ran along, as quick as I could, all the way to the border. 'Are you a soldier?' they asked me. 'Hell no,' I told them; 'I am a civilian refugee . . .' because I was afraid to be interned. But all the same I changed boots as soon as I could, because they might have recognized me by them. They let me get on board

ship at Vlissingen and from there I was able to get back to my
outfit.

"The second time that I was caught, I was with four civilians and a
chaplain. We were going into X. . . . We asked the women who were
at the windows: 'Are there any Germans hereabout?' And they replied:
'There aren't any' . . . because they had been commanded to answer
this and the Germans who were hidden in the houses would have finished them off if they had answered otherwise. When we were taken we
were led into a field with a sentry to guard us. Of course I had been disarmed, but they hadn't searched my hip pocket, where lancers keep
their revolver. And I kept my hand in that pocket, without stirring as
I lay close enough to the sentry to touch the bayonet on his gun. He
didn't stir either. He was lying down too and we were looking at each
other. Until eventually he takes out his tobacco and begins to roll a
cigarette. It didn't take long. I shot him right between the eyes. He
moved so little that the others could hardly believe he was dead.

"The third time I was taken prisoner by a fellow from the cavalry.
That is, there were two of them, but one had left his gun on the
ground. He had remounted. . . ."

Later on, X. discovers the reputation of people from L'ége: all great
talkers. There is perhaps not a word of truth in Houssonloge's tales.

Visit to the Louvre — desolation.
The end of a civilization?

Under the influence of chloroform the wounded relive the recent
anguish. Ghéon's wounded man muttering: "Oh, the cold! I can endure
anything but this cold!"

Jean Cocteau's story in which, as in everything he tells, it is hard
to distinguish the original germ of reality under the vast poetical exaggeration. In the hospital he was next to a soldier who whispered as
he held his hand: "You aim at the fellow on the right; I'll take care of
the one on the left. Hooray! We're holding. Now, old boy, shout:
'Victory! Victory!' and as loud as you can so the captain will hear you."
Then Jean Cocteau whispers in his ear so as not to attract the attention of the other beds: "Victory! Victory!"

"He can't hear you. You know he's deaf."

Then Cocteau, after two weak attempts, risks shouting: "Victory!"

The poetic Red Cross lady volunteer immediately opens the door
and repeats in a theatrical voice: "Victory! Victory! Victory!" stepping
gingerly forward as if approaching the footlights.

Worth examining closely: the Abed family, one of the most recently arrived, which wants nothing but a mattress and blankets (nine persons).

The Kl. family, sent to Magny — (the two sons, one named Ambiorix), the son-in-law and the daughter they keep out of the way. . . . Lamentable discovery of the trunk full of clothing they are lugging about with them.

The work of the Foyer Franco-Belge.

He gave to it, as he said in the few letters he wrote at that time, "all his heart and all his time"; that meager formula allowed him to skimp his correspondence.

How and why that work, in the beginning altogether charitable, gradually became administration.

Other charitable organizations, limited in their aims, function with ease. There are many refugees for whom food or lodging (or even the two together) are not suitable. One asks only for a bed; another family would be happy if only they could come by the cooking-utensils they can't afford to buy. Another who gets the dole does not need to be fed *and* lodged by a charitable organization; that would be a waste. Most organizations don't care; as they say elegantly: "That doesn't concern us." Mme X. comes to us after having been to the Cirque de Paris, which is sordid, to the Séminaire Saint-Sulpice, which is lamentable, to the Salle Wagram, which is full up; she is offered lodgings that she doesn't need since she is satisfactorily settled and can do her own cooking, for her six children; she is paying forty-five francs a month, sometimes even less. If she is offered meals, what good will that do her? All she needs is a small weekly installment allowing her to meet the situation; for example, an assurance that her rent will be paid. The dole will take care of the rest. The meals that are suggested would cost much more at the charitable organization and would force her and her children to go out in all weather. In addition, meals taken on the outside keep her from having "a home."

* * *

Well then, since we have this great good luck
That the old instrument's feeble twanging is broken,
Let us boldly make the best of it rather than
Stoop to pick up the pieces or save a token.

Since our libraries were full,
And our heads as well, to overflowing;
Since everything had been said and felt and known,
At least in the old way of knowing;

Since our worn cloak of ethics had become a shroud
And it is too early for us to go naked;
Since everything that was stifling in us cried aloud
Without having ever yet received any help;

Since in our heart of hearts we longed for the cataclysm,
The great gust to sweep away all impurity,
Praise God if, instead of coming from without,
It rises from the very depths of humanity!

This war is not like other wars;
We have more than a territory or patrimony
To protect. . . . No! a future is striving to be born,
A vast future, tearing its feet as it wriggles free.

Oh! how vigorously your heel thrusts
To leap forth, new world!
With love and with the hope
Of a longer-lived beauty,
May the soil you spurn forgive you!

❊

Poor wavering soul, you cannot take
Both the past and the future as your own.
You have either, weeping for dead ashes' sake,
To sink toward the tomb or else to awake
Young enough to spring into the unknown.[49]

---

[49] Alors, puisque nous avons cette chance immense
      Que l'ancien instrument qui vibrait encore soit brisé,
      Saisissons-nous intrépidement de cet avantage
      Et n'allons pas nous courber pour rien ramasser.

      Puisque aussi bien nos bibliothèques étaient pleines
      Et nos cerveaux, à ne pouvoir plus rien y loger;
      Puisque tout était dit, du moins selon l'ancien mode,
      Tout connu, tout vécu, du moins à l'ancienne façon;

      Puisque notre manteau de morale était usé jusqu'à la corde
      Et que pourtant il n'est pas encore permis d'aller nu;
      Puisque tout ce qui étouffait en nous criait miséricorde
      Sans avoir, jamais encore, rien obtenu;

      Puisque, dans le secret de nos cœurs, nous souhaitions le cataclysme,
      Le grand coup de vent qui balayât l'impureté,

Vive Dieu! s'il ne vient pas du dehors, mais s'élève
Du profond de l'humanité!

Cette guerre n'est pas pareille à une autre guerre;
Il n'est pas seulement question d'un territoire à protéger,
D'un patrimoine, d'une tradition. . . . Non! c'est un avenir qui veut
    naître
Énorme et se dégage en s'ensanglant les pieds.

Oh! quel coup de talon tu donnes
Pour bondir en avant, nouveauté!
Dans l'amour et dans l'espérance
D'une plus vivace beauté,
Que le sol écrasé te pardonne!

Pauvre âme incertaine, tu ne peux t'éprendre
A la fois de l'avenir et du passé.
Il s'agit de voir si tu veux rester pleurant sur des cendres,
Si vers la tombe enfin il ne te reste plus qu'à descendre
Ou si, dans l'inconnu, tu te sens assez jeune encore pour t'élancer.

1915

I tell you that a new civilization is beginning. Yesterday's was based too much on Latin civilization; that is to say, on the most artificial and empty culture. In contradistinction to the thoroughly natural Greek civilization. . . . But it must be admitted that its very shortcomings made Latin culture appeal to us.

24 September

Until then I wrote in the overflow of my joy. Through lack of expression, today my suffering is increased. I am awkward in grief. And I am even inclined to attribute to some secret fatigue any decrease in my happiness. How tired I am! . . .

25 September

I have recovered my balance only at the piano, where I am continuing to practice the Albéniz compositions. I know three of them by heart and more than half of a fourth. Picked up again in the same manner Franck's Prelude, Choral, and Fugue and some of Chopin's Études.

Paul A. Laurens takes advantage of the great leisure his canteen leaves him to "go back to school," as he says, and "to learn how to draw all over again." Together with two comrades, he requisitions a model and sits down to work for hours at a time. I cannot rejoice with him over this. A bad time to learn when everything is again being questioned. Besides, did he sin through lack of technique? I believe, on the contrary, that his originality might have been better seconded by a less ready technique, and even by a little clumsiness. Virtuosity never produced anything but banality. The only technique that is worth anything is the one that emotion itself has created and can invent again when need be. I want to write nothing except under pressure of necessity.

Sunday, 26 September

Keep this notebook from day to day: good discipline, which has always benefited me.

I finally finish *Gulliver*. I didn't enjoy it very much and am glad to have finished. It remains limited, harsh, and acrimonious. You constantly expect something better, something else, and the idea of what it might have been spoils for me the little it is.

Began yesterday, with great pleasure, *The Autobiography of Mark Rutherford,* which Bennett had suggested to me.[1]

This evening's communiqué fills me with anguish. Could it at last be the beginning of the dawn? . . . I hear their cries, up at the front; I see that mad rush and the bursting forth of their mortal hope. I think of little Jean-Paul Allégret and of E. D. It rained almost all night.

27 September

Suffocating communiqué this morning. Will the lid eventually be raised? It seems to me that at the first breath of fresh air I shall stifle. I should like to be with Em.

Card from Copeau last night, oddly out of time.[2] He speaks of Florence, of Angelico. . . . Does all that still exist?

28 September

Hope still hesitates, not daring to open wide its wings and take flight toward new skies. . . . What patience our waiting calls for! How long will I have to keep silent? And when the time comes will I have enough strength and time left to speak?

I am diverted from the Foyer and now go there only in the afternoon to find little to do. I am tired of it and constantly break away. I can't stick it. . . . Before my recent short trip to Cuverville I had again been completely absorbed by a new branch (the distribution of clothing) that had to be thoroughly reorganized. Right now the keeping of our list of grants, perfectly organized, does not call for any further initiative. The regular work on it has become almost entirely administrative. Perhaps I shall settle down for a while at rue Taitbout to keep an eye on the way the restaurant is functioning. Most likely it would be worth reconsidering many things there, but I fear that Charlie Du Bos might be hurt. I cannot half give my services or lend myself. For eleven months at the Foyer I managed to let myself be completely absorbed by my task and become utterly interested in it. Now that the machine is running properly, is it permissible for me to get away from it, as from a finished book? . . .

No. Nothing in the material world is ever finished. Everything goes on. And what you have once taken upon yourself has a claim upon you.

Darius Milhaud came yesterday, late in the afternoon, to play the symphonic poem he has just composed on one of the Tagore poems I

---

[1] This sincere work of spiritual self-probing by William Hale White first appeared in 1881.

[2] The last three words appear in English in the text.

translated. It was nothing but noise to me.[3] Then he played us most
delicately some rather ordinary melodies of Mendelssohn. The day before I had accompanied Marianne Delacre. She sang some Chausson
and some Duparc. A purpose or psychological meaning always bothers
me in music. For me it loses its real meaning when it tries to take on
too definite a meaning.

29 September

"It is hard to say whether one would like to get old in a hurry or,
on the other hand, make time stand still," Mme Lacroix, whose only
son is at the front, says to me this morning at the Foyer. The letter
she received from him yesterday is dated the 22nd. Will he go through
this hell and come out alive?

Day spent at Magny, where the Chaussons' auto takes me. Cold,
fog, and rain; as long as I retain a little animal heat, I stay in front
with the chauffeur, delightfully chilled by the crisp autumn air. At
Satory I join Mme Chausson, her two daughters, and Marianne Delacre
inside the car.

Pleasant hours spent with Raymond Bonheur, but the visit is prolonged a bit too much. We do not get back to Paris until dark. Although I am to dine, as Marianne Delacre is, with the Théos at rue
Laugier, where the auto drops us, I leave the others to dash to the
Foyer and pick up the Rutherford book that I had forgotten there in
the morning. My appetite for it cannot wait.

Returning home at half past ten, I am unwilling to take leave of
this empty day without having at least given it three quarters of an
hour of piano-practice (Albéniz) — muffling the sound out of consideration for the neighbors.

1 October

I almost left for England. I was already leaving the Théos' with my
bag and steamer-rug; I had an appointment to meet Mrs. Wharton tomorrow morning at the Gare du Nord. Henry James and Arnold Bennett were expecting me. Yesterday I had written to Raverat to announce my arrival and had taken leave of the Foyer. Fortunately I
encounter insurmountable difficulties at the prefecture. Before getting
my passport I have to go to the Invalides to regularize my military
status or at least to prove that it is regular; then to the local police station with two witnesses and my photograph; then to the British Embassy; then to the Ministry of Foreign Affairs. . . . And, since there

---

[3] Milhaud's *Melody* for voice and piano (rather than symphonic poem)
was inspired by the Tagore-Gide poem beginning: "*Les nuages s'entassent
sur les nuages.*" It has been published only once, by *La Revue Française de
Musique.*

was not enough time for all these formalities, I suddenly found myself extraordinarily relieved to give up the project altogether. If I got some pleasure from the idea of going away, my pleasure at the idea of staying was certainly much greater, and I enjoy this late afternoon, here, like someone who has just had a narrow escape.

I rushed to Mrs. Wharton's, for she was to get my ticket. Yet it would have amused me to travel with her. But this was not the moment.

2 October

Last night, on my way home to Auteuil, I risked knocking at Labasque's door. I found him seated on his bed reading, in the *N.R.F.* that Charlie Du Bos had allowed him to take from the rue Taitbout, the Whitman remarks so flatly translated by Bazalgette. Eager to show him the Goya drawings, of which I have the reproductions, I dragged him off to the Villa.

I have no idea what that strange youth seeks in painting; everything disappoints him. He hardly lent a little attention to the prints I showed him, which he had once been so eager to see. The other day he was on the point of getting enthusiastic about Redon, and now he has already dismissed him. Moreover he expresses his most unjustifiable condemnations with such modesty and such conviction that he almost makes them bearable and acceptable.

Dined, as the day before, on eggs and some sausage bought at Godefrain's.

Great intellectual fatigue still; a sort of gray oppression of all my thought. And yet . . .

Cuverville, 7 October

Arrived here Tuesday evening. At the Foyer I was no longer doing anything that mattered. Heaviness of head and dizzy spells.

I was planning to write up many things here, but my thoughts thicken and coagulate. Not even been able to finish Rutherford's book yet.

And nevertheless there is filling out and taking form the book I should like to write if . . . But the vastness of the amorphous substance crushes me; I don't know where to seize hold of it and wonder how I shall manage it, also whether I shall still have strength enough.

8 October

This evening I finish *The Autobiography of Mark Rutherford*. Wonderful integrity of the book. I do not know any literary work that is more specifically Protestant. How does it happen that the book is not better known? How grateful I am to Bennett for having told me about it! The exquisite qualities of Hale White's style (this is the author's real name) are the very ones that I should like to have.

9 October

Read with interest, in the *Revue de Paris* for 15 May lent by Ducoté, E. G.'s pages on the refugees.[4] Reasonable, cordial and very fair in tone. But how simple the problem becomes when presented thus by an authoritative representative of the administration. It is obvious that at the Foyer we see them in a very different light: all the cases that come to us, or at least those that get our attention, are precisely the ones that the administration was incompetent or unwilling to solve.

It is, alas, only too natural, with our electoral system, that the economy that is preached to the administration should be tried out chiefly at the expense of the refugees, of those who don't belong to the arrondissement or the commune and who are partially protected and supported by regional committees. E. G., of necessity, sees only those who get satisfaction; we, on the other hand, see only the others. And it's not so jolly!

Only by making a virtue of egotism can I manage not to think of them. I remember that summer when the thought of Jules Iehl's sufferings obsessed me, when, just to imagine him fading away in his dull office, made all work impossible for me; I could not get my mind off of him and was ashamed of my comfort. For eleven months at the Foyer I lived devoured by sympathy. I cannot yet say or even know what that period did to me. On certain days I came to believe that I should never get over it.

10 October

Yesterday, radiant weather. But all day long I drag myself about, my head unbearably heavy. Unable to write anything, but continued my practice of Albéniz's *Lavapiés*. Read *La Princesse Georges*, which rather happily surprised me.[5] Its cleverness often achieves elegance. But quite useless to speak of it.

Read thirty pages of Théophile Gautier's *Caprices*. I don't know anything more silly. A Kipling tale (*Second Jungle Book*) in English. And continued *The Lesson of the Master* by James.

11 October

Abominable numbness. I dream with a sort of anguish of the life that Cuverville holds in store for me and from which I don't see how

---

[4] The article, entitled "Scenes and Types of Refugees: Notes by a Sub-prefect," is signed Ernest Gaubert.

[5] *Princess George*, a play by Alexandre Dumas *fils*.

I can escape save by breaking bonds and loosing myself from the most venerated and cherished obligations. It is not freedom I seek, but rather being able to work in good healthy conditions, which I have never yet managed to achieve. It often seems to me that in more favorable conditions I should have been able to produce much more; and that thought tortures me like a remorse. But I am always timid when there are decisions to be taken. It is not toward the most attractive alternative that my temperament urges me, but rather toward the least costly. I am quite amazed to have been able at times to travel. Far from yielding to an impulse, each time I had to force myself to leave.

12 October

Back to Paris.

16 October

Having resumed my life as a philanthropist and parasite, I no longer have a moment to write in this notebook. At the Foyer morning and afternoon; I am caught again by the extreme interest of certain cases, by the atmosphere of affection and bewilderment that pervades that place, and the dangerous intoxication that self-sacrifice brings. Em. is to come to town Monday.

21 October

Frantically busy from morning to evening. These last few days we have had an avalanche of pathetic cases. Unable to note anything.

22 October

Yesterday, in *Le Temps,* an article by Souday in reply to the idiotic article by F. M. on Gobineau.[6] The day before yesterday I had stepped into Galignani's, possessed by the desire to buy Conrad's new book, which I am now reading with the greatest pleasure.[7]

Hardly a day goes by that one does not read in the papers, despite the censor, enough to make one wonder whether or not we really deserve to conquer. To tell the truth, neither of the two countries deserves to crush the other, and Germany, by obliging us to oppose her, committed a frightful mistake.

---

[6] Frédéric Masson had written a savage and ridiculous article on Gobineau in *La Revue hebdomadaire.* Souday refutes this article most scathingly in *Le Temps* for 22 October 1915.

[7] The book is doubtless *Within the Tides* (1915). Galignani's is a bookshop in the heart of Paris dealing in English books.

24 October

I have never produced anything good except by a long succession of slight efforts. No one has more deeply meditated or better understood than I Buffon's remark about patience.[8] I bring it not only to my work but also to the silent waiting that precedes good work.

All the same, by dint of waiting, I wonder if I have given all that I might have. At times it seems to me that everything I have produced up to now was only to prepare for the rest, merely to train my hand, and that everything important remains to be said. (I have already expressed this idea elsewhere, but I feel the need of repeating it as I do so often to myself.) At times it strikes me painfully that I have delayed too much and that many of the books that remain to be written should already have been written.

26 October

Yesterday both A. C. and Mlle Langweil were missing from the Foyer. I had to take charge of the information desk, from which I kept jumping up to handle the clothing-distribution as well. Nerve-racking day ending up in a meeting of the committee. Stormy session, for it becomes apparent that, while our desk that handles financial grants has succeeded in a fortnight in saving more than two hundred francs (despite the newcomers whom we admit every day), the two other desks, of L. and of C. Du B., have each gone up a hundred francs. This explains why the total result should be so unsatisfactory.

One cannot expect a very prolific people to show the same regard for human life and the same respect for the individual as a nation that is on the wane. To this consideration must be added the *idée fixe*, which dominates the German people, of the superiority of their race. They work according to the principles of the horticulturist, who teaches that a serious selection consists not only in preference and choice but also in the systematic suppression of all that is not chosen.

Confess that, if you were inhabited by the *idée fixe* of a possible amelioration of the human race, a practical and almost immediate amelioration, you wouldn't strive so enthusiastically to prolong the life of misformed people, degenerates, undesirables, etc., and to encourage, or even merely to permit, their reproduction! To permit this, sacrifice that. Nothing is more logical. Again, it is a question of knowing what deserves to win out.

How many times at the Foyer, caring for, consoling, supporting those poor human rags, capable only of moaning, infirm, without a

---

[8] Buffon is reported to have said: "Genius is but a greater aptitude for patience."

smile, without an ideal, without beauty, I felt rising within me the
frightful question: Do they deserve to be saved? The idea of replacing
them with other, more thriving examples of humanity certainly is a
part of the Germanic *philanthropy*. It is logical and, consequently,
monstrous.

27 October

People seem to think the game is won when they can fall back on
a cliché such as "France has the genius of improvisation," by which
they excuse and encourage improvidence.

Lauris, very touched yesterday by the death of Hervieu, told us
the sinister remark that is attributed to Count G.: "In 1870 people were
gayer."

30 October

Intense work at the Foyer. Great fatigue in the head, or at least an
almost constant headache, preferable nevertheless to the disintegration
and fading of thought, from which I have so often suffered.

Sunday

Yesterday gave Françoise a piano lesson; very satisfied with the
progress she has made. Marcel is on leave for a few days. Yesterday
evening after dinner spent two hours with him. The recollection of his
manifestations of indifference and harshness makes me always somewhat fear seeing him again; at once, however, all fear is drowned in a
flood of friendly joy; but very few moments have passed before I am
seized by a sort of mad impulse that urges me to say to him what is
most likely to harm me in his eyes. Uncle Charles and Édouard Widmer likewise make me talk nonsense: I know, I feel clearly, that each
of them is annoyed by the lack of preciseness of my information, and
this irresistibly leads me to want to cite figures. Why? . . . Likewise,
why did I have to tell Marcel yesterday that Ghéon "had taken part
in our advance in Champagne" although to all others inquiring after
him I have said that he was in "the mining region"? Thus it is that a
man trips on his way across a drawing-room just because he feels that
others think he is going to trip.

Tuesday

Yesterday, Marcel came to lunch, as well as Jeanne and the children. Marcel was in uniform. His face seemed to me more furrowed
than the other evening; he has aged much. After exchanging a few
remarks, he assumes a vacant look and his forehead wrinkles; one
hardly dares address a word to him, so distant he seems. Em. makes
virtuous efforts to bring him back into our group and obtains only a

brief sparkle. As for me, I give up; for too long now everything I can say to him irritates him without interesting him. Nothing is more painful to me than these meals, which were weekly last year, and as often as I could I avoided them.

Sunday, 7 November

Perhaps my slavery to the Foyer will relax somewhat with Mme Théo's return. Beginning this evening she is going to live at the Villa and tomorrow she will probably take up her work again at our desk for financial grants.

There are many things I should have liked to note in this notebook, but I didn't have time; it also happens that after first relating them to Em. my need to set them down here is diminished.

The sudden death of Hérouard, Georges's farmer, shocked Em. and again convinced her that she ought to be there. There are four Hérouard boys in military service, for whom the mother trembles every day since they are all equally exposed to danger. Until now nothing has happened to them; but a sister-in-law happens to die and, while Hérouard and his wife were returning together from the funeral, in the streets of Montivilliers, Hérouard suddenly sinks onto the sidewalk. Bursting of an artery, it is thought.

Until now Mme Hérouard had known only happiness; nothing could have flourished better than her farm, than her family. Mother of eleven children, all healthy, handsome, brave. And, just like our refugees, who all say: "We were not accustomed," it seems that today Mme Hérouard is all the more to be pitied and that misfortune has struck her even harder, from catching her less prepared.

There is certainly a familiarization with misfortune, an inurement to it, or rather a habit of contraction, a certain faculty of withdrawing within oneself, by which non-expansive natures offer hardly any sensitive surface to the blows of fate.

I should like to say to each of these once happy people: "It's your turn." No, there is no compensation nor advantage in that. Those who had sunk sluggishly into an egotistical comfort are incapable of deriving a lesson from misfortunes; and, as for the others, how can one blame them for having yielded to the invitation of happiness?

Thursday, 11

Hateful sluggishness. At times it seems to me that I have already ceased living and that I am bestirring myself in a sort of posthumous dream, a sort of supplement to life, without importance or meaning. This state of apathy is probably the natural result of the emotional strain of the Foyer.

Mme Théo is again giving herself to our organization and this permits me a little leisure; but I don't take real advantage of it and neither work properly nor rest properly.

Yesterday, at the Prisoner of War Organization where I had gone to get a piece of information, M. C. de W., who is the head, I believe, asked me if I had been able to resume my "little literary relaxations."

Friday, 12

I had had the absurd weakness to accept an invitation to dine at Mme Edwards's with the Philippe Berthelots; I come away quite upset. I don't understand very well why people invite me: not famous enough for it to be flattering to have me; my conversation remains desperately dull, and there is nothing to get out of me.

I got into rather hot water by suddenly taking up the defense of Souday, raising my voice and exaggerating my praise, through simple exasperation at the summary judgment of Philippe Berthelot and the others: "And to think that the war will not rid us of fellows like that!"

Philippe Berthelot utters aphorisms of paradoxical flavor and impeccable form, which denote his assurance of his superiority and that of his family, his friends, his tastes, etc. He affects a great calm like that of Renan, which is due, I believe, to an utter insensitivity. In his look, his voice, his gesture, there is something inhuman that paralyzes me. I am also bothered by the narrowness of his forehead; and since despite this he has a prodigious memory, it seems that his ideas must have lost one dimension in order to store themselves in his brain.

Mme Philippe Berthelot arrived in a sheath gown without any waist at all, a sort of silk slip of solid apple-green; excused herself, as she has done on every other occasion I have seen her, for wearing "a tea-gown"; and Mme Edwards, as on every other occasion, exclaimed: "But, my dear, I too am wearing a negligee." It had a very low neck prolonged by transparent gold lace, a cream-colored silk skirt, very short and edged with fur, and over it all a sort of broad-sleeved jacket, likewise edged with fur and considerably shorter than the skirt. These two women sit close together on a low divan with the manners of odalisques. Mme Edwards laughs and clucks and coos, puffing out her neck and letting her head roll on her bare shoulders. Sert is there, plumper and more sententious than ever. I try in vain to listen to him. He tirelessly lectures me on the superiority of "baroque" art and distills boredom as much as I do myself. It seems to me that, with all the time he has been living in France, he might have deigned to lose a little of his accent. F. is the sixth: thin, courteous, insignificant.

At table, the Heredia family is discussed: charming group, a bit noisy, but so amusing, so whimsical! . . . And Philippe Berthelot begins relating his earliest recollections of them. The eldest daughter was barely sixteen then; the youngest was merely a child. Was it the

first time that Philippe Berthelot had entered that drawing-room? I
don't know. . . . Two days before, the maid had had a slight "accident" which was now the young ladies' subject of conversation. One
of them suddenly announced that she was going to fetch the fetus,
went out, and shortly returned from the sixth-floor room with a jar.
And since, in the middle of his tale, Mme Edwards protests, Philippe
Berthelot insists, asserting that it was not a sham, that the fetus was
very definitely in the jar, where the young ladies, with the aid of a
long buttonhook, amused themselves by whirling it around.

The G. couple and the J. R. couple came after dinner. About books,
things, and people much nonsense was said; and if I said perhaps a
little less than the others, this is because I talked less.

I was asked with such insistence to play that refusing became most
difficult. To encourage me Mme Edwards sat down before a book of
Chopin and played some mazurkas with fluidity and charm, but in the
artistic manner, with that *tempo rubato* I dislike so much, or, to speak
more precisely, without paying any attention to the time and with sudden accents, stresses, and effects much more apt to show off the player's temperament than the excellence of the composition. This took
place between two drawing-rooms, in a tiny room hung with gold and
on a piano completely out of tune. The Philippe Berthelots having
left, I wanted to get away too, but since it was raining hard, Mme
Edwards insisted on having an automobile brought round for me and
led me meanwhile toward the piano in the other room, the large
drawing-room with the charming Bonnard decorations. I began the
Prelude in E-flat major. But just as it occurs to me when talking with
an Englishman to take on an English accent, I assumed, out of politeness, the same *tempo rubato* that Mme Edwards had just used and
stopped after twelve agonized bars.

The auto that was taking me home to Auteuil ran out of gasoline two
kilometers from the Villa, so that I had to walk in the dark and under
a driving rain. I was unable to close my eyes all night long, and all
today I shall go about with a headache and a grudge against yesterday's hosts and against myself.

Saturday, 13

Late in the morning yesterday I had gone to see J.-É. Blanche,
whom I find considerably aged and diminished. He leads me into the
little sitting-room and there remains standing, shifting his weight from
one leg to the other like a bear, or taking a few steps from one armchair to another by leaning on their backs, very ill at ease from the
truss he has been wearing for twelve days.

Their relatives from the south have come to stay with them. He does
not feel at home anywhere, and while the child, every evening, studies

beside Mme Blanche in the warm sitting-room, he, taking refuge in the much too large drawing-room, shivers and suffers from the drafts: he is sorely tried by the war.

Sunday, 14

Gloomy days; uninterrupted squalls. Two days ago I received at the Foyer this letter from little Teugels:

"I am writing you these few words to let you know that I shall not return to you, because I regret very much having left my regiment. Monsieur Gide, I ask only one thing of you, and that is that you let me take care of things myself. But, I beg you, don't do anything more for me, for I don't want you or the ladies to get involved in my conversations; for I must tell you that I don't live anywhere, for my friend has gone to Rouen to work. For, as for me, Monsieur Gide, there is only one thing for me to do, and that is that on this date, the 12th, I am going to drown myself in the Seine, and I say good-by and farewell to you. I have nothing more to say to you than these last words. Farewell, Monsieur Gide, and as for the ladies of the Foyer . . .

JEAN THE RASH
died 12 November at 5 p.m."

I put this strange letter into the Teugels file and set down the last interview I had previously had with him, his visit to the Foyer, the morning of the day when this letter was brought to us by a chance acquaintance, then my long wait, with that acquaintance, in the evening on the Place de la Concorde, through which Teugels had said that he would pass. All night long I imagined that poor creature without any place in our society, everywhere condemned and taking refuge in death.

In the garden a tame sparrow, which I had already noticed last year, is fluttering about. He has four or five white feathers on each wing.

Tuesday, 16 November

That thoughtlessness, that vague confidence made up of stupidity and presumption (to say nothing of the confidence based on a faith in Providence) — the worst events teach it nothing and in no way improve it. This or that little fact, this or that unfortunate decision is blamed. . . . "The evil goes farther back," alas! At the danger hour it is discovered that the entire edifice, from top to bottom, is tottering and that society altogether . . . But where were their eyes if they didn't see this long ago? On every level of society each individual is fleeing his rightful responsibility.

18

Shameful article by Beaunier in *Le Figaro* against Renan; Souday very properly takes up the challenge in *Le Temps*.

Yesterday Em. and I visited the little class that Mme Bouni-Reclus is teaching at our organization. When we came in she was teaching geography to ten boys and girls ranging in age from eight to ten, all studious, well-behaved, and healthy. In the next room the elementary class detained us for some time. Two teachers are applying to these kids the Montessori method, which at least has the advantage of keeping them quiet. Before beginning the lesson they are made to stand in a circle and then kneel down in front of a little unpainted wooden chest supporting a reproduction of the Virgin and Child by Botticelli. In chorus and repeating the words after the teachers, they chanted a sort of prayer and blew kisses at the image. All this very loud so that the unbeliever, Mme Bouni-Reclus, would miss nothing.

From 22 to 26 November, an automobile trip with Mrs. Wharton.

Hyères, 26 November

I have made the acquaintance of Paul Bourget. He received me most cordially at Costebelle, at his estate named Le P., to which Mrs. Wharton had taken me. He felt a great need to captivate someone he knows to represent another generation, another side of the fence, another point of view. The introduction took place in the garden.

"To enter here, Monsieur Gide," he said to begin with, "you have no need to go through *the strait gate*."

This didn't exactly mean anything but a way of showing his kindly attitude. And shortly thereafter he managed to allude to my *Immoraliste;* then, returning to the subject, after Mrs. Wharton had left us for a moment to go and see Mme Bourget, who was kept in her room by a slight indisposition:

"Now that we are alone, tell me, Monsieur Gide, whether or not your immoralist is a pederast."

And, as I seem somewhat stunned, he reinforces his question:

"I mean: a practicing pederast?"

"He is probably more likely an unconscious homosexual," I replied as if I hardly knew myself; and I added: "I believe there are many such."

At first I thought that he had taken this way of showing me that he had read my book; but he especially wanted to develop his theories:

"There are," he began, "two classes of perversions: those that fall under the head of sadism and those that belong to masochism. To achieve sexual pleasure both the sadist and the masochist turn to cruelty; but one, etc. . . . . while the other," etc. . . . .

"Do you class homosexuals under one or the other of these perversions?" I asked just to have something to say.

"Of course," he replied; "for, as Régis points out . . ."

But at this moment Mrs. Wharton returned and I never learned whether, according to him, the homosexual fell under the head of sadism or of masochism. I was sorry that he turned the conversation into another channel; it would have amused me to have Mrs. Wharton's opinion, if she had one.

Paul Bourget still seems extremely hardy for his age, as if gnarled and hewn out of chestnut. His least remarks are redolent of literature; he splatters you with literary allusions like the spaniel that shook off precious stones.[9] "You are welcome to — what is anything but Elsinore," he said as we left the garden to enter the house. In less than a half-hour he managed to speak of Régnier (Mathurin), Shakespeare, Molière, Racine (whom he confesses not to be very fond of), Baudelaire, Boileau, Zola, Balzac, Charles-Louis Philippe, etc., all this with an extraordinary lack of real literary taste, I mean an odd lack of appreciation of poetry, art, and style. It is this that allows him to admire such paltry productions as those of Psichari, for instance, for which he has just written a preface. He reads us a few pages from the Voyage du Centurion, from the proofs;[10] his voice catches as if he were on the point of weeping. Out of the corner of our eyes Mrs. Wharton and I glance at each other, not knowing which deserves more wonder, Paul Bourget's emotion or the mediocrity of those pages. He insists on our reading the whole book, of which he gives us the proofs. And a little later, as I am walking down the corridor of the Costebelle hotel with him, after tea and a short walk, then a new conversation in Mrs. Wharton's room, in which we talked of Pascal and of the Mystère de Jésus [11] . . . he takes me familiarly by the arm and, leaning toward me:

"So you will promise me to read the Voyage du Centurion?" And, in a whisper of solemn secrecy, he adds: "Believe me: it is worth the Mystère de Jésus."

On this odd declaration we separated.

Bourget told me also:

"I am a panpsychist! I no longer believe in matter."

---

[9] "The Little Dog Shaking Off Money and Precious Stones" is the title of the thirteenth tale in the third part of La Fontaine's Contes.

[10] The Centurion's Journey (1916) by Ernest Psichari.

[11] The Mystery of Jesus is a brief series of devotional reflections by Pascal, both profound and beautiful.

7 December

No sooner finished *Almayer's Folly* by Conrad, I plunge into *The Bible in Spain* by Borrow. Nothing could express the amusement and curiosity with which I hasten to a new English book by a good author whom I don't know yet; an amusement that, for some time now, French literature cannot provide for me since it does not hold in store any real surprises. As when I first read a Balzac novel (it was *Eugénie Grandet*).

8 December

My wonder as a child on seeing the first eucalyptus tree in blossom. We had just reached Hyères. I ran quickly to the hotel and was not satisfied until I had led my mother out to look at those wonderful flowers with me. I shall have to relate also the trips I made at that time to the islands; perhaps the most enchanted memory of my childhood is that of the moments, the hours, that I spent on Sainte-Marguerite (or Saint-Honorat), leaning over the rocks on the edge of the water, watching the fairyland formed, at that time, by the natural aquariums among the rocks. Sea-anemones, starfish, sea-urchins besprinkled the rock walls down to depths where the eye ceased to make them out clearly; everything was palpitating according to the rhythm of the waves, but there were shelters to which not even the slightest undulation reached; there creatures and flowers breathed indolently; by keeping still and quiet for a long time, one could see strange, almost a little frightening animals issuing from dark lairs. I would stay there without stirring, lost in a contemplation — or rather an adoration — that nothing interrupted until Marie's call, toward evening, in time to catch the return boat.

I am very much afraid that the shores of those islands, so charming in my childhood, have been as lamentably spoiled as the immediate surroundings of Cannes itself; as was also the coast of England of which Edmund Gosse speaks so eloquently in *Father and Son;* and as are all the most charming spots on this earth as soon as man begins to sprawl on them.[12]

13 December

I am anxious for this notebook to be finished; I am not writing anything worth while in it; but I shall not drop it until it is finished. . . .

---

[12] André Gide is speaking of the Iles de Lérins, off the coast of Cannes, and not of the Iles d'Hyères, as might be at first supposed.

20 December

(For the novel.)

X. went so far as to say that the best way to triumph over Prussian militarism was not to try to conquer Germany, but on the contrary — He was never allowed to finish. He would continue, a little later and in a somewhat lower voice:

"The best way to overcome them would be to make their whole attack useless. Their offensive increases in direct ratio to our resistance. Faced with a nation that did not defend itself, all the Krupp cannon wouldn't be any good. . . ."

The others swallowed their indignation and gave up trying to make X. understand in what way Christian renunciation (and that non-resistance which the Gospels teach us) becomes unbearably shocking as soon as a collectivity, rather than individuals, is involved — and even more so when the collectivity is a nation entrusted with a past. X. was not convinced by the little that they did say, however. He cited the early Christians and asserted that it was precisely through their non-resistance that they had triumphed over all oppressions. He maintained that a nation that does not defend itself is essentially invincible. "A nation of cowards!" exclaimed the others. He replied: "A nation of martyrs." He claimed that this would have been the real way to win out over Germany and that France would thus have conquered her without fail, as Christianity had conquered ancient Rome, and that it was mad to claim that our disorganized nation could win out otherwise over Germany's organization. The only victory toward which we could and should aim today, he concluded, is a mystical victory; and it is the only real one.

In vain they tried to make him see that for such a victory there would have had to be, throughout France, an agreement and organization, the lack of which was our greatest weakness.

"And if any party had been mad enough to propose such a thing," Marcel said, "the indignant revolt of the others would have brought on a revolution even more harmful than war."

"Harmful!" X replied; "are you quite sure? Yet you know very well that all the half-victories that the superhuman feats of our army allow us to hope for will hardly decrease the permanent danger threatening us, that France may exhaust herself."

"In that case I am for Corneille's 'He should die!'"[18] Marcel answered, "and I much prefer to end up sharp than to fizzle out. My two sons are at the front, where I have already lost three of my brothers

---

[18] In Corneille's *Horace*, Act III, scene vi, the father, when asked what he would expect his son to do in unequal battle against three opponents, heroically says: "*Qu'il mourût.*"

and I don't know how many cousins and nephews. We shall all die if
need be, but at least the world will see France die entire and we shall
be saving her from a survival due to some shameful compromise."

Immediately the others began to boo X. and to raise their glasses
(this takes place at the Café Vachette) in honor of France and of
Marcel, who had just spoken so eloquently.

27 December

Intellectually tired, apathetic; I no longer achieve anything. . . .

Ghéon, on a week's leave, reads us the poems he has just written;
some of them strike me as excellent. I deeply regret that his long piece
on Romain Rolland employs arguments that are often dubious. He repeats the story of the hands cut off the little children, even though
we have striven everywhere in vain to get back to a proved fact, even
though all the inquiries we conducted at the Foyer, with a view to
winning the huge prize offered by America to whoever could confirm
such atrocities, led only to ultimate denials.

This is the place and the occasion to set down the strange, pathetic
tale that Mme Théo has brought home from the Foyer. She has it directly from Mme Théâtre, a good, reliable woman of the lower classes
whose odd name amused us at first, but whose exaggerated reserve
kept her somewhat at a distance from us. Every week she would come
to our section to get her grant. A little boy three or four years old
usually came with her. I remember my faintness the first day when,
wanting to give the child one of the hard candies we always kept on
hand, I noticed that he didn't have any right hand: the sleeve of his
jacket hid as best it could a hideous stump, which did not however
show any sign of seam or scar; at wrist-level the arm simply stopped
short. . . . The mother, who was watching my eyes, told me then that
the child "was born like that." I was amazed, for I didn't think such a
thing possible; but I could only accept what the mother told me. And
now here is the story:

During the Germans' incursion into Reims, there was great confusion among the civilian population, rubbing elbows as it was with
enemy soldiers and officers. Chance brought Mme Théâtre into a
delicatessen where she had to queue up next to a German lieutenant;
she had her son in her arms. The lieutenant was to be waited on ahead
of her. Out of the silver coin with which he paid he was given back
two pennies. Eager to make a good impression, and perhaps also
through natural kindness, he turned around and held out the pennies
to the child. (I must add here that the mother, who now hides the
stump under a sleeve that is intentionally too long, then wrapped it
up rather awkwardly in a cloth that only served to call attention to it.

The child, as if to accept the offer, made a gesture that revealed his deformity.

"Then," says Mme Théâtre, "I saw the officer change color, his jaws set, and his lips tremble; he looked toward me; I felt that he wanted to speak but didn't know what to say; but I didn't need words to understand his question. Surely he was thinking: 'So it's true then, what they accuse us of? This is what we Germans have done?' . . . And I too was unable to find any words to tell him: 'No, it's not what you think.' I merely shook my head from left to right as if to say: 'No.' I thought he would understand. . . . But I must tell you that for several days I had been without news of my husband and thought him dead, so that my face had such a sad expression that he must have been misled by it. He hurried out of the shop, his hand before his eyes and shaken with sobs."

1916

Had a good night; got up at six thirty; if I could sleep well as a regular thing, I should like to get into the habit of getting up early (as Em. always does) and of putting myself right with myself before starting off for the Foyer. There is no reason to give up everything; from seven to eight I could practice the piano, for instance; or busy myself with a translation if I fear to wake M., who is our boarder for three weeks. In a short while I shall perhaps even be capable of beginning to write again.

This morning I go over the text of J.-É. Blanche's book before giving it to the printer.

My conversation with Copeau did me much good, the day before yesterday. My attention constantly brought back to ruins, in my life at the Foyer, it was hard for me to imagine that anyone could still aim to build something. I am aware that the atmosphere in which I have lived for more than a year is the most depressing possible. Faced with that uninterrupted parade of misfortunes constantly tearing my heart, I became ashamed of any superiority and repeated to myself the words of Montesquieu's Eucrates: "For one man to rise above humanity is too costly to all others."[1]

Yesterday I hoped to be able to spend my Sunday as I wished. A telegram from del Marmol calls me urgently to the Foyer, where I find C., Lauris, Boccon-Gibauld, and del Marmol gathered. It is the business of restoring to the general fund the special emergency fund (Langweil reserve), which has come up again. Mlle Langweil threatens to leave the Foyer; we are no longer surprised by her inconsistencies, whims, etc. . . . but this one can do us serious harm; we must parry it. I am asked to beg Mme Théo to write del Marmol an explanatory letter, which we spend the better part of the afternoon composing and which I go and take to del Marmol at rue Taitbout. Mme Théo, who has also come to this little secret gathering, has brought her books and explained all the figures; I believe our colleagues were satisfied.

We were unable to get home until eight thirty.

D. had come to dinner, hoping to go over afterward with me the translation by d'Humières that Mrs. Wharton had left with me; but I was too tired and feared that this might keep me from sleeping.

---

[1] The fictitious interlocutor speaks thus to the despotic Sylla in Montesquieu's *Dialogue de Sylla et d'Eucrate* (1745).

During Élisabeth Van Rysselberghe's stay, read with her and without her a number of Browning's poems.

Continued the second part of Rutherford and Macaulay's *Frederick II.*

17 January

Ghéon writes me that he has "taken the jump." It sounds like a schoolboy who has just taken a crack at the brothel. . . . But he is really talking of the communion table.

Shall I set down here the odd dream I had last winter?

Ghéon, until then a boarder of the Van Rysselberghes at rue Laugier like me, had just left for the front. I dreamt this: I was walking, or rather *floating*, beside someone whom I soon recognized to be Ghéon. Together we were advancing in an unknown countryside, a sort of wooded valley; we were advancing with delight. The valley constantly became narrower and more beautiful and my delight was reaching its height when my companion suddenly stopped and, touching my forearm, exclaimed: "No farther! Henceforth between us there is *that*." He did not point at anything but, lowering my eyes, I made out a rosary hanging from his wrist, and I suddenly awoke in unbearable anguish.

18 January

While writing to Ghéon, I reread the fifteenth chapter of the Gospel according to St. John and these words are suddenly illuminated for me with a frightful light:

"If a man abide not in me, he is cast forth as a branch, and is withered; and men gather them, and cast them into the fire, and they are burned."

Truly was I not "cast into the fire" and already a prey to the flame of the most abominable desires? . . .

19 January

Everything in me calls out to be revised, amended, re-educated. The trait I have most trouble struggling against is my sensual curiosity. The drunkard's glass of absinthe is not more attractive than, for me, certain faces encountered by chance — and I would give up everything to follow them. . . . Why, to be sure this involves such an imperious urge, such an insidious, such a secret counsel, so inveterate a habit that I often wonder if I can escape it without outside aid.

"I have no man, when the water is troubled, to put me into the pool." (John, v, 7.)

20 January

A day full of snares — which I got through . . . providentially, I may say, with my will playing but the weakest part. . . .

Joined Copeau at the eurhythmics class in the afternoon (Foyer in the morning); visited his children's class; went to see the maker of orthopedic instruments to take care of the bed to send to the F.'s. Visit to Van Bever. In the evening took D., Jean Schlumberger, Copeau, and Mme Théo to an innocent English play, *Kit*, a tale of espionage and detectives, etc. . . .[2] Full day — empty day. All I can say is that I got through it.

21 January

Forenoon at the *N.R.F.* with Copeau; no visits. All negotiations are suspended while waiting for G.; a telegram announces his arrival for Monday. We talk at length of the possibility of forming a small company of actors sufficiently intelligent, clever, and well trained to improvise on a given scenario and capable of reviving the *commedia dell' arte* in the Italian manner, but with new types: the bourgeois, the noble, the publican, the suffragette would take the place of Harlequin, Pierrot, and Columbine. Each of these types would have his own costume, his own way of speaking, his own bearing and psychology. And each of the actors would personify only one type, limiting himself to it and never getting away from it, but constantly enriching and amplifying it.

If this plan is realized, I foresee and long for an audience in complicity with the actors, urging them on and communicating enthusiasm to them. Very soon these performances (which I do not see as filling the whole program, but rather as preceding, following, or breaking the main show) would make the theater's success and would take on a bold importance; they would constitute a *satire of parties* — an excellent, healthy satire in the name of common sense.

The whole afternoon lost at that committee-meeting to which Mme B. called us — at which two deputies and twelve representatives of regional committees vied with each other in producing soporific eloquence and took an infinite amount of time to develop something that every one of us was convinced of in advance. I come away exasperated and exhausted; but, having gone to bed early, I can get up early and produce rather good work this Saturday morning.

---

[2] *Kit* was a three-act comedy by Worral and Terny, adapted by W. B. Périer and Verney. After considerable success at the Bouffes Parisiens, the play moved to the Théâtre des Variétés on 5 October 1916, with the famous comedian Max Dearly in the leading role.

22 January

René Widmer, a second lieutenant, told us how his sole preoccupation at the moment of the attack was to get his men back into their
units and to keep them from breaking ranks.

He was half stifled by a gas shell when he received the bullet that
went through his face.

He still has to cover several kilometers on foot, on the arm of X.,
to get to the dressing-station, where he spends the night. Beside him
a poor private from another detachment, his abdomen cut open, moans
as he lies dying. He says to René: "Will you give me your hand, lieutenant? I am suffering so horribly!" And all night long he holds René's
hand in his, at times squeezing it convulsively.

Sunday, 23

Yesterday evening I yielded, as one yields to an obstinate child —
"to have peace." Lugubrious peace; darkening of the whole sky. . . .

On my return to the Foyer I had to preside over a meeting in which
nothing was going satisfactorily. My annoyance was so great that I
feared to express it and forced myself to keep silent.

I no longer have any justification at the Foyer and don't like it
there. For more than a year charity kept it alive and throbbing; now
it is becoming a philanthropic undertaking in which I have neither intellectual nor emotional interest.

24

Yesterday an indescribably odd and beautiful sunset: sky filled
with pink and orange-tinted mists; I admired it especially, as I was
going over the Pont de Grenelle, reflected by the Seine heavy with
barges; everything melted into a warm and tender harmony. In the
Saint-Sulpice tram, from which I was watching this sight with wonder
in my eyes, I noticed that no one, absolutely no one, was aware of it.
There was not a single face that didn't look preoccupied with cares.
. . . Yet, I thought, some people travel to a great distance to find nothing more beautiful. But most often man does not recognize beauty
unless he buys it, and this is why God's offer is so often disdained.

This morning at Druet's funeral; he died the day before yesterday
of a sudden stroke. Shook hands with some twenty people; brought
Marcel Drouin back to lunch with me.

"What good does it do you to try to be smart?"

I imagine a novel of which the subject would be an illustration of
these words: *"The weight of my sins drags me down."*

Very bad night. I again fall as low as ever.

This morning, up before seven, I go out a moment and hear a black-bird's song, odd, so precociously springlike, so pathetic and pure that it makes me even more bitterly aware of the withering-up of my heart.

I read in Rutherford (Vol. II, p. 113) a passage about the devil and hell that just happens to back up my thought wonderfully: "The shallowest of mortals is able now to laugh at the notion of a personal devil. No doubt there is no such thing existent; but the horror at evil which could find no other expression than in the creation of a devil is no subject for laughter, and if it do not in some shape or other survive, the race itself will not survive. No religion, so far as I know, has dwelt like Christianity with such profound earnestness on the bisection of man — on the distinction within him, vital to the very last degree, between the higher and the lower, heaven and hell. What utter folly is it because of an antique vesture to condemn as effete what the vesture clothes! Its doctrine and its sacred story are fixtures in concrete form of precious thoughts purchased by blood and tears." [3]

For several days now I have been striving to free myself from the Foyer, to cease being interested in it. I have great difficulty in doing so, and the time I spend trying to interest myself in something else (not to say in myself) is put to poor use, almost lost. And since Saturday I have been again assailed by abominable imaginings, against which I am defenseless; I find no refuge anywhere. At certain moments, sometimes for hours, I wonder if I am not going mad; everything in me yields to my mania. Yet I strive to organize the struggle. . . . What patience and what deception it would take!

And this evening, however, an excellent letter from Ghéon brings me a little comfort.

Good! Once more I have managed to recover my balance. Ghéon's letter helped me. Last night a calm meditation prepared a restful night. I was able to get up early. At work at six thirty, filled with a strange inner peace. I did not try to pray, but my entire soul opened up to divine counsel like a body warming itself in the sun. Every hour of this day has followed the impulse of that first hour. Moreover, if a temptation had arisen, I don't believe that I should have resisted; but none arose and I reached the evening in peace.

Read for the Review W.'s manuscript and the one by J.-É. Blanche,

---

[3] Though André Gide gives his reference as to a second volume of the *Autobiography*, the passage is actually found in *The Deliverance of Mark Rutherford*. Gide quotes it in his own translation.

a little Rutherford; practiced the piano more than an hour. At the Foyer this afternoon.

28

I get up with a horrible disgust of everything and of myself. I felt so well yesterday! None the less the day was not too bad. At the Review in the morning; conversation with G., etc. . . . Nothing important to note.

I have no less trouble strengthening in myself now the idea of sin than I once had in weakening it.

Saturday, 29

Rather good day. Morning spent in setting down the story of Rilke's sequestration, of which I do not want to forget a single detail.[4]

My little niece came at eleven for her piano lesson; played a duet with her for the first time (Haydn's symphonies).

Afternoon at the Foyer. Committee.

On the way back with Charlie Du Bos, rather pathetic conversation. I walk with him as far as the Opéra. I shall try to note down elsewhere the curious evolution of the Foyer and for what fatal reason I am coming to be less and less interested in that organization which meant so much to me just a few months ago.

Back to Auteuil at eight o'clock. Drouin comes after dinner. I read a story by Maupassant (*Le Parapluie*[5]) and my reading is interrupted by the sound of one or more zeppelins. Right after Drouin leaves, the siren sounds; he returns to warn us. We stay on the watch rather late. Almost sleepless night; Miquette very ill.

Read last night (I have been at it for several days) Bossuet's wonderful pages on "Orison," taken from I don't know just what work and reproduced in the beginning of my little edition of the *Élévations sur les Mystères.*[6] But when I then tackle the first two elevations, I get tangled up in a succession of pseudo-reasonings, which, far from convincing me, again antagonize and disgust me. No, I cannot enter through that gate; there *is* no gate for me on that side. I can affect stupidity; I have tried it; but not for long, and soon I revolt against that impious comedy which I am trying to play on myself. If the

---

[4] Rilke left Paris for Germany shortly before war was declared. In April 1915 his furniture and library were sequestered in order to cover the unpaid rent. Gide, notified too late to save everything, managed to take charge of some papers for return to the poet after the war.

[5] "The Umbrella."

[6] *The Elevations on the Mysteries*, a series of metaphysical meditations, were composed for the Sisters of the Visitation in 1795.

Church demands that of me, this is because God remains far above
her. I can believe in God, believe God, love God, and my whole heart
inclines me to do so. I can make my heart dominate my mind. But, I
beg you, don't look for proofs and reasons. That is where man's imper-
fection begins; and I felt myself to be perfect in love.

Sunday, 30

If I had to formulate a credo, I should say: God is not behind us.
He is to come. He must be sought, not at the beginning, but at the
end of the evolution. He is terminal and not initial. He is the supreme
and final point toward which all nature tends in time. And since time
does not exist for Him, it is a matter of indifference to Him whether
that evolution of which He is the summit follows or precedes, and
whether He determines it by propulsion or attraction.

It is through man that God is molded. This is what I feel and believe and what I understand in the words: "Let man be created in
Our image." What can all the doctrines of evolution do against that
thought?

This is the gate through which I enter into the holy place, this is
the series of thoughts that lead me back to God, to the Gospels,
etc. . . . .

Will I some day succeed in setting this forth clearly?

For a long time already I have believed this without knowing it,
and now it becomes clear in me through a series of successive illumina-
tions. The reasoning follows.

Monday, 31

I am continuing the reading of Bossuet's *Élévations*. He proves the
existence of God by the sentiment of perfection that every man carries
in his heart: "What is error if it is not a privation of truth . . . and
what is ignorance if it is not a privation of perfect power? . . ." Then,
passing to God's prescience, he proves it by reference to prophecy.

All this is lamentable and dishonest. I can give up my reason, but
I cannot distort it. Read last night in the *Revue hebdomadaire* the
third or fourth part of Francis Jammes's *Rosaire*.[7] It is to real piety
what smut is to love.

Lunch at the Ducotés'. Disappointment not to find Édouard there,
he is at the hospital of the rue Lhomond nursing a violent outbreak
of furunculosis resulting from overexertion and intemperance at the
front.

---

[7] *The Rosary in the Sun*, a novel, was published serially in the *Revue
hebdomadaire* in January and February 1916.

Spent two hours with J.-É. Blanche patching up his manuscript, which is dreadfully weak in spots.

(Mme Blanche and he were lunching at the Villa. It was, I believe, the first time that we had invited them.)

Committee-meeting at the Foyer (we were seventeen) and small super-committee-meeting after the others had left and there remained only Lauris, Du Bos, del Marmol, Mme Théo, and I.

Can I get myself to note down the new phase into which our organization is moving? I should do so. The story is instructive.

1 February

I give up the reading of Bossuet's *Élévations* before my disgust overflows and carries away with it what I should like to keep. I have gone on as far as I could, but no reading is more likely to hurl me into the opposition, and I am stopping out of precaution.

I am trying to put aside a half-hour every evening and every morning for soothing meditation, self-analysis, and expectation. . . . "Remain simply attentive to that presence of God, exposed to His divine observation, thus continuing that devout attention or *exposition* . . . at peace under the rays of the divine sun of justice."

I long ardently to write that book of meditations or elevations which will balance the *Nourritures* and fuse in places with the *Conseils à un jeune écrivain* that I am preparing.[8] May I. . . .

Francis Jammes annoys me most when he believes, or pretends to believe, that it is through reasoning and an exaggerated need for dialectics that I withdraw and stand in opposition, whereas quite the contrary. . . . But what is the good of starting a discussion on this point? It is not ignorance, humility, or renunciation — it is rather falsehood that I detest. And that pretense by which the soul dupes itself and offers itself to God as a dupe.

2 February

Tried to write to Gosse in reply to his article on France. I spent the better part of my morning on it and produced nothing worth while. Practiced Albéniz.

Our cats break the most beautiful vase in the drawing-room, the only beautiful one: a large gray and blue Persian vase that I had got at an auction. Its narrow base gave reason to fear and I had taken care to weight it heavily with lead shot. In order to put some flowers from Saint-Clair into it, Em. recently removed the shot (otherwise, she says, it would have been too heavy to lift), but when she removed the flowers, she forgot to put back the shot. Right after the war, things like that will go on in this country.

---

[8] *Advice to a Young Writer* was never completed or published.

3 February

I have given up reading the Bible in English; my expectation must not be caught by words, even were it to enjoy them. Nevertheless I sometimes open the book to find the text I have just read in French. And at times a sudden new light is thrown on the text: "Except a man be born again." [9] All this morning I repeated these words to myself and I am repeating them this evening, after having measured all day long the frightful shadow that my past cast onto my future.

4 February

Last night the central-heating system burst; the water from the boiler flows out onto the hearth; I put everything out; and this morning at seven o'clock I rush to G., the contractor, so thoughtlessly that I first look for him at rue du Chemin Vert in Ménilmontant before finding him at rue du Moulin Vert. Consultation: the central pipe will have to be replaced; this will come to seven or eight hundred francs (war price) and will take about a fortnight. We give up and make the economical decision to spend our time only in the dining-room, with the possibility of installing a small stove in the drawing-room near the piano. Em. is clearly very much crushed by the event and I can foresee that she won't have much will to resist colds.

At lunch, as I am telling Em. what new life is given me by anything that upsets my habits, she replies: "That is because *you* are strong" — and immediately I hear again that knell that rings throughout the *Immoraliste*. Yet this is not quite true: certain natures are urged on by anything that gets in their way, while others are stopped. I remember the bicycle accident at Cuverville that amused Gérard so much and cast such a gloom over Marcel.

5 February

Wrote to Gosse in reply to his article on France that appeared in the *Edinburgh Review*:

". . . At least I want to tell you with what gratitude I congratulated you (in the article I was planning to write on this subject) for discerning under this new and so wonderful France the old France that has never ceased existing: 'Not a new France miraculously created, but the old France, *welded together,* and passed through the fire of affliction.' [10] That is excellent.

"And I am likewise thankful to you for being more indulgent, toward our old French shortcomings, than I can be. You generously

---

[9] The quotation appears in English in the original.

[10] The quotation from Edmund Gosse's article appears in English in the original.

cover them up because you know the French so well and because you
know what noble impulses motivate us even in our worst errors. In
general no one lives more for others, or hand in hand with others, or
in relation to others than does the Frenchman. Whence at one and the
same time his vanity, his politeness, his love of politics, the hold that
emulation can get upon him, his fear of ridicule, his interest in fashion,
etc. . . .

"On the first page of the *Petit Journal illustré* I admired the other
day a picture (which also exasperated me) representing the decorat-
ing of a seriously wounded soldier; lying on a hospital bed, he straight-
ened up as far as he could when the general approached to pin on
his medal and exclaimed (as the caption related): 'A man must be at
attention, general, to receive the *Croix de Guerre!*' then he fell back
dead, exhausted by this exhibition.

"This is wonderful and it is absurd, very much in the tradition that
already made Bossuet say: 'The maxims of false honor which have
brought so many among us to their death. . . .'

"Dear friend, how I like to hear you say: 'If France has of late
laughed less, her smile has on occasion been more beautiful than
ever.'"

6 February

Yesterday, following my visit to W. M. regarding Rilke, having
some time ahead of me before the committee-meeting at the Foyer, I
went into the Saint-Séverin Church and stayed there about a half-
hour meditating and reading the end of the Rutherford. I was sitting
on the right side of the church; there were only a few silent, worship-
ping women; the outside light reached me subdued and colored by
the stained-glass windows, and the sounds of out of doors were muf-
fled when they reached me. The peace in which I was bathed had nothing especially religious about it, or at least did not incline me toward
a particular devotion. I simply savored to what a degree contemplation is useful to me.

7 February

I have never been so modest as when constraining myself to write
every day in this notebook a series of pages that I know and feel to
be so definitely mediocre; repetitions, stammerings so little likely to
make anyone appreciate, admire, or like me.

Always have I been pursued by the desire to shake off all affections
but those of a quite exquisite and superior quality. If these notebooks
should come to light, later on, how many will they repell, even then!
. . . But what affection I feel for him who, despite them, or through
them, will still want to remain my friend!

I cling desperately to this notebook; it is a part of my patience; it helps keep me from going under.

8 February

Yesterday two very important committee-meetings; following the second one, at the Foyer, long explanation before del Marmol, Lauris, Mme Théo, etc. I shall tell of this elsewhere.

Dined at Darius Milhaud's. He asks my advice about the "cantata" he wants to make of my *Retour de l'enfant prodigue*.[11]

This morning at the *N.R.F.* I find on the office mantel a little volume (Romanica series) of the *Journal* of Maurice de Guérin — which I open at random to find this excellent page that I enjoy copying down here:

"7 September. I get lost in conversations. Most often I derive nothing from them but dejection and bitterness. In them I compromise my inner life, everything that is best in me. *In order to keep the conversation going, I throw into it my favorite thoughts, the ones to which I am most secretly and solicitously attached. My shy and awkward speech disfigures, multilates them, throwing them out into the bright light in disorder and confusion and only half-dressed. When I go away I gather up and hug to my breast my scattered treasure, trying to put back into place dreams that are bruised like fruit fallen from the tree onto rocks.*"

I have never very much liked, nor even carefully read, Maurice de Guérin, always irritated to be told that I resembled him. But it is true that I *feel* that page, even to the slightest detail of its rhythm and vigor, as if I had written it myself — and that I should have liked to write it.

Bothered also by the calligraphy of the *Centaure* and of the *Bacchante* (which are both almost unendurable to me), by the latent *whimpering* of his mind ("The loveliest days," he says, "the most absorbing studies fail to quiet in me that restless and *whimpering* thought which is the basis of humanity"), by his sister, by his friendship for Barbey d'Aurevilly, etc. . . .

9 February

See in the green cloth notebook, *Numquid et tu . . . ?* under this date.

I have resumed the reading of Pascal, of much greater advantage to me than Bossuet. I am beginning to feel the benefit of the daily

---

11 Milhaud's cantata using the dialogues of Gide's *Return of the Prodigal Son* was in fact composed in Rio de Janeiro in 1917. Written for five voices and twenty-one instruments, it has been executed in Paris, in Brussels, and at the Baden-Baden Festival of 1928.

meditation that I impose on myself every morning and evening. I am still lacking in strength, but calm; I do not pray, but I listen and wait and, for the moment at least, I do not wish for any other form of prayer.

My days continue to be miserably broken up. Obliged to remain with the others in the evening, I cannot be alone until after all have gone up to bed; I constantly lack time.

Friday, 11

Noted nothing yesterday. In the morning, work — or at least an attempt at work. But since the beginning of the week I have not yet managed to have a morning to myself. Little things to take care of arise at the last moment, and my equilibrium is not yet sufficiently assured so that I can resume my meditation as soon as the cause of this upset is gone. Yet I am better and keep myself in a state of vigilance. The best way of struggling against temptation is still not to expose oneself to it. One cannot hope to reach paradise in one single leap. It takes resolve and, even more, patience. Nothing could be less romantic, nothing could be more tiresome at times than the minute detail of this moral hygiene; no great victories; it is a constant struggle without glory, like the one that is being fought in the trenches.

Each defeat, on the other hand, is sudden and complete and seems to hurl you back to the lowest point. It is often delightful. At least it can be, and I keep telling myself this. And the Evil One is always ready to whisper in my ear: "This is all a comedy that you are playing to deceive yourself. With the first blush of spring you will pass over to the enemy. The enemy? What do you mean by enemy? You have no other enemy than your own fatigue. If it were more open, your sin would be glorious. Be frank, then, and admit that you use the word *sin* in this connection only because you find this dramatic effect convenient and a help in recovering that agility you were on the point of losing: namely, the free control of your flesh and mind. Today you take your physical fatigue for moral decay; soon, when you are cured, you will blush for having thought you had to have recourse to such means to cure yourself." Meanwhile I am still ill — and shall remain ill as long as I listen to that voice.

Monday, 14 February

The central-heating system out of order, the house ice-cold save only for the dining-room, where I can be alone only when Mme Théo is at the Foyer. Hence I have had to interrupt those morning meditations in which my soul was washed and from which it derived so much strength and amenity for the rest of the day. It is the hour when "the room is being done." Then later, immediately after breakfast, waiting for Mme Théo to leave for the Foyer—a selfish, exasperated waiting that leaves my nerves on edge and me upset and ugly—a fine state in which to sit down to work! All the advantage from the night's counsel is lost.

This, moreover, is why I have written nothing here for the last three days.

Yesterday several visits for the Foyer (at 87 rue Boileau) in the huge "low-priced housing project." But it does me no good. Too much sensuality is constantly slipping into my charity. My heart, my whole being go out unreservedly and I come away from those visits quite undone. Or else I remain utterly and painfully dry and would quite willingly suggest putting an end to the suffering by suppressing the individual who is complaining.

Who can understand that destitution can be as attractive as luxury and huddling in distress as attractive as the exaltation of love?

This is the point at which the highest heaven touches hell.

And this morning I read in Pascal: "We are full of things that push us outside.

". . . Our passions push us outside, even when no objects are present to arouse them. Outside objects tempt us by themselves and call us even when we are not thinking of them."

Indeed, Pascal, did you know such torments and anxieties as mine? Oh no! I am making your words serve my ends, giving them a precise meaning they do not have. You are speaking in an abstract and general manner. Or are you thinking of the period of your youth? Long ago the Holy Thorn purified and refined all that! [12]

And you go on:

"Thus to no avail philosophers say: 'Withdraw within yourself; there you will find your salvation.' We do not believe them, and *those who do believe them are the most empty and most foolish.*" That is what the Evil One tells me too.

16 February

The day before yesterday, relapse.

One seems to fall as low as ever and all the effort of these days seems lost.

But one's balance returns a bit more rapidly; the surrender is not so complete.

Hell would consist in continuing to sin, despite oneself, without deriving any pleasure from doing so. It is natural that the soul given

---

[12] Toward the end of Pascal's life the miraculous cure of his niece by a relic of the Crown of Thorns convinced him that his work was approved by God.

over to the Evil One should become, without any pleasure for itself, a docile instrument of damnation for others.

I am consciously using here, as I did earlier, a vocabulary and images that imply a mythology in which it is not absolutely essential that I should believe. The fact that it is the most eloquent to explain an inner drama is enough for me. And psychology can explain it likewise, just as meteorology has done for certain Greek myths . . . what does that matter to me! The deepest explanation can only be finality.

I have realized the profound truth of the words: "Whosoever shall seek to save his life shall lose it." To be sure, it is in perfect abnegation that individualism triumphs, and self-renunciation is the summit of self-assertion.

It is through self-preference, on the other hand, that the Evil One recruits and enslaves us. Who would dare to speak of liberation in this connection? From what laws? As if vice were not more imperious than any duty!

17 February

"One has merely to avoid seeking this relationship, to judge nothing and to remain simply *in the darkness of faith*," writes Fénelon (*Lettres spirituelles*, 2 October 1710), and he continues: "I should like, according to the rule of Blessed John of the Cross, 'to override' everything without judging of it and to remain in the *obscurity* of pure faith. . . . The obscurity of faith and obedience to the Gospels will never lead us astray."

Saturday

Piano-practice. It is useless, even harmful, to persist in working too long at one time over the same passage. It is better to return to it often; this is what constitutes real patience. Nothing is less romantic. To a vehement capture by assault, it prefers a slow and methodical siege.

Likewise, for profound difficulties in artistic creation. Likewise in piety and knowledge of God: the apparently most sudden revelation is preceded by a gradual, slow preparation. The work of art is always the result of an unsatisfied perseverance.

Monday

In the accounts (signed P. du B.) that the *Journal de Genève* is publishing of the frightful Serbian retreat, of which the horror is beyond everything, it says:

"Wounded men, not knowing where to go, sank to the ground anywhere whatever, in public squares, in gardens and ditches. There were panics alternating with sudden spurts of hope. *There were also strangely pleasant moments. Past, future, nothing counted any more,* and every minute was lived with all one's nerves. It was savored like a unique, incomparable thing.

"At first it rained. Then fair weather returned, a late-autumn fair weather with its vast muted skies, its wan sun, its too brief twilights. *And the landscape was as if transfigured.* All along the road, soldiers and refugees stopped to take one last look at the deep plain, its horizon of blue hills, its delicate curtains of trees, its broad, tranquil stream."

Tuesday

Is it truly counsel or authorization that you are seeking? Reread these lines of Fénelon:

"One must never suppose divine permission except in errors already committed; that permission must in no way decrease our hatred of sin or our self-condemnation" (*Lettres spirituelles,* 16 March 1696).

You who undertook, by suppressing remorse, to suppress sin!

I have so effectively put that word out of countenance that now I hesitate to use it; it shames me.

Thursday

We were to leave tomorrow morning for Cuverville; a telegram from L. warns us that the snow and ice keep him from sending a carriage to Beuzeville. Fear of difficulties about our Alsatian cook's passport, if we go by way of Havre, makes us put off our departure a day.

Yesterday Mme Théo went back to living in the Maus's apartment on rue des Belles-Feuilles. There she will await the return of Théo Van Rysselberghe, who is still tarrying at Saint-Clair. I feared for her the melancholy of that first evening alone and went to dine with her.

Friday

Finished the evening at the home of Marcel Proust (whom I had not seen since '92). I had promised myself to relate that visit at length; but I no longer have the interest to do so this morning.

It snowed heavily last night; our departure is put off indefinitely.

Friday evening

The joy of work, of calm, of equilibrium. Serene soberness of thought. Began to translate the poems of Kabir.

Saturday

Too brief days; the slow succession of hours. Snow outside; nothing to do and not even any letters to write, for I should not dare to mail them from Paris; no visit to fear since I am thought to be in Cuverville, where our mail is awaiting us. Day entirely spent in work, meditation, and reading. Far back into the past I should not find such a pure one.

I pick up *Jean-Christophe* again from the beginning and make a great effort at sympathy without my consideration for Romain Rolland, or for his book at least, being increased.

It breathes a sort of rough heartiness, vulgarity, and guilelessness — which will please the reader to whom the artist always seems to be putting on airs. But that's that.

What bothers me is the ease, the thoughtlessness, with which he makes a German of his hero — or, if you prefer, he makes his hero of a German. As far as I know, there is no other example of this, for even Stendhal takes care to point out that his Fabrice was born of a French father.[13] What more are we expected to see in this? The Germanic quality of his tastes, tendencies, reactions, and impulses, which allows Romain Rolland, if not to paint Jean-Christophe precisely in his own image, at least to infuse life into him through sympathy? Or else the illusion of a generous but uncritical mind abstractly creating in Jean-Christophe a creature who is no more German than he is French, a musician, a vague personality to whom he can attribute any sensations and emotions he wants?

Oh, how Germanic is that very psychological inadequacy! How inexpressive it is! [14]

2 March

Reached Cuverville the night before last at about midnight; considerably done in by an eighteen-hour trip, embellished by a collision at Serquigny; four or five dead and about twenty wounded. (See the papers.)

Both those who were giving aid and those who were receiving it behaved in seemly fashion, certainly having already learned their lesson from the war; enjoyed talking with people of all ranks. As for me, again noticed my great difficulty in taking tragically, even seriously, a chance accident. I remain amused, as at a show, or excited rather and ready to put forth a great reserve of sudden activity. Somewhat prevented, however, in helping to extricate the wounded and in giving them first aid by my anxiety for Em., accompanied by two maids,

---

[13] Stendhal, who wanted the false statement that he was a Milanese engraved on his tombstone, chose Italy as the scene of his famous novel *The Charterhouse of Parma*, of which Fabrice del Dongo is the hero.

[14] What I said no longer strikes me as just right today (21 May). When he made his hero a German, Romain Rolland was especially looking for a certain perspective that would allow him to judge French manifestations. [A.]

without counting the two dogs and five cats. The good wife of a sea captain clung to us, carrying in her arms a beautiful baby boy, two years old. We had to lug baskets and hand-baggage and help all these people to climb the embankment, etc.

We were, moreover, rather far from the crumpled cars, and the shock we felt was not very great; it did not give me any idea of how serious the accident was and hence I did not approach the scene until after the victims had already been extricated. I should have liked to be of greater help.

The extreme quiet of Cuverville, after the fatigue and late night, acted yesterday like a bromide on my mind. Read on the way and after getting here the second volume of *Jean-Christophe,* some of Nietzsche's *Thoughts out of Season* (wonderful beginning of the study on Strauss), the Lasserre on German influence, some excellent articles by Souday that I had gone to get the day before at the office of *Paris-Midi.*[15]

3 March

Lamentable intellectual restlessness, which, running as an undercurrent to everything I am doing, makes me wonder, whatever I undertake, if I should not do better to begin something else. This state of unrest generally precedes creation in my case; I keep repeating this to myself in order not to get too irritated against myself.

Wrote to Mrs. Wharton, to Gosse, and to a journalist who would like me as an honorary member of a committee with the propaganda aim of urging young writers to produce! He encloses with his letter a sort of prospectus outlining the purposes of the organization; hard to imagine anything more foolish. Lost an hour replying to him and getting out of it.

Edmond brings me a pair of new sabots. Worked with him pruning the plum trees.

Got ahead with *Catherine Furze.*[16]

During these periods of restlessness I ought deliberately to give up all reading, set nothing in front of me but blank paper. But I flee work, begin six books at a time, not knowing which one to hide behind so as not to have to reply yet to the demands. . . .

There is no more time to lose; I must convince myself of this and give myself formal notice beginning tomorrow. There is no good long-

---

[15] The Nietzsche work, referred to in French, is *Unzeitgemässe Betrachtungen;* the book by Lasserre is *Le Germanisme et l'esprit humain* (*Germanism and the Human Spirit*).

[16] A novel by Mark Rutherford (William Hale White), first published in 1894.

ing for the time when I could still make resolutions; I must still make them just as in my youth — and make up my mind rather to do nothing than to do something *else*.

Put off until later any other reading, translation, letter-writing — and *first* start my work again.

Saturday

Struck with gloom by the mediocrity of the notes I put in order this morning: I had greatly misled myself as to their quality. Almost nothing worth keeping. I felt not only disappointed but mortified, and wondered if I had not likewise exaggerated the importance of my idea. . . .

Read the appendix I find in my edition of the Vulgate on the authenticity of the Gospels. It is followed by a "Concordance" that it will be interesting to compare with Westphal's, for I am reading several pages of him every day.

Worked two and a half hours in the garden with Edmond.

Sunday, 5 March

This morning wrote a half a page of my *Chopin*.[17] In the afternoon finished putting my papers in order; that is, classifying in series the pages of old notebooks that seem to me worth keeping and tearing up all the rest. I tore up and tore up and tore up just as the day before I had cut and torn out the dead wood from the espaliers. How much there was! And how mediocre the little that I spared still seemed to me! Between certain covers I came upon very old piles. I recognized certain sentences that I had once thought full of strength and vigor, but from which the sap had completely withdrawn by now. I was ashamed of them and even suffered from the very appearance of the handwriting, so unsimple, so unnatural. . . . I do not like anything in me but what I achieve at the expense of the most modest, most patient effort.

Even the pages I have preserved will have no value unless they are completely melted down, completely *lost* in the ensemble.

My sight, during the last few days, has failed considerably.

6 March

How far can my intellectual humility go. . . . I have a horror for all rhetoric and romanticism and that verbal effort of the mind to try to "add an inch to one's height."

---

[17] The "Notes on Chopin" were not published until December 1931 in the *Revue musicale*.

Shrove Tuesday

Heavy fall of snow last night. The sound of little snowslides on the roof keeps us long awake. On awakening, the countryside is white; the big cedar looks like the Himalaya. Under their load of whiteness the bushes are prostrate. The least twig is supporting an enormous burden. The wire netting around the tennis court has become a sparkling wall. Above the immaculate plain shines a cloudless azure. Not a single bird singing; not a sound. It occurs to us that on the battlefield a like shroud must be spread, hiding the dead, smothering the dying, covering the horror.

The children have come, according to the local custom, to recite what they call "the farce" for us. They come along in little groups of two or three, each one carrying a large basket; they go from door to door and, in gratitude for their little song, everyone gives them an egg — or, for want of an egg, an apple, a penny, a piece of chocolate. I have set down several of their songs, almost amorphous, but which come from the depths of the past.

Unsatisfactory work. My eyes are too tired for me to read.

Bad ending to the day.

Wednesday

Yesterday evening wrote several pages of Memoirs.[18] This morning commentary on Christ's words to the Samaritan woman. The piano has come, an upright piano to save money and also because we should not have had enough men here to carry the other.

I am training myself to play with my eyes closed, for they hurt me. I doubt that I shall succeed and believe that I should give up if I were never to see again.

Thursday, 9 March

Thaw all day yesterday. The layer of snow, at first almost ten inches thick, has now sunk to the thickness of a wool blanket. But it still covers the earth everywhere, so that Em. and Georges said: "It hardly melted at all." I reminded Em. that, the first day, Miquette sank in up to her belly and had such a time that I had had to run to meet and carry her.

Practiced again the few preludes and fugues of the *Well-Tempered Clavichord* that I know by heart, and the Prelude in A minor of the organ suites.

---

[18] Under the title of *Si le grain ne meurt . . . (If It Die . . .)* the Memoirs were first printed privately in 1920–1 without name of publisher. They were finally published openly in 1926 by Librairie Gallimard.

Saturday

This is the day on which "the room is done." (I have got them to "do" the room in which I work only once a week.) Consequently I spent the whole morning at the piano (Granados).

In the afternoon Valentine and the two little girls arrived.

Since all the ashes were taken out of my fireplace while "the room was being done," the fire refuses to catch, and the little time left to me that I hoped to give to work I spend getting all out of sorts working over the fire.

Continued writing my childhood recollections. But, in connection with the walks in the Luxembourg Gardens with my father, I fall back into hesitations, erasures, and new starts, which kill all spontaneity. I must above all cure myself of this. I returned to the same passage more than six times and had to go to bed before having succeeded in getting it right.

I must dare to go right on, even if I have to write in the margin: "to be rewritten."

This morning, as soon as I got up, I wrote it all over rather easily, doubtless benefiting from yesterday's work.

Tuesday

Spent the day yesterday at Havre; examination of my eyes — reassuring on the whole, but I must get stronger lenses. Having plenty of time to waste, I walked along the quays behind the Bourse. The little square and the quays altogether are covered with bales of cotton, on which all the port urchins are running, jumping, and tumbling; many of the bales are badly done up or half-undone; the cotton falls out and gets mixed with the mud in the street and on the pavement; you walk on thick padded mud. This makes a most odd appearance; it looks as if the bales are melting; it's the cotton-thaw. It is enough to wring your heart and make you angry. Approaching the wharf, I saw several barges, one quite full of bales and the others half full; I thought they were being unloaded and wondered where this additional merchandise was going to be piled. But I realize, as I think it over, that this must have been, on the other hand, an effort to clear away. Those barges could never have crossed the ocean to bring the cotton; they are there to carry it away and are getting ready to go up the Seine as soon as the water falls enough to allow this.

Bought three big long notebooks, of an odd format, to write down my recollections.

Valentine, when I get home, warns me that I am going to find two guests in my room; they are two little hares, caught this afternoon in Hérouard's barnyard. With great difficulty I got them to drink a bit of warm milk with an eye-dropper or a spoon. I really think I should succeed in bringing them up, but, besides the fact that they would devastate the garden if they were let out in it later, it would be too hard in the meantime to keep them out of reach of the dogs and cats. So that, after mature deliberation, we go and put them back at night under the fallen branch of an apple tree where they were discovered and where their mother will certainly be able to find them.

Letter from Claudel, whom I had asked if he would write a preface for Unamuno's book that we are to publish in translation.[19] He scents heresy in it: modernism, Protestantism. . . . How could I be so misled by it? . . . Decidedly all roads do not lead to Rome and he alone who keeps his mouth shut can be sure of staying in the path of orthodoxy. It is better not to enter upon it; this is still the best way of not straying.

Day spent almost entirely in gardening: pruning plum trees, liming trees, sowing sweet peas — and giving Françoise her piano lesson.

Thursday

Wrote to Mrs. Wharton, to Ghéon, and to Edmund Gosse.

Wrote at length in the *Green Notebook*[20] concerning a reading of St. Luke.

Worked rather patiently on my childhood recollections.

Friday

Went to Criquetot to see the library of the late Justice of the Peace. Astounded by the number and choice of the volumes: ancient and modern literature, philosophy and especially religious controversy, criticism, art, natural history and history, travels, philology — there is the best in every field. I even find a rather large number of translations of English and Russian novels which I am going to try to buy.

On my way, went in to say hello to old Mme Freger. Her face against the white pillow seems even redder; she coughs, spits, and gasps, but no longer complains of her dead eye, which is now quite white, colorless, and hideous to see. Old Mother Michel, who is taking care of her, has only one eye likewise. When she was first suggested to Mme Freger, the latter refused: "Mother Michel! who watches over the dead! . . . Don't want her." And yet she had to give in since no one else could be found to take care of her.

---

[19] *The Tragic Sense of Life* was in fact published by Librairie Gallimard in 1917 in a translation by Faure Beaulieu.

[20] *Numquid et tu . . . ?* [E.] [Note supplied by the French editor. Such notes will hereafter be indicated by an E. in brackets.]

Sunday

Insomnia the last few nights, rather painful because of the nervous disorders that reappear — as they always do, alas, as soon as I begin working seriously. Yet I am being very good, observing a continence than it seems to me I have not known since my childhood, or except in very rare periods. I threw into the fire the day before yesterday two packages of cigarettes I had brought back from Havre. Smoking makes me dizzy almost at once; I light a cigarette from habit rather than out of pleasure.

The pruning of our fruit trees is dreadfully behindhand; the sap is rising. I have taken an active part in it and every day have spent almost four hours at it. I get furious with Mius when I discover the absurd arrangement of his espaliers. Since he sacrifices everything to appearances and since the least empty spot upsets him, he contrives to bring a branch forward from anywhere whatever to take the place of the missing one, which he should have known how to get the tree to produce. Impossible to describe the acrobatic contortions and odd arrangements my trees were forced to by that limited mind. His dream would have been to write his name everywhere in bent branches; on the espaliers I find the shape of every letter in the alphabet. And in order to achieve somewhat reasonable outlines again, I have to risk real havoc, which the trees won't get over for a long time.

22 March

One struggles effectively so long as one thinks it a duty to struggle; but as soon as the struggle appears meaningless and one ceases to hate the enemy . . . Yet I am still resisting, though less from conviction than from defiance.

Recovered myself at once.

Sunday, 26 March

It is beginning to snow again. Continued the pruning nevertheless with Edmond. I take an ever greater interest in this work as I gradually feel that I am doing it better. I even go back to certain trees that seem insufficiently cut back when I look at them again. How attentively I shall watch the spring growth!

But most of our trees are withered by a sort of blackish blisters, of which I fail to find a description in any book and which I think due to the cold winds and the excessive humidity. What a shame to have the climate and the exposure against one, the end of the plateau, where the garden is, sloping toward the north.

Went Friday to the auction of the things belonging to the Justice of the Peace. The library was apparently bought as a whole by a Rouen bookseller for an absurd amount (about two thousand francs);

but there was left over from that first sale a parcel of one-franc novels translated from the Russian and the English which I knew to be rather hard to find today (Dickens, Thackeray, etc.). I had put among them a translation of *Krotkaïa,* which has disappeared from my library;[21] but the Rouen dealer got hold of it — so that I came back with a very meager booty.

28 March

Indescribably gloomy days; uninterrupted rain and cold winds. Resumed writing out my Memoirs; translated a few poems of Kabir and went on with my reading of *Jean-Christophe.* I am beginning the fourth book. I confess that, at moments, the first ones had overcome my prejudices; a certain rather crude grace, a use of the right key, made up for the lack of style; but the third part of *L'Adolescence* (Ada) is excessively unpleasant in its awkward frankness and painfully inadequate in its means of expression.[22] Those tedious passages or rather that willful spinning-out of the material, that heavy rudimentary lyricism (Germanic, I dare say) — are all unbearable to me. And even the constant manifestation of the intention, which shocks me as an artistic immodesty, or lack of tact.

But I can understand that such a book should make friends, and many.

31 March

I have forsaken this notebook the last few days. Now that my work has got under way again, it has become less useful for me to write in it, and consequently more tiresome. I keep getting ahead in the writing of my recollections, often with many hesitations, backward glances, and fresh starts; but I refuse to reread what I have written and even to write out a clean copy, for fear of being disgusted with what I am writing and not having the courage to go on.

It is not so much doubt and lack of self-confidence that hold me up as a sort of disgust, a nameless hatred and scorn for everything I am writing, for everything I was, everything I am. Indeed, in going ahead with the writing of these Memoirs, I am performing a sort of maceration.

It is still very cold, but the weather has turned fair again. Despite the present distress, everything is bursting with extraordinary rapture, which overflows in the birds' singing; that singing had never struck

---

[21] A fragment of Dostoyevsky's *Journal* for November 1876, translated by Constance Garnett as "A Gentle Spirit."

[22] "Ada" is the third part of *The Adolescent,* which is in turn Volume III of *Jean-Christophe.*

me as so plentiful, so insistent, or so pathetic. I don't think this results only from the fact that the war inclines us to be particularly touched by whatever purity and joy still remain to us; no, the very maids and peasants notice it: "Did Madame hear the birds singing yesterday?" they ask. The birds are especially numerous here because of the fruit and because Em. is always feeding them. I believe also that the battle-zone has driven back into our region many species that we were not accustomed to see here, except perhaps very rarely. But, among them, a flock of jays; Valentine predicts that they will devastate all the nests. And the fact is that yesterday the children found, at the foot of the yew tree, a tiny nest fallen to earth full of cute little bluish eggs (blackbird eggs, I think) pierced and dry, which seems to indicate that the jays have begun their depredations.

2 April

Radiant weather since yesterday. Wonderfully limpid sky. For the first time I went out of the garden (for I don't count two or three trips to Criquetot) and went down to the valley; I hoped to see the Déhais children again, but they were doubtless at school. The brush is being cut on the hill; the landscape seems enlarged by this; the tall trees that have been left seem more graceful, more noble. A slight vapor gave distance to the various planes so that I hardly recognized this valley, and surprise was mingled with my delight. The air was still frigid as soon as it ceased to be very calm or as soon as one stepped out of the sun.

I have done almost nothing all day long, filled as I was with admiration; it entered me through every sense.

I worked at length on the trees; having asked Valentine to lime the trunks of those in the hothouse garden, I noticed that it would be wise to brush the trunks first. In the toolshed I discovered a brush with metal bristles and went at the job zealously. I cleaned off an unbelievable amount of moss, lichen, and dust, and the trunks of the young trees appeared smooth, shining, soft in color, and pleasant to the touch and to the eye. They looked like handsome naked athletes rubbed with oil, stalwart, and with muscles taut.

I am struck with wonder, as I was with Ghéon at La Roque, by the beauty of bark; and what a difference, from one tree to another, in grain, tone, and quality! The bark of the plum trees, which I took care of first, is pinkish gray, cut transversally with bright orange cracks, making a marvelous effect.

After this work and that of the day before (cutting out the dead wood), the big plum tree behind the tennis court is unrecognizable, transfigured.

4 April

I humbly beg God this morning:

My God, sustain me, guide me, protect me throughout this day.

13 April

Left for Paris. Arrived at nine thirty p.m.; found Copeau and Ghéon waiting for me.

(Extreme fatigue for two days.)

Went to rue des Belles-Feuilles to the Maus house, where Mme Théo was already settled and where Théo comes to join us. Friday morning: *N.R.F.;* lunch with Copeau and Ghéon.

Went to the Cirque Médrano, where I meet Copeau. Conversation with Fratellini, the clown (the elder).

Monday morning, back to Cuverville.

Tuesday, 18 April

I am changing to another notebook.

Returned yesterday from Paris, where I had gone to spend three days, called by Ghéon, who was on leave. Saw Copeau again too.

It did me good to renew contact with my worthy friends. The last days in Cuverville had been horrible. I fancy that not many can understand how far I can go in hostility toward myself. I have got to the point of not daring to speak, and the words that escape me are those of which I am not master and which I should like to recall at once. The closer I am to disavowing them, the more cutting, sharp, and peremptory is my tone of voice in pronouncing them, and the less inclined I am to put up with the slightest contradiction.

What is the reason for this strange *withdrawal of sap* to which my mind is so often subject and which leaves it cluttered with dead wood? And I think: a little sap and again this frightful dead wood would be covered with leaves and flowers. . . . But dead, it is frightful. I wish it in the fire and would gladly lop it off.

The man who is ever constant and the same knows nothing of this; and this is why too healthy people are most often rather poor psychologists.

19 April

I glimpse what might be a sort of mystical treatise as a pendant to my *Enfant prodigue,* which I should entitle: "L'Entretien avec Nicodème." [23]

---

[23] No such work as this "Conversation with Nicodemus" has ever been published; the other work is of course the prose poem of 1907, *The Return of the Prodigal Son.*

I reread everything concerning the man of whom only St. John speaks. The whole morning is spent thus, for I am stopped at each step by a new burst of light.

I kneel down and say aloud: "My God! My God, give me the possibility of praying to you again! Give me simplicity of heart."

20 April

I brought back from Paris all the papers, letters, and documents I could find that might quicken my recollections and help me to put them in order. But they get in my way and stifle my spontaneity.

Isabelle Rivière arrived yesterday and we began to go over together her translation of Conrad's *Victory*.

Easter Monday, 22 or 23

I get to the point of being unable even to understand, at times, to what I owe the friendship that certain people bear me. I countermand it . . . so unpleasant and exasperating do I find the things I hear myself saying. Without doubt, if I heard them from another, they would be enough to make me hate him. What poverty! what complacency! what a need to climb on top of others, to crush them! . . .

The evil is so deep and long-standing and carries such impetus that it upsets all the attention I give it, which consequently only succeeds in making my remarks seem more deliberate. I find a little relaxation only at the piano, at work, or in the garden.

26

A new letter from Lebrun, the victim of the judicial error, or at least of the too summary judgment I spoke of in my *Souvenirs de la Cour d'Assises*, and in whose favor I had intervened to get a commutation of his sentence.[24] In Paris I had seen him again when he got out of the hospital; a bullet had pierced his chest; he was returning to his depot and was only passing through Paris. In his uniform I didn't recognize him; and even in civilian clothes I should not have recognized in this shoddy big fellow the poor figure sunk down on the court bench. He had to tell me his name. "Ah! Lebrun!" and suddenly I saw again his affectionate, warm way of looking at one.

A letter from him, four days ago, brought me news. He had been wounded again, then sent to southern Tunisia, where he had caught the fever, then to El Kef, then sent back to the front. That very day I

---

[24] In *Recollections of the Assize Court* the man is called Yves Cordier, doubtless for reasons of discretion. Eighteen years old, he was accused with two others of having beaten up in October 1911 and robbed of ninety-two francs a sailor named Braz. His five-year prison sentence was commuted to three years through the intervention of André Gide, a juror on his case.

had mailed to the address he gave me, a letter and a money-order. Will he ever receive them? His letter of yesterday is a farewell. He has been picked to take part in a partial attack — one of those attacks you know that you are not to return from. Nothing could be simpler than these lines; nothing more moving.

3 May

The day before yesterday I had got up at six o'clock, although having gone to bed late, in an excellent state of mind for work; but soon a sharp neuralgic pain killed my enthusiasm. It was like a knife in my right side; the pain continued to get worse for three hours and brought on vomiting, then stayed about the same until four p.m.; at that time I was able to sleep a little, and on awakening it was all over. Nothing remained but a general fatigue and a slight tenderness on that side. The fatigue still subsists two days later. . . . Ashamed to have so little resistance to pain. Without doubt that attack was of the mildest type; and yet I don't know how I could have stood anything worse.

I read in a letter from my mother to my father: "André would be very nice if he didn't have a mania for standing a long time absolutely still at the foot of a tree watching snails."

The letter must date from '73 (the year of Isabelle Widmer's marriage, which it mentions earlier). I was therefore four years old.

Tuesday evening

"How happy you will be if you learn what the real occupation of love is!" (Fénelon: *Lettres spirituelles*, p. 111.)

15 June

I have torn out about twenty pages of this notebook; this broke the continuity and I have been unable to write anything in it for more than a month. I have given all my time to the Memoirs. If anyone is surprised that I can enjoy this work while the echo of cannon is still shaking the earth, I shall explain that it is just because any work of imagination is impossible for me, and any intellectual work. Without and within me I feel an immense upset, and if I am writing these Memoirs today, it is also true that I cling desperately to them.

The pages I tore up seemed like pages written by a madman.

16

Yesterday, at the request of the government, all clocks were advanced an hour. You could not imagine the number of stupid remarks to which that decision gave rise. People managed to talk about it for hours on end.

* * *

Cuverville, 15 September

I resume this journal, forsaken last June, in a new notebook. I had torn out the last pages; they reflected a dreadful crisis in which Em. was involved; or, more exactly, of which Em. was the cause. I had written them in a sort of despair, and since, to tell the truth, those pages were addressed to her, I tore them up at her request as soon as she had read them. Or rather, even though she discreetly refrained from asking it of me, at least I was too keenly aware of the relief it would be for her not to suggest it to her at once. And probably she was grateful to me for it; but yet I regret those pages; not so much because I think I have never written any like them, nor because they might have helped me to get out of an unhealthy state of mind that they sincerely reflected and into which I am only too inclined to fall again; but because that suppression interrupted my journal at once and because, deprived of that support, I have since wallowed in a terrifying intellectual disorder. I have made useless efforts in the other notebook. I forsake it half filled. In this one, at least, I shall not be aware of the gap.

I had left Cuverville in the first week of July; spent a month at the Théos'; left for Toulouse at the beginning of August. After a week at Bagnols, went with Eugène Rouart to the Mas, to Amélie-les-Bains, Perpignan, and Banyuls (where we were arrested because our papers were not in order). — Back to Paris; a week at the Théos'; then to Cuverville again. I have been here now for ten days, not knowing where to turn, devoid of hope, joy, and valor. I was waiting for the arrival of a promised fountain-pen to begin this notebook, in which I am going to try to reclaim myself.

16 September

I shan't succeed without a constant effort, an hourly effort, constantly renewed. I shan't succeed without deceit and attention to detail.

Nothing gained if I aim to note here only things of importance. I must make up my mind to write everything in this notebook. I must force myself to write anything whatever.

Last night was a bit better (frightful anguish the night before). During the evening I had read a few pages of Bossuet (first sermon on Providence), so copious and so charmingly true that I had gone to sleep quite calmed.

Late in the afternoon my headache returned; such an intellectual torpor that I need great courage not to despair. With great difficulty I managed to write a few letters (one of them to that odd fellow

Labasque); I went out; I hoped that walking would restore me, but it only increased my discomfort to the point of dizziness.

In this morning's *Temps* appeared an article by Souday ("*Le Pauvre Subjonctif*"),[25] containing fragments of the letter I had written him. I rather regret having asked him not to name me, for everything he quotes from my letter seems good to me. I always have a tendency to lay it on a bit too heavily. . . .

This morning Jean came to me, sent by his mother so that I could teach him his scales. The day before, I had already given him his first lesson despite the frightful scene his mother had made when I had unwisely asked her not to intervene. She immediately launched out against me like a fury: "I want everything for myself; I want to get all the credit for the lesson. And besides, she doesn't understand her own child better than I do! And furthermore he is much less advanced than I think. In addition, I never can put myself in the place of others," etc. Stupefying. Besides, the good T. is utterly incapable of teaching what she was just barely capable of learning. She gets out of her depth and out of patience every time the child hesitates; but her vanity and maternal love are at stake and she insists. She insists even though the child were to suffer from it, and after breakfast closets herself with him for stormy "lessons in *solfège*," from which they both issue flushed and absolutely furious. She does not leave the child an instant during the lesson I give him, sits right beside him and hurls herself with intellectual might and main athwart the questions and answers. It calls for archangelic patience.

17

Abominable torpor. I have great trouble convincing myself, if this state of imbecility continues, that my role is to shelter myself, to hold myself in reserve. As soon as my worth decreases, as soon as it ceases to appear clearly to me, I should like to be used in some more direct fashion, offer myself to some active service or other. And I know that I should be good at it. How can I believe that I am *better* by remaining here? Get thee to a depot!

Sunday

They deign to inform us today, after four or five days' delay, of the Bulgarian communiqué citing the number of Rumanian prisoners taken at Turtucaia. Even so, the *Journal de Genève* is the only paper to give it. This atmosphere of falsehood is stifling, poisoning, mortal. Our country deserved better.

Yesterday a stirring letter from Mme Mayrisch containing this passage:

---

[25] "The Poor Subjunctive."

"This brief note is chiefly to tell you how deeply I share with you the joy of seeing France rise again. You never spoke to me of these things without regret, but I was extremely conscious of your suffering and of the terrible feeling of impotence that seized hold of you every time you noticed that the country was slipping once more in another regard. To tell the truth, I never felt you absolutely at sea and without remedy except at such moments. With the circle of your happiness now closed at the single spot through which all joy might have escaped, how happy you must be, dear friend! I believe I am not exaggerating the importance of this, am I? And I flatter myself that I understand it as well as anyone. . . . You know how utterly I shared with you the anguish of two years ago; know, then, how completely I participate in the infinite hope of today."

Yes, I remember those conversations with her and Ghéon, in Asia Minor (one at Smyrna, particularly), about the slow decay of France, about the unused or squandered virtues, about the imminence of war — in which Mme Mayrisch refused to believe and which, several months before the declaration, Ghéon and I foresaw, predicted, almost longed for, since it seemed to us that war itself was a lesser evil than the abominable decay into which our country was gradually falling — and from which war alone could perhaps still save us. . . .

T., when she is in a conciliatory mood, tacks onto her most affirmative sentences a "you understand?" — which I find exactly the same in my Aunt Charles, who is equally obstinate and altogether impermeable to the feelings, thoughts, or intentions of others. Since, between my aunt and me, contradiction has never been very fierce, and since she would like to convince us, her "you understand?" expresses a slightly different meaning, becomes: "you don't seem to understand." For both of them, if you are not of their opinion, this is because you do not quite "understand" them; the lack of understanding, of intelligence, always belongs on the other side, as far as they are concerned; and they are active all right!

"Thus it is that, to punish the greatest sinners, as we learn from the divine apostle, he gives them over to their own desires; as if he said: He gives them over to the hands of the executioners. . . ."

"When we possess temporal goods, certain secret bonds are created that gradually tie the heart to the love of present things, and these ties are generally more dangerous the more imperceptible they are." (Bossuet: *Providence*, I.) [26]

---

[26] In his *Sermon sur la Providence*, preached in 1662, Bossuet handles a subject that constantly reappears throughout his work.

19 September

Yesterday, an abominable relapse. The storm raged all night long. This morning it is hailing heavily. I get up, my head and heart both heavy and empty, full of the entire weight of hell. . . . I am the drowning man who is losing heart and now struggles only weakly. The three calls have the same sound: "It is time. It is high time. It is no longer time." So that you do not distinguish one from the other and already the third one is sounding while you still think you are at the first.

If at least I could relate this drama; depict Satan, after he has taken possession of a creature, using him, acting through him upon others. This seems an empty image. Even I have only recently come to understand this: you are not only a prisoner; active evil demands of you a reverse activity; you must fight in the other army. . . .

This evening I am going to Paris; my pretext is to meet Gosse, whom Briand has invited here. Besides, I shall be extremely happy to see him again; and I am not doing anything worth while here, for I do not count my piano lessons to the children and my translation of *Typhoon,* which has progressed considerably of late.

The great error is to form a romantic image of the devil. This is what made me take so long to recognize him. He is no more romantic or classic than whomever he is talking to. He is as diverse as man himself; more so, because he adds to his diversity. He made himself classical with me, when it was necessary to catch me, and because he knew that I could never willingly assimilate to evil a certain happy equilibrium. I did not understand that a certain equilibrium could be maintained, for a time at least, in the worst. I took to be good everything that was regulated. Through measure I thought to dominate evil; and it is through that very measure on the contrary that it took possession of me.

20

Arrived yesterday evening in Paris. Read without stopping, during the trip, the first sixty pages of *The Return of the Native*.[27] This morning wrote to Em. Went to the Hôtel Crillon to see Gosse, but he does not arrive until this evening. Went to the Propaganda Headquarters to speak with Bréal about Lauris. Lunched with Mme Théo at the little bar on the rue Bassano. Came home to nap and write to Em.

A disgust, a frightful hatred of myself, sours all my thoughts the moment I wake up. The minute hostility with which I keep watch over every slightest impulse within me contorts it. Shortcomings or virtues,

---

[27] Thomas Hardy's novel.

I no longer have anything natural in me. Everything I remember about myself fills me with horror.

Friday

Wrote to Em. yesterday and the day before.

This morning, lunch with Gosse at the Crillon. More wearing than pleasureable. The conversation exhausts me. Gosse is exquisitely cordial. Nevertheless I felt, two or three times, that perhaps I was approaching a bit too closely.[28]

Ah! I should like to plunge into a deep bath of silence.

Saturday

Let myself be dragged off to Versailles by Mme Théo and Élisabeth. Glorious weather, calling for joy. But nothing in me can answer that call now.

Sunday

Empty day; lost. I drag myself through the hours and long for nothing but sleep.

Monday

But don't you see that you are speaking to a dead man?

Wednesday

Capture of Thiepval and of Combles.

I was to set out this morning for Offranville. But the auto that came to pick me up at eight o'clock was sent away. I felt so tired, after a night of coughing and restlessness, that I put the trip off.

Offranville, Friday

Constant fatigue and headache. This morning, on awaking, fine rain. The sky is uniformly gray, with no more blue or sunlight than there is in my mind. The sort of sparkling amusement that J.-É. Blanche takes in conversation, even when he is the only one to speak and I reduce my contribution to a few rare interjections, grips me at first by a sort of contagion.

Yesterday as I came out of the métro at the Louvre station, I saw a girl standing still in the passageway, or at least she was walking so slowly that to those who were hurrying around her she could have seemed motionless. She was reading an unbound book of rather large format, which didn't seem to be a popular publication. Her manner of dressing was respectable and her whole attitude suggested a de-

---

[28] See later entry. [A.]

lightful reserve. She seemed absorbed in her reading to the point of
forgetting the people around her and the place; and, out of curiosity,
I was about to approach her in an attempt to make out the title of the
book that was absorbing her to such a point when a big ungainly
workman, about forty years old, with a stroke of his hand, as he was
passing her, sent the book flying on the muddy pavement. A single
blow should have dispatched him to the same position. But one would
have had to be up to it. He was a big fellow and apparently of the
worst kind; he was a head taller than I; and moreover he was not
alone; another much younger workman was with him, he too a rugged
fellow, and in scoffing fashion he was getting great fun out of the
scene. Both of them looked like men ready to pull a knife; the older
one was barely master of himself. . . . In short I thought it wiser to
use my tongue rather than my arm. But I thought only of terribly inappropriate words: "That's certainly clever, what you just did!"

If I had said: "That's certainly smart!" it would have been all right,
but "clever" smacked deplorably of the bloated aristocrat and annoyed me with myself. "Clever" was greeted with a sly laugh and repeated in a tone that aimed to imitate my voice; then the man who
had knocked the book down said: "I get as big a kick out of that as
out of reading!"

To which there was no reply. I should have done better to help the
girl pick up the leaves of her book. But she had done this while I was
watching the workmen disappear.

I am writing this with boredom and a great effort. That is evident.

                                                           3 October

Back in Cuverville. I had left Paris Friday; spent a night at Offranville at J.-É. Blanche's, a night at Varangeville at the Godebskis', and
last night at Offranville. (Visit to Calmont.)

I had gone to meet Gosse at the Hôtel Crillon, where the Propaganda Ministry had reserved a very pleasant apartment of three rooms
for him. He was expecting me. I was taken up; it was on the third
floor. I found the same old Gosse barely a bit older-looking; slightly
shriveled, thinned out in spots. As in the past, his movements seemed
to me prompted perhaps a bit more by his mind than by his heart, or
at least by a sort of *self-respect*.[29] Intelligence, which with him always
has a weather-eye out, intervenes and checks him on the slope of surrender. He begins to catch himself at the moment when I was beginning to like him. Moreover, it is perhaps not so much me as himself
that he distrusts.

As soon as I come in, effusion; our four hands are joined for some

---

[29] This expression appears in English in the original.

time; then I sit down. And he, after a very brief silence, which seemed intended to catch his breath, as if yielding to an irresistible impulse (yet it was a trifle put on):

"Ah, dear friend, let us embrace once more!"

Seeing an invitation in these words, I rise from my chair and, rushing toward him, apply to both his flabby cheeks two big kisses in the French manner. He jumped a bit, drew back almost imperceptibly with a slight grimace immediately hidden, but from which I recognized that he intended to remain master of the situation and tell me just how far to go and no farther, that by taking literally his "let us embrace" I was forgetting that he spoke French only half well and that, in short, for the English, so chary of demonstrations, a prolonged handshake was better than any embrace. I can imagine Gosse later on asking Millet, his guide, or someone else: "But tell me, sir, when you want to shake someone's hand in the middle of a conversation, how do you say this in good French? Just imagine that the other day, having had the imprudence to say to Gide: 'Let us embrace,' I find him actually embracing me! It was absurd."

We lunched together at the Crillon; I was tired out in advance and also by the necessity I have just pointed out of skillfully mixing the most extreme cordiality with an imperceptible reserve. It would be less obvious on his part if we were speaking English; this would be entirely up to him since he speaks English in the clearest possible manner and I am sure I should understand him; but he is getting a little practice, for he is to lunch tomorrow at Briand's. He asks me what wine I prefer, suggests sauternes, and I have no sooner accepted than he orders a less expensive one he has just discovered on the card. Later on, he shows that he is slightly hurt that I have not drunk more of it.

At dessert he suggests: "A cigar?"

I refuse.

"What! You don't smoke?"

Then, as if in spite of myself, nervously:

"Why yes, a cigarette, if you wish."

And this is just what I know that I ought not to say, for Gosse, who doesn't smoke them, has none on him and is going to have to order some. The waiter, as might be expected, brings the most expensive packages on a tray. Gosse is not a miser the way X. is, but he is *close*, and all the more so since he is a guest of France and a discretion that is only common decency checks him. The amusing thing is his need of making me feel, subtly, what I am only too well aware of since it covers me with embarrassment:

"Take this little package as a souvenir of our lunch."

I had only to slip the package into my pocket with a few words that would have shown I was not taken in. I might have said, for example: "If I offer one, I shall do so in your name," or else simply: "I shall think of you when I smoke them," but I found nothing to say, I didn't even look for anything, filled to overflowing with a vast melancholy . . . which was like drowsiness. And the worst of it is that when we got up I left the package of cigarettes on the table.

I have set down other bits of our conversation in a letter to Em.

At the slightest material obstacle, whether it come from the ink or the paper, my thought contracts, stops. My fingers' numbness leads to the numbness of my brain. A scratchy pen and my style is embarrassed. Today I forbade myself the piano. I force myself to write despite my headache and that sort of stupor which so often paralyzes me here. At least my fountain-pen is all right. I am writing on a bench on the avenue. I am lost if I do not manage to catch hold of myself before winter. These summer months were hateful, full of utter waste of time, with no work accomplished. I do not think I have ever been farther from happiness. With ever the vague hope that, from the depths of the abyss, will arise that cry of distress that — no — I have forgotten how to utter. . . . One can, while being at the lowest ebb, still look toward the azure; no, however low I was, I always looked still lower. I gave up heaven. I ceased defending myself against hell. Obsessions and all the prodromes of madness. Truly! I frightened myself; and incapable in my own case of the advice I should have been so able to give to someone else.

Does this fact of already talking about my state indicate that I am already so sure of being cured?

There is in J.-É. Blanche something contented, facile, and light that causes me an indescribable discomfort. Blanche has too many trumps in his hand, and his oddest intellectual quirk is the need of proving to all and sundry that with a single trump less life is not worth living. His most sincere remarks begin: "I don't know how you can . . ." His house is surrounded by a beautiful garden: "I don't know how you can live in a street." During the fine weather he is in Normandy: "I don't know how you can spend the summer in Paris."

Occasionally this commiseration is veiled. He asks me where the Théos are now living. I reply: "Rue Claude Lorrain." And already in his manner of repeating: "Rue Claude Lorrain?" in his tone, in the ironic and painful interrogation of his eyebrows — which rise unequally so that the left one remains frowning while the right one goes way up — you can guess that he foresees that the rue Claude Lorrain must be an unmentionable, impossible street in an uninhabitable section of town. He adds: "I don't know it." (Now, he knows everything that it is proper to know.) "Where is it?"

"It runs into the rue Michel-Ange," I told him, "right after the Auteuil viaduct."

"In short, Billancourt."

This "in short," to judge from the tone, means "dare to say it," "confess it," and "this is just what I was expecting.". . . "How can anyone live in Billancourt?" [30]

If I were to write many novels, I should fill one with Blanche.

4 October

This morning it is raining pitchforks. Good weather for work; my night was not too bad. My head is cleared up, as it were.

Yesterday evening S. again intervened in the course of the lesson she had asked me to give Jean. I have all the patience needed for the child; but for the mother it takes more than for a class of twenty kids on the warpath.

S. admits that she can get nowhere with her son; he doesn't listen to her; both of them get irritated and tired. S. proceeds by affirmations, leaving nothing to the pupil to discover; she removes all flavor, all the essence from her teaching. Noticing the failure of her method, or lack of method, she calls me to the rescue; but at the very first words finds that I am not going about it in the right way, takes up the ruler again, and confuses everything. — Like the day when waiting for the results of a competition of the "Good Housekeeper" to know at last the best recipe for red-currant jelly, she exclaimed at the very first line:

"But that's not right at all!"

Late in the afternoon I had been to chat with M. Lechevalier, the school-teacher, by whom I had just read a remarkable study on the *non*-depopulation of this region. Perhaps he had been urged on to it by the questions I asked him last year; at my request, he had drawn up a statistical table of the Cuverville families that I could show to my Uncle Charles to convince him that the birth-rate is not declining equally in all parts of Normandy; that there were even certain regions in Normandy, among which was ours, that . . . etc. But the information that I went to ask of him yesterday was of quite a different nature; it was a question of providing Eugène Rouart with a table of prices brought by agricultural products before the war (grain, fodder, etc.) compared with those paid to farmers since the war through requisition. Eugène Rouart claims that the farmer is strangled by the war;

---

[30] Billancourt is a continuation, then an unfashionable one, of Auteuil.

and I hear it said here that the farmer, as a result of the war, is enjoying and unprecedented prosperity.

To explain this disagreement, I think it can be said:

1. That the requisition rates vary from one *département* to another.

2. That stock-farming, which brings in the greatest returns in Normandy, hardly exists in the Garonne Valley.[31]

3. That the Garonne Valley holds the record for depopulation and that, consequently, it is obliged to pay for labor that is furnished free to the farmer of the Caux district by his own children.

4. That fertilizers, so costly in the south, are used only in small doses in our districts where they are complemented by natural dressings resulting from the stock-farming. Etc. etc.

The statistics cited by M. Lechevalier tend to prove that the consumption of alcohol in our region (Caux district) is considerably less than in many others. I urge him to take into account, as an important factor in the problem of alcoholism, the inadequacy of nourishment in comparison with the consumption of alcohol, a factor that I have never seen taken into account and that I consider very important. Although consuming proportionately less alcohol, our peasants in the Caux district, very insufficiently nourished on the other hand, resist alcoholism much less than the gorged farmers of Calvados — just as a plant in poor soil and itself "sickly," as they say here, becomes more easily a prey to diseases, parasites, etc., etc.

Thursday, 5 October

Rainy day. After lunch Jeanne, Valentine, and the children set out for Étretat in a carriage. Delightfully calm afternoon with Em. I read her the first thirty letters of Dupouey, of which I had received the copy this very morning. The silence, the calm of the empty house, brought calm back to my heart. This morning I opened the green notebook again (*Numquid et tu . . . ?*) and wrote a few lines in it, but still heavy with unrest, with doubt, with melancholy. My nerves are so weak, so vibrant, that I believe they never relax a bit except in silence; yes, I have already noted how the slightest noise upsets me. I feel immediately better in silence.

The secret of better work is perhaps simply to sit down at my table at once instead of beginning my day with an hour of piano, as I used to do. I work in this way until eleven o'clock without worrying about the mail; then I go downstairs to give Françoise her piano lesson while my room is being done.

---

[31] Eugène Rouart had large farms in the southern *département* of the Haute-Garonne.

J.-É. Blanche possesses almost everything that can be possessed on earth, but the gardens of heaven remain forever closed to him. What keeps him from entering is not that he does not believe, for he has a pretty good suspicion that he is barred; what keeps him from entering is that he is rich. But I have discovered another reason, which is perhaps the chief one: it is that he lacks imagination.

He thinks he is charitable because he takes pity on many poor people, and he envies everything that he does not pity. He has a great deal of egotism and very little self-respect; I mean by this that he goes very little out of his way for the sake of anyone else.

6 October

Most likely I shall have neither the strength nor the constancy to write the wonderful novel I glimpse on this theme:

A man, equally capable of passions, even of dissipation, and of virtues, marries, when still young, a woman whose love exalts in him only nobility, disinterestedness, etc.; for her he sacrifices, without even being quite aware of it, everything ardent, adventurous, luxurious in his nature; or at least, he holds all this in reserve.

An abominable nostalgia seizes hold of him, soon after the death of that wife. He still feels young. He wants to begin his life over again, a different life which will give him everything of which the virtue, the reserve, the voluntary poverty of the first life deprived him. He hurls himself into a luxurious life. Disgust, scorn of himself that derives therefrom. . . .

"It is impossible to love a second time what one has truly ceased to love," says La Rochefoucauld. And this is true even when what one has ceased to love is oneself.

The subjects of my books, of each one of them, would have seemed idiotic if I had related them in this fashion. I am convinced that this one, however ridiculous it may appear in this bare state, could be most pathetically beautiful. It is the story of him who would deny his virtue.

7 October

A few words from Em. plunge me back into a sort of despair. As at last I make up my mind to speak to her of that plan of spending the winter at Saint-Clair:

"*I certainly owe you that,*" she said with an effort of her whole nature, which at once made her face so sad, so grave, that immediately I think only of giving up this plan like so many others, since it costs her so much and since I should have to buy my happiness at the expense of hers — so that it could therefore no longer be my happiness.

There was a time when I abominated all literature, all art, when it did not spring from joy, from an excess of *joie de vivre*. And my unnamable melancholy of today should now urge me to continue speaking?

9 October

I read in the *Revue des deux mondes* that the Yungs send us this morning Gosse's article on Anglo-French intellectual relations.

Gosse is playing with words. It was never a question of "European literature," as he claims, but of "European *culture*," which involves a participation of the various literatures of our old world, each of them powerfully individualized. And only the particularization of each literature, only its nationalization, could permit the Europeanization of culture. So that . . . and so on.

Received a letter from Souday, who complains bitterly that he is not given press copies of Péguy's works. I write to Souday; I write to Gallimard. I spend the better part of my day on this. I made a copy of my two letters.

I have no desire to dictate and don't want to give Gallimard a pretext for taking offense. I have no importance and do not want to have any. But, in order to avoid being made responsible for attitudes and acts that friendship alone keeps me from disavowing, it would be better to change the firm's imprint at the earliest opportunity and give up a compromising and misleading solidarity.[32] I believe with Copeau that it is right for Gallimard to make decisions and to do so alone; but then it becomes necessary that he should sign, alone, his decisions, that the Librairie de la *N.R.F.* should become Librairie Gallimard.

10 October

In the rare moments she manages to give me, I continue with Em. the reading of Dupouey's wonderful letters. I should like, if I can attain a pure enough ardor, to write a preface for the publication of these letters. Their beauty often sparkles before my eyes like a sword of ice.[33]

11 October

My regret is constantly reawakened that Georges Rondeaux could not make up his mind to keep a journal of the various slight incidents

---

[32] As is usual with French literary reviews, *La Nouvelle Revue Française* led to the foundation of a publishing house, which between about 1911 and the present has become one of the most important in France. The last name of its director, Gaston Gallimard, was eventually taken as the firm name.

[33] The letters were in fact published in 1916 with a preface by Gide.

of the Commune of Cuverville, of which he is the mayor. Georges was perfectly qualified for this work; the affairs of the Commune interest him and make up almost his sole occupation; the Commune is just large enough so that he can and must know and keep an eye specifically on each family; he is not new to the country so that he understands the manners and customs and dialect, and yet a certain perspective allows him to enjoy all the picturesque peculiarities. He is excessively attentive to shortcomings, flaws, physical and moral defects, but the sort of predilection he brings to them gives an odd flavor to his tales. I wonder at his memory and the quality of that memory which retains the particular by preference and down to the last detail. Finally, he can write. How will he spend his long winter evenings? In idleness.

It should be added that the Commune (quite apart from the war) has reached an especially lively chapter of its history; a tragic chapter just made to delight the gloomy mood of a chronicler; and that, from the episodic interest of that simple narration, an urgent general lesson would emerge.

Many a time, through regret at letting so rich a matter be lost, I have taken up the pen in his place; but, besides the fact that my intellectual preoccupation urges me elsewhere, I feel too constantly that Georges is better qualified than I for this job, that I am turning myself to it only as a substitute. After all, what I know of it is not direct; I have it from him; he is the one who sees the people, talks to them; my story is never anything but an echo.

Georges ought to tell the story of the Déhais family's moving and their settling in a new house, twenty yards away from the old one but on the other side of the road and therefore in another Commune. The new house is cleaner, healthier, gayer than the first one; but on the first rainy day Déhais, who has just thoroughly cleaned out the cistern, discovers that the rain-pipes, which the owner has just had repaired, lead backward; I mean that their slope drives the water to the opposite end from that of the down-spouts; and yet the work was paid for as if it had been properly done.

Negligence, incompetence, or stupidity? The best plans of the cleverest generals are torn to pieces on those miserable brambles with which the fields of France are sown. — More dangerous for us than the enemy's barbed wire.

12 October (?)

Not very sure of the date nor, therefore, of having obeyed yesterday the coercion I impose upon myself of writing a few lines in this notebook every day.

New losses are announced in the region; I told Em. yesterday how improper it seemed to me that the children, every time the weather permits, should roam the countryside, with Valentine, dressed in such gaudy and motley costumes that they look like a masquerade party, exaggerating their wealth and idleness in the eyes of these poor peasants in mourning who work and slave, bent double over the furrows.

13 October

I am struggling desperately, but at times melancholy takes the upper hand and submerges me. I have just reread the last chapter written of my Memoirs, which I promised myself to write right off and over which I have already labored so much. Nothing of what I should have wanted to put into it is there; everything in it strikes me as studied, subtle, dry, elegant, faded. And yet I have not even approached my subject, and one cannot even yet glimpse the introduction, or foresee the approach, of what was to fill the whole book, of that for which I am writing it. I have reached the point of no longer knowing whether or not I am to go on.

15 October

Slow decrease of ardor. Yesterday, abominable relapse, which leaves my body and mind in a state bordering on despair, on suicide, on madness. . . . It is the rock of Sisyphus, which falls back to the very bottom of the mountain he was trying to climb, which falls back with him, rolling over him, dragging him along under its mortal weight, and plunging him back into the mud. What? Shall I have to, once again and to the very end, repeat this lamentable effort? I think of the time when, in the plain and without any thought of ascending, I used to smile at every new hour, indolently seated on this rock that there was no question of raising. Alas! you took pity on me despite myself, O Lord. . . . But hold out a hand to me, then. Lead me yourself to that place, near you, which I am unable to reach.

"Poor soul, aiming to raise your sin up to me. . . ."

"O Lord! you know that I give up justifying myself against anyone. What does it matter that it is to escape yielding to sin that I yield to the Church! I yield. Oh! untie the bonds that hold me. Deliver me from the frightful weight of this body. Oh, let me live a bit! let me breathe! Tear me away from evil. Do not let me stifle."

17 October

Age is coming without my hoping to know anything more about my body. A happy equilibrium almost immediately followed my lapse and my distress. I should like to see in it a reply to my appeal, but at the moment that I was uttering that cry, I am well aware of it, the best of my distress was over. I was like the man who feels his fever falling at the moment of swallowing his quinine, but who swallows it just the same because, all the time that his fever lasted, he kept thinking: Oh, if only I had taken some!

I write this without any irreverence but because I believe both that the act of piety is not necessarily the result (the successful outcome) of the distress and that it is unseemly to seek to interest God in physical lapses that can just as well be cured by a better regime.

Received yesterday a circular letter signed by Copeau: "I am momentarily in relation with Ducros, the editor of *Les Marches de l'Est*,[34] a man invalided out of the service and at present commissioned by the French Government to take care of our press service in Switzerland. He is living in Berne and is working very actively and very intelligently, as far as I was able to see, to counterbalance the German effort in the German-language Swiss press. He asks me to furnish him a list of writers likely to give him good articles and capable of appealing to neutrals by the level-headedness of their reasoning and the authority of their thought.

"Can you, either on literary and artistic matters or on questions related to the war, furnish Ducros with copy, which would be translated into German and published in the most important Swiss newspapers? I believe this is something very important to do."

I replied to Copeau at once, giving him my approval and complete agreement. But, upon reflecting on it, I glimpse the ticklish element in the plan. I consider every premature effort toward reconciliation as worse than vain, as harmful, and believe that whoever speaks now in that direction wastes his voice, and what is worse, he discredits it.

And I should have kept silent until now only to resume speech in German! . . .

18 October

Somewhat better work. Yet I have still not been able to finish rewriting the previously written part of my Memoirs. Finished the first half of the translation of *Typhoon*. Got ahead with *The Return of the Native*.

20 October

Somewhat better work, the result of an enormous effort. I cannot believe that, under a slightly better physical regime, I should not succeed in furnishing a larger sum of work with less wear.

A draft of a letter by Dupouoy, found in his papers, is finally going to give me the occasion to write to Maurras:

---

[34] *The Eastern Border Provinces,* probably an allusion to Alsace and Lorraine.

"You cannot but be touched by the posthumous evidence of one of the most beautiful souls I have ever known. I copy these lines with a deep emotion and all the more gladly since I most heartily associate myself with them.

"PS. — Thank you for sending me *L'Étang de Berre*.[35] I rather regret that you maintained this title: 'the two fatherlands,' which runs the risk of misleading and even deceiving the reader, most disagreeably for my thought. . . . But perhaps, after all, it is not the mere title that would have to have been changed. Unless you added, as in your latest book, a 'twelve years later' along these lines:

"'I recognize that I was mistaken about A. G.'s thought; and this is doubtless somewhat his fault, for he is often careful to hide his thought, it seems, rather than to express it; but upon rereading him (and no longer 'from memory' as I once did and now recognize that it is not always wise to do), it strikes me that he never sought anything in his articles but French unity, nor proved anything except that that unity was naturally composed of the harmonious diversity of our provinces, and that this unity was realized, more specifically than in anyone else, in the man whose cross-bred heredity mingled the blood of Languedoc, for instance, with Norman blood as it happened in his case, or with Breton blood, as it happened in the case of Léon Daudet.'"

Outline of a second letter:

"No, my dear Maurras; there is nothing new there; and if you had deigned to lend my books, the same attention that you granted one day to my *Roi Candaule*, I suspect that you would have found in each one of them at least as many of those 'profound and subtle truths' (I believe these are your very words) as in the least important of my writings. Instead of which you have always let me be decried by your carping lieutenants. What do you expect? I do not write for fools, but I cannot demand that intelligent people should understand me without having read me. This is why I have never protested but have always remained, despite you and despite your followers, very close to your thought and, I assure you, most cordially yours. . . ."

[35] Maurras took the title for this book of essays, first published in 1915, from the name of a large lake in his native region, not far from Marseille. The essay to which Gide alludes, entitled "The Two Fatherlands or the Choice of a Burial-Place," was reprinted as it had originally appeared in 1902. Starting with Gide's assertion of 1897 that he had been born in Paris of a Norman mother and a father from Languedoc, Maurras claims that Gide will eventually reveal to which province he is most loyal when he chooses his final resting-place.

21 October

That morning, more specifically, he had waited for her — one can say "desperately" — in her room, where he had gone down the earliest he could, rushing his dressing and putting off both work and prayer. It must be said that the day before she had promised to be there, and it was as to a rendezvous that he hastened, with a new and joyful soul; it would act as a springboard for his whole day.

When he had entered, the room was empty; he had found, placed on the table, D.'s letter, which the day before she had promised to read to him. She had placed it there opened, as if to say: "Read it without me," which he did not do, for he found no pleasure in it. He sat down in the window-seat, opened a book he had brought with him; but he could not fix his attention on it. He kept thinking: where is she? what is she doing? what shall I say to her when she eventually returns? Obviously she is not inactive; I am willing to admit that some urgent problem may have called her as it constantly happens, all day long, every day. He made an effort not to be vexed and planned to say to her simply, sweetly: I was beginning to believe you had forgotten me; or: you had rather forgotten that I was waiting for you. . . .

At this moment he heard her step in the vestibule; but she still was not coming upstairs; she was going back and forth; she was busying herself about something or other; there were now but very few minutes before the bell that was to gather the household for breakfast. . . . Then it was that he heard her beginning to wind the clock. It was the big grandfather clock at the foot of the stairs; obviously as she was going by she had seen the clock stopped and, on the point of joining him, had stopped to set it. He heard it strike twice, then the half-hour, then three times. . . . The worst of it is that the clock, an old-style one, struck double. It was after eight o'clock; he calculated that he still had to hear it strike fifty-four times; and each one of these notes unbearably spaced out. . . . He couldn't stand it any longer and went out into the hall.

"I had left the letter on the table so that you could read it," she said as if it were the simplest thing in the world. "You see that I had things to do. When this clock is not on time, the whole house is late."

"I notice that; it is now twenty minutes that I have been waiting for you."

But she made no excuses; she remained so calm and he so upset that he began to think he had been wrong to wait for her and she right not to have come. He said nothing, but thought:

"My poor dear, you will always find clocks to set, along your way, whenever it is a question of meeting me."

Beautiful weather since yesterday; sharp cold. Insomnia until early morning because of the impossibility of keeping warm in bed. Sorry reward for the walk I had taken, for my health, to the La Motte farm on the other side of the valley; back by way of Déhais's farm and the village, where I go in a moment to ask for news of the Bertin boy.

In the evening I go out again with Em. to take iodine to one of the prisoners working in Mme Hérouard's fields. She says she is thoroughly satisfied with them. I had seen them as I went by at the beginning of my walk and one of them, to whom I had previously spoken, complained of a serious sore throat. I feared his effusions, but fortunately he barely thanked me.

Today I go and take the Bertin boy a large package of beans to shell; this is Em.'s excellent idea after I had told her my fears. I feared that that big fellow, who is deathly bored in the little room where his convalescence keeps him and who is terribly worried at not earning anything, might try to go back to work too soon; and this would finish him off. I wondered what distraction, what occupation I could take him. . . . He accepts with the most charming delight and I promise to take him another package to shell on Monday.

Somewhat better work. Prayer.

22

My upstairs room has become too cold; I settle in the office. Every evening with the children we play little cipher problems (provided by the covers of *Le Journal de la jeunesse,* of which we have old series [36]) in which we have become rather proficient. By whom is this sentence, offered by one of the problems: "It takes a great deal of philosophy to observe what is seen every day"?

I am furious to see badly conducted experiments and incomplete observations give credit to errors; for instance, this one: that as soon as two male dogs are left together, one can be sure that they will fight. And to avoid this a fence is put between them or one of the two is kept on a leash and this results, naturally, in infuriating him. His fury is born of the obstacle and not of the fact that they are both male dogs. If there is near them, between them, a bitch in heat, the whole question changes; and yet even then they do not always fight. But if between them there is no fence or bone or bitch, or if she is not in heat, the dogs do not quarrel; quite the contrary. And just from seeing Toby squirt three times against the fence separating him from the baker's dog enlightens me sufficiently as to his feelings.

---

[36] *Young People's Magazine.*

23 October

Out of fifteen members of a gun crew ten fall because it was considered useless to make a shelter for them. This takes place during the first days of the July offensive on the Somme; the position was looked upon as "provisional" and not needing a real installation. But the artillery preparation lasts a little longer than was planned; the gun is spotted and the men are at the mercy of the systematic shelling.

This is what comes out of the tale told by a *poilu* who comes to see us; a lad of the class of '15 or '16, wounded after a month at the front.[37] Excellent morale; desire to present the best side of everything. This boy, whom I did not know before, was born either out of wedlock or in adultery (I don't know just which). Black-listed until now. Excellent pupil of M. Lechevalier, who protected him, helped him, etc. . . . (Just now he is a clerk in Havre.)

The lamentable accident in which the priest's nephew met his death was due to negligence alone, it seems. A sentinel was not posted or did not happen to be at his post to prevent a mule loaded with hand-grenades from entering. The mule stumbles and falls; the grenades go off, leading to the explosion of a munitions depot installed there. The place was, it seems, a tunnel. . . . The accident, of which people kept from talking, is supposed to have caused the death of nine hundred men and a few officers, including a lieutenant-general. The tunnel having fallen in, it was impossible to rescue the men at once; the remains that were recovered four days later were completely charred.

Negligence; thoughtlessness; vague confidence in some good luck or other;[38] shall we ever correct these shortcomings?—which cost us as much in men as the skillful German "preparations."

24 October

Wrote to Mme Dupouey.—Constant headache. Unable to do almost anything all day long. Jeanne and the children have left. A letter from Mme Théo gives me news of Charlie Du Bos, from whom the attribution of the financial grants has finally been taken away. This should have been done long ago. I send a telegram to Mme Théo offering to resume work at the Foyer for three weeks, for I fear they may be overtaxed.

Went to take the Bertin boy some more beans to shell. I had gone to see and pay him; he is beginning to be tamed, it seems, and is

---

[37] In France, even in peacetime, every youth is called up for military service presumably at the age of twenty; the class of 1915 was therefore made up of those born in 1895.

[38] The expression *good luck* appears in English in the original.

gaining confidence. At his request, I take him two books: *Treasure Island* and *L'Intelligence des animaux* by Toussenel (?) [39] — which I skim through on the way and which seems to me idiotic, stuffed with terms incomprehensible to children, to whom it is supposed to be addressed. . . . I should have done better to bring a Jules Verne.

25 October

This whole war seems a demonstration of this: that with the finest virtues in the world nothing can be accomplished without method. This is what Maurras teaches; but it is what Germany practices.

Everything convinces me more and more that these questions of strategy, which are surrounded with so much mystery and for the solution of which it is claimed that very special knowledge is indispensable, are matters of ordinary common sense—that a mere direct, lucid, and ready mind is often more apt to solve than a number of old generals. It is much harder for the latter to get away from the routine in which their whole career has kept them than for a new mind to stay out of it altogether. People make fun of home strategists. . . . At least they are not dangerous. I am sure that among them there are a number of very clever ones who only lack data to reason perfectly. But when you read General L. or M., for instance, in yesterday's *Temps,* you shudder at the thought that before being retired that poor brain risked our country's fate.

One didn't have to be a genius to see that if Rumania really had only a very limited supply of arms, she was not going to risk it beyond her natural frontiers, which were excellent; at least not before being assured of aid.

"It is a fine achievement," it will be objected, "to predict things after they have taken place!"

But there is no question of achievement here at all. Do you believe that certain people waited for the seizure of Constanta to think what I have just written?

At the rate at which we are going, there will soon be formed a Germanophile party in France, which will be recruited not among anarchists and internationalists, but among those who will be obliged to recognize the constant superiority of Germany. They will judge, and rightly, that it is good, that it is natural, for superiority to govern. And perhaps they will reflect that something in France remains su-

---

[39] *L'Esprit des bêtes* (*The Intelligence of Animals*) is the exact title of this naïve book by Alphonse Toussenel (1803–85), which originally appeared some time before 1855. It is written by a hunter, and the animals are classified from the hunter's point of view.

perior to that very superiority; but alas! that something divine is powerless and mute. Would Germany be able to recognize that something? Would she strive to stifle it? Or would she not perhaps consent to exploit it? . . . Exploit that in which the enemy excells! What a fantasy! And indeed would that something permit itself to be exploited by the enemy?

26 October

Lapse the day before yesterday and yesterday. The best thing is not to be too upset about it. It is not good to keep rubbing one's nose in one's mistake.

28 October

There were no fewer than eleven Germans working yesterday in the Hérouards' beet-field, plus two territorials to guard them (?), who were likewise working. I was unable to speak to any of them; or more exactly had no desire to. The one to whom I had given a bottle of iodine was not there. I have been told that he is apparently rather seriously ill.

The rain is falling heavily and the rain-spouts are filled with dead leaves. But in order to raise the big ladder Edmond needed a hand. It is decided to call the help of the sole prisoner who is working next door, in the Fregers' barnyard. I had merely glimpsed him perched in an apple tree knocking down the apples with a pole. His appearance and the expression of his face had kept me from speaking to him. He is a Saxon, short and strapping, thirty-two years old. We learn from Valentine, who started conversation with him, that he is a farmer and the father of three young boys.

"'Future soldiers,' he told me right away," she added indignantly as she repeated this remark that seemed to have come straight out of Roman history. She added: "Never would a Frenchman have said that."—What a pity!

Valentine always seeks much more to be moved than to inform herself. When she is asked just what words the soldier used, she hesitates; she doesn't remember; we begin to wonder if she understood correctly.

Consequently we went to get that man. In that difficult and even rather dangerous maneuver, for the ladder was endless, he showed himself to be remarkably dexterous and strong. Edmond does not hide his stupefaction. Edmond has five sons in the service, yet it is obvious that he doesn't in any way dislike this "enemy." He expresses this to me in his hesitant, awkward, confused speech; it is obvious that he is afraid of saying something silly, afraid of expressing himself badly; and yet, feeling encouraged:

"He's so *fast!* He went too fast, even. . . . He's a farmer, it appears.". . . (A long silence.) "Yes, after all, a man like us." (Again a silence; then, slowly, smiling, yet sadly and as if tenderly:) "Those people don't want to die any more than we do. . . ."

Fearing that Edmond might get excessively soft, I repeat to him the Saxon's remark to Valentine, which at first he fails to understand. I explain:

"Yes, future soldiers. He means: *I* may be a prisoner; but I have sown for the future; I have left three over yonder who will some day replace me and avenge me."

But while I am explaining, I think of the smile that German gave us just a moment ago when he was doing us a service, of the look in his eyes — such a childlike smile, such a limpid look — that I decidedly doubt whether or not Valentine really understood him.

29 October

The newspapers exasperate me; their contemptible and old-fashioned optimism seems always to believe that victory consists in being unwilling to notice the blows one receives. It strikes me that they flatter and encourage one of the failings of the French mind that are most dangerous in wartime, for it is inevitably accompanied by unpreparedness. These are the same papers that denied the German peril before the war; today they seem to serve us up in detail, from day to day, the small change of that inept and ruinous self-confidence. No defeat will correct them. — This is why the reading of *La Dépêche de Rouen* comforts me, although I am not on their side. It is better to have an intelligent adversary than a foolish friend. — But to point out mistakes amounts to aiming at Briand. This is perhaps what explains and excuses the apparent silliness of the big governmental papers.

Yet it seems to me that there might be another tack to take and another tone. Isn't it always unwise to hold one's mask too far from one's face? The governmental papers might, without hiding the mistakes, recognize that Briand remains the best equipped to repair them, since after all it was he who committed them. . . .

In short, we are in a hole.

30 October

Arrived at Offranville yesterday evening at seven thirty. Five-hour trip, which did not seem to me too long, thanks to *The Return of the Native.*

It is what I say to him, much more than what he himself says, that I hold against J.-É. Blanche. I must have already written this somewhere and probably in the same terms: whereas we love certain persons because, by a sort of contagion, we exaggerate in their presence everything that is best in us, certain others (and J.-É. Blanche in particular) expect and draw from us only the least beautiful resonances. I am constantly amazed anew that J.-É. Blanche can find any pleasure whatsoever in seeing me; it seems to me that I should hate the person that I show myself to be to him if I met him somewhere.

31 October

Dined yesterday at the little auxiliary hospital of Veules that Miss Trevelyan directs with two friends, one English and the other American. Evening spent with the wounded; charades, etc.

2 November

Outline of a letter to Copeau. (Copied and put into the file.)

4 November

Got back to Cuverville at eleven p.m.

5 November

J.-É. Blanche says to you readily: "I do not understand what reasons other than mystical ones a person might have to refuse himself anything on earth. Now, I don't believe in anything.". . . Love, feelings of humanity, of justice, defiance, scorn, even pride, everything through which renunciation is achieved is equally lacking to him. And he does not know that it is lacking to him. He knows that he hasn't got it; he does not know that he is missing it.

Or, as it is vulgarly said: he doesn't miss it. J.-É. Blanche is a man who *doesn't miss anything*. He has no imagination.

Yesterday someone opened the barway of Mme Freger's enclosure. Ill-will or carelessness — no one knows. However, the seven heifers that were grazing in the enclosure got out. Mme Sandré saw them pass on the road at eight a.m.; then Loisel at ten o'clock; they entered X.'s pasture and he was satisfied to put them out. Mme Freger was not notified until four p.m. The poor woman had to beat the countryside in a driving rain. The animals are finally found, but one of them "has lost a horn," no one knows how, and a young cow that was expecting a calf gave birth along the road. The calf died. Now, Mme Sandré knew those animals to belong to Mme Freger, who lives a hundred yards from her house. Neither she nor anyone else who saw them pass had either the wits or the kindness to warn the owner, a very young woman whose husband is at the front and who is killing herself with work. This is simply monstrous, but in this district the monstrous is a daily occurrence.

6 November

The contaminated soldiers were so numerous that finally it was thought necessary to take measures. I have copied the confidential letter from the Under-Secretary of State to the general commanding the third region at Rouen, dated 11 October. The cases of syphilis, it is specified, which were fifteen hundred and forty in May and June, rose to seventeen hundred and sixty-eight during the two following months. Whence an invitation to the mayors to take the initiative and, if need be, open licensed brothels, where at least the prostitutes would be inspected by doctors. Tell the story of the farm of Saint-Aubin-sur-Scie.

Saturday, 16 December

Got back my fountain-pen this morning. This allows me to work again peripatetically and to return to this notebook.

Back in Cuverville for the last nine days after an absence that was to have been only a week and that lasted exactly a month. Prolonged my stay in Paris at first to see Jean Schlumberger again. Suddenly Verhaeren's death called me to Rouen, then taken as far as La Panne. Amazing trip, but one that I do not feel in a mood to relate.

Finished *The Return of the Native.* Began (here) practicing Beethoven's symphonies arranged by Liszt; a real discovery, and more particularly the beginning and the minuet of the one in F major (the Eighth) which struck me as having an extreme interest, an extreme novelty in its difficulty, and an extreme beauty.

I returned for two days to the translation of *Typhoon;* but I soon dropped it to give myself completely to that preface for a new edition of *Les Fleurs du mal* that Helleu (Pelletan) asked me for.[40] I labored dreadfully the first few days in a state of fatigue, stupidity, and unspeakable exasperation; but this evening, when I have just put the finishing touch to it, I am not too dissatisfied with the result — and especially to be able to pass to something else.

Wrote a quantity of letters.

Sunday

I reread this morning the beginning of the second notebook of my Memoirs, to try to start myself off again. Several anecdotal passages seem to me rather well turned; but most often the languid, lullaby tone is unbearable to me. I admire nothing so much as that friskiness

---

[40] Gide wrote an original and stimulating preface for a new edition of Baudelaire's *Flowers of Evil* published by Éditions Pelletan — R. Helleu, in 1917. The preface was later included in Gide's *Incidences* (*Angles of Incidence*).

of Stendhal in his letters, which I pick up immediately afterward in order completely to disgust myself with myself.

. . . .

(I am lost if I begin to cross out.)

I find on a bit of paper this remark by Grimm, which I did well to note down and which I want to pin up in front of me when I write (Mme d'Épinay quotes it in her *Mémoires*):

"But do not work at it," he told her, "except when you have a real desire to do so, and, above all, always forget that you are writing a book; it will be easy to put in transitions later on; that air of truth cannot be given when it is not there at the first spontaneous writing, and the most gifted imagination cannot take its place." (Vol. II, p. 312.)

Tuesday morning

Again black torpor in the middle of the day; and at night discouraging insomnia. I make up my mind to get up very early and go to bed likewise.

The day before yesterday this succeeded rather well; not that my night was much better; but, at work at five thirty, I managed to keep myself all day long in a state of tension and joy that I ordinarily know only when traveling.

The difficulty of my narration (I was copying out the scene of the unexpected return to rue de Lecat that served me for *La Porte étroite*), a difficulty that had first stopped me, two months ago, and at which I had stuck, seemed to melt before me. Without any effort I found the best and simplest solution. . . . I wrote, moreover, only very little; busy rather with cleaning up.

Replied to some letters and advanced the translation of *Typhoon*.

In the evening, before dinner, encouraged by this favorable wind, I am emboldened to the point of beginning reading my Memoirs to Em. — with such palpitations of the heart that, at moments, I am forced to interrupt myself.

Wednesday, 20 December

This morning I was unable to get up before six thirty. Very bad night, but without any nervous troubles.

Obliged to go out for an hour (for the first time since my return here; and for the first time the weather is splendid).

Rather great intellectual fatigue, which forces me to give up my new regime. My eyes hurt and I dare neither to read much nor to work much.

Saturday

With a very great emotion finished reading to Em. the first four chapters of my Memoirs; gave her the beginning of the fifth to read. My work has just happened to stop at the story of my furtive visit to rue de Lecat. . . . To tell the truth, the impression from this reading is not bad and even of such a nature as to encourage me greatly. But, to my taste, it is all overwritten, in too precious, too conscious a style. . . . . I always write better and more easily what I have not carried too long in my head; as soon as my thought precedes my pen, it checks my hand.

Yesterday, late in the day, great fatigue and depression to the point of making me think I shall have to interrupt everything. But this morning, after an almost sleepless night, I get up in fairly good fettle.

Saturday, 31 December

Went to spend two days at Havre in reply to the invitation of Émile Vandervelde. Visited with him the factories of Sainte-Adresse, Gunéville, and Harfleur. Read yesterday with great interest Pierre Hamp's new brochure.[41] I have the greatest difficulty in getting back to my work, which, at moments, seems to me completely empty of meaning, of justification. No desire, either, to continue this notebook. Oh, not to be able to liquidate all that past this last day of the year of disgrace 1916! . . .

[41] Either *La France, pays ouvrier* (*France, Land of Labor*) or *Le Travail invincible* (*Invincible Work*), both published in 1916 by Librairie de la N.R.F.

NUMQUID ET TU . . . ?

To Charles Du Bos
Allow me, dear Friend — whose affection
sustained me in difficult hours — to write
your name at the head of these few pages.
Indeed, they would have remained in a
drawer were it not for the attention you
kindly granted them.

(1916–1919)

"Numquid et vos seducti estis?"
(John, vii, 47)
"Numquid et tu Galilæus? . . ."
(John, vii, 52) [42]

What do I care about the controversies and quibbles of the doc-
tors? In the name of science they can deny the miracles; in the name
of philosophy, the doctrine; and in the name of history, the facts. They
can cast doubt on His very existence, and through philological criti-
cism throw suspicion on the authenticity of the texts. It even pleases
me that they should succeed in doing so, for my faith in no wise de-
pends on that.

I hold this little book in my hand, and no argument either sup-
presses it or takes it away from me; I hold it fast and can read it when
I will. Wherever I open it, it shines in quite divine fashion, and any-
thing that can be brought against it will do nothing against that. This
is where Christ escapes the very ones who have come to lay hold of
him, and not through cunning or force; and where they, back among
the chief priests, when the chief priests and Pharisees ask them: Why
have ye not brought him? — Quare non adduxistis illum? — reply: Nun-
quam sic locutus est homo. — Never man spake thus — sicut hic homo
— like this man. (John, vii, 46.)

I read, in the preface to the Gospels in my Vulgate, that if "in-
stead of making of the apostles witnesses who are reporting what they
have seen and heard, one tried to make of them, as the rationalists
suppose, writers who are inventing what they say, it would be appro-
priate to say with Rousseau that the inventor is much more surprising
than the hero." I did not know that Rousseau had said that, but I think
it also, and that it is not so much a question of believing in the words
of Christ because Christ is the Son of God as of understanding that he

---

[42] "Are ye also deceived?" and "Art thou also of Galilee?"

*is the Son of God because his word is divine and infinitely above
everything that the art and wisdom of man offer us.*

*This divinity is enough for me. My mind and heart are satisfied
with this proof. Anything you contribute in addition obscures it.*

*It is because Christ is the Son of God, they have said, that we must
believe in his words. And others came who ceased to bear his words
in mind because they did not admit that Jesus was the Son of God.*

*O Lord, it is not because I have been told that you were the Son
of God that I listen to your word; but your word is beautiful beyond
any human word, and that is how I recognize that you are the Son
of God.*

*Through what absurd modesty, what humility, what shame have I
put off writing until today what has for so many years been impatient
within me? . . .*

*I was always waiting for more wisdom, more study, more knowl-
edge, as if the wisdom of men were not folly before God.*

*O Lord, I come to you like a child; like the child that you want me
to become, like the child that becomes whoever yields to you. I resign
everything that made up my pride and that, in your presence, would
make up my shame. I listen and surrender my heart to you.*

*The Gospels are a very simple little book, which must be read very
simply. There is no question of explaining it, but merely of accepting
it. It needs no commentary and every human effort to throw light
upon it only dims it. It is not addressed to learned men; science pre-
vents one from understanding anything in it. Access to it can be gained
through poverty of spirit.*

It is true, this opening of the Epistle to the Romans is confused,
full of repetitions, annoying to anyone who is not aware of the pathetic
effort of the apostle to bring forth so novel a truth, which he feels
with all his soul, and not confusedly, but which eludes his grasp and
wrestles with him like an angel and struggles.

Not the law but grace. It is the emancipation in love — and the
progress through love to an exquisite and perfect obedience.

One must feel here the effort of the tender young Christian doctrine to burst the tight swaddling-clothes of Semitism that enfold it.
This cannot be fully understood before having first grasped the Jewish spirit.

*For I was alive without the law once: but when the command-
ment came, sin revived, and I died.*

To be sure, it is only too easy to distort the meaning of this extraordinary word and to lend to St. Paul an intention that was never his. However, if one grants that the law precedes grace, cannot one admit a state of innocence preceding the law? *For I was alive without the law once.* This sentence is lighted up and filled, despite St. Paul, with a fearful significance.

Except a man be born again.[43]
See everything with novelty; is it not true that the Kingdom of God is nothing else? The innocence of the little child: *If you do not become like unto these* — these little children who *are naked and feel no shame.*

For I was alive without the law once. Oh, to achieve that state of second innocence, that pure and laughing rapture!

The Christian artist is not he who paints saints and angels, any more than edifying subjects; but rather he who puts into practice the words of Christ — and I am amazed that no one has ever sought to bring out the *æsthetic* truth of the Gospels.

Oh, to be born again! To forget what other men have written, have painted, have thought, and what one has thought oneself. To be born anew.

9 February (1916)
If ye were blind, ye should have no sin: but now ye say, We see; therefore your sin remaineth. (John, ix, 41.)

How could you fail to be conquered in advance, poor soul, if in advance you doubt of the legitimacy of the victory? How could you fail to resist feebly, when you doubt whether you must really resist?

There is, besides, much more craze than real desire in your case — the craze of the collector who *owes it to himself* not to let this item escape — as if his collection of sins could ever be complete! As if one more were necessary to complete his perdition!

My time is not yet come: but your time is alway ready. The world cannot hate you. (John, vii, 6.)

Journalists *alway ready* and ready for anything whatever at any time whatever. *The world cannot hate you.*

15 February
That Christ should have cried out: *Now is my soul troubled,* this is what constitutes his greatness. This is the point of debate between the man and the God.

---

[43] This line appears in English in the original.

And when he goes on: *Father, save me from this hour,* this is still the human speaking. When he finishes: *But for this cause came I unto this hour,* the God prevails.

The words that precede throw light on this one: *Except a corn of wheat fall into the ground and die* . . . and again: *He that loveth his life shall lose it.* Here Christ renounces man; here truly he becomes God.

18 February

The predominance of the mediocre and the sudden advantage of the second-rate is expressed and explained in the book of Genesis (vii and viii) with extraordinary eloquence. In equal quantities, in seven couples each, all the "clean" animals are preserved in the Ark; they issue from the Ark and immediately Noah takes a levy from among the best; the best are sacrificed, offered as a sacrifice to the Eternal. What faith, what belief in progress this sacrifice implies! At the very moment that he escapes disaster with what he has been able to save, at the moment that he sets foot on dry land and in this terrestrial life, of the little that remains to him, of these few unique representatives of each species (and what a value each one had for him!), of these irreplaceable individuals he at once offers the best. . . . No, the sacrifice of Isaac, more atrocious though it may be, is not more eloquent to my mind. I find here again that confidence that everything progresses toward the best and in spite of everything, and even because of the perpetual sacrifice of this best, to which the chain of beings reaches. It leads to renunciation, joyous and voluntary. It is in the negation of self that springs up and takes shelter the highest affirmation of self.

(On rereading more carefully chapter viii of Genesis, I notice that this selection is not specified. It is said that Noah took, to offer them in holocaust, *of every clean beast, and of every clean fowl* — now it was said in chapter vii that God had enjoined to take with him in the Ark *seven* couples of each of the latter and only *one* couple of the others — the unclean beasts — which the sacrifice does not touch, does not seek. But they are the most prolific.)

Et nunc . . .

It is *in eternity* that right now one must live. And it is *right now* that one must live in eternity.

What care I for eternal life without awareness at every instant of the duration?

Just as Jesus said: *I AM the way, the truth,* He says: *I am the resurrection and the life.*

Eternal life is not only to come. It is right now wholly present in us; we live it from the moment that we consent to die to ourselves, to obtain from ourselves this renunciation which permits resurrection in eternity. *He that hateth his life in this world shall keep it unto eternal life.* (John, xii, 25.)

Once more, there is neither prescription nor command here. Simply it is the secret of the higher felicity that Christ, as everywhere else in the Gospels, reveals to us.

If ye know these things, happy are ye, says Christ later. (John, xiii, 17.) Not: *Ye shall be happy* — but: *happy ARE ye.* It is right now and immediately that we can share in felicity.

What tranquillity! Here truly time stops. Here breathes the Eternal. We enter into the Kingdom of God.

20 February

Knowing the time, that now it is high time to awake out of sleep: for now is our salvation nearer than when we believed. (Romans, xiii, 11.)

Strange word — I should like to know apropos of what it was pronounced. Forcibly it preserves, and ever takes on more, present-day interest; every day it postpones the promise a bit further.

The important thing is that for many a soul, in many a different epoch, it assumed a particularly urgent character. But how far it is from the permanent and eternal character of Christ's words! We are plunged back into time. *The night is far spent, the day is at hand.*

21 February

... But not to doubtful disputations.

For one believeth that he may eat all things: another, who is weak, eateth herbs. Let not him that eateth despise him that eateth not; AND LET NOT HIM WHICH EATETH NOT JUDGE HIM THAT EATETH: FOR GOD HATH RECEIVED HIM. (Romans, xiv, 1–3.)

And why not pursue the quotation farther:

Who art thou that judgest another man's servant? to his own master he standeth or falleth. Yea, he shall be holden up: for God is able to make him stand.

This chapter xiv of the Epistle to the Romans is moreover unanswerable throughout. A little farther this can be read:

I know and am persuaded by the Lord Jesus, that there is nothing unclean of itself: but to him that esteemeth any thing to be unclean, to him it is unclean.

Obviously this concerns foods; but to how many other passages of the Bible has a double, a triple meaning been assigned? (*If your eye,* etc. . . . Multiplication of the loaves.) There is no need of quibbling here; the meaning of that word is broad and deep: the restriction must not be dictated by the law, but by love; and St. Paul formulates it immediately afterward: *But if thy brother be grieved with thy meat, now walkest thou not charitably.*

My Lord, preserve me from everything that can wither up and divert my heart.

And Paul continues, and this enters me like a sword: *Destroy not him with thy meat, for whom Christ died.*

What! for a little pleasure shall I deny the death and mercy of Christ! *For meat destroy not the work of God.*

For the kingdom of God is not meat and drink; but righteousness, and peace, and joy in the Holy Ghost.

And this is the final word, the boundary-stone against which my whole intellectual protest stumbles:

Happy is he that condemneth not himself in that thing which he alloweth.

I must return to this.

25 February

And these things I speak in the world, that they might have my joy fulfilled in themselves. (John, xvii, 13.)

That they might have in them my perfect joy, says the Segond translation.

I pray not that thou shouldst take them out of the world, but that thou shouldst keep them from the evil one.

Segond says: *from evil,* which is much less eloquent. And it is not a matter here of a simple literary effect. Whereas evil expresses only the absence of good, or a personal state of sin, the Evil One is an active power, independent of us.

Si quis vult me sequi deneget semetipsum (in Matthew: *abneget semetipsum) et tollat crucem quotidie, et sequatur me.*

Qui enim voluerit animam suam salvam facere, perdet illam; nam qui perdiderit animam suam propter me et Evangelium, salvam faciet eam. (Matthew, xvi, 24; Mark, viii, 34; Luke, ix, 23.)

4 March

This text is suddenly made clear by virtue of another version. (John, x, 17.)

The Segond translation has: *Je donne ma vie, afin de la reprendre* (I give my life in order to take it back).

Here is the text of the Vulgate:

Pono animam meam ut iterum suman eam.

Wonderful word — to be compared with: *Whosoever shall seek to save his life shall lose it*, etc.

One would have to see the Greek text.

Whereas the two French versions I have at hand (Segond and A. Westphal) and the English all speak of *life*, the Vulgate says *soul*, more expressly. The meaning becomes something like this: I renounce what makes up my life, my soul, my personality, to assume it anew, to renew my mastery over it — and it is for this that the Father cherishes me: *Propterea me diliget Pater.*

That life, that soul, no man taketh it from me by force. Of myself, quite willingly, I lay it down. For it is in my power to lay it down; it is in my power likewise to seize hold of it again. Such is the commandment I received from my Father:

Nemo tollit eam a me; sed ego pono eam a me ipso, et potestatem habeo ponendi eam, et potestatem habeo iterum sumendi eam: hoc mandatum accepi a Patre meo.

This is the mysterious center of Christian ethics, the divine secret of happiness: the individual triumphs in the renunciation of the individual.

Quicumque quæsierit animam suam salvam facere, perdet illam: et quicumque perdiderit illam, vivificabit eam. (Luke, xvii, 33.)

(Notice that the text of the Vulgate always gives *anima* and not *vita.*)

And this finally, in which Christ's thought is clarified and strengthened:

Qui amat animam suam, perdet eam: et qui odit animam suam in hoc mundo, in vitam æternam custodit eam. (John, xii, 25.)

He who loves his life, his soul — who protects his personality, who is particular about the figure he cuts in this world — shall lose it; but he who renounces it shall make it really living, will assure it eternal life; not eternal life in the future, but will make it already, right now, live in eternity.

Amen, amen, dico vobis, nisi granum frumenti cadens in terram, mortuum fuerit, ipsum solum manet: si autem mortuum fuerit, multum fructum affert. (John, xii, 24.) Resurrection in total life. Forgetfulness of all particular happiness. Oh, perfect reintegration!

This is likewise the teaching to Nicodemus: *Amen, amen, dico tibi, nisi quis renatus fuerit denuo, non potest videre regnum Dei.* (John, iii, 3.)

6 March

Unumquemque sicut vocabit Deus, ita ambulet. (1 Corinthians, vii, 17.)

Unusquisque in qua vocatione vocatus est, in ea permaneat. (Ibid., 20.)

*Unusquisque in quo vocatus est, fratres, in hoc permaneat apud
Deum.* (Ibid., 24.)
    . . . *ut sim fidelis.* (Ibid., 25.)

12 March

Oh words of Christ, so completely misunderstood. Eighteen centuries have passed, and this is where we are in regard to you! And
some people go about saying: "The Gospel has ceased to live: it no
longer has either meaning or value for us." *They blaspheme that of
which they are ignorant,* and I want to shout to them: the Gospel still
awaits us. Its virtue, far from being exhausted, remains to be discovered, to be constantly discovered.

The word of Christ is always fresh with an infinite promise.

The cross appears in the Gospels well before the executioners bring
it in. (Luke, xvi, 27; Matthew, x, 38.)

3 April

There is always a danger in defining precisely the meaning of the
words of the Gospel, for in doing so one limits their implication.

Thus I read in Westphal, apropos of Christ's word: *Signum non
dabitur ei, nisi signum Jonæ prophetæ* — this note: ". . . Jesus refers
the Pharisees of his generation, proud and scornful, to 'the sign of
Jonas'; in other words, to the lesson given all of us by the story of
that faithless servant brought back to duty by chastisement and dis-
concerted witness of the return to grace of a condemned city." That
is simply comical.

The miracle of Jonah — there is no shilly-shallying about it — is
Jonah issuing alive from the whale after having spent three days in
its belly. A mystical comparison has been established between this and
Christ's disappearance in the tomb for three days, but this remains
none the less the most enormous, most unbelievable, most monstrous
of miracles.

The divine virtue of Christ's words is recognizable by the fact that
they are addressed, over the crowd of Pharisees and Sadducees before
whom they were pronounced, directly to each one of us: You ask for
a miracle to convince you. If only a sign came from heaven, something extraordinary, then you think you would believe. I offer you, to
rest your reason, an unheard-of miracle, in which your reason refuses
to believe, which you can verify neither with your senses nor with
your mind, something absurd and nothing else. *No other sign shall be
given you but that of the prophet Jonah.*

It is not *because of* that that you can believe, that you must believe,
poor soul! It is *despite that.*

—No, I shall not help you to believe. You know well that on the contrary . . . so that there may be nothing but what is absurd and loving in your faith; and so that it may be withdrawn from the learned and permitted to the humble.

Faith is made of confidence in God and renunciation of self.

7 April

I reproach Westphal likewise for reducing the solemnity of the text for the sake of a certain familiarity that he considers appropriate not to frighten his readers. He attempts to establish a text on the ground floor, which can be entered without effort, and which does not contrast sharply with everyday life. Thus it is that he translates: *The opportune moment has not come for me. For you whom the world cannot hate, the occasion is good at all times; but the world hates me because, etc. . . .*[44] allowing only the most accidental interpretation of this dazzling word: Tempus meum *nondum advenit, tempus autem* vestrum semper est paratum. (John, vii, 6.)

What! I meet you here again, Nicodemus! you who first came to Jesus by night, *nocte primum* — and who later on will bring aromatics to embalm him, for you are rich and you think that without your riches Christ would rot. . . .

Phariseus, princeps Judæorum: such you appeared to me at first; such you remained, although you deserve already that it be said to you: *Numquid et tu Galilæus es? — Art thou also of Galilee?* But with you at least it is possible to talk. If you take up the defense of Christ, you do so in the very name of the law you represent. You say: *our law* and you ask those who want to lay hands upon Him: *Doth our law judge any man before it hear him?* You like to listen and you like to be listened to. You know how to talk; you have an open mind; you listen to Christ; what am I saying? you even question him. But you are not among those at least who allow themselves to be led astray. *Numquid et vos seducti estis?* (John, vii, 47.)

When Christ said to you: *Except a man be born again . . .* you exclaimed: *How can a man be born when he is old? can he enter a second time into his mother's womb?* After having talked, you are the same as before, so that, even in your presence, Pharisee and prince in their midst, it can be said: *Have any of the rulers or of the Pharisees believed on him?* (John, vii, 48.)

---

[44] "*Le moment opportun n'est pas venu pour moi. Pour vous que le monde ne peut haïr, en tout temps l'occasion est bonne; mais le monde me hait, moi, parce que, etc. . . .*"

Too long have I cherished your hesitations, your marks of integrity, your scruples — the display of your cowardice.

Sed turba hæc, quæ non novit legem, maledicti sunt.

From word to word of this sacred text I see sparks of light. . . .

But this people who knoweth not the law are cursed.

Give me, O Lord, to be among these latter, and cursed by the orthodox men, by those "who know the law."

Search and look, they say to Nicodemus, *for out of Galilee ariseth no prophet.*

A Galilæa propheta non surgit. (John, vii, 52.)

This is what they are still saying, those who believe in nations, in races, in families and fail to understand that the individual constantly rises up to give them the lie.

And every man went unto his own house. Et reversi sunt unus-quisque in domum suam. (Ibid., 53.)

O Lord! he who comes to You no longer has a house.

20 April

Amen, amen, dico vobis: quia omnis qui facit peccatum, servus est peccati. (John, viii, 34.)

Sin is what one does not do freely.

Deliver me from that captivity, O Lord!

Si ergo vos Filius liberaverit, vere liberi eritis.

If the Son therefore shall make you free, ye shall be free indeed.

And the Evil One whispers to my heart:

What good is that liberty to you if you cannot use it?

It is with these words in his heart that the Prodigal Son ran away.

23 April

Unus autem ex illis, ut vidit quia mundatus est, regressus est, cum magna voce magnificans Deum. (Luke, xvii, 15.)

The translators give: "when he saw that he was healed" — which hardly renders the *mundatus*.

Osterwald dares: *cleansed.*[45] I am not going to quibble; but this morning the words: *ut vidit quia mundatus* act upon me with a strange power.

Frightful blemish, oh stain of sin! Ashes left behind by that impure flame, slag. . . . Can you cleanse me of all that, O Lord? that I may glorify you.

"How happy you will be if you learn what is the occupation of love!" (Fénelon: *Lettres spirituelles.*)

---

[45] *Nettoyé.*

28 April

The Bible of Crampon gives in a note the Greek word of the text of Luke (xvii, 33) that it was so important for me to know.

And the whole text is illuminated by it.

Whosoever shall seek to save his life shall lose it, and whosoever shall lose his life shall find it, Osterwald's version gave, thus emptying that word, in which would soon be seen nothing but a balancing of the thought, a somersault paradox such as "the first shall be last" or "blessed are the unhappy"; but this is making it too easy for the enemy. The Greek word is: ζωογονήσει, for which Crampon proposes *will regenerate,* or literally: *will engender him to life.*[46] Here indeed is the *be born again.*[47]

It is likewise in chapter xvii of Luke that is specified: *regnum Dei intra vos est.* And Crampon, who translates like Osterwald and Westphal by: *The kingdom of God is among you,* at least feels the need of adding in a note:

"Among you in the sense: The kingdom of God has therefore come to you in the person of Christ and his disciples. Others translate: *it is within you,* in your heart, thereby indicating the inner and spiritual nature of this *kingdom.*"

12 May

Written nothing further in this notebook for the last fortnight. Gave up my readings and those pious exercises which my heart, utterly dry and listless, had ceased to approve. See nothing in it but a comedy, and a dishonest comedy, in which I convinced myself that I recognized the hand of the demon. This is what the demon whispers to my heart.

O Lord! Oh, do not leave him the last word. I do not wish any other prayer today.

2 June

Period of indifference, of dryness and unworthiness, my mind wholly concerned with ridiculous anxieties that fatigue and dim it.

This morning I read in St. Paul (I did not go back to my Bible until yesterday): *And if any man think that he knoweth any thing, he knoweth nothing yet as he ought to know.*

But if any man love God, the same is known of him. (I Corinthians, viii, 2–3.)

16 June

I am no longer able either to pray or even to listen to God. If he perhaps speaks to me, I do not hear. Here I am again become com-

---

[46] *L'engendrera à la vie.*

[47] These three words appear in English.

pletely indifferent to his voice. And yet I scorn *my* wisdom, and, for lack of the joy He gives me, all other joy is taken from me.

O Lord, if you are to help me, what are you waiting for? I cannot, all alone. I cannot.

All the reflections of You that I felt in me are growing dim. It is time that You came.

Ah, do not let the Evil One in my heart take your place! Do not let yourself be dispossessed, Lord! If you withdraw completely, he settles in. Ah, do not confuse me completely with him! I do not love him that much, I assure you. Remember that I was capable of loving You.

What! Am I today as if I had never loved Him?

17 June

It is never of Christ but of St. Paul that I run afoul—and it is in him, never in the Gospels, that I find again everything that had driven me away. . . . I believe in miracles more easily than I follow this reasoning: *But if there be no resurrection of the dead, then is Christ not risen.*[48] Here it is he who denies the miracle exactly as if he said: "If water does not become wine naturally, Christ did not perform the miracle of the wedding-feast at Cana." I am willing not to reason; but here it is he who reasons; and it is precisely that lame reasoning that leads him to this conclusion where my heart and mind balk:

If in this life only we have hope in Christ, we are of all men most miserable. (I Corinthians, xv, 19.)

Atrocious remark and which St. Paul succeeds in making true—to which fortunately all the Gospels are opposed.

Nothing could be more foreign to the Gospels than: *If the dead rise not, let us eat and drink; for tomorrow we die.*[49]

22 June

Gratuitousness of the gift. Gift beyond question.

Surrender of mortal anxiety.

Oh, paradisaical fruition of every instant!

To share in that immensity of happiness, yes, I feel that You in-

---

[48] Worthy counterpart of this other: *Doth not even nature itself teach you, that, if a man have long hair, it is a shame unto him?* (I Corinthians, xi, 14.) [A.]

[49] My remark no longer strikes me as quite correct. Does not St. Paul wish simply to invite us to see in the resurrection of Christ a guarantee of our own resurrection and of our eternal life? It is on this belief that he aims to base all possibility of real joy. (January 1934; written while correcting the proofs of this text.) [A.]

vite me, Lord! And sometimes I remain on the watch, trembling at the immediate promise of so much joy.

If therefore I do not reply better to your voice, do me violence. Seize a heart that I am incapable of giving you.

Your lightning love, may it consume or vitrify all the opacity of my flesh, everything mortal that I drag after me!

I am bored with everything in which I do not feel your presence and recognize no life that is not inspired by your love.

23 June

Be not amazed to feel melancholy; and melancholy because of Me. The felicity I offer you excludes forever what you used to take for happiness.

Joy. Joy. . . . I know that the secret of your Gospel, Lord, lies altogether in this divine word: Joy. And is not that just what makes your word triumphant over all human teachings? — that it permits as much joy as the strength of each heart proposes.

Any Christian who does not attain joy renders the passion of Christ useless and thereby augments it. Wishing to carry Christ's cross, longing to assume his sufferings — does this not amount to slighting his gift? At least, Lord, at the memory of your adorable suffering let my heart weep with gratitude and love. Lamb of God, you who cancel the sins of the world, who else but God himself would have had the power and the right? Our sins nailed you to the cross, Lord, but your crucifixion redeems us. That God should offer himself, son of man, for the redemption of our sins, that he should thereby hurl his love into agony. . . . Contemplate, my soul, this ineffable mystery.

"Go, *and sin no more,*" says Christ to the woman taken in adultery. The truly Christian soul conceives a horror for sin, which caused Christ his suffering.

26 June

I was happy; You have spoiled my happiness. Jealous God, You have poisoned with bitterness all the springs where I used to quench my thirst, so that I have no thirst but for the water that You offered to the woman of Samaria.

"God himself is the enemy of those whose covetousness he troubles," I read this morning in Pascal.

". . . Cupidity makes use of God and enjoys the world; the contrary is true of charity."

"Can it be therefore that you do not believe in his miracles?"

"Do not drive my reason to resist. You know that I do not attack with it. If it were proved to me today that Christ did not accomplish

his miracles, my confidence in his voice would not be shaken; I should
believe in his teaching just the same."

"In short, you do not believe in his miracles."

"What! it is His miracles that make you consider Him divine?
What! you too need a miracle to believe in Him? Like the 'evil and
adulterous crowd' that said: 'Master, we should like to see a sign
from You.'"

"In short, you do not believe. . . ."

"I leave you the last word."

3 October

His hand forever stretched out, which pride refuses to take.

"Do you then prefer to sink ever, slowly, ever more deeply into the
abyss?"

Do you think that this rotten flesh will fall away from you by itself? No, not unless you tear yourself away from it.

"Lord! without your intervention it will first rot on me utterly. No,
this is not pride; you know it! But to take your hand, I should like to
be less unworthy. My filth will soil it before its light will whiten
me. . . ."

"You know well . . ."

"Forgive me, Lord! Yes, I know that I am lying. The truth is that
this flesh that I hate, I still love it more than You Yourself. I am dying
from not exhausting all its charm. I beg you to help me, but without
any true renunciation. . . ."

"Miserable one who aims to marry heaven and hell in you. One
cannot give oneself to God except wholly."

Are you really surprised if, after having left God for so long, you
do not attain, as soon as you turn to Him again, to felicity, to communion, to ecstasy? One can attain these only through intimacy.

20 October, in the evening

My God, make me awake tomorrow morning fit to serve you, and
my heart full of that zeal without which I am well aware that I shall
never again know happiness.

21 October, in the evening

Lord, grant me that I may have need of You tomorrow morning.

22 October

Lord, remove from my heart everything that does not belong to
love.

It is the image of God that we must purify in ourselves.

Lord, may my prayer, like that of very pure souls, be but a reflection of You returning to You when You look upon me.

Lord, do not interrupt your grace, so that I may not cease to pray to You.

26 October

Raise me up, Lord, for I bend down before You.

It is at the joints of our love that the Evil One attacks us.[50]

29 October

(After reading a *Lettre spirituelle* by Fénelon.)

My Lord, I come to You with all my sores that have become wounds; with all my sins under the weight of which my soul is crushed. . . .

7 November

My Lord, grant me not to be among those who cut a figure in the world.

Grant me not to be among those who succeed.

Grant me not to count among the fortunate, the satisfied, the satiated; among those who are applauded, who are congratulated, and who are envied.

20 June (1917)

After seven months of neglect, I take up this notebook again, which S. A., to whom I had lent it, gives back to me yesterday. The few words she says to me after her reading enlighten me at one and the same time as to the meaning of these pages and the boldness that certain people might find in them — but also, but above all, as to their inadequacy. To push farther the affirmation of one's thought, to give it form in a satisfying expression — one waits for age and maturity of mind; one hopes that that maturity will be ever greater; but in its place come fatigue and that sort of submission to the rule and to established conventions, made up less of modesty perhaps, than of fear, weakness, and cowardice.

I now find the trace of old trails I cut, which I allowed to be covered over by a thousand branches, and which I did not even blaze.

It was when my thought was boldest that it was truest. I was frightened, not by it, but by the fear that certain friends had of it. O my heart, harden yourself against that ruinous sympathy, counselor of all compromises. Why did not I always remain unchanged and always obstinate in following my line!

[50] Surely the expression *défaut de l'amour* is suggested, perhaps unconsciously, by *défaut de l'armure* ("joints in the harness"); alone, *défaut* means "lack, flaw, deficiency."

15 June (1919)

The English version suddenly opens my eyes as to a verse of Matthew that (as it happens then) takes on an extreme importance for me:

And he that taketh not his cross, and followeth after me, is not worthy of me.[51]

The three French versions that I have at hand translate: *He who does not take his cross* AND DOES NOT FOLLOW ME *is not worthy of me.* And yet is that really what Christ means? Is it not rather: *He who does not take his cross* AND WHO FOLLOWS ME — that is to say, he who would follow me without first taking up his cross? I turn to the Vulgate. Yes, that is it: *Et qui non accepit crucem suam, et sequitur me, non est me dignus.*

Lord, it is only weighed down with one's cross that one can follow You.

But did you not likewise say: *Come unto me, all ye that labor and are heavy-laden — and I will give you rest; for my yoke is easy and my burden is light.*

It is pleasure that bends the soul, and everything that one is alone in bearing; the weight of the cross straightens it up, and everything that one bears *with You.*

One of the gravest misunderstandings of the spirit of Christ comes from the confusion frequently established in the Christian's mind between future life and eternal life.

The eternal life that Christ offers, and in which all his teaching invites us to share, that eternal life has nothing future about it. It is not beyond death that it awaits us; and indeed, if we do not attain it at once, there is no hope that we may ever achieve it (find again the very beautiful passage by Mark Rutherford on this subject, Vol. I, pp. 108–10).[52] The words of Christ are divinely luminous and it has taken

---

[51] This verse is quoted in English.

[52] The passage, which Gide does not quote, is probably this one: "The dissolution of Jesus into mythologic vapour was nothing less than the death of a friend dearer to me then than any other friend whom I knew. But the worst stroke of all was that which fell upon the doctrine of a life beyond the grave. In theory I had long despised the notion that we should govern our conduct here by hope of reward or fear of punishment hereafter. But under Mardon's remorseless criticism, when he insisted on asking for the where and how, and pointed out that all attempts to say where and how ended in nonsense, my hope began to fail, and I was surprised to find myself incapable of living with proper serenity if there was nothing but blank darkness before me at the end of a few years. As I got older I became aware of the folly of this perpetual reaching after the future, and of drawing from to-

nothing less than all the ingenuity of man to dim or change the obvious meaning. But they shine anew for whoever rereads them with a new heart, with a childlike spirit.

It is to eternal life, it is to participate at once in the eternity of life, it is to enter the kingdom of God that Christ invites Nicodemus when He says to him: *Except a man be born again, he cannot see the kingdom of God* — for *whosoever shall seek to save his life shall lose it,* but whosoever is born again, whosoever surrenders up his life to be reborn, whosoever renounces himself to follow *Him,* makes his soul truly living, is reborn to eternal life and enters the Kingdom of God.

And is this not likewise what Christ teaches, on the edge of the well, to the woman of Samaria: *But whosoever drinketh of the water that I shall give him shall never thirst?*

Once more, the meaning of this teaching, for an unprejudiced mind, is so obvious that, rereading the story this morning in the Crampon translation, I was struck by these words: *the water that I shall give him shall be in him a well of water springing up* INTO EVER-LASTING LIFE.[53] What? could I have been mistaken? Does Christ speak of eternal life, just as it is generally taught, as a future state? This *jusqu'à* implies that; but isn't it a mistranslation? I open the Vulgate and read: *Sed aqua quam ego dabo ei, flet in eo fons aquæ* SALIENTIS IN VITAM ÆTERNAM.[54]

(The Segond translation and the Osterwald translation say likewise: *une source d'eau qui jaillira* JUSQUE DANS *la vie éternelle.* The meaning of these words is thereby falsified.)

But the hour cometh, AND NOW IS, says Christ right after this. *Venit hora,* ET NUNC EST. Whoever waits for that hour beyond death waits

---

morrow, and from tomorrow only, a reason for the joyfulness of today. I learned, when, alas! it was almost too late, to live in each moment as it passed over my head, believing that the sun as it is now rising is as good as it will ever be, and blinding myself as much as possible to what may follow. But when I was young I was the victim of that illusion, implanted for some purpose or other in us by Nature, which causes us, on the brightest morning in June, to think immediately of a brighter morning which is to come in July. I say nothing, now, for or against the doctrine of immortality. All I say is, that men have been happy without it, even under the pressure of disaster, and that to make immortality a sole spring of action here is an exaggeration of the folly which deludes us all through life with endless expectation, and leaves us at death without the thorough enjoyment of a single hour."

[53] The Crampon translation gives *jusqu'à la vie éternelle,* which suggests "until eternal life."

[54] It is thus that A. Westphal translates, and most happily. But the Latin *in* could, if need be, justify *jusqu'à.* I must have recourse to the Greek text. [A.]

for it in vain. From the very hour at which you are born again, from the very moment at which you drink of this water, you enter the Kingdom of God, you share in eternal life. *Verily, verily, I say unto you,* Christ repeats everywhere, *He that heareth my word and believeth on him that sent me* HATH (not: *will have,* but *already has*) EVERLASTING LIFE . . . *he is passed from death unto life. Transiit a morte in vitam.* (John, v, 24.)

FOREWORD TO THE 1926 EDITION

A collection of intimate writings, you told me. Under such conditions I am willing that this little book should be reprinted.

If words that have once been whispered should happen to be shouted, their intonation is distorted.

I hold that there is nothing secret that does not deserve to be known; but intimacy does not endure broad daylight. I hold also that the soul's recesses are and must remain more secret than the secrets of the heart and of the body. If it happened to me to be "converted," I should not endure that that conversion be made public. Perhaps some sign of it would appear in my conduct; but only a few intimate friends and a priest would know it. And should it be bruited about, this would be against my will, offending and wounding my modesty. I hold that this is no matter to be amazed at or to joke about. It is entirely a matter between God and me. This at least is my own feeling; and I have no intention, through these words, to throw blame on some very much discussed conversions.

Were I a convert, I should probably not speak thus. A convert, I should seek to convert, through my writings and my example, just like our famous converts. I am neither a Protestant nor a Catholic; I am simply a Christian. And as a matter of fact, I do not want anyone to make a mistake as to the testimonial value of these pages. Most likely I should still sign them today quite willingly. But, written during the war, they contain a reflection of the anguish and confusion of that period; and if, probably, I should still sign them; I should perhaps not still write them.

I do not claim that the state that followed this one is superior to it; it is enough for me that it is not quite the same. It is only fair to warn the reader.

One word more:
I had taken care, when rereading the notebook from which the pages of *Numquid et tu . . . ?* were extracted, to let none appear that the most orthodox Catholic, it seemed to me, could not approve.

My desire was one of conciliation rather than of discord; good faith and good will guided me. I thank Monsieur Massis for having shown me that his religion could not be mine. There can be no further doubt in that regard, thank God.

DETACHED PAGES

"He believes neither in God nor in the Devil."
(*Popular saying*)

Until then I had never realized that it was not necessary to believe in God in order to believe in the devil. To tell the truth, the devil had never yet appeared before my imagination; my conception of the devil remained utterly negative; I condemned him by default; I limited his contour by God; and since I extended God everywhere, I did not let the *Other One* begin anywhere. In any case I admitted him only as a metaphysical entity and merely smiled at first that autumn evening when suddenly Jacques Raverat introduced him to me.

❊

But I was full of scruples, and before I surrendered, the demon who addressed himself to me had to convince me that what was asked of me was permitted me, that this permitted thing was necessary to me. Sometimes the Evil One reversed the propositions, began with the necessary; he would reason thus — for the Evil One is the Reasoner: "How could it be that what is necessary to you should not be permitted you? Just consent to call necessary what you can't do without. You cannot do without that for which you thirst the most. Just consent not to call sin what you cannot do without. You would acquire great strength," he would add, "if instead of wearing yourself out struggling against yourself in this manner, you only struggled against the external obstacle. For anyone who has learned to struggle, no obstacle can hold up. Go, learn to triumph over yourself at last and over your own sense of decency. Haven't I taught you to see a hereditary habit in your uprightness, and the mere prolongation of an impetus; shyness and embarrassment in your modesty; less decision than carelessness in your virtue . . . ?"

In short, he drew argument and advantage from the fact that it cost me more to yield to my desire than to continue curbing it. To be sure, the first steps I took on the sloping path required, to risk them, a certain courage and even a certain resolve.

It goes without saying that I did not understand until much later the diabolic element in this exhortation. At that time I thought I was the only one to speak and that I was carrying on this specious dialogue with myself.

I had heard talk of the Evil One, but I had not made his acquaintance. He already inhabited me when I did not yet distinguish him. He had made me his conquest; I thought myself victorious, to be sure; victorious over myself because I was surrendering to him. Because he had convinced me, I did not feel myself to be conquered.[55] I had invited him to take up his residence in me, as a challenge and because I did not believe in him, like the man in the legend who sells his soul to him in return for some exquisite advantage — and who continues not believing in him despite having received the advantage from him!

I did not yet understand that evil is a positive, active, enterprising principle; I used to think at that time that evil was simply a lack of good, as darkness is a lack of light, and I was inclined to assign all kinds of activity to light. When, in 1910, my friend Raverat first spoke to me of him, I merely smiled. But his words entered my heart no less deeply. "I began," he explained to me, "by believing in the devil. . . ." (We were in the office at Cuverville, and a reading together of Milton in the afternoon had brought our conversation to the subject of Satan.) "And it is believing in him, *whom I actually felt*, that led me to believe in God, whom I did not yet feel." And since a great deal of irony was mingled with my amazement, and since I feared that he himself was not altogether serious: "Satan's great strength," he went on soberly, "comes from the fact that he is never just the way you think he is. You have already accomplished considerably against him when you are convinced that he is there. To recognize him properly it is better never to lose sight of him."

It took all my great friendship for Jacques Raverat to make me pay attention to his words. Henceforth I bore them in me, but like those seeds which germinate only after a long stratification; to tell the truth, they did not sprout until the beginning of the war, when, having given myself completely to a relief organization, I was able to see the face of the Evil One more sharply against this background of philanthropy.

The great mistake, which allows him to slip incognito into our lives, is that, ordinarily, people are willing to recognize his voice only at the moment of the temptation itself; but he rarely risks an offensive without having prepared it. He is much more intelligent than we, and he hides most often in reasoning; if we were more humble we should

---

[55] There is an untranslatable play here on the words *convaincu* and *vaincu*.

recognize him in the *Cogito ergo sum*. That *ergo* is the cloven hoof.[56]
He knows that there are certain souls that he cannot conquer in open
battle and that he must persuade.

I know that to many minds it might seem absurd, as it would still
have seemed the day before yesterday to my own, to go out of one's
way to postulate this existence, this presence of the demon in order
to explain by upheaval what cannot be explained through logic; a less
lazy or more subtle psychology would succeed in again putting this
phantom out of countenance, they say. These are the same minds that
think that the evolutionary explanation has succeeded in supplanting
God. What shall I reply except that I had no sooner *assumed* the demon
than my whole biography was at once made clear to me: that I suddenly understood what had been most obscure to me, to such a point
that this assumption took on the exact shape of my interrogation and
my preceding wonder.

What is more glorious than a soul when it liberates itself? What is
more tragic than a soul that makes itself a prisoner just when it thinks
it is liberating itself?

I am utterly indifferent, afterward, as to whether or not this name
of demon is the right name for what I mean, and I grant that I give
it this name out of convenience. If someone should come along later
and show me that he lives not in hell but in my blood, my loins, or
my insomnia, does he believe that he can suppress him thus? When I
say: the Evil One, I know what that expression designates just as
clearly as I know what is designated by the word *God*. I draw his outline by the deficiency of each virtue.

And since he is more intelligent than I, everything he thought up
to hurl me toward evil was infinitely more precious, more specious,
more convincing, more beautiful, more clever than any argument I
could have brought up to persevere in honor. I should never have
stumbled upon such arguments by myself. *Cogito ergo Satanas.*

Now, this is how He proceeds:

"To begin with, thank you for having brought me into being! Yes,
you are well aware that your kindness creates me. You are well aware
that I didn't exist, but probably you needed to take off from me in
order to believe in God—a God that might help you to fight me."

"Good Lord, how complicated all this is! I believe in God. The
existence of God alone matters to me, and not yours; but the proof
that you exist is that you want to make me doubt it."

"Come! Come! You are not so stupid as all that! You created me
in order to make me responsible for your doubts, your dejections, your

---

[56] A good pun is lost here on *ergo* and *l'ergot du diable*, "the devil's
spur."

fits of boredom. Everything that bothers you is I, everything that holds you back. If your pride protests against the bent of your mind, it is I. It is I if your blood boils, if your mood is flighty. When your reason balks it is I. When your flesh revolts, it is I. Your hunger, your thirst, your fatigue are all I. Your inclination is I. In short, you give me such a wonderful role that I wonder if sometimes you do not confuse me with God. The amusing thing, I tell you, is that henceforth you cannot believe in One without the Other. Just listen to the fable of the gardener. . . ."

"By heaven! I knew it: you too know how to talk in parables."

"Oh, I'm not limited to just one form of expression."

"This is because you speak in turn to the mind, to the heart, to the senses; and since, while protecting myself on one side, I am always uncovering myself on the other, you, who keep moving around me, always address yourself to the unguarded side."

"How well we know each other! You know, if you wanted to —"

"What?"

"What good friends we should be! . . ."

1917

Weather excessively foggy and melancholy. This morning we have to endure the respects of all the good people of the township.

Yesterday evening I was shocked by the tremendous amount of work that revising the translation of *Victory* would require.[1] I cursed out Isabelle Rivière and her childish theories about how *faithful* a translation must be — which makes her present hers studded with errors, awkward expressions, cacophonies, ugly passages. Yet I hoped to have finished with this job and to have only to reread. . . . But now this ages me a fortnight.

5 January

Rather disturbing intellectual fatigue; dizzy spells, etc. Nevertheless, rather good work. I envy Em. considerably, for, at my side, she is reading the *Grüne Heinrich;*[2] but I repulse everything that might distract me from Conrad. The reading of the newspapers already takes a lot of time that it often seems to me I might use better. I find some intellectual satisfaction only with Maurras and the *Dépêche de Rouen* (articles by Destain). The yelping of the other papers is shameful (naturally I make an exception for the *Journal de Genève*).

The latest issues of the *Mercure* are most interesting. It is odd how that review has taken on weight since Gourmont has ceased to be with it!

Learned by heart, these last few days, the Preludes in E minor (of which I already knew the end), in A-flat major from the first book, in C minor from the second, the Fugue in E major from the first (from *The Well-Tempered Clavichord*). Practiced in octaves the Fugue in E minor from the first book (Busoni).[3] Went over the *Lavapiés* by Albéniz.

6 January

Translation. However backbreaking it may be, this work amuses me. But how much time it takes! I count, on a average, and when all

---

[1] André Gide had undertaken the supervision of the translations of Conrad to be published by Librairie de la *N.R.F.* Isabelle Rivière, the wife of Jacques, then a prisoner in Germany, had translated *Victory.* The biographer of Conrad, G. Jean-Aubry, shared responsibility with Gide.

[2] *Green Henry*, by Gottfried Keller, is a novel of a youth's adaptation to life.

[3] These are all compositions by Bach.

is going well, an hour to half a page (of the Heinemann edition — I
am speaking of *Typhoon*). I think the result will be very good; but
who will be aware of it? . . . No matter.

Read the day before yesterday long passages of *Le Crime de Syl-
vestre Bonnard*.[4] This semi-academic manner irritates me. What delicacy! what simpering! . . . Between Sterne and Xavier de Maistre.
. . . If I had to take up criticism again, it would make me burst.

7 January

Withheld a letter I was about to write to Maurras; which I had
already written last night in the indignation caused by a paragraph
of the *Action Française* against Souday, in reply to an article by him
in the postdated *Temps* of the same day.[5] I cut all this out and pinned
it together with the draft of my letter. But why should I take up arms
for Souday? — just to be told that I do so out of gratitude for his
article and in the hope of others? Furthermore, am I sure that Souday,
because he defended a few ideas that I think right, deserves that I
should defend him? Putting the best supposition on it, what would
Maurras do? He would write me: "My dear Gide, your generosity
honors you, but we do not need your warnings. We are acting with
full knowledge of the affair; what shocks you, ever changing nature
that you are, is the straightforwardness of our line of conduct: there
are certain domains that we need to expropriate, through straightforwardness, and certain creatures that we need to crush. *You* pay attention only to the creature who is being crushed; *we* pay attention only
to walking straight. Etc. . . ." I know the theory; and at times I begin
to think that it is needed to save France. But what good is it to save
her life if one loses her soul? And occasionally a nameless melanchoy
sweeps over me as I watch that shining mirror that was France become dull.

Meanwhile, and none the less, Maurras's articles every day are
excellent.

11 January

For several days I have been seeking what title to give to these
Memoirs; for I should not exactly like *Mémoires* or *Souvenirs* or *Confessions*. And the awkward thing about any other title is that it allows
of a meaning. I am hesitating between: *Et Ego* . . . but which limits
the sense, and *Si le grain ne meurt* . . . but which slants it, while en-
larging it.

I believe, however, that I shall decide on the latter.

---

[4] An early novel by Anatole France.

[5] *Le Temps*, officially a morning newspaper, always appeared in the
evening under the date of the following day.

18 January

Rather good work, whence this notebook's silence.

Read to Em. the day before yesterday the fifth chapter of the Memoirs, which I had just written out afresh. (There are still a few slight changes to make.)

Oh, how poor that translation by Isabelle Rivière is, and how much time I am forced to give to it. I count an average of an hour to each typed page. Yet since, out of regard for her vanity, which is immense, I am leaving as much as possible of her version, I doubt whether the result can ever be a happy one; I do not think I shall let my name be used on it. Most likely Conrad himself will never know, or ever suspect, the trouble I have got into simply through affection for him, for his book, and for the "well-done job."

The effort and time I give to *Typhoon* are still greater; but in that case it is my own work, freely chosen, and I shall gladly sign it.

19 January

Toby died last night. I reproach myself for not having noted from day to day the phases of his illness. I have just written to the Criquetot pork-butcher, who has assumed the veterinary's functions since the mobilization, to come with the necessary instruments to perform an autopsy. I have no idea of what he died . . . ? Of a tumor, says Mathilde Roberty. Whatever the complaint was, it was strangely complicated by his nervous state. He was certainly the most neurasthenic dog one could possibly imagine. He had every possible phobia: hugged hedges and walls; always took the longest way around to come to a call; was seized with dizziness as he climbed the stairs; dared to eat only when no one was looking. He adored sugar; but if you offered him a piece, he would let it fall on the floor and go off into a corner to play the martyr. Whence it was impossible ever to reward him; untrainable, you could have got him only through hunger, and even then — I believe he never forgave me the spoonful of sugared coffee that I had made him take just after his arrival, when I did not yet know him and thought I could tame him. But the least approach to a blow put him in a snarling mood, or else he would run miles away as soon as I would raise my cane, or else he would squirt on the ground. It was just as impossible to help him; if you wanted to take a tick off of him, you had to put on gloves or else muzzle him; even then I had to give up more than once. And with his mania for rubbing up against old walls and bushes along the way, he swept up everything bad on his path; even to comb him required a thousand precautions and I had to give up combing his belly. How often he bit me like a mad dog!

With other dogs he tried to be dashing and would offer himself

to their caresses. Although excited to the point of frenzy by the odor
of our bitch in heat, he could never achieve anything with her, any
more than with any other bitch whatever and any more, it goes without saying, than with our old cat, although she nevertheless excited
him as much as a bitch and, on her side, would provoke and pursue
him as much as if he had been a tomcat. You cannot imagine a more
absurd and more dumbfounding game; Toby would wear himself out
after her for hours and days on end.

He would spend most of the day seated, like a macaque, on his
lumbar vertebræ with his legs and his whole hindquarters paradoxi-
cally brought forward between his front legs and sporting his cock
like a rosette of the Légion d'Honneur on a lapel.

Porto-Riche had given him to me after having learned from Copeau, who frequented him, that we had a bitch of the same breed.
Most certainly he wanted to get rid of him. Probably after having seen
him at work, he had named him Joseph.

And for the last six weeks Toby had refused to eat. Em. kept him
alive with pieces of sugar, which, I believe, stopped the diarrhea that
he had first had very seriously. We thought he was going to die of in-
anition, when suddenly — But I shall tell that after the autopsy has
been made.

It is possible to write properly, it is possible to think properly only
what one has no personal interest in thinking or in writing. I am not
writing these Memoirs to defend myself. I am not called on to defend
myself, since I am not accused. I am writing them before being accused. I am writing them in order to be accused.

20 January
We are reading aloud, with Mathilde, *Le Retour d'Alsace* by Giraudoux, of which the first pages delight us.[6] Yet one cannot but be
embarrassed, eventually, to see those pathetic events painted with the
brush of a miniaturist. But, he could reply, so long as we remained
ignorant of the events in Alsace, what we were living had nothing
pathetic about it and was just as I have depicted it. — Of course, and
that is just the most pathetic aspect of the affair; but one feels it despite Giraudoux. I confess that right up to the very end I hoped for
some more virile pages, which might have put all that prettiness in its
proper place.

---

[6] The delicate war-recollections entitled *The Way Back from Alsace*
formed one of Jean Giraudoux's first writings. Later they were published as
a part of his *Adorable Clio*.

The pork-butcher did not come, so we had to bury Toby without finding out what killed him.

The *Journal de Genève* points out the lugubrious silence that the Allies' reply to America maintains on the subject of the Armenians. It was hardly worth while writing your bombastic articles, O Barrès, on your return from Asia Minor. I recall the exasperation those articles caused me, for I had just come back from there too. It seemed to me that very little common sense was needed to see how precarious and uncertain (not to say desperate) our work and our influence were there.

Any effort suffices when you are carried by the current; but when the tide withdraws, when you have to struggle against the current . . . any effort that is not sufficient becomes ruinous.

21 January

Mathilde Roberty is leaving this evening. While she was here I interrupted the writing of my Memoirs. I am eager to get back to them. So far I have not yet broached, not even hinted at, what makes me write them. Perhaps I shall tarry excessively over these trifles in the vestibule. Furthermore, the idea of death never leaves me, and not a day passes that I do not ask myself this question: if suddenly, this very day, in an hour, right away, I had to stop everything, what would remain, what would be visible, of all I had to say? By dint of precautions and shilly-shallying, and with my mania for always saving the best for better times, it seems to me that *everything* remains to be said and that up to now I have merely prepared the way. And yet I have no confidence in life, in my life; that fear never leaves me of seeing it end suddenly . . . just when I was finally beginning to dare to speak out and say some essential and true things. Nothing must distract me further from this.

22 January

Marie Macquin writes to Em. about her brother Ghéon:

"His zeal is wonderful. He has gone beyond me. I get out of breath following him."

L'Action Française, in its account of the last meeting of the Chambre, naturally skipped over M. Abrami's intervention. It does not say (what we learn from *Le Temps* of the same day) that "this young deputy went to the front at the beginning of the war as a private, that he had a year and a half at the front, was five times cited for bravery, once at Verdun, received the Croix de Guerre; and furthermore that he knows Greece thoroughly since he lived there seven years." (It was on the question of the government's attitude toward Greece that he challenged the minister.) His speech, measured, clear, and without useless eloquence, is of the kind that can most enlighten opinion; of the kind, consequently, that it is essential to skip over if you want to keep on molding opinion. Pressemane's utterly ridiculous and awkward question, on the other hand, is reported at length. It is of no importance in itself and Briand's reply led the vote to reject it right away; but it is likely to set people against the Parliament, and this is always good!

If Valentine or Ghéon, for instance, had read Abrami's speech, no doubt they would have been stirred and their confidence in Briand would have been somewhat shaken. But this is just why *L'Action Française* does not allow them to read it. This is right if it is good for Briand to remain in power; this is wrong if it is desirable that he should yield his place. But that is just where the question lies. And these papers never try to enlighten opinion; they strive to form it. A reader like Valentine is at their mercy. It is obvious that if I knew that meeting of the Chambre only through *L'Action Française* I should be of exactly the same opinion as Valentine.

23 January

In Mathilde's presence, again, that same paralysis seized me that congeals me, at the piano, as soon as I am aware that someone is listening to me. My very memory stumbles over the first measures of the piece I know best. In vain I tried the easiest preludes (in F-sharp minor of the first book and in C minor of the second), which I have been playing impeccably of late; I produce nothing that is not hesitant, jerky, confused; the very piano, under my unsubtle touch, had frightful sonorities; it was the playing of an ungifted child of twelve.

The other day, in the presence of Darius Milhaud, the same inhibition when I wanted to show him the passage of Chopin's scherzo to which my notes alluded.

25

Work, cut by headaches, not very painful but very tiresome, and which try my patience. I know now that it is not wise to try to work anyway and that a serious fatigue might result from doing so. I temporize, I maneuver; I try to convince myself that tomorrow will be better if I make up my mind to sacrifice today to it. The important thing is not to lose heart or let myself become gloomy.

The time when my mind, *lauter* and *munter*,[7] sailed on an ocean of gaiety. . . .

---

[7] Clear and wide awake.

30 January

I resume *Jean-Christophe*. I have reached *Le Buisson ardent,* of
which the beginning is certainly remarkable.[8] At times it strikes me
that this barbarous, rough-hewn book, without art, without grace, and
possessing qualities apparently so un-French, remains the most important or at any rate the most typical thing produced in France by
our generation. If I did not have such a headache, I should write
further on this subject.

1 February

I am striking out of my Memoirs, of this first part at least, all the
reflections and considerations thanks to which one earns the reputation
of a "thinker." They do not seem to me to be at home here; and everything, for me, yields to the artistic consideration.

This is likewise what makes me strike out in my preface to the
Fleurs du mal the few paragraphs that, yielding to Helleu's invitation,
I had eventually added.

8 February

The ground has been covered with snow for about ten days now.
It does not thaw even in the middle of the afternoon, and the wind
has swept the snow so high on the other side of the embankments that
trenches have had to be dug in the roads. All the sunken roads are
filled to the level of the surrounding fields. When you follow their
course you sink in to the hips; you disappear; you have to walk in the
fields themselves, considering yourself happy if you can make out
their limits; for if you don't you roll into the sunken road. Yesterday
evening I contemplated at length and took Em. to see the almost imperceptible but constant work of the wind on the snow; the entire
plain is blurred as it were by the thin veil of moving snow-dust; it
rushes along the surface just like the sand of dunes; the setting sun
made it iridescent.

Yesterday, went to take to the Aubins two big bundles of firewood
too heavy for the two little girls who had come to get them. I had
taken the wheelbarrow, but the wheel sank into the snow and I had
some trouble getting there. The three other children, younger, were in
the room where the mother received me. She protested considerably
that she had not done up her hair, explaining most volubly that "mea-
sles" obliged her to wear her hair down. It fluffed out around her like
a clown's wig. Nothing could be more sordid than that dwelling. The
children have broken six panes out of ten and cretonne has been hung
over the gaps.

---

[8] *The Burning Bush* forms Part III of Romain Rolland's novel *Jean-
Christophe.*

The three little ones are crouching barefoot on the hearth, where a tiny fire is trying desperately to keep alive; they are scurvied, scrofulous, rickety, but still manage to smile a mocking smile. One feels that the three of them, huddled against each other like a nest of young hares, are almost snugly wrapped in their poverty. Mme Hérouard cooks for them and brings them a "pot-au-feu," which the poor idiot of a mother would be incapable of preparing herself with the meat that Em. gives them.

Cuverville, 27 February

Yesterday back from Paris, where I had gone to spend a week. A telegram from Jeanne had called me urgently, the freezing water having burst a water-pipe in the Villa, flooded the cellar and the back stairs, etc. Great intellectual fatigue as I left here, dizzy spells, etc. The distraction of Paris rather rested me. Certainly it was good to interrupt my work and that intellectual hypertension it involved. I advanced my Memoirs as far as the end of chapter four; that is to say, about a hundred and eighty manuscript pages of large oblong format. Finished the translation of *Typhoon* (only a few pages are still lacking) and learned by heart a number of fugues and preludes (*Well-Tempered Clavichord; Inventions; Suites*).

My principle was that nothing rests one better from a fatigue than a different fatigue; but perhaps in this case the effort I demanded of my memory was too close to that of translating (which also calls upon the memory).

A few hours before my arrival Em. had been brought a little hare three weeks old that had been found in the farmyard, huddling behind a bundle of firewood. Em. thought that I could perhaps raise it; but I still have a sorry memory of my experience of four years ago. Yet I tried, first with a spoon, then with an eye-dropper, to make him take a little warm milk. The baby hare did not struggle, but simply contracted his throat so that one could make him swallow almost nothing. I had put him into a basket half full of wood-shavings near my room. Last night, hearing him stir, I got up to try to feed him again; and while I was warming the milk over a candle, I heard outside strange animal cries, which I am certain must have been a doe-hare's cries. It occurred to me that the baby hare heard them likewise and that this was what made him stir. Despairing of the possibility of nourishing him, I went out, taking him in my pocket, and having climbed the fence, put him back in about the place where he had been found during the day. (It was two a.m.) How I should like to know what he did! The night was unfortunately very cold; this morning hoarfrost silvered the grass; I fear he was unable to come through. . . .

1 March

Extreme difficulty in getting back to work. Everything I have written of my recollections seems to me, when I think it over, deplorably *profane* and light. That pendulum movement to which my mind yields, despite all resolutions, would plunge me back into extreme license if only outside circumstances and my physical state permitted greater exaltation. It strikes me that I was foolish and guilty to bend my mind artificially so as to make it better understand the Catholic teaching. That is where the real impiety lies. I recognize that *tendency toward veneration,* which was doubtless a fortunate attitude in my youth but which is quite out of place today; in which I am now willing to see only weakness, deplorable modesty, inept confidence in the superiority of others, doubt of myself, surrender of my own thought simply because it is mine, repudiation.

There is no question of humility before God, but rather of that humility before men which has always been my secret malady, which, moreover, I find likewise in Dostoyevsky and Baudelaire. Something that a Francis Jammes, for example, could never manage to understand, who sees danger only on the side of pride, and of modesty knows only the outward simpering. (This comes from the fact that he knows nothing of and denies everything in which he does not show himself to be superior.)

7 March

Passing through another desert region. Atrocious, idle days, utterly devoted to growing older. Outside, icy wind, rain. War.

With an enormous effort I extract from myself in a few hours a new page of the Memoirs, for which a few moments would have been enough in a period of joy. And, like a painter who fears to mess up his canvas, I decide that it is wiser to give up for a time and to wait for a better disposition.

Reading *Le Feu* by Barbusse;[9] excellent so long as he is willing not to be intelligent; deplorable in the last chapters, in which he prides himself on thinking and slants the dialogues toward ends that are, as it were, his conclusions about the war. There are, for instance, the pseudo-mystical remarks of a certain aviator that are simply laughable. Obviously that is what Barbusse holds dearest in his work. Wonderful, on the other hand, certain chapters such as "The Leave," "Volpatte and Feuillade."

Mme de Sévigné's letters, which I was seized by an irresistible desire to reread and which I have just bought for twenty-seven

---

[9] The brutal realism of the war novel *Under Fire* won the Goncourt Prize for Henri Barbusse in 1916 and brought him fame.

francs in the pleasing Teschener edition, in eleven volumes, on my way through Paris.

8 March. Evening

The thought of death did not leave me once all day. It seems to me that it is right here, close beside me.

10 March

Yesterday, after a somewhat better day, during which I at least succeeded in working a little, a strange dizziness overcame me in the evening, just as I was going to go up to bed — yet without nausea and, if I may say so, without discomfort, but so violent that I wondered whether or not I should be able to get out of the armchair in which I was seated.

This morning I am quite unable to stand up; since, when I tried to, everything began whirling around me, I first thought I was going to fall on the floor and barely had time to get back to bed — where I am writing this, more for the sake of filling up the time than through a need to write. I am like a man who has been bled white.

Paul A. Laurens, when we were together at Biskra, already used to blame me for giving too much meaning to certain words of the Gospel, or at least of addressing to everyone what obviously, he said, could be applied only to priests. I do not know whether or not he would have had the approval of the Church in this; yet I doubt if he was speaking on his own. — Yet, quite on the contrary, I never open the Gospel without feeling myself called upon directly and individually, and I hold that Christ's teaching is completely misunderstood when its urgency is diverted or deferred.

Thus it is that, taking up again yesterday my Bible, which I had so long forsaken, I open it by chance to the meeting between Christ and the woman "which had a spirit of infirmity eighteen years." How could I fail to recognize myself in this woman "bowed together, and could in no wise lift up herself"? [10]

I ought to write this in my green notebook; but I am too lazy to go and get it; besides, it is too long since I have written anything in it.

Monday

Night haunted, devastated, laid waste by the almost palpable phantom of X., with whom I walk for two hours or in whose arms I roll on the very steps of hell. And this morning I get up with my head empty, my mind distraught, my nerves on edge, and offering an easy access to evil. Yet last night I did not quite yield to pleasure; but this

----

[10] Luke, xiii, 11.

morning, not even benefiting from that repulsion which follows pleasure, I wonder if that semblance of resistance was not perhaps worse. One is always wrong to open a conversation with the devil, for, however he goes about it, he always insists upon having the last word.

Tuesday

Equilibrium almost recovered. Rather good work. Last night, great disappointment at discovering, in an article by Sainte-Beuve, that I am not reading Mme de Sévigné's letters in a good edition. Yet it is hard for me to leave her and to wait for the large Paris edition. Is there anything better than her reflections on death in the letter of 16 March 1672? It is turned out in a way that could not be equaled.[11]

We are reading aloud *Mr. Britling Sees it Through* by Wells.

22 March

Until the week before last, I got as far ahead as I could in the writing of my Memoirs (pathetic conversation with Albert Jalaguier — I changed the name — and the reflections that followed it).[12] But there

---

[11] The following is the passage, which Gide does not quote:

"You ask me if I am as fond of life as ever: I must own to you that I experience mortifications, and severe ones too; but I am still unhappy at the thought of death: I consider it so great a misfortune to see the termination of all my pursuits that I should desire nothing better, if it were practicable, than to begin life again. I find myself engaged in a scene of confusion and trouble: I was embarked in life without my own consent, and know I must leave it again: that distracts me; for how shall I leave it? in what manner? by what door? at what time? in what disposition? Am I to suffer a thousand pains and torments that will make me die in a state of despair? Shall I lose my senses? Am I to die by some sudden accident? How shall I stand with God? What shall I have to offer to him? Will fear and necessity make my peace with him? Shall I have no other sentiment but that of fear? What have I to hope? Am I worthy of heaven? or have I deserved the torments of hell? Dreadful alternative! Alarming uncertainty! Can there be greater madness than to place our eternal salvation in uncertainty? Yet what is more natural, or can be more easily accounted for, than the foolish manner in which I have spent my life? I am frequently buried in thoughts of this nature, and then death appears so dreadful to me that I hate life more for leading me to it than I do for all the thorns that are strewed in its way. You will ask me, then, if I would wish to live forever? Far from it; but if I had been consulted, I would very gladly have died in my nurse's arms; it would have spared me many vexations, and would have ensured heaven to me at a very easy rate; but let us talk of something else." (Letter 189 in the Carnavalet Edition, Vol. II; no translator mentioned.)

[12] In *Si le grain ne meurt . . . (If It Die . . .)* Albert Jalaguier bears the pseudonym of Bernard Tissaudier.

is a certain point of exertion I know it is unwise to go beyond. I long for a diversion that would take me outside myself for a time, away from my desk, from my piano, where my memory is likewise worn out by the effort I demand of it. I had decided to leave for Paris, but various reasons kept me from day to day — among which my anxiety at leaving Em. alone here. So that, for a week now, day after day, I exercise patience and grow impatient, neither daring to work seriously nor able to distract myself sufficiently. The weather is frightful; the air frigid; for the last two days it has been snowing.

I am eagerly reading Sainte-Beuve with unequal pleasure — discover his profession of faith, so important (or more exactly his program) in the second part of his article on Chateaubriand (*Nouveaux Lundis*).[13]

23 March

Heavy fall of snow last night. Anguish at the thought of our soldiers without shelter as a result of that German withdrawal, which, the more one considers it, seems ever more — But I had promised myself to stop talking of the war here. This morning the sky is radiant. I leave Cuverville at four o'clock, without knowing exactly where I am going, and leave this notebook here.

A most touching letter from Ghéon. But, despite a few rare, stray impulses, my soul remains inattentive and closed — too enamored of its sin to consent to follow the path that would take it away from that.

Trip to Toulouse (Bagnols-de-Grenade).
Carcassonne.
Les Sources.

19 April

Back to Cuverville by the mail train at about four o'clock yesterday. Wrote at once to Van Bever (kept a copy) asking him to substitute for the article on Théophile Gautier and Baudelaire, painfully extracted from my lecture for his review, the *Preface to the "Fleurs du mal"* (Pelletan's new edition), with which I am rather satisfied.

---

[13] The entire second part of the article entitled "Chateaubriand Judged by an Intimate Friend," which appeared in Vol. III of *The New Mondays*, outlines Sainte-Beuve's method "in examining books and talents." He begins: "Literature, literary production, to me is not distinct, or at least separable, from the rest of the man and his organization; I can enjoy a work, but it is impossible for me to judge it independently of my knowledge of the man himself; and I am wont to say: *as the tree is, so is the fruit*. The study of literature thus leads me quite naturally to the study of character." He then shows the importance, in this study, of the background, upbringing, parents, brothers and sisters, children, friends, and even disciples of a writer.

This morning splendid weather — at last.

Little André Allégret. The most *born-in-exile* [14] child I know. Forced to hypocrisy. The School of Falsehood. How many of his features remain mysterious to me! I asked him what he wanted to be when he grew up. With deep conviction he answered:

"An ambassador."

I fear that my astonishment, which I was unable to hide, may have hurt him.

Returned to and practiced again the Sonata *"Pathétique"* — a certain passage of which obsessed me during almost my whole trip. On a good piano I could now play it in such a way as to satisfy myself; but Beethoven's pathos moves me much less deeply right now than Bach's contemplative adoration.

What a trap I was caught in yesterday evening! J.-É. Blanche, at whose house I was lunching with the charming Princesse Murat (one of the few *ladies* whom I think I should enjoy frequenting), said to me.

"Come this evening to Boylesve's; he knows you are in Paris and would be pleased to see you."

At about five o'clock I ring at his door. In the entrance hall already a pile of silken wraps warns me; I ask the old manservant if there are many people.

"Not many."

"Ladies?"

"Some ladies." And as I make a gesture to leave: "Oh, Monsieur needn't worry!" then, without paying attention to my hesitation, he introduces me — I ought to say pushes me — into the drawing-room. And I find myself in a real gathering of chatterboxes; there were ten of them and Boylesve the only man, completely surrounded.

"You know," he says to me, "all these ladies"; and vaguely he names, after Mme Boylesve, who rushes toward me: Mme Mühlfeld, Mme Paul Adam, Mme Capiello, Mme Blanche, Mme Chaumeix, Mme Edmond Jaloux, etc. I am wearing my traveling clothes, heavy tan shoes, yesterday's collar, no cuffs. . . . Mme Mühlfeld none the less seizes hold of me at once and forces me to be *too* nice, for fear of being impertinent. We take tea; we talk in low voices and little groups; occasionally one catches some stupidity pronounced in a somewhat louder tone. Jaloux comes in, already full of assurance and solidly established in the social life of Paris. A few ladies leave and the conversation becomes general; that is to say that everyone begins talking of religion. Someone asks, as in a parlor game:

---

[14] The expression *born in exile* appears in English.

"And you, madame, do you believe in God?"

Jaloux declares that, as for him, he does not believe in God but in the Pope; and several times he repeats: "Yes! I do not believe in God, but in the Pope. I told you, madame, that it is not in God I believe, but in the Pope."

One has to have escaped for some time from the drawing-rooms of Paris in order, when plunged suddenly back into them, to feel all their inanity.

When Jaloux came in, a movement had taken place among the ladies; they all changed places as in the game of musical chairs, so that when I took leave I was unable to recognize them and, shaking or kissing hands at random, or neglecting to shake others, I doubtless committed a number of blunders. But after all! nothing could be more uniform or more set than the tone of voices, the costumes, the attitudes, the arrangement of those gowns, those hats, those smiles.

21 April

I plunge into the translation of *Antony and Cleopatra* with rapture.[15] Made the last changes on the typescript of *Typhoon* (first part).

25 April

Good work (exclusively translation of *Antony and Cleopatra*) and piano. I am beginning to practice the Albéniz compositions I had learned by heart last year.

Went over the whole first book of Beethoven's Sonatas. I do not know why people pretend at present to scorn the first ones; certain ones among them are irresistibly spontaneous, with a novelty and truth of accent that overthrows all objections. But I am beginning to look with horror upon the pathos and the repetitions.

29 April

Regularly good work these last few days. Translated three long scenes of *Antony and Cleopatra* with the greatest interest. Went over and perfected the Albéniz compositions. — Then suddenly, yesterday afternoon, resumption of the dizzy spells and of the headaches. Am I again going to have to cling to this notebook?

30 April or 1 May

Wrote to Copeau yesterday; today to Conrad. The air is getting warmer and the sky is radiant. How young I should still feel if I did not know that I shall soon be fifty! — But the anguish of events has

---

[15] André Gide's translation of Shakespeare's tragedy was first published in 1921.

us by the throat; I do not allow myself to speak of them, but I can think of nothing else.

We continue to read *Britling* aloud.

Already in the last weeks of 1914 I wrote in one of my notebooks: There are many chances that if the war goes on, as many claim, for several years, each country will eventually be back on its own frontiers, exhausted.

Just the same it takes a certain dose of mysticism — or of something — to go on speaking, writing, when you know that you are absolutely not being listened to.

From top to bottom, and starting from the ground up, I see nothing but negligence, thoughtlessness, and dishonesty. In the midst of which the mere honest man appears as a hero — or as an easy mark.

The feeling of duty, or to speak in more secular fashion: of the law, has relaxed to such a degree that just a slightly strict application of the law would make people cry tyranny. What is more ridiculous than the word "enforcement" of a law!

The pleasure of corrupting is one of those which have been least examined; this is true likewise of everything we begin by stigmatizing.

3 May

All the brilliance of the sky does not make these days any less gloomy. The upset of the recent offensive, in vain hidden by the press, weighs frightfully on the whole nation. . . .

I am less and less inclined to believe that the decision can be won by arms. Since the Russian Revolution it seems to me clear that this enormous war is itself going to be swallowed up by social questions. I have ceased despairing of seeing Germany as a republic.

"Well then, England too?"

"All the states of Europe as republics; the war will not end otherwise. For neither will Germany triumph over us, nor shall we triumph over her; and even if we do triumph, we shall be unable to keep ourselves from being even more stricken by our victory than she by her defeat. The question today is: just how far on the road toward death shall we go because we do not want to admit this?"

There enters into a nation's resistance a great deal of virtue, and certainly of the most admirable kind, but also obstinacy and even a little stupidity. It is beautiful to want to perish and to prefer perishing in order not to surrender one's virtue. But it is absurd not to un-

derstand that one is dying. This is just why so many souls take refuge
in mysticism today, whom reason brings to bay and who could not
otherwise escape reason.

Arrival in Paris, 5 May, Saturday evening
. . . Such a calm I had not known for months, years even. A real
bit of reasoning is required not to call this happiness. If only I had not
been wakened several times during the night by the disturbances of
the Villa (leaks, doors beating in the wind, etc.), if only I had been
able to sleep my fill — it seems to me that I should have awakened ten
years younger. Even after this middling night I did not feel any particular fatigue or especially that profound upset of the mind and the
flesh which almost always follows imperfect satisfactions.

Marvelous fullness of joy.

19

I refrain from speaking of the single preoccupation of my mind
and flesh. . . .

Noteworthy decrease in virtue these last days, resulting from a
rather serious grippe, which, as ever, drags on and on and which I am
at last barely able to throw off.

I was thinking of Ghéon the day before yesterday when he came
to see me. Without exactly expecting him, I knew that he was hoping
for a leave soon. He talks to me at length of this latest offensive and
prolongs his visit until Em.'s return. Then come Jeanne (and the children) and in their presence, during the bustle attendant upon the
preparation and serving of tea, Ghéon tells his story over again, but
much less well.

Ghéon has taken on a resemblance to the good vicar of Cuverville.[16] That resemblance strikes both Em. and me separately. The
same intonations; the same absentminded and benevolent attention;
the same provisional agreement followed by the same withdrawal;
even the same indefinable absence.

That day we did not approach any of the problems that have arisen
between us.

But yesterday on the other hand, for more than an hour, I applied
to our friendship all the motions of artificial respiration, all the rhyth-
mical tractions that are customarily practiced upon drowned people
in an effort to bring them back to life. And at one and the same time
I tried to convince him and to convince myself that we still thought
the same and yet to yield nothing that I should later have to retract.

After that conversation I see a bit more clearly, it seems to me: that
is, to begin with, that the saints are always against the Church. But

---

[16] Henri Ghéon had but recently been converted to Catholicism.

against the Church it is impossible not to be wrong; you must make up your mind in advance to this and accept being conquered. The Church recognizes as holy only those who have surrendered. This goes without saying.

This is monstrous, like Germania, and organized in an equally impregnable way. All this out of precaution and a need to protect material interests. At one and the same time Catholicism condemns society and comes to terms with it. . . .

I stop . . . *ab irato*.

I stiffen myself against grief, but it seems to me at times that Ghéon is more lost to me than if he were dead. He is neither changed nor absent; he is confiscated.

6 August

Enough vigor (I feel) to take the train at six fifty a.m. From Berne I shall send a telegram to Rivière announcing myself for five p.m., or three hours ahead of the train that I was first supposed to take.

This is because the Chanivaz camp closes five days earlier than I had been told and I am jealously counting the hours separating me from M. I should have left Paris three days earlier if I had known.

Overcast, gray sky; rain. It is almost cold.

* * *

From Geneva to Engelberg

Although he is too taciturn, I like traveling with Fabrice. He says, and I believe him, that at forty-eight he feels infinitely younger than he was at twenty. He enjoys that rare faculty of starting off anew at each turning-point in his life and of remaining faithful to himself by never resembling anything less than he does himself.

Today when he is traveling first-class (this hadn't happened to him for some time now), in new clothes of an unaccustomed cut and under a hat that is wonderfully becoming, he is amazed when he encounters himself in the mirror, and he charms himself. He says to himself: "New creature, today I can refuse you nothing!" Just because he has indulged in a box of delicate Oriental cigarettes, he immediately feels like more of a millionaire than Barnabooth.[17] Heavens! what beautiful weather it is. Having compressed itself this morning for rain, it is now bursting. All alone in this empty region of the Swiss first-class carriages, he walks up and down the corridor with a triumphant air — favored by the German script that has been rife since he left the Valais.

---

[17] Valery Larbaud's hero, the imaginary multimillionaire A. O. Barnabooth, traveled throughout Europe in great luxury analyzing his soul.

He confessed to me that he had first experienced a strange disappointment on meeting Michel at Chanivaz. He hardly recognized the
youth. After barely a month's absence could this be? The fear of seeing the adolescent grow up too rapidly constantly tormented Fabrice
and precipitated his love. He loved nothing so much in Michel as the
childlike qualities he still preserved, in his tone of voice, in his ardor,
in his caressing ways — all of which he recaptured shortly afterward,
wild with joy, when the two of them stretched out beside each other
on the edge of the lake. Michel, who lived most of the time with his
collar wide open, had bundled himself up that day in some stiff collar
or other that changed even his bearing; and this is why Fabrice did
not recognize him at first. Furthermore, it must be confessed that
Michel had already let himself be deeply marked by Switzerland. And
Fabrice began to detest that raw and starched element that Helvetia
adds to every gesture and every thought. Were it not for this, one
might have thought oneself at Oxford or in Arcady.

9 August

Michel was at the age when one is still ignorant of almost everything about oneself. His appetite was barely awakening and had not
yet measured itself with reality. His curiosity seemed turned only in
the direction of barriers; this is the disadvantage of a puritan upbringing when it is applied to someone who is not inclined to be hedged in.

Michel's soul offered Fabrice rapturous perspectives, which were
still clouded, it seemed to him, by the morning mists. To dissipate
them the rays of a first love were needed. It was of this, not of the
love itself, that Fabrice felt he might be jealous. He would have liked
to suffice; tried to convince himself that he might have sufficed; he
grieved to think that he would not suffice.

Lucerne, 10 August

What cleanliness everywhere! You dare not throw your cigarette
into the lake. No graffitti in the urinals. Switzerland is proud of this;
but I believe this is just what she lacks: manure.

In the morning, Geneva, on a bench on the Bastions

One of Fabrice's most disconcerting intellectual peculiarities for
his neighbors (I mean for his companion of the present moment, whoever he might be) was to break away from himself constantly. — From
himself? No, I have expressed it badly: Rather, to break away from
circumstances. Without resolve or defiance, his whole soul would slip
beyond, and the event would no more manage to seize him than Jason

did in taking Proteus prisoner. Adversity exalted him rather; he yielded only to fatigue; but he was often fatigued.

Saas-Fée, 19 August

I am striving to read Tolstoy's *Intimate Journal*, which I had had sent here on the advice of Igor Stravinsky — but I get no pleasure, no profit, from it.

21 August

My mind enamored of everything, even of ugliness. . . .

They always head toward the easiest, and even desire does not urge them far forward.

I believe that Michel's affectionate appearance covers a refractory, saucy nature, always ready to rebel. It is difficult to obtain from him what he does not grant spontaneously through love.

On certain days that child took on a surprising beauty; he seemed clothed in grace and, as Signoret would have said, "with the pollen of the gods." From his face and from all his skin emanated a sort of blond effulgence. The skin of his neck, of his chest, of his face and hands, of his whole body, was equally warm and gilded. He was wearing that day, with his rough homespun shorts, only a silk shirt of a sharp, purplish red, swelling out over his leather belt and open at the neck, where hung amber beads. He was barefoot and barelegged. A scout's cap held back his hair, which otherwise would have fallen tangled on his forehead, and, as if in defiance of his childlike appearance, he held in his teeth the brier pipe with an amber bit that Fabrice had just given him, which he had never yet smoked. Nothing could describe the languor, grace, and sensuality of his eyes. For long moments as he contemplated him, Fabrice lost all sense of the hour, of the place, of good and evil, of the proprieties, and of himself. He doubted whether any work of art had ever represented anything so beautiful. He doubted whether the mystical vocation of the man who used to accompany and precede him in pleasure would have held firm, and his virtuous resolve, before so flagrant an invitation, or whether, to adore such an idol, the other would not have declared himself a pagan again.

* * *

The ground we have conquered by escalade, they think they are imitating us when they advance into it on the level, but it seems to me that by this very fact something of our joy is refused them. Oh, how eager I am to talk of them again with you! As if to protect myself against liking them too much, I should like to indict them. But how hard it is to come to grips with the indecisive, the undeveloped!

At times I reach the point of wondering whether what I like in this is not so much music as piano-practice and whether I do not urge myself on specifically because of a need to achieve perfection in something.

19 September

Returned to Cuverville last night. Trip from Beuzeville in a carriage, watching all the way the wonderfully starry sky, whose immensity had perhaps never been so apparent to me.

Ill-spent day; wrote nothing but a few letters; read nothing but a few specious stanzas of *La Délie*, which has just appeared in the collection of *Les Textes français*, and a few pages of *La Tentation* in the edition I bought for Eric Allégret.[18]

The sentences of *La Tentation* seem to me as beautiful as they did on first reading, but I am less sensitive today to the most beautiful form of style than to its limpidity and the movement of the soul that is evident through the words. Faguet's preface is not bad; if I had to write one, I should make an effort to bring out Antoine's relationship to Bouvard and Pécuchet, which strikes me, after all, as more important than that between Antoine and the second Faust.[19]

20 September

What good is it for me to resume this journal if I dare not be sincere in it and if I hide my heart's secret occupation?

21 September

Almost uninterrupted dizziness all day today. But rather good work — if the clearing away of a pile of correspondence can be called work. Letters to Alibert, to Lady Rothermere, who is translating my *Prométhée*,[20] to Ida Rubinstein about the contract to be drawn up for the translation of *Antony and Cleopatra*, etc., etc. I read the first of Walter Pater's *Portraits* (Watteau) with the greatest pleasure, which is unfailingly accompanied by a desire to translate.

---

[18] *Délie* (anagram of *L'Idée*) is a Renaissance collection of Petrarchian and Platonistic poems by Maurice Scève; it was issued in a scholarly edition by the Société des Textes Français Modernes. *The Temptation of St. Anthony* is of course Flaubert's famous work.

[19] Gide is thinking of the two naïve and well-intentioned characters of Flaubert's later ironic novel *Bouvard et Pécuchet*.

[20] *Prometheus Ill-Bound* did in fact appear in a translation by Lady Rothermere in London (1919).

How beautiful it is! The sky is pure. My mind soars and floats in
the calm air. At one and the same time I think of death and cannot
convince myself that I have only a limited number of summers to live.
Oh, how little my desires have diminished and how hard it would be
for me to reduce them! I cannot consent to put my happiness in the
past. And why should I? Never did I feel younger and happier than
last month — to such a point that I was unable to write anything about
it. I could only have stammered. . . .

23

The joyful state in which I lived more than a month strengthened
me doubtless and gave me confidence again. I should have liked to
plunge back into work immediately afterward. Since my return I have
barely been able to write anything but letters, letters, letters. Each
mail mortgages me anew. English translation of the *Prométhée* (to go
over), Spanish translation of *La Porte étroite*. Rights for my translation of *Antony and Cleopatra* to be discussed; the project of a translation of Locke to be examined and new translators who are offering
themselves for Conrad. — This year will have seen appear my edition
of *Les Fleurs du mal*, my reprintings of *L'Immoraliste* and of *Les
Nourritures*. Is the little success this represents worth the effort it
costs me?

I began again to suffer considerably from my nerves all day today.
This evening I made up my mind to read to Em. the pages of Memoirs
written in Paris at the beginning of the summer. Rather satisfied with
certain passages; but the word often calls too much attention to itself
and makes too apparent my desire to write well.

I should like now a more abrupt, less obliging way of speaking. I
cannot dream of getting back to it so long as Cuverville is not emptied
of its guests; I long to be alone here with Em., as last winter.

24 September

Radiant weather; but my headaches have returned. This morning
wrote a page of Memoirs (Anna's death), but I cannot manage to get
back to work seriously. It is better to put it off until later, resolutely.

I leave tomorrow for Offranville.

25 September

Blanche takes me into his room to amuse him while he shaves and
finishes dressing. He sponges his face with wads of absorbent cotton
that he takes out of a metal tube. He asks me to rub his back with a
moist, soapy towel: "Right there, between the shoulders; I can't reach
it. My wife usually rubs me every morning. But since you are here

. . ." And while I curry him, he repeats to me Barrès's indignation on reading my *Préface aux "Fleurs du mal."*

26

To Dieppe in auto. Went up the Polet Valley to a camp of Kaffirs (?). It is six o'clock; the work-day over, this is the recreation period. Amazing animation in the field on the edge of the road. Beside a football game, a strange round began to the sound of makeshift instruments. And, all around them, the Norman landscape withdraws and effaces itself before this torrid recall of the desert. . . . What a sweet smile these ferocious blacks have! An instinctive and almost animal attraction draws the most secret depths of my being toward them, while their elementary music voluptuously overwhelms my mind.

28 September

The *Revue de Paris* for 15 September announces the novels it plans to bring out. *Typhoon* is left out. My most natural impulse would be to take it away from them, as I had done for *La Porte étroite;* but I follow the advice of my hosts and of Mme Mühlfeld and write to Marcel Prévost asking him to tell me his intentions.

Paris, 1 October

Back from Dieppe yesterday with Mme Mühlfeld. In the train I gave her to read, to make the time pass, *Le Prométhée,* which she had never read and of which I was lugging about a copy to correct Lady Rothermere's translation. At every page, rapturous admiration of Mme Mühlfeld, who naturally declares that she has never read anything more beautiful.

Went to the Gare de l'Est to meet the Élie Allégrets. Spent the night at the hotel opposite the Gare Saint-Lazare, where I had had to take a room because of the impossibility of getting anyone to take me to Auteuil at once. The following morning (yesterday) to the Gare de l'Est to pick up the eight hundred pounds of luggage that had been left there the day before. Slept at the Villa.

Today glorious weather. My inner sky is even more radiant; a vast joy softens and exalts me.

22 October

Returned to Cuverville yesterday.

I have lived all the time of late (and, altogether, since 5 May) my head swimming with happiness; whence the long empty space in this notebook. It reflects only my clouds.

25 October

I am no longer mistaken about it: Michel loves me not so much for what I am as for what I allow him to be. Why should I ask more? Never have I enjoyed life more, nor has the savor of life seemed more delicious to me.

I have not yet advanced in my Memoirs, but I am copying into the oblong notebook the part (chapter vii) that I had not yet put into final form. I have got back to the translation of *Antony and Cleopatra* — and above all I have written letters, a pile of back letters that were obstructing the horizon for me. I am reading *Phèdre* [21] to the little girls. I prolong the evening in my bed until midnight (for three nights now and I haven't felt any the worse), reading, deciphering with difficulty the book sent by W., *Sons o' Men* by G. B. Lancaster — a rather remarkable book but written in a New Zealand dialect that is almost incomprehensible to me.

28 October

Excellent work. Joy; equilibrium and lucidity. I am reading in my spare time Brunetière's *Histoire de la littérature française classique* [22] (rereading) with great interest; and in the evening, to the little girls, *Les Fourberies de Scapin.* [23]

I am eager to have finished copying chapter vii of my Memoirs in order to get on with them.

29 October

Letter to Guillaume Lerolle in reply to his translation of Santayana:

". . . Until now I saw but two possible attitudes toward the great Germanic philosophers: either consider them responsible for this war (like Louis Bertrand and numerous imbeciles) or oppose them to it (and I confess that this is rather my view). The position that Santayana takes is ingenious; he reveals an extraordinary breadth and suppleness of mind; and, if he does not quite succeed in convincing me that Nietzsche was altogether wrong, this is after all because he is not quite so convinced of it himself.

". . . It is not yet proved, alas, that the great writers he is *discrediting* are leading Germany to ruin (even if you admit that she is inspired by them today). I am absolutely sure that after the war we shall rush toward everything German — especially if we are the victors — and shall see that nothing could better magnify our victory than to magnify our enemy. We shall examine him with the greatest curiosity — and only then will begin the real influence of Nietzsche in France

---

[21] Racine's tragedy.
[22] *History of French Literature of the Classic Period.*
[23] *The Impostures of Scapin,* a comedy by Molière.

—just as Goethe's influence began only after 1870 and despite everything that Barbey d'Aurevilly wrote against him. I fear that, ten years from now, certain of Santayana's smiles may evoke smiles from his readers."

30 October

I rest myself with Keats, resuming his letters with infinite delight: "Better be imprudent moveables than prudent fixtures." (*Letters*, II, p. 80.) [24]

Never have I aspired less toward rest. Never have I felt more exalted by that excess of passions which Bossuet considers the attribute of youth, in his wonderful *Panégyrique de Saint Bernard*,[25] which I was rereading this morning. Age cannot manage to empty either sensual pleasure of its attractiveness or the whole world of its charm. On the contrary, I was more easily disgusted at twenty, and I was less satisfied with life. I embraced less boldly; I breathed less deeply; and I felt myself to be less loved. Perhaps also I longed to be melancholy; I had not yet understood the superior beauty of happiness.

31 October

Dramatic character: the despised bastard who discovers that he is the son of a king. His re-establishment above his brothers, legitimate sons.

Fictional character: the man whom the doctors give only a year to live. And at the end of that year he finds himself ruined, but healthier than ever—and resolute, having got the *habit of happiness* (lack of preoccupation with the future).

1 November

At moments it strikes me, and as if in a sudden flash, that I have only a little time still to live, and that this is why I take such a lively interest in everything I read, that everything I see seems so beautiful to me, and that I enjoy life so completely.

I received from Michel yesterday a letter full of exquisite fancy and grace that lighted up all my thoughts. Half of the day was given, alas, to correspondence. Read considerable English (Santayana—chapter on Browning, on the Platonism of the Italian poets, and on Shakespeare's lack of religion—in *Poetry and Religion*, which Guillaume Lerolle lent me; and *Simon the Jester* by Locke); got ahead with the rewriting of the Memoirs; went over a chapter of the translation of *End of the Tether*.[26]

---

[24] The quotation appears in English.
[25] *Panegyric of Saint Bernard.*
[26] This is another work by Conrad.

Read this evening to the little girls a few pages of the *Panégyrique de Saint Bernard*.

Education is liberation. This is what I should like to teach M.

3 November

Less a painter than a musician, it is certainly movement in preference to color that I wished my sentence to have. I wanted it to follow faithfully the palpitations of my heart.

6 November

Read the wonderful portrait of La Harpe in the *Mémoires d'Outre-Tombe*.[27] Numerous chapters of Santayana (*Poetry and Religion*). I drop *Simon the Jester*, which had at first delighted me but whose company soon becomes tiresome. Received *Les Écrits nouveaux* (first number), containing a fragment of my lecture on Gautier and Baudelaire. Everything that I did not use again in my *Préface aux "Fleurs du mal"* strikes me as rather poor. Poor the whole review and positively poisonous the dialogue of André Germain against J.-É. Blanche. I ask the editor (whose name escapes me just now) to remove my name from the list of contributors.

Greatly advanced the translation of Shakespeare. Wrote piles of letters.

8 November

Valentine and the two little girls (and a dozen trunks) left us yesterday. Immense joy to find myself alone with Em. again at last.

Like the "lame minds" of Pascal, Val. annoys because she thinks you are the one who is lame. She considers me a quibbler because I cannot endure illogic; but, like many women, she cannot endure being corrected. Conversation with her is no more than a defense of positions; it is enough for you to touch hers, even as a friend, for her to attack yours, or what she thinks to be yours. After a few days of this regime my head is all at sea, my brain bewildered, and during meals I long only to withdraw to my room — or to flee Cuverville, if it were not for the child's piano lessons.

You feel that she never seizes an idea any more firmly than she does that large number of proper names which she never succeeds in pronouncing properly.

---

[27] Chateaubriand's *Memoirs from beyond the Grave*.

12 November

Unbroken work; but I have dropped the rewriting of the Memoirs to devote myself entirely to the translation. I embrace Shakespeare's text with rapture and am extremely satisfied with certain pages.

Went out yesterday and today for the first time since my return.

Reread Boileau's last epistles —

   The Orpheuses are seen to pant under the laurels [28]

— and, every evening, a few pages of Bossuet's *Oraisons funèbres*. I doubt whether he ever wrote anything more beautiful than the sentences about the Reformation, at the beginning of the *Oraison funèbre de Henriette de France:*

   When God looses from the well of the abyss, etc.[29]

Went over my translation of Whitman and wrote a stack of letters.

I am learning Beethoven's maddening little Sonata in F (in the form of a minuet) from a sense of mortification, and its finale in the form of a toccata. Many exercises of trills, with, nevertheless, some progress over last year.

I watched at great length this morning a bumblebee's struggle with a snapdragon that did not want to give up its honey. The insect besieged the whole circumference of the corolla, stabbed it frequently, bit it, and then tore it with a rage that was at first impotent and eventually triumphant. . . .

For the last week I have been anxiously and impatiently waiting for a letter from M.

---

[28] *"On voit sous les lauriers haleter les Orphées"* is line 78 of Boileau's *Epistle XI,* addressed to his gardener. The Orpheuses are the poets in pursuit of the Muses.

[29] The whole passage, from the *Funeral Oration of Henriette de France,* is:

"When God looses from the well of the abyss the smoke that darkens the sun, according to the words of the Apocalypse, that is to say error and hypocrisy; when, in order to punish scandals or to awaken his peoples and his ministers, he allows the spirit of seduction to mislead noble souls and to spread abroad a vain dissatisfaction, a wanton curiosity, and a spirit of revolt, he determines in his profound wisdom the limits he intends to set upon the lamentable progress of error and upon the sufferings of his Church. I am not undertaking, Christians, to tell you the destinies of the heresies of recent times nor to designate the fatal limit by which God resolved to circumscribe their course; but, if my judgment does not deceive me; if, recalling the memory of recent centuries, I make an equitable report at the present stage of development, I dare to believe, and I see wise men agree with this sentiment, that the days of blindness have run their course and that it is henceforth time for light to return."

16 November

The thought of death pursues me with a strange insistence. Every time I make a gesture, I calculate: how many times already? I compute: how many times more? and, full of despair, I feel the turn of the year rushing toward me. And as I measure how the water is withdrawing around me, my thirst increases and I feel younger in proportion to the little time that remains to me to feel it.

18 November

The above lines will seem prophetic if I am to die in a short while; but I shall be really ashamed if it is given to me to reread them fifteen years from now. If I could simply not know or forget my age, how little I should be aware of it! I ought never to remind myself of it except to urge myself to work.

Somewhat tired these last few days, having slept less well. Rather out of patience also with this job of translating and revising the translations of others, which takes almost all my time. I hope to be rid of it before the end of the year (even before my forthcoming departure for Paris, perhaps) and to be able to concern myself solely with the Memoirs.

One of the Hérouard sons, the youngest of those who are in military service, has just been killed. Em. went this morning to Cuverville to attend the funeral service for Georges's deputy mayor, old Crochemore. As people were preparing to leave the church, an old woman began to shout in a high-pitched voice:

"There's God! There's God!"

Em., who is afraid of crazy people, ran out terrified, while her neighbor reassured her:

"Don't be afraid, Mam Gille! She's seized like that every time."

And for some time we amuse ourselves by imagining the panic caused by the arrival of God in the church.

20 November

I cannot go on; I am out of patience and strength and expectation. I am still working, as best I can, which is to say almost a great deal.[30] But I have lost sleep and a certain feverishness upsets my body and mind.

23 November

In the train — *going to Paris.*[31]

What to do? I can kill myself more easily than stop my life — I mean: than limit it, reduce it.

---

[30] I have almost finished my translation of *Antony and Cleopatra*. [A.]

[31] These last three words appear in English.

Every moment it seems to me that I am beginning to live and that my appetite is at last awakening.

I shall die by bursting, as Mme Théo used to say.

Cuverville, 30 November

Scarcely back here and I am recalled by a telegram from Eric Allégret.

The day before leaving, the 22nd, I had finished my translation of *Antony and Cleopatra* — of which I gave a reading to Ida Rubinstein at Bakst's.

Immense delirium of happiness.

My joy has something untamed, wild, incompatible with all decency, all propriety, all law. Through it I return to the stammering of childhood, for it offers my mind nothing but novelty. I need to invent everything, words and gestures; nothing of the past satisfies my love any longer. Everything in me blossoms forth; is amazed; my heart beats wildly; an excess of life rises to my throat like a sob. I no longer know anything; it is a vehemence without memories and without wrinkles. . . .

Long contemplation before the hearth. Occasionally, from amidst the living embers [32] a tiny brand throws out a whiter, stronger flame that continues, becomes even more intense, until the moment of falling in ashes. Just as the coal springs to life and whitens if it receives its fill of oxygen. . . .

Cuverville, 8 December

Yesterday evening back from Paris, for which I had left on the 1st. A vast, singing joy did not cease to fill me; nevertheless, the day before yesterday, and for the first time in my life, I knew the torment of jealousy. I tried in vain to defend myself against it. M. did not come in until ten p.m. I knew he was at C.'s. I was all on edge. I felt capable of the maddest things, and from my anguish I measured the depth of my love. Moreover, it did not last. . . .

The next morning C., on whom I called, reassured me completely by telling me, according to his habit, every last word and gesture of their evening.

Sunday, 9 December

Read last night in bed until midnight according to my new method, which assures me a rather good sleep. And it is in bed that I am writ-

---

[32] The words "living embers" appear in English.

ing this. I have resumed work with the greatest satisfaction. Wrote to
Maurras about a remarkable letter on Barbusse's book that appeared
in *L'Action française*. Began the preface to Dupouey's letters. Read
with Em. the first chapter (wonderful) of *Under Western Eyes* while
going over the manuscript translation that is offered me. Practiced
the *Goyescas* with delight.[33]

10 December

What a novel, what a drama could be written under the title
"PROPTER VITAM," in which life would be bought only at the expense
of honor, honor only at the expense of life.

Em., who is finishing reading *Les Mémoires d'Outre-Tombe*, shows
me the extraordinary paragraph on civil war:

"Whatever may be said, civil wars are less unjust, less revolting,
and more natural than foreign wars. . . ."[34] Civil wars are at least
founded on individual outrages, on confessed and recognized aver-
sions; they are duels with seconds, in which the adversaries know why
they have sword in hand." Etc. (Vol. V, p. 369.)

13 December

Slowly I construct that preface for the letters of Dupouey. Good
practice of Granados.

We are reading aloud *Under Western Eyes*, in which we admire
such prophetic reflections about the Russian soul.

Why should I note all this? . . . But what else could I note down
here if I forbid myself to speak of political events or of the war — and
at the same time of what nourishes my ardor?

15 December

Ride to Criquetot. The sky was overcast, very dark, heavy with
showers; a great sea wind swept the clouds. The thought of M. keeps
me in a constant state of lyricism I had not known since my *Nourritures*.[35] I no longer feel my age, or the horror of our time, or the
season, unless to draw from it a new source of exaltation; were I a
soldier, with such a heart, I should meet death joyously.

I believe I have ceased to prefer "the fine weather" to these late-

---

[33] *Under Western Eyes* by Conrad first appeared in 1911. *Goyescas* are
piano compositions by Granados, on which was based his later opera of the
same name.

[34] *"When the latter are not undertaken to save national independence,"*
he takes care to add. [A.]

[35] Written largely in 1895, *The Fruits of the Earth* was published in
1897.

autumn skies, so pathetic, so serious in tone, so tragic in sonority. Vast flights of crows spread madly over the plain.

As soon as I got home I wrote at one breath the preamble to *Corydon*, as a reaction to the *Préface aux Lettres de Dupouey*, which I had finished that very morning. Then I practiced the irritating toccata (finale) of Beethoven's little Sonata in F major, which, almost completely mastered, becomes charming.

Read with Em. *Under Western Eyes* and corrected the rest of *End of the Tether* (soon finished).

16 December

Labored over *Corydon* all day yesterday and today. I lose myself in the accumulation of notes, outlines, and rejects that I had left pretty much topsy-turvy — and I am angry with Marcel Drouin for having stopped me in my work at the moment when the iron was hot. It seems to me, however, that what I had to say is important. I repeat to myself Ibsen's remark: "Friends are to be feared, not so much for what they make us do as for what they keep us from doing." It's a pity, but I shall succeed.

Outside it is snowing; all the rays of sunlight are dead on the desperate plain. . . .

18 December

. . . It is true that for some time, and well before the war, I was obsessed by the abominable idea that our country was dying. Everything revealed to me her exhaustion, her decadence; I saw them everywhere; it seemed to me that one would have to be blind not to see them. If something can save us, I used to think, it can only be a tremendous crisis, such as our history has already witnessed, a great danger, war. . . . And at the beginning of this war I let myself be eagerly overwhelmed with hope. The Nation seemed to catch hold of herself. We would have all given our blood to save her. Then this war made us see at close hand all our insufficiencies, all our disorders, paid for by a tremendous expenditure of virtues. . . .

Today people accuse the war; but the evil came from farther back.

The Germans have everything to take from us. We have everything to learn from them.[36] — Does not this formula sum up rather well? . . .

22 December

The day before yesterday funeral service for little André Hérouard, who just fell "gloriously." The whole family is in tears. The little

---

[36] The play on the words *prendre* (take) and *apprendre* (learn) is unfortunately lost in translation.

church of Cuverville is quite full on the women's side and half empty on the men's side. I sit under a window that gives me a head-cold through a broken pane. It is bitterly cold and the officiants' mouths steam like censers. In front of me, the elder Hérouard sons; I am lost in contemplation of their ears; I wonder if that organ is not particularly revealing; according to it the Hérouard boys are still very close to the animal (none the less excellent lads both of them). Their ears spring out sharply from the skull, rise almost vertically and cupped like those of domestic animals; they look as if they were mobile; and the faint outline of a convolution is on the outside of the lobe in their case. . . .

Then I contemplated the vicar's admirable head; but he is wrong to keep on his pince-nez when serving Mass; it is almost shocking. And I thought of Flaubert and of all the injustice of his art—the result of a deplorable theory and of an urgent need of maceration (which, with his enthusiasm, remains the best part of him, perhaps).

We finished yesterday revising *End of the Tether* (or at least there remain only three pages now). I am fed up with this petty corrector's job. It exasperates in me that need for verbal logic toward which my mind is already only too inclined. But all the same it is not without profit.

Got considerably ahead in *Corydon*.

And now I am again recalled to Paris—for the third time since this autumn. I am leaving this evening.

1918

Back in Cuverville since the first of January. Worked on *Corydon*.

Read yesterday and the day before various passages of my Recollections in the presence of Mathilde Roberty, who came to spend a week with us. Great dissatisfaction with almost all I have written of them. It all lacks tremor, elasticity, richness. The often happy expressions appear to have been sought out. It seems to me that I see better, now, how the rest should be written.

In Paris I reread to Jean-Paul Allégret a few pages of Proust—dazzled.

I write to Lady Rothermere upon sending her a copy of *Prétextes*, of which she would like to translate some passages:

"The chief difficulty comes from the fact that my sentence constantly suggests rather than affirms, and proceeds by insinuations—for which the English language, more direct than the French, feels rather a repugnance. It has always seemed to me that in my writings the thought mattered less than the movement of the thought: *the gait.*" [1]

Monday, 14

Forsaken this notebook for a week. I get no pleasure, or profit, from writing in it; if I open it again today this is because my work is slackening. I have almost finished *Corydon;* at least, to advance it further I shall need a bit of perspective; but the most important part is done.

I wanted to harness myself to the Memoirs again, but I have no further taste for them; the few passages that I read aloud in the presence of Mathilde Roberty disappointed me; and the comparison I made between them and the pages of Proust's marvelous book, which I was rereading at the same time, overwhelmed and finished me off.

Could the reserves of health and joy that this summer accumulated in me be exhausted now? A secret relapse makes me fear this. I am already thirsty to plunge into life anew.

Practice of Beethoven and Granados.

17

I have absolutely no idea as to the value of what I am writing now. Under a somewhat different form from the one I originally thought of giving it, it is that *Castor et Pollux* or *Traité des Dioscures* that I have

---

[1] The expression in italics appears in English.

been carrying in me for almost twenty years.[2] If I am sufficiently satisfied with it, I shall probably dedicate it to Pierre Louÿs in recollection of his *Léda,* which he dedicated to me years ago.

Wrote a number of letters the last few days. Very good piano-practice.

Read Tagore's *Reminiscences.* But that Indian Orient is not made for me. With rapture I resumed reading Meredith's *The Shaving of Shagpat.*

20 January

Went to Étretat the day before yesterday; out of training, I was done in by the ride; I thought I should fall from fatigue on the way and did not return until night. The sky was overcast and purplish gray; no pleasure in seeing the sea again; from one cliff to another and all the way to the horizon it was dull and monochrome as a child might have painted it.

But, tired as I was last night when I got home, and despite my bad night, this morning I should have liked to start out again. The already warm wind, moaning in the trees of the avenue, raises all my desires. I am fed up with tranquillity, with comfort. . . .

Oh! I shall always understand you, friend — even if you were to kill. But in crime too there is a sort of virginity that can never be recovered and the loss of which invites you to look upon crime with ever greater ease. One now knows, *once and for all,* that one is capable of committing it.

24 January

I leave again tomorrow for Paris, full of anxiety after Jean-Paul's letter of yesterday, in which he tells me his suspicions about his brother. I hope still to find him there, as well as André, who is joining up and leaving Saturday.

12 February

My stay in Paris was prolonged until yesterday. The day before yesterday signed the contract with Ida Rubinstein.[3]

13 February

Is the winter over already? The air is warm. The buds are swelling with hope. The birds are exulting and the robin that comes to get

---

[2] Nothing was ever published under the title of *Treatise of the Dioscuri* or *Castor and Pollux,* but the long-matured project eventually produced the *Considerations on Greek Mythology.*

[3] For the production of his version of *Antony and Cleopatra.*

little bits of meat on the edge of my window no longer flies away when I approach.

I have just seen Em. serving the poor children of the Commune with the soup they come and get at noon in Mius's abandoned house since the bread tickets have cut their rations. Without this I have no idea how they could get along; but thanks to this they are all happy and healthy-looking. There are seventeen of them this morning; the table is scarcely large enough; and tomorrow there will be nineteen. Em. lighted a fire in the room and put flowers on the table.

Yesterday one of them stopped eating because he thought he had seen a "carpeleuse" (caterpillar) in his plate. I did not know this word, probably related to the English word "caterpillar." [4] To reassure him, Em. threw away the plate of soup — though, if I had been there, I should certainly have eaten it in their presence.

15 February

I am beginning to think that our Commune is the only one in France in which the rules are observed. As mayor, Georges did not think he could grant himself more than two hundred grams of bread a day. And he has restricted Em. and me to this same minimum allowance. People are poking fun at us. The mayors of the neighboring communes began by granting themselves the lion's share. We are a subject of ridicule. . . . But I do not mind being made fun of.

Each time a new ruling is imposed on France, every French citizen begins worrying not as to how he can follow it but as to how he can escape it. I keep coming back to this: people talk of a lack of organization when it is a lack of conscience they mean.

20 February

For the last four days I have been plunged into that tale of *L'Aveugle* which has been inhabiting me for so many years and which I was giving up hope of writing.[5] I am striving to write it without a rough draft and have immediately written some twenty pages. I should like not to reread and polish it until I work on the typed copy.

I am reading with rapture the story of *Bhanavar* in *Shagpat,* and Tristan's *Mariamne.*[6]

---

[4] The usual French word is *chenille.*

[5] Later become *La Symphonie pastorale.* [E.] *The Pastoral Symphony,* which Gide here calls *The Blind Girl,* was published in 1919.

[6] The tragedy of *Mariamne* by Tristan L'Hermite, which had a great success in 1636, marks an important stage in the development of the French classical drama.

22 February

It is hard for you, you say, to assert that God is. But tell me if it isn't still harder for you to assert that God is not?

I am reading Ghéon's notebooks with an indescribable sorrow and even disgust.[7] Only now does it appear to me clearly to what extent his mind was marked, alas, by my influence during all the time that I frequented him. I took such delight in feeling him burn with the same ardor that I balked at the evidence, which was obvious to many.

And I protested the day before yesterday when Eugène Rouart exclaimed: "You shall see! You shall see how rare are those who, with age, are not won back by the influences of their early childhood, in spite of all the effort they originally made to get away from them." And he was actually thinking of Ghéon.

23

I write for Ghéon:

"It appeared to me clearly last night that your book should have been: not retrospective — but a sort of day-to-day account of your successive states of mind. That would have been poignant from one end to the other, just as it becomes poignant every time you paint the state in which you *are* — and ceases to be every time you report the state in which you *were*.

"Yes, this mosaic work shocks and annoys me; not that I blame you for minimizing what we shall call if you wish the devil's share; but, by devaluating your preceding thought, you depreciate correspondingly your victory over it and force people to think: Why, naturally! the empty values that Life, Art, Beauty, even Pleasure were for him previously, it is not hard to throw them overboard. But, for certain minds, you are well aware that they represent something more than that. Your way of speaking, for instance, of the work of art's *refusal to come to a conclusion* is frankly impertinent. What agreement do you expect to win by this, save from just those against whom you fought yesterday? But is it really for them alone that your book is written? You know well that for Shakespeare, Eliot, Ibsen, Dostoyevsky, the refusal to come to a conclusion is in no wise an example of art for art's sake, as you seem to invite your readers to think, but rather a sense of intellectual loyalty.

"It is of the word *impartiality* that you should have taken hold, and that is what you should have sought to overcome; but you could

---

[7] The manuscript of *L'Homme né de la guerre* (*The Man Born of the War*), which relates Ghéon's conversion to Catholicism in early 1917, was published in 1919.

not have done so except with a pathetic *partiality*. That impartiality, which is but *intellectual honesty,* is what allowed George Eliot, for example, to paint a figure like that of Hetty Sorrel, capable of inspiring the Christian soul of your sister.

"'There is no longer any question,' you might have said, 'of my being impartial' — any more than there is any question for any of us, in this war, of remaining neutral . . . etc. . . .'"

It is always the same story in life: there are those on whom you count, whom you need, who do not do their duty; so that those who continue to do theirs look like easy marks and seem to have been duped.

One must set one's stake higher.

1 March

Very bad nights the last four days. It is very hard for me to prolong more than a fortnight the benefit of the diversion of Paris.

I read to Em. last night the first forty-five pages of *L'Aveugle*. Oh, how I should like to have finished it! . . .

Tristan's *Mariamne,* in spite of some wonderful lines, greatly disappointed me. You feel, as you so often do, that Tristan (like so many others) could have done much better; but that they lack application. Yes, I think that application is much more often lacking than the gift of writing. Insufficient application often stems from a doubt as to one's own importance; but it is even more frequently due to an excessive self-confidence.

3 March

Lucien Maury, with whom I was lunching the other day in Paris, is greatly worried about the wave of socialism he feels rising, which he foresees as submerging our old world after we think the war is over. He believes revolution inevitable and sees no way it can be opposed. When I speak to him of the resistance organization that *L'Action fran-çaise* is working to form, he becomes indignant. Maurras exasperates him and Léon Daudet makes his blood boil.

"I can understand," I told him, "that they should not satisfy you. But you will be forced to side with them if you are anxious to resist. There will be no third choice. It will be like the Dreyfus affair: you will have to be *for* or *against,* willy-nilly. You don't like the *Action française* group? It is not so much that I consider it the best — *but it is the only one.*"

After a good night (or at least somewhat better) today I feel quite refreshed. I write this so as to be able to read it in my hours of distress and anguish: never have I felt as if I had a more active, more lucid mind, a more supple body, a warmer heart. Never have I felt happier. Never has the air filled my breast more voluptuously. Never has the suffering or the joy of a friend — what am I saying? — even of any stranger I meet on my way — found greater sympathy in me — nor the nation's anxiety greater echo. Never have I felt greater strength in me or more desire to embrace or more breath to inspire.

4 March

Insomnia again; anguish, exasperation, and finally surrender . . . not so much through excess of desire as to be able to get rid of it and go back to sleep. . . . But sleep cares nothing for that paltry satisfaction, followed by relaxation. I awake in a daze (for none the less, toward morning, I had finally gone to sleep). Oh! I cry for that health, that happy equilibrium, which I enjoy in M.'s presence and which makes even chastity easy for me when I am with him, and my flesh smilingly at ease.

I succeed nevertheless in keeping myself in a state of joy; in spite of the headache that I drag around with me all day long.

Was present at the seventeen children's meal and helped Em. to serve them.

Went to the Criquetot station to meet D. (who was not there); cold wind, overcast black sky. I walked along briskly, winged with the hope of my forthcoming liberation and imagining M. at my side.

On the way back, just as I was getting out of Criquetot, I encountered the little Aubin girl bent under a sack of bread heavier than she, which I carried to the main gate.

Wrote to Ruyters a rather important letter on Dostoyevsky and the Gospel (of which I regret not having kept a copy).

6 March

Read to Em. the recently written pages on Greek mythology; quite amazed to find so bad the passages that I thought the best and so good the passages with which I was least satisfied. — In general, at the point I have now reached, I should be much more willing to let myself go. What I write best today is what I write with the least effort. Yes; yield to my nature. Yesterday's application suffices.

Drew up the table of contents of selected passages for the Swedish translation.

Examined with Em. the accounts of which she has just finished making the statement. The item *Gifts* absorbs about a quarter of the annual expenditures (which, moreover, considerably exceed the "in-

come"). Happy to see Em. approve that expenditure as much as I. I
know that if she let herself go, she would give even more — even to
the point of depriving herself completely. Oh! I should like to succeed
in giving still more. I should like to succeed in giving everything away,
to enjoy only what I gave or what I received from others.

8 March

Recalled to Paris again. . . .

Em. can never know how my heart is torn at the thought of leaving her, and in order to find happiness far from her.

Domi takes me away. He came to Cuverville to say farewell to
Em. before leaving for the front. This morning he helped serve the
soup to the poor children of the Commune; afterward he said a few
words to them in a manner that was both playful and serious, which
brought tears to the eyes of all of us. That little farewell ceremony, so
short and simple, was, for Em. and me at least, upsetting.

18 April

Returned to Cuverville yesterday — after two sojourns in Paris —
interrupted by a week at Carantec, with M. — at Godebski's.

"Yes, I am very fond of Mme E.," said Cocteau, "and I admire her.
She is so sincere. Just take this for instance — she went to see Debussy's body laid out; but when, later on, she was asked: 'Well, how did
he look?' 'Why, I don't know,' she replied; 'I didn't see him at all. *I* see
nothing but colors.' And that's true. Isn't that wonderful: she sees
nothing but color!"

Nothing is more foreign to me than this concern for modernism
which one feels influencing every thought and every decision of Cocteau. I do not claim that he is wrong to believe that art breathes freely
only in its newest manifestation. But, all the same, the only thing that
matters to me is what a generation will not carry away with it. I do
not seek to be of my epoch; I seek to overflow my epoch.

Propose this definition of *sin*: everything that involves the injurious.
This is simply displacing the question, not answering it. Often a
superior good is obtained only at the cost of a particular injury.

20 April

Frigid weather. Completely done in by a cold.

I occasionally wonder if I am not quite wrong to try to correct M.;
if *I* have not more to learn from his shortcomings than *he* would profit
from acquiring the virtues I should like to teach him. I inherit from

my mother that mania for always wanting to improve those I love. And yet what attracts me in M. is also what I call his shortcomings — which are perhaps only poetic virtues: thoughtlessness, turbulence, forgetfulness of the hour, complete surrender to the moment. . . . And how could that bold self-affirmation which I like so much in him go without some egotism?

23

Written a number of letters the last few days; this evening for the first time I feel free enough to turn my attention back to my work; I have the greatest difficulty getting back to it and heating enough to achieve a perfectly soldered joint.

25

Finished yesterday *The Shaving of Shagpat,* one of the books of which I am most jealous, which I should most like to have written!

I reread this morning Ruyters's study of me (still in manuscript) taken from his lecture. It does not satisfy me any more than Rivière's. The æsthetic point of view is the only one from which to speak of my work soundly.

26 April

Excellent disposition of mind — if only I could take it upon myself not to smoke any more. Read yesterday Balzac's stupefying *Vautrin.* Had I already read it? If so, how absentmindedly I read it, not to be aware until now that it is there, rather than in *Le Père Goriot* or *Les Illusions perdues,* that he must be taken by surprise and that he confesses himself most significantly. I have underlined all the passages (in particular the dialogue with Raoul de Frescas) suitable for quoting.

28

Period of dissolution; haunted by the memory and the need of M. Need of the beyond, of wearing out my demon and exhausting my desire. I ought to be crushed and on the contrary, this evening, my mind is clear, fresh, fit — to such a point that I go up after dinner (a thing I haven't done for a long time) in order to get back to work.

30

Enticed by *Vautrin,* I am reading *Les Ressources de Quinola,*[8] which contains a rare stupidity.

4 May

Sawing wood, then taking a tub, have put my body in a state of happy equilibrium. But the prolonged silence of S. A. worries me to

---

[8] *The Resources of Quinola,* like *Vautrin,* is a play by Balzac.

the point of anguish. Getting along without M. has already ceased to seem possible to me. All my youth is in him.

9 May

What a wonderful subject for a novel:

X. indulges in a tremendous effort of ingenuity, scheming, and duplicity to succeed in an undertaking that he knows to be reprehensible. He is urged on by his temperament, which has its exigences, then by the rule of conduct he has built in order to satisfy them. It takes an extreme and hourly application; he expends more resolve, energy, and patience in this than would be needed to succeed in the best. And when eventually the event is prepared to such a point that he has only to let it take its course, the let-down he experiences allows him to reflect; he then realizes that he has ceased to desire greatly that felicity on which he had counted too much. But it is too late now to back out; he is caught in the mechanism he has built and set in motion and, willy-nilly, he must now follow its impetus to its conclusion. The event that he no longer dominates carries him along and it is almost passively that he witnesses his perdition. Unless he suddenly gets out of it by a sort of cowardice; for there are some who lack the courage to pursue their acts to their conclusion, without moreover being any more virtuous for this reason. On the contrary they come out diminished and with less self-esteem. This is why, everything considered, X. will persevere, but without any further desire, without joy and rather through *fidelity*. This is the reason why there is often so little happiness in crime — and what is called "repentance" is frequently only the exploitation of this.

Rather languishing, the interest of Fielding's *Amelia,* which I am reading aloud to Em. Eager to look for the possible connection (or rather the similitude of tone) with *Gil Blas,* I pick up in the latter *L'Histoire de Scipion* and am above all amazed to find it better.[9]

10 May

The newspapers, according to their criminal habit, have aimed only to chloroform the nation. Long articles have been scattered everywhere making fun of the elephantine proportions of the German tanks, baptized, they claim, with a six-syllable name as awkward as the instrument itself; an instrument of bluff, they concluded, unusable in practice. Henry Bidou's article of yesterday lets it be seen that besides these heavy tanks they used, against the English forces, tanks of another model, extremely rapid and light on the contrary, which did the

---

[9] *The Story of Scipio* is a section of the picaresque novel *Gil Blas* by Lesage, published in sections from 1715 to 1735.

greatest harm to our allies. The latter were likewise surprised by a new type of bomb-thrower, easily transportable and wonderfully suitable for sustaining an infantry attack. The English, not being forearmed against these new inventions, had to yield. . . . Everything convinces me that the victory, if there can ever be one, will be owing not to this or that's being used more judiciously, nor to aviation, nor to the superior valor of the troops — but rather to something or other that we don't yet know and that will cut up the adversary by surprise. Each successive German advance was always due to a surprise. We were first surprised by their machine-guns, then by their asphyxiating gases, etc., etc. The English could have obtained an extraordinary result if they had known better how to employ their tanks instead of gradually accustoming the enemy to them. For there is no device however subtle or strong against which one side or the other does not manage to defend itself. The victory will be due to an invention, to something surprising or other; and not so much to the army as to the scientist and the engineer.

But the maddening thing is to think that France is the home of inventors! One always gets back to this: we do not know how to take advantage of our resources.

But what is the good of writing all this?

11 May

If I could be sure of living twenty-five years more, it seems to me that then I should have enough; but that I shall not be satisfied with less.

17 May

Ah! it is already midsummer. My heart is nothing but a vast hymn of joy. . . .

I have worked a great deal these last few days and finished almost the first part of *L'Aveugle*.

19 May

Pentecost. I leave tomorrow for Paris. The countryside is overwhelmingly beautiful.

Saw M. for two days at Limoges, whence I return bursting with happiness. I am awaiting him.

31 May

Back to Cuverville by the first train from Les Ifs, where I spent the night.

1 June

I sometimes think, with horror, that the victory all our hearts wish France to have is that of the past over the future.

In Paris I read (in part) Douglas's abominable book, *Oscar Wilde and Myself.* Hypocrisy can go no further, nor falsehood be more impudent. It is a monstrous travesty of the truth, which filled me with disgust. Merely from the tone of his writing it seems to me that I should be aware he is lying, even if I had not been the direct witness of the acts of his life against which he protests and which he claims to whitewash. But even this is not enough for him. He claims that he was ignorant of Wilde's habits! and that he upheld him at first only because he thought him innocent! Whom will he convince? I do not know; but I hope not to die before having unmasked him. This book is a villainy.

2 June

The Germans are at Château-Thierry. Days of abominably anxious expectation. The fine weather has not ceased to favor them, the wind to blow against us. At times it seems as if there were something impious and desperate in our resistance, and this above all breaks my heart. Oh! I am speaking without mysticism. I mean that that *Liberty* we claim to represent and defend is most often but the right to have our own way, to please ourselves, and would be better named: insubordination. All around us I see nothing but disorder, disorganization, negligence, and waste of the most radiant virtues — only falsehood, politics, absurdity. Nothing is put in its place, nothing is properly employed, and the rarest elements and most worthy of triumphing become, through their misuse, suspect, harmful, and ruinous.

8 June

Busy these last few days perfecting *Corydon.* Most likely I shall still have many slight changes to make in the proofs and numerous additions to the appendix — but such as it is I could hand it over to the printer. I should have liked to have thirteen copies printed — not one more — and should have taken care of this at once if Gouchtenaere (Méral) were still in Paris and if his printer had not been upset by the bombardment.

I should likewise like to bring out before the end of this year:
A new edition of *Les Nourritures;*
The big edition of *Typhoon;*
The letters of Dupouey;
A third volume of *Prétextes;*
And an edition of three hundred copies of *Le Prométhée.*

Perhaps also my translation of *Antony and Cleopatra*. And finally I hope very much to have finished my *Symphonie pastorale*.[10]

18 June

I am leaving France in a state of inexpressible anguish. It seems to me that I am saying farewell to my whole past. . . .

* * *

Grantchester, 3 July

I took two puffs too many from the cigarette that is now burning out in the ashtray at my elbow; but the dizziness is not painful in which my mind whirls vaporously with the bluish volutes of smoke rising toward the white ceiling. I had the hideous photographs and prints taken down that covered the walls of this little room where nothing belongs to me and which I inhabit the more willingly the more completely my past is annihilated. My hostess has put some orange-colored lilies in the bowl where yesterday some flowers of which I don't know the name were wilting. On the mantel that clock which I vainly tried to stop is making a frightful tumult. The air is warm, the sky pure; time flies. I light another cigarette.

How much I like this remark of Hobbes which Aubrey repeats: "If I had read as much as others, I should not have known any more than they."

15 July

Returned the day before yesterday to Grantchester, which I had left on the 9th to meet Raverat. Talked at great length with him; read a great deal of poetry — I liked Marlowe's and Herrick's most of all.

Cambridge, 2 September

I have been living at Merton House for a fortnight. In all my life I have never been better set up, except of course at Cuverville and at the Villa. Norton, whose guest I am, is absent.

* * *

[10] A new edition of *The Fruits of the Earth* did appear in 1918, as did the translation of Conrad's *Typhoon* and the *Œuvres choisies* (*Selections*) of Walt Whitman. The *Lettres du Lieutenant de Vaisseau Dupouey* did not come out until 1922 and *Antoine et Cléopâtre* until 1921. A new edition of *Le Prométhée mal enchaîné* (*Prometheus Ill-Bound*) with thirty drawings by Pierre Bonnard was issued in 1920. *The Pastoral Symphony* was indeed finished in 1918.

Cuverville, 10 October

Back in harbor for several days now. I don't know whether or not I shall recover the constancy to keep this journal unbroken — as I did before my trip to England? . . .

Some difficulty in getting back to work; the books I have brought back from London interest me more than those I might write. Deplorable, but a passing state. Browning especially, of whom I am just finishing the biography (study by Chesterton [11]) and whom I am tackling everywhere at once. Amazing *Mr. Sludge, the "Medium"* — the short piece *Prospice* particularly touches me, and the wonderful opening of *The Worst of it*. Read likewise some poems from the end.

Laziness in making my thought explicit; tendency to prefer it left in the poetic state — I mean: nebulous. Struggle against this.

Obsessive fear of death and that the ground may suddenly give under my steps. I love life passionately, but I have ceased to have confidence in it. And yet this is necessary.

11 October

Spent considerable time yesterday evening with the beehive, which the bees have abandoned but which none the less contains several honeycombs heavy with honey.

Went on with *Sludge* and read to Em. the glorious *Prospice*. Reread the first hundred pages of the third volume of the *Littérature anglaise*.[12] I shudder at the thought that, later on, some Taine will judge our society according to the plays of Bernstein and Bataille, according to the Malvy and Steinheil trials, etc.[13] Written elsewhere some reflections on this subject.

12 October

Went over and corrected, these last few days, all I had written of *La Symphonie pastorale*. I have a good impression of it; but I find it harder to harness myself to it again in proportion as the subtle and

---

[11] Some very perspicacious remarks drowned in a flood of dialectic; exasperating need to convict some imaginary adversary of absurdity. A large number of his paragraphs begin thus: "This is a truth little understood in our time," etc. . . . , or "None of the students of Browning seems to have noticed . . ." sentences by means of which he seems to want to give rarity to what are often the most banal of remarks. I cannot endure this bluff. [A.]

[12] Taine's *History of English Literature*.

[13] In 1909 the trial and acquittal of Mme Japy Steinheil for the murder of her mother and husband caused a sensation throughout the world. In 1918 the Radical Minister of the Interior since 1914, Malvy, was tried for high treason and eventually convicted of malfeasance in office with a sentence of five years' banishment.

nuanced perfection that the subject demands is far from what I dream
of and long to realize today. I grow somewhat impatient against this
work that I must first finish.

Read with satisfaction Valery Larbaud's preface to the Whitman.[14]

13 October

It is from the point of view of art that it is most fitting to judge
what I write — a point of view the critic never, or almost never, takes.
And if, by a miracle, someone takes that point of view, he has the
greatest trouble getting his readers to accept it. It is, moreover, the
only point of view that does not exclude any of the others.

16 October

Eric Allégret and Domi, both on sick-leave, came to surprise us the
morning before yesterday. Gave Domi to read *How They Brought
the Good News from Ghent to Aix.*

Yesterday dragged around a rather severe headache all day long.
Yet I got back to my work. Perhaps I should not have been so willing
to leave it, last June, if I had foreseen that it would be so hard for me
to pick it up again. But was I capable, at that time, of reasoning, of
weighing, of calculating? . . . An irresistible fatality urged me on
and I should have sacrificed everything to meet M. — without even being aware that I was sacrificing anything to him.

Today I have the greatest difficulty getting interested again in the
state of mind of my minister, and I fear that the end of the book may
suffer from this. In an effort to give life to his thoughts again, I have
gone back to the Gospel and Pascal. But at one and the same time I
long to recapture a state of fervor and I do not want to be taken in by
it; I pull on the reins and wield the whip at the same time; and this
produces nothing worth while.

Reopened the piano and played some fugues from the *Well-
Tempered Clavichord* with the greatest contentment.

19 October

Reading and work. I am somewhat worried to see myself reach so
quickly the end of my *Symphonie pastorale;* I mean that I shall have
exhausted my subject while the proportions and equilibrium of the
book called for a more extended development. . . . But perhaps I am

---

[11] In 1918 Librairie de la *N.R.F.* published a selection of poetry and
prose by Walt Whitman entitled *Œuvres choisies* and translated by Jules
Laforgue, Louis Fabulet, André Gide, Valery Larbaud, Jean Schlumberger,
Francis Vielé-Griffin. Larbaud wrote the preface.

wrong; and, besides, the sudden change of situation could stand some expanding.

Read considerable Browning. Perhaps I shall use as an epigraph for the second part of my Memoirs this stanza from *By the Fire-side:*

> *My own, confirm me! If I tread*
> *This path back, is it not in pride*
> *To think how little I dreamed it led*
> *To an age so blest that, by its side,*
> *Youth seems the waste instead?* [15]

20

I am reading the life of Cardinal Manning in Lytton Strachey's *Eminent Victorians,* and Renan's *Souvenirs.* I can endure neither the flaccidity of his thought nor the amenity of his style. But this book nevertheless seems to me of great importance.

23

Read Browning's *Ivan Ivanovitch* and *Bishop Blougram's Apology.*

26

And while reading Browning (*Saul, Fra Lippo Lippi, Andrea del Sarto,* etc.), I thought: but we have Victor Hugo. Consequently, this morning, I pick up *La Légende des siècles* (Volume II of the little definitive edition) [16] and make a great effort to read *Eviradnus.* Appalled by the gigantic silliness of those sublime lines. Just imagine a foreigner plunged into that! Beyond the technical interest, what remains? — begging Souday's pardon. Beautiful lines, admirable lines (the envelope of the song of *Eviradnus* is extremely beautiful — and even particularly rare in quality), but of a beauty that is almost solely verbal and sonorous. One can imagine nothing more empty, more absurd . . . nor more splendid. [17]

DETACHED PAGES

I

All great works of art are rather difficult of access. The reader who thinks them easy has failed to penetrate to the heart of the work. That

---

[15] No epigraph is used for either Part I or Part II of *Si le grain ne meurt.* . . .

[16] Hugo's *Legend of the Centuries* is a collection of narrative poems on legendary and historical subjects.

[17] The poem *Eviradnus* is a heavy melodramatic narrative of medieval knights. Lines 640–710 contain a song in lyric stanzas together with four stanzas forming a frame for the song and setting the mood.

mysterious heart has no need of obscurity to defend it against an over-
bold approach; clarity does this well enough. Very great clarity, as it
often happens for the most beautiful works of French art, by Rameau,
Molière, or Poussin, is, to defend a work, the most specious girdle;
you come to doubt whether there is any secret there; it seems that you
touch the depths at once. But ten years later you return to it and
enter still more deeply.

It is for the same reasons that the French language at first seems
childishly easy to learn, then more and more difficult as you begin to
hear it better.

❊

Obviously what shocks me in the case of Romain Rolland is that he
has nothing to lose as a result of the war: his book (*Jean-Christophe*)
never seems better than when translated. I shall go further: he can
only gain by the disaster of France, by the disappearance of the
French language, and French art, and French taste, and all of those
gifts which he denies and which are denied him.

He is animated by such perfect good faith that at times he almost
disarms you. He is an unsophisticated person, but an impassioned unsophisticated person. He early took his frankness for virtue and, since
it is somewhat summary, he considered hypocrites those who were
less rudimentary than he. I am sure that too often his attitude was
permitted by a lack of sentiment and taste, even of comprehension
that the mind brings to art, to style, and to that sort of Atticism that
now has no other home but France. Nothing is more amorphous than
his book; it is a Kugelhupf [18] in which you sometimes encounter a good
raisin. No affectation, no artifice; I am well aware that this is why
some like him.

❊

The day that La Rochefoucauld bethought himself of referring and
reducing the impulses of our heart to the instigations of self-esteem,[19]
I doubt whether he so much revealed an extraordinary perspicacity or
simply nipped in the bud any attempt toward a more indiscreet investigation. Once the formula had been found, people held to it and
for over two centuries they lived with that explanation. The psychologist seemed most experienced who showed himself to be most skeptical and who, when faced with the noblest and most exhausting
gestures, was best able to expose the secret egotistical incentive.
Thanks to which everything contradictory in the human soul escapes

---

[18] A Kugelhupf is a German cake.
[19] Gide uses La Rochefoucauld's term: *amour-propre.*

him. And I do not blame him for exposing "amour-propre"; I blame
him often for stopping there; I blame him for thinking he has done
everything when he has exposed "amour-propre." I blame especially
those who came after him, for having stopped there.

One will find more profit in meditating this remark of Saint-
Évremond (which I deeply regret not finding in the selection published by the *Mercure* any more than in any anthology):

"Plutarch judged man too coarsely and did not think him so different as he is from himself: wicked, virtuous, equitable, unjust, hu-
mane, and cruel; *whatever seems contradictory to him he attributes to
outside causes*," etc. . . .

This is a wonderfully educative remark.

No theory is good unless it permits, not rest, but the greatest work.
No theory is good except on condition that one use it to go on beyond.
Darwin's theory, Taine's, Quinton's, Barrès's. . . . Dostoyevsky's greatness lies in the fact that he never reduced the world to a theory, that
he never let himself be reduced by a theory. Balzac constantly sought
a theory of passions; it was great luck for him that he never found it.

The most important discoveries are most often due only to *taking
into consideration* very small phenomena that had been previously
noticed only because they threw calculations off slightly, insensibly
crippled forecasts, imperceptibly tipped the arm of the scale.

I am thinking of the discovery of those new "simple bodies" in
chemistry, so hard to isolate. I am thinking especially of the decompo-
sition of elements, of "bodies" that chemistry considered as "simple"
until today. I am thinking that in psychology there are no simple feelings and that many discoveries in the heart of man remain to be made.

How much I like what Saint-Évremond says of Plutarch: ". . . I
think he could have gone further and penetrated more deeply into
human nature. There are recesses and deviations in our soul that
escaped him. . . . If he had defined Catiline, he would have presented him to us a miser or a prodigal: that man *alieni appetens, sui
profusus*,[20] was beyond his knowledge, and he would never have un-
tangled those contradictions that Sallust separated so well and that
Montaigne himself understood much better."

※

---

[20] "Avaricious of another man's property, extravagant of his own."

DIALOGUE BETWEEN RACINE AND FATHER BOUHOURS: [21]

BOUHOURS: "It is certainly regrettable that you were not able to remedy that repetition of sonorities that I already pointed out to you at the time of your first reading:

> *Vous mourûtes aux bords où vous fûtes laissée.* [22]

"Can it be that this does not bother you, who have sometimes been praised for your. . . ."

RACINE: "Grammar before harmony, my friend."

BOUHOURS: "Need you teach *me* this? And yet do you not think that you might conciliate them here?"

RACINE: "You know that in vain I strove to do so. I am speaking of the very line that grieves you, which, I confess, caused me much trouble at first."

BOUHOURS: "I suggested to you *'vous trouvâtes la mort'* instead of *'vous mourûtes'* [23] — or on the other hand to modify the second hemistich. Certainly you would have succeeded in doing so if you had not first told yourself that this was not possible."

RACINE: "I did not convince myself that this was not possible; but, as I sought to change the line in such a way as to spare delicate ears that repetition of sonorities of which you complain, I came to wonder whether or not it was really necessary to go to so much trouble in an effort to avoid a repetition resulting from the most prompt and most natural way of expressing oneself. Even more, I soon became convinced that some might find in that very repetition a certain charm; and I confess that I myself, by dint of repeating the line over and over, eventually found some in it."

BOUHOURS: "One can convince oneself of anything one wishes."

RACINE: "Do not push me too far or I shall soon tell you, and shall in fact convince myself, that I wrote that line precisely for the repeti-

---

[21] "Corneille and Racine followed the rule; they did not make it. If, later on, through the influence of their genius, they became linguistic authorities, in their lifetime they humbly corrected themselves, one to satisfy Vaugelas and the other out of respect for Father Bouhours, official corrector of the noble style." Brunot, Preface to *Histoire de la langue française* (*History of the French Language*), p. xv. [A.]

[22] "You succumbed on the shores where you were abandoned." Spoken by Phædra about her sister Ariadne, this is one of the lines of Racine's *Phèdre* most famous for their beauty.

[23] This change would substitute "you found death" for the more direct "you died" or "you succumbed." In the original dialogue both speakers, but particularly Father Bouhours, speak in a fashion that seems rather stilted today.

tion, on the contrary, and that it is that repetition that I particularly like in it."

BOUHOURS: "If you have gone that far, you have no further use for my advice."

❅

I believe that there is in the formation of a great man something particularly *well timed* [24] and that his work often owes to its timeliness a share of its greatness. In our time Molière would perhaps have made fun of Verlaine, and that would have been unfortunate; whereas it was good that he made fun of Vadius.[25] His admirable qualities were particularly to be appreciated at a time when they were the ones that were needed (but isn't common sense always needed?). And that sort of joy, full of a rather trivial wisdom, a rather crude art, a rather heavy wit (which I like so much, in him), I do not say that they would be less fashionable today, but I doubt that they could produce, today, works of art as accomplished as they could in his time, and likely to win the approval of the best and most various minds.

I say all this, but, while I am writing it down, I am less sure of it; for after all if Mirbeau is not Molière, it behooved him not to show us this so clearly. — All one can say, probably, is that the great man is the one whose qualities are most favored by the epoch, and that there exists between it and him a sort of complicity.

❅

In these lines of Baudelaire:
> *Là, tout n'est qu'ordre et beauté,*
> *Luxe, calme et volupté,*[26]

in which the inattentive reader sees only a cascade of words, I see the perfect definition of the work of art. I take each one of these words separately, next I admire the garland they form and the effect of their conjunction; for no one of them is useless and each of them is exactly in its place. I should quite willingly take them as titles of the successive chapters of a treatise on æsthetics:

1. *Order* (logic, reasonable disposition of the parts);

---

[24] This expression is in English in the original.

[25] In *Les Femmes savantes* (*The Learned Ladies*) Molière ridicules the pedantic poetaster of his time in the person of two characters named Vadius and Trissotin.

[26] *There, all is order and beauty,*
Luxury, calm, and voluptuousness.

These lines form the refrain of the famous *Invitation au voyage*, which has been several times set to music.

2. *Beauty* (line, dash, profile of the work);

3. *Luxury* (disciplined richness);

4. *Calm* (tranquilization of the tumult);

5. *Voluptuousness* (sensuality, adorable charm of matter, attractiveness).

❈

The novelist does not long to see the lion eat grass. He realizes that one and the same God created the wolf and the lamb, then smiled, "seeing that his work was good."

❈

I have not read M. V. de Pallarès's book against Nietzsche; but, in *La Coopération des idées,* on the subject of this book, a few pages by M. G. Deherme, who approves it while wondering, to begin with, whether Nietzsche is important enough to make it worth while speaking of him: [27]

"In order properly to appreciate the work of Nietzsche, one must first know what the man was. M. de Pallarès shows us Nietzsche as a prodigal son (or child prodigy?), a disciple of Schopenhauer and Wagner, a critic turning furiously against his master, against his friend of yesterday, suffering in every nerve, a megalomaniac, an evangelist, a Zarathustra, then sinking into complete madness twelve years before dying. Impulsive, unstable, obsessed, neurasthenic, a drug-addict, he was a weak man and an aboulic type. This is why he speaks exclusively of what he most lacks: strength and will."

This is the accusation that was hurled at the Crucified One: "If thou art the Christ, save thyself!" I recognize it. I am not comparing Christ with Nietzsche — even though M. Binet-Sanglé showed us some time ago that the Nazarene too was simply a sick man and a madman! — I am merely comparing that absurd accusation which is hurled against them and which proceeds from the selfsame lack of understanding. It is customary in our epoch to seek a physiological cause for intellectual impulses; and I am not saying that this is wrong; but I am saying that it is wrong to try to invalidate thereby the intrinsic value of the thought.

It is *natural* that any great moral reform, what Nietzsche would call any transmutation of values, should be due to a physiological *lack of balance.* In well-being thought is at rest, and so long as the state of things satisfies it, thought cannot propose changing it. (I mean: the

---

[27] In 1894 Georges Deherme, who was to found popular universities for free discussion and the promulgation of his positivist doctrines, started a publication entitled *Intellectual Co-operation.*

inner state, for as to the external, or social, state, the reformer's motive is quite different; the former are chemists, the latter mechanicians.) At the origin of a reform there is always a discomfort; the discomfort from which the reformer suffers is that of an inner lack of balance. Densities, positions, moral values are different as he sees them, and the reformer works to reconcile them again; he aspires to a new equilibrium; his work is simply an attempt at reorganization, according to his reason, his logic, of the disorder he feels within him; for a disordered state is intolerable to him. And I am not saying, of course, that it is enough to be unbalanced to become a reformer — but rather that every reformer is, to begin with, unbalanced.

I do not know that there can be found a single one among those who have offered humanity new evaluations in whom these Messrs. Binet-Sanglés cannot discover, and quite rightly, what they would perhaps call a blemish — what I should like to call simply: a provocation. Socrates, Mahomet, St. Paul, Rousseau, Dostoyevsky, Luther — M. Binet-Sanglé has only to enumerate them, to suggest still others; there is not one of them that I should not recognize as abnormal.

And of course it is possible *after these men* to think as they do without being unbalanced oneself; but it is an unbalanced state that in the beginning brought these thoughts to our rescue, which the reformer needed to re-establish in him the broken equilibrium. It was necessary in fact that, in the beginning, one should be ill to permit, later on, the health of many. Rousseau without his madness would have been only a crude Cicero; and it is precisely in Nietzsche's madness that I see the certificate of his authentic greatness.

Concerning Maurice Barrès

What he calls the "Protestant spirit" is that "dangerous" spirit of equity that made the Jansenists write:

"To whatever order or nation you belong, you must believe only what is true and what you would be disposed to believe if you belonged to another nation, another order, another profession. . . ."

And again:

"We judge of things, not by what they are in themselves, but by what they are in regard to us: and truth and usefulness are for us but one and the same thing." (*Logique de Port-Royal,* Part III, chapter xix, § 1.) [28]

What the great Arnauld deplores as he notes it Barrès uses as the basis of his ethics.

---

[28] *The Logic of Port-Royal* by Antoine Arnauld is one of the capital documents of the Jansenist movement of the seventeenth century, which was so bitterly opposed by the Jesuits until its beliefs were declared heretical.

For greater utility Barrès depicted as Kantian and German, or as Protestant and anti-French — and consequently to be shunned — that form of thought which is properly Jansenist and more profoundly French, on the other hand, than the Jesuit form of thought in opposition to which it is always pictured.

II

IN AN ALBUM . . .

To the memory of Émile Verhaeren

February (1918)

A little country whose vast horizon pushes its frontier to the edge of the sky and whence the soul springs forth with ease; a sky, and often a fog that forces one to seek the sun within oneself, in which the impassioned wind reigns supreme; a black soil, rich in latent ardor, in secret fervor, and in concentrated energy; an excessive toil that keeps the muscles taut and makes man find his greatest beauty in effort; and then nevertheless comfort but without flabbiness; luxury but without complacency; voluptuousness without languor.

And you, great overpopulous cities, crowded harbors, and especially you, well-off, clean little towns, well painted and well drawn, still quiet just yesterday, at peace with men and trusting God — today ground down, painful, having had to pay for imaginary debts, having an immense injustice and a bad quarrel to settle. . . .

I see all this again in your living eyes, Verhaeren, great departed friend, more living today, more vivid by your absence than when we knew you to be among us — I hear a great love singing, and a great indignation, in your more active voice, which knows nothing of death.

❋

You would like to know what to believe in regard to my political opinions. It seemed to you that too often, to the right or the left I took one step forward only to take two backward immediately after, so that nothing was less trustworthy than the declarations I might have made. This is just why I did not make any, knowing full well the indecision of my mind, but nevertheless believing that indecision preferable to inconstancy.

To tell the truth, political questions do not much interest me; I have trouble convincing myself that one regime is preferable in itself; and if I get to the point of wishing France a king, even if he were a despot, this is because everything proves to me, alas, that of all the peoples I know, the Frenchman is the one who most lacks a feeling of the public weal and of that solidarity without which a republic results in the greatest prejudice to all.

Yes, political questions interest me less, and I believe them less important, than social questions; and social questions less important than moral questions. For after all I hold it a fact that the "bad organization," of which people are constantly complaining here, can be most often imputed to the negligence or lack of conscience of the employees, from the most modest to the highest, in the exercise of their functions. It is not so much the system as man himself that must be reformed, and Paul Valéry seems to me on the right track when he protested, the other day, that the most important ministry was that of education.

I am well aware that if the very stuff of the mind is bad, nothing good can be embroidered on it; but it is not proved that the stuff is bad. It seems to me that here, as so often in France, it is not so much the scarcity that is to be deplored as the bad utilization of what we have.

⁂

The French nationalist can be recognized by his love for what is Spanish. Happily he can be recognized by a few other signs as well.

The nationalist has a broad hatred and a narrow love. He cannot stifle a predilection for dead cities. His most violent hatred is directed against the French literary provinces that do not belong to France — I mean Belgium and Switzerland in particular. He regrets that all French Protestants are not Swiss, because he has a mind that likes simplification and he hates Protestants as much as he does the Swiss.

The nationalist is quite willing to believe that Christ was a Catholic.

If you have any love for your country, you will find in yourself more than one idea in common with them, but the nationalist cannot endure having any idea in common with you.

⁂

MORÉAS

In the whole history of our literature there is perhaps no example of a more secretly musical poetry and one of which the personal resource seems to depend more intimately on the French language itself.[29] If Moréas had been unrecognized, I should have enjoyed devoting to Les Stances abundant praises, in which my heart would have spoken as freely as my brain.

Today when our unbalanced country is letting itself be led by its southern provinces and expects to find its salvation in that depolarization, it is doubtless hard to bring out all the strangeness that poetry

---

[29] Born in Athens as Iannis Papadiamantopoulos, Moréas was inspired with a love of French literature by a French governess; he did not settle in France until he was over twenty.

contains for a specifically French mind. All the harder, since professional nationalism, exaggerating its hostility toward northern influences, reviling for this reason a Verhaeren, a Vielé-Griffin, is powerless to resist whatever comes from the south. And I am well aware that we have never received from Greece but what was pure and harmonious (just as, of late, nothing has come from Italy but tinsel); but that very harmony, so suave, is permitted only by the sacrifice, or disdain, or ignorance, of some other French qualities, indispensable to the equilibrium of France: the very ones that are represented by our lost provinces.

And this is indeed the saddest result of that loss; not only are those qualities or virtues insufficiently represented in France at present, but also France is no longer aware of her lack, is learning to get along without them, is denying them. The very genius of France lay in that equilibrium which constituted our greatness, our beauty; such a rare realization of equilibrium that was just as completely broken by the enormous victory of the French Empire and its dangerous additions as, since 1870, by the loss of an indispensable province – a province of the French spirit.

※

I consider liberty as a fearful and disastrous thing that one must try to reduce or suppress in oneself first – and even, if one can, in others. The frightening thing is imposed slavery, to which no consent is required; the excellent thing is self-imposed slavery; and for lack of something better: the slavery to which one submits. Oh, voluntary servitude!

When a Francis Jammes relies on Catholicism, this is because he finds nothing in himself capable of dominating his license, I mean his exuberance of gifts.

I like to serve; I do not like to be a slave; slave to my past, slave to my future plans, slave to my faith, to my doubt, to my hatred, or to my love.

If I like to serve, whether a creature or a thought, and to renounce myself through love, I intend that the lease, freely consented to, should be constantly renewable and that reason or love should constantly dictate the clauses to me anew.

※

CORYDON

I do not feel any imperious attraction (toward this book). It is undeniable that I am writing it out of season and when I have ceased to have any need to write it. This is what I explained yesterday to

Marcel Drouin, fearing that he might see in it some almost unhealthy obsession, an impossibility of getting my mind off this subject. But, on the other hand, the difficulty comes rather from the fact that I must artificially revive a problem to which I have found (as far as I am concerned) a practical solution, so that, to tell the truth, it no longer bothers me.

All my will-power is needed to keep me at this work, in which I seek no advantage. (Likewise for *La Porte étroite*. Only what has ceased to serve is a suitable subject for art.)

What made me undertake it at first, or at least gave me the first rudimentary idea of it, was the disavowal of that false holiness with which my disdain for ordinary temptation clothed me (in the eyes of J., for instance, and which she used to help crush M. by comparison).

You meditate for months; in you an idea becomes flesh; it palpitates, it lives, you caress it; you adopt it intimately; you know its contours, its limits; its deficiencies, its reliefs, its recesses; at once its genealogy and its descendants (?). As soon as you present in public some exposé of this prolonged meditation, immediately a critic rises up to declare in peremptory fashion that you know nothing about it, and he does so in the name of common sense, that is to say of the most general opinion, that is to say the most conventional — to get away from which your entire effort tended.

Had Socrates and Plato not loved young men, what a pity for Greece, what a pity for the whole world!

Had Socrates and Plato not loved young men and aimed to please them, each one of us would be a little less sensible.

If only, instead of getting angry, people tried to find out what is being discussed. Before discussing, one ought always to define. Most quarrels amplify a misunderstanding.

I call a *pederast* the man who, as the word indicates, falls in love with young boys. I call a *sodomite* ("The word is *sodomite*, sir," said Verlaine to the judge who asked him if it were true that he was a *sodomist*) the man whose desire is addressed to mature men.

I call an *invert* the man who, in the comedy of love, assumes the role of a woman and desires to be possessed.

These three types of *homosexuals* are not always clearly distinct; there are possible transferences from one to another; but most often the difference among them is such that they experience a profound disgust for one another, a disgust accompanied by a reprobation that in no way yields to that which you (heterosexuals) fiercely show toward all three.

The pederasts, of whom I am one (why cannot I say this quite simply, without your immediately claiming to see a brag in my confession?), are much rarer, and the sodomites much more numerous, than I first thought. I speak of this on the basis of the confidences I have received, and am willing to believe that in another time and in another country it would not have been the same. As to the inverts, whom I have hardly frequented at all, it has always seemed to me that they alone deserved the reproach of moral or intellectual deformation and were subject to some of the accusations that are commonly addressed to all homosexuals.

I add this, which may seem specious but which I believe altogether exact: that many heterosexuals, either through diffidence or through semi-impotence, behave in relation to the other sex like women and, in an apparently "normal" pair, play the role of true inverts. One is tempted to call them *male Lesbians*. Dare I say that I believe them to be very numerous?

It is the same as with religion. The kindest thing those who have it can do for those who don't is to pity them.

"But we are not to be pitied. We are not unhappy."

"All the more unhappy since you don't know that you are. We shall cease to pity you, then. We shall detest you."

We are accepted if we are plaintive; but if we cease to be pitiable we are at once accused of arrogance. No, not at all, I assure you. We are merely what we are; we simply admit what we are, without priding ourselves on it, but without grieving about it either.

That such loves can spring up, that such relationships can be formed, it is not enough for me to say that this is natural; I maintain that it is good; each of the two finds exaltation, protection, a challenge in them; and I wonder whether it is for the youth or the elder man that they are more profitable.

M. taxes me with having badly economized my appeal to the emotions since I exhaust it in the beginning of the book, so that I cease to stir as soon as I try to persuade. This is because I am addressing myself and wish to address myself to the head and not to the heart; this is because I do not seek to win over the reader's sympathy, which would run the risk of becoming indulgence; and it is precisely because, as I am well aware, certain words springing from the heart would touch the reader more deeply than all these more or less specious reasonings — it is precisely for this reason that I have kept from using those words. Compare the device of the lawyer who tries to pass off his client's crime as one prompted by jealousy. I do not

want any of that. I intend that this book should be written coldly,
deliberately, and that this should be evident. Passion must have preceded it or at most be implied in it; but above all it must not serve as
an excuse for the book. I do not want to move to pity with this book;
I want to EMBARRASS.[30]

⁎

FRANCE AND GERMANY

The nationalist parties, on both sides of the frontier, vie with each
other in exaggerating the differences of temperament and mind that,
according to them, would make any understanding between Frenchmen and Germans impossible. It is certain that differences do exist;
they are known moreover; some writers have detailed them master-
fully and I do not have to speak of them here. I believe, however, that
they are less fundamental and native than jealously magnified by the
family upbringing, the teaching of the schools, and finally the press.
During the war I saw the people of our countryside get along very
well with the German prisoners employed in agriculture. On the other
hand, it is rare that a Frenchman traveling in Germany was not struck
and charmed by the graciousness of the people toward him, regard-
less of the social class to which they belonged. In the domain of culture, just as much in the sciences as in arts and letters, the shortcomings and advantages on both sides are complementary to such a degree
that there can only be advantage in an understanding, and prejudice
in a conflict.

I cannot, alas! forget that the present problem does not concern
simply direct relations among individuals. To be sure, a writer does
not have the competence necessary to establish the precise conditions
of a political agreement between states, but he has the right and the
duty to state to what a degree that understanding seems to him desirable; let me go farther and say: *indispensable* in the present situation of Europe.

There is no more fatal error today, both for nations and for individuals, than to believe that they can get along without one another.
Everything that sets the interests of France and Germany in opposition to one another is injurious to both countries at once; beneficial,
on the contrary, everything that tends to bring those interests closer
together.

It is properly the dispute between the colossal and the individual,

---

[30] The fact that this paragraph is found among the "Detached Pages"
following the year 1911 is an example of the slight errors in dating that
crept into the Paris edition.

as it has been said. Everything French tends to individualize itself; everything German, to dominate or to submit.

Many inanities have been said and written against individualism — by those who did not understand or were unwilling to recognize that the triumph of the individual is in the divine word of the Gospel: "Whosoever shall seek to save his life shall lose it; and whosoever shall lose his life shall preserve it."

As soon as the cliché of "localized invasion" had been hit upon, events began to look better. Before that, people had said: "to hold out is to win," and a little later: "the German army absorbed by France."

I heard a Belgian lady near me express her annoyance at those five thousand francs promised to the first soldier to capture an enemy flag.

"To win a flag they would be willing to lose a battle. Oh, the others are well aware of that! It's just like the Mulhouse business; any other nation would have avoided such a thing. Three quarters of the mistakes made in France are due to love of the dramatic remark or gesture. Oh, don't get the idea that such motives mean anything to them! *They* are practical, and *you* are romantic. Ah, you certainly deserve Rostand! The white plume, champagne, whatever suits that incurable triviality which makes you joke under a rain of bullets and never admit that the others are prepared . . . and besides, you count too much on chance. Self-confidence is a good thing, but especially when it is justified." [31]

To tell the truth, the duties toward the state are those that I took longest and had the greatest difficulty to learn. For a long time I remained in regard to them in that naïve state of confidence of the child who fancies that his morning chocolate reaches his daily table hot by virtue of some cosmic necessity. It is good for the education of the child that, as a result of some family disturbance, his chocolate should from time to time be upset. The fear of not having any more chocolate at all is salutary.

France nevertheless has had great navigators. She does not lack Bougainvilles and La Pérouses. But it seems that our schoolboys are ignorant of them, and the virtue of the adventurers had not until very recently awakened any great echo in our literature. The sea wind that I breathe deeply in so many English-language books (and I do not say simply English books in order not to exclude probably the most

[31] The preceding three paragraphs, which reproduce almost textually a passage already given under date of 4 September 1914, illustrate the slight disorder in classifying the wartime pages that has been mentioned in the initial "Note."

glorious of all, *Moby Dick*), that air loaded with strange perfumes, with storms and near-shipwrecks and sprays. . . .

Specifically French remarks:

"All the misfortune of men comes from a single thing, which is not knowing how to remain at rest, in a room." [32]

"Henceforth I'll not stir, and I'll be a hundred times better off." [33]

"What the devil was he going to do in that galley?" [34]

"Let us cultivate our garden." [35]

"How can one be a Persian?" [36]

"Man . . . always bears the punishment for having wanted to change places." (Ironic in Baudelaire.)

"The earth and the dead." [37]

"He didn't *have* to go there." [38]

Etc. . . .

RELIGION

Catholicism has linked to the figure of Christ and to his teaching a whole procession of ideas and a whole set of attitudes, so closely that it is today very difficult to reject the one without the other, and so exclusively that any other thought that does not belong to the procession, that any other attitude that does not enter the order of the ceremony, immediately seems injurious to Christ Himself; so that without being a Catholic one cannot be a Christian. Yet as for these attacks against Christianity, Christ never deserved them, but the Church did; and everything I think against it today, I do so with Him.

I have often said to Claudel:

"What withholds me is not freethought, but the Gospel."

"Withholds you from what?"

"Why, from entering the Church, of course! Catholics do not know the Gospel. And they not only don't know it, they don't know that

---

[32] Famous maxim by Pascal.

[33] The conclusion of "The Man Who Chases after Dame Fortune" and returns home empty-handed after braving the perils of travel and distant risks in La Fontaine's *Fables*, VII, 12.

[34] The refrain of the father's lament in *Les Fourberies de Scapin* by Molière when Scapin tells him that his son was taken hostage while visiting a Turkish galley.

[35] The last words and moral, as it were, of Voltaire's *Candide*.

[36] The summary of the Parisian attitude to the Persian visitor in *Les Lettres persanes* (*The Persian Letters*) by Montesquieu.

[37] The most famous slogan of Barrès's nationalism.

[38] Refrain of a popular song.

they don't know it; they honestly believe they know it, so that they continue not to know it."

"It is," Ghéon said to me with the zeal of a neophyte, "the great error of Protestantism to want to limit revelation to the Gospels alone, not to understand that God continues to be in direct relation with listening humanity. The word of God is not confined to the Gospels, and God continues to explain himself, expressing himself just as much in the Pope's latest encyclical as in the very words of Christ; and the Church does not cease to be divinely inspired. Seeing an opposition between this and that proves that one has understood neither one nor the other," he says.

The Church is in possession of the Gospels. She alone is qualified to decide as to the meaning of Christ's words. She reserves and arrogates to herself the right of interpreting, and declares any man a heretic who listens to God directly.

I do not know whether or not the words that P. S. attributes to Maurras are authentic (very poor article in the *Journal de Genève* of 19 February 1917) — in any case they are very significant:

"I shall not leave this learned retinue of Fathers, of councils, of popes, and of all the great men of the modern élite *just to trust myself to the Gospels of four obscure Jews.*"

They throw light upon and give weight to the conversation I had last autumn with Ghéon:

"What you call specifically 'the word of Christ' I cannot consider as any more important or any more authentic than the whole tradition that followed it. The word of Christ is *all that* at one and the same time, and I cannot admit that he speaks more or better in the Gospels than he does in any encyclical whatever."

Ghéon passed through Paris again. Last night he came to dinner at rue Claude Lorrain, where I have been a boarder of the Théos for three weeks. I was expecting encouragement, support, consolation from this meeting; it brought me only sorrow, a profound and secret sorrow like a loss one could not admit. Everything in his words and gestures, to me who know him so well, breathed resolve, restraint, a cue, and the advice of a "superior."

"But shan't you be led by a parallel development to consider hell as immanent so to speak and already find in present life the immediate realization of its horror?"

"I grant that every clear-sighted sinner can immediately taste the complete presentiment of hell. And isn't it already hell just to know the place of rest, to know the way there, and the gate, and to remain excluded? to feel the bright light of love grow dim, the screen of flesh grow thicker, that flesh constantly grow heavier and oneself become ever more attached to it. In regard to hell, people always speak of stagnation and make of that absence of progress the last degree of the horrible. . . ."

Hell — as well as paradise — is within us. Milton expresses it admirably in this line, when he makes Satan himself say:

Which way I fly is Hell; myself am Hell.

(*Paradise Lost*, iv, 75.) [39]

❈

"One of the worst intellectual dishonesties is to play on words, to present Christianity as imposing almost no sacrifice on the reason and, by means of that artifice, to draw to it people who do not know to what they are binding themselves after all. That is the illusion of secular Catholics who claim to be liberal. Knowing neither theology nor exegesis, they make of adherence to Christianity a mere adherence to a coterie. They take what they want and leave the rest; they admit this or that dogma and reject another, and then later on they get angry when they are told that they are not true Catholics." (RENAN: *Souvenirs*, p. 300.)

❈

Somewhat disappointed by your article. But no, my friend, alas no! The problem is not so simple as you make it. You denounce only the most elementary form of religion. No, it is not always that. The noble and disinterested forms are even more dangerous and perfidious, for they are addressed to the élite. The idea of bargaining never entered into the religion I knew; no, not even the idea of a simple reward. And I recall that this is precisely what Claudel complained of after reading *La Porte étroite*. This, according to him, was just where the Protestant error lay; he did not consent to see in that very disinterestedness anything but pride.

---

[39] The quotation appears in English.

1919

Long explanation-plea with André Ruyters, whom I had the extraordinary luck to find alone. Glad to have finally been able to talk to him, but not altogether satisfied with the manner.

The point of view of almost every one of my friends changes extraordinarily with age; they all have a tendency to blame me for my constancy and the fidelity of my thoughts. It seems to them, naturally, that I was unable to learn anything from life, and because they thought it prudent to grow old, they consider my *imprudence* as madness.

A sentence from Eugène Rouart's letter that I have just received is revelatory: "I am pleased," he says, "that Ghéon, without any close family responsibilities, has been able to recover the tradition of his fathers, and . . . (illegible word) wisely; he had to find his limits," etc. Oh, how sad all this is! What sophisms to hide from oneself one's failure! My God, preserve me from intellectual wrinkles! And above all keep me from not recognizing them as wrinkles!

                                                                  22

Luncheon at Armenonville with Mme Mayrisch, Mme Théo Van Rysselberghe, Lady Rothermere, and Paul Méral. The last is surely intelligent, but human matter is for him without weight and without pain, a mere object of speculation, like all the rest. He does not experience enough difficulty pushing his thought to its logical conclusions. As for me, I feel that I have done nothing until I have dragged my reader along with me with all his load of reticences and objections.

It is the same here as with the mountain-climbing trips on which little Gérard was amazed that I wanted Em. to accompany me. — "You would go so much farther if you were willing to go alone," he used to tell me, and in her presence. — Of course, I know that; but what matters to me is not going far myself, but rather taking someone else along.

                                                                  23

Jean Schlumberger came to the Villa yesterday to give a reading of his novel, in the presence of Mme Mayrisch and Mme Théo.

Jean is certainly more embarrassed than aided by the abundance of his memories. To be sure, he arranges them and dresses them up adroitly; but he has not sufficiently digested all that.[1]

---

[1] I have reread the book since. It doesn't seem to me that what I wrote above is quite fair. The whole book strikes me as much better today than at

26 July. On arriving at Dudelange

Not a day passes but what I say to myself: all the same, old man, take care, for tomorrow you might wake up mad, idiotic, or not wake up at all. That marvel which you call your body, that even more astonishing marvel, your mind — just think what a little accident would suffice to put their machine out of order! Already I am full of admiration when, without holding onto the bannister, you go down the stairs; you might stumble, bash your head in, and that would be the end. . . . The idea of death follows my thought as the shadow follows my body; and the greater the joy, the light, the blacker the shadow.

7 August

I have abandoned this notebook for the other one, in which I am noting, inch by inch,[2] each progress of my novel.[3]

Drama at the A.'s; storm that was waiting only for E.'s return before bursting — or rather, for this is not fair: I had to open his eyes; his blindness was such. . . . To what a point the vision of suprasensible things can take you in with regard to the daily realities! Shall I speak of the *dazzlement* of faith? No, that is saying too much; there is rather a progressive deadening of the critical sense. It is just as hard for certain minds, accustomed from childhood to regard as established and indisputable certain moral and social ideas, to consider them as arbitrary — as for the musician, raised from childhood in the habit of the diatonic scale, to tell himself that that succession of sounds is not fatal, does not exist outside of him, and that, after all, those intervals according to which he constructs his symphony are conventional, and that the need he feels of hearing the leading note be followed by the higher half-note of the tonic is something acquired.

"But," it will be argued, "all music is built upon that."

"Yes, my friend, that of your country, of your epoch, but go to China or Egypt and you shall see that a different music can be built upon a scale with different intervals. No natural law is involved here, such as that of gravity, which the architect cannot escape. There is no law of harmony that the musician *cannot* escape; there is no 'moral law' that the real psychologist must and can accept as *given*."

first — and even a most remarkable book. [A.] The book in question is doubtless *Un Homme heureux* (*A Happy Man*), first published in 1921.

[2] This expression appears in English.

[3] *Le Journal des Faux-Monnayeurs* (*The Counterfeiters' Daybook*). [A.]

1920

Left Cuverville at dawn. Rather dull trip. Read some excellent pages of Walter Pater in his *Renaissance*.

Stopped at the Allégrets'. Received the last proofs of *Si le grain ne meurt. . . .*[1]

Sunday, 9 May

Went to take my trunk to the Villa. Afternoon spent with the A. M.'s, who drag us to a luxurious and deadly cinema where we bore ourselves to death for two hours. M. meets Emmanuel Faÿ there, a friend worthy of M. and of whom I should like not to be jealous. Go away crushed by the stupidity of the film and the irritating mannerism of the star, Mary Pickford, whose praises M. sang.

At the Villa, where I go to spend the first night, nothing works properly. This morning I had to hurry and get the plumbers in order to have gas.

I am noting all this in order to prime this notebook again. Do not know whether or not I shall have the constancy to carry it on very far. It seems to me that, at the present moment, this mirror gets in my way instead of being a help.

Tuesday

Yesterday came home too tired to write anything. I had lunched at the Drouins', then attended the first stage rehearsal of *Antoine et Cléopâtre*. The actors' monotonous delivery equalizes the text and sandpapers it, so to speak. It does not seem that any of them is sensitive to the beauty of words in themselves. It is like the roller that is pushed over the clods of earth after plowing. I am surrounded by twenty-five men who would be my enemies if it were *my* play that I had to defend. Yet each one of them is charming and is obviously doing his best. But I am once more convinced of the impossibility of making a play a work of art.

I shall attend all these rehearsals, for my education; but the gap is too great; they can do what they want with the play; its staging bores me and I have completely lost interest in that "realization."

Today went after Drésa, whom I had not found in his studio yesterday. There is a misunderstanding between Ida Rubinstein and him as to the costumes; as to hers at least, for she claims to be delighted with all the others. It is a question of letting Drésa decide as to the tones of the gowns that Worth is to design and make. I make some

---

[1] His Memoirs, entitled in English *If It Die. . . .*

diplomatic efforts between them, while not giving a damn about the result.

This morning at the *N.R.F.*, where Trevelyan, with whom I am lunching, picks me up. Then rehearsal. Then visit, with Ida, to the business man who is to handle the dispute. All this takes a dreadful amount of time. I should most likely have done better to go away on a trip.

While waiting for M., I am rereading Baudelaire's intimate journals. Incomparable distress of that soul, every one of whose efforts is a desperate one. Souday, the other day in *Le Temps,* tried to prove that Baudelaire is only a "false thinker." Why "false"? Baudelaire is not a "thinker" at all. Obviously, seen from that point of view, not a line of these journals that is not lamentably silly. Baudelaire's value is above all of an emotive nature.

Sunday

Letter from Ghéon in reply to the one I wrote him from Cuverville. He argues in favor of the "Christian sentiment" he claims to find in Shakespeare's drama. His good faith is complete. (I was able to chat with him that same evening.) A second part of his letter deplores affectionately the fact that I have not yet produced the "great work" of which he knows me to be capable. His reflections on this subject, to which we returned in the conversation we had in the evening, stir me rather deeply, but leave me perplexed; for, after all, I see what he means by a "great work" and that, for instance, Montaigne's *Essais* do not have a right to this designation.

I read in Montesquieu's *Correspondance* (Vol. II, p. 592): "There is a radical vice in France in this domain (education), and that vice is ineradicable because it stems from women. They who get mixed up in everything, they who eventually spoil everything, destroy everything. A child is soon corrupted in their hands, from the age of two to the age of six." See the rest.

Paris, 3 October

I pick up this notebook again after a very long interruption. Back in Paris for three days now; settled fairly well in the Villa; obliged to go out for my meals, busy from morning until night, I succeed only with great difficulty in saving a few moments of solitude and leisure. Yet never have I felt more fit, and the very evening of my arrival, despite my fatigue (or perhaps because of it), I should have written all night long if I had not forced myself to sleep.

Finished *Crochet Castle* by Peacock and began *The Old Wives' Tale.*[2]

---

[2] By Arnold Bennett.

Obtained the six-thousand-franc fellowship for Rivière.[3]

I pick up this notebook without trying to go back to yesterday; I am writing today as if I had written in it the day before.

Tuesday, 4 October

Lunched with Charlie Du Bos. Talked at great length of Henry James and of himself. Spent the late afternoon at the Villa going over with M. the photographs from the museums of Vienna and Berlin. I love that attention, ever greater the more informed it is, with which M. looks at everything, and I already admire the sureness of his taste and judgment. The day before we had been to the Cluny Museum in the morning, and to the Jacquemart-André Museum in the afternoon.

5 October

Lunched at Martin du Gard's with his friend Marcel de Coppet, on his way through Paris and about to return to the Chad region, where he has already spent four years in succession. Handsome face of a bishop with already completely white hair. His calm in contrast to our bustle. Most interesting conversation (which Gallimard joined, after the meal), that I should have noted down that very evening.

The 6th, day of my departure for Cuverville, Roger Martin du Gard comes to the Villa at nine thirty. He brings back *Si le grain ne meurt . . .* of which I had taken him a copy two days before. He informs me of his deep disappointment: I have side-stepped my subject; from fear, modesty, anxiety about the public, I have dared to say nothing really intimate and only succeeded in raising questions. . . .

Since I have been here, received from him a long, excellent letter in which he goes over all the points our conversation had touched upon. Yet I feel that I have related of my childhood everything of which I have any recollection and as indiscreetly as possible. It would be artificial to put more shadow, more secret, more deviation into it. Perhaps, however, Jacques Raverat is right when he tells me (he came yesterday from Montivilliers) that often my account, in an effort to be clear, simplifies my acts a bit too much, or at least my motives — and that it is true here as it is of all my books, each one of which taken by itself falsifies my figure. "In order to have a somewhat lifelike portrait of you," he told me very correctly, "one would have to be able to read them all at once. As soon as one knows you well, one understands that all of the states which, out of regard for art, you depict as successive can be simultaneous in you; and this is just what your Memoirs do not make one feel."

[3] Jacques Rivière received in 1920 the General Pershing Fellowship offered by the Fondation Blumenthal (6,000 francs a year) to a French citizen having contributed signally to French thought or art.

Cuverville, 11 October

The children (Odile and Jacques) have left two goldfish here; Em. put them, with a big stone and a bit of moss, in a crystal bowl in the room I am occupying and, while I work, I watch them from the corner of my eye. Yesterday they took a little bread I had broken up for them. This morning old Virginie tells Em.:

"Monsieur is wrong to give them bread. A fish, you know, lives on his excrements; or on human flesh."

28 October

Calm at last; alone in this big Villa, which I should perhaps not be so mad to have had built if only I could live in it.

I let all these last few days be devoured by errands, visits, etc. The necessity of going and getting my meals outside, or at least of going after supplies, left me very little time for work; for it to be good, it is important not to lose sight of it.

Yesterday evening I took out all my youthful "journals." I cannot reread them without exasperation — and were it not for the salutary *humiliation* I find in reading them, I should tear up everything.

Each progress in the art of writing is bought only by the surrender of a self-satisfaction. At that time I had them all and used to approach the blank page as one does a mirror.

1 November

I cling to the Villa but, without service, continue to lose a considerable time in household cares. This evening Mme Théo arrives, who is going to help me "keep house." I am struggling with the intermediary chapters of my Memoirs, which are to be placed between the printed book and what I wrote this summer (trip to Algeria with Paul A. Laurens). I should like to succeed in satisfying Martin du Gard's exigencies. I should especially like to get myself to use a more nervous, more incisive, drier manner of expression; no longer yield to that need of giving cadence to my sentences, whose rocking motion I am beginning to hate. To hate the honeyed, sticky poetic coating. . . .

At Ruyters's yesterday evening, with Marcel Drouin and Ghéon. Jean and Marc Schlumberger came to join us after dinner. Ghéon read us the first two acts of *Le Mort à cheval*,[4] one of the three plays he has brought back from this summer. He has worked relatively little. If he had worked longer, he would have written more; but nothing would have been any the riper. His requirements, without his suspecting it, have ceased to be any but moral or religious ones. He considers himself satisfied if his work is edifying. What he read us yester-

---

[4] *The Dead Man on Horseback.*

day is alarming. But he will no longer listen henceforth to any but those who approve him, and his friends of yesterday are forced, today, either to be silent or to help him deceive himself.

3 November

Invited to lunch by Mme Mühlfeld, with Paul Valéry and Cocteau; I go to join them. I had not exchanged three sentences when I was already exasperated. Whatever subject the conversation drifted to, the minds of Valéry and Cocteau strove to disparage; they vied with each other in lack of comprehension, in denial. Repeated, their remarks would seem absurd. I can no longer put up with that sort of drawing-room paradox which shines only at the expense of others. Péguy used to say: "I am not judging; I am condemning." In this way they executed Régnier, Mme de Noailles, Ibsen. Octave Feuillet was brought up and they agreed in granting him more talent than Ibsen, whom Valéry declared "tiresome." Seeing me reduced to silence – for what would have been the good of protesting? – Cocteau declared that I was in a "dreadful mood." I could not have seemed "in good form" except on condition of joining their chorus, and already I was blaming myself enough for having come to hear them.

Yet each one of them, taken separately, is charming; and for Valéry in particular, if I esteemed him less, I should not suffer so much from his negative attitude. How could it be surprising if, after having disenchanted the world around him, after having strained his wits to lose interest in so many things, he is bored!

8 November

Dined yesterday at Ruyters's, with Ghéon.

Apropos of D., the conversation at table turned on young people. Mme Ruyters, André R., and Ghéon declared that before twenty-five a young man was concerned only with himself and wasn't interested in anything; that furthermore D.'s lack of curiosity, which so saddens me, was altogether affected and that that very affectation was typical of his age. When I attempted to give a sentimental explanation for this, Ghéon exclaimed:

"But it's not so simple as that!"

And this is really the first time that I have happened to be accused of seeing things too simply. Coming from Ghéon, that accusation might have seemed comic, but I was touched by it only because it made it apparent how far away Ghéon had got from me. Then all three of them, and against me, began to reconstruct abstractly a psychology of the adolescent, without examples and entirely conventional, to which ran counter everything I might have said and which, out of prudence, I did not say. I remembered that, when faced with L.'s extravagances, Mme Ruyters had said to Mme Théo: "We know what it is, don't we? We were all like that."

23 November

On leaving the Palais de Justice (I find the Law Library closed, where I had been planning to work), I meet Duhamel on the Place Saint-Michel and he walks up the boulevard with me and, through the Luxembourg, as far as the Lion de Belfort (I was on my way to lunch at the Allégrets'). Excellent conversation about the novel. Like me, he is struggling against Martin du Gard's criticisms. He protests that I was not wrong to write *first* those monographs which Martin du Gard regrets not seeing fused together and confused in one thick cluster; and that those little purified tales that Martin du Gard criticizes have more hope of enduring than the complex novel that I now long to write.

When one tries to set down the substance of a conversation (as I am doing here), nothing remains; the very words themselves are needed — just as the resurrection of the flesh is needed to permit that of the spirit.

22 December

Spent two days at Clermont, at Roger Martin du Gard's, for he calls me in consultation for his novel, of which he reads me the first six chapters and outlines the general plan.[5] Uninterrupted conversation, which I believe to have been most profitable to both of us. He greatly encourages me to continue writing my Memoirs and to dare to write of my life everything that I relate to him.

But it is especially toward the novel that I now turn. I open the brown notebook and want to get in the harvest of these last few days.[6]

I enjoy keeping this journal up to date only when I have hope of writing in it almost every day, even if only a few lines.

Time flies and each day escapes me without my succeeding in embracing anything. I envy Martin du Gard and his calm solitude at Clermont.

End of December

Miquette's death.[7] Long blind, deaf, frightfully swollen, she seemed to remain attached to life only through fidelity to her mistress.

---

[5] The novel in question is *Les Thibault* (*The World of the Thibaults*), of which the first part was to appear in 1922.

[6] The brown notebook must be *Le Journal des Faux-Monnayeurs* (*The Counterfeiters' Daybook*).

[7] Miquette was a dog belonging to the Gides.

1921

Cuverville, 1 January

Arrived last night at Cuverville. All the way down I read *The Breaking-Point* by Artsybashev; strongly recommended by Roger M. du G., but I do not like it much. As for raw material, it is better to seek it in life; in books it is craft that interests me especially — and in this one, no more of one than of the other. Shall I go on?

I played myself the trick of not bringing any cigarettes (in Paris I was getting to smoke much too much), but this morning I am maddened.

In a tremendous effort of virtue, I force myself this morning to do the gymnastic exercises recommended by Roger M. du G.; plus, this afternoon, an hour's walk, to the detriment of the piano.

I have ahead of me the preface to *Armance*,[1] the intermediary chapter of *Si le grain ne meurt . . .* , and that enormous novel that I must begin to block out.

Before my departure, went to see *Parade*[2] — of which I don't know what to admire the more: pretense or poverty. Cocteau is walking up and down in the wings, where I go to see him; aged, contracted, painful. He knows that the sets and costumes are by Picasso, that the music is by Satie, but he wonders if Picasso and Satie are not by him.

The *Contes russes* delighted me.

3 January

Atrocious days. Insomnia; relapses into the worst; bad work in which, without any fervor whatever, I try to take advantage of a little remaining momentum.

. . . .

[1] Gide wrote a highly original preface for Stendhal's novel, *Armance*, which appeared in the edition of Stendhal's works published by Librairie Champion, after having appeared in the *Nouvelle Revue Française* for August 1921.

[2] A satirical ballet (book by Jean Cocteau, music by Erik Satie, scenery and costumes by Pablo Picasso, choreography by Leonide Massine), *Parade* was first presented by the Diaghilev company in Paris on 18 May 1917. Together with it, a ballet named *Contes russes* (*Russian Tales;* music by Anatoly Liadov, scenery and costumes by M. Larionov, choreography by Massine), made up of Russian folk tales, was given.

8 January

Better sleep; better work. I make up my mind to extract from my-self a *Lettre à Angèle,* which will make certain of my friends pursue me with invective, yet I owe them frankness.[3]

I am learning all over again the *Lavapiés* and the *Eritana* of Al-béniz, which I used to play currently by heart three years ago and which I have some trouble getting back into my head; but consid-erable pleasure also — and I certainly play them better today.

Read aloud a series of short stories by Chekhov in the English version; with the greatest interest.

11 January

I am giving up reading *The Breaking-Point* at page 260 (as I had once given up *Sanine*[4]). I have rarely encountered a book more dis-agreeable to me. It is brutal without being really strong.

Literature for medical students.

12 January

When the path your mind begins to follow saddens unto death creatures who are infinitely dear to you, you can, at one and the same time, believe that that is the path you must follow and yet advance in it tremblingly; remain with a divided heart; know hesitations and backings — in which Ghéon would see the mark of an irresolute mind, though it is only a matter of heart and sympathy. It is not constancy that I lack; it is ferocity.

"I am well aware that he is happy" (Ghéon), "that he has found rest and happiness."

"It is up to you to enjoy the same."

"You yourself told me: man is not born for happiness."

Likewise, Ghéon says: "I hate *'arrière-pensées.'* "

Yet there are certain cases in which, on the contrary, only *"arrière-pensées"* would seem acceptable to him — but then he would give them another name. He would call them "the voice of conscience."

14 January

There is taking place in my inner being what happens with "little countries": each nationality claims its right to existence and revolts

---

[3] In the late nineties and early years of this century André Gide com-mented on literature and art in *L'Ermitage* in the form of letters to an imag-inary Angèle. Later he occasionally revived this form in the pages of the *Nouvelle Revue Française* — notably in the issues of March through June 1921.

[4] *Sanine* is the novel that established Artsybashev's fame.

against oppression. The only classicism admissible is the one that takes everything into account. Maurras's classicism is hateful because it oppresses and suppresses, and I am not sure that what he oppresses is not worth more than the oppressor. Today it is time to hear what has not yet spoken.

I like this praise, in C. Du Bos's article on me: "infinitely respectful of the sensitivity of others."

16 January

I am reading Wells's articles on bolshevism (in *Le Progrès civique*) with the greatest interest and that sort of intellectual illumination when you recognize in another your own still uncertain thought clearly stated, strengthened, and sobered down.

Merezhkovski's reply is most ordinary.

26 January

I am leaving Cuverville tomorrow. The physiological and moral conditions in which I find myself here are most depressing and my work has suffered considerably therefrom.

. . . .

Practiced the piano on an average of three hours a day; perfected especially the *Eritana* and the *Lavapiés* of Albéniz, which I play by heart and in the right tempo — on condition that no one is there to hear me.

Cleaned up the two supplementary chapters of the first part of my Memoirs.

Note on Browning, introduction to the translation of *Sludge*. Re-read *Armance* with rapture.

Read aloud nineteen tales by Chekhov (English version), of unequal length, none of which is indifferent and some of which are remarkable.

How and why does it happen that Andler in his book on the precursors of Nietzsche does not speak of Dostoyevsky?

I note this sentence from Andler's book — which I am reading with the greatest satisfaction:

"It is easy for petty people to call weakness an unrest in which must be seen above all the torment of a more vibrant and more extended sensitivity. If they lack energy (he is now talking of the others) at the first moment, this is because their attention is solicited in several directions at once; and they must extract from a multiple passion a richer will, of which the constancy had to be laboriously constructed." — That is very good and deserved to be better expressed.

Paris, 4 May

One might say that there are two kinds of attention: one intense, and the other half listless and discursive; it is the latter that one is most inclined to lend; I really believe that most people are capable of the former kind only in case of danger and when it can serve as a warning. But, not having any gift whatsoever at telling stories, when I begin to tell a story aloud I am always afraid that it will be too long and that people will not listen to the end; I have often had even this mortifying experience (if, suddenly, I had to cut my story in the middle) of waiting in vain for a voice to say: "And so? . . ."

And perhaps indeed the lack of confidence that results from this, that fear of not being able to retain the reader's attention (even much more than my "impatience," as has been said), is the cause of that contraction or shrinking of the end of my books. — Just a moment more, gentlemen, and I shall have finished.

It is because I do not count on that prolonged attention, the second kind, that I appeal to the first kind, intense attention, infinitely rarer, harder to obtain, and granted more sparingly — but without which one cannot penetrate my writings.

Related elsewhere (in the gray notebook of the novel) the story of that little schoolboy from the Lycée Henri IV — whom I surprised yesterday in the act of stealing.[5]

7 May

Seized last night by strange fits of dizziness, accompanied by almost no discomfort, but so strong that surely I should have lost my equilibrium if I had been standing. I had just gone to bed; I turned on the light again; the field of my vision did not so much turn around as it was violently shaken up and down. It seemed to me that at the slightest movement I might make to turn over in bed, I should run the risk of being sick.

This morning the same dizziness is there, ready to reappear and reappearing intermittently, forcing me to sit down quickly in order not to fall. I am striving not to attach any importance to it, other than the embarrassment that results from it and immobilizes me this morning (Sunday).

13 May

Hateful period, which I do not believe I can get over without tearing myself away from here. I am working (on the preface to *Armance*)

---

[5] This true incident, told in the *Journal des Faux-Monnayeurs,* reappears transposed in the novel of *The Counterfeiters.*

with extreme difficulty. . . . Useless to leave the record of my lapses
in this notebook. Spells of dizziness, heaviness of all my thoughts.

14 May

Spent an hour of yesterday evening with Proust. For the last four
days he has been sending an auto after me every evening, but each
time it missed me. . . . Yesterday, as I had just happened to tell
him that I did not expect to be free, he was getting ready to go out,
having made an appointment outside. He says that he has not been
out of bed for a long time. Although it is stifling in the room in which
he receives me, he is shivering; he has just left another, much hotter
room in which he was covered with perspiration; he complains that
his life is nothing but a slow agony, and although having begun, as
soon as I arrived, to talk of homosexuality, he interrupted himself to
ask me if I can enlighten him as to the teaching of the Gospels, for
someone or other has told him that I talk particularly well on the subject. He hopes to find in the Gospels some support and relief for his
sufferings, which he depicts at length as atrocious. He is fat, or rather
puffy; he reminds me somewhat of Jean Lorrain. I am taking him
Corydon, of which he promises not to speak to anyone; and when I
say a word or two about my Memoirs:
"You can tell anything," he exclaims; "but on condition that you
never say: *I.*" But that won't suit me.
Far from denying or hiding his homosexuality, he exhibits it, and
I could almost say boasts of it. He claims never to have loved women
save spiritually and never to have known love except with men. His
conversation, ceaselessly cut by parenthetical clauses, runs on without
continuity. He tells me his conviction that Baudelaire was homosexual:
"The way he speaks of Lesbos, and the mere need of speaking of it,
would be enough to convince me," and when I protest:
"In any case, if he was homosexual, it was almost without his knowing it; and you don't believe that he ever practiced. . . ."
"What!" he exclaims. "I am sure of the contrary; how can you
doubt that he practiced? He, Baudelaire!"
And in the tone of his voice it is implied that by doubting I am
insulting Baudelaire. But I am willing to believe that he is right; and
that homosexuals are even a bit more numerous than I thought at first.
In any case I did not think that Proust was so exclusively so.

Just from having heard, at Darius Milhaud's, Mlle X. dash off with
extraordinary assurance and charm, to perfection, a number of compositions by Chabrier and Debussy (particularly the *Études*) and
(very poorly these) by Chopin — I remained discouraged, not daring
to open my piano for twelve days. Small wonder after that that I don't

like pianists! All the pleasure they give me is nothing compared to the
pleasure I give myself when I play; but when I hear them I become
ashamed of my playing — and certainly quite wrongly. But it is just
the same when I read Proust; I hate virtuosity, but it always impresses
me, and in order to scorn it I should first like to be capable of it; I
should like to be sure of not being the fox of the fable. I *know* and
feel for instance that Chopin's *Barcarolle* is to be played much more
slowly than Mlle X. does, than they all do — but in order to dare to
play it in the presence of others as *leisurely* as I like it, I should have
to know that I could just as well play it much more rapidly and especially feel that whoever hears me is convinced of this. Played at that
speed, Chopin's music becomes *brilliant,* loses its own value, its
virtue. . . .

15 May

Dizzy spells, perhaps a bit less definite, but more and more frequent. This morning they haven't left me since my awakening. Perhaps the abuse of tobacco has something to do with it, for yesterday
evening, dining at M. du G.'s and spending the evening with him, I
again let myself indulge in too much smoking.

However, my work for the last two days has been rather good
(preface for *Armance*).

. . . .

Wednesday

Last night I was about to go up to bed when the bell rang. It was
Proust's chauffeur, Céleste's husband, bringing back the copy of *Corydon* that I lent to Proust on 13 May and offering to take me back with
him, for Proust is somewhat better and sends a message that he can
receive me if it is not inconvenient for me to come. His sentence is
much longer and more complicated than I am quoting it; I imagine he
learned it on the way, for when I interrupted him at first, he began it
all over again and recited it in one breath. Céleste, likewise, when she
opened the door to me the other evening, after having expressed
Proust's regret at not being able to receive me, added: "Monsieur begs
Monsieur Gide to have no doubt that he is thinking constantly of him."
(I noted the sentence right away.)

For a long time I wondered if Proust did not take advantage somewhat of his illness to protect his work (and this seemed quite legitimate to me); but yesterday, and already the other day, I could see
that he is really seriously ill. He says he spends hours on end without
being able even to move his head; he stays in bed all day long, and
for days on end. At moments he rubs the side of his nose with the
edge of a hand that seems dead, with its fingers oddly stiff and sep-

arated, and nothing could be more impressive than this finicky, awkward gesture, which seems the gesture of an animal or a madman.

We scarcely talked, this evening again, of anything but homosexuality. He says he blames himself for that "indecision" which made him, in order to fill out the heterosexual part of his book, transpose "*à l'ombre des jeunes filles*"[6] all the attractive, affectionate, and charming elements contained in his homosexual recollections, so that for *Sodome*[7] he is left nothing but the grotesque and the abject. But he shows himself to be very much concerned when I tell him that he seems to have wanted to stigmatize homosexuality; he protests; and eventually I understand that what we consider vile, an object of laughter or disgust, does not seem so repulsive to him.

When I ask him if he will ever present that Eros in a young and beautiful guise, he replies that, to begin with, what attracts him is almost never beauty and that he considers it to have very little to do with desire — and that, as for youth, this was what he could most easily transpose (what lent itself best to a transposition).

28 May

Lunched the 26th at Versailles at the Princesse de Bassiano's; her auto with Mme Mühlfeld and Paul Valéry already in it came to pick me up. An hour's reading or piano-practice is pleasanter to me than the most sumptuous dinner in the world; this one was exquisite moreover; nothing to say about the conversation. Yesterday dined with Mme Mayrisch, Mme Van Rysselberghe, Valéry, and Rivière. Valéry, amazing as always, but in whose cosmos I cannot breathe.

In finished the day before yesterday my preface for *Armance*, which caused me considerable trouble, for I have been very tired of late. I feared it might be very bad, but I read it with pleasure to Roger M. du G. this morning, then this afternoon to Mme Mayrisch and Jean S. I now no longer have anything standing between me and my novel — except the end of the chapter of my Memoirs, which I should like to give to the printer in a month.

I am reading *As You Like It* — astonished to understand it so well, but without any great pleasure.

2 June

Invited by Piot, yesterday I went to the Opéra for the last rehearsal of *Les Troyens*. I remembered my rapture of fifteen years ago,

---

[6] *A l'ombre des jeunes filles en fleurs* ("In the shadow of blossoming girls") is the original title of the second part of Proust's long work, which Scott-Moncrieff freely translated as *Within a Budding Grove.*

[7] *Sodome et Gomorrhe* (*Cities of the Plain*) forms a fraction of Part IV and all of Part V of Proust's work.

at the Théâtre Sarah-Bernhardt, when Delna had the role of Dido in
Les Troyens à Carthage, of which the first act has become the third
in this hybrid performance.[8] All that is left is conventional, dull, tiresome. (I am not speaking of the musical text, but of the execution.)
A much too large orchestra covers the insufficient voices. Impossible
to feel the slightest emotion, despite all my efforts to recapture the
emotion I once felt. And at times I recognized measure for measure.
. . . I left at the third act, sick with boredom.

3 June

Good piano-practice the last few days. Have been able to devote
three hours to it daily. Went back to Chopin's *Barcarolle,* which it is
not so hard as I thought to play more rapidly; I manage to do so (I
let myself be intimidated much too easily by others' *brio*) — but when
I do, it loses all character, all emotion, all *languor;* and that is above
all what this wonderful piece expresses: languor in excessive joy. It
seems that there is too much sound, too many notes as soon as one
ceases to understand the complete meaning of each one. Any good
execution must be an *explanation* of the piece. But the pianist, like the
actor, strives for the *effect;* and the effect is generally achieved at the
expense of the text. The player is well aware that I shall be more impressed the less I understand. But that is just what I want — to understand. Being impressed, in art, is worth nothing unless it yields at
once to emotion; and most often it stands in the way of emotion.

8 June

How much I like this that I read in Sainte-Beuve (*Les Cahiers*): [9]
"The Latins, in their language, did not dislike a certain vagueness, a
certain lack of determination of the meaning, a touch of obscurity.
. . . Take it as you will, they seem frequently to say: understand it
in this sense, or in this other sense which is close to it. — You have a
certain latitude of choice. — *The principal sense is not absolutely exclusive of another.*" (I am underlining.) Delight in feeling myself to
be very Latin, in this regard.

* * *

Cuverville, 10 July

Arrived here the 2nd. Wonderful, unchanging weather. All nature
is panting and begging pity. Insufficient work, interrupted by correspondence. A sort of resignation benumbs my will, my mind. I have

---

[8] Hector Berlioz's opera *The Trojans* he later broke into two operas, *The
Siege of Troy* and *The Trojans at Carthage.*

[9] *The Notebooks,* a posthumous publication.

recourse to this notebook, once again, in order to learn to demand more of myself.

11 July

It seems to me that I desire everything less fiercely since there has begun to withdraw from me that felicity I had hoped for from a complete communion with her.

12 July

Everything I have read by the Tharaud brothers has seemed to me of the best quality; the only reproach I think can be made against their books is that they are never dictated by any inner necessity; they do not have those deep and necessary relations with the author in which a destiny is pledged.

14 July

Finished the third chapter of the second part of *Si le grain ne meurt* . . . — that is to say, all that I plan to have printed now. I doubt whether I shall be able to pursue further the writing of those Memoirs. And yet what interest they would have!

Finished *Green Mansions* by Hudson; it contains a rather pleasant but insufficient exoticism, which yields too often to a comic-opera sentimentality.

I am reading aloud to Em. *Une Ténébreuse Affaire* with amazement.[10] *Outline of Psychology* by William James.

20 July

Struggle against that impulse to pour personal experiences into the novel, and particularly those which have made one suffer, in the fallacious hope of finding some consolation in the treatment one gives them.

"They appear particularly interesting to us only because they happen to us."

"No, no; on the contrary, that is the sophism: everyone has the adventures he deserves; and for choice souls there are privileged situations, special sufferings, of which vulgar souls are simply incapable."

21 July

I should long ago have ceased to write if I were not inhabited by the conviction that those to come will discover in my writings what those of today refuse to see there, and which nevertheless I know that I put there.

---

[10] *A Shady Affair*, a novel by Balzac.

The declarations of the nationalists too often make me think of the protestations of Lear's daughters. The deepest love does not leap so easily to the lips. I hold for the silence of Cordelia.

28 July

It is not exactly that sensation is getting weaker; no, but by a sort of transposition it seems that it no longer concerns me directly. I am as if I had already been dead for some time, as if already I were no longer involved. And look . . . above all it seems to me that nothing more of what I do or what I feel involves my moral responsibility. Yes, that is it. I am already dead, and what I am living now is a sort of unimportant supplement which *commits me to nothing*.

X., who wanted to commit suicide, sometimes gets to the point of wondering if, in reality, he has not already done it.

> *Since now at length my fate I know,*
> *Since nothing all my love avails,*
> *Since all, my life seemed meant for, fails.*[11]

Since the day when . . . I have never again become completely conscious of my moral continuity.

Colpach, 28 August

A blind man could imagine colors more easily than an insensitive person could imagine the mysterious charm emanating from the appearance of a body. How could he understand that agitation, that need of enveloping, of caressing, that commandeering of our whole being, and desire's errant lack of precision? . . .

Spent a few charming days on the beach of Hyères, where Elisabeth Van Rysselberghe comes unexpectedly to meet me. Discovered with her, during a walk in the pine forest, an extraordinary little village, near the abandoned salt-marshes — Le Pesquier, I believe — which one would have thought Polynesian: sheltered, hidden, buried under the trees, and suggesting such an odd felicity that immediately you long to live there, to end your days there. I go back there the same evening with Roger Fry, met by chance; and, three days later, with Copeau.

La Bastide, 12 September

Rereading for the last time the proofs of my *Morceaux choisis*, for which the *N.R.F.* is waiting, I am especially struck by the insistence, the monotony, the repetitions.[12]

---

[11] From *The Last Ride Together* by Browning.

[12] A little volume of *Selections from André Gide*, containing a few unpublished fragments, was brought out by Librairie Gallimard in 1921.

Paris, 29 September

I note this sentence from Grimm's letter on Rousseau (Vol. IX, p. 141):

"Nevertheless, such was the effect of the dispute" (about the *Discours* crowned by the Dijon Academy) "that that opinion, which was not his and which he had embraced only to be unusual, became his own by dint of defending it." [13] Sentence that can so well be applied to Barrès at the moment of the Dreyfus affair.

30 September

I am rereading the book of *Maximes* with the greatest admiration. [14] It seems to me that the position I tried to take with regard to La Rochefoucauld could not be maintained without injustice. My first mistake was to try to assimilate what he calls "amour-propre" to egotism. Despite everything, the maxims having to do with self-esteem are of less interest than those that are not linked to any theory, to any thesis, and some of which are singularly penetrating and *turned* in a way that can be imitated but which belongs only to him; or at least if it can be found in the drawing-rooms of the classical period, *he* carries it to perfection.

3 October

Back to Cuverville.

Spent three to four hours relearning pieces 1 and 4 of the *Goyescas* (and I am far from completely possessing the first). I ought now to tackle *Les Faux-Monnayeurs;* but through timidity, through indolence, through cowardice, I welcome every distraction that offers itself and do not know how to embrace my subject. I advise myself to walk back and forth in my room for an hour, forbidding myself any reading whatever. And repeat this like a novena, preferably before going to bed. Without letting oneself be discouraged if one sees no results the first few evenings.

I write, almost without any difficulty, two pages of the dialogue with which I hope to open my novel. But I shall not be satisfied unless I succeed in getting still farther from realism. It matters little, moreover, if, later on, I am to tear up everything I write today. The important thing is to get accustomed to living with my characters.

4 October

The weather is so miraculously beautiful that one can no longer recognize the country. I am writing these lines on the bench in the

---

[13] Rousseau's first work was a *Discourse on the Arts and Sciences*, which takes the paradoxical view — according to some, prompted by Diderot — that artistic and scientific progress corrupt society.

[14] The famous collection of La Rochefoucauld's *Maxims*.

avenue facing Valentine's beech grove. The sun is about to set. In vain
I seek an epithet to describe the extraordinary luminosity of the sky.

6 October

Third day without smoking. Too much time at the piano (three
or four hours every day); insufficient work.

7 October

Good piano-practice; but very poor work. I am trying to write an
article on the resumption of intellectual relations with Germany. Every clause seems to go at cross-purposes and the least call of the out-
doors distracts me. Every sound, every song is a call to me.

I am reading the *Oraison funèbre de Le Tellier*[15] and Donne's
Divine Poems, from which I pick out these admirable lines:

> *Take mee to You, imprison mee, for I*
> *Except You enthrall mee, never shall be free. . . .*[16]

12 October

I had the cowardice to go the day before yesterday, Sunday, to the
village and buy a package of tobacco. But I experience no pleasure in
smoking this coarse black tobacco, the only one I could find; and this
is so much the better, for it helps me to keep from smoking.

After three days of agony, yesterday I finished an article on the resumption of intellectual relations with Germany; sent at once to
Rivière.[17]

. . . .

Every summer I reread in part *Les Caractères;* not that I particularly admire La Bruyère; there are ten authors of his time whom I
prefer to him and who amaze me more; but it just happens that there
is none of them whose star is more reassuring. Very often, and chiefly
in the first book, one wonders whether or not what he says was really
worth saying, so simple and reasonable it seems; but one is grateful to
him for saying it nevertheless, and so simply. He tries neither to amaze
nor to please, but to express reasonably what he is sure of. (A good
mind, he says, expects to write reasonably.)

---

[15] *Funeral Oration of Michel Le Tellier, Chancellor of France*, by Bossuet.

[16] Gide quotes the lines in English and then translates:
> *Empare-toi de moi, Seigneur, et m'emprisonne,*
> *Car je ne puis goûter de liberté que dans tes chaînes.*

[17] *Les Rapports intellectuels entre la France et l'Allemagne* by Gide appeared in the *Nouvelle Revue Française* for November 1921.

I am tormented by the desire to re-do the *Caractères;* there would probably be no immodesty in attempting it; I should adopt the outline of the book and try to express with the same simplicity the new aspects of our epoch, and everything that an *"honnête homme"* of today[18] can reasonably think about manners, about society and the various elements that go into it, about literature, about religion and the arts. I should say just as simple things and just as simply as this:

Probably less patience and less effort are needed to bring an art to maturity than are later needed to keep it from spoiling.

15 October

Em. tells me about the young postman I was interested in and whom I helped to find a new position. His sister, with whom he was living, left him suddenly last month, abandoning at Goderville the mail-wagon she was driving that day, to jump into the Rouen train, where she joined the son of a Criquetot innkeeper. . . . She took away the three thousand francs that she claimed her brother owed her and that the brother was keeping and including in the common purse, never supposing that his sister could have any secrets from him.

"Oh no, she is not thinking of getting married either," he said just recently; "we get along very well together as we are; a brother and sister can live very well together."

So that his first thought must have been, when he learned of her flight: "What! she wasn't happy, then?"

Certainly she hid from him all her desires, all her ulterior motives, just as she would have done with a husband.

All the unconfessed egotism that entered into the fraternal devotion suddenly came to light. In his indignation, he had the girl traced and the police finally found her in Rouen in a miserable furnished room. She and her lover, whom she wants to marry, were at the end of their resources; that is, only ten francs were found on them. She had no problem proving that she had taken from the common purse only what was legitimately hers, so that, after two days in prison, she was set free.

The oddest part of the story is the sudden decision the little postman took of getting married immediately too, to balance his sister:

"Since that's the way it is, she'll see! . . ."

16 October

Leaving Cuverville this time was like dying.

---

[18] The ideal of the seventeenth century, the *"honnête homme,"* can probably best be translated by "all-around man."

17 October

I cannot shake off an abominable fatigue and melancholy. All humanity seems to me desperately ugly and soiled. What bestiality, what egotism in the expression of all these faces! What an absence of joy, of real life! Is it to redeem each of these that a Christ died?

1 November

Arrived yesterday evening at Roquebrune. . . . As the moment of leaving her approached, I felt more painfully everything that attached me to her and I came to wonder if reason really counseled this departure. How hard I find it not to prefer the austere, or at least not to believe in its superiority! Instinctive distrust for everything that pleasure adorns.

26 November

Returned to Cuverville the evening of the 24th. It seems to me now that I dreamed this trip . . . Pisa, Siena, Orvieto, Rome; perfect weather, if it had not been taken from work. Immediately I plunge into it again, cursing that lecture on Dostoyevsky for which Copeau, on my way through Paris, extracted the promise.

Yesterday evening reread Browning's *Ivan Ivanovitch* and considerable Coleridge. I am waiting until I have brought my correspondence up to date before getting back to the piano.

29 November

Big article by Massis in *La Revue universelle* on (or rather: against) me. Massis sets up against my books a remark of Claudel: "Evil does not compose." As if it were by lack of composition that my books sinned!

All together, the article, although denouncing my influence as a public danger, is full of unconfessed admiration. What rather irritates me is seeing Massis ascribe to me not only sentences by me but also sentences written by others about me. Even then the quotations he makes are not always exact, and the reader is never warned when it is merely a character from one of my novels speaking; I must take responsibility for everything indifferently; everything that can harm me. He does not try to sketch a lifelike portrait, but simply to prejudice his readers against me.

This article, prepared in advance, appears the very day that the volume goes on sale; as already, some time ago, when he demolished *Les Caves*. When shall I ever see such haste in praise? But for Massis it was a matter of sounding the keynote for the critics.

For the last four months that I have resubscribed to the *Courrier de la Presse,*[19] I have received nothing but violent attacks. It is enough to make one think that I am paying for them. A Spanish critic, obviously well informed, goes so far as to speak of my hardness of heart and my avarice. The article is, besides, rather funny; but what a caricature it draws of me! Will it be possible, later on, to make out my real features under such a heap of calumnies? Three quarters of the critics, and almost all those of the newspapers, form their opinion, not according to my books themselves, but according to café conversations. I know moreover that I have on my side neither the cafés, nor the drawing-rooms, nor the boulevards; and these are what make successes. Consequently it is not that kind of favor which I seek, nor which I have ever desired. I shall let my books patiently choose their readers; the small number of today will form the opinion of tomorrow.

I do not want to pretend to be stronger or more self-assured than I am, and some of these misjudgments are extremely painful to me; but finding in my *Morceaux choisis,* as I reread them, a sentence that does not satisfy me would affect me much more. I have difficulty in not yielding to that tendency of mine to agree with criticisms; but I am often reassured by the fact that the accusations made against me contradict one another. Then too, I think of Baudelaire and that most of these accusations are the very ones that were likewise directed against him.

Only today have I returned to the piano. I am rereading *The Idiot* and have again plunged with intoxication into *The Ring and the Book,* which I understand much more easily.[20] There is nothing headier than Browning, not even Dostoyevsky. Yet perhaps I should get less excited if I knew his language perfectly. The slight fog that occasionally floats between the lines lends them imaginary depths.

1 December

Wrote about thirty pages of my book this week; I am writing it right off without hesitation (and this is the way *this* book must be written); but I don't know where I am heading and fear to be stopped soon.

Finished the first volume of *The Idiot;* my admiration is no longer quite so great. The characters grimace excessively and *coincide,* so to speak, too easily; they have lost much of their mystery for me; I am almost inclined to say that I understand them too well; that is to say that I understand too well the use Dostoyevsky plans to make of them.

---

[19] A clipping-service.

[20] *The Idiot* is the novel by Dostoyevsky; *The Ring and the Book* is a long narrative poem by Browning.

There are in this book incomparable passages, charged with an extraordinary educative value; finally, certain characters are amazingly successful; or rather (for all the portraits are admirable) certain of their dialogues — particularly between General Ivolgin and the wife of General Epantchin. — But my impression is confirmed: I prefer *The Possessed* and *The Brothers Karamazov*, perhaps even *A Raw Youth* (without mentioning certain shorter tales). But I think that *The Idiot* is particularly likely to please the young, and of all Dostoyevsky's novels it is the one I should advise them to read first.

I have returned to the piano; am amazed to play Beethoven's sonatas so easily now — at least the ones that I once worked over considerably and then left. But their pathos exhausts me, and what is most satisfying to me today is Bach, and perhaps his *Kunst der Fugue*,[21] of which I never get tired. It has almost nothing human left in it, and it awakens not emotion or passion, but adoration. What calm! What acceptation of everything superior to man! What scorn for the flesh! What peace!

2 December

I stiffen my will as best I can; but Ghéon's desertion causes me an almost unbearable and constantly renewed grief. His article in *L'Action Française*, the first in a series on literature, is still intelligent but already quite *slanted*. He rises up against the notion of the "gratuitousness" of the work of art and maintains that no work of art worthy of the name was ever created except with a utilitarian aim and the intention of serving. (And he dares to cite as an example the *Fables* of La Fontaine!) I recall our latest conversations. My sorrow at leaving him made me yield to him as much as possible; but in this whole article I feel a protest against my thought, against me.

Meanwhile Massis deigns to see in my work, from one end to the other, nothing but a desire to influence. . . . They had better get together; they will eventually hit it off.

I have read Proust's latest pages (December issue of the *N.R.F.*) with, at first, a shock of indignation. Knowing what he thinks, what he is, it is hard for me to see in them anything but a pretense, a desire to protect himself, a camouflage of the cleverest sort, for it can be to no one's advantage to denounce him. Even more: that offense to truth will probably please everybody: heterosexuals, whose prejudices it justifies and whose repugnances it flatters; and the others, who will take advantage of the alibi and their lack of resemblance to those he portrays. In short, considering the public's cowardice, I do not

---

[21] *The Art of the Fugue.*

know any writing that is more capable than Proust's *Sodome et Gomorrhe* of confirming the error of public opinion.

5 December

Remarkable fragments of Amiel's *Journal intime* in the December *N.R.F.* But his style, both hesitant and finicky, is absolutely unbearable to me.

"While seeking the exact nuance of my thought," he says in another fragment, "I go over the whole gamut of synonyms, and, very often, my pen proceeds by triads." Then he adds: "The single expression is an intrepidity that implies self-confidence and clairvoyance. To achieve the unique touch, one must not doubt, and you are always doubting." That is excellent, but not always correct, it seems to me. The "unique touch" is not necessarily a proof of intrepidity; it can result just as well from an *acceptance of sacrifice*. Every choice implies a sacrifice; and it is impossible to draw well without choosing.

Charlie Du Bos comments on this passage excellently. (Quoted in the October *N.R.F.*)

7 December

Every evening I plunge again, for a half-hour, into the *Kunst der Fugue*. Nothing I said of it the other day strikes me as quite exact now. No, one does not often feel in it either serenity or beauty, but rather an intellectual torment and an effort of the will to bend forms as rigid as laws and inhumanly inflexible. It is the triumph of the mind over figures; and, before the triumph, the struggle. And while submitting to restraint—through it, in spite of it, or *thanks to it*—all the play of emotion, of tenderness, and, after all, of harmony that can still remain.

10 December

This stagnation poisons me. I stifle in calm waters. Like the trout, I enjoy swimming upstream.

11 December

Several articles about my *Morceaux choisis*, or rather about Massis's article. Much more is said about that article than about my book itself. And the little that is said of it is moreover so stupid that I am reassured to see it directed against me.

Sunday

I am rereading Suarès's *Dostoïevsky*.[22] It is by far the least good
of the three studies in this book. (I have just reread some excellent
pages by him on Pascal.) The opening, the introit, irritates me. I
know that what he says there is not true; he has not yet spoken of
Dostoyevsky, not at all because he was "reserving" him, but simply
because he didn't know him. The evening when I spoke to him of
Dostoyevsky, he told me he had so far read only *The House of the
Dead* and *Crime and Punishment*. In Russian literature he still saw
only Tolstoy. And his whole study reflects this; he wrote it very rapidly in order to balance my lecture and so that it could not be said
that anyone had taught him something. The knowledge he rapidly as-
similated of the other novels of Dostoyevsky was too recent (and to
what oratorical tricks he has recourse to hide this!) for him to be able
to talk very well of them. His remarks, however just they may be, are
those one makes on a first reading. A more prolonged frequentation
would have urged him to bring out much more important features.
The "witty remarks" he quotes (in particular) are precisely those that
strike one at first; but I have no doubt whatever that those are not
the ones Suarès would still quote today. Doubtless he would even find
them (as I now do) not of the best quality, rather "theatrical witticisms," witticisms that get their effect, the kind that easily win the approval and applause of the half-lettered people, of the half-fools. (The
type: "Forgive us our happiness.")

And, toward the end of this study, everything he says of Nietzsche
is monstrous. I can understand, moreover, that he later felt the need
of writing a retraction.

Speaking of the time Dostoyevsky spent in prison, he cannot keep
himself from adding in a note: "And I too have my hell!" And I likewise, and I too . . . at each new feature in the portrait he is painting
one feels that he would like to say this, that he would especially like
one to think this without his saying it, for he is aware that saying it
is a weakness. Oh, what a different accent this has from the *personal
cry* of Michelet, in the second volume of his *Histoire de France:* "As
for me, my passion began the day that my soul fell into this miserable

---

[22] Suarès's *Trois Hommes* (*Three Men*), originally published in 1913,
contains studies of Pascal, Ibsen, and Dostoyevsky. When Gide speaks of
his own lecture (which was given in 1921), he may be confusing it with his
brochure *Dostoïevsky d'après sa correspondance* (*Dostoyevsky According to
his Correspondence*), which was issued in 1908 and again in 1911, or with
his article on *The Brothers Karamazov* in *Le Figaro*, 4 April 1911. See *The
Journals of André Gide*, Vol. I, p. 340.

body, *which I finish consuming by writing this.*" (I am quoting from memory, like Proust.) [23]

12 December

Insomnia, I am struggling as best I can; force myself to "take exercise"; to walk; to take a cold tub as soon as I return from a "health walk.". . . Nothing does any good; each night is a bit worse than the preceding one and makes me lose a bit more of the health acquired this summer. I am like the circus clown taking off his waistcoats one by one; and I wonder at the provision I had made.

14 December

I am continuing Suarès's *Dostoïevsky.* It seems to me very clear that he has not yet read *The Possessed.* And if he knows *The Eternal Husband,* how can he call that wonderful book a "poor book"?

15 December

Yesterday found Jean S. when my train arrived. I had notified him by telegram. Went to the Lutétia, for greater convenience. This is the first time that I have stopped in a hotel in Paris, at least with the intention of staying there. Saw that same evening Copeau, Roger Martin du Gard, M. and Loup,[24] the last during an intermission at the Vieux-Colombier.

Very tired, I spoke feverishly and much too much, as almost always happens after a rather prolonged retreat. The very sound of my words intoxicates me, dazzles me, and I talk without rhyme or reason. (This is not altogether fair. I am intoxicated rather with sympathy.)

"M. Gide does not even represent a literary school, not even the review in which he writes. His work is the most flagrantly unpunished intellectual and moral scandal of the century," I read in *La Revue française* that the Argus clipping-service sends me this morning. It is signed René Johannet.

This is the two hundred and eighth clipping (I paid the bill six weeks ago). In addition to advertisements, I receive nothing but savage attacks.

Paris, Lutétia, 16 December

Yesterday, Thursday, began my day calmly in this sixth-floor room where I am really comfortable. Wrote to Em. and to the good little René Michelet, from whom I had finally just received a letter. Then

---

[23] Here is the exact beginning of that sentence: "Each of us has his cross and his stigmata. Mine date from the day when . . ." etc. (Vol. II, chapter ix.) [A.]

[24] "Loup" is Mme Mayrisch.

went to the *N.R.F.* to talk with Prunières, Allard, Gallimard, and Jean Schlumberger. The atmosphere is now very pleasant there and the disorder has ended, almost. Lunched at the Allégrets'. I had hoped to take M. with me, but we didn't lunch until one o'clock and furthermore it was the little girl's birthday. Exasperating waste of time. Before lunch I had managed to have a rather long conversation with André about his engagement; it seems to me that he is making a mistake and I tried to open his eyes. Nothing is more dangerous than the role I played in this case . . . and without any result, besides.

Went to pay a bill at Foinet's, the picture-framer's. Excellent call on Paul Laurens. Then rue Vaneau, to the hospital where Nicole has just had her appendix removed. Valentine was with her. Nicole glowing with grace and beauty.

Back to the hotel, where Mme Mayrisch and M. are to meet me. Wrote to Alibert while waiting for them. Took tea with them; then all three set out on errands. I return alone to the Lutétia; dined in my room on the slice of pâté and hard-boiled eggs that Em. had put into my bag. Then at eight o'clock to Roger Martin du Gard's, where I stay until one in the morning, reading him the beginning of my novel, commenting on it and criticizing it, and talking to him of Browning.

Why should I note all this? . . . As a specimen of the way I spend a day in Paris; and to teach me to waste less time today.

Sunday, 18 December

I shall not succeed in writing my book until I have got away from the conviction that it is my last book, that I shall not write any others. I shall more easily suppress the parasitical elements if I feel sure of being able to place them elsewhere. In the matter I have piled up before me, there is enough to nourish a half-dozen novels.

Last night went to see *The Kid* [25] with M. du G. Talked considerably on the way home (on foot); then insomnia until four or five a.m.

Wednesday, 21 December

Seen much of M. du G. the last few days, with an ever equal pleasure, interest, and profit. (Read him the other evening the amorphous beginning of my book.) Lamentable cutting up of my days.

26 December

Prolonged insomnia. Never have I felt my mind so active. Last night, if I had had a secretary at hand, I should have dictated a quarter of a book. My thought succeeds in formulating itself much more easily and clearly than it used to do. I believe that I could speak "ex-

---

[25] Charlie Chaplin's film.

tempore" before an audience whose sympathy I felt sufficiently. Last
night I imagined a sort of course on Dostoyevsky: lectures interrupted
by readings, which I should have given myself; for actors, who are
generally chosen to present such extracts to the public, never read
them in a satisfactory way (not even Jacques Copeau, despite his intelligence and his gifts). They remind one of the stage and not of
reality; one is aware that for them a book is written for the theater
and is only a substitute; they are like those clever pianists, those bad
pianists, who are anxious only to imitate an orchestra and constantly
make you feel the want of one. They are like those illustrated books
which make you see the characters, but not always in the way you
would have wished. The art of the stage is a continuous illustration;
but, on the other hand, the art of reading must leave the hearer's imagination, if not altogether free, at least able to think it is free. Mere
allusions, hints, often are enough, if, of course, they are just right; it
is no good to begin laughing when it is written that the speaker laughs
at that moment; any more than if he walks, to begin walking; any
more than, in the fashion of Mayol, to evoke the image of objects.
Reading Poe's *The Pit and the Pendulum,* he must not imitate the
swinging of the pendulum with his arms, but rather simply the anguish
of the unfortunate subject following it with his eyes. It is less a matter
of making people see than of making them feel.

What I am saying here in no way tends to diminish the worth of
actors, but merely to bring out that "reading" and "acting" belong to
two different æsthetics. I shall even say that the better an actor is, the
worse he will read, or that I should be very suspicious of an actor
who reads too well. Here is Dullin reading a tale taken from *The
House of the Dead;* you see the husband's ferocity; you hear the wife's
groans as she is beaten . . . but he forgets, and makes one forget,
that the one who tells the tale is but a brute utterly unaware of the
pathos of the scene he is describing, and that the tragic element comes
from the very fact that he doesn't know that what he is telling is tragic;
he ought to go in the contrary direction to his story; and he is the one
that it is important not to lose sight of. The listener will be all the
more moved the less he is himself, etc. . . .

This is just the kind of thing I should say "extempore" much better than I am writing it here.

The effort toward a new state of affairs always seems anarchy at
first in the eyes of the conservative. What could be more revolutionary
than the Gospel?

It has been said that I am chasing after my youth. This is true.
And not only after my own. Even more than beauty, youth attracts

me, and with an irresistible appeal. I believe the truth lies in youth; I
believe it is always right against us. I believe that, far from trying to
teach it, it is in youth that we, the elders, must seek our lessons. And
I am well aware that youth is capable of errors; I know that our role
is to forewarn youth as best we can; but I believe that often, when
trying to protect youth, we impede it. I believe that each new generation arrives bearing a message that it must deliver; our role is to help
that delivery. I believe that what is called "experience" is often but
an unavowed fatigue, resignation, blighted hope. I believe to be true,
tragically true, this remark of Alfred de Vigny, often quoted, which
seems simple only to those who quote it without understanding it: "A
fine life is a thought conceived in youth and realized in maturity." It
matters little to me, besides, that Vigny himself perhaps did not see
all the meaning I put into it; I make that remark mine.

There are very few of my contemporaries who have remained
faithful to their youth. They have almost all compromised. That is
what they call "learning from life." They have denied the truth that
was in them. The borrowed truths are the ones to which one clings
most tenaciously, and all the more so since they remain foreign to our
intimate self. It takes much more precaution to deliver one's own message, much more boldness and prudence, than to sign up with and
add one's voice to an already existing party. Whence that accusation
of indecision and uncertainty that some hurl at me, precisely because
I believed that it is above all to oneself that it is important to remain
faithful.

DETACHED PAGES

CONVERSATION WITH RATHENAU

X. claims that the Germans' lack of tact is a French invention. So I
show him the letter I receive from Franz Blei, with whom I had rather
good literary relations before the war (it is the first letter to have
come to me from Germany since the war): "Why don't you come to
Munich?" he asks. "You would be received with open arms and would
certainly experience, on getting away from France for a moment, the
same relief that we Germans feel when, in Switzerland for example,
we escape the terrible oppression weighing on our country. . . ." What
can I reply to that? Nothing, of course. I did not reply.

On the other hand, after having read M. Raphaël's book,[26] I felt
a desire to talk with Rathenau, whom I did not yet know, and, taking
advantage of a stay with my friends the Mayrisches, in Luxemburg,

---

[26] *Walter Rathenau, ses projets et ses idées d'organisation économique*
(*Walter Rathenau: His Plans and Ideas for Economic Organization*), by
Gaston Raphaël, appeared in 1919.

had them write him and suggest his coming to meet me at their house.
This was in 1920, when Rathenau no longer occupied any governmental position and had for a time withdrawn from politics.

The two full days I spent at Colpach with Rathenau left me a
clear enough memory so that, a year later, I can note down fragments
of his conversation as readily as I could have done at the time.

I was somewhat embarrassed at first by the extreme affability of
that enormous man, who immediately took me by the arm and led me
along the paths of the estate. He revealed great emotion. "It is the
first time since the war," he told me, "that I have left Germany — at
least for pleasure, for anything other than business — the first time, it
seems to me, that I can breathe freely." He expressed himself in
French with hardly a mistake and, it can really be said, with no accent
whatever.

"I attach to our meeting," he went on, "the greatest importance
and consider it as significant as all the political arrangements between
our two countries." I found no reply available at first and tried to put
into my silence the distance he did not allow me to respect materially.
I had thought that we should converse seriously without ceasing to
feel between us the frightful gap the war had just left. But at the very
first instant, as I say, he had seized my arm, my body, with as much
cordiality and warmth as an old friend would have shown upon meeting me after a long voyage.

In spite of myself I thought, before the mysticism of some of his
remarks, of what Groethuysen used to say to us at Charles Du Bos's.
In the book he was writing before the war on the German character,
he was trying to show that the German — composed of two extremes:
a soul and an automaton — almost never succeeds in filling up the
intermediate space, in being commonly and simply *human. From "Parsifal" to the Goose-Step* was to be the title of the study. It was Parsifal
speaking now.

I remember particularly what he said to me of America, which, he
claimed, "has no soul," has not deserved to have one, for she has not
yet "deigned *to plunge into the abyss of suffering and sin.*"

That same day he outlined to me at length the financial state of
Germany, whose wealth, he said, was not monetary but entirely in
her productive power and in the hard-working qualities of her people,
so that she would not begin to get back on her feet, he was sure of
it, until the value of the mark should be reduced to zero, thus forcing
her to begin anew, on a real rather than a conventional basis.

Some of his theories, and the very ones with which I was most inclined to agree, seemed to me so contrary to the spirit of the Jewish
race that I could not resist showing my amazement. He did not reply
directly, but, approaching the question from the reverse and by a long

detour: "Have you noticed," he asked, "that when certain qualities are too profusely" (this is not the word he used) "distributed among a people, in a race, that people, that race, does not succeed in producing an individual in whom those qualities are very particularly concentrated. In Italy, for instance, if there is no great musician, it is because everybody is a musician. Germany, on the other hand, in the time of Bach, was not at all generally musical. And that is what permitted Bach—" And suddenly he stopped, leaving me to conclude. Certainly he wanted to imply that certain qualities were no less specifically Jewish just because they were not distributed among all the representatives of his race; and that those qualities just happened to be the ones that I was wrongly surprised to find in him.

*

The *Souvenirs de Banville* was one of my greatest literary disappointments. I like to excess that delicate, perspicacious, charming spirit, full of poetic mischievousness. At moments he is almost Ariel. I like him for himself, and I like him against Gautier, one of the most useless speechifiers with whom any literature can be encumbered. With what emotion, what a happy tremor, I opened this little book of *Souvenirs;* with what regret I had to close it soon afterward!

What did I not hope for from those portraits?

What did I find? Praise; still more praise; and such kindness in criticism that . . . jam in which, under the abundance of sugar, the special flavor of each fruit disappears.

*

It is from Balzac that Boylesve descends; not from the best or most important novels; from *Ursule Mirouet* or from *Le Curé de Tours,* for example.[27] It is noteworthy that Balzac's great masterpieces have been less prolific than the lesser works of *La Comédie humaine,* in which the matter, less surely or less minutely treated, left more to be rounded off. It is, in a more general way, interesting to note that the progeny of great men is always doubtful and, so to speak, *oblique,* that it is never the accomplished masterpiece or, better, the accomplished aspect of each work that a disciple will imitate or be inspired by, but on the contrary the shortcoming; just as, in nature, the parasitical prolificness develops on the shady side and not on the sunny side. In any work of art the shortcoming, the weakness, gets by, thanks to the perfect; it is the imperfect that the disciple seizes because that is all he can hope to advance further (this is very badly stated—to be

[27] *Ursule Mirouet* and *The Priest of Tours* are novels that Balzac classified as "Scenes of Provincial Life."

rewritten). Thus what Baudelaire's disciples took from *Les Fleurs du mal*: the macabre, the bizarre, etc. (see Rollinat), never that very perfection which is of the highest price. Likewise for Michelangelo, etc. . . . Much to be said. — It is rare that an artist, however great he may be, develops to perfection all the parts of himself; and when this does happen (Goethe, Racine, Poussin), one can say that he has no followers, for he has blocked all the paths.

✻

The reasons that make those stars wane are perhaps the very ones that linked them, according to Bourget, to the generation preceding mine.[28] For the moral dispositions of one generation are not at all the same as those of the following generation. Bourget extolled them as apostles of pessimism. And it is toward the constellation of the Lion that we feel impelled today. Nothing can be done about this: what we seek in our masters is not discouragement. If Stendhal and Baudelaire still hold a very high place in our firmament today, this is because the rays emanating from their work have still other virtues from those Bourget recognized in them. To tell the truth, it is because, of the whole pleiad cited in the *Essais de psychologie contemporaine*, they alone are perfect artists, and only perfect art is proof against aging.

✻

I am rereading Volume III of Flaubert's *Correspondance* and, whether it be latent or loudly stated, the blasphemy against life, that permanent blasphemy on the part of a writer I love, causes me great pain. I feel the *duty* to be happy, higher and more imperious than the factitious duties of the artist. I pray, I cry from the depths of my soul's distress: My God, give me the faculty to be happy — not with that tragic and fierce happiness of Nietzsche, which I nevertheless admire too, but with that of St. Francis, with that adorable, beaming happiness.

✻

Take care not to confuse art and manner. The manner of the Goncourts, which made them seem so "artistic" in their time, is the cause of their ruin today. They had delicate senses; but an insufficient intelligence made them go into ecstasies over the delicacy of their sensa-

---

[28] In the two volumes of his *Essais de psychologie contemporaine* (*Studies in Contemporary Psychology*), which appeared in 1883 and 1885, Paul Bourget examined the literary idols of the youth of that day: Baudelaire, Renan, Flaubert, Taine, Stendhal, A. Dumas *fils*, Leconte de Lisle, E. and J. de Goncourt, Turgenyev, and H.-F. Amiel.

tions and give importance to what should be subordinated. It is impossible to read a page by them where that good opinion they have of
themselves does not burst out from between the lines; they yield in-
fallibly to that self-satisfaction which makes them think: "Ah, what
artists we are! Ah, how crude other writers are!" Manner is always the
indication, and it soon becomes the penalty, of a self-satisfaction. The
most subtle, the strongest and deepest art — supreme art — is the one
that does not at first allow itself to be recognized. And just as "real
eloquence doesn't give a rap for eloquence," so true art doesn't give
a rap for manner, which is but its caricature.

❊

I hold that the composition of a book is of the first importance and
that it is by a lack of composition that most works of art sin today.
Certain ultra-modern schools protest against this, but the effort at
composition that they reveal was often unable to mask a somewhat
artificial resolve. I am going to reveal to you my whole thought on
this subject: the best thing is to let the work compose itself and give
itself its order, and above all not to *force* it. And I use this word likewise in the sense that horticulturists give it: forced cultivation is a
cultivation that makes a plant blossom prematurely.

I believe that the major shortcoming of writers and artists today is
impatience: if they knew how to wait, their subject would automatically compose itself slowly in their mind; by itself it would cast off the
useless matter and everything that impedes it; it would grow like a
tree whose leading branches are developed at the expense of . . .

It would grow *naturally*.

It is through composition that a painter gives depth to his canvas.
Without composition a work of art can offer only a superficial beauty.

It is necessary and it suffices. The work of art . . . in which whatever serves no purpose is harmful.

❊

I had the excellent good luck, while still very young, of being
called upon to read, as a regular thing, to a group of people of different ages, of great common sense though of average culture, and of
most varied reactions. The gift of sympathy that throughout my life
has been my torment and my open sore allowed me to feel — with
amazing perspicacity and without its being expressed — the degree of
assent or boredom of each of my listeners. Without always accepting
their tacit judgments, I recognized their cogency. "It is true: this pas-

sage is too long. The author has gone to a lot of trouble, and this is
too evident. . . ."

❋

I do not yet know whether I have more envy or scorn for those
very direct men whose personality without secret is revealed and completely expressed in every gesture, whose figure could all be represented on a single plane.

As for me, I am constantly aware that my qualities prejudice one
another. They are complicated. Yet I do not want to examine into
either the detail or the total number of them; I wish to enjoy only the
harmony that . . .

I intend to have everything within reach. A certain restlessness accompanies this desire.

❋

How could I fail to speak with difficulty? I have new things to say.

❋

Fear that sort of balancing of the sentence (indulgence toward
which I am only too inclined), that fatal number — which has nothing to do with rhythm and the natural expression of the movement
of thought.

I have always had more understanding, more memory, and more
taste for natural history than for history. The fortuitous has always
interested me less than the necessary, and it has always seemed to me
that one could learn more from what is repeated every day than from
what occurs but once. (External inevitability — intimate inevitability.)

❋

H. C. accused me one day of coquetry in the arrangement of my
sentences; nothing could be more false. I like only the strict and bare
necessity. When I began to write my *Nourritures*, I realized that the
very subject of my book *was* to banish all metaphor from it. There is
not a movement of my style that does not correspond to a need of my
mind; most often it is but a need of order. The writer's eloquence must
be that of the soul itself, of the thought; artificial elegance is a burden
to me; likewise all added poetry.

❋

The wise Sainte-Beuve denounces, I do not remember where, that
frequent intellectual failing of urging oneself by preference, and seek-

ing invitations, in the direction in which one is already most inclined
by nature. And this is what makes me so often deplore the fact that
parents should be given the care of children who already naïvely resemble them and find in them the example and encouragement of their
secret dispositions; so that, to tell the truth, family education rarely
straightens them up but simply helps them to bend in one way or another, and the sons of set parents are even more set themselves, bent
over to the right or the left and often unable to recover the vertical
position without a revolt that is full of risks. If I were not a lover of
brevity, I should write a whole book on this subject, but one that would
make people cry shame; for after all, out of some forty families I have
been able to observe, I know hardly four in which the parents do not
act in such a way that nothing would be more desirable for the child
than to escape their influence. Some people are indignant at the alco-
holic teaching his son to drink; but they, according to their lights, do
not act differently.

※

X. begins one day to reread some of his old letters (to his dead
mother), amazed to discover that, formerly, he had already gone
through a crisis identical with the one he is now going through (a
crisis he did not remember), and that he acted then exactly as he is
doing now, just as stupidly — that is to say, that he becomes aware
that he cannot act otherwise — and he remembers that he had never-
thless promised himself then never to be caught in this again. (See,
for instance, Paul Laurens, who irresistibly "chooses the noblest" decision.) He reflects that each one of us is constantly repeating the
same gesture; or that, more exactly, there is in the character of each
one of us a propensity toward a particular gesture that determines the
conduct of his whole life.

※

"No, I am saying simply that death is easier to face than life. Just
imagine Roger, capable of facing a thousand deaths to free his An-
gelica; his courage will fail him if he sees, as a reward for his prowess,
a lifelong slavery beside his mistress, on the wave-washed reef."

As soon as desire is involved in it, love cannot hope to last.

※

If good sentiments were enough to make a good book, *La Pâque
des roses*[29] would be one of the best. But alas! "the qualities of the
heart are as independent of those of the mind as the faculties of genius

---

[29] *The Easter of the Roses* by Touny-Lerys.

are of the soul's nobilities," wrote Balzac. Oh, what pale ink and what
an awkward pen Touny-Lerys has to express his affections! — affections
so recommendable that disarmed criticism dares only encourage and
smile affectionately.

✳

The man subject to afterthoughts buys a vase for the pleasure of
giving it to a friend who desires it. Between the buying and the giving
he has time to reflect; complicated scruples convince him that it is
indelicate to give this too expensive vase (ostentation of his wealth,
putting his friend in a false position, etc.). He takes it home.

Meanwhile the friend goes to the shop to buy the vase and, not
finding it there, thinks the other bought it to keep it from him.

This judgment forms and becomes fixed in his mind. When the
man with the vase comes to give it to him, it is too late; he conflicts
with the other's conviction that, if he is giving it away, it is because
he has ceased to like the vase and that it has a flaw. He doesn't have
to look long for it; it is a defect that completely depreciates the vase
in his eyes. The man with the vase swears that he had not seen it. The
conversation becomes bitter — and the vase is broken at the same time
as their friendship.

And the worst of it is that the man with the vase becomes what the
other claims him to be, makes him be. Useless to insist thereon.

✳

I admire, as I continue reading Flaubert's letters, the force of the
man's grip.

The difficulties he plans to overcome are all on the same plane; and
he always finds to reduce them the same common denominators.

✳

It must, however, be admitted that writers have never been more
anxious about perfection than when . . . subordinated and modest. ·

A certain decadence in craft follows a social infatuation.

Of the danger of sitting in the first rows.

✳

I call "journalism" everything that will be less interesting tomorrow
than today. How many great artists win their cases only on appeal!

✳

Notes for a study of Francis Jammes

A poet — not an artist.

And I am not trying to establish here, like an idle talker, some empty, subtle distinction. I consider it as very important that, coming after a school that pushed the adoration of art to the point of scorning poetry (I mean just as much Heredia as Mallarmé), Jammes, in order to overcome that excess, had to preserve an almost total blindness in regard to art; nothing upset his belief in himself, since he had eyes for nothing but that. I do not say that Henri de Régnier and Vielé-Griffin were any less the poet (I can, however), but they were certainly more the artist. Francis Jammes was a poet and was solely that. Music, painting, philosophy (I speak of it here as of an art), and I was on the point of saying literature, are to him closed gardens to which he has not the key; he hardly notices his lack; he, whose senses are as delicate as those of a wild thing, remains in front of a painting, a symphony, an idea, like his dog in front of the flowers; they are not his game.

I know that he can become enthusiastic about a Cranach, but that is because he thinks he sees, in its apparent clumsiness, a sort of negation of art.

Francis Jammes expresses, less ironically I believe than M. H. C. claims, but with that sort of intentional naïveté which he carefully cultivates in himself, the perfect subjectivism of his poetic convictions and of his sentimental landscape. That he should feel *out of his element* as soon as he gets outside his fold goes without saying; Barrès wrote excellently some time ago that there are souls capable of a single landscape. And I do not hold this against Jammes; his strength at least lies in having understood that culture, getting outside his element (either physically or intellectually), would, with his nature, produce nothing good. But how little the hares care about this! And how little anxious they are to know whether their doe-hare comes from a seat in the Pyrenees, a Norman field, or a Thuringian furrow! And the drops of water of the streams! each one of which can say, thank God, with Terence: *"Aqua sum,"* and *"lympha fugax,"* [30] and "none of the properties of water is alien to me." And the heart of man! and all *natural things!* . . .

I like Francis Jammes; but I prefer truth. (I have forgotten how that is said in Latin.)

Francis Jammes sees God with a beard, like his; I, who see him

----

[30] "I am water," and "running stream."

smooth-shaven, this embarrasses me considerably in the admiration I should like to have for *Monsieur le Curé d'Ozeron;* [31] because I keep thinking that the beard is artificial. And everywhere in the book I keep seeing the beard.

An amused indulgence for his most extreme peculiarities and the hope (which soon became assurance) that what is considered a fault in the shy state will be taken for a virtue when emboldened. But if someone other than he unwisely ventured to think the same, you should have seen him! He would accept as sincere and natural only what resembled him, and only in a domain in which he remained indubitably superior.

In Jammes, no, it was not exactly pose, but a very self-satisfied surrender to himself — that made him, for instance, just as we were to set out on an excursion (organized by him, at Hendaye), sink onto a chair because a certain breath of air had just brought him a certain scent of jasmin that reminded him of Mamore.

Jammes has often been compared to La Fontaine, and I find them, indeed, alike in more than one regard (a certain ingenuity, roguishness even, in their way of seeing, followed by a naïveté in the expression — just the contrary of what ordinarily occurs), alike to the point that one can think of Jammes what Chamfort wrote of La Fontaine:

"When La Fontaine is bad, it is because he is careless. . . ."

But Jammes is carried along by an epoch that, in matters of art, intends to make a virtue of negligence. And I shall attempt to explain . . . just how far his natural gifts are exaggerated.

(The authorizations this provides. — Flattery. — A dynasty of poets without art.)

Create "associations." According to Wordsworth, this is the highest faculty of the human mind. (*The Prelude,* Book XIV.)

. . . I believe the kindness of a Gustave Flaubert to be just as great, just as responsive, but I understand through what sort of modesty he hides it, and I feel that Jammes's poetic compassion would have irritated him.

The only thing one can say here is that Jammes cries out readily, and the only thing that should matter to us is that he cries out beautifully. He was frequently satisfied to do so readily; and the deplorable

---

[31] *The Vicar of Ozeron,* a novel of Catholic inspiration by Jammes (1918).

thing is that a great number of young girls and old maids have been
most grateful to him for just this.

Often the label *influence* is applied to the simplest authorization.
The influence of Nietzsche has been seen in the most shameful uncon-
straint of egotism; many finding authority in . . . (quote Pascal's
sentence about the example of Alexander).[32] Likewise, numerous po-
etasters, flatteringly fancying that Jammes's poetry consisted in his
negligence and his loose form, resolved to be poets merely by casting
off all constraint.

I should be glad to say, somewhat generalizing my thought, that
all examples of casting off the reins are pernicious. One had to be
Jammes — that is to say, *one of God's signal successes* — to allow oneself such license; those who feel thereby authorized today to sing like
pure birds are lost. And yet I should not dare to say that the influence
of Jammes is pernicious; at least it is not solely pernicious. (The
epoch.)

One cannot imagine a more exquisitely aerated poetry.

There are certain poets, of whom Jammes is perhaps the only one
among us today, who, it seems, would have written their work just the
same in whatever period they had been born (and whatever might be
their ignorance of others' literature).

I feel keenly that a Whitman, for instance, could only have been
born an American, but I mean that, once born, he would have written
anywhere whatever and at any time whatever his *Leaves of Grass,*
even if Homer, Shakespeare, and Longfellow had not existed. Likewise, with nevertheless a little bit of literature added, Jammes could
have got along without reading; I hope for the honor of France that
he could only have been born a Frenchman — but all the same I can
see him writing his *Élégies* at Tibur under Augustus, his *Jean de
Noarrieu* anywhere whatever; he has a very definite local savor, it is
true, but in China he would have had a Chinese savor; he speaks
uniquely well of the countryside of his district, but there is nothing

---

[32] Pascal's reflection, which Gide does not quote at this point, is number
103 in the Brunschvicg edition of the *Pensées:* "The example of Alexander's
chastity has not made so many continent men as that of his drunkenness has
made intemperate ones. There is no shame in not being so virtuous as he,
and it seems excusable to be no more vicious than he. We think we have escaped the vices of the common run of men when we see ourselves indulging
in those of great men; and yet we do not take care that in that regard they
belong to the common run. We are linked to them by the end through which
they are linked to the mass; for however high they rise, they are still joined
to the least of men at some point. They are not suspended in air, quite cut
off from our society. . . ."

very particularly Pyrenean about him. His spirit is the spirit of Jammes, not of Orthez; nothing is less motivated in him than himself.

He has the petulance, the melodious outburst, the sudden imprecation, the charming lack of understanding of a bird.

I have always suspected him of confusing poverty and frugality and of having no trouble in finding the latter poetic. Moreover, real poverty is that of cities, because it is such a close neighbor to the excesses.

The more unequal a poet is (which is the same as saying the more spontaneous he is), the less he accepts anyone's preferring this or that part of his work; the less patiently he suffers criticism. This is because it seems to him, all his work emanating from the same source, that everything in his work must be of equal quality—which, on the contrary, can be true only of an extraordinarily polished work. That facile self-satisfaction would run the risk of leading the artist into an infinite presumptuousness, but Catholicism is there at hand: the pride that offers itself to God takes on an appearance of modesty. He proud? You see for yourself that he is kneeling.

"I have always thought that the critical faculty is rarer than that of invention." (Beardsley.)

Quote this as an epigraph to the study on Francis Jammes.

I have never met in all literature perhaps, and I find it hard to imagine, a writing creature in whom the critical sense is more wondrously lacking. More deliberately; more unconsciously also.

"There are to be sure these two lines," he told me on showing me a long poem he had written during the night, ". . . which don't seem to me very good."

"Well, correct them."

"I don't dare. I believe I no longer have the right to."

And if I had been naïve enough to ask: Why? "Because last night," he would have replied, "if they seemed to me good when I was inspired, now I am consequently not so good a judge."

In his earliest writings, a great taste for the artificial (which in him is confused with a taste for exoticism): *Mr. de Voltaire, Le Mangeur de poissons, Sinbad,* etc.,[33] and if he repudiates that later on, there remained in his mind that strange confusion between artifice and art which made him repudiate one with the other.

----

[33] *Mr. Voltaire, The Fish-Eater, Sinbad.*

Study in Jammes what Lasserre calls "the sagging of the reason under spontaneity, the dispersion in sentiment through the abdication of the organizing and constructive energies." (*Romantisme*, pp. 158–9.)

Even though many of Jammes's compositions balance in perfection even the happiest productions of the most accomplished art, it is always unseemly, in connection with Jammes's poetry, to speak of art.

"The purely poetic gifts were thenceforth augmented in him by a very keen, very sure sense of observation," says Edmond Pilon speaking of Jammes.

Jammes has, on the contrary, one of the least observing minds I know; his intuition proceeds by sudden leaps; he has the genius, the demon of analogy. His contemplation or his emotion simply *takes advantage* of the object.

To be unable to take facts and people for what they are, there is no more foolish error. Wishing Ingres a warmer palette or Delacroix a more correct draftmanship can no longer dare be done, since it was too much indulged in for two generations. At most one can, like Montesquieu, say: "Turenne had no vices; and perhaps if he had had any, he would have carried certain virtues farther." (VII, p. 165.)

Deploring the excesses of the Renaissance, the homosexuality of Greece, slavery in ancient Rome, is possible only if one threw away the rest; but isn't it wiser to realize that this all remains in a very close correlation, that the superabundance of life in the Renaissance could not overflow into literature without at the same time overflowing into manners, that without homosexuality Greece would not have deserved her sculpture, that, as it has been said before me: the Roman slave permitted the free man — and that Jammes's lack of intelligence favored his poetry.

❋

EVOLUTION

"What!" he said. "You uphold and prove that whole successions of centuries passed before man could be formed; and, for the Supreme Being, you do not admit that even more time is needed? Understand that God is the end-result, not the point of departure, of the whole creation. And this, moreover, would not prevent the whole creation from being his work. But he was not realized until after us. All evolution must lead to God."

1922

Yesterday Roger Martin du Gard came to read me the part of *Les Thibault* that I did not yet know. Martin du Gard incarnates in my eyes one of the highest and noblest forms of ambition: that which is accompanied by a constant effort to perfect oneself and to obtain, to demand of oneself, the most possible. I don't know whether I do not admire, even more than the finest gifts, an obstinate patience.

2 January

Yesterday, morning and luncheon alone; a bit sad; or let us say rather: grave. Reading and attempt at meditation; correcting proofs.

Around four o'clock, went to the Drouins', where I find Valentine and her daughters. Then to Charlie Du Bos's, where I find him alone. The conversation immediately takes on an extraordinarily enveloping and penetrating turn: it is an 'Οαριστὺς of thoughts. It seems that he hides away there all the precaution of his affection, the diversion of his voluptuousness.

I urge him insistently to continue his *Journal intime,* in which he will surely reveal the best of him, which too often escapes his articles.[1]

I finish this New Year's Day at Mme Mühlfeld's, where, after the other guests have left, Fargue and Valéry amuse themselves by reciting great obscenities that are not very new. Then I return to the Villa to dine alone.

In the evening, opening La Bruyère at random, I read this passage I did not know (or at least to which I had not given sufficient attention):

"The wise man is cured of ambition through ambition itself; he aims at such great things that he cannot limit himself to what are called treasures, positions, fortune, and favor; in such paltry advantages he sees nothing good and solid enough to fill his heart and deserve his anxieties and desires; *he even must make an effort not to disdain them too much.* The only possession capable of tempting him is that sort of fame which should be born of virtue pure and simple; but men rarely grant it, and he does without." (*Mérite personnel,* p. 43.)[2]

---

[1] *Extracts from the Journals of Charles Du Bos were in fact published in 1931. Only in 1946 was the complete publication undertaken posthumously.*

[2] *Concerning Personal Merit is one of the sections of The Characters.*

3 January

I planned to devote my morning yesterday and the best part of
the day to work; a *pneumatique* [3] from Rathenau, expressing his desire not to leave Paris without having seen me, made me rush to the
Crillon, where he was still staying one day more. I wanted neither to
take the first step nor to leave his call unanswered. He received me
in his private drawing-room and, for an hour, we talked in a rather
serious way. It is very hard for me not to be embarrassed by his over-
cordial manner of seizing hold of one; his hand hardly left my arm
once during the whole conversation, of which the refrain was "all
Europe is rushing toward the abyss." Haguenin came to interrupt us
and I yielded my place to him.

Lunched at Martin du Gard's and, right after lunch, launched into
a criticism of his novel, or, more generally, of his manner — which carried us very far. He shows himself to be extraordinarily anxious and
desirous of acquiring certain qualities that are quite opposed to his
nature: mystery, shadow, strangeness — all things that the artist derives from certain dealings with the Devil. And for more than an
hour we talked of the *indirect presentation* of events. I planned to
note this all down this morning, but M. came and rang at my door
rather early; and, besides, I feel as if doped by a dreadful night. Last
evening I had thought at length of *Les Faux-Monnayeurs;* tremendous
effort to vivify my characters and *relate* them among themselves; after
which, impossible to find sleep.

Em. writes me: "I am greatly worried by the campaign of vilifica-
tion opened up against you. Of course it is the force of your thought
and its authority that has instigated this. Oh! if only you were in-
vulnerable, I should not tremble. But you are vulnerable, and you
know it; and I know it."

Vulnerable . . . I am so, I was so, only through her. Since, it is
all the same to me and I have ceased fearing anything. . . . What
have I to lose that is still dear to me?

5 January

My good days of work are those I begin by reading an ancient
author, one of those that are called "classics." A page is enough; a
half-page, if only I read it in the proper state of mind. It is not so
much a lesson one must seek in them as the *tone,* and that sort of being
out of one's element which sets the present effort in proper proportion,

---

[3] The Paris post offices provide a special-delivery service connecting all
the offices by pneumatic tube; letters so sent are called *pneumatiques* or
petits bleus (because of the small blue form on which they must be written).

without divesting the moment of any of its urgency. And this is the way I like to end my day too.

This morning I copy out La Bruyère's passage on true and false greatness. (II, 42.) [4]

8 January

Working this morning in front of the triple window of the drawing-room, I observe the strange gardening operation that the birds, warblers as well as sparrows, practice on the sallow-thorn bushes in my little garden. They peck at and pinch off the nascent buds from each branch; but the branches, too flexible, provide a perch only at their base, so that the birds can reach with ease only the first buds, the lowest ones, those nearest the trunk. Those on the end of each tigella are consequently preserved; and it is precisely toward those that the sap rushes naturally; so that the shrub opens up and stretches out and widens as much as possible. The terminal buds always develop at the expense of the others, even to the point of completely atrophying them. Yet those sacrificed buds are, or would have been, quite capable of development too, but their possibilities remain latent; were it not for pruning which, protesting against the too great lateral extension of the shrub, drives life back to them; but this can be done only at the sacrifice of the terminal buds.

16 January

Charlie Du Bos sends me *The Marriage of Heaven and Hell*,[5] which I had told him I wanted to read, sure as I was of finding in it a revelation and a confirmation of certain thoughts that have long been stirring within me. My meeting with Blake is of the greatest importance to me. Already I had glimpsed him, during the first year of

---

[4] The passage, which Gide does not include in the *Journal*, is:

"False greatness is cold and inaccessible; aware of its weakness, it hides itself or at least does not reveal itself boldly, letting only enough of it be seen as is necessary to impress and to keep from appearing what it really is: simply pettiness. True greatness is free, easy, and familiar, letting itself be touched and handled. It loses nothing from being seen at close range; the more it is known, the more it is admired; through kindness it stoops to the level of inferiors and effortlessly returns to its original position. At times it yields, neglects itself, gives up its advantages, always able to pick them up again and make the most of them. It can laugh, joke, and play, but always without loss of dignity. It is approached with freedom and restraint together; its character is noble and open, inspires respect and confidence, and makes princes appear to us as great and even very great without making us feel that we are small."

[5] By William Blake.

the war, in a book of *Selections* from Élisabeth Van Rysselberghe's library, rue Laugier, where I was then living with the Théos. Like an astronomer calculating the existence of a star whose rays he does not yet perceive directly, I foresaw Blake, but did not yet suspect that he formed a constellation with Nietzsche, Browning, and Dostoyevsky. The most brilliant star, perhaps, of the group; certainly the strangest and the most distant.

21 January

Jules Delacre asks me for a few lines of introduction for his first program. He is opening with *Le Chandelier*.[6] I reread the play with rapture.

Sunday, 28 January

Last night, leaving the Godebskis' with M., we walk together toward the Madeleine métro station. It had rained considerably during the day; now a strong wind was blowing, drying the sky and the streets. It was a pleasure to walk, and M. was in an excellent mood. Opposite the Olympia we notice an old hawker of newspapers, bent double, with a whitening beard, talking to himself in an undertone. We accost him and buy a paper; and right away the conversation begins. I ask him how much he earns and whether or not he does anything else but sell papers all day long; whether he has ever done anything else in his life. He tells us that when he was younger he was a clerk in a business house, but he didn't have the health he should have had; he had to give up that trade.

"And since that time you feel stronger?"

"Why, I can say, sir, that my strength has decupled rather than centupled."

On this fine phrase we leave him.

4 February

Every day, and all day long, I ask myself this question — or rather this question asks itself of me: Shall I find it hard to die?

I do not think that death is particularly hard for those who most loved life. On the contrary.

Freud. Freudianism. . . . For the last ten years, or fifteen, I have been indulging in it without knowing it. Many an idea of mine, taken singly and set forth or developed at length in a thick book, would have made a great hit — if only it were the only child of my brain. I cannot supply the initial outlay and the upkeep for each one of them, nor even for any one in particular.

---

[6] *The Beacon,* one of Musset's comedies.

"Here is something that, I fear, will bring grist to your mill," Rivière said to me the other day, speaking of Freud's little book on sexual development. I should say!

It is high time to publish *Corydon*.

8 February

I am preparing the six lectures on Dostoyevsky that I have promised. Very good work since Élisabeth has left me. But the last three days the cold has been curling me all up. I felt very well, perhaps better than I have ever been. And suddenly, yesterday, dizzy spells again. They resumed last night. This morning I cannot succeed in formulating a single idea.

10 February

"One must first seek to know oneself," I read in the interview with Henri Bordeaux (*Annales politiques et littéraires*). Odd advice! Knowing himself is the very last thing to which the artist should aspire; and he can achieve it only through his works, by producing them. This is at least the case of all great artists. And this explains the coldness of certain works: when the artist "knew himself."

The best means of learning to know oneself is seeking to understand others.

18 February

Yesterday, first lecture on Dostoyevsky. Too many quotations; far too many. A certain intellectual shyness, modesty, urged me to let Dostoyevsky speak as much as possible; it was also the fear of falling short that made me prepare those quotations like so many safety-islands — which I had to use, even after they had become useless. All together, rather dissatisfied with myself; and even very dissatisfied when I think of what it might have been. But this will be a lesson for the next one.

1 March

Every time I go for some time without writing, I am seized with the fear of having forgotten how. Was ever a writer as unsure of himself? And yet the sentence that satisfies me is the one that comes as from the outside and without my looking for it, or that rises up from within me spontaneously. But this welling up is not continuous, and it is just because it is spontaneous that I fear it may dry up.

17 March

Relapse; fatigue and apathy. The dizzy spells have become so frequent that I no longer dare make any appointment. I delivered my fourth lecture, last Saturday, in such a state of discomfort that I wondered whether or not I could get through it; the theater walls swayed before my eyes; but my thoughts swung back and forth even more. I began each sentence without having any idea how I should finish it; without even knowing with what I could fill it. It goes without saying that that lecture was "the best" if I can believe those who complimented me on the way out.

In the evening I made a great effort to go to the d'Harcourts' for they have just come back from Lima with a collection of old Mexican vases that they want to show to a few friends.[7] I had promised to go and was to find there Paul and Jeannie Valéry, the Ghéon-Macquins, the Lacostes, etc. I myself was taking Jean Schlumberger, with whom I had dined. But as soon as I was in the d'Harcourts' drawing-room (and, besides, particularly embarrassed by the reproachful look of Paule Gobillard, whom I had neglected calling on for much too long), I felt so ill at ease that I skipped out without taking leave of anyone.

Went to consult Dr. Chiron; rather flattered by his amazement when I held out to him the analysis-report I had just had made.

"It's not at all surprising that you felt so tired."

22 March

Constant dizziness; fatigue. Return of winter; we are shivering. Everything takes on a frightful taste of ashes.

I do not understand very well what they call "my influence." Where do they see it? I don't recognize myself anywhere. It is what differs most from me that I prefer and I have never tried to push anyone save in his own path, in his own joy.

A good teacher is constantly concerned with teaching his disciples to get along without him. But because I say to Nathanaël, at the end of my book: "And now throw this book away; leave me," they get angry.[8]

Sadness is almost never anything but a form of fatigue in my case. But I must confess that there are moments, of late, when I feel mortally sad.

28 March

Gave, last Saturday, my last lecture on Dostoyevsky. In view of my great fatigue, and fearing that I might lack presence of mind, I had written down almost all of it.

---

[7] Raoul and Marguerite d'Harcourt were collectors of and authorities on the arts of ancient Mexico and Peru.

[8] In the Envoi of *Les Nourritures terrestres* (*The Fruits of the Earth*).

I now have ahead of me an article on Valéry I promised for the special number of *Le Divan;* a brief notice on Vannicola, which the mayor of Capri requests for a publication that will make it possible to give poor Vannicola a decent tomb; an important article for the *Revue de Genève* (on the present state of Europe). And finally, this evening, Rivière asks me to do a note on Morand's charming book.[9] All this distracts me dreadfully from my novel. I cannot get back to it, moreover, until after the presentation of *Saül,* of which the rehearsals are soon to begin.[10] During them I shall scarcely be able to do more, probably, than dictate my lectures to the stenographer I have engaged for the month of April.

I have felt somewhat better for two days. I should like to work only in joy; that joyful activity of the mind which I knew last autumn and which took the place of happiness.

This afternoon heard Honegger's music for *Saül.* I fear that it may stand out too much and that the whole demoniac part may be enlarged out of all proportion.

Finished reading *Othello,* swooning with admiration.

22 April

Left with Copeau to spend three days at Montigny, in the charming little house of P. A. Laurens and his wife, which I did not yet know. And as soon as we get back, we begin the rehearsals of *Saül.*

I should feel well if it were not for these dizzy spells that seize me every day on awakening. Worked too much of late, urged on by the presence of the secretary I engaged for two months and to whom I am dictating my lectures on Dostoyevsky. I was able to get through the first two before my departure. They cause me considerable trouble and I get lost in the abundance of notes I took. I should like to finish this work before summer; I am eager to get back to my novel. But everything I find a means of saying through Dostoyevsky and apropos of him is dear to me and I attach a great importance to it. It will be, just as much as a book of criticism, a book of confessions, to anyone who knows how to read; or rather: a profession of faith.

[9] Gide's article appeared in *La Revue de Genève* for January 1923 in a symposium on "The Future of Europe" to which Keyserling, Middleton Murry, Pareto, Merezhkovski, and Unamuno also contributed. The book by Paul Morand is probably *Ouvert la nuit* (*Open All Night*), but Gide did not review anything by Morand at this time.

[10] Gide's drama *Saul,* though published in 1903, was never produced in France until Copeau put it on at the Vieux-Colombier on 16 June 1922 for nine performances.

8 May

One completely overcomes only what one assimilates.

It is in order to leave the skim milk for the weak that the healthy stomach takes the cream.

OSSIA: [11] If the vigorous man did not take the cream, the weak man would not have the skim milk.

5 June

Finished, very painfully, the revision of my lectures. Finished the translation of Blake.[12] The rehearsals of *Saül* still keep me in Paris. Great need of rest; almost incessant dizziness; great desire to flee.

Attended the other evening the opening of Ghéon's play: *Le Débat de Nicolagie et de Sainte Anne.*[13]

It seems to me that Ghéon is playing the role of "the helot drunk with God."

Hyères, Monday, 11 July

Left Porquerolles yesterday, where I spent twelve days with the Martin du Gards.[14]

We left the island together and separated only a little before Hyères, at the station whence the train was to take them to Toulon.

The wind that considerably enlivened our crossing calmed down completely toward evening. . . . (God! how that sentence will annoy me if I happen to reread it later on! This translation of *Hamlet,* which is obsessing me right now, keeps my nose close to words. How could the mind give itself plenty of room when it is constantly drawn backward? — That translation is enough; what do I care about writing well here? It is against that that I have most to struggle. A certain need of number, an indulgence toward eurythmy, bends my style. I should like less polish, more broken edge and accent.)

Yesterday, after dinner, the moon rose exactly opposite the hotel (which is on the edge of the sea), so full, so tremendous, and so yellow that one wondered at first if it was really the moon. . . . But what else do you expect it to be? The sun had just barely set; the colors had not yet disappeared; the sea, quite smooth now, lent its azure to the bronze reflections of the sky to produce an indescribable green, which seemed chemical or vegetable. One would have said that the moon

---

[11] *Ossia* is the Italian for "or else."

[12] Gide's translation of *The Marriage of Heaven and Hell* was first published in 1923.

[13] *The Debate between Nicolagia and St. Anne.*

[14] Porquerolles is the largest of the Iles d'Hyères, off the Mediterranean coast of France.

herself contributed to the gilding of the west; in the still luminous air it cast no rays; it seemed a large colored but non-luminous object and it cast on the sea's jade surface only discreet gold spangles, like a carpet covering a narrow pathway for a Savior walking on the waters. It was only much later that it took possession of the sea, spreading out at great length a dazzling sheen, no longer gilded, but silvered, for the moon itself, while it was becoming more luminous, was losing all color as if it owed its brightness to its excessive pallor. . . . Enough!

Eleven o'clock

I have already been in the water twice today; the second time, naked, followed by a long sun-bath on the sand.

12 July

What I should like to write now is *Les Nouvelles Nourritures*.[15] And I can write it properly only in spite of myself. It must be as unconcerted as anything can be.

This pine grove would be charming, which stretches out along the beach, which is broken up by dunes, and where cistus, lentiscuses, briers, and sallow-thorns form the underbrush. I never meet anyone here, but no god inhabits it either, since the trace of man has so profaned, disenchanted, soiled it. Everywhere old tin cans, rags, eggshells, nameless rubbish, greasy papers, turds, toilet-paper, broken bottles. Everywhere the image of selfishness, of overfamiliarity, and of gluttony.

12 July

I go off to Le Pesquier to see the poor old man I had promised to visit. He is eighty-six. His sister is seventy-five; she lives with him and I had taken her for his wife. It is now twenty years that he has been living at Le Pesquier. This is where he landed after having wandered everywhere, gone around the world several times. He tells what Le Pesquier was like when he first came there: a few huts, wonderful cork-oaks (there is only one left now), and an abundance of mesembryanthemums, which he calls "witches."

On my way back I find in the sand, not far from the shore, an extraordinary huge lily, greenish white, on a rather short stem, which is indeed one of the strangest flowers I have ever seen in this region.[16] On the beach, little golden-brown tiger-beetles.

---

[15] *New Fruits of the Earth* did not appear until 1935.

[16] Doubtless the lily of which Moréas speaks:
Je naquis au bord d'une mer . . . etc. . . . (I was born on the edge of a sea . . . etc. . . .) [A.]

13 July

You ask the child who is in the water: "How is the water this morning?" He replies: "The same like yesterday."

Obviously that is more satisfactory to him, seems to him more precise and in a better style, than to say: "Like yesterday."

14 July

I finish translating, this morning, the first act of *Hamlet* and give up proceeding further. I have spent three weeks on these few pages, at the rate of four to six hours a day. The result does not satisfy me. The difficulty is never completely overcome, and in order to write good French, one has to get too far away from Shakespeare. (It seems to me that this is peculiar to *Hamlet*, that the text of *Antony and Cleopatra* was much less thorny and allowed one to follow it better. And even though the very subject of *Hamlet* is stranger, richer, more subtle, and touches us more deeply right now, I did not for a moment experience those swoons of rapture that shook me all through the reading of *Othello*.) Marcel Schwob's translation, exact though it be, is obscure, almost incomprehensible in spots, amorphous, arhythmical, and as if unbreathable. Is it really this text that we heard at Sarah Bernhardt's? — without changes, without cuts? How it must have embarrassed the actors! Certain of Shakespeare's sentences are as wily as the devil, full of redundancies . . . I should like an Englishman to explain their beauty to me. Faced with Schwob's sentences, which strive to sacrifice neither a repetition nor a turning, you think: it must be very beautiful in English. But *Hamlet* has long been a sacred text and we admire without questioning.[17]

15 July

Is it a shortcoming of my mind? The explanations I hear given of this or that literary difficulty rarely seem good to me — or at least it seems to me that I could suggest a better one. Thus it is that Thibaudet, in an article, which is moreover very interesting, on Jarry, assimilating the character of *Ubu* to Flaubert's *Garçon*, claims to see the origin of the latter in that bombastic and stupid way the Norman bourgeois has of saying *"mon garçon"* to call those whose name he doesn't know: "How goes it, my boy?" And Thibaudet quotes, as supporting evidence, a letter from some colleague or other suggesting the idea that Flaubert must have suffered at being hailed in this manner

---

[17] André Gide's translation of the first act of *Hamlet* was published in the Paris bilingual review *Échanges* in December 1929. His entire translation of the tragedy, completed many years later, was first published in New York in 1945 by Pantheon Books.

by some imbeciles, during his childhood. — This all seems to me su-
premely silly.[18]

I have always thought, and still think, that Flaubert took the idea
of his character from the expression: *"mener la vie de garçon"* (live a
bachelor's life), which was current then. Little Gustave and his friend
Ernest Chevalier must have been struck by that expression, and by
other similar ones: "an old bachelor," "a bachelor apartment." They
must have wondered what that "bachelor's life" could be like, in-
trigued by the insinuations it implied; and, inspired doubtless by some
"bachelors" they knew (or at least their parents knew), who were
said to be living that mysterious "bachelor's life" in Paris, they built
in the realm of the fantastic, as indeed the schoolboys of Rennes did,
with Jarry, for Papa Ubu.

And now in the preface to *Hamlet* (Schwob, p. xix), which I am
reading this morning, there is an explanation of the vulgar jokes that
Hamlet addresses to the ghost: "true-penny . . . old mole." According to Taine: "He tries to joke as a child whistles in the dark, in order
not to be afraid." To begin with, it is noteworthy that Hamlet does
not permit himself these jokes at the beginning of the encounter. The
individual meeting with the ghost has already taken place, and Hamlet
when he is *alone* with the ghost does not permit himself anything of
the sort. He is, on the contrary, excessively solemn, like the ghost himself. He risks these jokes in questionable taste only afterward, once
in possession of the secret, and back among the other students. It is in
their presence that he dares them; he wants to swagger in their presence; the jokes are for them and are already a part of the comedy he
is getting ready to play; they are the first attempts at that "antic disposition" he plans to "put on."

I have scarcely known, throughout my "career," anything but flops;
and I can even say that the flatness of the flop was in direct ratio to
the importance and originality of the work, so that it was to *Paludes,
Les Nourritures,* and *Les Caves du Vatican* that I owed the worst ones.
Of all my books the one that on the contrary brought me the warmest,
most substantial, and promptest praises is the one that (not the least
well turned out perhaps) remains the most outside my work, that
interests me the least (I am using the word in its most subtle sense),
and that, all things considered, I should be most willing to see disappear. After this, how could I be surprised that *Saül* should have

---

[18] Alfred Jarry's famous farce of *King Ubu* was originally composed
when he was a schoolboy; it is an absurd and pointed satire. The name *Garçon* that Flaubert gave to one of his characters means both "boy" and
"bachelor."

been so coldly received by the critics? They saw nothing but declamation in it, as they saw nothing but words in my *Nourritures*. Are you then unable to recognize a sob unless it has the same sound as yours?

La Bastide, Saturday, 22 July

It seems to me that each of my books was not so much the product of a new state of mind as its cause, on the contrary, and the original provocation of that mental and spiritual disposition in which I had to keep myself in order properly to elaborate the book. I should like to express this more simply: that the book, as soon as it is conceived, disposes of me wholly, and that, for its sake, everything in me to my very depths tunes up. I no longer have any other personality than the one that is suitable to that work — objective; subjective? These words lose all meaning here; for if it happens that I use myself as a model (and sometimes it seems to me that there can be no other exact way of painting), this is because I first began by becoming the very one I wanted to portray.

I am rereading aloud with Mme Théo and Élisabeth Van Rysselberghe the seventh book of *The Ring and the Book* (Pompilia). Abnegation can go no further.

26 July

Browning's canto finished, eager for a more current book to read, we tackle *A Laodicean* by Hardy. Unable to go any further than the hundredth page. What is one supposed to see in a book so desperately mediocre?

27 July

The reasons that impel me to write are multiple, and the most important ones, it seems to me, are the most secret. Perhaps this one above all: to have something secure against death — and this is what makes me, in my writings, seek among all other qualities those upon which time has the least grasp and by which they escape all passing fads.

In order to appear affected, there is nothing like trying to be sincere.

It is almost always out of vanity that one reveals one's limits — while trying to go beyond them. . . .

Carry-le-Rouet, 4 August

Back from Avignon, where I had gone to meet Alibert and where I arrived completely intoxicated by the reading of Walter Pater (*Greek Studies*), of which I translate a few pages to Alibert.

Upon leaving Dostoyevsky, how good it is to touch these shores again. . . .

> On desperate seas long wont to roam,
> Thy hyacinth hair, thy classic face,
> Thy Naiad airs have brought me home
> To the glory that was Greece,
> And the grandeur that was Rome.[19]

At Brignoles I lived among the Scythians with Bunin. His *The Village* is admirable. — Read aloud *The Devil's Disciple* by Bernard Shaw, with rapture. A quantity of English poetry.[20]

Jules Romains's *Lucienne* fell from my hands at the fiftieth page. There is nothing involuntary in this book; every sentence his heroine speaks is dictated by a desire for modernity.[21]

It is not a fear of being wrong, it is a need of sympathy that makes me seek with passionate anxiety the stimulus or the recall of my own thought in others; that made me, in my article on Germany, support my opinion by quotations from Thibaudet and Curtius; that, finally, made me translate Blake and present my own ethic under cover of Dostoyevsky's. If those in whom I recognize my thought had not been there, I doubt whether it would have been much hampered — but its expression would perhaps have been different. It is useless to go back over what has been well said by others. — Nothing is so absurd as that accusation of *influence* (in which certain critics excel every time they note a resemblance). — How many things, on the contrary, I *have not said* because I later discovered them in others! Nietzsche's influence on me? . . . I was already writing *L'Immoraliste* when I discovered him. Who could say how much he got in my way . . . ? how my book was shorn of all I disliked to *repeat.*

At La Bastide I reread some pages of *Candide.* Simplicity of style amazes me, and I can admire it, only by reason of the complexity of the relations involved. It is not difficult to state simple things simply. Voltaire begins by simplifying his thought; he makes the game too easy for himself.

---

[19] Gide quotes one line of Poe's *To Helen* in Mallarmé's translation, adding in a note: "I have not the text at hand; it would probably be appropriate to look up and complete the quotation (in a footnote)."

[20] The last two words appear in English.

[21] *Lucienne* is the first novel of the trilogy entitled *Psyché.*

5 August

However irksome that work may have been (the translation of
Hamlet), now I miss it. My idle mind slips toward melancholy despite
my effort to brake it on the slope. . . .

I have always had a horror (or fear) of liberty and, the gods having granted it to me in almost as complete a form as any living creature could wish, I have always striven to limit, to compromise, and
to reduce it. What I do most gladly is dictated by sympathy; I belong
to melancholy only as soon as work ceases to absorb me.

Carry-le-Rouet, 7 August

Great penury of reading-matter; fierce boredom. I go this morning
to Marseille, whence I bring back a book by Gebhart, an anthology of
sixteenth-century poets, and Galsworthy's *The Patrician*.

13 August

Preface to *Corydon:* quote Ibsen's remark (from the *Correspondence*).[22]

What has sometimes been taken for a certain timidity in my
thought was most often only the fear of saddening someone who is
dear to me. Who could say for how many hesitations, delays, and
reticences sympathy is responsible? I do not regret such examples of
tardiness, judging that the artists of today often sin through a great
lack of patience. I hold, contrary to Alceste, that, in art at least, "time
has much to do with the matter,"[23] and that what is served up to
us today would often have improved by ripening. Often a thought
that at first fills our mind begins to wilt tomorrow. This is why I have
waited long. I wanted to be sure that what I put forth in *Corydon*,
which perhaps seemed to me venturesome, I was not soon to deny.
But in this case my thought has only grown more vigorous, and what
I now reproach my book with is its prudence and timidity. Ten years
have passed; I have taken on more assurance. Examples, new arguments, bits of evidence, everything has come to corroborate my theories.
What I thought yesterday I think even more firmly today, and the
indignation that this little book may cause (what can I do about it?)
will not keep me from thinking that the things I say in it deserve to
be said. Not that I hold that everything one thinks must be said and
published; but just precisely this, and that one must dare to say it
today.

---

[22] "Friends are dangerous, not so much for what they make us do as for
what they keep us from doing." [A.]

[23] In Molière's *Le Misanthrope* the hero protests when Oronte boasts
that he wrote a sonnet in a few minutes: "Time has nothing to do with the
matter."

This does not mean that this book satisfies me. If I had to rewrite it, I should do so quite differently. But such as it is, I cannot rewrite it. What I above all blame it for is its timidity. The precaution I thought I had to take of giving the best arguments to the adversary strikes me today as a somewhat cowardly device; and awkward, for it can deceive no one and yet runs the risk of making people think I wanted to deceive.

Colpach, 3 September

Ten-day session at Pontigny — from 14 August to the 24th.[24] The fourth I have attended — one of the most interesting — not so much because of what is said there as because of the various elements brought together and the unexpected relationships. I was wonderfully surrounded by friends; Mme Théo, Mme Mayrisch, Mme Bussy, Élisabeth, Martin du Gard, Jean Schlumberger, M., Rivière — and even Jaloux, who had come for the first time. . . . And Charlie Du Bos, the life of the party; ineffably suave and tractable and eloquent. Paul Desjardins, on his behalf, had invited the charming Maurois, the author of a jolly little book (*Les Silences du Colonel Bramble* [25]) that I had read with great amusement at Cambridge; he is a charming, alert, courteous mind — and very nicely cultivated, which never does any harm and which offered many possibilities of understanding between us.

De Traz, Prezzolini, Tielrooy, and Curtius — represented respectively Switzerland, Italy, Holland, and Germany. The absence of Bennett, of Bunin, of Lytton Strachey was deplored; in short, too few countries were represented and next year we shall have to make better preparations. But I doubt whether more representative and better-chosen elements can ever be brought together. There should be added the excellent Dr. Chauveau, Mr. Raverat, three young men preparing for the École Normale Supérieure, Miss Strachey, an exquisite Scottish girl, three young women schoolteachers, etc. — thirty-five in all.

Brussels, 5 September

Read at Colpach a number of the short studies by Lytton Strachey collected in his latest volume.[26] The one on Racine, remarkable on the part of an Englishman, does not satisfy me however. He does not clearly establish Racine's starting-point and, admiring him very much,

---

[24] Paul Desjardins organized summer discussion groups in the abandoned Abbey of Pontigny, which gathered writers and artists from all over Europe. Each *décade*, or ten-day session, was devoted to a specific topic.

[25] *The Silences of Colonel Bramble*, Maurois's first work.

[26] *Books and Characters*.

does not perhaps admire him just as one should. Seen through him, Racine appears, despite him, gray, timid, cramped. The quotations he makes could be better chosen, more typical. If one does not bring out Racine's perfection, the smallness of his orchestra, just like Mozart's, might seem poverty.

I prefer Lytton when he speaks of Shakespeare's last plays. Everything he says here is penetrating and persuasive. He also speaks excellently of Beddoes and of Blake. . . .

Reread Mérimée's *La Chambre bleue* and *Il Viccolo di Madama Lucrezia* with interest but without admiration.[27] Each problem of style and presentation is solved in the most elegant fashion, but the elements he plans to put into his tale and into his sentences are always of the same nature and cohabit too easily. One exhausts all the mystery at once, and the first astonishment awakens no secret echo in us.

But with what admiration I read aloud with Élisabeth Defoe's *Colonel Jack*! It is as beautiful as life itself; the art that presents and covers life could not be more discreet or more transparent.

Colpach, 10 September

Hateful days of idleness and listlessness. . . . Each morning I wake up with my brain heavy and more numbed than the day before. Forced, in the presence of the others, to play a comedy of joy and pleasure — while I feel all real joy slowly cooling in my heart.

. . . .

Read Hermant's *Confessions d'un enfant d'hier.*[28] The book is not good and seems to me even less good since it should be his best. The anecdotal part, by far the most successful, remains peculiar to him and awakens but few echoes; the theoretical part, with which the book opens, is pasty, heavy, badly licked into shape, and has almost no connection with the narrative that follows it.

In Francis Jammes's *Mémoires* appears above all his extraordinary lack of sympathy. It is to this, even more than to his limited intelligence, that must be attributed his lack of understanding of others. The puppets he presents are always seen from the outside; he catches nothing but the mannerisms of people. And that he should be sensitive to that first, to that above all, I can admit — the annoying thing is that he stops there. More intelligent, or less vain, he would try to go beyond, but he feels at home in that very lack of understanding as in a sort of ignorance that, divesting him of any point of comparison, magnifies him. It is odd that, in the three convert artists I have known

---

[27] *The Blue Room* and *Madame Lucrezia's Alleyway* are two short stories.

[28] *Confessions of a Child of Yesterday.*

best — Ghéon, Claudel, Jammes — Catholicism brought only an encouragement to pride. Communion infatuates them.

I am rereading in book-form Cocteau's *Le Secret professionnel*,[29]
which R. Martin du Gard had made me read in *Les Écrits nouveaux*.
How could I have considered it good? Wounded vanity never produces anything but grimaces.

Finished *L'Italie mystique*[30] by Gebhart and began his much less
good *Botticelli*.

> *Cuverville, 21 September*

Arrived yesterday evening. House still full. Very happy to see
Marcel again, who, in return, seems happy to see me.

Not accomplished much this first day. But I know that I shall need
about a week to get hold of myself and liquidate the back correspondence. — Finished correcting the proofs of my translation of Blake.

Have ahead of me the revision of Pushkin's *Queen of Spades*,[31] an
article on Valery Larbaud, and that essay on the state of Europe
which I promised to de Traz and which I don't know how I shall
turn out.

> *8 October*

Yesterday I finished the article for the *Revue de Genève*. At last I
get back to *Les Faux-Monnayeurs*.

> *10 October*

It is necessarily easier to work, as Ghéon does, for a public that is
already formed and to provide it exactly the product it demands than
to anticipate the demand of a still unformed public.

Rivière's novel (*Aimée*), which I am reading in proof, exhausts
me, flabbergasts me. I understand now why he likes Marivaux so much.

As I finish that reading, I am almost on the point of making a
resolution never again to write in the imperfect.

> *11 October*

Em. reminds me of this remark of Rivière ("reminds me" is a mere
convention, since I had completely forgotten it) which he made to us
at Cuverville: "I was born to write very beautiful things, which will
bore everyone and which no one will read."

---

[29] *The Professional Secret* is an essay on the criticism of art and poetry.

[30] *Italy of the Mystics,* a history of the religious renaissance in the Middle Ages by Émile Gebhart.

[31] Mérimée translated this story, with others by Pushkin and Gogol, as
La Dame de pique. Gide wrote a preface for a new edition.

Reading aloud of *Madame Firmiani*.[32]

In Paris from 14 October to the 23rd.

Cuverville, 24 October

André Ruyters has entered the Banque d'Indo-Chine. Sore at heart to have to go to China. He does not like the Chinese because they do not have religion and consequently "cannot break away from it."

25 October

I do not write for the coming generation, but for the following one.

I read: "It would be better for you that I went away altogether" (Gissing, translation).[33] The action of going remains in the present despite the tense of the first verb. "That I go away" is called for. And only if it is all put into the past: "It would have been better for you that I went away."

I read: "The style of X. is more *numerous* than that of Flaubert." No, this cannot be. An audience is more or less *numerous*, but a sentence, a style is *numerous* or else it is not. The sentence has *number*. It cannot be a question here of more or less.

27 October

I pick up again this morning, interrupting my rereading of the *Provinciales*,[34] the *Lettres spirituelles* of Fénelon. How can I resist copying:

"You need to have the continual outbursts of your too lively imagination checked: everything amuses you, everything dissipates you, everything plunges you back into your nature" (p. 160).

Hardly a day passes that I do not challenge everything anew.

28 October

As a result of the column in *Le Temps* (fiftieth anniversary of Gautier's death), I write to Paul Souday:

"I am astonished and somewhat saddened, I confess, to encounter in your column that imputation of 'puritanism' that Eugène Montfort invented some time ago with the obvious intention of discrediting my judgment and doing me harm. Do you really think one must be a

---

[32] *Madame Firmiani* is a tale by Balzac.

[33] This whole paragraph turns on the sequence of tenses in French, particularly when the subjunctive is involved.

[34] Pascal wrote his *Provincial Letters* (or *Letters to a Provincial*, more properly) as brilliant polemic to defend Jansenism against Jesuit attacks.

puritan not to enjoy Gautier's art, or do you think that in Gautier's art
there is nothing shocking save for a puritan?"

Wasted two hours on this — and, naturally, I do not send it.

A straight path never leads anywhere except to the objective.

29 October

Finished *New Grub Street*.[35] — Rather less good than a good Rosny,
than *Nell Horn* for instance. Glad to have read it, in order not to have
to read it.

It is through his contradictions that a creature interests us and
reveals his sincerity. Sensuality gives Francis Jammes's piety its savor;
his love of hunting exasperates, by contradicting it, his pity for animals,
and his pride swells his modesty.

I was not fair to this book by Gissing, annoyed perhaps by the bad
translation (for I was not reading it in English). It is none the less a
beautiful book.

6 November

Interview with Philippe Soupault and Drieu La Rochelle in *La
Revue hebdomadaire*. "I return to André Gide," writes the latter. "I
could never like the man; but I respect the author and his patience;
it's a pity if his prudence is turning into a vice." This, then, is the idea
people have of me. . . . Prudent to the point of a vice. . . . I write
Drieu a rather long letter, which I fortunately keep myself from sending, according to my custom. I should have sent it nevertheless if the
article had seemed better to me (it was only after having written that
I finished reading it); but no, doubtless he is wrong about me and is
completely misunderstanding what sort of man I am, but, from me to
him at least, I feel that an affinity is so little possible that he is probably right in believing that it is no more possible from him to me.

It is true that he adds: "I am infinitely grateful to him for the
studious example he gives me . . ." etc., etc. . . .

It is not up to me to correct him.

8 November

One artist is often no less gifted than another who crowds on all
his sail and seems about to revolutionize art. It is often through sympathy that one does not express one's thought fully — that one with-

---

[35] *New Grub Street* is a bitter fictional satire of writers and their public
by George Gissing (1891).

holds it cautiously halfway up the slope where those can catch up without whom one does not enjoy advancing.

Sunday, 12 November (?)

Leaving for Paris tomorrow, where I am going to spend a week. Altogether, worked rather well of late. Wrote the first thirty pages, more or less, of *Les Faux-Monnayeurs*. Went over *Corydon* and wrote the *Préface*.[36] Learned by heart the three odes of Keats (*To a Nightingale, To Psyche, To Autumn*). Reread *Les Provinciales, La Double Méprise*, and aloud *La Maison Nucingen* and *Les Secrets de la Princesse de Cadignan*.[37]

I am reading rapidly, but with a rather lively interest, *Les Mystères de Paris*[38] and, with the most complete and firm adherence, Sainte-Beuve's *Port-Royal* (but I turned at once to the third volume to accompany my reading of *Les Provinciales*).[39]

Back at Cuverville, 26 November

Never take advantage, for any new work, of the impetus from the preceding one.

Likewise, win over for each new work a new public.

30 November

From that moment (when she had burned T.'s letters) she felt released, at the same time, from all her duties toward him.

3 December

Jacques Rivière constantly seeks to caress himself in others. His extraordinary pursuit of affinities and his predilection for what resembles him. His admirations always have an element of flattery and self-indulgence.

7 December

Art is prudence. When you have nothing to say, or to hide, there is no need to be prudent. The timorous are not prudent, but cowardly.

15 December

Three hours at the piano;
An hour of correcting proofs (*Si le grain ne meurt* . . .);

---

[36] Probably the preface for Pushkin's *Queen of Spades*.

[37] *The Double Mistake* is by Mérimée; *The House of Nucingen* and *The Secrets of the Princess of Cadignan* are by Balzac.

[38] *The Mysteries of Paris* by Eugène Sue.

[39] Sainte-Beuve's *Port-Royal* is a detailed historical and critical account of the Jansenist movement, which had its seat at Port-Royal.

An hour of Shakespeare (*Cymbeline*);
An hour of Sainte-Bevue's *Port-Royal*
— this is my daily menu.

Ordinarily my correspondence takes about two hours more — and I often give six hours to the novel. — A half-hour or an hour's exercise — and, with the wasted time, my too short day is filled.

I do not succeed, despite my ardent desire, in devoting much more to work.

From 16 to 17 December

Visit from Maurois, who reads me what he has done with Shelley.[40] It does not seem to me that he has sufficiently re-created his character, and, besides, it is hard to see what connection with him, Maurois, made him choose this subject. He does not take sides with Shelley and does not seem to confess himself through him, as Pater would have done at once, for example. But it is a very workmanlike job.

For three days now I have had such tense and vibrant nerves that I don't know whether or not I shall be able to keep on much longer — I mean: pursue my work much farther.

"It is a region," said Maurois of the neighborhood of Elbeuf, and quoting the remark of an old peasant, "it is a region in which, if you want to see people at the windows, it is better to shout 'fire' than 'help'!"

21 December

In Christianity, and each time that I plunge into it again, it is always she that I am pursuing. She feels this perhaps; but what she feels above all is that I do so to tear her away from it.

24 December

Forced to interrupt work. Intellectual fatigue and nervous hypertension.

Continued the third volume of *Port-Royal*, in which I find at every turn of the path marvelously sagacious remarks and insights. I copy this note (p. 341): ". . . it was hypocrisy above all that lodged deeply in man during those *covered centuries*" (those that followed the ruin of the ancient world). "A great Jesuit preacher of the eighteenth century, Father de Neuville, wishing to denounce that plague of hypocrisy hidden in the heart of each of us, even the best, said: 'There is not a man who does not prefer to be completely unknown rather than completely known. . . .' That so Christian remark of Father de Neuville

[40] This is Maurois's *Ariel*.

is as far as can be imagined from the ancient feeling, when generals struggled openly for glory, and when the shining oil of the palæstra was the only clothing of nudity. — It was while thinking of these last results of Christianity, of *these* REPRESSED *results* that, as it were, became fixed in the organization and *affected the whole man,* that another moralist of a very modern school, and a cousin of the preceding,[41] could say: 'Christianity, like its elder, Buddhism, was a great relative good, a remedy for a decadence, born of that very decadence; but it belonged to it. The principal evil passed, *who will cure us henceforth of the remedy* — of the remedy's aftermath?'"

Do not those "repressed results" already announce Freud?

I copy this passage on the eve of Christmas. Sunday.

Monday, Christmas

Forty children around a tree; very pretty, the tree; and the children very ugly. The emotion their faces are least capable of expressing is joy. Besides, I did not feel that they were having a very good time. Constrained, stiff, and mute, they all stayed around the tree, forming a circle; no advance succeeded in putting a little more ease into their stilted manner.

Wednesday

I am leaving for Paris — whence I hope to bring back Martin du Gard on the 4th or 5th. For a week now nothing has worked right. I am a fish of the rapids and stifle in these too calm waters.

Stopped at the Terminus. With M. and his mistress, B., spent one of the dullest evenings, at the Casino de Paris, where everything seemed to me frightful. Silliness, vulgarity, bad taste, idiotic and hideous display of costumes.

Yesterday, Thursday, at the Vieux-Colombier with the Martin du Gards. The new play by Vildrac, *Michel Auclair,* was being played. The first act seemed to me rather bad; but the second, almost excellent in spots. The third reflects excessively the indigent philosophy of the school.

30 December

Almost empty day. At ten o'clock Sichel, whom I had met two days before at Martin du Gard's, came to read me (in my room at the Lutétia) his article on *Paludes,* which he declares to be the book of mine he prefers. Lunched at the Allégrets'; Élie, suffering from paludism and an excess of fatigue, received me for a moment at his bedside. He is taking advantage of this rest to read. When I was a

---

[41] One must obviously recognize Sainte-Beuve himself here. [A.]

child, I admired his faculty of devouring in two hours a book that would have kept me two weeks. But today I am suspicious of people who read quickly. . . . Élie Allégret has just dashed through in this manner *La Chartreuse de Parme,* which he vaguely remembered having already read in his youth.[42] His judgments on the book are childish. He questions me, asking me to explain what sort of influence Stendhal has had. . . . Etc. . . .

Nothing could be more demoralizing than the shoddy waste of hours at the Allégrets', on a holiday. I left rather soon after the meal.

Went back to the hotel to sleep an hour.

Went to see Copeau, whom I find harassed and very low. He complains of the solitude for which he has worked so obstinately. He thrust aside all advice and behaved so that his best friends withdrew from him. "I'll hang on to the end; but don't talk to me." Now he could accept having people talk to him. . . . He feels utterly abandoned. One cannot but abandon a mystic.

Met Paul Valéry at Adrienne Monnier's. Walked back with him at length. He claims to be embarrassed, even exasperated, by the false situation he owes to his success.

"People expect me to represent French poetry. They take me for a poet! But I don't give a damn about poetry. It interests me only by a fluke. It is quite accidental that I wrote poetry. I should be exactly the same if I hadn't written any. That is to say that, in my own eyes, I should have the same value. That has no importance to me. What does matter to me I should like to say. I believe I might have said it, that I could still say it if I had leisure and tranquillity . . . but I have ceased to belong to myself. The life I am leading suppresses me."

Dined at the Martin du Gards' — delightful all three of them. Spent the evening chatting with Roger.

------

[42] Stendhal's novel, *The Charterhouse of Parma.*

1923

The question of gifts. . . . There is no day when I feel less inclined to give them. It is not that I always hate the expected, the anticipated — which often, moreover, is confused with the *was ziemt*.[1] But I do not want to be, in life, the artisan or provider of it. I don't feel as if I were in the right role.

If I were Paul Valéry, I should say: "Odd how the habit of giving gifts is lost . . ." in the same tone with which he said, before his return to poetry with *La Jeune Parque:* [2] "Odd how much less poetry has been written in the last fifteen years!"

Lunched yesterday at Copeau's. In the presence of Agnès and the children he outlines to me his new plans.

Went back to rest (or try to) at the hotel — thought that the relaxation would be greater at the baths of the rue P.L. — where I took a half-dozen showers and stayed more than an hour.

Left there in a state of unbelievable physical lightness somewhat recalling the one I describe in *Si le grain ne meurt*. . . . But immediately afterward I made the great mistake of smoking, which right away turned my euphory into something banal and benumbed.

Went to see Uncle Charles, then the Drouins. Marcel was not there. He was to go that evening to *Les Deux Orphelines*.[3] I bet he dilly-dallied, arrived late, and found no seats left. That is what is called "having bad luck."

Dined alone beside the Gare Montparnasse, then spent an hour at the P. A. Laurenses' — very gay with their . . . friends (?), who were very nice, besides.

Then to the Allégrets'. I knew through M. that his mother had just read *Silbermann*,[4] which I had sent the day before to Élie, and that she was indignant about the book and about the exact portrait it draws of the Protestant character. I should have liked to talk with her about it; I had prepared my position. I was ready to tell her that she couldn't know "the Protestant environment" — because she had never left it —

---

[1] What is fitting.

[2] After distinguishing himself in literary circles in the nineties, Valéry gave up poetry for nearly twenty years. It was André Gide who persuaded him, during the first World War, to return to poetry; he then composed his long poem *The Young Fate*.

[3] *The Two Orphan Girls* (1874) is a popular melodrama by Adolphe Philippe Dennery.

[4] A novel by Jacques de Lacretelle about the unhappiness of a Jewish boy in a Paris school.

just as one cannot understand the French character (or at least what constitutes its peculiarity) unless, through some familiarity with foreign countries, one is in a position to perceive how the Frenchman differs from others.

But I was not able to see Suzanne Allégret *alone*.

Élie is exhausted; the hollows of his cheeks seem to meet in the middle. One of the elements of his "absorbing activity" is a great need to lose himself, to cease seeing himself, which is perhaps not exactly abnegation. He deceives himself on this score, as well as on many others. . . .

2 January

Young Sichel comes to work every morning from my head. He takes the only two hours of the day when I could hope to work. Furious over that interruption . . . which is perhaps, after all, salutary.

Spent the end of New Year's Day at Charlie Du Bos's. I had taken along the typed copy of *Les Faux-Monnayeurs*, of which I gave a reading. Mlle des Garrets came to join Z. My great habit of reading aloud permits me to feel very rapidly and exactly the listener's impression — and these try-outs are very useful to me. I was able to note all the holes, false notes, etc. . . . But, altogether, excellent impression.

Dined at the Drouins' with Mme B., Valentine, and my two nieces — charming.

Dined at the Valérys'. Paul tells me (as I already suspected) that *La Pythie* issued entirely from one line:

Pâle, profondément mordue.[5]

He sought the rhyme, then the rhymes. They dictated the form of the stanza, and the whole poem developed without his knowing at first how it would be nor what he was going to say in it.

He is more and more incapable of listening to others and of taking into consideration what would interrupt his thought. His speech is more and more rapid and indistinct. I often have great trouble understanding him and have to ask him to repeat one out of every four sentences.

He talks again of his "*tædium vitæ*," which at moments becomes a physical suffering, an unbearable nervous and muscular anguish. What am I saying? — at moments? . . . This is a state in which he finds himself, he says, nine days out of ten. He grants that this anguish had completely left him when traveling, particularly in England. He exclaims:

"Oh, if only I had enough money not to have to bother with writing at all! . . ."

_____

[5] "Pale, and most deeply stung," is the fifth line of *The Pythoness*, one of the most characteristic poems of Valéry's collection, *Charmes*.

3 January

At the Cirque Medrano with Roger Martin du Gard, Bronja, and M. Walked home.

9 January

Last Saturday (it is now Wednesday) I took Martin du Gard back with me to Cuverville, where he stayed three days. His presence distracted me from this notebook in which however I should have liked to note different recollections of my stay in Paris. In particular a conversation with J.-É. Blanche, whom I had gone to see in his studio.

10 January

Francis Jammes sends me his volume *Choix de poèmes.*[6] Some of them, at the beginning, remain exquisite. But the dominating note, alas! is silliness, false naïveté, self-satisfaction. There is nothing prouder than his modesty; whence his refusal to learn anything, his belief in the divinity of his inspiration, his self-indulgence. Infatuation is always accompanied by stupidity.

"Bookish" is a reproach that is often directed at me; I lay myself open to it by my habit of always quoting those to whom my thought seems related. People think I took that thought from them; this is false; that thought came to me of itself; but I enjoy, and the more so the bolder the thought is, thinking that it has already inhabited other minds. When, reading them later on, I recognize my thoughts in them, as it happened with Blake, I go crying their name everywhere and publishing my discovery. I am told that I am wrong. I don't care. I take pleasure in quoting and persuade myself, like Montaigne, that only in the eyes of fools do I appear any less personal for it.

Those on the contrary who gather the ideas of others take great care to hide their "sources." — There are examples of this among us.

11 January

I say a few words to Em. of the "drama" that calls me to the side of E.

I have no reason to hope, or even to wish, that Em. should ever be able to consider what she glimpses and imagines of that story otherwise than as a most lamentable catastrophe. And yet I have the greatest difficulty keeping from protesting when she concludes, from the little I dare tell her: "I have always thought it was unfortunate that El. had been raised without religion."

(For it goes without saying that El. is not happy, cannot be happy, has not the right to be happy — and here I cannot rectify without im-

---

[6] *Selected Poems.*

prudence; but I suffer intolerably from these false ideas that I know
to derive from those false premises whereby falsehood finds support
in what should on the contrary overcome it.) Thus it is that all the
events of life, as the events of the war did likewise, serve only to push
each person farther in his own direction, so that nothing is more empty
and illusory than what is commonly called "experience." — An experience teaches only the good observer; but far from seeking a lesson in
it, everyone looks for an argument in experience, and everyone interprets the conclusion in his own way.

If my head were not so tired, I should write much longer on this
subject. And this must be the subject of several pages of *Le Journal
d'Édouard:* [7] "Concerning the interpretation of events." This exclama-
tion: "A religious upbringing would have kept her from doing that,"
can be said in a tone of regret, of blame, as well as of approbation, and
imply either: "What luck! How fortunate that . . . !" or "What a
shame!"

I am reading some of Alain's *Propos* with very great admiration. [8]
I prefer him, and even by far, to Maurras and do not see where
Maurras could be said to be superior to him — unless in his deafness.
Maurras is a deaf man, as England is an island; whence his strength.

Si le grain ne meurt . . . Supplement:
I used to provide my aquarium with diving-beetles, with boat-flies,
with dragonfly larvæ, and became passionately interested in observing
their combats at length. But what charmed me even more was the unknown race that awakened and crawled teeming in the clump of
mud surrounding the roots of the water plants I used to tear up from
a pond and bring back dripping in the bottom of my botanizer's box.

Sunday, 14 January
Leaving for Roquebrune, for Genoa, for the unknown. — I never
leave Cuverville without a sort of heartbreak.

Paris, 16 January
Went yesterday to the Vieux-Colombier, where Dullin's company
was giving *Antigone,* or "Sophocles's lady," by Cocteau. [9] Suffered un-

[7] Édouard is one of the principal characters of *The Counterfeiters,* and
his *Journal* has an important role in the book.

[8] The philosopher Émile Chartier always wrote in the form of informal,
brief *propos* (remarks) on literature and philosophy, war, society, religion,
art, etc. For many years he had a few such pages in nearly every issue of the
Nouvelle Revue Française.

[9] With Louis Jouvet, the actor Charles Dullin was one of Copeau's
chief associates in his new theater. In 1921 Dullin founded his own group,
known as *L'Atelier.*

bearably from the ultra-modern sauce in which was served up that wonderful play, which remains beautiful more in spite of Cocteau than because of him. One can understand moreover what tempted him here, and he has cooked it up with consummate cleverness; but those who applaud him are those who to begin with considered Sophocles as a great bore and who have never drunk of "the true, the blushful Hippocrene." [10]

Cocteau's play is not at all *blushful*. It reflects the same feeling that made Stravinsky say he would gladly collaborate on *Antony and Cleopatra*, but only if Antony were given the uniform of an Italian "*Bersagliere*."

Patina is the reward of masterpieces.

Roquebrune

Nicholas must be accustomed early to emptying his slop-jar himself, for fear that later on he may assume the air of a martyr or look to himself like a saint if by chance he happens to have to clean a pot.

23 January

I write to Suzanne Allégret:

"You do not doubt, when you speak to me in your letter of the importance of Christianity, that I am convinced in advance. In the whole history of humanity I know nothing more important. I return to it constantly and know that there are two teachings whose virtue man will never exhaust: that of Christ and that of the 'Greek legend.' And that Christ's is of an infinitely superior kind I hope one day to convince certain of your sons. . . . I have less hope of ever seeing you consider the gods of Olympus otherwise than as 'false gods' — even though they always avenge themselves on those who fail to recognize them, as Greek tragedy teaches us — and the daily spectacle that makes you frequently say: 'But, André, how can you explain that these children . . .'"

A letter that I judge it wiser not to send.

23 February

Leaving Rapallo for Annecy.

The day before my departure I had a wonderful climb into the mountains.

A week at Annecy with E. Charming little Savoie hotel, of which, given the season, we are the only guests. Read aloud Shakespeare's *Merry Wives* and *The Vicar of Wakefield*, which delights us. I finish

---

[10] The quotation from Keats appears in English.

at Annecy Keats's wonderful *Endymion,* which I did not yet know and which kept me intoxicated for days on end.

The exactingness of my ear, until the last few years, was such that I should have warped the meaning of a sentence for its rhythm.

10 March

Arrived at Cuverville yesterday evening after two and a half days in Paris. I accept the invitation to accompany Paul Desjardins to Morocco—invited by Lyautey. Departure set for the 25th of this month.

Wednesday, 28 March

Stop at Tangier, where we disembark at about seven o'clock. Wonderful first rays of the sun, which, as soon as they have passed the hill, animate and gild the white city. Despite my tremendous joy at being back on Arab soil, rather a bit disappointed. We go to the Kasba— but I cannot moderate my gait sufficiently to stay in step with my two companions. Hamp is completely refractory; the Moslem nonchalance gets on his nerves. These people who "don't do a darned thing" escape *man's affliction* and are outside his visual range.[11] But I am astonished by his fear of contacts, contaminations, lice, his flat refusal to sit down on the bench of a Moorish café, to taste Moroccan cakes. I drop my companions. Leaving the town, I start out along a sandy avenue edged with very old Indian fig trees and cutting through a suburb more exotic than all the rest of the town; huts and low shanties—like those of the Paris "zone" beyond the fortifications.—Glad to leave again.

Thursday

The air is light; the heat bearable; the sky radiant. Casablanca, where I was expecting only amorphous warehouses, delights me. I don't regret that it does not have a more native character.

Marrakech, Saturday

What keeps Hamp from exasperating me more is that he exasperates Desjardins even more. It is his self-assurance that is shocking; he is not stupid, but he lets nothing into his mind that is not indubitable and that he cannot check at once. One would like to get him to read Montaigne, and one loses hope for him upon learning that his favorite reading is the *Essais.* Yet he is charming; I like his grumpy cordiality;

---

[11] Many of Pierre Hamp's books are grouped under the general title: *La Peine des hommes*—the expression Gide uses here.

he is even not incapable of good-heartedness and his humor is colorful. But up to now he can make nothing of the Arabs; he gets irritated
by their slowness and vainly applies his scale of values to their calm
felicity. The *Utinam ex vobis unus* [12] never whispers in his heart.

Back in Paris 21 April, at Cuverville the evening of the 26th.
Violent attack (in *Les Nouvelles littéraires* [13]) by Henri Béraud,
the author of *Le Triomphe de l'obèse* [14] — who cannot forgive me my
thinness. Very diverting. — All the same, Massis's articles were of a
very different type; this fellow gives every impression of being an idiot.

2 May

This morning, in *L'Action Française,* I have the great surprise of
seeing Léon Daudet take up my defense against Béraud — very nicely,
I declare — and speak of me as a "terrible and penetrating" writer. . . .
On the other hand, a little paragraph in the next column informs
me that for the last fortnight Béraud has been fulminating against
L'Action Française. [15]
But already I wonder that they do not make it up at my expense.
Under their blows and by the violence of their attacks, I become
aware of my *ruggedness.*

Great movement among the bees of our hive, ready to swarm. This
morning I have seven of them wearing themselves out at the one
window of my room that I always keep closed; the other window is
wide open; the bee would merely have to make a slight detour to recover freedom; but it butts against the glass and would think itself
lost if it left the light for an instant; and since there is no exit in that
direction, it soon falls exhausted. It is the story of the fish in the net.
It is the story of the French in the Ruhr.
In order to let the bees out, I am obliged to have the double window
opened.

I am reading with less difficulty and more pleasure a number of
poems by Donne.

Cuverville

Brief sojourns in Paris. Simultaneous correcting of proofs of my
Dostoïevsky, of *Corydon,* and of *Si le grain ne meurt* . . . Hypertension and fatigue.

[12] "Would that I had been one of you," from Virgil: *Bucolics,* X, 35.
[13] *Les Nouvelles littéraires* (*The Literary News*) is a weekly founded in
1922.
[14] *The Triumph of Obesity.*
[15] And the *N.R.F.* has just published a book by Charles Maurras. [A.]

Martin du Gard comes for four days here and reads me the third volume of *Les Thibault*. Nothing, more effectively than that reading and the conversations that ensue, disposes me again toward work.

Léon Daudet and Paul Souday unexpectedly take up my defense, and Henri Béraud's awkward attack turns against him. I cannot believe him to be altogether in bad faith; obviously he believes that I somewhat resemble that absurd character to whom he gives my name and against whom he strives to stir up his readers. He is well aware that he is not painting my portrait; but at least thinks he is drawing my caricature; but he only succeeds in drawing his own — and the pack he groups around him is made up of those who have been refused by the *N.R.F.* He claims to have received the congratulations of X., Y., and Z., quotes ten names of which eight belong to authors we have blackballed.

17 May

I have taken M. to spend four days at Annecy-Talloires.

This morning, solitary walk, climbing up to the break in the rocks (on the right as one turns one's back on the lake) through which falls a very beautiful cascade.

A long, wide ribbon of azured, silvered coolness that loses itself suddenly in a black, bottomless gulf.

Water? Not exactly; but foam, or at least water so divided, so aerated, and become so light that it falls quite slowly. The rather vertiginous path I am following overhangs the gulf and is itself overhung by immense rocks that half close over, forming a vault, but a broken vault like that of Agrippa's Pantheon, which allows a glimpse of the sky.

Odd: I do not like mountain-climbing, but — explain it as you will — every path that climbs draws me, and I rise as naturally as water descends.

In the train, yesterday, heard this charming sentence:

"At the price matches have reached today, it becomes interesting when they don't burn."

18 May

Read in the train Jean Cocteau's *Le Grand Écart*,[16] with a great effort toward approbation and praise; during the first quarter of the book I managed, through goodwill, to deceive myself, amused as I was by the extreme ingenuity of the images and the burlesque brusque-

---

[16] *The Splits*, a novel of adolescent life in Paris. Published in the United States as *The Grand Écart* (1925).

ness of certain presentations. But soon irritation dominates before so
constant and so avaricious an anxiety to lose nothing, such a wary
turning to account. In this book art is constantly degenerating into
artifice. If Cocteau let himself go, he would write light comedies.

Mme Van Rysselberghe pointed out yesterday (and very judiciously) how the richness of vocabulary of contemporary writers discouraged the effort of syntax. The syntax remains banal and lifeless
when the labor of depicting and animating is entrusted to the choice
of words. But no one notices this, and when a Boulenger gets alarmed
at the corruption of the language, it is always useless and inoffensive
neologisms that he condemns, words borrowed from abroad — and very
rarely errors in syntax. Thus I have never seen anyone pick up the
"pour ne pas que" which is becoming commoner and beginning to be
accepted to such a point that I give up deploring it.[17]

24 May

In an interview in *Les Nouvelles littéraires* Abel Hermant unexpectedly takes up my defense with a courtesy and generosity that
touch me deeply. Béraud replies at once in *L'Éclair* — very long, nasty
article in which treachery takes the place of wit.

"No one will be grateful to M. Hermant," he says, "for having descended into the arena — not even M. Gide; for gratitude, if one is to
believe those close to him, is not his strong point."

29 May

The triumph of objectivity is allowing the novelist to borrow the
"I" of others. I have misled by succeeding too well in this; some have
taken my books for a series of successive confessions. That abnegation,
that poetic depersonalization that makes me feel the joys and sorrows
of others more keenly than my own, no one has described so well as
Keats (*Letters*).[18]

---

[17] "In order not that . . ." as in *Pour ne pas qu'il le fasse* for *Pour qu'il
ne le fasse pas.*

[18] Gide was doubtless thinking of the following passage from a letter to
R. Woodhouse dated 27 October 1818: "As to the poetical Character itself
(I mean that sort of which, if I am any thing, I am a Member; that sort distinguished from the wordsworthian or egotistical sublime; which is a thing
per se and stands alone) it is not itself — it has no self — it is every thing and
nothing — It has no character — it enjoys light and shade; it lives in gusto, be
it foul or fair, high or low, rich or poor, mean or elevated — It has as much
delight in conceiving an Iago as an Imogen. What shocks the virtuous philosopher, delights the chameleon Poet. It does no harm from its relish of the
dark side of things any more than from its taste for the bright one; because
they both end in speculation. A Poet is the most unpoetical of any thing in

14 June

Reread La Fontaine's *Épîtres* with an indescribable rapture — at least those to Mme de la Sablière and to Huet.

17 June

I went to see Valéry yesterday. Found Marie Laurencin at his house (exquisite in a sort of very open sweater, gray and artichoke-green [19]) and Sert, come to announce her success. The painters' jury has just awarded her the first prize (fifteen thousand francs). Very glad to be there to congratulate her at once. They give way to a band of journalists. I wonder that Valéry does not throw them out at once. But he doesn't know how to refuse anything, or at least refuse himself to anything, and when I express a certain indignation that he allowed himself to be named a member of the Catulle Mendès Committee (!), he says laughing: "One must never refuse the ladies," then adds, as always: "Besides, you know, you are right; but I don't give a damn."

The *good writing* I admire is that which, without calling too much attention to itself, checks and delays the reader and forces his thought to proceed slowly. I want his attention to sink at every step into a rich soil that is deeply broken up. But what the reader generally looks for is a kind of endless belt that will carry him along.

What I should like this novel to be? a crossroad — a meeting of problems.

. . . in this world where one can no longer find anything pure — not even stupidity.

---

existence; because he has no Identity — he is continually in for and filling some other Body — The Sun, the Moon, the Sea and Men and Women who are creatures of impulse are poetical and have about them an unchangeable attribute — the poet has none; no identity — he is certainly the most unpoetical of all God's Creatures. If then he has no self, and if I am a Poet, where is the Wonder that I should say I would write no more? Might I not at that very instant have been cogitating on the Characters of Saturn and Ops? It is a wretched thing to confess; but is a very fact that not one word I ever utter can be taken for granted as an opinion growing out of my identical nature — how can it, when I have no nature?" (*The Letters of John Keats*, edited by M. B. Forman, I, 245.)

[19] I notice that there are a number of words to designate the tones of all the other scales: "plum, *tête de nègre*, snuff, puce, salmon, flesh," etc.; but that for the scale of greens one must always repeat this word together with the specifying word: "apple-green, emerald-green, spinach-green, Nile-green," etc. [A.]

Metaphors that constantly lift the sentence toward the outside.

18 June

Mme D. Simon Bussy writes me: "I shall never be a saint (like you, I mean); I don't even want to like the *Créateur* better than the creature — or rather 'at the moment I covet, my soul does *not* cease to be aware of God. . . .' In fact those are the only moments in which I enjoy the kingdom of Heaven." [20]
How good that is!

Those persons (such as I) are dangerous because the sense of property, and *consequently* of responsibility, escapes them. I had not bethought myself of that at first — but . . .

Since he wants her to accompany him everywhere, he no longer dares go anywhere.

29 June

English poetry, richer, more abundant than French poetry; but the latter, it seems to me, occasionally reaches a higher point. I cannot like all the facilities the English poet grants himself, and that absence of rigor; the strings of his lyre, almost always, seem to me insufficiently taut.

30 June

Certain sentences of Saint-Évremond are so well formed that I doubt if, even in the *Caractères,* one would find comparable ones. Sharper-pointed than those of La Bruyère, they penetrate more deeply. But I am speaking here of the best, and often one wonders whether what Saint-Évremond expresses was worth the trouble of being said (I wonder about this sometimes for La Bruyère too); that author who has left so little, one is almost ready to find him too fulsome. He judges everything with sagacity and delicacy, but he seems to lack inner pressure, and one does not always feel that he had a great need to write the little he writes. He must have been a charming talker.

Ghéon sends me the new edition of his book "augmented by unpublished fragments and a spiritual notebook." Whether one believes or does not believe, one cannot deny that the Christian (or let us say more precisely: the Catholic) religion invites to a more attentive introspection. But what annoys me in *L'Homme né de la guerre* [21] is the

---

[20] The whole letter is given in English but for the clause within single quotation marks, where Mme Bussy is turning a sentence by Gide into the negative.

[21] *The Man Born of the War* is the record of Ghéon's conversion.

constant effort Ghéon makes to deceive himself. Its psychology remains quite arbitrary and conventional and Ghéon does not speak of himself any more *truly* than he does of the devil or of God.

The dialogue of the second chapter, between the Christian and the artist, could be beautiful if it were authentic; but, from the very beginning, everything is falsified.

"You have, then, lived twenty years in this desert? Without God and without need of God?" the Christian begins, and the other replies:

"And what is more, without anxiety, in a sort of pagan plenitude, *to such an extent does the Prince of this World excel in lulling the conscience to sleep, in gilding and garlanding sin.*"

It is not the artist who replies here; he could not express himself thus; it is still the Christian speaking. That is not fair. And the rest is no more so.

Four days ago, at Les Baux, in sandals, I was twenty years old. That evening, at Arles, seated on a bench along the boulevard with my two traveling-companions, we listen to this drunken dialogue:

"I tell you I don't need you."

"P'rhaps not. . . . But you need — not to need — me."

A minute later they take off their coats and threaten to "floor" each other.

31 June

It seems to them that one has ceased to advance as soon as one no longer advances in their direction.

The thought, falsified, falsifies the style: "*Since* nineteen hundred years that Christ taught and his doctrine has been interpreted, *I come* and declare that, for nineteen centuries, all those people were wrong." (This is a remark that Ghéon attributes to me.) Everything they cannot reduce seems to them tainted with pride.

I am rereading *The Merchant of Venice* in English. It is one of Shakespeare's plays that I prefer. Something winged, fluttering, from one end to the other of its texture, makes one forget its flagrant shortcomings. No relation (or else one that is so subtle as to be imperceptible) between the story of the "bond" and that of Portia's three coffers; in the fourth act the complication of the rings is grafted on as an extra, without any relation to the rest. One almost gets to the point of forgetting Shylock; he is no longer involved and thus one accepts the frightful injustice that is smilingly imposed on him. If Shakespeare were animated by Christian sentiments, what a fine occasion to show them here! But no, Portia's clemency does not for a moment become

that of the Gospels, and it is by no means in the name of Christ that
the Duke sets up a doctrine of forgiveness in opposition to the Jew's
legitimate and fierce intransigence. His daughter and his fortune are
taken from him; never for an instant is it admitted that the feeling of
his legitimate right is confused with his desire for revenge. He is
ruined, deserted, flouted; and they want to force him to become a
Christian! — to recognize the superiority of a religion that has tricked
him! But there is no question of religion (and very fortunately) in
this play; simply of an easy ethic that allows laughter, friendship, and
love, and it is to sheer cupidity that these fine sentiments are opposed.
One would like Antonio's generosity not to stop with Shylock, and,
since everyone's desires are satisfied at the end, that the Jew should
at least recover his money.

1 July

Nothing irritates certain Catholics more than to see us attain naturally to a renunciation that they, with all their religion, have such
difficulty achieving. They almost accuse you of cheating; virtue must
remain their monopoly, and whatever you achieve without saying
your beads doesn't count. Likewise, they do not forgive us our happiness; it is impious; they alone have the right to be happy. It is, moreover, a right they rarely indulge.

Saint-Martin-Vésubie, 3 July

First evening of work (continuation of the *Journal d'Édouard*);
obtained with great difficulty; demanded of myself. But, afterward,
frightful night; choking and my body shaken with nervous trembling.
I can really not get ahead until I have rested more. Incomprehensible
torpor, at any hour of the day, makes sleep more attractive than reading, than work, than life. I sink into abysses of indolence, of thoughtlessness, of emptiness.

This morning, despite the heat, hoisted myself, first through mead-
ows and thickets, then from rock to rock, and finally going up the bed
of a mountain torrent, to a waterfall under which I rushed as soon as
I could undress. The icy water, falling from a height, stung like hail.

My more or less happiness, today, depends solely on the more or
less perfect functioning of my body. This torpor is often unbearable.
But I believe that nothing has done more to make me understand people of modest intelligence than these depressions, these weaknesses.
Valéry is missing something because he has never waked up almost
idiotic on certain mornings.

5 July

Lost this morning, on the mountain slope where I was looking for Louis, a little selection of the *Lettres* of Voltaire that I was rereading with delight.

The great majority of people, and I am speaking of the cultivated ones, are able to see only what has already been depicted. It is especially on reading Voltaire that one understands the importance of Rousseau. Voltaire expresses with considerable grace and delicacy what one did not perhaps exactly need him to feel. His famous letter to Rousseau remains a marvel of affectionate playfulness, of good grace, and of amenity in the fairest criticism.[22] He has reason on his side; but Rousseau has something else, more important than reason, that Voltaire does not grasp.

9 July

Found my Voltaire letters; I resume the reading of them; but at once they strike me as less excellent. His pen is too fine; it succeeds only in the "upstrokes."

As I congratulated Édouard Champion on the excellent luncheon he served us the other day:

"Nothing to it! Nothing to it, dear Monsieur Gide. When you come again, you will have the same thing."

But as I insisted and recalled in particular a marvelous salmon trout:

"It is true that our cook isn't bad. For a long time we had a chef, but really he didn't cook any better; and with this woman we are saving a thousand francs a month."

Unpleasantly disappointed by *Le Terrain Bouchaballe*, which I so much wanted to like.[23] At the two extremities Suarès and Max Jacob: one who is interested only in himself and is interesting only when he talks of others; the other who is interested only in others and is interesting only when he talks of himself.

10 July

Since that evening of work followed by an infernal night, had a miserable life: dizzy spells, shivers, heaviness of head, boredom. The

[22] Upon reading Rousseau's *Discourse on the Origin of Inequality among Men*, Voltaire wrote him a very witty letter, dated 30 August 1755, beginning: "I have received, sir, your new book against the human race. . . ."

[23] *The Bouchaballe Plot of Land* by Max Jacob.

hard thing is not to achieve fervor, but rather to stay there. This morning, after a not too bad night, I drop my indifferent work for adventure; unfortunately my watch is an hour slow and I don't start out until eight thirty. And I don't reach the real mountains until around noon. Losing and finding again the trails used by the flocks, leaping from rock to rock or forcing my way through clumps of rhododendrons, wearing sandals on my bare feet, and shorts, for my duck trousers got too much in the way of my jumping. The flora has suddenly changed; on a carpet of close-cropped grass, gentians, heavenly blue myosotis of a variety I didn't know before, and a great many little echeverias of three types, some of them an exquisite pink. A small lake in which I bathed; and, later on, I plunged under a waterfall again; fields of snow; extraordinary amphitheater of abrupt rocks. The sky is threatening and it is too late for me to think of reaching the pass whence I think I might see the *département* of the Hautes-Alpes. Twice a bird's cry, sharp, fierce, and surprisingly loud makes me shudder. An eagle? I do not manage to see it.

On the way up, just before the waterfall and the hotel of Le Boréon, I encountered a group of eight harvesters. Among them suddenly I recognize Louis. A marvelous smile burst forth on his face. For a moment I hesitated whether to follow him; I should certainly have done so if he had been alone; but the others began talking to him and I feared to obtrude myself on him. Shall I find him again? I didn't remember that he was so handsome.

11 July

I am reading *Les Gaîtés de l'Escadron* and rereading *Boubouroche*.[24] I do not know the play drawn from the short story, but the latter does not strike me as one of the best; there are others, by Courteline, that I much prefer. If it seems particularly successful, isn't this because the subject is particularly thin? *Une Canaille* is in no way inferior to *Boubouroche* and its matter is more solid. *Le Fils* could have been treated by Dostoyevsky.[25]

Courteline is too inclined to let himself indulge in an easy truculence that he attributes indifferently to all his characters. But, most likely, the more vulgar the humanity he depicts, the less appropriate it is for its representatives to be differentiated.

In *Les Gaîtés de l'Escadron* a certain generosity that I like is visible through his cynicism.

---

[24] *The Squadron's Escapades* and *Boubouroche* are both comic stories by Georges Courteline, the former dealing with soldiers doing their military service and the latter with a classic cuckold.

[25] *A Scoundrel* and *The Son* are both short stories by Courteline.

18 July

Yesterday set out at six thirty; went back up the valley of the Boréon; went through the pass of Les Ladres; came back down to Saint-Martin by way of the valley of the Madone. Got back at three thirty.

Took off my sandals for the fun of walking barefoot across a stretch of snow; thought I could not endure the bite of the cold to the end. Showered under a waterfall. Lunched at the refuge of the Madone. Glad to feel still up to the mark.

Finished rereading for the third time from cover to cover the collection of Shakespeare's *Sonnets*. And I read each sonnet twice in succession. Many among them are exasperating; but there are many whose suavity appears only on rereading. To be sure, I admire them; but I also admire myself considerably for having got to the point of admiring them. (There are numerous ones that I have certainly reread twelve times.)

21 July

Spent last night at Nice; arrived at Hyères-Plage yesterday. Swim yesterday; swim today, after which an extraordinary well-being. I breathe better than at Saint-Martin; here I find the air lighter and the temperature less overwhelming. The sea is indescribably beautiful. And no flies!

At Nice spent the morning playing with a wonderful child of four, brown as a nut, laughing and saucy, and talking with his eighteen-year-old sister, as dark as he, gay and visibly naked under her loose black dress. She lets me take the little fellow to the Galeries Lafayette, where I buy him a pistol with darts. For love of them I should have been glad to stay in Nice and almost missed my train.

Finished *The Tempest*.

25 July

When desire subsides so does my whole being.

When beauty no longer excites in us any need of approach, of contact, and of embracing, the state of calm that you were fool enough to long for at a time when an excess of desires tormented you, that state no longer seems to you anything but apathy and deserves to be praised only because, perhaps, it makes the idea of death less atrocious, by taming you to it.

(A Henri Béraud would probably consider "tame to" as an error; I doubt that the expression is correct, but doubt that any other one is so good.)

26 July

Strange article by Barrès in the *Nouvelles littéraires:* "*Salut à de jeunes écrivains.*" [26] In it can be read: "Love the gold, the azure, and the flame.". . .

I detest that way of writing, that way of thinking. It would have exasperated both Stendhal and Flaubert. It smells of the tenor and the odalisque. It lacks both sinew and muscle; it is floating, vague, and swelled with wind like a flag.

28 July

Feeling somewhat better, I got back to work and overcame, I believe, rather considerable difficulties. But, at once, here my insomnia begins again. Happy equilibrium, paradisaical crest to which I can attain; of what marvels would I be capable if only I could stay there!

29 July

Both at Saint-Martin and here I have seen, among the guests of the hotel, none but faces exuding stupidity, egotism, and vulgarity. (Except for a Greek boy of twelve with a marvelous face and body, wonderfully svelte; but excessively aware of his beauty and, consequently, quite stupid with self-satisfaction.) Yet at the next table to the one where I am writing, and turning her back to me, a girl, "barely beyond childhood," with great elegance in her outlines, whom M. would like. I do not tire of looking at her; she notices this and, I believe, is amused by it. But already one can foresee just where her features are going to thicken and become heavy.

And the conversations! I listen to them in spite of myself, fascinated like Saint Antoine in front of the catoblepas and saying: "Its stupidity attracts me." [27]

At Saint-Martin there were five children, the eldest of which happened to be this little Greek. Mme Théo and I amused ourselves by counting the number of their sentences that did not begin with "I. . . ." The sole anxiety each of those children had was to discover some superiority over the others.

But how can one hope that stupid parents should bring up their children intelligently? And already these little ones resemble them.

3 August

Excellent work these last few days, despite the presence of André Allégret. But I doubt whether these dialogues I am writing so rapidly have sufficient density.

[26] "Hail to Some Young Writers."

[27] The catoblepas is described in Flaubert's *Temptation of Saint Anthony* as so stupid that it gnaws on its own front feet.

I am taking Élisabeth Van Rysselberghe and André Allégret to
Corsica. We embark this morning for Ajaccio.

Vizzavone, 5 August

Wonderful Monte d'Oro; one of the most beautiful peaks I have
seen. Long walk this morning; reached the crest opposite the mountain, then came down through the narrow valley inhabited by pines
of an unknown variety that look like cedars and give a Chinese look
to the landscape. Bathed twice in deep basins while following the bed
of the torrent. Ah, how much less young I felt at twenty!

6 August

Climbing Monte d'Oro. But we tackle it too much on the right and
do not reach the main peak. After an exhausting climb in the sun, we
lose the path, which dives under a snow-field. For more than an hour
we scale rocks and rather painfully reach a very narrow pass, on the
other side of which we have the surprise of finding ourselves exactly
opposite the hotel. It is too late to start out anew and we are too tired.
Rather amusing descent on sloping granite slabs; then it becomes exhausting, after we have got back to the forest, through the ferns and
on the slippery pine-needles. We get back at seven thirty, having
walked twelve hours without stopping, done in, extremely amused by
our endurance, but exasperated by the mountain. Not for a minute
did the landscape reward us for our trouble. Bathed three times on
the way.

8 August

Corte, Piana. Back to Ajaccio by a public auto. Wonderful road
along the sea. A short stop at Sagone; just time enough for me to
plunge into the most tepid and most transparent water. The auto starts
up and I run after it without having been able to take time to dress.

11 August

Back to Nice on the 9th. Yesterday traveled by night. Stop at
Carnoules from three a.m. to six. We sleep on a bench. Splendid night.
Behind the station, to the left, a tremendous forest fire lights up the
sky; to the right, high in the sky, a thin sliver of a moon.

I am reading with rapture Benjamin Constant's wonderful *Lettre
sur Julie*, which I did not yet know.[28] I do not think I have ever read

---

[28] The *Letter about Julie* is a beautiful description of a charming woman
who had recently died and who had been a great lover of liberty and of the
principles of the French Revolution. It is usually published in the same volume with Benjamin Constant's novel *Adolphe*.

anything by him that I prefer. The beauty of the style is closely linked
to that of the thought and it would be impossible to write better.

23 August

A few days at La Bastide; a meeting with Eugène Rouart and a
day with him in Marseille; a long and excellent visit to F. Paul Alibert
at Carcassonne; then, the 18th, I joined the group at Pontigny. I am
writing these lines, at eight a.m., on the bank of the Givry River,
seated on a beam that, when the sun strikes it, will soon be covered
with that sort of red bedbugs of which I don't know the exact name
and which I had never before seen except in small groups; here they
formed thick bunches; in spots the wood was completely covered
with them.

Entrancing: this is a word I should like to invent anew in order
to glorify the azure of this radiant morning. On the river-bank the
covered wagon of some itinerant basket-makers. Eight children. Four
of them come and sit or stretch out beside me. Exquisite girl of
fourteen.

Pontigny from 23 August to 2 September. M. comes to join me the
last day. We leave that same evening for La Bastide; then, the 4th, at
Marseille we embark for Tunis.

Cuverville, 9 October

Back here the 7th. Back from Tunisia. On the platforms of the
P.L.M. station [29] as in the Marseille station, groups of emigrants lying
down, rolled helter-skelter in many-colored blankets. Pinned on their
chests, they are wearing a sort of label, a disk of red cardboard on
which I manage to read: *Cherbourg.*

"They are Syrians," a station employee tells me, "who, under the
auspices of the Cunard Line, are going to get work in Mexico."

Reread *Adolphe* (back from Tozeur) with the greatest admiration [30] — and with delight chapter v of the third volume of Montaigne's
Essais.

There was waiting for me in Tunis a very beautiful letter from
Paul Claudel, which moves me very specially — all the more so since
the newspapers were announcing almost his death, or at least, after

---

[29] More commonly called the Gare de Lyon, this is the Paris station for
the line known as P.L.M. or Paris — Lyon — Méditerranée.

[30] *Adolphe* is a keenly analytical novel of love by Benjamin Constant
(1816).

the catastrophe in Japan, let it be understood that he had probably perished in the earthquake.

10 October

We are reading aloud *The Scarlet Letter*.[31]

I should like to read everything, at one time. Danger of dispersion.

Browning, Marvell; continued Logan Pearsall Smith's excellent *The English Language;* went back to William James's psychology; *L'Histoire des variations* by Bossuet,[32] etc.

In addition I take out again *L'Étui de nacre*[33] in order to be sure that I was not misjudging Anatole France. *Aziyadé* and *Le Maroc* by Loti.[34] But the best part of my time is taken up with back correspondence.

Certain days, at certain moments, I completely lose the notion of reality. It seems to me that at the least misstep I shall slip into the other side of the scenery.

What they want is a criterion that will allow them not to need taste when judging.

Perhaps add to that passage in *Si le grain ne meurt* . . . where I relate my religious dissatisfaction and thirst for something else which the lessons of M. Couve left in me:

"If someone had then given me to read *L'Histoire des variations*, I really believe that my Protestantism would have been seriously shaken; but I did not until much later make the acquaintance of that revolting and admirable book; moreover, at that time would I have been capable of understanding it? I do not believe so; but only of revolting against it."

Cuverville, 5 November

Great offensive on the part of Massis in *La Revue universelle* – of which the spring offensive was only the prelude. It is not so much those who attack me who strike fear into me as those who are going to defend me.

----

[31] Hawthorne's novel.

[32] *The History of the Variations within the Protestant Churches* is a study of the different rebellious sects, and hence a work of theological controversy.

[33] *The Mother-of-Pearl Box* by Anatole France is one of the novels of the series entitled *Contemporary History*.

[34] *Aziyadé* is a novel of Turkish life and *Morocco* is a volume of travel impressions.

21 November

Went to see Bernard Faÿ, who talks to me at length of his brother Emmanuel, M.'s friend. He has just died in New York. He did not kill himself, but it's the same thing: he let himself die; he made himself die. He said to his brother, one of the last days:

"One has no heart in playing, in a world in which everyone is cheating."

Mme Simon Bussy accuses me of cheating with the devil.

4 December

Interview with Rivière.

Points to bring up in mine, if it is ever to appear:

What Rivière means by "globalism";

Never paint from nature;

Make one's preparations from nature; but do not inform the reader of one's preparations;

Analysis must always precede synthesis; but from analysis to the work of art there is all the difference that there is between an anatomical drawing and a statue. All the preparatory work must be reabsorbed; it must become invisible although always there.

Just as "it is impossible to write well without skipping over intermediary ideas" (as Montesquieu said), there is no work of art without short cuts.

14 December

"How is Souday with you?"

"He has been successively cold and boiling, according to whether he thought me to be a royalist or a republican. Since he has grasped the fact that I am neither one nor the other, he has become tepid; he grants me a certain value as an artist, but 'as a thinker' considers that I am worth nothing."

21 December

Jacques Maritain came then Friday morning, 14 December, to the Villa on the stroke of ten, as it had been agreed. I had prepared a few sentences, but none of them was of any use, for I understood at once that I did not have to play a character in his presence, but on the contrary simply reveal myself, and that this was my best defense. His curved, bent way of carrying his head and his whole body displeased me, and a certain clerical unction in his voice and gesture; but I overlooked this, and pretense seemed unworthy of us two. He tackled the question at once and declared straight out the purpose of his visit, which I knew and which was to beg me to suspend the publication of a certain book that François Le Grix had described to him as imminent and of which he begged me to recognize with him the danger.

I told him that I had no intention of defending myself but that he must be aware that everything he could think of saying to me about this book I had already said to myself, and that a project that resists the trial of the war, of personal losses, and of all the meditations that ensue runs the risk of being too deeply anchored in the heart and mind for an intervention like his to hope to change it. I protested that, moreover, there had been no obstinacy in my case and that even, after a first reading to a friend (Marcel Drouin) ten years ago, of the first two chapters of this book, on the advice of that friend I had interrupted my work; that I had almost given it up despite the profound upset that renunciation caused me; that if, on the other hand, at the end of the second year of the war, I had picked it up again and completed it, this was because it appeared clear to me that this book had to be written, that I was uniquely qualified to write it, and that I could not without a sort of bankruptcy release myself from what I considered my duty.

We both spoke with extreme slowness, anxious to say nothing that might misconstrue or go beyond our thought. He transmitted to me Henri Massis's fear of having, by the provocation of his articles, hastened that publication. I begged him to leave Massis all his fears and regrets and remorse and spoke of the wonderful letter Claudel had written me, about my *Dostoïevsky* likewise, in which I felt at least the impulse of a truly Christian thought, which I in nowise recognized in Massis's articles. Maritain then told me that Massis might have made a mistake, and as I pointed out to him certain points in those articles that obviously revealed a desire to falsify my thought: "He may not have understood it properly. . . ." I protested that he was too intelligent on other points not to force me to consider that falsification as conscious and voluntary.

"I have," I told him, "a horror of falsehood. That is perhaps just where my Protestantism lurks. Catholics cannot understand that. I have known many; and indeed, with the single exception of Jean Schlumberger, I have nothing but Catholics as friends. Catholics do not like truth."

"Catholicism teaches the love of truth," he said.

"No, do not protest, Maritain. I have too often seen, and with too many examples, what compromises were possible. And even (for I have that intellectual failing, which Ghéon used to reproach me with, of too easily putting words into my adversary's mouth and of inventing arguments for him) I see what you might reply to me: that the Protestant often confuses truth with God, that he adores Truth, not understanding that Truth is but one of the attributes of God. . . ."

"But don't you think that that truth, which your book claims to make manifest, can be dangerous? . . ."

"If I thought so, I should not have written the book, or at least I should not publish it. However dangerous that truth may be, I hold that the falsehood that covers it is even more dangerous."

"And don't you think that it is dangerous for you to say it?"

"That is a question that I refuse to ask myself."

He then spoke to me of the salvation of my soul and told me that he often prayed for it, as did several of his friends who were convinced like him that I was marked out by God for higher ends, which I sought in vain to evade.

"I am inclined to believe," I said to him smiling, "that you are much more concerned with the salvation of my soul than I am myself."

We spoke at length, on this subject and likewise of the Greek equilibrium and the Christian lack of equilibrium. As the hour was advancing, he made as if to rise.

"I should not like to leave you before — Will you allow me to ask you something?"

"Go ahead and ask," I said with a gesture indicating that I did not guarantee a reply.

"I should like to ask you a promise."

"? . . ."

"Promise me that when I have gone you will put yourself in a state of prayer and ask Christ to let you know, directly, whether you are right or wrong to publish this book. Can you promise me that?"

I looked at him at length and said:

"No."

There was a long silence. I continued:

"Understand me, Maritain. I have lived too long and too intimately, and you know it, in the thought of Christ to agree to call on him today as one rings someone up on the telephone. Indeed, it would seem to me unworthy to call on him without having first put myself in a state to hear him. Oh! I do not doubt that I can succeed in doing so. I know, moreover, just how that state is achieved; I have the recipe. But on my part there would be, today, a certain element of pretense; I am loath to do it. And moreover, may I tell you this: never, even at the time of my greatest fervor, even at the time when I used to pray — I do not say only every day, but at every hour, at every moment of the day — never was my prayer anything but an act of adoration, a thanksgiving, a surrender. Perhaps I am very Protestant in this. . . . And yet no, I do not know why I say this. It is, on the contrary, very Protestant to ask advice about anything. There are some who would consult Christ to know how to lace a pair of shoes; I

cannot; I will not. It has always seemed to me unworthy to ask anything of God. I have always accepted everything from him, with
gratitude. No, do not ask that of me."

"I shall then be obliged to leave you disappointed?" he asked sadly
as he held out his hand.

"At first," I replied, putting into these words all the hidden meaning that I could, without moreover knowing just what meaning. And
thereupon we separated.

I am writing this immediately upon my return to Cuverville and
while my memory of it is still fresh.

DETACHED PAGES

(Recovered Pages)

I

"Have you noted," said Édouard, "the sort of moral anchylosis produced in M. by his assumption of never being in the wrong? It is an
assumption that many people make; I made it too in my youth, and if
now I am so sensitive to it in others, it is because I myself had the
greatest difficulty getting rid of it. My parents had accustomed me to
act, not according to my inner urge, but according to an ethical rule
outside of me, which they considered applicable to all men, so that,
in the same circumstances, any creature whatever, no matter how different from me, would have seen the same moral postulate rise up before him, which he could not escape without flinching and without in-
curring the blame of others (which would still be bearable), but also
some self-reprobation or other that my upbringing in fact had striven
to make unbearable to me. Not to have acted, in whatever combina-
tion of circumstances, precisely as I was expected to act seemed to me
abominable to such a point that all inner peace was immediately
compromised, that peace without which I believed that I could not
live — while on the contrary . . . but at that time could I admit, could
I suspect even, that whatever is newest in each creature and most
peculiar to him is perhaps not the most detestable?

A great error is revealed here: minds accustomed to live according to the rule cease to recognize, as soon as someone escapes the
rule, any other domination than that of one's own sweet will; a
person seems to them a slave as soon as he is a slave to his passions,
and, as he escapes the passions when he lives according to duty, he
ceases to seem to them a slave and it seems to them that he is free the
moment the slavery to which he submits is a moral, banal, and commonly accepted slavery. They cry out: "O Lord, deliver us from our-

selves," and their way of delivering themselves is to bend their thought, their will, their whole being until they desire nothing to which their moral being cannot give complete assent, so that they have an illusion of acting freely while already their choice has ceased to be free, and that constraint to which they submit and the very difficulty they experience in submitting to it are at once a pledge of the error into which their nature hurled them and of the truth of that rule which forces and counterfeits their most sincere impulses.

But the rigorous puritan upbringing by which my parents had fashioned my childhood, but the habit and need of a discipline, allowed me to glimpse, once escaped from the common rule, something quite different from a mere surrender; and this allowed me to shrug my shoulders when I heard myself accused of listening henceforth only to the invitation of pleasure. To rediscover, underneath the factitious creature, the unspoiled self was not, or so it seemed to me, so easy a task; and that new rule of life which was becoming mine: to act according to the greatest sincerity, implied a resolution, a perspicacity, an effort that strained my whole will, so that I never seemed more moral to myself than at the time when I had decided to cease being moral; I mean: to be moral henceforth only in my own way. And I came to understand that perfect sincerity, the kind that, in my opinion, leads to the most valor and greatest dignity, sincerity not only of the act itself but of the motive, can be achieved only through the most constant, but also the least bitter, effort, only with the clearest vision (I mean: the least suspect of self-satisfaction), and the most irony.

It soon became apparent to me that I had gained almost nothing; that I was still acting only according to the best motive, so long as I made my acts measure up to that approbation which implied, before acting, a sort of deliberation and weighing in imagination, whence the action was delayed and blocked. The promptest, the most sudden action henceforth seemed to me preferable; it seemed to me that my act was all the more sincere since I had swept away before it all those preambles by which I used to attempt to justify it to myself. Henceforth, acting in any way whatever and not giving myself time to reflect, my least acts seemed to me more significant since they were no longer reasoned out. At the same time I delivered myself from anxiety, perplexity, and remorse. And perhaps that intimate gymnastic to which I had first submitted had not been altogether useless and helped me to achieve that state of joy which made me recognize my act to be good solely from the pleasure I took in doing it.

The Greeks, who, not only in the multitude of their statues but also in themselves, left us such a beautiful image of humanity, recognized as many gods as there are instincts, and the problem for them was to keep the inner Olympus in equilibrium, not to subjugate and subdue any of the gods.

It is not so much by his acts that a lover of humanity makes himself useful as by his example. I mean: by his very figure, by the image he offers and leaves behind, and by the happiness and serenity it radiates.[35]

II

T. explains:

. . . There is a certain indulgence by which every sentiment we experience is exaggerated; and often one does not suffer so much as one imagines oneself to be suffering.

I have never been able to renounce anything; and protecting in me both the best and the worst, I have lived as a man torn asunder. But how can it be explained that this cohabitation of extremes in me led not so much to restlessness and suffering as to a pathetic intensification of the sentiment of existence, of life? The most opposite tendencies never succeeded in making me a tormented person; but rather perplexed — for torment accompanies a state one longs to get away from, and I did not long to escape what brought into operation all the potentialities of my being. That *state of dialogue* which, for so many others, is almost intolerable became necessary to me. This is also because, for those others, it can only be injurious to action, whereas for me, far from leading to sterility, it invited me to the work of art and immediately preceded creation, led to equilibrium and harmony.

It must, however, be recognized that, for a number of souls, which I consider among the best tempered, happiness lies not in comfort and quietude, but in ardor. A sort of magnificent using up is all the more desirable to them since they are constantly being renewed by it and do not so much suffer from the wearing away as they rejoice in their perpetual re-creation. As for me, I can tell you that I have never so keenly felt myself growing old as in that very quietude to which your rule of conduct invites one, but which you are less likely to achieve the more earnestly and nostalgically you strive to attain it. Your belief in the survival of souls is nourished by the need of that quietude and your *lack of hope* of enjoying it in life.

Shall I tell you what keeps me from believing in eternal life? It is that almost perfect satisfaction I enjoy in effort itself and in the immediate realization of happiness and harmony.

---

[35] "A cheerful intelligent face is the end of culture, and success enough," says Emerson. "For it indicates the purpose of nature and wisdom attained." [A.] This passage, which Gide quotes in French, is found in Emerson's *Conduct of Life* (1860) in the chapter entitled "Culture."

III

I was like the prodigal son who goes squandering his possessions. And that imponderable treasure which the slow virtue of my fathers, from generation to generation, had patiently accumulated on my head, no, I was not unaware of its value; but the unknown I could hope for by renouncing it seemed to me even more precious. The words of Christ rose up luminously before me like the column of fire that guided the chosen people in the night, and in the heavy darkness in which I decided to adventure I kept repeating to myself: "Sell all your goods and give them to the poor." My heart was filled with apprehension and joy, or more exactly: with the apprehension of my joy. For, thought I, it is not a question of interpreting the divine words to attain complete happiness; it is a question of accepting them without reservations, of understanding them "in spirit and in truth"; and then at last, and then above all, to put them into practice, for, as it is said in the Gospel, "every one that heareth these sayings of mine and doeth them not . . ."

I began then to seek out which, among the thoughts, opinions, and tendencies of my soul and mind that were most familiar to me, were the ones that I most certainly derived from my ancestors, from my upbringing and puritan formation, which at first had constituted my strength, from that sort of moral atmosphere in which I was beginning to stifle. And doubtless, pushing that relinquishment to the extreme, to the absurd, I should have ended up in complete impoverishment — for "what have you that you have not received?" — but yet it was complete impoverishment that I coveted as the truest possession. Resolved to give up in this manner every personal possession and convinced that I could not hope to dispose of everything except on condition that I possessed nothing in my own right, I repudiated every personal opinion, every habit, every modesty, my very virtue, as one throws off a tunic in order to offer an unveiled body to the contact of the wave, to the passing winds, to the sun. Strengthened by these abnegations, I soon felt my soul only as a loving will (yes, this is the way I defined it to myself), palpitating, open to all comers, like unto everything, impersonal, a naïve confusion of appetites, greeds, desires. And if perhaps I had been frightened by the disorder into which their anarchy led me, was I not able to reassure myself at once by recalling these words of Christ: "Why should you be troubled?" I surrendered then to this provisional disorder, trusting in a more sincere and natural order that would organize itself, I thought, and believing moreover that the disorder itself was less dangerous for my soul than an arbitrary and necessarily artificial order, since I had not invented it. Divine ray! I exclaimed, isn't what is opposed to you above all that false wisdom

of men, made up of fear, lack of confidence, and presumption? I resign everything to you. I surrender myself. Drive out all shadow from
me. Inspire me.

Considering later on that nothing separates one more from God
than pride and that nothing made me prouder than my virtue, I began
to detest that very virtue and everything on which I could pride myself, everything that allowed me to say: I am not like you, common
run of men! And I am well aware that this excess of renunciation, this
repudiation of virtue through the love of virtue itself, would appear,
as merely an abominable sophistry to the pious soul who reads me.
Paradox or sophistry that thenceforth bent my life, whether or not the
devil prompted it I shall examine later on. It is enough for me to say
for the moment that I advanced boldly on this path that was so new.
What am I saying: path? Every step I took forward was a venture into
the unknown.

1924

I am reading for the first time in English Stevenson's *Dr. Jekyll and Mr. Hyde* — with an admiration, alas, that is somewhat diminished. Too ingenious, too organized; it lacks grandeur. Wonderful subject; but I wonder if it is not a mistake to have made Jekyll "at peace" precisely after having got rid of Hyde — "his face seemed to open and brighten." — *It ought to be just the contrary.*

It is thanks to Hyde that Jekyll should be able to find tranquillity.

5 January

Finished the Stevenson. Jekyll's confession is wonderful and what I wrote yesterday is absurd.

If I do not tear out this page, it is for the mortification of rereading it some day.

I have gone back to William James's *Psychology*, but drop it after reading two chapters (among which the one on instinct) and assuring myself of its mediocrity.

7 January

Georges, while reading Chekhov, exclaims:

"How remote those Russians are from us!" Nothing annoys me more than that conviction in which the nationalists (and many others) keep the mass of French readers — that they are forever incapable of understanding foreign nationalities. Far from trying to recognize in them what remains human despite the differences and through which they could strike up a fellow-feeling, they pay attention only to the differences. This is so obviously true that I should not note it here; but there is added to it this reflection which, this morning, strikes me as rather new.

Are not the differences from one people to another strangely emphasized by the habits that lead them, each in his own literature, to bring out certain parts of his character that others are accustomed to hide, or at least not to present in the raw — just as for dress and, through dress, certain shiftings of the boundaries of modesty.

The habit and the need, among the ancient Greeks, to reveal themselves naked, to reveal themselves "in the raw" — nothing seems less natural to us today.

I have no doubt that there is a subject for reflections in this.

In each literature the first question to ask is: What does it hide of man?

(The question: What does it reveal? is relatively less important.)

Paris

The need of writing novels is not, it seems to me, always very spontaneous in many of the young novelists of today. The supply follows the demand here. The desire to depict from nature the people one has met I believe to be rather frequent. It turns to account a certain gift of the eye and of the pen. But the creation of new people becomes a natural need only in those who are tormented by an imperious inner complexity and are not satisfied by their own deeds.

It is very bold to assert that you would have thought just the same without having read certain authors who will later seem to have been your initiators. Yet it seems to me that had I not known Dostoyevsky, Nietzsche, Freud, X., or Z., I should have thought just the same, and that I found in them rather an authorization than an awakening. Above all, they taught me to cease doubting myself, not to be afraid of my thought, and to let myself be led by it, since moreover *I found them in it.*

26 January

Wrote yesterday a rather long letter to Massis (of which I have kept a copy), but I sent it to the wrong address and fear that it will not reach him. And since it was not registered, it will not be returned to me.

13 February

If my journal is published later on, I fear that it will give a rather false idea of me. I have not kept it during the long periods of equilibrium, health, and happiness; but instead during those periods of depression when I needed it to catch hold of myself, in which I show myself as whining, whimpering, pitiable.

As soon as the sun reappears, I lose sight of myself and am completely absorbed by work and life. My journal reflects none of this, but only my periods of despair. I haven't known any for a long time now.

14 February

Because I publish little, it is thought that I write slowly. The truth is that I go for rather long periods without writing. As soon as my brain is in good form, my pen or pencil cannot go fast enough. I wrote the whole last act of *Saül* in one day (at Arco). I am apt to write in

the train, in the métro, on a bench along the quay or along the boulevards, on road embankments, and those are my best pages, the most
truly inspired. One sentence follows another, is born of the other, and
I feel as I see it being born and growing within me an almost physical
rapture. I believe that this artesian welling up is the result of a long
subconscious preparation. I am apt subsequently to make a few changes
in this first sketch, but very few.

Only the work of joining is often very painful and demands a great
intellectual concentration.

It happens that my rough drafts have many sentences written between the lines, but this comes from the profusion of thoughts and the
difficulty of putting them in order and fitting them together.

Cuverville, 1 March

Plunged into Bossuet's *Sermons,* the six volumes of which were
waiting for me here. In both the excellent and the worst they surpass
all my hopes.

Thibaudet on Bergsonism; after having taken a great interest in the
preface (all the greater since I know almost nothing of Bergson), I am
losing contact.[1]

What I dislike in Bergson's doctrine is all I already thought without his saying it, and everything in it that is flattering, even caressing,
to the mind. Later on, his influence on our epoch will be thought to
be seen everywhere, simply because he himself belongs to the epoch
and constantly yields to the trend. Whence his *representative* importance.

Cuverville, 4 March

I leave tomorrow again, my nerves at the end of their tether. Not
accomplished all I had planned to do during this ten days' retreat.
Great need of relaxation and aeration.

Constantly renewed difficulties of a book that is nourished by *invention* alone and that will take advantage of no impetus.

Returned to the piano (Bach and Granados). Typing the manuscript.

Reading Bossuet (*Histoire des variations* and *Sermons*).

Brignoles, 19 March

What is called today "objectivity" is easy for novelists without an
inner landscape. I can say that it was not in me that I was interested
but in the conflict of certain ideas of which my soul was merely the
theater and in which I functioned less as an actor than as a spectator,
a witness.

---

[1] Albert Thibaudet wrote a two-volume study entitled *Le Bergsonisme.*

27 March

In order to judge something properly, one must get a bit away from it, after having loved it. This is true of countries, of persons, *and of oneself.*

Abominable fatigue. All the springs of my being are unsprung.

Reread three cantos of *The Ring and the Book.* Admirable.

Vence, 28 March

I buy in the Carnoules station *Les Bijoux indiscrets,* which I am reading with rapture. I believe, however, that I prefer *Jacques le fataliste.*[2]

Roquebrune, 7 April

Read with great pleasure Anatole France's *Histoire comique.* Encouraged, I pick up again *Le Jardin d'Épicure;* but I recover my original disgust when faced with that benevolent and tepid drink.[3]

15 April

Read *Les Dieux ont soif.*[4] Certain pages, certain chapters are excellent. It is, all together, a very good book.

I am asked, for a special number devoted to the glory of Anatole France, for some notes "that certainly I must have in a drawer."

But what could I dare write after the praise I read in *Le Quotidien* signed by the Comtesse de Noailles? — It ceases to be criticism, even full of praises; it's a rave. Such an excess, such immoderation, such an inflation of words, feelings, and thoughts, devaluates anything reasonable and sensible one could say subsequently.

15 May

I had carelessly read Pourtalès's letter summoning me to the first meeting of a Benjamin Constant Committee. I arrive an hour too early in front of the bar on the Champs-Élysées, where I am to meet with Barthou, Bourget, Du Bos, Boylesve, etc.

I am writing these lines seated on a bench of the avenue after having walked in the gardens surrounding the Grand-Palais. Very tired

---

[2] Both *The Indiscreet Jewels* and *Jacques the Fatalist* are philosophic tales by Diderot.

[3] *The Comic Story* and *The Garden of Epicurus* are both novels by Anatole France, whose eightieth birthday was widely celebrated on 6 April 1924.

[4] *The Gods Are Athirst,* Anatole France's novel of the French Revolution.

these last few days, today's fine weather has restored me. If only I didn't have this meeting, I should be almost joyous. Since I have broken loose from myself, joy or sorrow have ceased to have any but physiological causes in me.

30 May

Good work yesterday evening, after a rather empty afternoon at Longchamp, then at the fair on the quay between the Invalides and the garden of the Tour Eiffel.

I believe I have satisfactorily sketched out the important visit to La Pérouse after his unsuccessful suicide.[5] Unfortunately I left in Cuverville (?) some papers I shall need to finish it.

I am rereading Goethe's *Elegies,* and here is something that touches me more than the Béraud attacks: I discover that I have until now been guilty of a misinterpretation in the first line of the second Elegy:

Nun bin ich endlich geborgen.

Until now I have been reading *geboren* and once translated it (in my lecture on Influence): "at last I am *born,*" instead of "I am safe, escaped, under shelter.". . .

31 May

This notebook will not be the confidant of my sorrows. My whole being calls out all its strength and stiffens under pain. I even find a sort of salutary exaltation in it, and my horror of those adulterated pleasures that are taking M. away from me leads me back to work.

3 June

I intend to give to those who read me strength, joy, courage, defiance, and perspicacity — but I am above all careful not to give them directions, judging that they can and must find them only by themselves (I was about to say: "in themselves"). Develop at one and the same time the critical faculty and energy, those two contraries. Generally we find among intelligent people nothing but the stiff-jointed, and among men of action nothing but fools.

17 June

Eager to get back to the study of German, which I have completely abandoned since the war — or more exactly since I began to study English (1909) — I take up again Goethe's *Elegies* and the *Venetian Epigrams,* and I have the surprise and joy of understanding them much

---

[5] In *Les Faux-Monnayeurs* (*The Counterfeiters*).

better than I once did; and not only the meaning of the words, but also their rhythm and poetic quality.

19 June

Off for Cuverville. In the train I read various articles in the special number of the *Disque vert* devoted to Freud.

Ah, how embarrassing Freud is! And how easily it seems to me we would have discovered his America without him! It seems to me that the thing I should be most grateful to him for is having accustomed readers to hearing certain subjects treated without having to protest or blush. What he especially brings us is daring; or, more exactly, he spares us a certain false and embarrassing modesty.

But how many absurd things in that imbecile of genius!

If it were as thwarted as the sexual appetite, mere hunger would be the great provider of Freudianism (just as we see thirst prompt the dreams of those without water in the desert). In other words: certain forces owe their violence to the lack of an outlet. It is true that the sexual desire, when not directly satisfied, is liable to multiple hypocrisies — I mean: of assuming the most varied forms — as the other hunger can never do. The point on which my assiduous investigations (if I were a doctor) would bear is this: what happens when, for social, moral, etc. reasons, the sexual function is forced, in order to find satisfaction, to leave the object of its desire; when the satisfaction of the flesh involves no assent, no participation of the rest of the person, when it is thus divided with a part of itself remaining behind? . . . What remains subsequently from that division? What traces? What secret forms of revenge are then prepared by that part which had no share in the feast?

21 June

On the advice of Bernard Faÿ, I am reading *Les Pléiades* by Gobineau. Impossible indeed not to take into account the tales of the three Calenders when judging *Le Bal du Comte d'Orgel.*[6] Gobineau's influence on Radiguet is undeniable (*Les Pléiades* was his favorite reading-matter), and it can even be said that the passage from one book to the other is almost imperceptible. But the publisher's ballyhoo will result in Radiguet's being read much more than Gobineau has ever been read, so that this imitation will go unnoticed.

---

[6] *The Pleiades* by Gobineau appeared in 1874; *The Count's Ball,* a novel by Raymond Radiguet, appeared in 1924 after the death of its author at the age of twenty.

23 June

I am copying out for Champion a chapter of *Si le grain ne meurt.*
. . .⁷ Shocked to discover in it a number of grammatical errors, am-
biguities, bloomers. If it were not already printed, I should cut out
three quarters of it.

They are much too anxious to know *my* thought; my only care was
to reveal theirs to them.

I have the least pugnacious temperament, the most conciliatory
mind there is; but when faced with bad faith, I have the greatest difficulty in remaining calm — and perhaps even more if someone else's
interest is endangered — yes, even more than when my own is concerned. But there is a certain injustice in regard to ideas to which I
fear too few people are sensitive, and which arouses in me the greatest indignation.

Déhais, to designate hoar-frost, uses the expression *"blanc rimé,"*
which I do not find in Edelestan's Norman dictionary. In Skeat's ety-
mological dictionary I don't find any trace either of this old Norman
word — which is certainly the "rime" of the English — in which Agnès
Copeau recognizes the Danish *"rim."*

24 June

It is not enough for the Dadas that I have written a book they like
(*Les Caves*).⁸ In addition, I should not write, or have written, anything but that. They do not rise to the point of realizing that it might
be amusing for us too to displease, and to displease just such as they!
Each of my books turns against those who were enthusiastic for the
preceding one. That will teach them to applaud me only for the right
reason and to take each of my books simply for what it is: a work
of art.

26 July

What proves that his appetite was not very lively is that he claimed
to prefer "nothing" as soon as he couldn't get the exquisite. Montaigne

---

⁷ Édouard Champion published privately a series of little brochures
with the general title of *Les Amis d'Édouard* (*Édouard's Friends*), to which
there was a limited number of subscriptions. Gide's chapter appeared in this
series, as did earlier his *Numquid et tu . . . ?*

⁸ The Dada movement, founded by Tristan Tzara in 1916, was a negative revision of literary values and a challenge to rational thought. After
1924 it was absorbed in surrealism.

blames this concern for choice in the young; he prefers to see them a bit greedy rather than epicures.

27 July

Whoever acts like everyone else necessarily gets annoyed with whoever does not act like him.

I read in the Introduction to *The Scarlet Letter* by Hawthorne these two sentences to be put into the Barrès file: "Human nature will not flourish, any more than a potato, if it be planted and replanted, for too long a series of generations in the same worn-out soil. My children have had other birthplaces, and, so far as their fortunes may be within my control, shall strike their roots into unaccustomed earth."

Paris, 6 August

Left Cuverville this morning, annoyed to have to leave my work. I hope to be able to return the day after tomorrow. Delight at finding Drouin conciliatory and accessible; yet I am not misled as to the large share of affectation in his apparent affability, but want only to yield, for, after all, my liking for him sweeps everything else aside. It sweeps everything before it — and me too — to the point of imprudence. In vain I remind myself that I have always had to repent for every confidence I have allowed myself to make him. Drouin asks me to read him *Les Faux-Monnayeurs*. Am I going to be able to face his frown? He speaks to me of *Corydon* with a kindness and indulgence that touch me — for I know how far he is from approving of the book; but yet he does not show any excessive reprobation. I must say, besides, that I have become much less sensitive to blame. The launching of the attacks of the last few months has toughened my skin.

Dined yesterday evening with Copeau. Under a driving rain he takes me to an excellent little restaurant near Montparnasse that Suarès had told him about, where we enjoy a tasty lobster and a heady Burgundy. Copeau is in funds, in luck, in verve, and he communicates his fancy to me.

10 August

I do not know any worse trial than to read a work to my excellent brother-in-law. Yet I have warned him of the discouragements that his apparent inattention or insensitivity causes me. If he had not begged me to, I should not have shown him anything of *Les Faux-Monnayeurs*.

He comes to the reading already yawning; takes care to warn me that he doesn't know whether or not he will be able to remain attentive for long. At the end of every sentence I am afraid to see him fall

asleep, so that I speed up my reading more and more and have only
one anxiety: to reach the end of the chapter before he drops off. After
which, the dullest silence; an arid desert in which one's thirst seeks
a water-hole everywhere, the least little trickle of curiosity, interest,
or liking. Though I tell myself that this absence of manifestation is a
part of his rule, I remain crushed.

Paris, 17 August

My fatigue can be recognized by these musical obsessions which,
on certain days, never leave me for hours on end and wind their way
through every thought I manage to have.

Despite my resistance, I have to recognize and name each note; in
spite of myself I pursue the motif from tone to tone until my exasperation is pluperfect.

I left Cuverville early this morning. Marcel had not understood
that I was leaving today. Yesterday evening he seemed very sorry
about it and to have put off from day to day the conversation he had
promised me about my book. "I'll talk to you about it when I have reread it," he had told me.

I *knew* that he would get to it too late, as he always does.

But I doubt if, after a rereading, he would have talked any better about it than he did when caught short, somewhat embarrassed to
have let himself be taken by surprise.

His remarks are most intelligent (as always) and there is not one
of them that I am not anxious to take into account. I shall note them
down in the notebook I have devoted to the novel.

He always takes the same care not to pay me any compliment; but
now at least I know enough not to let myself become gloomy over it.
There was a time when his silence in regard to praise flattened me out.
I told him so and I am grateful to him for not changing his manner on
that account. Moreover, he could not.

I do not know anyone more intelligent than Marcel Drouin save
Valéry . . . and even then.

His weaknesses are all due to his temperament, and almost of a
physiological sort. They are none the less intolerable to anyone who
knows him well.

"To be right" . . . Who still wants to be? . . . A few fools.

Chartres, 6 September

Unadulterated awe; and not only in front of the cathedral. This
warm morning of soft azure I wander in the old quarter of the lower
town, on the edge of a charming, grassy, shady canal and of a stream

of which I don't know the name. A bit worried at the thought that perhaps Roger Fry, who is with me, is waiting for me in the hall of the hotel. But *there is a spell upon me,*[9] and I need solitude. I persuade myself that he does too. How young I should still feel if I did not know that I am not!

Some people work over themselves to obtain the unity of their person. I let myself go.

9 September

Back to Cuverville after two days in Elbeuf, at Maurois's with the Du Boses and Anne Desjardins.

As if the world were an enigma of which we had to find the key!

3 October

Back to Paris to get ready for my trip. Before leaving, worked over again the character of Vincent, very insufficiently sketched. As to Lady Griffith, it is better not to give her too much existence.

The parts that join certain dialogues strike me as rather colorless. But perhaps it is better that they do not stand out too much.

Many ideas are abandoned almost as soon as they are launched, but it seems to me that I might have taken better advantage of them. Chiefly those that are expressed in the *Journal d'Édouard;* it would be good to bring them up again in the second part. It would then be all the more surprising to see them again after having lost sight of them for some time — like a first motif in certain of Bach's fugues.

They have besmirched their praises to such a point that the self-respecting artist considers their curses as incense.

26 October

At Cuverville the last three days. Departure for the Congo put off. Reasons: M.'s examinations; finishing of *Les Faux-Monnayeurs.* Insufficient preparation, etc. . . . Leaving in November, I thought to be back in April. Six months are too little for this trip. Leaving in July, it will probably be for a full year.

Shall I be able to finish my book between now and July? I doubt it.

I have spent the last three days mending the last chapters — read to Martin du Gard on my way through Paris. The last one in particular (the evening of the banquet); but now I am stalled.

Plunged into Bach again (*Suites for Organ* and *Art of the Fugue*).

---

[9] The words in italics appear in English.

In the train began *The Egoist*,[10] which I continue with an increasing irritation.

A letter from Gosse informs me that I have been "unanimously" named an honorary member of the Royal Academy to replace Anatole France.[11]

Some people head toward an objective. Others simply go straight ahead.

As for me, I do not know where I am going; but I am making progress.

I am perhaps merely an adventurer.

It is only in adventure that some people succeed in knowing themselves — in finding themselves.

It is true of my *Faux-Monnayeurs* as it is of piano-practice: it is not always by plugging away at a difficulty and sticking at it that one overcomes it; but, rather, often by working on the one next to it. Certain people and certain things require to be approached on an angle.

Article by Ghéon in *L'Action Française*. One of the least good that I have read by him. "I cannot forget that Gide wrote *Philoctète*," he says.[12] Others cannot forget that I wrote *Les Caves*. Still others, *Les Nourritures*. But none of them can forgive me for having written all of this together.

6 November

Day on which we were to leave. The weather is beautiful.

7 November

"You ought to get married. Try to make another person happy . . . you would see how unhappy you can be . . . both of you; yes, both of you. But it is instructive."

8 November

Rather good work; and it is, indeed, for this reason that I have not written anything in this notebook. I open it only when the weather turns bad and my sky darkens.

For the last two days, less good sleep. No matter; since 26 October

---

[10] This is George Meredith's novel.

[11] Anatole France had died on 12 October 1924.

[12] Gide's drama, *Philoctetes, or the Treatise of the Two Rules of Conduct*, was first published in 1899.

I have written chapters x and xi of my second part; begun xii; and I see a bit more clearly for the rest.

Good piano-practice. Bach, Albéniz, and Chopin. Very little reading.

Llona informs me of a request to publish *Corydon* in New York. Very amused to see that America is the first to declare herself.

10 November

The important thing is to find a way (or an absence of way) of life that will preserve at one and the same time the savor of the object and our own greed. Progressive disenchantment of the whole universe on the one hand, and satiety on the other: it seems that this is the aim we set ourselves; and there is none more easily nor more commonly achieved, alas!

11 November

Attacks of insomnia the last three days; the night leaves a sort of dregs in my mind that choke it. Yesterday, incapable of work, even at the piano. I make up my mind to leave Paris (if only for a few days), for I have no hope of climbing back upward if I remain.

Cuverville

Doctor X., a friend of Henri Béraud, wrote his *Anti-Corydon* in three days, it seems. Why did he not use this time to read my book more carefully? He would then have given up any thought of writing his.

It is quite natural that you jostle as soon as you cease to follow the current.

Each new idea you propose *must* find opposition.

The opposition does not prove, moreover, that the idea is right.

"The more difficulty one has had in obtaining something, the more one clings to it; this is the reason why fools are so obstinate; they are not willing to give up any of their ideas, because they had so much trouble conceiving them."

I enjoy reading this excellent remark in the *Handbook of Criminal Investigation,* in which I am absorbed.[13]

Les Nouvelles littéraires is perhaps not very far-sighted in conducting an "inquiry" on the influence of present-day French literature

---

[13] By Hans Gross — translated from the German. [A.] Gide quotes the title in French.

abroad. Replies have come in from England, Germany, and Russia (pending those of other nations) that henceforth that influence is non-existent. One thought as much.

However great was the fame of Anatole France, of Maurras, and of Barrès across the Channel and across the Rhine, I doubt that they did very much for our reputation. By presenting them as the most perfect representatives of the French genius, we encouraged the belief that nothing new could be hoped for from our country. Skepticism is now out of date; nothing further can be expected from it. This takes care of France; and as for Maurras and Barrès, what interest could their theories have for foreigners?

The anthology Duhamel has provided for Germany does us a disservice. It justifies that reputation, too often deserved, which has been built up for us, of being a nation of mere orators. By preference he has chosen from each author the most oratorical passages, etc. (I shall have to return to this), from Hugo in particular.

The qualities that make people revile me in France today are the very ones that have brought me that reputation abroad which infuriates Henri Béraud. And the interest in my books abroad derives precisely from what makes them seem boring to him. Too numerous in France today are those who are interested only in outworn ideas and idle talk.

If only that inquiry could open our eyes. But in advance I can hear "good Frenchmen" concluding: "decidedly there is no way of understanding one another from one country to another"; and sink deeper into their error.

It is the separation of art from ethics, its detachment, its lack of interest in moral questions, that today allows religion to seize hold of art. (Could be better said.)

> *Mitis in apricis coquitur vendemia saxis.*
> (On the sunny rocks
> Ripens the mellow vintage.) [14]

To be inscribed on the façade of a work of art.

The dog baying at the moon takes it for the sun and bemoans his loss; the entire universe seems to him to have become icy, deserted, drab.

So does the lover who laments and misjudges love on the basis of a whore's love.

---

[14] Virgil: *Georgics,* II, 522. Gide has translated the line into French.

When he writes that he cannot be interested in anything I write, H. de Régnier is perhaps sincere (I consent to see malevolence only when I cannot do otherwise), but this is just the unfortunate part of it.

Back to Paris.

For *Les Faux-Monnayeurs:*
There is what you know and what you don't know. Between the two what you suppose. I wonder at certain novelists who are never at a loss. As for me, rather than to invent, I prefer to confess: I don't know.

I listen to my characters; I hear what they say; but what they think and what they feel? As soon as I infer, I draw them my way. As soon as a person differentiates himself, he does so much more than one supposes. Only the masses understand the masses; community of thoughts and feelings belongs to ordinary people.

So long as Bernard kept talking I had only to listen to him; but as soon as he falls silent he eludes me; I don't know where I am.

It is certain that if *I*, the novelist, have in me the character of the novelist Édouard, I must have also the novel he is writing.
(Scene of the interception of the counterfeit coin.)
P.'s "sublime remarks";
"It is by dint of praying that you come to believe."
Make the minister say in his prayer:
"My Lord, my Lord, my Lord . . . why do you withdraw from me? Are you deaf to my prayer because I am not calling you by the proper name? Must I cease believing in you, or must I believe that you are acting against me? Nothing of what I have put under your charge has prospered. I loathe thinking that when I rely on your promise I am wrong. I have put my whole family under your protection and you ignored them. I had entrusted my children to you; they grew up to curse you, and all my fidelity could not restrain their blasphemy. If I have not deceived myself, You have deceived me."

19 November
Returned to Paris yesterday evening.
I have read to Roger Martin du Gard the last chapters I have written. The reflection of my book in a brain so different from mine makes its shortcomings, and even its qualities, stand out better. Roger's remarks and criticisms are excellent and I cannot ignore them. How much work still ahead of me to complete what I have already worked on so much!

I am finishing, in big draughts, *The Egoist*. I doubt whether a novel has ever bored me more. Before twenty years have passed, our grandchildren will be amazed at the interest certain people among us took in it. I refuse to see in it Meredith's "masterpiece."

21 November

I should like to use as an epigraph for *Les Faux-Monnayeurs* this sentence by Vauvenargues which I read this evening in Sainte-Beuve (first article in the *Lundis*):

"Those who do not get outside of themselves are all of a piece." [15]

ANDRÉ WALTER

I began to write before knowing French very well — and, above all, before knowing how to make good use of it. But I was bursting. Today I experience a continual discomfort while rereading that book. I intended, at that time, to dominate language. Only much later I understood that . . .

26 November

Insomnia again; whence less good work. After a few days of patience, however, I managed to draw forth the conversation between Passavant and Strouvilhou, or rather the latter's monologue. Wrote it almost at one sitting and am perhaps not dissatisfied with it. It seems to me nevertheless that in a better state of health I might have given it a more mordant quality, a more fantastic aspect, and, above all, worked it better into the texture of the story.

I am writing this in the dining-room of the Hôtel des Bains at Étretat, which I reached on bicycle. A strong wind was blowing and I had frequently to get off.

Plunged into Plotinus's *Enneads*. All those who turn man against life become my personal enemies.

30 November

Read with considerable amusement Brousson's book on Anatole France.[16] He does not seem to me to betray his subject and I do not think France was very different from the way he is shown here, nor that there were any secret strata in him. I have written elsewhere what I thought of France, and this book only confirms my opinion. A clever and fluent man, just as incapable of music as of silence.

---

[15] This remark does not appear as an epigraph in the book.

[16] *Anatole France en pantoufles* (*Anatole France at Home*), by his former secretary.

What I am blamed for today is what I shall be praised for later on. The complaints made of me could be made of Montaigne; he would be reviled if he reappeared among us.

3 December

New attacks by the little Gourmont in this month's *Mercure* (apropos of the reprinting of Rivière's *Études*).[17] He blames my writings for being "full of tears and moonlight," to which, he claims, I owe my success among society people. Which is more worthy of wonder: his silliness or his bad faith? If he is convinced, how stupid he is! If he is intelligent, how false he is!

I hope that some critic, later on, will gather together these attacks and some of the perfidious shafts that certain reviews shoot at me the first of every month. Since no friend steps up to protest, any more than I do, the legend is gaining credit little by little. The public knows nothing of me but the caricature, and since it does not invite anyone to know me better, people don't go any further. What am I saying? If some people have enough curiosity to read me, they do so with such a prejudiced mind that the real meaning of my writings eludes them. They will eventually see in them what they have been told was there, and not see anything else. My sincerity is taken for a grimace, and for affectation everything that contradicts the monster they have been persuaded I am.

The essential thing is not to write anything that one wouldn't have written without these attacks, nor to write it differently; it is to go on being what one is, just as simply as if this weren't being questioned. It would be a miracle if a singer who constantly heard that he didn't have a strong voice did not get to forcing a strong voice. Furthermore, I tell myself that after all there is a greater danger for talent in praises; as Blake would have said, they relax one; in attacks there is something "bracing" that I do not mind. The trying part of it is that they are so awkward that I have trouble recognizing that they are aimed at me. People don't strike me; they strike the artificial hump they had first rigged me up with.

To be pursued by a little simpleton who is dominated by his late brother and to whom no one listens doesn't matter. But Massis, but Béraud especially, kick up a devil of a row. . . . Their attacks have made me more famous in three months than my books had done in thirty years.

---

[17] The little Gourmont is Remy's younger and less distinguished brother, Jean de Gourmont. Rivière's *Studies*, containing essays on Claudel, Gide, etc., had originally appeared in 1911.

3 December

Point out to Charles Du Bos, in the ninth volume of *Les Nouveaux Lundis,* an article by Sainte-Beuve about the *Réminiscences* of M. Coulmann, where he talks of Benjamin Constant (pp. 154–5). He quotes a rather curious and significant conversation with Béranger about B. C.[18]

5 December

Arrived in Paris the day before yesterday in the evening. Delight at finding M. at the Villa. He had lighted the heater, prepared tea, and, while waiting for me, was reading *Les Cinq Sens* by Delteil.[19] He is right in being very severe toward this book, which I picked up the following morning with a certain disgust. To be sure, all the amusement of *Choléra* is found in it, but somewhat diluted. Let us be wary of whatever flatters the current taste.

I am finding a relief from Meredith in Dickens.

Went back to *Our Mutual Friend,* of which I had but a too vague memory.

Paris, 8 December

I am struggling against the grippe. Sore throat and shivers. Outside, fog and icicles. . . . I close myself in with *Les Faux-Monnayeurs* and spend a tremendous amount of time filing and polishing Douviers's visit to Édouard. No welling up; nothing artesian. In a state of physical felicity I should have written without any trouble and at one sitting these three pages I have been struggling with for five days.

I read in Diderot's letters to Falconet: ". . . Ofttimes more is owed to an unusual error than to a common truth" (p. 166).

[18] This is the conversation, which Gide does not reproduce: "Benjamin Constant was not among those of whom he made an exception, for, M. Coulmann having told Béranger that Constant planned to come and see him [in prison]: 'Yes,' replied Béranger, 'I am sure he will come; he will not overlook this opportunity for popularity. I commented Sunday that he must be saying to himself, when everyone was flocking around me: "I should like to have written the songs and be sentenced in this way." He is envious of any triumph whatever. That provides him with sensations. He thought he loved Mme de Staël, whereas he loved only the emotions she gave him. He is so worn out that he has to borrow from others the feelings he has ceased to find in himself. His passions are quite artificial. When he used to display the passion he thought he had for Mme de Staël, he was wont to listen to the words he addressed to her; she would reply, likewise seeking in her eloquence for any sentences she might put advantageously into one of her novels. Everything was artificial between them. She claimed to feel a *physical dislike* for him. . . .' "

[19] *The Five Senses* is by Joseph Delteil, as is *Choléra.*

13 December

He (the demon) creates in us a sort of reverse repentance of an abominable sort, a regret not for having sinned, but for not having sinned more, for having let some opportunity for sinning slip by unused. And just as the regret for one's missteps and tears of repentance wash away earlier impurities, it sometimes happens that the soul's present corruption spreads out and overflows onto spotless pages, and that the demon wins back what had eluded him.

Kept at the Villa by grippe. Physical and moral numbness. Apathy.

Read Conrad's *Falk* and much Diderot. When he is good, he is bewitching.

20 December

Kept to my room the last few days. Not too painful confinement, thanks to M., who came to keep me company in the Villa. But my soul was wrapped in a fog that his good humor, good grace, and fancy barely succeeded in piercing. Visit from Martin du Gard every second day. He has just telephoned me for the sole purpose of asking if I have noted down our conversation of yesterday. He did not hang up until I had promised to do so at once. I wanted to convince him that *he* should do so, but he is too busy. One is more inclined to note someone else's remarks than one's own. Still, it is not so much the expression that matters here as the very substance of the conversation.

I believe what brought us to it was what I told Martin du Gard of my difficulty in recognizing people, of which I gave him a few fresh examples. . . . (In particular, I told him the story of a certain substitution of persons that I should not have noticed if Ghéon, who was present, had not warned me.)

"No," I went on, "this cannot be attributed to any lack of attention or of interest. My interest for each individual remains very great. . . . I believe it comes rather from my lack of a certain *sense of reality*. I can be extremely sensitive to the outer world, but I never succeed completely in believing in it. What I am saying has nothing theoretical about it. . . . I can imagine that a very learned doctor would be able to discover that some 'internally secreting gland,' some 'adrenal capsule' is atrophied in me. And furthermore I believe that that gland, if it exists, functions very unequally according to the individual. I even believe that this sense of the exterior world varies greatly according to the animal species. A cat is accustomed to an apartment; but were he, upon leaving this dining-room, to find next to it, instead of the long room, a virgin forest, he would not be too much surprised. I have seen my animals on certain days after a fall of snow; the landscape, even the ground, was unrecognizable; they seemed to find this quite natural and entered into that new world as if nothing had happened. It seems to me that I too. . . . If upon opening that door I were suddenly to find myself facing — well, the sea. . . . Why yes, I should say; that's odd! because I know that it ought not to be there; but that is a rationalization. I can never get over a certain amazement that things are as they are, and if they were suddenly different, it seems to me that that would hardly amaze me any more. The physical world always seems to me a little fantastic. I began to be aware of this a long time ago. It was during a trip in Brittany that I took at the age of eighteen. I had hired, at Douarnenez I believe, a little one-seater carriage, a sort of strange gig driven by a little old coachman who was thrown from his seat by a bump; he began to slip, to slide down, beside the seat, without saying a word and without dropping the reins; he hung on for a few moments, dangling in the void I don't know just how. I had not noticed the accident at once, absorbed as I was in my reading. When I raised my eyes from my book, there was no more coachman. I leaned forward; he was on the point of falling under the wheels. I seized the reins, though this was not very easy, pulled on them, and managed to stop the horse. It was just in time. . . . But if I tell you this, it is because I recall the strange state in which I found myself. It was a sort of sudden revelation about myself. I did not feel the slightest emotion; simply I was extraordinarily interested (*amused* would be more exact), very ready moreover to avert an accident, capable of the proper reflexes, etc. But taking part in all that as if at a show *outside of reality*. And if the accident had occurred to me, it would have been exactly the same; for I don't want you to see in this a mark of insensitivity. It has happened to me . . . why, in the gondola in Venice when the gondolier who had taken me into a deserted canal at midnight put out his lantern and, standing in front of me, asked for my wallet, I experienced quite clearly the feeling that my life was in danger. Well, I could not manage to take it all 'seriously.' I acted as if I did, with complete presence of mind and in a state of extreme nervous tension and hypersensitivity . . . but I was as if at the theater, amused, simply amused. For naturally fear, real fear, becomes impossible at such moments. This is a fact: I can no longer manage to be afraid. . . . You were worried the other day to see me living in the Villa alone."

"At least, you lock your door at night?"

"No, not even when the cellar door remains open. Why, the other evening I tried to frighten myself; I was alone in the Villa; it was very late; I was seated at my table and, opposite me, behind the large glass door through which I could see only a black abyss, I made an effort to imagine the head of a burglar. I managed to make my heart beat a little faster; but it was mere amusement, nothing more. Yet I have known what fear was; when I was a child I was extremely funky; I used to have frightful nightmares from which I would wake bathed in sweat. . . . And suddenly the gland ceased to function. At present I can have horrible dreams, see myself pursued by monsters, knifed, cut in bits . . . but it never becomes a nightmare. Ah! German philosophy found in me a favorable soil. When I read Schopenhauer's *The World as Will and Idea,* I thought at once: so that's it! But already a certain remark of Flaubert's had given me the cue. It is, I believe, in the preface to the poems of Bouilhet. I recall the revelation it was for me when Pierre Louÿs read it to me (we were still in our next to last year). It is 'advice' that Flaubert is giving to a young man who is planning to write. He says (I do not take responsibility for quoting it exactly): 'If the external world has ceased to appear to you as anything but an illusion to be described . . .' And I do not indulge in metaphysics. I forbid myself to be a mystic, and my intelligence does not give complete assent either to Kant or to Plato. It's something else. I am not worried to know whether or not I believe in the external world: it is the *feeling of reality* that I haven't got. It seems to me that we are all moving about in a fantastic show and that what others call reality, that their external world, has not much more existence than the world of *Les Faux-Monnayeurs* or of *Les Thibault.*"

That last sentence is inexact; it narrows down and slightly falsifies the meaning of what precedes by reducing it to Balzac's witty remark to Sandeau: "Let's get back to reality; let's talk of Eugénie Grandet."[20] It is to be compared rather with what Keats says in a wonderful letter.[21]

---

[20] Eugénie Grandet is the heroine of Balzac's novel of the same title.

[21] Can this be the passage to which Gide is alluding? — "The roaring of the wind is my wife and the Stars through the window pane are my Children. The mighty abstract Idea I have of Beauty in all things stifles the more divided and minute domestic happiness — an amiable wife and sweet Children I contemplate as a part of that Beauty, but I must have a thousand of those beautiful particles to fill up my heart. I feel more and more every day, as my imagination strengthens, that I do not live in this world alone but in a thousand worlds. No sooner am I alone than shapes of epic greatness are stationed around me, and serve my Spirit the office which is equivalent to a King's body guard — then 'Tragedy with scepter'd pall, comes sweeping by.' According to my state of mind I am with Achilles shouting in the Trenches, or with Theocritus in the Vales of Sicily. Or I throw my whole being into Troilus, and repeating those lines, 'I wander, like a lost Soul upon the Stygian Banks staying for waftage,' I melt into the air with a voluptuousness so delicate that I am content to be alone. . . . You see there is nothing spleenical in all this. The only thing that can ever affect me personally for more than one short passing day, is any doubt about my powers for poetry — I seldom have any, and I look with hope to the nighing

time when I shall have none. I am as happy as a Man can be — that is in myself I should be happy if Tom was well, and I knew you were passing pleasant days. Then I should be most enviable — with the yearning Passion I have for the beautiful, connected and made one with the ambition of my intellect. Think of my Pleasure in Solitude, in comparison of my commerce with the world — there I am a child — there they do not know me, not even my most intimate acquaintance — I give into their feelings as though I were refraining from irritating a little child. Some think me middling, others silly, others foolish — every one thinks he sees my weak side against my will, when in truth it is with my will — I am content to be thought all this because I have in my own breast so great a resource. This is one great reason why they like me so; because they can all show to advantage in a room, and eclipse from a certain tact one who is reckoned to be a good Poet." (To George and Georgiana Keats, October 1818, in *The Letters of John Keats*, edited by M. B. Forman, I, 261–2.)

1925

Some of those young men make great and somewhat ridiculous efforts to stifle the contradictions they have felt rising within them or before them, without understanding that the spark of life can flash only between two contrary poles, and that it is larger and more beautiful the greater the distance between them and the richer the opposition with which each pole is charged.

God's effort to produce the triangle from Himself.

And no more than the Christian must seek to reconcile two contradictory truths, such as God's prescience and individual free will: likewise we must protect in us all the natural antinomies and realize that it is only thanks to their irreducible opposition that we are alive. And as for those antinomies, I believe them to be all imaginary (and first of all the one I mentioned, which comes from this false postulate: God is prescient — God is), but the mere fact of living calls them up, creates them.

Everything that André Breton makes me say in his false interview [1] is much more like him than like me. The form of ambition he ascribes to me is absolutely foreign to me; but it is the form of ambition that he is most inclined to understand. There is not one of the sentences he puts into my mouth that I do not disavow; I say this for simplicity's sake — for the extreme perfidy of his article comes from the fact that not a single one of those sentences can I swear never to have said; but it is presented in such a way as to distort its meaning throughout. The very sound of my voice is falsified.

And I see in this camouflage, alas, rather a perfidious cleverness than any awkwardness. I cannot believe that Breton, very much concerned about the influence he plans to exert over young minds, did not aim to discredit me, to kill me. And it must be recognized that he has achieved a very consistent and very hideous portrait of me.

See the little blue notebook kept (very badly) at the hospital where I am operated on for appendicitis.

---

[1] In his volume of essays *Les Pas perdus* (1924), André Breton included an imaginary interview entitled "André Gide Discusses His Volume of Selections." The interview, supposed to have taken place in a bakery-shop on the rue de Grenelle, is savage by implication.

Saturday, 10 January

It is now just fourteen days since I was operated on. I am to leave the hospital this afternoon. Martin du Gard and M. are coming to pick me up in an auto and take me back to the Villa — which I hope soon to leave for Cuverville.

Received a number of letters and visits.

Meditated a great deal; read a great deal.

I believe I am sincere in saying that I clearly envisaged death. That is to say that, before the operation, I made myself ready not to come out of it; and I did so quite naturally. I should like this "thought" of Pascal to be apocryphal: "Neither the sun nor death can be looked at fixedly." It is unworthy of a strong soul and even of a well-trained mind.[2]

Read these last few days:

Two volumes by Fabre;

A considerable amount of Brehm (mollusks, worms, insects);

A number of Ruskin's *Præterita;*

Souvenir d'un jardin détruit by Boylesve;

Conrad's *Secret Agent;*

Erewhon Revisited (Larbaud translation);[3]

and finally Gibbon's *Memoirs,* which delighted me as much as the *Præterita* irritated me. Excluding the large Brehm, which interested me for quite other reasons and taught me something, I got no real pleasure, indeed, from any but the last book (Gibbon), aware more of the shortcomings than of the qualities of those who precede in the above enumeration. Unable to finish *The Secret Agent* or *Præterita.*

Back on 23 January 1925 to Cuverville, which I had left on 2 or 3 December.

Without strength, without appetite, without joy.

Very far from heaven; and even, simply, from the earth.

28 January

I have the greatest difficulty harnessing myself to *Les Faux-Mon-nayeurs* again. The last chapters (written in Paris during my grippe) seem to me to lack sap and savor. They remain outside the action.

Too much piano-practice; it distracts me and numbs my mind like opium.

---

[2] Besides, it is by La Rochefoucauld. [A.]

[3] Boylesve's *Recollections of a Devastated Garden* is a novel first published in 1924. Larbaud translated most of Samuel Butler's works, *The Way of All Flesh, Erewhon,* etc.

Suddenly recalled from Roquebrune — where I had been for six days and was beginning to work — by the shocking death of Rivière.

21 February

I set out for Marseille again after having spent exactly a week in Paris.

Marseille

A frightful number of hours pass without bringing either profit or pleasure. They constitute an interval and it seems that one might just as well not have lived through them. Too tired to work, I have sought nothing but dissipation since morning. Empty day. A cold that freezes up all lyricism and brings tears to one's eyes.

Wandered in the Arab quarter, which I did not know before. Sordid poverty and melancholy. Some Sicilian workmen are fighting and rolling in the gutter. Children in rags, chilled to the bone.

"Black does not exist in nature," said a painter, who, to prove it, never used anything but blue ink.

La Bastide, late March

Need of interrupting my work. A few readings which help me to judge *Les Faux-Monnayeurs* better.

Finished *Our Mutual Friend* by Dickens (rereading).

Returned to *L'Éducation sentimentale.* The third volume of *Sodome et Gomorrhe, Sarrasine,* and a dozen chapters of *Le Rouge et le noir. L'Abbesse de Castro;* excellent.[4]

It does not seem to me that *Our Mutual Friend* is up to *Great Expectations.* A certain need to surpass himself, to write a super-Dickens — the rope too taut. Striving after effects: the little invalid girl who treats her father like her child; the anatomy-laboratory assistant and his relations with the man who sold him his leg; a victim who is taken for his own assassin; a rich heir who, through love, pretends to be a poor man, etc. Excessive picturesqueness, not always genuine. Many dialogues reek of fabrication. Despite everything, amazing resource. The art of always presenting his characters in movement and ready for some change. — Alas! never has Dickens's psychology been more conventional, his heroes' sensibility and the motives of the acts more worn out.

The Proust struck me as among the least good, and very indifferently written.

---

[4] *The Sentimental Education* is a novel by Flaubert; *Sodome et Gomorrhe* is Proust's *Cities of the Plain; Sarrasine* is a short story by Balzac; *The Red and the Black* and *The Abbess of Castro* are by Stendhal.

All *Bouvard et Pécuchet* is in germ in *L'Éducation*.[5] Strange need of debasing everything. Epic of disgust.

Sarrasine has no value save in the realm of the absurd. Its pasty method of painting hides a great poverty of draftsmanship.

By contrast *Le Rouge et le noir* seemed to me masterful. Every sentence is stretched like the string of a bow; but the arrow always flies in the same direction, and toward an ever visible target — which helps one to see that it hits it.

Hyères-Plage, 3 April

L'Éducation sentimentale holds in suspense a passionately interesting problem: is the least particular the most representative? Because of this it is a great book. It seems to me that there are still things to be said about Flaubert.

15 May

Yesterday evening, call on Claudel. He had asked me to come and was waiting for me. At number 80 rue de Passy, an apartment set back and not giving onto the street. I go through two rooms, the second of which is rather large, and find myself in a third one, still larger, which he uses as a bedroom and workroom. Open army couch in a corner; a low book-case goes around two sides of the room; many objects, brought back from the Far East, decorate it.

At my ring, Claudel came to meet me and holds out his hand. He seems to have shrunk. A short, swansdown-lined jacket of coffee-colored silk makes him look still thicker. He is enormous and short; he looks like Ubu.[6] We sit down in two armchairs. He completely fills his. Mine, a sort of chaise-longue, has such a low back that to be comfortable in it I should have to get too far away from Claudel. I give up and lean forward.

In the presence of Claudel I am aware only of what I lack; he dominates me; he overhangs me; he has more base and surface, more health, money, genius, power, children, faith, etc., than I. I think only of obeying without a word.

Cuverville, end of May

Visit from Paul Valéry. Cleaning up and typing of five chapters of *Les Faux-Monnayeurs*. A deadly chore, which, however, fits my apathy. I have given up counting on anything but the Congo to get me out of it. Preparations for this trip and the expectation of new landscapes have disenchanted the present; I am experiencing how true it was to

---

[5] Both titles are novels by Flaubert.

[6] The grotesque hero of Alfred Jarry's farce *King Ubu*.

say that happiness lies in the moment. Nothing seems to me anything but provisional now. (The hope of eternal life likewise excells in this.)

My sight has weakened considerably of late. Spectacles relieve this deficiency. Would that the brain could wear them too! Difficulty my mind has in "focusing" the idea it is examining; analogous to my eye's difficulty today. The outlines remain fuzzy.

8 June

Finished *Les Faux-Monnayeurs*.

14 July

Departure for the Congo.[7]

DETACHED PAGES

NOTES FOR MAETERLINCK'S BOOKS

I do not say that our explanations are always good; but since our logic has been formed according to nature and since we see nature according to our brain, it seems to me that if we lived in a world in which two and two made five, we should not be at all shocked, because in our brain likewise two and two would make five. A *naturalist* is not so much a man who is concerned with nature as a man for whom things are natural — or, if you prefer, who understands phenomena *naturally*.

It is not good writing to let one's prose be shot full of Alexandrines. For this creates a hybrid style of ambiguous charm. They are perhaps not good lines of verse; but surely it is execrable prose. And I shall even say that the better the line of verse is, the worse the prose is; for the rhythm of verse is not that of prose, and the rhythm of verse breaks that of the prose.

But an isolated Alexandrine and a succession of lines that will shock any ear slightly sensitive to music are two different things.

THE INTELLIGENCE OF FLOWERS.[8]

It is easy to imagine even greater complications, even more finicky means of fecundation, which Maeterlinck would have considered ever more marvelous — and which would have had less and less chance of survival.

---

[7] From July 1925 to June 1926 the *Journal* is to be found in *Le Voyage au Congo* and *Le Retour du Tchad*. [E.] Both these works are published in English in *Travels in the Congo*.

[8] Maeterlinck wrote a naïve book entitled *L'Intelligence des fleurs*.

Imagine a species that has died out — a marvel of "intelligence" — having *needed* an insect, which has died out too.

Recall the Goncourts at the Jardin des Plantes.[9]

The *romance* of nature — unbearable. What *is* forever remaining the limit of what *might have been*. Why see *virtue* in something that, without that virtue, would not exist?

The tree that clings to the soil and leans toward the light — good heaven! — it is essential to be able to; everything that *could* not has been swept away by the torrent.

I see in nature a lesson of intelligence (of adaptation); I refuse to see in it a lesson of virtue.

(Pathetic dressing-up of the problem for the reader who feels God or nature only through man. Christianity is there for this; it is enough that Virtue should become flesh, that God should become man; why should one want to anthropomorphize Nature and construct the whole Cosmos in the image of our intelligence?)

Grandville = the marriage of hydrogen and oxygen.

Considering the dandelion "intelligent" for having such volatile seeds — is like considering the duck *intelligent* because it has webbed feet for swimming. Or like admiring the bird for surrounding its egg with a shell.

Anthropomorphism. — For whom this book is written:

1. Poetic but ignorant people;
2. Learned people ignorant in matters of literature.

How it is done. Take up Huber's little book. Easy stupefaction about *natural* things. The bees' cells, hexagonal. A *single* bee never begins alone; its wall is a party wall from the start. *Necessity* urges the bee to do it, not *calculation*.

Life of the plants. The least manual of botany. Examples of the seed of alfalfa (*useless* form); of the poppy. (But the corn poppy too.) Poetization that commits the *crime* of removing their meaning from things. It is *uselessly* that the poppy, etc. . . . *uselessly* that the alfalfa. . . . There is PRODIGALITY of *forms* in Nature, as there is prodigality of seeds. The SUPERFLUOUS is what is disconcerting, but it is also what we must admit.

This plant which would have tremendous expanses of dunes to cover and which has invented no means of propulsion to scatter her seeds far from her. . . . I conclude that this flower was stupid; unless, I thought, the family instinct dominated in her the anxiety for

---

[9] See *The Journals of André Gide*, Vol. I, p. 103.

the health and well-being of her children, as so often occurs among men; and I thought for several minutes of the fine book that could be written on "the heart of plants," in which one would reveal the touching example of those in which that hypertrophied organ doubtless prevented the development of the brain — which made no inventions in aerostatics or ballistics, but preferred to the joys of invention the very pure joy of keeping their children right close to *them*.

That plant literally drops its seeds under itself. It answers to the vulgar name of *Bon-Henri*.[10] In learned language it is a member of the Chenopodia. "Bon-Henri"; even in Latin this name sticks to it; and, meditating on the origin of that odd appellation, suddenly this ridiculous explanation occurred to me:

"No, it is not stupidity, O blind man!" I exclaimed. "Learn to see, in this disdained plant, a real family love."

I even have, when I see Maeterlinck swooning like this, some trouble considering him as intelligent as his flowers.

The tree and the plant have every interest in not having their offspring grow too close to them, because they would be stifled by it — or, if you prefer, the offspring of a tree has every interest in not growing too close to the paternal tree, because it would be stifled by it. While one is about it, one can just as easily accept the fact that the intelligence is in the seed.

The third way — the two first are: (1) the force of propulsion that puts the intelligence in the plant; (2) the volatility, motility, mobility, etc., of the seeds, which put the intelligence in them — a third way consists in endowing the seed, though inert, with an attraction such that an animal takes it and after having eaten it, in whole or in part, drops it in a spot sufficiently far from its point of origin; this is, I believe, the nature of all berries and all fruits that are heavy *but* wrapped in flavor. I say *wrapped in flavor* (pear, strawberry, cherry, fruits with pips or stones), and not having flavor themselves (almond, chestnut, etc.), which the animal destroys as he eats them. Those fruits . . . etc., foreseeing the animal's taste; foreseeing man's taste.

Why not admit that the plant, too, knows *sensual pleasure*? That shocks me infinitely less than believing in its "intelligence."

. . . the intelligence of wheat would be even more remarkable since, being gifted with no ballistic faculty, it foresaw that man's

---

[10] The plant in question is strawberry blite or strawberry spinach.

hunger was going to call upon its flour, so that this plant, quite unarmed and inert, speculating on our industry, thanks to our appetite,
has won over tremendous expanses. There would moreover be much
to be said about cultivated plants; it occurs to me that some among
them, naturally weak and not very prolific, would almost have disappeared from the surface of the earth, at least would occupy only rare
and limited spaces, if they had not had the touching idea of making
themselves useful in order to call on our reciprocal aid. And what can
one think of the forage plants? which, even more wily, by a more
crafty means, managed to adapt themselves, if I may say so, to the
hunger of one of those animals we have domesticated. Among the so-
called vegetables, I wonder at the fact that many species (which
nevertheless might have served to feed us) are neglected because
others won out in that struggle for life which here takes the form of
an effort toward succulence. Tobacco's behavior I like less, for it reveals a less kindly nature. I wonder at all the so-called industrial plants
that managed to foresee our needs, plants that sometimes we did not
come to understand until very late and in an already very advanced
stage of civilization; and this proves how far behind theirs was the
intelligence of men; others that, trusting in the progress of industry,
like hemp, managed — through a foresight that seems almost paradoxical — to take the place of others with a more naïve and, I should add,
impulsive imagination (I am thinking of the obsolete calamus and
papyrus).

Finally I am thinking that the Greeks, when they dedicated the
olive tree to Minerva, showed that they had glimpsed in that tree what
the tree had sensed in man — a parallel effort toward light, which we
also feel today in the colza. I could go on, for it occurs to me that
perhaps the humble grass on which I am walking is waiting, possessor
of a secret, for man to formulate at last the question to which it will
be the reply. Absurdity!

※

Completely revolted by your conversation of yesterday evening. In
that case, hooray for religion!

What makes the conversation difficult is that you are constantly
seeking to catch me out.

Your effort tends toward what? Toward proving to me that there
is nothing . . . or rather that, since there is nothing, everything is
allowed, etc., which strikes me as monstrous. What! as soon as *everything depended on man, he would not be held to anything?* What! it
was only a mystical fear that stopped you? When you were a child, did
you need the paternal clout to force you to do your home-work right?
And as soon as I use the expression: "do it right," you exclaim: "You

see how you come back to our notion of *right* and *wrong!*" Yet I am
obliged to use the only words our language has at its disposal. My
entire effort, since I escaped from my first Christian wrapping, has
been to prove to myself that I could get along without it. (You, quite
the contrary.) I have sought to draw up a list of specifications completely independent of the idea of sanction and of absolute imperative.

In this world: real sufferings; imaginary sufferings. The first can
be attenuated; the second almost suppressed. They most often result
from a belief in *idols* — or in *bogeymen*. The former are constructions
that are venerated and do not deserve to be. The latter are phantoms
that are feared and do not deserve to be.

❄

X. would perhaps not be insensitive, but he is ignorant; he is im-
mensely ignorant. And then he lacks the imagination to visualize, when
he is in the room where supper is served, what is going on in the cellar
and the kitchen. He has a soft heart, I know; he cannot endure injustice within his sight; but his sight does not carry far. That thou-
sands of people have labored to assure him comfort — he needs to go
on being ignorant of this in order to continue being happy.

❄

Note for the "Thousand and One Nights"

"It is the imagination that interests him passionately in games of
chance, by showing him future wealth and the delights it promises, in
such flattering colors . . . etc.

"It is certain that the Moslem peoples would have preceded him
in that path if from the beginning the Koran had not made the prohibi-
tion of gambling the safeguard of Islamism, and if it had not directed
the Moslems' imagination toward the *discovery of hidden treasures.*"
(Burckhardt: *Renaissance,* II, p. 194.)

Very important to note, in fact, the absence of *gambling* in *The
Thousand and One Nights.*

❄

Modulations

Do not ask me how we passed, by what sudden leap or what unforeseen modulation, from the district of F sharp to that of F natural.
It seemed to us right away that all nature became humanized, lost
with its too great vividness that sort of vibrant tartness of the greens
that both delighted us and held us at a distance. F natural, I repeated;
and nothing could be more natural than that tone of F! The landscape
was becoming tempered. It was good to live there. Already I ac-

customed my thought to it; I meditated on it; I was loving with ease
there, when suddenly, undeniable, the E flat, as with a stroke of a fairy
wand, like a sudden ray falling through a gap in the clouds, like the
unexpected return of a friend, suddenly came to bend our joy softly
toward more tenderness and piety. We were entering B flat.

❄

TAINE

Not only are certain geniuses not *formed*, carried, supported by the
epoch that produces them, but, to borrow Dupouey's expression
(*Notes sur Rossetti*, p. 39),[11] they remain as different from it as the
rocks from the tide that submerges them. They are opposed to the
epoch, and their strength lies precisely in their lack of up-to-dateness.

And let it not be argued that, on closer inspection, it can be seen
that that opposition is only apparent — because by dint of "closer inspection" one can succeed in seeing anything one wants. Let it not be
said: from the welcome that was extended them a little later one can
estimate how great was the unconscious expectation of them, etc., because everything is in man and the epoch remains vacillating like the
Roman crowd, in Shakespeare's *Coriolanus* or *Julius Cæsar*, at the
mercy of the impulse given to it by the *opponent*.

The most tiresome aspect of that theory of Taine — which was perhaps a good method of study and, as one would be glad to say, was
able to provide a few awkward minds with a convenient instrument
of criticism — is that it managed to deceive some artists, to teach them
to seek guidance in the epoch, while their whole effort should have
been to *distinguish* themselves from it.

His theory: that artists are the products of their epoch, leads him
to consider in them only the reflection of that epoch, leads him to
neglect all those who do not surrender to the current. Now, it so happens that those are just the ones that matter; and sometimes it happens
that some of them mislead him, for the epoch, modeling itself on them
at once, lives according to them, so that at a short distance it is impossible to tell easily what precedes from what follows. That is to say
that the epoch and manners (he will say) often were impatiently waiting for the voice that the artist finally furnishes them. Not always.
There are, among the greatest, those who, far from following the
epoch, are opposed to it; who, as Wilde said, bring answers to questions that have not yet been asked. Their anachronistic importance is
often not recognized until long afterward. Doubtless they embarrassed
Taine; but more simply they eluded him. The very quality of the

---

[11] Lieutenant Dupouey, whose letters Gide prefaced, had previously
written *Notes on Rossetti*.

artist and the reason why his individuality stands out and the reason why his heart matters, Taine strives to pay no attention to these things and I doubt, after all, that he was very sensitive to them. Some of his judgments are monstrous. He wantonly confuses Farquhar, Vanbrugh, and Congreve to such a point that when he quotes them he neglects even to name them and that, almost throughout the chapter, you don't know of which of the three authors he is speaking.

It seems to me that it would be fairer to say — if one wanted to theorize — that at every epoch many of the most various artists are born; but that the only ones to succeed are those who swim with the epoch and are supported by the current. Can one imagine Cézanne under Louis XIV? What is the good of asking: what would he have produced then? For there is reason to believe that he would have produced nothing at all or that, if he had produced, no one would have known anything about it.

The determinism from which it seems clear that our mind, any more than our body, cannot possibly escape is so subtle, corresponds to such diverse, multiple, and tenuous causes, that it seems childish to try to number them, and even more to get rid of them. And I admit that man is never free; but the simplest and most honest thing is to act as if he were. In this fashion there is less risk of being mistaken than by constantly trying to make out in his every gesture a coarse motivation and the influence of his race and heredity, of the epoch and the climate.

※

Gospel! Gospel! What peace you promised the world! . . .
. . . those men of goodwill, your disciples, whom you recruited among the humblest.

※

Marcel Schwob occupied, when I first met him, a very odd half-story apartment, rue de l'Université, sandwiched between the second and third floors; this explains why it had an extremely low ceiling. I believe there were only two rooms; the one in which he used to receive was encumbered with books and papers; I can understand why he was obsessed with a constant desire to travel, for one felt dreadfully cooped up in the apartment. There was, as far as I can recall, a small fireplace in that room; in any case there was, above that fireplace or some piece of furniture, a mirror, and that mirror was almost completely covered with cloth and papers. Schwob soon explained to me that he detested mirrors, or at least encountering the reflection of his face; perhaps he suffered to see himself ugly. He was not handsome, to be sure, but his eyes had a charming softness in perfect harmony with the tone of his voice. He was very short and not exactly fat but as if stuffed with sawdust; he was flabby. Toward the end of his life, after having suffered dreadfully from illness, he seemed not so much thin as emptied.

His kindness was exquisite. He took great care to direct the intellectual curiosity of his friends toward what he thought might satisfy them. I shall never forget that it was he who made me read Ibsen; but he was wrong in advising me to begin with *The Lady from the Sea*.

At one of the first visits I paid him, I met Jules Renard, whom he introduced to me; but at that moment I had not yet read anything by Renard and his name meant nothing to me. I remember that he begged Renard to deign to read *Anna Karenina* [12] and that Renard refused in an obstinate manner, insisting that nothing could interest him that was not of French origin. And I believe that Renard did not depict himself as any more limited than he was in reality.

I met Renard once more at Schwob's; it was a long time after. At that time Schwob was living, rue de Valois (?), in an extremely gay apartment of which the windows opened onto the gardens of the Palais-Royal. Renard was with his wife that day. He was already about to leave when I came in. And as he and his wife were heading toward the door, Schwob said: "It's a pleasure to see a husband and wife of exactly the same height." Then Renard, turning only his head, said over his shoulder: "Yes, in bed we cross our toes!" then opened the door and went out, pushing his wife before him.

[12] Tolstoy's novel.

1926

Back at last from a long trip, I take cognizance of Isabelle Rivière's letter that appeared in the May *N.R.F.* I read this: *Gide asserts that this Catholic, a practicing Catholic until the age of sixteen, "had never opened the Gospel."*

Already, soon after the special number of the *N.R.F.*[1] in which these incriminated lines appeared, Isabelle Rivière, when I met her again, protested against what she considers in her letter of yesterday a "gross inexactitude."

It is too late for Gide to make a correction, Mme Rivière says a little farther on in the same letter. Perhaps not; and since this letter invites me to do so, I shall try to clarify what I meant.

A short while before the war I had had long conversations with Jacques about the Christian religion. We did not succeed in coming to an agreement, Jacques sharply dismissing the questions that seemed to me of the highest importance, I mean ethical questions, and declaring that, if he felt drawn by the Church, he felt, on the other hand, no love, nor even any curiosity, for the person or teaching of Christ.

"I feel nothing but boredom in connection with all that," he repeated to me; a particularly painful assertion for the simple Christian I was then — and still am.

I eventually asked my friend if he were sure of knowing Christ, for some of his grievances against Christ seemed to me to be wide of the mark.

When I insisted, he asked me in what translation I advised him to read the Bible. I replied to that question by sending him the translation by Abbé Crampon, which I consider one of the best and which I am most likely to read. I knew, besides, that the Protestant translations are suspect in the eyes of many Catholics and didn't want to risk the reproach of influencing.

I must recognize that this first direct contact with the Gospel did not have on Jacques Rivière the almost dazzling effect I was hoping for and that I know it can sometimes have on certain souls, even if they had been long ago catechized. I believe that Jacques remained for a long time embarrassed by the word of Christ that I constantly opposed to him: "No man cometh unto the Father but by me." His reticence, or resistance, on this score is still clearly marked, it seems

---

[1] Rivière had been chief editor of the *Nouvelle Revue Française* from 1919 until his death in 1925; the issue of the review for March 1925 was devoted to him.

to me, in a certain passage of his prison notes, written after reading
the Gospel according to St. Mark. (But is this passage, which he had
read me, reproduced in the book? I do not know. I am writing this at
Cuverville and do not have *A la trace de Dieu* at hand.[2])

14 June

I feel again that odd numbness of the mind, of the will, of my
whole being, which I rarely experience except at Cuverville. Writing
the least note takes an hour; the least letter, a whole morning.

. . . .

I was still full of fervor just a few days ago; it seemed to me that I
could move mountains; today I am crushed.

The difficulty comes from this, that Christianity (Christian orthodoxy) is exclusive and that belief in *its* truth excludes belief in any
other truth. It does not absorb; it repulses.

And humanism, on the contrary, or whatever other name you give
to it, tends to understand and absorb all forms of life, to explain to
itself if not to assimilate all beliefs, even those that repulse it, even
those that deny it, even the Christian belief.

Culture must understand that by trying to absorb Christianity it is
absorbing something that is mortal for it. It is trying to admit something that cannot admit it; something that denies it.

15 June

With great effort I succeed in turning out a few letters — to *Le
Progrès civique*, to a minister who, in *Le Christianisme social*, had
gone to some length to maltreat me, to Claudel, etc.

I have put order into my papers and tried, but in vain, to start my
report to the Minister.[3] Went over a part of my travel notes. If I produce my *Journal* in continuous form, the tragic parts, which it is important to bring out, will be drowned under the abundance of descrip-
tions, etc. I do not know what decision to make.

Strange state of mind. No desire to open any book. Could this be
the result of the trip? My library is disenchanted.

[2] *In Search of God* (1925) had been written during Rivière's four years
in a German prison camp.

[3] Doubtless the Minister of Colonies, to whom Gide was to report on
his trip to the Congo and the Chad.

28 June

Back to Paris. Conversations from morning till night. Exhausting. However tired I am, I must conquer.

Georges Rondeaux:

I bring him the little collection of *Anas* published by the *N.R.F.*, telling him:

"You will be disappointed."

"I don't mind that," he replies.

1 July

X. will say:

"The slow progress of Catholicism on her soul; it seems to me that I am watching the spreading of a gangrene.

"Every time I come back, after having left her some time, I find new regions affected, deeper, more secret regions, forever incurable. And, if I could, would I attempt to *cure* her? That *health* that I would offer her, mightn't it be mortal to her? Any effort exhausts her.

"What a convenience, what a rest, what a minimum of effort is offered her by that carefully dosed piety, that fixed-price menu for souls that cannot spend much!

"Who could have believed it? — Could God himself have expected it? What! everything that attached me to her, that rather vagabond mood, that fervor, that curiosity, all that did not really belong to her, then? What! it was only out of love for me that she clothed herself in it? All that comes undone, falls off, reveals the bare soul, unrecognizable and fleshless.

"And everything that constitutes my *raison d'être*, my life, becomes foreign and hostile to her."

11 July

I add at the top of the preceding page:

X. will say:

"Am I retracting?

"I have merely realized that what I wrote above is not quite exact. But it could be. And perhaps it will be. Reality furnished me with the direction and the impetus; my imagination did the rest. It invents nothing, but is constantly working to get the most out of the *facts as given.*"

Chitré, 14 July

Swimming in the Vienne, and canoeing. Auto excursions. Visit to several beautiful churches.

They exaggerate piety to such absurd excesses that they force common sense to revolt and throw us into blasphemy and anarchy.

25 July

Back to Cuverville after six exhausting days in Paris. Élie Allégret's departure for Tahiti. I cannot get myself to give up smoking, and I smoke more, the more tired I am — and this tires me even more. — Wonderful film about the Samoan Islands: *Moana.* The fishing and swimming scenes are particularly successful; I have never seen anything more voluptuous.

29 July

Very painful nervous fatigue. A sort of continual trepidation shakes my inner being. Urgent need of rest. Here I can do nothing but work. I am leaving tomorrow.

6 August

Paris. Exhaustion that lets up only when I have nothing to do. Everything strikes me as provisional, and since I have been back here I have done nothing except to be rid of something. Oasis: Jules Renard's *Journal,* which I am sipping slowly. Already it is beginning to be clear to what a degree that *whole* epoch will smell artificial and musty. Ah, how well I did to get away!

Em. has informed me of J.'s fears about Jean T. and my ascendancy over him. She begs me to do nothing to attract Jean. She fears my "influence." I had to promise to "give him the cold shoulder." This is absurd. I am sure that I could do that child good and perhaps spare him serious mistakes. He is at the age when one has the greatest need of advice. It is thought that mine could only be bad. Just try and protest! Yet it would suffice to have a look at what became of the young men in whom I have really been able to take an interest. Those on whom I was able "to have an influence." There is not one of them that I tried to draw in my direction. Quite the contrary: my constant care has been to push them in their own direction. There is not one of them of whom I haven't the right to be proud. As for Jean T., I should like merely to warn him. He is going ahead in life like a scatterbrain and will probably acquire experience only after burning his fingers painfully. But no one pays any attention to my disinterestedness and to the respect of others that prompts my advice in every case.

Goethe's greatest good luck was perhaps Eckermann. But most likely he would not be of this opinion and would see in those "conversations" nothing but a constant betrayal of his thought.[4]

[4] Eckermann brought out his famous *Conversations with Goethe* after the great man's death.

Absurd misprint in my translation of *Antony and Cleopatra: vilence* instead of *vilenie.* Impossible to imagine a more complete change in words, in accent, in number of syllables, etc., resulting from that mere substitution of a letter.

Arnold Naville, who corrected the proofs, sought in vain what *vilence* might mean; and, eventually, kept the word, thinking it was perhaps a neologism.

Renard's *Journal:* it is not a river; it is a distillery.

9 August

"It is not enough to be happy! in addition it is essential that others should not be," writes Renard. I fear that there is in this more affectation of sincerity than true sincerity.

Little Catherine:

"There are 'gooseberries' and 'duckberries.'"

"An *'écruche'* and an *'autre cruche,'*" she says as she takes two ostriches out of her Noah's ark.[5]

She says: "Do you know what the rooster likes best? — Sitting down on the hens."

10 August

In Renard's *Journal,* many extremely just observations:

"The great error of justice is imagining that the accused always acts logically."

13 August

J. Renard: The sentence strangles the thought. He produces the right note, but always as a pizzicato.

15 August

The poor old woman who is called "Grandma" here is eighty-six. So humpbacked, or at least so bent double (for her back is straight) by constant gardening that she cannot straighten up and walks with her rear higher than her head, very slowly, leaning on a cane. She has always worked, always labored. From Hyères she went to Saint-Clair, whence Mme Théo brought her here out of pity and rather than let her enter the poorhouse. Her hands are completely deformed by rheumatism; it seems that her feet are worse. At night she suffers so that she cannot sleep. From morning till night she is working in the garden,

---

[5] The word for ostrich in French being *autruche,* it is easy to see how a child could hear it as *autre cruche* ("other jug"). Her other remark, in the original, plays upon the adjectives *gros* ("big") and *petit* ("little"), the word for gooseberries being *groseilles.*

for she is always afraid of being dependent and insists on earning her living. She pulls up the weeds — and sometimes the flowers too, but with such zeal that no one dares correct her. She is told: "Grandma, take a rest. It's Sunday." But when she is not working, she is bored. She envies those who know how to read. She remains seated on the canal embankment, her eyes half-closed, turning over old memories in her mind. I approach her, for she claims that she is bored and that she enjoys chatting. But when she complains, says that she would like to die, that life is nothing but one long suffering for her, and "yet I can't kill myself . . ." and then adds: "I'd like to, though" — I don't know what to say.

It is for such creatures, to help them endure their suffering, to put up with life, that rosaries exist, and prayers, and belief in a better life, in the reward for one's labors. Skepticism, incredulity, are all right for the rich, the happy, the favored, those who don't need hope and for whom the present is enough. And that is just the saddest part of it: poor Grandma does not believe in God, or that anything beyond death will make up for her sorry life.

She says: "Do you want me to tell you? If there is a God, well, he's an idiot — or a bad one. . . . He takes away young Madame Flé, who wanted nothing better than to go on living and whom everyone liked. And I want nothing better than to die, but he prolongs me. . . ." All this said with the accent of the Midi.

Some nights sleep is like a timorous animal that flees at your approach and that you try to tame.

True kindness presupposes the faculty of imagining others' sufferings as one's own. I mean that without imagination there can be weakness, but not true kindness.

Jules Renard's garden could do with a little watering.

Nothing is more provoking than those critics who claim to prove that what you write is not what you wanted to write.

Niska, when she is in heat, flees the dogs that are attracted by her odor and refuses herself to them; but she chases after Bellone and, when they are left to play together, and excite each other, her period of heat is indefinitely prolonged.

20 August

Renard's *Journal.* Odd, that life which becomes progressively narrower. His blindness with regard to foreigners allows him to admire

Rostand, G., etc. He primps over his limitations, spruces up his egotism, and curls his baldness. From page to page one can observe — and therein lies the great interest of this journal — the progress of that emotional, and even intellectual, inhibition brought on by the exigence of sincerity.

He writes, right after having exaggerated his admiration for Rostand's play:

"In Coquelin's dressing-room I tell Rostand:

"'I should have been very happy if we could both have been decorated the same day. Since it it not possible, I assure you that I congratulate you without envy.'"

And he adds:

"That is not true; and as I write these lines, I begin to weep!"

And farther on, after having insisted on the low quality of his envy, he backwaters:

"Now, that is exaggerated. Ah, perhaps never has man spoken a single *true* word!"

Instead of noting ingenuously that there is no feeling so simple that it is not immediately complicated and falsified by introspection.

There is no worse enemy of thought than the demon of analogy.

"A freshly shaved field."

What is more tiresome than that mania of certain writers who cannot see an object without thinking at once of another?

"I limit myself as best I can," says Renard.

Believing that you can achieve perfection in anything whatever, by having no attention for anything but *that*, is an indication of a small intelligence.

"Don't take me away from my dear little grotto" (where she was living surrounded by her excrements), said the sequestered girl in Poitiers. — Her secretions poison her soil.[6]

Without the motes that it lights up, the ray of sunlight would not be visible.

22 August

We reached Auxerre by auto from Brignoles. Spent the first night at Grenoble. Modernized city; nothing left of the charm of the Place Grenette in 1890, when André Walter was looking for an inn where

---

[6] In *La Séquestrée de Poitiers* (*The Poitiers Incarceration Case*) Gide wrote up the true story of a girl who was for years locked up by her family.

he could settle down and write his *Cahiers*.[7] The square was full of life, but not noisy as it is today. As far as I can remember, it was surrounded with old houses. There were blossoming orange trees in tubs. A heady perfume floated in the air in front of the café terrace where I sipped a coffee ice, white with milk (such as I have never tasted since). I did not yet know Stendhal.[8] I did not yet smoke. My glance was chaste and did not disturb, or but rarely, my peace of mind. The hotel was dear and I was afraid of not having enough money.

Exhausting landscape of the Grenoble environs. We stopped at Les Mées to have a close view of the very odd alignments of rocks with unexplainable erosions.

The second day, spent the night at Bourg. The tame fox belonging to the hotelkeepers. His amorous play with the dogs. The following day was market day (Wednesday). Amazing produce of the farms; each farmer's wife, well dressed, in line with her hand placed on the basket in front of her, which was full of butter, eggs, vegetables, and sometimes a little bouquet of centauries or garden flowers.

Church of Brou. Overloading: useless and cosmopolitan luxury. Bought, imported art, come from a distance. The marvel of Florence is that the art is born of the very soil. The only really Christian art is that which, like St. Francis, does not fear being wedded to poverty. This rises far above art as adornment. Nothing is less Christian, less spiritual than the ornamentation of Brou. Very beautiful, however, but profane. Preciosity begins with useless expense.

All our writers of today (I am speaking of the best) are *precious*. I hope to acquire ever more poverty. (Paradox.) In destitution lies salvation.

Cluny. One has not the right to be consoled for this crime. The church sold, becoming a quarry for ready-cut stones. The exploitation of others' work.

Amazing Cluny stud-farm. Wonderful neck and withers of the work-horses. Those in the Renaissance drawings were not at all exaggerated, then. The animal — a work of art. Between the bars of their stalls we twice see stallions rub their noses together, knock their teeth together, one of them seize and suck the other's tongue, all with delight and undeniable signs of sexual pleasure. I stay rather long watching them. The stable-master as he passes says: "They are trying to bite each other. When they are too vicious they sometimes have to be

---

[7] Gide's first published work was entitled *The Notebooks of André Walter*.

[8] Born in Grenoble, on the Place Grenette, Henri Beyle (Stendhal) spent his childhood there.

separated." Is he deceived? or, out of propriety, is he trying to deceive us?

Spent the night at Beaune, at the hotel where I had dined with Copeau two years ago. Rather early the next day, visit to the Copeaus at Pernand. Jacques Copeau in very good form, but no time to talk. I regret seeing Copeau enjoy and encourage his son's shortcomings. He shows me with indulgence a sheaf of large brown sheets on which Pascal has pasted photographs of political figures cut out of periodicals — and carefully, cleverly chosen to throw the most unfavorable light on the "government." With such a device one could make Christ himself ridiculous.

When I ask Jacques if it wouldn't be painful to him to see such a *treatment* inflicted on us, and if he is quite sure that we would come off any better, he replies: "We would always have more nobility." But I do not believe this. I have just seen, among M.'s photos, certain portraits of me back from the Chad that would delight Béraud and Massis; and Copeau himself doesn't always look like a "great man."

Spent the night at Semur.

Auxerre — then Chablis, where I am writing this.

23 August

The London Royal Society of Literature, of which I was elected a member, eighteen months ago, to take the place of France (or Loti?), asks me today what titles and decorations are to follow my name in the list of Honorary Fellows that is "about to appear."

I reply: "Honors began by fleeing me. Later I fled honors. On the list of Honorary Fellows of the Royal Society my name is not to be followed by any title. The F.R.S.L. will only stand out the better."

The most important things to say are those which often I did not think necessary for me to say — because they seemed to me too obvious.

Pontigny, 24 August

Dog-tired, I go to bed early and go to sleep at once. But soon this first sleep, nibbled at by the thousand sounds of the others going to bed, yields and bursts in all directions. It is all over with my rest for the whole night.

The tiring thing, at Pontigny, is not being able to follow up each thought that the discussion awakens in you; impossible to recapture it later on. This is what has always made me prefer the book to the lecture or the speech. The orator overcomes objections because he does not give them time to take shape; or else one cannot follow him. It is necessary to drop either them or him. The book is *fairer*.

Whence that fear I have, on occasion, of letting myself be convinced by speech. . . .

26 August

Finished correcting the proofs of *Les Nourritures* (Aveline edition).[9] Fear of self-indulgence leads me to take a severe view of that book. The constant use of dashes (I am suppressing more than three quarters of them) annoys me, and even more of certain words, particularly the *"après,"* of which I make an improper and excessive use.[10] But, despite myself, I must recognize the importance of this book. And, after all, it is such as it had to be, and successful. It is even well composed, and all the disaggregation of the middle was inevitable and necessary. The last part brings this out and, in its very dissatisfaction, announces something different and leads farther. I read there the permission of becoming — and almost the announcement of my subsequent books, of what I have become. For anyone who is willing to read carefully and without prejudice, there is the criticism of the book in the book itself, as is fitting.

It does not seem to me possible that, some day, a critic shall not come along and notice all this on his own. And that it would have been madness to write *this* book with more wisdom.

I understand moreover what Lebey disliked here. "It is from this point onward that you must write." But it so happens that this book (the middle of this book at least) had to be stammered. And the least precious epithet, the least attempt at an effect, all effort toward literature, had to be banished from it. It went against everything that "symbolism" liked. It was with this book that I was to begin to get myself reviled.

29 August

Dreadful fatigue. The Pontigny discussions are getting more and more specialized. Only professional philosophers can take part in them. I wonder at the outlay of subtlety on the part of those who, without any creative power, exhaust the unrest of their strong minds in the examination and critical analysis of others' works. Just because, in a few words, I tried to bring Montaigne a little closer to reality, to *his* reality, just because I tried to descend a bit from those abstract regions in which the air was becoming almost unbreathable for many among us, I am now looked upon as an enemy of philosophy.

---

[9] A new edition of *Les Nourritures terrestres* (*The Fruits of the Earth*) was brought out in 1927 by Claude Aveline, Éditeur, with an important new preface by Gide dated July 1926 and two appendices: one containing an enthusiastic letter from Albert Samain dated 1897 and the other reproducing the original publisher's inventories, which show that exactly five hundred copies were sold during the first ten years (1897–1908).

[10] Gide must be referring to the independent use of *"après"* in the sense of "later on."

Tunis, 15 September

Got on board on the 13th — arrived this morning at six.

Indescribable boredom; everyone is ugly. I would give this whole trip for a few hours of practice at a good piano. Reduced to practicing Chopin's mazurkas in imagination; not without advantage, moreover. Formidable waste of time, at an age when . . .

26 September

The best recollection of Tunis: a few hours spent at the excellent little Pleyel piano belonging to the bookseller Tournier. Alone in the apartment, I go over Fauré's nocturnes and barcarolles, which I hardly remembered at all.

I am rereading *Les Caractères* of La Bruyère.[11] So clear is the water in these basins that one must lean over them for some time to appreciate their depth.

I am writing these lines seated on the terrace of the little hotel of Hammamet, where I am waiting for René Michelet, Herman de Günsel, and his mother, who are to come on the train from Tunis. M. was ill all night long. I think only of leaving again. Lack of appetite and lack of curiosity; torpor.

Paris, 2 October

The devil take those people in whose presence you can't even sniffle without their immediately asking you:

"Have you caught cold?"

12 October

Arrived at Cuverville on the 8th. Daily piano-practice until I can play no longer. Between six and seven hours every day. Reviewed Chopin's Sonata in B-flat minor (minus the funeral march), a number of études and preludes, Bach's two Prestos in G minor (Brahms), and the *Lavapiés* by Albéniz. Went over likewise a number of compositions by Schumann that I still know by heart — and tried to reconcile myself with him. But his "developments" are unbearable to me, however exquisite the motif may be, and there are few of his compositions of which I would not be glad to drop half. The best ones are, most often, the shortest ones.

Delight at still knowing completely by heart all the *Symphonic Études* (at least I recover them altogether after two hours of practice) — minus the middle of the finale, which I give up.[12]

[11] *The Characters* are keen philosophic reflections on men and manners, after the fashion of Theophrastus.

[12] The *Etüden in Form von Variationen* or *Symphonische Etüden*, Op. 13, by Schumann.

16 October

Paris again. Tumult. I feel myself becoming unsociable. No desire
to chat any more. And more absolutely: no desires. Conversation with
Adrienne Monnier, who does not like *Les Faux-Monnayeurs*. In general there is taking place with this latest book what has already taken
place so many times with the preceding ones. The most recent one is
liked only by those who hadn't yet liked the others, and all the readers
who had been won over by the preceding books declare they like
"this one much less." I am accustomed to it and know that it is enough
to wait.

Adrienne Monnier talks to me for some time and rather eloquently
of the coldness and fundamental *unkindness* that this book reveals and
that must be my hidden nature. I don't know what to say, what to
think. Whatever criticism is made of me, I always acquiesce. But I
know that Stendhal likewise was long accused of insensibility and
coldness. . . .

1927

There is not a single declaration of this type (profession of fidelity in the preface to *Les Nourritures*[1]) that does not seem to me to ring a little false when I reread it a short time afterward. What is the good of saying one was sincere when writing it? There is no character so simple that it does not involve complicated byways. The peculiarity that seems to win out is the one on which attention centers; the mere beholding eye already distorts and enlarges. One loses sight of the whole physiognomy, and a certain feature that one causes to dominate is not perhaps the dominant feature.

Because it has always been easier for me to choose and to reject in the name of someone else than in my own name, and because I always feel I am impoverishing myself when I limit myself, I am quite willing to have no well-defined existence if the individuals I create and draw from myself have one.

Sainte-Maxime, 6 February

Through a great need for solitude, I left Saint-Clair this morning, for a day. Accustomed for several years now to leaving all initiative up to M., I have the greatest difficulty deciding on any move whatsoever. I need to be paced; but society distracts me; need of a springboard of boredom from which to plunge into work. I had left Paris with the hope of getting rather far ahead with this new novel, of which I wrote the first pages so gaily and easily at Cuverville, without a rough draft, almost without erasures.[2] Upon rereading them they don't seem to me so bad. The too pleasant society of the Simon Bussys at Roquebrune, and the impossibility of being alone, killed my impetus. I shall return home without having written a line; or, at least, nothing but letters and a few changes and additions to my travel-account.[3]

[1] "I am commonly judged on the basis of this youthful book, as if the ethics of *Les Nourritures* had been mine throughout life, as if I had not been the very first to follow the advice I give to my young reader: 'Throw my book away and leave me.' Yes, I immediately left the man I was when I wrote *Les Nourritures;* to such a point that, when I examine my life, the dominant feature I find in it — far from being inconstancy — is fidelity. That profound fidelity of heart and mind I believe to be infinitely rare. Those who, before dying, can see accomplished what they had planned to accomplish, I ask you to name them, and I take *my place among them*."

[2] Probably *L'École des femmes* (*The School for Wives*), which came out in 1929.

[3] *Le Retour du Tchad* (*The Way Back from the Chad*, which appeared in English as a part of *Travels in the Congo*).

Great fatigue and indescribable boredom.

Saw Eugène Rouart again; he came to pick me up at Saint-Clair and take me to Toulon, where I spent the night before last. He has managed to sketch out and construct his mask; it partakes of the virtuoso, of the clown, and of the statesman. Something unclassified, unclassifiable, and, I must say, highly successful.

To say the simplest and most ordinarily reasonable things, his brow wrinkles and his whole body screws up as if he were painfully extracting a secret from his depths. He certainly used six times in one hour the extraordinary word "insistative," which he believes to be heavy with thought. He speaks of the "insistative character of *Si le grain ne meurt . . .*" and of the "insistative policy of Mussolini."

> *Saint-Clair, 8 February*

Everything I might write to explain, exonerate, or defend myself I must refuse myself. I often imagine such a preface for *L'Immoraliste,* for *Les Faux-Monnayeurs,* for *La Symphonie pastorale* — one, above all, that would set forth what I mean by fictional objectivity, that would establish two sorts of novels, or at least two ways of looking at and depicting life, which in certain novels (*Wuthering Heights*, Dostoyevsky's novels) are joined. The first, exterior and commonly called objective, which begins by visualizing others' acts and events and then interprets them. The second, which begins by paying attention to emotions and thoughts and runs the risk of being powerless to depict anything that the author has not first felt himself. The resources of the author, his complexity, the antagonism of his too diverse possibilities, will permit the greatest diversity of his creations. But everything derives from him. He is the only one to vouch for the truth he reveals, and the only judge. All the heaven and hell of his characters is in him. It is not himself that he depicts, but he could have become what he depicts if he had not become everything himself. It was in order to be able to write *Hamlet* that Shakespeare did not let himself become Othello.

. . . Yes, I could set forth all this. But haven't I already said it or let it be sufficiently understood when speaking of Dostoyevsky? What is the good of repeating? It is better to say to the reader: read me more carefully; reread me; and go on to something else.

One of the great rules of art: do not linger.

Nothing is accomplished if I have not truly been able to become, to the point of deceiving myself, this character that I am assuming and to depersonalize myself in him to the extent of being blamed for never

having managed to portray anyone but myself — however different
from one another may be Saul, Candaules, Lafcadio, the minister of
my *Symphonie pastorale,* or La Pérouse or Armand. It is returning to
myself that embarrasses me, for, in truth, I no longer really know who
I am; or, if you prefer: I never *am;* I am *becoming.*

Paris, 11 February

All that Hirsch found to quote in the account of my travels in the
Congo was the paragraph having to do with elephantiasis of the gen-
ital organs, so frequent among the natives — a juicy morsel for the
readers of the *Mercure;* and in the commentary preceding and following the quotation Hirsch went to great lengths to ridicule me — and
this is always easy when speaking of someone you don't know. Now,
I am known to the readers of the *Mercure* only by Jean de Gourmont's
invectives and by Hirsch's silences. I warned Vallette that more than
I was involved; that it was inadmissible for the *Mercure* to pass over
in silence so legitimate a claim; that Hirsch ought for a time to declare
a truce, even if he is to resume his silence and hostility right afterward.
And this month Hirsch disarms, quotes me at length, and even claims
to "regret" his irony of the preceding month. It is so disagreeable to
me to hear my "humanity" praised by him that it makes me, too,
"regret" his irony and silence. The only praise that touches me comes
from those I can esteem.

But I am writing all this only for the sake of writing something
and of getting back into the habit of chatting with this notebook.

12 February

Call on L., who offers me 24,000 francs to bring out a new edition
of a thousand copies of *Si le grain ne meurt.* . . . No other reason
to let him do it but "the profit motive." I resist. He will tell himself
that he did not offer me enough. He will never know that it was above
all his son who killed the deal, a fat fellow of about thirty who talks
in a cynical manner and regrets not having a sister "who could give
him money." When Mme L. declares that she approves men who deserted from the army because they were antimilitarists, he exclaims
that he approves even more "the militarists who deserted in spite of
that." Etc.

13 February

"The approbation of a single mere *respectable man,*" she told me
"is the only thing that matters to me, and that your book will not get."
But whoever approves my book ceases to appear respectable in her
eyes.

Likewise, before some of the most important acts of my life she would write me: "Nothing good can come of it," and consequently would refuse to recognize as good anything that might ensue. — These are final judgments.

18 February

I have not been able to keep my promise to myself. Distracted from this notebook — but by work.

26 February

Exasperated by the life I am leading and by all those who make me waste my time. Exasperated against myself for not knowing how to defend myself better. I no longer take any pleasure in conversations, even when I shine in them. — Paul Valéry writes me a heartbreaking letter. Will it be like this until death, and shall we never again know leisure? "O fecund laziness!" — People trespass frightfully on one another.

Yesterday dined with Bennett and his wife, then evening at Godebski's, where Sert, etc., etc., come to join us.

Sert's violent outburst against Barrès, in whom he sees a descendant of the Spanish gypsies, to whose ethnological type he belongs, asserts Sert. His *El Greco* annoys Sert particularly, and just the mere fact of seeing in that "Greco-Venetian half-caste" the father of Spanish painting.

1 March

Long conversation with Roger Martin du Gard — ensconced in his materialism like a wild boar in its wallow. Le Dantec and Taine are his gospels; in every objection I make to him he insists on seeing a manifestation of my Christian heredity. It appears, after a short while, that one of his Thibaults is inhabiting him, so that it is less Roger speaking than Antoine; this reassures me, but very little, for it does not seem to me that the author, in this case, is dominating his character, or that he can get far away from him. He wants to write a monologue of Antoine in which the leitmotiv or refrain would be "In the name of what . . . ?" He does not admit that anything can stop man on the slope of his instincts, except the fear of a policeman-god, in which he does not believe. The basis of all ethics can only be religious, he asserts, and is amazed and annoyed by the refutations of his thesis provided by the mere manifestations of his own self, so naturally good and respectable.

On the train going to Cuverville, 5 March

How well I should be if it were not for all these people shouting that I am ill!

They insist on seeing in *Les Faux-Monnayeurs* an abortive book. The same thing was said of Flaubert's *Éducation sentimentale* and of Dostoyevsky's *The Possessed*. (I remember that what made me read *The Possessed* and *The Brothers Karamazov* was the retreat of that great ninny Melchior before these "apocalyptical and sinister" books.[4]) Before twenty years are up it will be recognized that what people now hold against my book is precisely its qualities. I am sure of this.

> *Cuverville, 6 March*

Too many projects in my head. And desire to work on all of them at once. My brain has never been more active. But the idea of death never leaves me a minute. I had written: the fear of death; but it is not a fear . . . or else it is merely that of not having enough time to do my duty toward myself (another day I should write: toward God). That idea of God is perhaps useful to establish the edifice; but like the support that in the beginning upholds the vault; once the vault is finished, it can do without a support. Moreover the idea we are able to have of God remains so vague and so *personal* that it matters little whether one denies it or believes in it. To me God is the great stopgap. And I can well shout with Hugo:

> *Il est! il est! il est! il est éperdûment.*[5]

But what good is that if I don't know *What* He is! Our very adoration remains on a human scale. Why be upset by this?

> *7 March*

Prélude, Choral et Fugue. It is Overbeck. — No matter.[6]

It is perhaps not very skillful to swell *Le Traité des Dioscures* with the religious question? To be looked into.[7]

Great difficulty in taking my new novel seriously.

"The interviewer's visits."[8]

---

[4] Gide is referring to Eugène-Melchior de Vogüé in *Le Roman russe* (1886), which introduced Russian fiction to France.

[5] "He is! he is! he is! he is desperately," is a line from the Conclusion of Hugo's long poem *Religions and Religion*.

[6] The *Prelude, Chorale, and Fugue* is by César Franck (1884). Friedrich Overbeck (1789–1869), a German painter who was inspired by the Italian primitives, was appreciated in his time for his mystic sentimentality.

[7] *The Treatise of the Dioscuri* was abandoned as such and became the *Considerations on Greek Mythology.*

[8] In the early years of this century Gide had occasionally expressed his ideas in the form of imaginary interviews, a form to which he was to return in 1941 and 1942 during the German occupation of France. He did not employ this device during the twenties and does not know now to what he was referring in this passage.

And I must go over once more the account of my travels — second part.[9]

I should like to write also my *Nouvel Œdipe* and a *Dialogue avec Dieu*.[10]

8 March

Wrote the little column of News Items for the April number. I am reading with rapture Jules Renard's *Journal* (1903–5). Less shriveled up than the preceding volume. At moments one comes on excellent, perfect touches, and sometimes even, oh surprise, on a compassionate note.

Le Tertre, 25 March

Certain evenings after which one would like to beg everyone's pardon. It is usually in the presence of a new face that this disaster occurs.

Roger's brother brings Hélène Martin du Gard from Paris. The car he is driving drops them on the doorstep after eight o'clock. We hardly know each other; that is to say that there is no precedent between us. One is working on a blank canvas where the least brush-stroke counts. What happens then? It is as if the trap of the abyss were opened in me, as if all hell gushed out in me. What is that steam that rises from the depths of the self, that clouds your vision and inebriates you? The ego swells, inflates, spreads out, exhibits all its hideous contents. With the aid of fatigue, you lose all control over yourself; your voice rises and gets out of key, you hear yourself self-satisfiedly uttering thoughtless words you would at once like to recall; you witness, powerless to do anything, that miserable parody of a hateful creature who takes your place, plays your role, and whom you would like to (but cannot) disavow . . . for he is yourself.

I said nothing yesterday that was not hateful, absurd, and such that if I could break off relations with myself, I should.

This morning I am trying to get all these monsters back into their cage.

. . . The passage from: everything one could do, to: everything one could have done.

4 April

Went to see the doctor. All the springs of my being are unsprung.

. . . .

[9] *Le Retour du Tchad.*

[10] The *New Œdipus* is the play *Œdipe*, which came out in 1931; nothing entitled *Dialogue with God* has ever appeared.

14 April

Went to hear *Le Venin* by Bernstein (whom I almost asked yesterday for a defense of *Les Faux-Monnayeurs* for the book that *Le Capitole* is preparing).[11]

Characters frightfully limited to themselves.

S. S. has got into the habit of not getting up until ten o'clock. It
is not because her health requires this, but:

"I'm at least that much to the good," she says.

Lausanne, 19 April

Metropolis. German film in utter bad taste and colossally stupid.
Must have cost very much to make; impossible to stop thinking of this.

Yesterday, at Neuchâtel, saw *The Gold Rush* again.

Suarès is cool toward Charlie Chaplin out of pride. Unjustifiable
resistance. Unique case in which one can share the popular opinion.
And no misunderstanding about it. You and I laugh at and are amused
by the same thing. It would be a shame to miss this possibility of communion. It is so good to be able not to scorn what the crowd admires!

Back from Zurich to Neuchâtel, 1 May

Town benumbed in a silvery fog that the sun dissipates toward
noon. Everybody at church, since it is Sunday. I sit down on a bench
facing the lake; this morning the opposite shore was hidden by the
fog, which gave it a — North Sea aspect. (For some time I seek in vain
a four-syllable epithet that would fit.) I should be glad to live in
Neuchâtel, where the memory of Rousseau is still alive, and where the
children are more beautiful than anywhere else (those under sixteen
are not admitted to the moving pictures). The ground is so clean in
town that I don't dare throw my cigarette anywhere.

All the thoughts of these people walking by, with their "hymnal
and psalter" under their arm, are washed and ironed by the sermon
they have just heard and carefully piled in their heads as in a clean
linen-closet. (I should like to rummage in the bottom drawer; I have
the key.) Bells are ringing. Is it time for a new service or for lunch?
The quays empty.

---

[11] *The Venom* is a typical comedy by the successful dramatist Henry
Bernstein. He did contribute an article to the volume entitled *André Gide*
published in 1928 by Éditions du Capitole.

Interview with De Traz in *Les Nouvelles littéraires.* It is amusing to see Lefèvre spread out more and more and invent new authors. Let's launch each other mutually.[12]

"What is the *acte gratuit?*" he makes De Traz say.[13] "Isn't there a false profundity in it?" — No, not at all, my dear L., there is no profundity in it at all. I merely meant that the *disinterested* act could well not always be charitable; but once this is said, you are free, with La Rochefoucauld, not to believe in disinterestedness at all. Perhaps I don't believe in it either, but I claim that the individual's potentialities and his inner meteorology remain a bit more complicated than you ordinarily make them, and that what you call the bad potentialities are not all egocentric. This is stated quite ridiculously; but I am writing in haste, and plan to insist on this point soon — apropos of curiosity perhaps; the individual's perdition, but without it no progress would be possible.

Zurich, 5 May

Some rot and others ossify; all get old. Nothing but a great intellectual fervor can overcome the body's fatigue and withering. With M. my whole youth left me; I doze while awaiting his return and waste my time as if I still had a great deal to waste. I sleep too much, smoke too much, digest badly, and am hardly aware of the spring. The creature surrenders when he has no one to think of but himself; I strive only through love; that is to say, for someone else.

> *Ah! would that it would return —*
> *The time of falling in love!* [14]

---

[12] For some time almost every issue of *Les Nouvelles littéraires* contained an interview by Frédéric Lefèvre, one of the editors, entitled *"Une Heure avec . . ."* They were later published in book-form.

[13] As a result of Gide's *Caves du Vatican,* the gratuitous or disinterested act became a burning question. Gide had already approached the problem in 1899 in his *Prométhée mal enchaîné.*

[14] In

> *Ah! que revienne*
> *Le temps où l'on s'éprenne!"*

Gide has "adapted" the lines from Rimbaud's *Chanson de la plus haute tour* (*Song of the Highest Tower*):

> *Ah! Que le temps vienne*
> *Où les cœurs s'éprennent.*

In Rimbaud's *Une Saison en enfer* (*A Season in Hell*) the lines appear as:

> *Qu'il vienne, qu'il vienne,*
> *Le temps dont on s'éprenne.*

6 May

Lunched with Strohl, whom I had gone to pick up at the university, where he shows me various collections of shells, shellfish, corals, insects — of the greatest interest; visit somewhat spoiled, in my memory, by my need of showing off my knowledge — but it was also to encourage Strohl, whose conversation can become most exalting. He always says exactly what can be most valuable to me, and I listen to him tirelessly. A pity that his study of me is so awkward in expression![15] He takes me to lunch in a little restaurant in old Zurich made precious by the memory of Gottfried Keller. I insist on paying for the meal; but, through awkwardness, "modesty," stinginess, I leave an insufficient tip, the memory of which is enough to poison the rest of the day for me.

Yesterday Strohl had taken me on a wonderful auto ride, in a landscape extraordinarily full of flowers: unbroken conversation that teaches me more than the reading of a pile of books.

7 May

What annoys me is not being able to understand why I left an insufficient tip. — Could it be because I felt that Strohl was watching me?

Yes, perhaps.

(See Ubu's admirable remark to Mme Ubu: "You are very ugly today. Is it because we have guests?"[16])

Whether I believe or don't believe?

What does that matter to you?

And what does it matter to me?

It is no more possible for me to think sincerely your credo than to believe in the sun's rotation around the earth. But, believers, I have known your state. *Et ego.* I know that that monstrous idea, planted in the core of our mind, by the very limitation it sets upon each of our thoughts, leads us to that pathetic state of which the work of art can take advantage. And what can make one think that art itself is essentially religious, what can make the believer believe that art and artistic creative power are dependent on faith, is not only the increased eloquence the artist owes to his faith, but also the increased receptivity on the part of the believing auditor or spectator when faced with a work of art of religious inspiration; it is the mystic communion between artist and public, which only that common belief allows. One

---

[15] Jean Strohl's study of Gide entitled "Reflections on the Relations between Art and Science" appeared in the volume of homage called *André Gide* and published by Éditions du Capitole in 1928.

[16] In Alfred Jarry's farce *Ubu Roi* (*King Ubu*).

is in collusion. The sets are already up, the instruments tuned, the tears ready. Everyone feels that he belongs to the flock, to the family; between the actor and himself (the author modestly effaces himself), everyone feels a secret connivance.

"That's my dish."

As for me, I want a work of art in which *nothing is granted* in advance, before which everyone remains free to protest.

Even the masks of central Africa, the native sculptures, are the product of a religious sentiment. Primitive mentality is more religious than ours and, in this regard, the Negro is more than a match for us.

"How can they *believe* in that?" you wonder, you who believe. My sorry amazement in regard to your faith is of the same nature as your amazement in regard to theirs.

The palace of faith. . . . You find consolation, assurance, and comfort there. Everything in it is arranged to protect your laziness and guarantee your mind against effort.

"Brought up in this palace, I know its ins and outs." [17] (There are even such charming ones that I am still nostalgic for them.) . . . One has to check too many things in the cloakroom. I am willing to give up my purse, but not my reason — my reason for existing.

One enters there with eyes closed; with eyes blinded. This is indeed the way Œdipus enters.

Œdipe, or the triumph of ethics.

I have related the story of the play to Martin du Gard.

I should have done better to write it.

We are wallowing in the approximate.

For a long time I have not experienced anything intense. Not even self-disgust or boredom.

                                                              8 May

No, no, it is not my doctrine that is wrong. The principles were good, but I have not followed them.

I remember having heard Wilde tell me: "It is not through excessive individualism that I have sinned. My great mistake, the error I cannot forgive myself, is having, one day, ceased to persist in my individualism, ceased to believe in it in order to listen to others, ceased to believe that I was right to live as I did, doubted myself."

You blame my ethic; I accuse my inconsistency. Where I was wrong was when I thought that perhaps you were right.

[17] An echo of line 1424 from Racine's *Bajazet,* Act IV, Scene vii: *"Nourri dans le Serrail, j'en connais les détours."*

The best of my thoughts were those of my youth, those of which I doubted, out of sympathy, and which I should like to recapture.

What I admire most in Valéry is perhaps indeed his constancy. Incapable of real sympathy, he never let his line of conduct be broken, never let himself be distracted from himself by anyone else.

Zurich, 9 May

My landlady — a woman about thirty-six years old — works from eight a.m. until midnight. (She must even get there at seven thirty if she wants to take advantage of the servants' breakfast.) One day of rest per week (the law requires it, so it seems), but, on the other hand, one other day she works from four a.m. till midnight. (A few days from now, for one week, her hours will be from four thirty to nine.) Two hours' rest per day, which she uses to make up the rooms (her place is ten minutes from the station). And a half-hour during the day to catch her breath, sit down, wash.

She has been doing this for five years, but declares that she cannot keep it up. Yet she plans to go on until next spring — unless she falls ill.

The restaurant employees are not paid, but with their tips make rather good wages.

Add to the work of this poor excellent woman the wash — her own and that of her nineteen-year-old son, an apprentice pastry-cook in Geneva, who does not yet earn more than one hundred francs a month.

I have not set down here any figure that she did not assure me to be exact — and that I was unable to check, for each night I hear her come in at a quarter past twelve — and start out around a quarter past seven in the morning. I offered to make my own bed, but I saw that this offended her and that she finds a certain satisfaction in cleaning and putting in order her four rooms.

I learn from Dr. Fischer, who occupied these two rooms before me and with whom I dined at Lucerne last night, that she had married a blind man, out of pity. That man, not quite honest, had hidden from her the fact that he was covered with debts and, by successive seizures, the bailiffs had taken all the furniture from her first home. After that she had divorced him.

You cannot imagine a gentler, more obliging, more patient, more serenely resigned creature. "There's no other way." This is all she has to say when she speaks of her servitude.

Did not return until midnight from a wonderful auto ride; we reached Engelberg by way of Lucerne and went on into the valley as far as the auto could go (against the law).

I took the greatest pleasure in that long, thirteen-hour ride; but somewhat exhausting. Dined near Lucerne, on the edge of the lake, with Dr. Fischer and my auto companions.

10 May

Last day in Zurich. Yesterday I had gone to meet Strohl at the university. Second visit, with him, to the zoological galleries. You cannot imagine a better guide, nor more interested himself, more exalted by the interest he sees me taking in everything he shows me. The visit lasts almost two hours; but the galleries are cool; I am lightly dressed, without a coat. . . .

"Do you want me to run and get it for you? . . ."

"Don't be silly! Certainly not; but I fear catching cold if I tarry here as I should like to do."

In short, we go out and I start running as soon as I have left him. It is seven o'clock.

At nine thirty Strohl comes back from Zollikon on purpose to find out whether I have caught cold. He brings the makings of a toddy: rum, sugar, lemon-squeezer — and Antipyrine.

I suspect him of having the other day (6 May) purposely left his umbrella in the little tavern where we had lunched. He had probably noticed the insufficiency of the tip I left and wanted to have a pretext for returning soon after and giving, behind my back, a supplementary tip. Extraordinary refinement of delicacy, discretion, and kindness.

Not: *Le Nouvel Œdipe* — but rather: *La Conversion d'Œdipe.*
The title strikes me as excellent.[18]

Many opium-smokers and addicts of cocaine in Zurich. Some of them, Rychner tells me, begin to give themselves injections while in the last classes of the Gymnasium; that is, in their sixteenth or seventeenth year. He knows one personally whom the professors caught using the syringe during a final examination (similar to our *bachot*). Cornered, he confessed that he had acquired this habit in class.

"You don't think anyone can endure the boredom of X.'s lectures without injections, do you?" he added, laughing.

Basel, 11 May

Retrospective exhibit of Böcklin. Enough to make one think that there is no real school or tradition of painting (in our day and for

---

[18] Eventually Gide entitled the play neither *The New Œdipus* nor *The Conversion of Œdipus,* but simply *Œdipus.*

some time now) except in France. Today all the foreign painters of value come to Paris to be informed. Böcklin is worth nothing save by his intentions. The hell of art is paved with them. Nothing distinguishes some of his canvases from the most vulgar daubs, except a certain assurance that impresses and that apes *maestria*. What vulgarity! What presumptuousness! Poverty of draftsmanship. Bumptiousness of the color.

Heidelberg, 12 May

The game is lost, which I could win only with her. Lack of confidence on her part, and great assumption on mine. It is no good to recriminate, or even to regret. What *is not* is what *could not be*. Whoever starts out toward the unknown must consent to venture alone. Creusa, Eurydice, Ariadne, always a woman tarries, worries, fears to let go and to see the thread break that ties her to her past. She pulls Theseus back and makes Orpheus look back. She is afraid.

One by one I recapture each thought of my youth.

The want of logic annoys. Too much logic bores. Life eludes logic, and everything that logic alone constructs remains artificial and forced. *Therefore* is a word the poet must not know, which exists only in the mind.

"Infinite" conversations with Ernst-Robert Curtius. I often feel closer to him than perhaps to anyone else; and not only am I not embarrassed by our diversity of origin, but my thought finds an encouragement in that very diversity. It seems to me more authentic, more valid, when, in contact with his, I become aware that there was no need for this or that particular culture to produce it and that, having both set out from such different places, we meet on so many points. Finally, I find in him, in his eyes, in the tone of his voice, in his gestures, a gentleness, amenity, and kindness that are as if evangelical and to which my confidence responds more and more.

I always acquiesce to criticisms made without animosity; and, in self-defense, I always dislike an element of self-interest. But I cannot subscribe to what Charles Du Bos says: that I yield in *Numquid et tu. . . ?* to the temptation to interpret the Gospel in my own way. Constantly, on the other hand, I provide arms against myself, and it is often what condemns me that I consider, and with the most insistence. Why, otherwise, should I have gone out of my way to look for the hidden meaning of the word: "And he that taketh not his cross, *and followeth after me,*" — unless precisely *against* myself?

To win one's joy through struggle is better than to yield to melancholy.

Need of asserting this, after reading some *"Notes en marge des Voyageurs traqués"* by Montherlant [19] — who, as it just happens, informs me of his return and says he wishes to see me:

Arrogance and boredom are the two most authentic products of hell. I have done everything to defend myself against them and have not always succeeded in keeping them at a distance. They are the two great provinces of romanticism. It is always easier to yield to them than to overcome them, and it is impossible to achieve this without some deceit. It is important to know when to prefer being a dupe, lending oneself to delusion, and the cleverest man, in this regard, is surely not the one "who cannot be imposed on," but who on the contrary enters into the game, above all anxious to maintain his joy.

No, I do not want anything to do with a felicity that can spoil clairvoyance. It is essential to be able to find happiness *beyond*. Acceptation; confidence; serenity: virtues of an old man. The age of struggling with the angel is over.

Cuverville, June

They talk of constructing a system. Artificial construction from which all life immediately withdraws. I let *my* system grow up slowly and naturally. What eludes logic is the most precious element in us, and one can draw nothing from a syllogism that the mind has not put there in advance. I let the most antagonistic proposals of my nature gradually come to agreement without violence. Suppressing the dialogue in oneself really amounts to stopping the development of life. Everything leads to harmony. The fiercer and more persistent the discord had been, the broader the reconciliation blossoms.

It is as natural for him who borrows his thought from another to hide the source as it is for him who recognizes his thought in another to proclaim that meeting of minds.

The most original artists are not necessarily the most uncultivated.

However rare and bold a thought may be, it is impossible that it should not be related to some other; and the greater an artist's solitude in his own epoch, the greater and more fecund his joy at finding relatives in the past.

---

[19] The issue of the *Nouvelle Revue Française* for January 1927 carried some reflections by Henry de Montherlant entitled *"Les Voyageurs traqués"* ("The Hunted Travelers"), and the June issue some "Supplementary Notes to 'The Hunted Travelers'" to which Gide is alluding here.

Youth attracts me, and even more than beauty. A certain freshness, an innocence, one would like to recapture. . . .

3 July

This morning, as soon as I awake (much too early) my brain, despite me, begins to construct sentences. Some of them are quite well turned out, but mean nothing. There are some that I should like not to lose, that I try to learn by heart, to remember; and it is all up with sleep.

Good God, how complicated everything is becoming! Lines in all directions; and no guidance. No way of knowing what to believe, what to think! . . .

Cuverville

Unhealthy torpor. The constrictions and pains in the esophagus (?) are becoming almost continuous and unbearable. I take refuge in sleep like a sulky child withdrawing from the game.

Reread *La Jeune Parque*.[20] Despite some charming movements that artifice alone could not invent and in which Valéry shows himself to be truly a musician, I cannot prefer this long poem to certain other ones, more recent and shorter, of *Charmes*. Not yet sufficiently detached from Mallarmé; marking time; abuse of the return to oneself, of the meander. . . .

A work by Claparède on Bonnet, which Jean Strohl has sent me.[21] I find in it a number of thoughts that, parallel to those of *Corydon*, had been brought forth by the mere observation of animals (on maternal love in particular). The healthiest of those thoughts are never the ones you find, after the fashion of Gourmont, in books, which always smack of their verbal origin. — The account of an observation, however faithful, impartial, and detailed it may be, is never worth the fact itself, which perhaps I should have observed differently and with a different purpose in view. To the true naturalist book knowledge can never be enough; he has no use for interpreters; he understands at once the language of nature and questions it directly.

---

[20] Paul Valéry's long poem, *The Young Fate*, which marked his return to literature. The title *Charmes* contains a play on the Latin *Carmine* and the word *Charms* in the sense of *spells*.

[21] *La Psychologie animale de Charles Bonnet* (*The Animal Psychology of Charles Bonnet*) by Édouard Claparède, published in Geneva in 1909. Charles Bonnet (1720–93) was a Swiss philosopher and naturalist; Édouard Claparède (1873–1940) was a Swiss psychologist and founder of the Institute J.-J. Rousseau.

Cuverville, 18 July

Exasperated by this travel-account (second part) from which I am unwilling and unable to get away, which monopolizes and clings to my every thought. I am trying to read right to the end of *Les Données immédiates;* [22] I have great trouble. . . .

Peira-Cava, August

"I am very far from being entirely of my own opinion." (Mme de Sévigné, 15 January 1690.)

I read in Proust (*N.R.F.*, August, p. 225):

". . . it was only out of her presence" — which I consider as a deplorable error; but I cannot consider as an error the use of "realize" in this sentence (p. 227):

"And moreover was it not in order to tend to them that I lived far from those who would complain of not seeing me, in order to be more deeply concerned with them than I could have done in their presence, in order to strive to reveal them to themselves, to *realize* them." It seems that Proust, by thus outlining the limits of the word, was careful to prepare an example for a future Littré.

To realize — to make real. Despite all the Soudays, I should dare to write: "Yes, I have gone into mourning, to be sure; but I do not realize this mourning in my heart."

The word will live; it expresses, and very well, an idea without which one cannot get along any better than without the word that creates it.

10 August

. . . Capable of every act of treachery and of every act of graciousness, the latter serving only to prepare or to get himself forgiven for the former, M. does not blame himself for having acted badly, but for "not having known how to go about it."

11 August

It is a mistake to intend to write only very important things in a *Journal*. That is not its justification. I want to write in it this evening what I should write if I had kept it up the last few days.

Great fatigue of the heart, yesterday and especially today. Done nothing that matters.

In the morning wrote some letters; read with Élisabeth Van Rysselberghe the beginning of the twelfth canto of the *Purgatorio*, which I finish alone a little later. How have I been able to abandon Dante

---

[22] Bergson's doctoral dissertation (1889), *Essai sur les données immédiates de la conscience*, was translated into English as *Time and Free Will*.

for so long?—(I like Élisabeth's application, and her patience, and her horror of the approximate.) In the evening a chapter of the *Grüne Heinrich*. But I feel devoid of vigor, devoid of virtue.

13 August

I drag myself around all day long.—How many times have I already written that sentence! Yet, this morning, rather good work. M. helps me considerably; and I am cowardly about letting myself be helped, ready to accept any idea, any sentence that is offered me. I am astonished that I can differ from myself to this extent.

I cannot cease thinking of this work on the big Concessionary Companies, and so long as I have not finished it, I shall not feel as if I belong to myself.[23] How difficult everything seems to me! I progress step by step, laboring, out of breath, of joy, of fervor. Can anything good come out of such an exertion of all the faculties? But I will not, I cannot, let go. It seems to me that I shall never see the end of it. And all day long I keep repeating to myself: *It must be done,* and it will not be done by anyone else.

Théoule, 18 August

Indescribable boredom; fed up with everything and everybody. Work alone can get me out of the swamp in which I am sinking. . . . The day before yesterday, with the aid of M., I finished the article on the Concessionary Companies. This evening I reread the first pages of it with disgust. I have never written anything more amorphous. Everything is to be rewritten; but later on, when I am less tired and when I have lost sight of it all for some time.

All the best I have written was well written from the start without labor, fatigue, or boredom.

My *loathing* today is perhaps sentimental in origin and comes from the worry M. is causing me.

19 August

I regret not having made more reservations about Thibaudet's study of me, in the *Revue de Paris*. It is always so disagreeable to me to protest, to balk, and to seem to be defending myself that in the letter I wrote him I picked out only that startling imputation of "hatred" in regard to my poor Uncle Charles—which would have hurt him cruelly—and which, in any case, was comparable to issuing counterfeit notes, so little credit and assent did it awaken in my heart.

The pages that Thibaudet rewrote, in reply to my objections—that

---

[23] A reference to an article for the *Revue de Paris*, in which he reveals the abuses of those companies in exploiting the African natives.

is to say, the opening ones — are manifestly better than the following ones, too rapidly written and thought out, in which he reveals more ingenuity than intelligence and real understanding. Not that he lacks that intelligence by any means, but throughout that long article he uses it much more to oppose me in a defense of Barrès than to understand me. He always judges me in relation to Barrès, and consequently he condemns me, or at least disapproves of me.

Characters seen from the outside; that is what they call objective portrayal.

He says: *"By seeking,* I found it."

Excellent; you could not invent that.

But too subtly comical; extremely difficult to get the best out of it. Never would a "scholar" have said that, for, to him, it goes without saying. But to Eugène Rouart it does not go without saying at all; the "by seeking" comes down to "by seeking in others," and the natural sentence would be: "I found at X.'s, the last time I called on him, an odd watering-system that . . ."

He says, with a great glow of enthusiasm: "But, my dear fellow, falsehood is an absolutely sacred thing. . . ."

J.: "Is your husband home?"

V.: "Jean, I'll not put up with your talking of your father that way. . . ."

Excellent opening of a scene, but hard to continue.

I can now put up with the society only of those in whose presence I can be silent and who, if I am silent, do not feel obliged to talk. It is very rare that what they say to me seems to be worth that thought I had, which their voice drives away, and which I cannot, later on, recapture. The pin that Stendhal used to stick in his lapel to get silence from his companions — I should rarely take it out. This was the charm of those long days of traveling through the brush in the Congo; for hours on end I could cultivate a single thought calmly, let it unfold all its branches in me; I doubt whether even Descartes's "stove" would have been more propitious than the *tipoye* [24] and walking. Cultivation in a heated room always involves a bit of forcing; I never lost contact with the outer world, with reality, which I deliberately intend to inhabit.

Met on the boulevard Drieu La Rochelle. Since he announces to me that he is going to get married in five days, I consider it proper to invite him into a bar for a glass of port.

---

[24] The *tipoye* is described by Gide in *Travels in the Congo* as a sort of armchair suspended from poles and carried by four bearers.

"Yes," he tells me; "it is an experiment I want to make. I want to know whether or not I shall keep at it. Up to now I have never been able to maintain a friendship or a love-affair more than six months."

All these young men are frightfully concerned with themselves. They never know how to get away from themselves. Barrès was their very bad master; his teaching leads to despair, to boredom. It is to get away from this that many among them hurl themselves headlong into Catholicism, as *he* threw himself into politics. All this will be very severely judged twenty years from now.

1 October

Maurois speaks of Wilde with elegance; the witticisms he quotes are well chosen; but this little study — very much a "lecture before a ladies' club" — leaves me dissatisfied.[25] One feels that he does not *possess* his subject. The "figure in the carpet" eludes him; or is he pretending not to see it?[26] I believe to be utterly false what he repeats after so many others, or what he lets be assumed: that Wilde's way of life was a dependence of his æstheticism and that he merely carried over into his habits his love of the artificial. I believe quite on the contrary that this affected æstheticism was for him merely an ingenious cloak to hide, while half revealing, what he could not let be seen openly; to excuse, provide a pretext, and even apparently motivate; but that that very motivation is but a pretense. Here, as almost always, and often even without the artist's knowing it, it is the secret of the depths of his flesh that prompts, inspires, and decides.

Lighted in this way and, as it were, from beneath, Wilde's plays reveal, beside the surface witticisms, sparkling like false jewels, many oddly revelatory sentences of great psychological interest. And it is for them that Wilde wrote the whole play — let there be no doubt about it.

Try to let some understand what one has an interest in hiding from all. As for me, I have always preferred frankness. But Wilde made up his mind to make of falsehood a work of art. Nothing is more precious, more tempting, more flattering than to see in the work of art a falsehood and, reciprocally, to look upon falsehood as a work of art. That is what made him say: "Never use *I*." The *I* belongs to the very face, and Wilde's art had something of the mask about it, insisted on the mask. But never did he mean to say thereby: be "objective." Always he managed in such a way that the informed reader could raise the mask and glimpse, under it, the true visage (which Wilde had such good reasons to hide). This artistic hypocrisy was imposed on him by

---

[25] The study appeared in *Études anglaises* (*English Studies*).

[26] Gide uses Henry James's title in English.

respect, which was very keen in him, for the proprieties; and by the need of self-protection. Likewise, moreover, for Proust, that great master of dissimulation.

How much more flattering it is to see a critic, out of malice or spite, force himself to disparagement than, out of cliquishness, to indulgence!

2 October

Get in the habit of gathering the idea as soon as it is formed; and cease to let it ripen too long on the branch. Some of them, under this treatment, have become soft. When the brain that bears them is itself ripe, all its fruits are ready to be gathered.

Yesterday, burlesque effort to light the heater. No watch. Alone in the Villa. I got up much too early (as always). It was hardly light. I go down to the cellar with a candle and waste a tremendous amount of time looking for kindling, logs, and the instruments that the furnace men, who have come since my last being here, have misplaced. The fire catches, but without flame, and it sends off such a smoke that, my face covered with tears, blinded, asphyxiated, I have trouble reaching a little window, then another, and thus organizing a draft. I light many newspapers to start the flame. But probably the damper is closed. Groping and covering myself with soot, I manipulate the chain, swing the damper, and become aware only then that the main pipe is lacking. The furnace men have taken it away to repair it, as M. had written me; I had forgotten it.

I take no pleasure in writing these things and do so only by forcing myself, for the training.

M. arrived yesterday at about eleven o'clock, back from London, more lively, more confident, more exquisite than ever. Dined with him, Yves, and Rosenberg, whom I had gone to pick up at the Marcels'. P. comes in an auto to join us and takes us off to the Ursulines cinema, where a new and rather successful film by Cavalcanti is being shown, together with a pretentious German drama, full of poetic, psychological, and philosophical intentions, an exhausting thing.

This morning started out rather early after a few exercises on the piano. An auto took me to the Ministry of Colonies, where I had the luck to find the very pleasant Besson, a friend of Coppet. He tells me that at the international conference in Geneva where the possible clauses of a ruling on native labor were being discussed, my book, the only document on the question of manual labor in the Congo, served as a basis for the discussion, as is shown in the report to the minister that he read me. Dropped in at the *N.R.F.* to pick up my mail; at the

Société Générale to get some money and have some sent to É.; then at Crès's to take him a manuscript page to be printed at the head of his reissue of my *Dostoïevsky;* then at the Crès firm, rue Hautefeuille, for an illustrated reprinting of *Amyntas;* then at the *Mercure,* where I enjoy meeting Duhamel, whom I had not seen since my return from the Congo. Very cordial conversation. I go back to the *N.R.F.* to submit various projects to Gallimard; then to the *N.R.F.* bookstore to get various bits of information from Roland Saucier. Meanwhile I had stopped under the galleries of the Odéon, where I hoped to find the *Goyescas* or Albéniz's *Iberia,* which I wanted to give to Rosenberg; but unable to find either one.

Amusement at seeing Rasmussen's window, boulevard Saint-Germain, entirely filled with my books and M.'s photographs. In the middle of the display, a large map of the Congo with our itinerary traced on it. Lunched at P.'s. Left almost immediately afterward.

Went to rue Drouot, to the Flammarion office, to inquire about the publication date of *L'Immoraliste.* To the M. Bank, to inquire of E. G. about my "situation" with the L.'s. Same thing at V.'s. Then to the L.'s to get my keys, my watch, and the mail that V. brought back from Cuverville. Then to Perret's to inquire about the progress of the work going on at the rue Vaneau (where I also went this morning). Went home to telephone to Thiébaud that I was counting on new proofs from the *Revue de Paris.* Finally able to practice the piano for a full hour. Went over the Preludes in D-sharp minor from the first book, in B major from the second book, the end of the Fugue (the part in semiquavers) in B minor from the second book, and made progress in the Prelude in F-sharp major, which I don't yet know entirely by heart.[27]

I am writing this while dining and am going to stop at the D.'s before going home. While walking, just now, I read Lalou's study that is to serve as a preface to my *Dostoïevsky,* and which Em. has just sent me from Cuverville.

I am writing all this in detail: Sample of a "day in Paris." Whence my desire to get away again.

The best way of getting someone else to "share" your conviction is not always to proclaim it.

5 October

How to get into a novel that impression felt as I entered the D.'s the other evening? First it would take the gradual portrayal of a young, good, intelligent person, often capable of the best, but clumsy when it comes to getting someone to love him, or rather hardly even

---

[27] These are all compositions by Bach.

aiming for this, out of misanthropy, disdain, pride; courageous, but timid in the face of life; full of withdrawals, and seeming, even in broad daylight, covered with shadow; capable of resolve, but without enough enthusiasm to make his way; already crushed by petty cares.

When, after dinner, I enter their little living-room, he is smoking his pipe beside a gramophone that he is playing probably not so much for his sake as to amuse his young wife and his sister-in-law; she lives with them to help in the housekeeping; the three of them are there in that little room to which he returns after the day's work. This is the only time he has to himself. And this time even, when he could catch hold of himself, is completely taken up by the family. In order to live on the same level as "his family," he comes down from his level, sets himself on that modest plane. Could he, with greater financial resources, spend more time by himself? I don't believe so. I believe he would not try to. These evening hours he owes to his young wife, whom he has not seen all day. He feels mediocrity sweeping over him. But what can he do about it? He has ceased struggling; sacrifices himself, hiding within him his ambitions, his dreams, his hopes, everything that would compromise that domestic felicity. — The chapter would be entitled:

CONJUGAL HAPPINESS
Et tibi magna satis . . .[28]

And no possible way out; no escape that does not appear cowardly, egotistical, impious . . . to the weak person.

9 October

At Cuverville again. Arrived yesterday on the evening train after a very reassuring visit to Dr. A., who informs me of the result of the X-rays I had taken four days ago. Those spasms of the esophagus, from which I suffered during my last stay in Cuverville, do not have the terrible organic cause I had feared. Due probably to ill-regulated reflexes caused by hypertrophy of the liver. And most likely my recent spells of insomnia have no other cause either.

A rather good night and this morning, at my awakening, radiant weather. A sky such as we have not seen all summer.

I took care to leave in Paris all the files relative to the Congo, to get rid of it, at last.[29] (My article on the Concessionary Companies is to appear in a few days in the *Revue de Paris*.) More loaded down with projects than ever.

---

[28] "And large enough for you . . ." from Virgil: *Bucolics*, I, 47.
[29] The last seven words appear in English.

Finished learning the Prelude in F-sharp major from the second book.

These last few days in Paris, I should have written excellent pages if only I had had the time. To what a degree I can be upset by "others," they will never know.

Do not pose in your own presence. *Id est:* do not affect the qualities and virtues you would like to have but have not.

But the human being is so extraordinarily perfectible (Amiel would first have written: malleable, alterable, etc.) — that often you become what you want to be, and you eventually really experience the feeling that you began by pretending to experience; that is, if you are not playing that comedy for others. And how many people, just because they thought themselves devout or in love, soon became sincerely devout or in love! How many, on the other hand, by doubting their sentiments, prevented them from developing! It is not bad, on occasion, to trust yourself. It is almost always good to trust another, for the credit he sees extended to this or that virtue binds him and encourages him to take on what he would not have been able to maintain if left to himself. Certain persons keep themselves in the path of virtue only in order to resemble the opinion they know, or hope, that others have of them. Nothing can be more harmful, for certain people, than trying to achieve sincerity, which inclines them to doubt of what are often their best sentiments, to consider themselves sure only of the worst. I never *am;* I am *becoming.* I am becoming the person that I believe (or that *you* believe) I am. There is in every human being a little bit of the irresistible and a great deal of as you will. And even the share of irresistible can be reduced.

(It is easier to think this at the age of fifty-eight than at twenty.)

If it is still fanciful at the age of sixty to think you know yourself thoroughly; it is dangerous at twenty to try to know yourself thoroughly.

My desire, doubtless, is sincere; but my desire to overcome it is no less so. But that is not the important thing, and it matters little to me to weigh the authenticity of one or the other. The important thing is to know whether I am right to try to overcome that desire, whether I am struggling out of fear or virtue, out of fear of others or of myself, etc., etc. Questions, moreover, that I never ask myself any more. The novelist who makes his hero ask himself these things one after another is not following truth; or else his hero is a mere hypocrite. One begins instinctively by solving all these questions; one asks them of oneself only later on and only if one is a quibbler. They do not so often precede action as they substitute for it.

The sentence that begins with: "I know myself . . ." always ends with a negative. "I know myself: I . . . not. . . ."

11 October

Radiant weather, projection of my inner serenity. Read the sermon on "the rich man" — or "final impenitence." [30] Some Herrick.

Made a bit more progress in my new novel, for which I have not yet found a title.

12 October

Everything is ready for work; I cleared up everything yesterday in order to get at it as soon as I get up; but here is the mail: no less than fifteen letters; and in addition I have left four on my mantel that have been awaiting a reply since my return here.

From Paris I write that I am leaving for Cuverville; from Cuverville, that I am soon to return to Paris. . . .

13 October

I am leaving Bach and Chopin for a time, or at least the exclusive study of them, and am going back with the greatest profit to the Minuet of the Symphony in F major (Beethoven-Liszt). Smiling and affectionate serenity; equilibrium in power; self-possession; perfection. And Mozart's concertos (Hummel).

Whatever the composition is, my sole way of working at it is to learn it by heart.

Wasted a tremendous amount of time at the radio that J. has set up in the dining-room. I think of La Fontaine's remark, which I have copied (from *Psyché*, I believe):

"If a lute played itself, it would make me flee, though I like music extremely."

Reread *Le Curé de Tours*.[31]

15 October

Very amused to find, in a note to the *Troisième Lettre de la Montagne* — and by Rousseau himself: [32]

"Someone having objected that Jesus Christ had been present at the wedding-feast of Cana and that he had even deigned to perform his

---

[30] Bossuet's *Sermon on the Evil Rich Man or on Final Impenitence*, inspired by Luke xvi, was preached before the court during Lent of 1662.

[31] *The Priest of Tours*, one of Balzac's novels classified as "Scenes of Provincial Life."

[32] Rousseau wrote his *Letters from the Mountain* (1764) as a vigorous protest against his political persecution at the hands of the Republic of Geneva; the work was condemned and burned by the Parliament of Paris.

first miracle in order to prolong the gaiety of the feast, the priest, somewhat embarrassed, replied grumpily: 'That's not the best thing he ever did.'"

Charming remark, but which had been reported to me as by Barbey d'Aurevilly and said about the pardoning of the woman taken in adultery. It is much better this way.

16 October

"Common sense." One of those convenient expressions that hide only what you want to put into them. And yet I know very well what I mean by this expression. "Common sense" consists in not letting oneself be dazzled by a sentiment or an idea, however excellent they may be, to the point of losing sight of everything else. Never *isolate* arbitrarily or indulgently anything, nor yet oneself.

It remains extraordinary and almost incomprehensible that Descartes considered common sense "the one thing in the world that is most widely shared" and "naturally equal in all men." I hold it on the contrary to be one of the rarest qualities . . . or else I understand Descartes badly.

18 October

How many people seem to us interesting only because they are in a sorry state! Love of the poor lives on this illusion, and love of the sick; it seems to me that Christianity (I did not say Christ) speculates a bit too much on this.

20 October

My grandmother Rondeaux, likewise, had saved up for the end the best of what she had to say, the last instructions and recommendations she wished to leave with her children. When she felt that the solemn hour was approaching, she gathered them all round her, but at that moment was seized with a paralysis of the tongue and, instead of a sublime speech, could only utter a tremendous scream. Such a loud scream, Albert told me as he related this recollection, that it was heard all the way to the end of the garden. This took place at La Mivoie.

That is perhaps what lies in store for me if I delay too much.

I cannot be satisfied with Roger Martin du Gard's absolute nihilism. I do not sidestep it, nor repulse it, but intend to go beyond, to pass through it. It is beyond, what I want to rebuild. It strikes me as monstrous that man should need the idea of God in order to feel steady on earth; that he should be forced to accept absurdities in order to construct something solid; that he should recognize himself incapable of demanding of himself what religious convictions obtained from him artificially, so that he lets himself go to nothing as soon as his heaven is empty.

The best thing Sisyphus can do is to leave his rock alone and to climb up on it in order to "dominate the situation." But, for this, it is still essential that the rock should be of good quality. How many of these young writers, who make so much of their writhings, are pushing only a cardboard rock, or have nothing to lift but a bookcase.

This image of Sisyphus is very good, but I believe I have already used it. It's a pity. But it is better to use it twice than to let it be lost.

23 October

All the thoughts that desire once nourished, all the anxieties it provoked, ah, how difficult it becomes to understand them when the source of lust dries up! And how can one be surprised by the intransigence of those who have never been led by desire? . . . It seems, with the coming of age, that one had somewhat exaggerated its demands and one is astonished to see younger men letting themselves still be tormented. The waves subside when the wind drops; the whole ocean falls asleep and reflects the sky. Knowing how to wish for the inevitable, this is all wisdom. All the wisdom of the aged.

Among the mistakes that pepper, alas, my works, a distinction must be made for those of the typesetter, for which I am in no way responsible: *"préexcellence"* for *"précellence,"* *"vilence"* for *"vilenie"* (in *Antoine et Cléopâtre*). Etc., etc.

Those for which I accuse myself and present my excuses are mistakes of ignorance, of negligence, of inadvertence. But there are certain audacities, certain turns of expression, that I maintain despite purists and pedants; certain "mistakes" that are not mistakes to my way of thinking, or that are conscious and voluntary mistakes (there is a certain piquancy in the fact that H. B. finds nothing to blame me for but these) — *"distingue s'approcher sa mère"* in *Le Retour de l'enfant prodigue* — a recollection of that wonderful line of Chénier:

> *Sur l'arène immobile il l'admire couler* [33]

— and, after several nouns, subjects of a single verb, the agreement of the verb solely with the last of the nouns — of which many examples in the classics.

Etc., etc. — As for the agreement of the subjunctive, I hold that it

---

[33] It is considered wrong in French to admit a pronoun object or reflexive when the verb has a dependent infinitive.

is absurd systematically to use the so *showy,* so embarrassing imperfect after any verb whatever that happens to be in the past; that the ear and reason are the only competent judges in this matter; that it is good to say:

"*Je voudrais qu'il devienne un honnête homme*" [34] — and not "*qu'il devînt,*" and keep this tense to indicate that this desire or wish has ended, that one has ceased to hope.

"*J'aurais voulu qu'il devînt un honnête homme — mais (il a mal tourné).*" [35] Indispensable shade of meaning.

A mother will say: "*Je souhaitais qu'il fasse ses devoirs avant d'aller se promener,*" expressing a wish that might still be realized — and "*qu'il fît ses devoirs avant d'être allé se promener*"; but in this case it is better to say: "*J'avais souhaité qu'il fît ses devoirs avant de . . .*" [36]

So that it can be said that the imperfect subjunctive remains optional and up to the individual after the imperfect indicative and the conditional — that it is *required* only by the pluperfect indicative or by the past conditional.

1. *Je veux qu'il fasse;*

2. $\begin{cases} \textit{Je voulais} \\ \quad \text{or} \\ \textit{Je voudrais} \end{cases}$ *qu'il fasse — or — qu'il fît;*

3. $\begin{cases} \textit{J'avais voulu} \\ \quad \text{or} \\ \textit{J'aurais voulu} \end{cases}$ *qu'il fît.*

25 October

I believe that in every circumstance I have managed to discern rather clearly the most advantageous decision I could come to, which is very rarely the one I did come to.

We are beginning to glimpse the end of the mythological era.

I have ever been as cautious as possible to keep my books from owing their success to anything else but their value.

Paris, 26 October

What interests them in a soul is the position it has taken, not the sound it makes.

---

[34] I should like him to become an honest man.

[35] I should have wished him to become an honest man — but (he went wrong).

[36] Contrast between: "I wanted him to do his home-work before going for a walk" and "I wanted him to do his home-work before having gone for a walk."

27 October

Montherlant is rather indiscreet, for my taste, in vaunting his noble title.[37] And, besides, he is borne along by the current. When I was writing *Les Nourritures* I was alone, and had gone through (there is no doubt about it) much more.

What I like in him is an accent of undeniable authenticity (to leave the word *sincerity* alone) that I likewise feel in Jouhandeau; but most of those who don't have to wonder: "What shall I write?" are mere followers, without knowing it.

28 October

I do not believe the future will be grateful to us for all the care we take with our books; quite the contrary, too much care might well cool them off sooner than others.

The habit of reading, from past centuries, only the books that deserved to survive does not give us much idea of why the others perished. Without going very far back, there is something to be learned from reading, for instance, Feydeau's *Fanny,* which many contemporaries of Flaubert considered a masterpiece. I believe that, later on, *Le Nègre* [38] by Soupault — which I have just read in the train taking me to Carcassonne — will not encounter any more indulgence, and that the very virtues of the book will seem, above all, examples of self-satisfaction, a sort of assent to oneself and to the epoch. . . . But nothing is harder than to get outside one's epoch enough to perceive the shortcomings common to a whole generation.

I am writing this very badly, tired out by a sleepless night. Arriving in Carcassonne before six o'clock, I had nevertheless been sleeping since Toulouse and got out of my compartment in such haste that I left in it a hat that was as dear to me as Lafcadio's beaver to him.[39]

Carcassonne, 30 October

How charming Alibert was yesterday when he exclaimed: "I would give all the symphonies of Beethoven, yes: all the symphonies for a single ballade by Chopin!"

Never younger, more intelligent, more lively, more delightful. One of the very rare people who have not let themselves be misled, or intimidated. Much more intelligent than his work suggests; there is no psychological, ethical, social, literary question on which you cannot

[37] Henry de Montherlant took every occasion to let it be known that he was a Count and descended from an old family of Catalan-French nobility.

[38] *The Negro.*

[39] In *Les Caves du Vatican* (*Lafcadio's Adventures*) the hero loses his new beaver hat in sensational circumstances on a train.

talk with him endlessly and in the most amusing way, for he knows how to laugh and make others laugh, and knows how not to laugh when it is appropriate to be sad or anxious. I haven't a single friend with whom I feel more perfectly at ease; that is to say, with whom I have to be less wary in talking. Conversation, under such circumstances, far from being a strain and an acrobatic feat, is restful, and one lets oneself go as to a natural impulse.

He is surprised to see me like Chardin so much. It was natural that, but little gifted to like painting naturally, I should attach myself particularly to a painter whom I could like only quite specifically for the qualities of which I had been most peculiarly deprived. In the beginning I may have had to apply myself, but, certain of liking him for the right reason, there are few painters who more authentically taught me to enjoy painting.

4 November

Having to look up a date in Simonson's *Bibliographie*,[40] I am amazed to see the exquisite epigraph: *"Cantaret Amyntas"* reproduced thus: *"Cantaret augustas"* — which, alas! has a meaning, so that the absurd and so profoundly, so psychologically discordant error goes unnoticed.[41]

But was it Simonson who made the error? Or was he only reproducing it? I dash to the volume. But I no longer have a copy of the first edition. In the reprint, alas, they have dropped the epigraph.

I beg my future publishers to restore it to the book, of which it explains or at least motivates the title.

Montherlant is charming. Neither Rivière nor I was mistaken as to his rare qualities, when he sent his first manuscript to the *N.R.F.*

But I do not like the *Fontaines du désir*.[42] There is prancing and pawing of the ground in it; it smacks of the thoroughbred horse and the "rearing stallion"; but also somewhat of the circus, the sawdust ring, and the audience's startled gaze, to which he is constantly appealing. What utter idleness, what egotism, this display and these games hide!

Daniel Simond, from Lausanne, whom I meet the day before yesterday on the boulevards and invite to lunch this noon, tells me that

---

[40] Raoul Simonson made several bibliographies of Gide's works.

[41] *Cantaret Amyntas* comes from Virgil: *Bucolics*, X, 11. "If I were only an Arcadian shepherd, Phyllis would make garlands for me, Amyntas would sing for me." *Cantaret augustas* has no relevant meaning. Literally it is: "He would sing of empresses."

[42] *Aux fontaines du désir* (At the Fountains of Desire).

his professor has suggested to him as a thesis-subject: the influence of
Nietzsche on my work. It is flattering; but to what can it lead? To
seeking out, in my *Immoraliste* for example, everything that might recall Zarathustra and paying no attention to what life itself taught me.

The book was entirely composed in my head and I had begun to
write it when I made my encounter with Nietzsche, who at first got in
my way. I found in him, not an instigation, but rather on the contrary
a hindrance. If Nietzsche stood me in good stead in this case, it was
subsequently by purging my book of a whole theoretical side that
could not but have overweighted it.

I have reflected considerably about this question of "influences"
and believe that very gross errors are committed in this regard. The
only thing that is worth anything in literature is what life teaches us.
Everything we learn only from books remains abstract, a dead letter.
Had I not encountered Dostoyevsky, Nietzsche, Blake, or Browning,
I cannot believe that my work would have been any different. At the
most they helped me to disentangle my thought. And even then? I
took pleasure in hailing those in whom I recognized my thought. But
that thought was mine, and it is not to them that I owe it. Otherwise
it would be valueless. The great influence perhaps that I have really
undergone is that of Goethe, and even then I am not sure whether or
not my admiration for Greek literature and Hellenism would not have
sufficed to counterbalance my original Christian formation.

Furthermore, I feel rich enough never to have tried to pass off as
mine the thoughts that belonged to someone else.

Alibert told me that he wondered if one ought not to see precaution, prudence on the part of Racine's wife, much rather than the indifference that is generally imputed to her, in her refusal to read or
see any play by her husband. Shouldn't one see in it respect for the
work and a need of giving assurance wholeheartedly in a domain that
escaped her competence? [43]

This is about what Alibert told me; but I have just reread in the
biographical notice (at the head of the Grands Écrivains de la France
edition) what Paul Mesnard wrote on this subject, which does not
contribute, it must be admitted, to these suppositions. Perhaps Alibert
outlined that thesis to me only because he was thinking more of Cuverville and of me than of Racine, and perhaps he was attempting,
under this pretext, to show me discreetly how capable he was of understanding the modesty and secret wisdom of such a feminine re-

---

[43] I believe today that one must see in it a quite Christian horror of
what belongs to the demon, and that Mme Racine had much to do with her
husband's silence. (Added in 1929.) [A.]

serve. In Racine's household it accompanied Racine's renunciation and almost the disavowal of his thought.

6 November

I am an unbeliever. I shall never be an ungodly man.

Those who claim to act according to rules of life (however beautiful those rules may be) strike me as idiots, or at least blunderers, incapable of taking advantage of life — I mean: of learning from life. In any case unbearable people.

9 November

One must resign oneself to it: rather than to remain sullen, deign to say a few banalities, a few stupidities. Moreover, this puts the other at ease.

Under whatever form it appears, there is no worse enemy than mysticism. I have reason to know. And I should like my deep knowledge of the subject, through repeated personal experience and through sympathy (for theoretical, or philosophical, or historical, or scientific knowledge of the mystical state scarcely informs one at all), to give some weight to my evidence. It is too easy to jump with Souday to the conclusion that every swerve in that direction implies a certain lack of gray matter. Sympathy — yes, sympathy, detachment and diffidence, and modesty can intervene. I claim to be much better qualified to denounce or accuse mysticism than someone who has never had to deal with it.

"But what do you mean by 'mystical'?"

"Whatever presupposes and demands the abdication of the reason."

10 November

Three hours of practice at the piano, regularly every day since my return to Paris — that is, since the 2nd; continuing moreover the Cuverville practice. I believe that nothing has ever given me a more immediate pleasure. Gladly, if I didn't have all the rest, I should devote the whole day to it. I bought under the Odéon arcades Liszt's transcriptions of Schubert's melodies, but enjoy playing only the Barcarolle and the *Erlkönig*. I am particularly working over Chopin's scherzos (abandoned for some time now), and especially the last one, the Barcarolle and the ballades.

There is a certain point of maturity of thought on either side of which the sentence that clothes it overstrains itself or becomes wrinkled. It is essential to gather it at the right moment.

Unbearable mania Jean Prévost has of always wanting to appear
more intelligent, and better educated, and better balanced and more
. . . etc., than the person of whom he is talking. Whether it be Pascal,
or Descartes, or Dostoyevsky.

11 November

And besides there is something absurd about this long practice
that leads to nothing and in which every day I use up the best of my
time, of my fervor. And if occasionally, after the second hour, I succeed in really satisfying myself, I probably experience less delight in
achieving perfection than sorrow at not being able to maintain it.

But this is not only true for the piano.

A poor woman comes to tell Eugène MacCown her troubles, the
sorry life that her lover, a young writer by the name of M. (I believe),
makes her lead. He beats her. This is because he is influenced by me.
"He goes to see Gide every day" (this woman tells Eugène), "tells
him that he has beaten me, and Gide says to him: 'Bravo; you did
right!'" Moreover, she is not taken in, and even before he has confessed it, she can tell by his look: "You have just been to see André
Gide."

With a few bits of malicious gossip of this type my reputation is
well established.

17 November

At moments I feel like complaining. Out of pride I manage to
check that desire. But my silence is not natural. I should often have
been better off to express my protest, which, repressed in this way,
poisons me. Yet what keeps me from speaking is that, if I did so today,
I should still be far from settling accounts. There is too much out-
standing. The little satisfaction I should get on one point would hu-
miliate me rather, so paltry would it appear to me.

The day will soon come when my *Corydon* will be found to be
very timorous. People will hardly be grateful to me for the desire for
justice that constantly tempers my thought. And I am hardly grateful
to myself for it. Everything constantly tells me and proves to me that
I was even more right than I thought. The examples I have at hand
constantly contribute new proofs to what I put forward timidly.

These words of Emmanuel Faÿ, which his brother repeated to me,
these words which were almost his *novissima verba*, haunt me, obsess
me: "There is no fun in playing in a world in which everyone is
cheating."

21 November

Back from Chartres, where M. and I had gone to see his brother Yves, who began his military service ten days ago.

I find old Céline somewhat haggard from boredom, fatigue, and fear. She was unable to sleep, imagining all night long that she heard the telephone ringing (she would have been utterly incapable of answering). The weather, moreover, has been lugubrious: "It never once *deceased* raining," she keeps saying.[44]

Nothing more lugubrious than such an old age, such a meaningless prolongation. "I don't know what's the matter with me," she says; "my eyes keep closing. . . . Ah! I am ready to be buried." And again: "It's probably my illness. The doctors told me I had—how do they call it now? You see, it escapes me—I don't know the name of anything any more. Oh yes: pains. . . ."

I fear she may be cold in the kitchen. "Oh, no, not so long as I keep moving. It's more in the evening if I try to read the paper for a bit. But then I go up to bed." And I tell her to come and read it in the dining-room; but she prefers her bed with a hot-water bottle.

"Well, Céline, don't you feel like going out a bit? It's Sunday."

"Ah! what would I do outside?"

24 November

B. sends me a series of American newspaper and magazine articles on the translation of *Les Faux-Monnayeurs*.

Sad to note that there is not one of them that is not better than the best of the articles that appeared in France.

With one or two exceptions, when a French critic wants to write an article about me, he strives not to explain or understand me, but to take up and maintain a position against me.

25 November

Is it because I have become more exigent? At the piano I feel farther from my aim than I did a few years ago. I believe that this is where the effect of age is most obvious: my gift of sympathy is decreasing and I am less inclined to assimilate the emotion of the musician I am interpreting; very complicated way of saying that I play less well.

Doubtless this decrease in sympathy comes also from the fact that I am becoming more clearly conscious of myself and my value; complicated way of saying that old age invites to egotism.

Noting the progressive decay of age requires the most difficult form of sincerity to obtain from oneself. A journal that kept track of it would

---

[44] There is no such word in French as the *décessé* she uses.

be vastly interesting. Moreover I do not believe that that decay is un-
avoidable, and, were it not for a slight weakening of my senses (sight
especially), I should barely feel touched by age; if I did not see it in
the mirror and if I did not constantly repeat it to myself, nothing in
me would remind me that three days ago I entered my fifty-ninth
year. But perhaps it is one of the privileges of age not to be too conscious itself of what is a glaring fact to everyone else.

> *Cuverville, 30 November*

I spend two mornings replying to the study (if one can use this
word) of my work by a certain Victor Poucel that appeared in
"*Études* — a Catholic review of general interest." And finally I do not
send my letter. What is the good? There is no chance of re-establishing
the truth. There is not one of my features that, voluntarily or involun-
tarily, is not falsified. But, after all, he is right, they are right to look
upon me as the enemy. The amusing thing is that I am likewise looked
upon as *the enemy* by their adversaries. It is essential not to let oneself
be crushed, or saddened, or exasperated, or conceited, but on the other
hand to find a certain equilibrium of the heart and mind in the balancing of these hatreds. And to keep *oneself* from hating.

> *13 December*

I receive a prodigious letter from the Jesuit Father Victor Poucel
in reply to the letter I made up my mind to send him after his two
long articles (*Études* — October-November). Ah, how I should like all
this to be published later on, for the greater edification of the reading
public! [45] He protests, most courteously moreover, against the expression "bad faith" that I had used. But his entire letter leads me to go a
bit farther in my thought: *good faith* is an essentially secular virtue,
which simple faith replaces.

> *Cuverville, 23 December*

They want to make of me a frightfully anxious person. I have no
other anxiety than that of seeing my thought misinterpreted.

Finally all hope is lost of saving the unfortunate prisoners of the
sunken submarine. Until yesterday they gave signs of life, and the
divers who, most dangerously, through the storm and the paralyzing
cold, went down to them, communicated with them by knocking

---

[45] Two letters from Gide to Father Poucel were published in *La Nouvelle Revue Française* for July 1928 and again in Volume XIV of Gide's
Œuvres complètes. The recipient also published them, together with his letter mentioned here (which he had asked Gide not to publish), in his little
book issued in 1929: *L'Esprit d'André Gide* (*The Mind of André Gide*).

against the hull; but day by day the answering knocks became weaker. Heroic, superhuman efforts were undertaken to get oxygen and light to the trapped men; but in vain. All that could be done was to tell them that they were being prayed for. Then, yesterday, the cable linking the submarine to the world of the living broke.

One cannot imagine a more horrible agony, in the cold, in the darkness, and among the dead and dying. . . . But even more horrible seem to me the prayers in this case. Their wives, their children, their friends, a whole nation was praying for them, was still praying, distractedly. What did those prayers say? "Father, we implore you; we beg you to save them — but . . . may your will be done." Did people hope to soften the wrath of an angry God, whatever forced him to take punishment through these cruel deaths . . . ? Urge him to reconsider the decision of his justice, of his wisdom . . . ? And, if he did not calm the storm, was this because He was not powerful enough or because they were not praying loud enough . . . ? or because the trapped men did not deserve this reprieve?

I should like the soul to be raised in such a way that it did not feel pushed to despair on learning suddenly that God has failed it. It is better to be sure of this in advance; and the best means of keeping Him from failing us is to learn to get along without Him.

There are doubtless very few lovers who do not feel, at certain moments, dreadfully imprisoned by their love.

DETACHED PAGES

If the book had not already appeared,[46] I should take care to add to the appendix several considerations that the excessive zeal of some may arouse.

Nothing more prejudicial to a cause, however excellent it may be, than certain exaggerations on the part of its defenders. The adversaries of that cause easily turn this into a weapon, which they turn against the cause, retaining and presenting to the public only the very exaggeration of certain claims, in themselves, however, thoroughly justified.

In the almost total ignorance of the public in regard to colonial questions, it is only too easy to mislead opinion in one direction or the other. No possible check. In case of a conflict, the victory most often goes to the one who speaks loudest, or longest, or last.

I should merely like to indicate here the few reflections I have had as a result of the polemics opened up concerning the abuses my book denounced.

---

[46] Voyage au Congo and Retour du Tchad (Travels in the Congo). [E.]

It seems to me, to begin with, that the famous question of portage, which has been especially brought up, has not been examined calmly. Were I to astonish or even to inspire indignation in some people, I must confess, to be frank, that I cannot denounce the custom of portage. Its abuses are frightful. In itself I cannot consider it an evil. Besides, it seems to me inevitable. Some people write, rather thoughtlessly: the railway, trucks, and boats must everywhere take the place of portage. That is easy to say. But for the railway tremendous construction work is required; for trucks, motor roads are needed; and as for the boats themselves, since the Congo becomes navigable again only at a great distance from its mouth, it is necessary — it was long necessary at least (see *The Heart of Darkness* [47]) — to transport through the jungle, on human backs, the heavy dismantled parts of any boat whatever.

Portage will therefore be, for a long time at least, necessary. The African native, moreover, submits to it without any protest, if the load that is imposed on him is not too heavy, and especially *if he is not taken too far from his village — and if it is a time of year when the cultivation of his crops, which must assure his family's life, do not require his presence.*

But one cannot go through a village in those equatorial regions without noticing the habit of the natives, from their earliest age, of carrying loads. . . . I dare not say for their amusement or pleasure, but quite naturally. Just think that they have neither wheelbarrows nor hand-carts, nor yet any beast of burden. I am willing to believe, even, that it is to that habit of carrying rather heavy weights on their heads that the natives — men as well as women — often owe the nobility of their bearing and posture. At least, I remember that the remark was made about the ancient canephori. But it goes without saying that it is not æsthetic reasons that I should like to have prevail. Children when still very young (the little girls especially) carry on their back, on their hip, a brother or sister just a little younger. This on the other hand, it will be said, runs the risk of deforming them. Not at all. I add this, in reply to exaggerated and unseasonable commiserations: the load we impose on our soldiers in the field is considerably higher than that which it is customary to impose on bearers. That load must not normally excede forty-four pounds. So it is not exactly there that the abuse lies. And, once more, one runs the risk of compromising the most just cause by protesting at random.

Everywhere where the administration has been able sufficiently to regulate the functioning of the halting-places, they are properly spaced, and the relays are organized in such a way as not to take the native

---

[47] A powerful story by Joseph Conrad (1902), which is laid in the Congo. Gide cites it frequently in his *Travels in the Congo*.

more than four, five, or six days at most from his home point. The administration, in addition, sees that the natives are paid, rather little to be sure, but, after all, sufficiently. If there is some abuse, the conscientious administrator can and must clear it up. So it is not there that the evil lies.

But, it cannot be too often repeated, in order to persuade those who are left unmoved by a question of mere humaneness, that all the abuses in our equatorial colonies have in common this particularly deplorable aspect, that, to make a greater profit, the Companies are ruining the colony. The natives die or desert in great numbers, and labor cannot be found for the most useful, most urgent undertakings. This consideration ought to touch the most obstinate, since it is addressed to their most sensitive part: the purse.

Care has been taken to shout aloud that my attacks were directed against our colonial administration; and this is utterly false. It was hoped, thereby, to ruin the value of my evidence. I met down there many remarkable administrators, accomplishing an extraordinarily difficult task with intelligence, patience, and courage; and, as for the others, they were chiefly lacking in help. Many abuses and exactions would be made impossible if only the supervision were better conducted, if the administrators were more numerous. Often overwhelmed by an amount of work he cannot handle, a minor official loses courage, isolated in the jungle and not feeling himself to be part of an organization.

Glossary of Persons

MENTIONED IN VOLUME II
OF THE JOURNALS

N.B. Not all the names listed in the Index are to be found in this Glossary. Servants, tradesmen, chance acquaintances, and others sufficiently identified in the text — together with the most famous in all domains — have been omitted here. Other names have simply resisted research.

Originally intended to identify the specifically French names that are presumably known to the author's compatriots, the Glossary has grown in the making to include all the persons about whom English-speaking readers might have questions.

André Gide and his friends have been most helpful in supplying information.

Certain names included in the Glossary of Volume I are reproduced here because they are mentioned again in this Volume.

J. O'B.

ADAM, PAUL (1862–1920), French novelist of manners and history (*La Force, Le Lion d'Arras*) and dramatist.

ALAIN (pseud. of Émile Chartier, 1868–), French essayist and philosopher whose influence for realism and liberal independence spread to a whole generation through his teaching and his superior journalism.

ALBÉNIZ, ISAAC (1860–1909), Spanish composer often inspired by folk themes.

ALIBERT, FRANÇOIS-PAUL (1873–), French poet of Virgilian temper, strongly influenced by Mallarmé.

ALLARD, ROGER (1885–), French poet.

ALLÉGRET, ANDRÉ, second son of Élie Allégret, with whom André Gide traveled in Corsica (1923).

ALLÉGRET, ÉLIE, Protestant minister, tutor of André Gide and best man at his wedding. Founded the French mission at Talagouga in the Gaboon and later became director of the Center of French Protestant Missions. Of his five children, André Gide adopted the third, Marc.

ALLÉGRET, ÉRIC, fourth son of Élie Allégret.

ALLÉGRET, JEAN, eldest son of Élie Allégret; died of tuberculosis at Arcachon.

ALLÉGRET, MARC, third son of Élie Allégret; adopted by André Gide, whom he accompanied on trip to the Congo (1925–6). Excellent scenario-writer, author of *Lac aux dames*.

ALLÉGRET, SUZANNE, wife of Élie Allégret, who accompanied him to the Congo when he went as a missionary.

AMIEL, HENRI-FRÉDÉRIC (1821–81), Swiss introspective author of an *Intimate Journal.*

ANDLER, CHARLES (1866–1933), French professor of history and political economy, who specialized in the subject of modern Germany.

ARNAULD, ANTOINE (1612–94), French theologian, defender of Jansenism against the Jesuits, friend of Pascal and Racine.

ARTSYBASHEV, MIKHAIL PETROVICH (1878–1927), Russian novelist, playwright, and essayist of violent scenes and erotic inspiration, best known for the novel *Sanine.*

AVELINE, CLAUDE (1901–   ), French novelist, essayist, and publisher.

BAKST, LÉON (1866–1924), Russian painter, particularly designer of theater scenery and chief painter of scenery for the Russian ballets of Diaghilev.

BANVILLE, THÉODORE DE (1823–91), French poet of *Odes funambulesques* and dramatist of *Gringoire.* Disciple of Théophile Gautier and exponent of art for art's sake.

BARBEY D'AUREVILLY, JULES (1808–89), French poet, novelist, and critic of originality and colorful personality.

BARBUSSE, HENRI (1874–1935), French novelist of naturalistic tendency, whose war novel *Under Fire* was a great sensation in 1916.

BARRÈS, MAURICE (1862–1923), French novelist who early won a place of distinction through his youthful "cult of the ego" and then evolved into a traditionalist and advocated "the cult of the earth and the dead"; his novels of Alsace-Lorraine preached a return to regionalism and expressed his ardent nationalism.

BARTHOU, LOUIS (1862–1934), French statesman and writer, several times Minister of the Third Republic and twice Premier, in 1913 and 1930.

BASSERMANN, DIETER, German translator of *Les Caves du Vatican* (1922).

BASSIANO, PRINCESSE DE (1882–   ), née Marguerite Chapin, of New York, wife of Roffredo Caetani, first Prince of Bassiano; patroness of art and literature, who subsidized, among other works, the quarterly review *Commerce.*

BATAILLE, HENRY (1872–1922), French dramatist of popular comedies of the psychology of love, such as *Maman Colibri* and *La Marche nuptiale.*

BAZALGETTE, LÉON (1873–1928), French literary critic and translator of Whitman, Pinero, etc.

BEAUNIER, ANDRÉ (1869–1925), French novelist and critic, who for many years wrote most of the literary criticism in the *Revue des deux mondes.*

BEARDSLEY, AUBREY VINCENT (1872–98), English illustrator in black and white and editor of the *Yellow Book.*

BEDDOES, THOMAS LOVELL (1803–49), English dramatist, essayist, and poet of macabre inspiration, best known for *Death's Jest-Book,* a play in the Elizabethan manner.

BELOT, GUSTAVE (1859–1929), French moral philosopher, and professor at the Graduate School for Social Studies.

BÉRANGER, PIERRE JEAN DE (1780–1857), French writer of popular songs.

BÉRAUD, HENRI (1885–   ), French journalist and novelist.

BERGSON, HENRI (1859–1941), French philosopher of "creative evolution," who exalted the faculty of intuition over the pure intellect.

BERNARD, TRISTAN (1866–1947), French comic dramatist, famous especially for *L'Anglais tel qu'on le parle, Le Petit Café, Triplepatte.*

BERNHARDT, SARAH (1844–1923), French actress.

BERNSTEIN, HENRY (1876–   ), French dramatist of great force and wide popularity (*Le Secret, La Jalousie, Judith*).

BERTHELOT, PHILIPPE (1866–1934), French diplomat who after numerous successful missions became director of political affairs (1919) and general secretary (1920) of the Ministry of Foreign Affairs.

BERTRAND, LOUIS (1866–1941), French novelist of the Mediterranean area and exponent of Latin imperialism; elected to the French Academy in 1926.

BEVER, ADOLPHE VAN (1871–1927), French literary historian, anthologist, and critic, secretary of the Théâtre de l'Œuvre (1893–6) and of the *Mercure de France,* 1897–1912).

BIDOU, HENRY (1873–1943), French historian and critic.

BINET-SANGLÉ, CHARLES (1868–   ), French psychologist who studied religious psychology and wrote, among others, a book entitled *The Madness of Jesus.*

BLANCHE, JACQUES-ÉMILE (1861–1942), French painter, known especially for his portraits, who also wrote his interesting recollections.

BLEI, FRANZ (1871–   ), Austrian writer who, besides other translations from English and French, translated Gide's *Bethsabé, Prométhée,* and *Roi Candaule* into German; founder of the review *Hyperion.*

BLUM, LÉON (1872–   ), critic, essayist, and political figure. Member of the Council of State (1895), president of the Socialist Party; director of the newspaper *Le Populaire* (1921–40); Prime Minister (1936–7, 1938, and 1946).

BOCCON-GIBAULD, lawyer who worked very effectively in the Foyer Franco-Belge during the first World War; great friend of Edith Wharton.

BÖCKLIN, ARNOLD (1827–1901), Swiss painter.

BOILEAU, NICOLAS (1636–1711), French poet of the classic age, best known for his *Art of Poetry* and his *Satires*, which established him as the critical arbiter of the reign of Louis XIV.

BONHEUR, RAYMOND, French composer, great friend of Carrière, Samain, Jammes, etc. André Gide wrote the first act of a light-opera scenario for him, but the project was dropped before completion.

BONNARD, PIERRE (1867–1947), French painter and illustrator of the impressionist school.

BORDEAUX, HENRY (1870–   ), French novelist of conservative, Catholic fiction. He became an Academician in 1920.

BORROW, GEORGE (1803–81), Scottish novelist of picaresque, auto-biographical tales such as *Lavengro* and *The Bible in Spain*.

BOSSUET, JACQUES BÉNIGNE (1627–1704), French bishop and famous preacher at the court of Louis XIV.

BOUGAINVILLE, LOUIS-ANTOINE DE (1729–1814), French mathematician, diplomat, and military man, fought under Montcalm at Québec, explored the South Pacific, fought in the American Revolutionary War, and became a Senator under Napoleon. The relation of his *Voyage around the World* was made famous by Diderot's philosophic "Supplement" to it.

BOUHOURS, FATHER (1628–1702), French literary critic and arbiter of style at the height of the classic period.

BOUILHET, LOUIS (1822–69), French poet of mixed romantic and realistic tendencies, popularizer of Oriental exoticism, and friend of Flaubert.

BOULENGER, JACQUES (1879–   ), French literary historian and critic.

BOUNI-RECLUS, MME, sister of Élisée Reclus, the famous geographer and theoretician of anarchism; she devoted herself to the Foyer Franco-Belge during the first World War.

BOURGET, PAUL (1852–1935), French novelist, dramatist, and essayist, who with Anatole France and Maurice Barrès dominated the literary scene before the first World War. His most characteristic novels are the psychological study *Le Disciple* (1889) and the sociological thesis *L'Étape* (1902).

BOYLESVE, RENÉ (1867–1926), one of the masters of the French psychological novel (*La Becquée, L'Enfant à la balustrade*).

BRÉAL, AUGUSTE, son of the eminent philologist Michel Bréal; French painter who studied under Gustave Moreau, and author of a penetrating study of Velázquez.

BREHM, ALFRED-EDMOND (1829–84), German traveler and naturalist, author of an *Illustrated Life of Animals*.

BRETON, ANDRÉ, (1896–), French poet, novelist, and critic who founded and led the surrealist group.

BRIAND, ARISTIDE (1862–1932), French statesman, who repeatedly occupied the most important ministries and was twelve times Premier, working consistently from the Armistice until his death for international peace (Locarno, Thoiry, and the League of Nations).

BRONTË, EMILY (1818–48), English poet, and novelist of *Wuthering Heights*.

BROUSSON, JEAN-JACQUES (1878–), French writer who based his sensational *Anatole France Himself* on his recollections as secretary to the famous writer.

BRUNETIÈRE, FERDINAND (1849–1906), scholarly French critic and historian of literature, who applied theories of evolutionism to literary genres such as the novel, poetry, criticism, the theater.

BRUNOT, FERDINAND (1860–1938), French linguistic historian and honorary dean of the Paris Faculty of Letters, whose monumental *History of the French Language* in 15 volumes appeared from 1905 to 1935.

BUFFON, GEORGES LOUIS LECLERC, COMTE DE (1707–88), French naturalist.

BUISSON, FERDINAND (1841–1932), French Director of Primary Education from 1879 to 1896 and editor of a dictionary of pedagogy.

BUNIN, IVAN (1870–), Russian novelist and writer of short stories who carried on the tradition of Tolstoy and Chekhov. Since the Revolution he has lived in France; he received the Nobel Prize in 1933.

BURCKHARDT, JACOB (1818–97), German historian, author of *The Civilization of the Renaissance in Italy*.

BUSONI, FERRUCCIO (1866–1924), Italian-German pianist and composer known especially for his arrangements of Bach.

BUSSY, DOROTHY, English translator of André Gide (*The Immoralist, Strait is the Gate, The Counterfeiters*, etc.), sister of Lytton Strachey and wife of the painter Simon Bussy.

BUSSY, SIMON (1870–), French painter, pupil of Gustave Moreau in whose studio he worked contemporaneously with Matisse, Rouault, Marquet, and others. His works in oils and pastels consist of landscapes, pictures of animals, and portraits, notably of Valéry and Gide.

BUTLER, SAMUEL (1835–1902), English novelist of *The Way of All Flesh* and vigorous satirist of *Erewhon*, etc.

CAPIELLO, MME, sister of Mme Mühlfeld and of Mme Paul Adam.

CASTAGNO, ANDREA DEL (1390?–1457), Italian painter of the Renaissance.

CAVALCANTI, ALBERTO (1897–), Brazilian-born film director and producer who has worked chiefly in Paris and in London.

CÉZANNE, PAUL (1839–1906), French painter, who broke with impressionism to create a solid new style.

CHABRIER, ALÉXIS (1841–94), French musician and composer, especially of operas and operettas.

CHAMFORT, NICOLAS-SÉBASTIEN ROCH, called DE (1741–94), French moralist.

CHAMPION, ÉDOUARD (1882–1938), French literary historian who has worked on Stendhal, Gérard de Nerval, Chateaubriand, etc.

CHARDIN, JEAN-BAPTISTE SIMÉON (1699–1779), French painter especially appreciated for his *genre* scenes and still-lives.

CHATEAUBRIAND, FRANÇOIS-RENÉ (1768–1848), French poet, novelist, essayist, and political figure who ushered in the romantic movement and left examples of a noble style for future generations.

CHAUMEIX, ANDRÉ (1874–), French literary critic, who wrote regularly in the *Revue hebdomadaire*, the *Revue de Paris*, and the *Revue des deux mondes*. He was long editor-in-chief of the *Revue des deux mondes* and a member of the Academy.

CHAUSSON, ERNEST (1855–99), French composer, pupil of César Franck.

CHAUVEAU, DR. CLAUDE (1861–?), French specialist in nose and throat diseases, Senator, and author of studies in the laws of social insurance, etc.

CHEKHOV, ANTON (1860–1904), Russian *conteur* and dramatist of moods and inner action expressed in suggestive understatement.

CHÉNIER, ANDRÉ (1762–94), French poet, whose work, published after his early execution by the revolutionary tribunal, seemed to the romantics a powerful romantic outburst, but was in reality soberly classical.

CHUQUET, ARTHUR (1853–1925), French historian of the nineteenth century and literary historian.

CLAUDEL, PAUL (1868–), French poet and diplomat (Ambassador to Tokyo and to Washington) whose odes and verse dramas (*L'Annonce faite à Marie* and *Le Soulier de satin*) struck a new note of genius. Elected to the Academy in 1946.

CLEMENCEAU, GEORGES (1841–1929), French political figure who occupied the highest positions, organized the Allied victory in 1918, and negotiated for France the Treaty of Versailles.

COCTEAU, JEAN (1892–   ), French poet, novelist, and dramatist long associated with all advanced artistic movements.

COMBETTE, BERNARD, French author of a collection of short stories and a novel, *L'Isolement* (1929), both published by Gallimard.

CONGREVE, WILLIAM (1670–1729), English dramatist of comedies of manners such as *Love for Love* and *The Way of the World*.

CONSTANT, BENJAMIN (1767–1830), French statesman and author of a powerful novel of psychological analysis, *Adolphe*.

COPEAU, AGNÈS, Danish-born wife of Jacques Copeau.

COPEAU, JACQUES (1879–   ), French critic and theatrical producer, who, after founding the *Nouvelle Revue Française* with Gide and others in 1909, revolutionized the French theater in 1913 by creating the Théâtre du Vieux-Colombier with its new style of simplicity and sincerity.

COPEAU, PASCAL, son of Jacques Copeau. Distinguished himself in the Resistance to the German occupation of France.

COPPET, MARCEL DE, French colonial official who served first as Governor, then as Governor-General in French Equatorial Africa. Gide and Marc Allégret went to meet him in the Chad when he had just been named Governor. He took as his second wife the daughter of his old friend Roger Martin du Gard.

COQUELIN, CONSTANT (1841–1909), French actor, famous for tragic roles.

COURTELINE, GEORGES (pseud. of Georges Moinaux, 1860–1929), French satirist in drama and fiction, who ridiculed officialdom in civil and military life.

CRANACH, LUCAS (1472–1553), German painter and engraver.

CURTIUS, ERNST-ROBERT (1886–   ), German philologist and critic who has taught French history and literature at Bonn, Marburg, and Heidelberg.

DAUDET, LÉON (1867–1942), French novelist and polemicist who entered politics as a disciple of Maurras and representative of the royalist party.

DEBUSSY, CLAUDE ACHILLE (1862–1918), French composer, whose new harmonies and literary associations (as a faithful member of Mallarmé's group he composed lyric poems inspired by Verlaine, Mallarmé, Louÿs, Rossetti, etc.) led to the apotheosis of symbolism in music in his opera *Pelléas et Mélisande* (1902).

DEHERME, GEORGES (1867–1937), French sociologist, believer in positivist doctrines, and founder of popular universities (1898) providing reading-rooms, game-rooms, discussion-rooms, evening lectures, and Sunday concerts for working men.

DELACROIX, EUGÈNE (1799–1863), French painter of the romantic school, famous for his brilliant color.

DELACRE, JULES, French actor and director of a Belgian theatrical company.

DELCASSÉ, THÉODORE (1852–1923), French political figure who several times occupied the Ministry of Foreign Affairs.

DELTEIL, JOSEPH (1894–   ), French novelist of light satirical works such as *Joan of Arc, The Poilus,* etc.

DENNERY or D'ENNERY (pseud. of Adolphe Philippe, 1811–99), French popular dramatist and novelist, known chiefly for his melodramas.

DESJARDINS, ANNE, daughter of Paul Desjardins, who became Mme Jacques Heurgon.

DESJARDINS, PAUL (1859–1940), French moralist whose *Devoir présent* (1892) proclaimed the necessity for a moral awakening, which he worked to achieve in founding the same year L'Union pour l'Action Morale, later L'Union pour la Vérité, and finally the Entretiens de Pontigny, which embraced in a spirit of inquiry all the great literary, social, æsthetic, political, and religious problems of the age.

DESMAREST, ALBERT, French painter, and first cousin of André Gide.

DIAGHILEV, SERGEI PAVLOVICH (1872–1929), Russian impresario of the modern ballet who produced *Boris Godunov* in 1908 with Chaliapin in the cast, in 1909 inaugurated the Russian ballets in Paris, and became one of the most important figures in the history of the ballet.

DIDEROT, DENIS (1713–84), French philosopher, critic, dramatist, etc., who edited the great *Encyclopédie;* a fecund writer and one of the great forces of the age of Enlightenment.

DOUGLAS, LORD ALFRED (1870–1945), English poet famous for his relationship with Oscar Wilde, which led to the notorious trial in which Wilde sued Douglas's father, the Marquess of Queensberry.

DREYFUS, ALFRED (1859–1935), French officer convicted of treason in 1894, whose case was eventually reopened after a vigorous campaign; in 1906 he was acquitted and released from prison.

DRIEU LA ROCHELLE, PIERRE (1893–1944), French novelist, essayist, and dramatist whose work reflects the unrest of the twenties and a sincere form of fascism that made him an intellectual collaborationist during the German occupation.

DROUIN, DOMINIQUE, son of Marcel Drouin; he spent much time in Ethiopia.

DROUIN, JACQUES, son of Marcel Drouin and nephew of André Gide.

DROUIN, JEANNE, née Rondeaux, sister of Mme André Gide and wife of Marcel Drouin.

DROUIN, MARCEL (1870–1946), French professor of philosophy in Alençon, Bordeaux, and Paris and, under the pseudonym of Michel Arnauld, essayist and critic. As a classmate of André Gide and Pierre Louÿs, he founded with them *Potache-Revue* and *La Conque* (1891); in 1908, after a brilliant record at the École Normale Supérieure and sojourns in Germany, was instrumental in founding the *Nouvelle Revue Française* with his brother-in-law, André Gide.

DRUET, E., French photographer, who established an art gallery dealing in such modern painters as Bonnard, Rouault, Vuillard.

DU BOS, CHARLES (1882–1939), French literary critic of great taste and penetration, who devoted much of his interest to foreign literatures (notably English); he wrote a book on André Gide at about the same time that he was being reconverted to Catholicism.

DUCOTÉ, ÉDOUARD (1870–1929), French poet, who became editor of *L'Ermitage* (1897–1906), grouping around him Gourmont, Ghéon, Claudel, Gide, Jammes, Copeau, etc.

DUHAMEL, GEORGES (1884–   ), French novelist (incidentally poet, essayist, dramatist), who won fame for his depiction of suffering humanity as seen by a military surgeon and proceeded to paint a picture of modern society (*Pasquier Chronicles*). After being a most effective editor of the *Mercure de France,* he was named perpetual secretary of the French Academy.

DUKAS, PAUL (1865–1935), French composer of *The Sorcerer's Apprentice*, etc.

DULLIN, CHARLES (1884–   ), French actor and theatrical producer, who after distinguishing himself as a member of Copeau's theater founded his own artistic and highly successful Théâtre de l'Atelier in Paris.

DUMAS, ALEXANDRE, *fils* (1824–95), realistic and social dramatist of *La Dame aux camélias, La Question d'argent*, etc.

DUMAS, GEORGES (1866–?), French psychologist internationally known for his studies in mental pathology.

DUPARC, HENRI (1848–1933), French composer of songs, pupil of César Franck.

DUPOUEY, PIERRE DOMINIQUE (1877–1915), French naval officer, a close friend of André Gide from 1903 until his death at the front. He became converted to Catholicism, and his example was the dominant factor in Henri Ghéon's conversion. Gide and Ghéon published his fervent letters in 1916.

DUVERNOIS, HENRI (1875–1937), French novelist and dramatist of psychological finesse.

ECKERMANN, JOHANN PETER (1792–1854), German amanuensis of Goethe and author of the famous *Conversations of Goethe with Eckermann.*

EDWARDS, MME, sister of Cipa Godebski and later Mme José-Maria Sert. Took an active part in the literary and artistic movements of the late nineteenth and early twentieth centuries, promoting, for instance, the Ballets Russes of Diaghilev.

EM., *see* Gide, Mme André.

ESPINAS, JEANNE, daughter of the economist Charles Gide and wife of Pierre Espinas.

ESPINAS, PIERRE, mining engineer, son-in-law of Charles Gide.

ETCHEVÈRE, MME D', Gide's secretary for several months; took an active part in the Foyer Franco-Belge in 1914.

FABRE, JEAN-HENRI (1823–1915), French arithmetician, physicist, chemist, and naturalist, who because of his famous studies of entomology has been called "the insects' Homer."

FABULET, LOUIS (1862–1933), French translator of Kipling.

FAGUET, ÉMILE (1874–1916), French literary historian and vigorous critic, who also wrote philosophical and sociological studies.

FALCONET, ÉTIENNE MAURICE (1716–91), French sculptor.

FARGUE, LÉON-PAUL (1878-1947), French poet in verse and prose of the delicate world of imagination and hallucination.

FARQUHAR, GEORGE (1678–1707), English dramatist of manners (*The Beaux' Stratagem*, etc.).

FAURÉ, GABRIEL-URBAIN (1845–1924), French composer, who wrote for the piano, chorus, chamber orchestra, and full orchestra as well as for the church and the stage. With Debussy he contributed to the rebirth of French music, and he renewed the classic tradition of Couperin and Rameau.

FAŸ, BERNARD (1893–   ), French historian specialized in American matters and in Freemasonry; condemned to life imprisonment in 1945 for collaboration with the enemy.

FAŸ, EMMANUEL, French painter who died young in New York; brother of Bernard Faÿ and great friend of Marc Allégret.

FÉNELON, FRANÇOIS DE SALIGNAC DE LA MOTHE (1651–1715), French bishop, royal tutor, and exponent of quietism, for which he was condemned by Rome at the instigation of Bossuet; his most famous work is the *Aventures de Télémaque.*

FEUILLET, OCTAVE (1821–90), French idealistic novelist, whose *Roman d'un jeune homme pauvre* (1858) was widely read.

FEYDEAU, ERNEST (1821–73), popular French dramatist and novelist, author of *Fanny* (1858).

FONTAINAS, ANDRÉ (1865–), Belgian-born symbolist poet and disciple of Mallarmé, interpreter of English-language poets such as Shelley and Poe, and sensitive art critic.

FONTAINE, ARTHUR (1860–1931), French sociologist and economist.

FRANCE, ANATOLE (1844–1924), French novelist and story-teller (who began his career as poet and literary critic), famous for his limpid style, delicate irony, and skepticism (*Penguin Island, The Revolt of the Angels*, etc.).

FRANCK, CÉSAR (1822–90), Belgian composer.

FRANCK, HENRI (1888–1912), French poet and intellectual leader, who left a long poem, some scattered essays, and a stimulating correspondence with his friends. Studied at the École Normale Supérieure (1906–9), then contributed to *La Phalange* and the *Nouvelle Revue Française*.

FRANÇOISE, *see* Gilbert, Françoise.

FRATELLINI, PAUL (1877–), FRANÇOIS (1879–), and ALBERT (1886–), circus clowns long popular at the Cirque Medrano and Cirque d'Hiver of Paris.

FRY, ROGER ELIOT (1866–1934), English art historian and critic.

GALLIÉNI, JOSEPH-SIMON (1849–1916), French general and administrator who distinguished himself in the Sudan, in Madagascar, and as Governor of Paris in 1914, when he engineered the Marne victory.

GALLIMARD, GASTON (1881–), French publisher, who became administrator of the *Nouvelle Revue Française* when founded in 1908–9 and later of the publishing house; also acted as business manager of Copeau's Théâtre du Vieux-Colombier.

GARNETT, CONSTANCE BLACK (1862–1946), English translator of Chekhov and Dostoyevsky.

GAUTIER, THÉOPHILE (1811–72), French poet and novelist, who, heading the school of art for art's sake, acts as a pivot between romanticism and naturalism.

GEBHART, ÉMILE (1839–1908), French historian of the Renaissance in Italy and France.

GÉRARD, *see* Gide, Paul.

GERMAIN, ANDRÉ (1881–), French poet of mannerist tendency and literary critic.

GHÉON, HENRI (1875–1944), French novelist, dramatist, and critic, who began writing tragedies of the people (*Le Pain, L'Eau de vie*) and, after his conversion to Catholicism in 1917, revived the miracle play (*Le Pauvre sous l'escalier*). Closely associated with the early *Nouvelle Revue Française* and with the Théâtre du Vieux-Colombier.

GIDE, MME ANDRÉ (?-1938), née Emmanuèle Rondeaux.

GIDE, CATHERINE (1923-), daughter of André Gide.

GIDE, CHARLES (1847-1932), younger brother of André Gide's father; famous professor of economics in Paris, who wrote more than a score of studies on political economy.

GIDE, GÉRARD, pseudonym for Paul Gide.

GIDE, PAUL, son of the economist Charles Gide and cousin of André Gide. (He figures in the *Journals* under the pseudonym Gérard.)

GILBERT, FRANÇOISE, daughter of Marcel and Valentine Gilbert and niece of André Gide.

GILBERT, NICOLE, daughter of Marcel and Valentine Gilbert and niece of André Gide.

GILBERT, VALENTINE, née Rondeaux, sister of Mme André Gide and wife of Marcel Gilbert.

GIRAUDOUX, JEAN (1882-1944), French novelist and dramatist, possessed of an original and beautiful style, who revived preciosity in literature.

GISSING, GEORGE ROBERT (1857-1903), English novelist famous chiefly for *The Private Papers of Henry Ryecroft*.

GOBILLARD, PAULE (?-1946), French painter who studied with her aunt Berthe Morisot and with Renoir; elder sister of Mme Paul Valéry and close friend of Mallarmé, Redon, Degas, etc.

GOBINEAU, JOSEPH-ARTHUR DE (1816-82), French diplomat and writer responsible for certain modern race theories.

GODEBSKI, CIPA, Polish-born art-lover who gathered painters, musicians, and writers at his house; brother of Mme Edwards, who later married José-Maria Sert.

GOGOL, NIKOLAI VASILIEVICH (1809-52), Russian novelist of satirical works, such as *Dead Souls*.

GONCOURT, EDMOND DE (1822-96), with his brother Jules (1830-70), was a leader of French naturalism in both the documentary novel and the theater. He also ranks as an art critic through his studies of Hokusai, Utamaro, and eighteenth-century art. The 9 volumes of *Journals* depict the society of their time. By his will he founded the Goncourt Academy.

GOSSE, SIR EDMUND (1849-1928), English critic, biographer, and poet, best known for his scholarly studies of Scandinavian and English literature. He was librarian of the House of Lords, 1904-14.

GOURMONT, JEAN DE (1877–1928), French novelist and literary critic; younger brother of Remy de Gourmont.

GRANADOS, ENRIQUE (1867–1916), Spanish composer of piano pieces and of the opera *Goyescas*.

GRANDVILLE, JEAN-IGNACE-ISIDORE (1803–47), French draftsman and caricaturist, who generally combined human and animal characteristics in his figures and may well have inspired Lewis Carroll in this regard.

GRIMM, MELCHIOR (1723–1807), German chronicler of Parisian intellectual life, whose correspondence records the achievements of the *philosophes*.

GROETHUYSEN, BERNARD (1880–1946), German-born and French naturalized philosopher, critic, and historian of ideas. Of Dutch and Russian parentage, he had the European spirit. A close associate of many French writers and artists, he was an ardent communist.

GROSS, HANS GUSTAVE ADOLPH (1847–1915), German author of practical handbooks on *Criminal Investigation* and *Criminal Psychology*.

GUÉRIN, MAURICE DE (1810–39), French prose-poet of romantic period strongly Catholic in sentiment.

GYP (pseud. of Marie de RIQUETTI de MIRABEAU, Comtesse de Martel de Janville, 1849–1932), French novelist and dramatist of manners.

HAGUENIN, ÉMILE (1872–1924), French professor of modern literature, a close friend of Marcel Drouin at the École Normale. From 1901 to 1914 he taught at the University of Berlin and after the war was head of the information service of the Reparations Commission in Berlin.

HAMP, PIERRE (1876–), French novelist of the working man (*Le Travail, Le Rail, La Peine des hommes*) and the hardships of the various trades.

HEREDIA, JOSÉ-MARIA DE (1842–1905), French poet of the Parnassian movement, whose single volume of sonnets, *Les Trophées* (1893), won him election to the French Academy.

HERMANT, ABEL (1862–), French novelist and dramatist of manners, appreciated for his wit. Elected to the Academy in 1927, he was excluded from that assembly in 1945 as a propagandist for the Vichy regime.

HERRICK, ROBERT (1591–1674), English poet of the *Hesperides* (1648).

HERVIEU, PAUL (1857–1915), French dramatist of social ideas, best known for *La Course du flambeau* (1901).

HEYWOOD, THOMAS (?–1650?), English dramatist, perhaps best known for *A Woman Kilde with Kindnesse* (1603).

HIRSCH, CHARLES-HENRY (1870–), French novelist, dramatist, and short-story writer.

HIRSCH, MAURICE, BARON DE (1831–96), German-born Austrian financier and philanthropist who enriched himself through Near East railway concessions and speculations in sugar and copper.

HOBBES, THOMAS (1588–1679), English philosopher of nature and man, whose *Leviathan* (1651) expounds his political philosophy.

HONEGGER, ARTHUR (1892–), French composer of Swiss-German parentage who wrote music for Gide's *Saül*.

HUBER, FRANCOIS (1750–1831), Swiss entomologist known for his valuable observations on bees, which he carried on, because of his blindness, through a conscientious secretary.

HUDSON, STEPHEN (pseud. of Sydney Schiff, ?–1944), English novelist of *Richard Kurt* (1919) and *Tony* (1924) and translator of the last section of Proust's work, *Time Regained* (1931).

HUDSON, W. H. (1841–1922), American-born British naturalist and novelist of the South American pampas, best known for his *Green Mansions* (1904).

HUET, PIERRE-DANIEL (1630–1721), French erudite critic, opponent of Descartes, theorist of the novel, and Bishop of Avranches.

HUMIÈRES, ROBERT D' (1868–1915), French translator of Kipling, who was killed at the front.

IEHL, JULES, Alsatian novelist and great friend of Charles-Louis Philippe; in 1909 his first book, *Cauët*, was highly praised by discerning critics. When Gide met him he was a clerk in an express office, but Eugène Rouart helped him to become justice of the peace at first at Albi and then at Poitiers, where he later held more important judicial offices. In 1910 André Gide made his trip in the Pyrenees and in Andorra with Iehl and Eugène Rouart. Some time between 1909 and 1912 he took the pseudonym of Michel Yell.

INGRES, JEAN-AUGUSTE DOMINIQUE (1780–1867), French painter famous for the perfection of his draftsmanship.

JACOB, MAX (1876–1944), French poet and painter, who revitalized modern poetry with a new vision and elegance. A Jew converted to Catholicism, he died in a concentration camp.

JACQUES, *see* Drouin, Jacques.

JALOUX, EDMOND (1878–), French novelist of subdued atmosphere and literary critic of sound judgment, who entered the French Academy in 1936.

JAMES, HENRY (1843–1916), American novelist of *Portrait of a Lady, The Golden Bowl,* and *The Ambassadors.*

JAMES, WILLIAM (1842–1910), American philosopher of pragmatism and psychologist, brother of Henry James.

JAMMES, FRANCIS (1868–1938), French intimist poet, who sang of his native Pyrenees with a childlike sensuality and an increasingly orthodox Catholic faith.

JARRY, ALFRED (1873–1907), French humorist in novel, drama, and poetry, whose fantastic works such as *Ubu Roi* foreshadowed surrealism.

JAURÈS, JEAN (1859–1914), French political figure and vigorous journalist; one of the leaders of the Socialist Party, he was assassinated by a fanatic on the eve of the first World War.

JEANNE, *see* Drouin, Jeanne.

JEANNIE, *see* Valéry, Jeannie.

JOFFRE, JOSEPH-JACQUES-CÉSAIRE (1852–1931), French marshal who commanded the French army from 1914 to 1916.

JOHANNET, RENÉ (1884–   ), French literary critic and student of nationalism.

JOUHANDEAU, MARCEL (1888–   ), French novelist whose bitter probings into the recesses of the soul have won him a special place in modern literature.

JOUVET, LOUIS (1887–   ), French actor and theatrical producer who distinguished himself in Copeau's theater and then founded his own very successful theater, where he has staged works by Giraudoux, Romains, Achard, etc.

KABIR, Indian mystic of the fifteenth century who taught a monotheistic religion.

KELLER, GOTTFRIED (1819–90), Swiss novelist of realistic fiction in German.

KEYSERLING, COUNT HERMANN VON (1880–1946), German philosopher, author of popular works such as *The Travel Diary of a Philosopher* (1925).

KIPPENBERG, ANTON (1874–   ), German editor and publisher long associated with the Insel-Verlag of Leipzig.

LA BRUYÈRE, JEAN DE (1645–96), French moralist of the classic age, famous for his *Caractères,* modeled after the observations of Theophrastus.

LAFORGUE, JULES (1860–87), French poet of the early symbolist movement, famous for the ironic vers libres of his *Complaintes.*

LA HARPE, JEAN-FRANÇOIS DE (1739–1803), French poet and literary critic.

LALOU, RENÉ (1889–　), French critic, best known for his *History of Contemporary French Literature.*

LANCASTER, G. B. (pseud. of Edith J. Lyttleton), Australian novelist whose first work appeared in 1908. She wrote of Australia and New Zealand; her first work was the novel *Sons o' Men* (1904).

LANUX, LILI DE, French musician and composer, granddaughter of Marc de la Nux, who moved to America definitively in 1915 after a first visit in 1914.

LANUX, PIERRE DE (1887–　), French essayist and journalist, at one time secretary to André Gide and, briefly, to the editorial board of the *N.R.F.;* in charge of the Paris office of the League of Nations (1924–34).

LA PÉROUSE (pseud. used for Marc de La Nux, 1830–1914), André Gide's piano teacher, whom he always venerated. Born on Réunion Island in the Indian Ocean, he was brought to France at eleven to receive a musical education. At twenty married the daughter of Anaïs Descombes, of the Nîmes Conservatory, where he studied. Pupil of Liszt (through whom he met Chopin), he taught in Paris for over sixty years and right up to his death knew all the Beethoven sonatas by heart. (The same pseudonym figures in *Si le grain ne meurt . . .* and in *Les Faux-Monnayeurs.*)

LA PÉROUSE, JEAN-FRANÇOIS DE GALAUP, COMTE DE (1741–88), French navigator who, after taking part in the Revolutionary War, rounded Cape Horn and navigated the Pacific.

LARBAUD, VALERY (1881–　), French poet, novelist, and essayist especially appreciated for his penetrating *Journal d'A. O. Barnabooth* (1913), which introduced into literature a new cosmopolitanism, and for his sensitive translations of Samuel Butler, W. S. Landor, Walt Whitman, etc.

LA ROCHEFOUCAULD, FRANÇOIS, DUC DE (1613–80), French writer of the most famous collections of *Maxims.*

LA SABLIÈRE, MME DE (1636–93), intellectual Frenchwoman who fostered science and letters in her *salon* and sheltered La Fontaine for twenty years.

LASSERRE, PIERRE (1867–1930), French literary critic of conservative tendency, who studied French romanticism and also contemporary writers.

LAURENCIN, MARIE (1885–　), French painter and illustrator, long a member of the group surrounding Picasso and Apollinaire.

LAURENS, PAUL-ALBERT (1870–?), son of Jean-Paul Laurens; painter and professor at the École des Beaux-Arts; intimate friend of André Gide, whom he accompanied on first trip to Africa (1893). His portrait of Gide is in the Luxembourg Museum.

LEBEY, ANDRÉ (1877–1938), French poet, then sociologist and historian; abandoned symbolism in favor of studies of Freemasonry and of the Bonapartes.

LE CARDONNEL, LOUIS (1862–1936), French Catholic poet of the symbolist movement.

LECONTE DE LISLE, CHARLES (1818–94), French poet of the Parnassian school, whose work is steeped in classical culture.

LE DANTEC, FÉLIX (1869–1917), French biologist and philosopher.

LEFÈVRE, FRÉDÉRIC (1889–), French journalist and literary critic who founded the weekly *Nouvelles littéraires* in 1922 and for years conducted interviews with the literary great, published as *Une Heure avec. . . .*

LE GRIX, FRANÇOIS, French literary critic and one of the editors of *La Revue hebdomadaire.*

LEMARIÉ, MME, faithful friend of the *Nouvelle Revue Française* and of the Théâtre du Vieux-Colombier.

LÉON, XAVIER (1868–), French philosopher, editor-in-chief of *La Revue de métaphysique et de morale,* and authority on the philosophy of Fichte.

LEPINE, LOUIS (1846–1933), Prefect of Police for Seine-et-Oise in 1893 and again from 1899 to 1912; great organizer and executive.

LESAGE, ALAIN-RENÉ (1668–1747), French realistic novelist of *Gil Blas* and *Le Diable boiteux.*

L'HERMITE, TRISTAN (1601–55), French poet and dramatist.

LHOTE, ANDRÉ (1885–), French painter and art critic.

LIMAN VON SANDERS (1855–1929), German officer who was named general and overseer of the Turkish army in 1914. During the war he attempted to organize the Turkish army and fought in the Near East.

LOCKE, WILLIAM JOHN (1863–1930), English architect and novelist, whose *Simon the Jester* (1910) interested André Gide.

LORRAIN, JEAN (1855–1906), French novelist of manners.

LOTI, PIERRE (pseud. of Julien Viaud, 1850–1923), French novelist of the sea and of far places, famous for *Pêcheur d'Islande* and *Aziyadé.*

LOUCHEUR, LOUIS (1872–1931), French industrialist and political figure representing the Nord *département,* several times Minister under the Third Republic.

LOUŸS, PIERRE (1870–1925), French poet and novelist of *Chansons de Bilitis* (1894), *Aphrodite* (1896), and *Les Aventures du roi Pausole* (1900).

LYAUTEY, LOUIS-HUBERT (1854–1934), French marshal and colonizer, who organized the French protectorate in Morocco. Member of the Academy, 1912.

MACQUIN, MARIE, sister of Henri Ghéon.

MAETERLINCK, MAURICE (1862–   ), Belgian poet and lyric dramatist of *Pelléas et Mélisande,* who evolved in the direction of a mystic rationalism and moral optimism.

MAISTRE, XAVIER DE (1763–1852), French writer, author of the *Voyage autour de ma chambre* and brother of the more famous Joseph.

MALLARMÉ, STÉPHANE (1842–98), French poet, whose intellectual purity and hermetic style influenced a whole generation of writers despite the limitation of his first *Complete Poems* to forty copies. His weekly receptions in his Paris apartment (1886–98) gathered the artistic élite of the Continent in fascinating conversation.

MANNING, HENRY, CARDINAL (1808–92), English churchman who, converted to Catholicism, became Archbishop of Westminster and Cardinal.

MARGUERITTE, PAUL (1860–1918), and VICTOR (1867–1942), French novelists who collaborated on novels of manners concerning the tragic events of 1870–1.

MARITAIN, JACQUES (1882–   ), French theologian and philosopher, inspired first by Bergson, then by Thomas Aquinas. Known primarily as a metaphysician, he has also contributed to æsthetics, ethics, and politics. French Ambassador to the Holy See (1946–   ).

MARIVAUX, PIERRE CARLET DE CHAMBLAIN DE (1688–1763), French dramatist and novelist of great sensibility and psychological penetration, whose name (*marivaudage*) stands for witty banter about love. His journals were inspired by Addison, and his novels in turn influenced Richardson.

MARMOL, DEL, Belgian director of the Foyer Franco-Belge during the first World War; André Gide was assistant director.

MARTIN DU GARD, HÉLÈNE, Mme Roger Martin du Gard.

MARTIN DU GARD, ROGER (1881–   ), French novelist and dramatist whose vivid realistic novel in many volumes, *The World of the Thibaults,* won the Nobel Prize in 1937.

MARVELL, ANDREW (1621–78), English poet and satirist.

MASSIS, HENRI (1886–   ), French literary critic and essayist, defender of the Latin inheritance in his *Defence of the West,* who severely criticized Renan, Gide, Duhamel, France, and Benda in the nationalist *Revue universelle.*

MASSON, FRÉDÉRIC (1847–1923), French historian and prolific writer, who served as perpetual secretary of the French Academy.

MAUPASSANT, GUY DE (1850–93), French novelist and short-story writer of the naturalist school.

MAUROIS, ANDRÉ (pseud. of Émile Herzog, 1885–   ), French novelist, biographer, and essayist, whose facile clarity made his lives of Shelley, Disraeli, and Byron world-famous and opened the French Academy to him in 1938.

MAURRAS, CHARLES (1868–   ), French poet, essayist, pamphleteer, and political leader of the Action Française movement; exponent of decentralization and a return to monarchy, who was tried in 1945 as the ideologist of the Vichy government and sentenced to life imprisonment.

MAURY, LUCIEN (1872–   ), French literary critic, translator from the Scandinavian languages, and co-editor of the *Revue bleue* (since 1934).

MAUS, OCTAVE (1856–1919), Belgian writer and lawyer, who was one of the founders of the advance-guard literary review *L'Art moderne* (1881) and later of La Libre Esthétique, the society before which André Gide lectured in Brussels.

MAYRISCH, MME ÉMILE (?–1947), wife of the director of the great Luxemburg metallurgical syndicate named Arbet. A woman of great culture in French, English, and German, she received poets, philosophers, painters, and sculptors in her château of Colpach in Luxemburg, which became a meeting-place of French and German cultures. She traveled in the Orient with the late director of the Musée Guimet and in the Near East with André Gide.

MELVILLE, HERMAN (1819–91), American novelist of *Typee, Omoo,* and *Moby Dick.*

MENDELSSOHN-BARTHOLDY, FELIX (1809–47), German composer.

MENDÈS, CATULLE (1843–1909), prolific French poet and dramatist.

MÉRAL, PAUL (pseud. of Gouchtenaere), young Belgian protégé of Lady Rothermere, who made vain efforts to succeed in literature and the theater.

MEREZHKOVSKI, DMITRI (1865–1941), Russian novelist, poet, and essayist, leader of the symbolist movement in Russia and proponent of a neo-Christianity.

MÉRIMÉE, PROSPER (1803–70), French novelist, dramatist, and, chiefly, writer of short stories, such as *Carmen* and *Colomba,* famous for their objectivity and artistry.

MESNARD, PAUL (1812–99), French professor and literary historian, known for his *History of the French Academy* (1857) and for his solid editions of Racine and Molière.

MESSIMY, ADOLPHE (1869–?), French political figure, Minister of War in 1911 and again in June-August 1914 (Viviani Cabinet).

After resigning at the end of August 1914, he served as a general of reserves. Later Senator from L'Ain and interested in colonial problems.

MICHELET, JULES (1798–1874), French historian, who joined poetic intuition to scientific research and in his voluminous work consistently defended the lower classes.

MILHAUD, DARIUS (1892–   ), French composer, one of the earlier experimenters with jazz forms.

MILLERAND, ALEXANDRE (1859–1943), French political figure who was both Premier and President in 1920.

MIRBEAU, OCTAVE (1850–1917), French novelist, dramatist, and critic, famous for his social satire and outspoken manner.

MONNIER, ADRIENNE, French poet, essayist, and publisher who founded in 1917 a bookshop and publishing-house on the rue de l'Odéon which has been a meeting-place for the greatest writers of the period.

MONTESQUIEU, CHARLES LOUIS DE SECONDAT DE (1689–1755), French political philosopher, best known for his *Lettres persanes* and his analysis of political constitutions, *De l'esprit des lois.*

MONTFORT, EUGÈNE (1877–1936), French novelist, editor of *Les Marges* (which he wrote entirely himself from 1903 to 1908), and author of a tableau of modern French literature.

MONTHERLANT, HENRY DE (1886–   ), French novelist and essayist who first epitomized the restless and cynical youth of the twenties and then produced a series of cruel novels of great power and technical skill.

MORAND, PAUL (1888–   ), French novelist and journalist of travel; his short stories *Open All Night* and *Closed All Night* established his reputation in the twenties as a clever juggler of images characteristic of the restless age.

MORÉAS, JEAN (pseud. of Jean Papadiamantopoulos, 1856–1910), Athens-born French poet, who founded within the symbolist movement (which he had been the first to name and defend) the "Romanesque school" and achieved a vigorous return to classicism.

MUHLFELD, MME, widow of the literary critic Lucien Mühlfeld, maintained an important politico-literary *salon* in Paris that was frequented by Régnier and Valéry.

MURAT, PRINCESSE (1867–   ), née Cécile Ney d'Elchingen, wife of Joachim-Napoléon, fifth Prince Murat.

MURRY, JOHN MIDDLETON (1889–   ), English literary critic, prolific essayist, and editor of the *Adelphi* (1923–30), perhaps most appreciated for his study of *Keats and Shakespeare.*

MUSSET, ALFRED DE (1810–57), French romantic poet and dramatist of lyric quality.

NAVILLE, ARNOLD (1879–), Swiss financier, early interested in the work of André Gide, on which he published biographical notes in 1930; long a close friend of the author.

NOAILLES, COMTESSE ANNA DE (1876–1933), French poet and novelist of delicate talent and vibrant sensitivity.

NORTON, HARRY, English mathematician and Fellow of Trinity College, Cambridge, great friend of Maynard Keynes, Rupert Brooke, Lytton Strachey, etc.

PARETO, VILFREDO (1848–1923), Italian sociologist and economist.

PASCAL, BLAISE (1623–62), French Catholic polemicist and philosopher, famous for the vigor, conciseness, and beauty of his *Pensées*, composed as an apology of Christianity.

PEACOCK, THOMAS LOVE (1785–1866), English poet and writer of satiric romances; intimate friend of Shelley.

PÉGUY, CHARLES (1873–1914), French poet and essayist, who exerted a very great influence through such works as his *Jeanne d'Arc, Notre Patrie,* and *L'Argent,* as well as through the review he founded and edited, *Les Cahiers de la Quinzaine* (1902–14).

PHILIPPE, CHARLES-LOUIS (1874–1909), French realistic novelist of the simple life, who left several masterpieces.

PICASSO, PABLO (1881–), Spanish-born painter who has been one of the most vigorous innovators and influences in modern French painting since the epoch of cubism.

PILON, EDMOND (1874–), French poet in vers libre, and art and literary critic whose regular fortnightly column in *La Plume* was remarkable for its impartiality.

PIOT, RENÉ (1869–1934), French painter, illustrator, and designer for the theater who renewed the art of the fresco in the early years of the century.

PLOTINUS (*ca.* 203–262 A.D.), Greek mystic philosopher who interpreted Plato's thought in Rome, converting his disciples to the loftiest spiritual life.

POINCARÉ, HENRI (1854–1912), French physicist and philosopher of eminence.

POINCARÉ, RAYMOND (1860–1934), French lawyer and political figure, President from 1913 to 1920 and several times Premier.

PORTO-RICHE, GEORGES DE (1849–1930), French dramatist noted for his psychological plays of love.

POUCEL, VICTOR (1872–), French Jesuit priest, teacher in the

Collège St. Joseph at Avignon, and essayist who wrote a study of André Gide in 1929.

POURTALÈS, GUY DE (1881–), Swiss biographer and music critic of French Protestant origin, known for his *Life of Liszt, Richard Wagner,* etc.

POUSSIN, NICOLAS (1594–1665), French master of classical painting.

PRESSEMANE, ADRIEN (1879–), French political figure, Deputy from the Haute-Vienne, and painter on porcelain.

PRÉVOST, JEAN (1901–44), French novelist and essayist of brilliant but hasty works reflecting the unrest and insatiable curiosity of his generation.

PRÉVOST, MARCEL (1862–1941), French novelist and dramatist of psychologically penetrating works of moralizing tendency. Elected to the French Academy in 1909.

PREZZOLINI, GIUSEPPE (1882–), Italian man of letters and critic, editor of such Florentine reviews as *Leonardo* and *La Voce,* and later bibliographer of Italian literary criticism. Professor at Columbia University since 1930.

PROUST, MARCEL (1871–1922), French novelist whose one great work in sixteen volumes is a masterpiece of psychological penetration and of poetic re-creation of the past through the involuntary memory.

PRUNIÈRES, HENRY (1886–), French music critic and historian, who founded *La Revue musicale* in 1919 and edited the complete works of Lulli (1930).

PSICHARI, ERNEST (1883–1914), French soldier and writer of Catholic inspiration; grandson of Renan.

PUSHKIN, ALEXANDER (1799–1837), Russian poet and liberal whose *Yevgeny Onyegin* and *Boris Godunov* are internationally known.

QUINTON, RENÉ (1866–1925), French biologist, noted for his study of *Sea Water as an Organic Milieu,* and pioneer in aviation.

RADIGUET, RAYMOND (1903–23), French poet and novelist of striking, precocious works of classical inspiration.

RAMEAU, JEAN-PHILIPPE (1683–1764), French musical theorist, composer, and organist.

RAPHAËL, GASTON, French professor at the Lycée Lakanal, Paris, and author of several books on German subjects, notably a book on Rathenau that interested Gide.

RATHENAU, WALTER (1867–1922), German statesman and industrialist, head of the A.E.G. electrical company, and organizer of German industry during the first World War.

RAVERAT, JACQUES, French artist whose father was one of the original patrons of the Pontigny gatherings. In 1911 married Gwendolen Mary Darwin, the granddaughter of Charles Darwin. Early disabled by illness, he died in Vence, where he and his wife had gone to live about 1921.

REDON, ODILON (1840–1916), French painter and engraver of the post-impressionist group, who painted his visions in a new color-scheme and created a highly personal art, instinct with thought and literature.

RÉGIS, EMMANUEL (1855–1918), French psychiatrist known for his clinical work and for his *Précis de médecine mentale*.

RÉGNIER, HENRI DE (1864–1936), French poet and novelist of great delicacy and fluidity, one of the leaders of the symbolist movement, elected to the French Academy in 1912.

RÉGNIER, MATHURIN (1573–1613), French satirical poet.

RENAN, ERNEST (1823–92), French philologist, historian of religions, and philosopher, most famous for his unorthodox *Life of Jesus*.

RENARD, JULES (1864–1910), French satirist in both novel and drama, author of *L'Écornifleur, Poil de Carotte*, etc.

RETINGER, JOSEPH H. (1888–   ), Polish author of a book on Conrad, a history of modern French literature, a study of the Mexican labor movement, *All about Poland*, etc.

RICHEPIN, JEAN (1849–1926), French poet and dramatist of vigorous popular subjects.

RILKE, RAINER MARIA (1875–1926), German poet, born in Prague, who lived long in Paris in close association with the sculptor Rodin. His elegies and other poems are works of philosophy and of great artistry.

RIMBAUD, ARTHUR (1854–91), French poet of great originality, whose two works revolutionized modern poetry. Abandoning literature entirely at the age of nineteen, he ended his life as an adventurer and business representative in Abyssinia.

RIVIÈRE, ISABELLE (1889?–   ), sister of Alain-Fournier, became Mme Jacques Rivière in 1909. Mother of two children. She has translated Conrad and others from English and written several books, of which the most interesting concern her famous relatives.

RIVIÈRE, JACQUES (1886–1925), French critic, and editor of the *Nouvelle Revue Française* from 1919 to 1925 after having been identified with the review from 1909. His vivid correspondence with Alain-Fournier and with Claudel is famous.

ROBERTY, MATHILDE, daughter of the Rouen minister who officiated at André Gide's marriage at Étretat and friend of Mme Gide.

Later she presided over a horticultural school near Neuchâtel in Switzerland.

ROLLAND, ROMAIN (1866–1944), French novelist, dramatist, and biographer, famous for his *Jean-Christophe*, his lives of Tolstoy, Beethoven, etc., and his pacifism.

ROLLINAT, MAURICE (1853–1903), French poet, known less for his elegies than for his macabre poems inspired by Baudelaire and Poe.

ROMAINS, JULES (pseud. of Louis Farigoule, 1885–), French poet, novelist, dramatist, and essayist, who invented Unanimism, achieved great success on the stage with his farce *Knock*, and wrote a cyclic novel of 27 volumes entitled *Men of Good Will*. He was elected to the French Academy in 1946.

RONDEAUX, GEORGES, brother of Mme André Gide and long mayor of Cuverville.

ROSENBERG, FÉDOR, Russian from Livonia, whom André Gide met in Florence during his wedding trip (1895).

ROSNY, the brothers (pseud. of Joseph-Henri Boëx, 1856–1940, and Justin Boëx, 1859–), French novelists of manners.

ROSSETTI, DANTE GABRIEL (1828–82), English painter and poet of the Pre-Raphaelite school.

ROSTAND, EDMOND (1868–1918), French poetic dramatist, whose *Cyrano de Bergerac* renewed the romantic drama brilliantly at the end of the century.

ROTHERMERE, LADY, née Mary Lilian Share, English wife of Lord Rothermere, the proprietor of the *Daily Mail* and other London newspapers; she translated Gide's *Prometheus Ill-Bound*.

ROUART, EUGÈNE, son of a famous industrialist and collector of modern French paintings; he married one of the daughters of the painter Henri Lerolle. As a graduate of the School of Agriculture at Grignon, he directed various large agricultural enterprises, and, entering politics, was elected Senator from the Haute-Garonne. Great friend of writers and painters, he contributed to the early interest in Francis Jammes. He and Jammes joined André Gide at Biskra in 1895 and Gide dedicated his *Paludes* to him. He himself wrote a novel, *La Villa sans maître*, which did not enjoy much success despite the interesting psychological problem it sets forth.

RUBINSTEIN, IDA, Russian-born dancer who danced with the Diaghilev company and put on performances of her own in works by Valéry, d'Annunzio, Gide, etc.

RUTHERFORD, MARK, *see* White, William Hale.

RUYTERS, ANDRÉ (1876–), Belgian writer and banker, who was one of the founders of the *Nouvelle Revue Française*. He went to

Addis Ababa as a bank director, then managed the Far Eastern branches of the Banque d'Indochine. He has long lived in China.

SAINTE-BEUVE, AUGUSTIN (1804–69), French critic belonging to the romantic school, whose "Monday Chats" and "Literary Portraits" have outlived his poems and single novel.

SAINT-ÉVREMOND, CHARLES DE SAINT-DENYS DE (1610–1703), French essayist, known for his voluminous, witty correspondence written during his forty-year exile in England.

SALMON, ANDRÉ (1881–), French poet, novelist, and critic who began as a cubist disciple of Apollinaire, later joined Dadaism, and distinguished himself as a critic of modern painting.

SAMAIN, ALBERT (1858–1900), French symbolist poet influenced by Verlaine and Heredia.

SANDEAU, JULES (1811–83), French novelist best known for *Mlle de la Seiglière*.

SANTAYANA, GEORGE (1863–), Spanish-born American philosopher of naturalist tendency.

SATIE, ÉRIK (1866–1925), French composer, member of the group known as "Les Six."

SAUCIER, ROLAND (1899–), director of the bookshop of the Librairie Gallimard, boulevard Raspail, since 1920.

SCÈVE, MAURICE (1510?–64?), French poet of the Renaissance school of Lyon, known for his subtle, often obscure lyrical poems.

SCHLUMBERGER, JEAN (1877–), French novelist of psychological insight and one of the founders of the *N.R.F.*

SCHOEN, WILHELM VON (1851–1933), German diplomat, Minister to Copenhagen, St. Petersburg, and (1910–14) Paris, and briefly Secretary of State.

SCHWOB, MARCEL (1867–1905), French prose-poet of the symbolist period, whose great erudition, visual imagination, and ironic, flexible style gave him a significant place in modern letters.

SCOTT-MONCRIEFF, C. K. (1889–1930), translator of Proust, Stendhal, Pirandello, and others into English. His translation of Proust, which he left unfinished, is most appreciated.

SERT, JOSÉ-MARIA (1876–1945), Spanish painter, best known for his vast murals in France and America. He drew an illustration for Gide's *Bethsabé*.

SÉVIGNÉ, MARIE DE RABUTIN-CHANTAL, MARQUISE DE (1626–96), French noblewoman famous for the vivid letters she wrote to her daughter.

SHACKLETON, ANNA (*ca.* 1830–84), talented Scottish girl who entered the Rondeaux family in 1850 as tutor to the seventeen-year-old Juliette (André Gide's mother) and remained her great friend until death. Her angelic disposition, her great interest in botany, and her intimate knowledge of English and German deeply influenced André Gide's childhood.

SICKERT, WALTER (1860–1942), English painter and illustrator, who frequented Aubrey Beardsley, Oscar Wilde, Charles Condor, etc.

SIGNORET, EMMANUEL (1872–1900), French poet of Wagnerian and Parnassian inspiration, whose poems André Gide collected in one volume in 1908.

SKEAT, WALTER WILLIAM (1835–1912), English philologist.

SMITH, LOGAN PEARSALL (1865–   ), American-born English essayist best known for his delicate *Trivia*.

SOUDAY, PAUL (1869–1929), French critic, who from 1912 until his death wrote the regular literary criticism in *Le Temps*.

SOUPAULT, PHILIPPE (1897–   ), French poet, novelist, and essayist who abandoned Dadaism and surrealism in favor of adventure novels of a poetic nature and political analysis.

STRACHEY, GILES LYTTON (1880–1932), English historian and critic best known for his *Eminent Victorians, Queen Victoria,* and *Books and Characters*.

STRAUSS, DAVID FRIEDRICH (1808–74), German materialistic philosopher, author of a *Life of Jesus, The Old Faith and the New,* etc., on whom Nietzsche wrote in his *Thoughts out of Season*.

STRAVINSKY, IGOR (1882–   ), Russian composer of great originality and variety.

STROHL, JEAN (1886–   ), Swiss biologist, Dean of the Faculty of Sciences, University of Zurich, and author of studies in the history of natural sciences and in teratology.

SUARÈS, ANDRÉ (1866–   ), French poet and essayist of flamboyant nature and broad views, whose studies of Wagner, Dostoyevsky, and Pascal are penetrating and original.

SUE, EUGÈNE (1804–59), French novelist and dramatist of thrillers such as *The Wandering Jew* and *The Mysteries of Paris*. His total work comprises about 200 volumes.

TAGORE, SIR RABINDRANATH (1861–1941), Bengali poet of the *Gitanjali,* who translated his verses into English prose.

TAINE, HIPPOLYTE (1828–93), French historian, critic, and philosopher, most widely known for his *History of English Literature*.

THARAUD, JÉRÔME (1874–   ), and JEAN (1877–   ), French novelists, who have always written in collaboration and handled a wide variety of fiction. Their most famous works are *Dingley, l'illustre écrivain,* and *La Maîtresse servante*.

THIBAUDET, ALBERT (1874–1936), French literary critic whose studies of Bergson, Mallarmé, Valéry, and Flaubert and regular articles in the *Nouvelle Revue Française* won him a place among the keenest and most stimulating French critics.

THIÉBAUT, MARCEL, French literary critic and long-time editor of the *Revue de Paris*.

TIELROOY, JOHANNES BERNARDUS (1886–), Dutch professor of French literature at the University of Utrecht, literary critic, and essayist on modern French literature.

TOUNY-LERYS (pseud. of Marcel Marchandeau, 1881–), French poet influenced by Verhaeren and Jammes; founded several reviews of poetry and in 1909 the movement known as *Primitivisme*.

TRAZ, ROBERT DE (1884–), Swiss essayist and vigorous editor of the cosmopolitan *Revue de Genève*.

TRONCHE, Frenchman employed by the *Nouvelle Revue Française* in the early years.

TURENNE, HENRI DE LA TOUR D'AUVERGNE, VICOMTE DE (1611–75), French marshal under Mazarin and Louis XIV, who also wrote interesting memoirs.

TZARA, TRISTAN (1896–), Rumanian founder of the Dada movement in Geneva in 1916, who has continued to write poetry in French.

UNAMUNO, MIGUEL DE (1864–1936), Spanish philosopher and essayist of *The Tragic Sense of Life*, whose universal culture and liberalism revitalized modern Spanish literature.

VALENTINE, *see* Gilbert, Valentine.

VALÉRY, JEANNIE, Mme Paul Valéry, née Gobillard.

VALÉRY, PAUL (1871–1945), French poet and essayist, who began his career when as a law student he met Pierre Louÿs and André Gide, then Mallarmé, whose chief disciple he became. After a brilliant start he abandoned literature for twenty years and was persuaded to return in 1917 by André Gide. His mature career was crowned by his election to the French Academy in 1925.

VALLETTE, ALFRED (1858–1935), French writer who was one of the founders and, from 1890 until his death, the editor of the *Mercure de France*. He was instrumental in the growth of that important review from a 32-page brochure of symbolist literature to a powerful force in modern letters, with its own publishing house.

VAN BEVER, *see* Bever, Adolphe van.

VANBRUGH, SIR JOHN (1664–1726), English dramatist of comedies of manners and architect of Blenheim Palace, the Haymarket Theatre, etc.

VANDERVELDE, ÉMILE (1866–1938), Belgian statesman, one of the leaders of the Socialist Party, Minister of State in 1914, delegate to the Peace Conference in 1919, and Foreign Minister (1925–7). Also the author of numerous publications.

VANNICOLA, GIUSEPPE (1877–1915), Italian poet and essayist of great spirit but little achievement, who suffered for many years from illness and poverty.

VAN RYSSELBERGHE, ÉLISABETH, daughter of Théo Van Rysselberghe and mother of Catherine Gide.

VAN RYSSELBERGHE, THÉO (1862–1926), Belgian painter of landscapes and portraits.

VAN RYSSELBERGHE, MME THÉO, wife of the preceding and, under the pseudonym of M. Saint-Clair, author of memoirs and delicate literary portraits.

VAUGELAS, CLAUDE FAVRE, SIEUR DE (1585–1650), French lexicographer and arbiter of style, whose *Remarks on the French Language* and work on the *Dictionary* of the Academy continued Malherbe's purification of the classical language.

VAUVENARGUES, LUC DE CLAPIERS, MARQUIS DE (1715–47), French moralist who left a collection of *Maxims* almost as famous as those of La Rochefoucauld.

VERHAEREN, ÉMILE (1855–1916), Belgian poet of the cult of humanity and the tumultuous forces of modern life.

VERLAINE, PAUL (1844–96), French symbolist poet, distinguished for the musical quality of his verse and his rather disreputable life.

VERNE, JULES (1828–1905), French novelist of fantastic adventure stories based on scientific developments like the airplane, the submarine, etc.

VIELÉ-GRIFFIN, FRANCIS (1864–1937), American-born French poet of nature, who, inspired by the Greek classics, the Scandinavians, and Walt Whitman, contributed a new breath to the symbolist movement.

VIGNY, ALFRED DE (1797–1863), French romantic poet of philosophic turn who, like Hugo, also wrote fiction and drama.

VILDRAC, CHARLES (1882–), French poet and dramatist, best known for his play *The Steamer Tenacity*.

VILLEROY, AUGUSTE, French dramatist whose works were played by Jacques Copeau; later became a member of Gaston Baty's theatrical group.

VIVIANI, RENÉ (1863–1925), French political figure who was Premier at the beginning of the first World War.

VOGÜÉ, EUGÈNE-MELCHIOR DE (1850–1910), French novelist and introducer of Russian literature.

WATTEAU, ANTOINE (1684–1721), French painter and engraver.

WERTH, LÉON (1879–   ), French novelist.

WHARTON, EDITH (1862–1937), American novelist of manners and keen psychological analysis.

WHITE, WILLIAM HALE (1831–1913), English writer of a sincere self-analysis who wrote under the pseudonym of Mark Rutherford.

WIDMER, ÉDOUARD, French chief engineer of the Western Railways; he married André Gide's cousin Isabelle Desmarest.

WIDMER, ISABELLE, André Gide's cousin, née Desmarest, who became Mme Édouard Widmer.

WIDMER, RENÉ, son of Édouard Widmer and second cousin of André Gide.

ZOLA, ÉMILE (1840–1902), French novelist of the naturalist school best known for his vast series of novels of contemporary life, *Les Rougon-Macquart.*

THE WORKS OF ANDRÉ GIDE

POETRY IN VERSE AND IN PROSE

Les Cahiers d'André Walter (Librairie de l'Art Indépendant, 1891)	The Notebooks of André Walter
Les Poésies d'André Walter (ibid., 1892)	The Poems of André Walter
Le Traité du Narcisse (ibid., 1891)	The Treatise of the Narcissus
La Tentative amoureuse (ibid., 1893)	The Attempt at Love
Le Voyage d'Urien (ibid., 1893)	Urien's Travels
Les Nourritures terrestres (Mercure de France, 1897)	The Fruits of the Earth
El Hadj (ibid., 1899)	El Hadj
Amyntas (ibid., 1906)	Amyntas
Le Retour de l'enfant prodigue (Vers et Prose, 1907)	The Prodigal's Return
Les Nouvelles Nourritures (Gallimard, 1935)	New Fruits of the Earth

TALES

L'Immoraliste (Mercure de France, 1902)	*The Immoralist (Alfred A. Knopf, 1930)
*La Porte étroite (ibid., 1909)	*Strait Is the Gate (ibid., 1924)
*Isabelle (Gallimard, 1911)	*Isabelle (ibid., 1931; in *Two Symphonies*)

N.B. Since 1935 the author and his French publisher have ceased classifying Gide's works in categories. The translator therefore assumes full responsibility for this pigeonholing.

* The titles preceded by an asterisk have been published in English translation.

*La Symphonie pastorale
(ibid., 1919)

*The Pastoral Symphony
(ibid., 1931; in *Two Symphonies*)

*L'École des femmes
(ibid., 1929)

*The School for Wives
(ibid., 1929)

Robert
(ibid., 1929)

Robert

Geneviève
(ibid., 1939)

Genevieve

SATIRICAL FARCES

Paludes
(Librairie de l'Art Indépendant, 1895)

Morasses

*Le Prométhée mal enchaîné
(Mercure de France, 1899)

*Prometheus Ill-Bound
(London, Chatto & Windus, 1919)

*Les Caves du Vatican
(Gallimard, 1914)

*The Vatican Swindle
(Alfred A. Knopf, 1925) or *Lafcadio's Adventures*
(ibid., 1927)

Thésée
(ibid., 1946)

Theseus

NOVEL

*Les Faux-Monnayeurs
(Gallimard, 1926)

*The Counterfeiters
(Alfred A. Knopf, 1927)

CRITICISM

Prétextes
(Mercure de France, 1903)

Pretexts

Nouveaux Prétextes
(ibid., 1911)

Further Pretexts

*Dostoïevsky
(Plon-Nourrit, 1923)

*Dostoievsky
(Alfred A. Knopf, 1926)

Incidences
(Gallimard, 1924)

Angles of Incidence

Le Journal des Faux-Monnayeurs
(ibid., 1926)

The Counterfeiters' Day-book

*Essai sur Montaigne
  (Éditions de la Pléiade, 1929)

*Montaigne
  (Horace Liveright, 1929)

Divers
  (Gallimard, 1931)

Miscellany

*Interviews imaginaires
  (New York, Pantheon Books, 1943)

*Imaginary Interviews
  (Alfred A. Knopf, 1944)

DRAMA

Philoctète
  (Mercure de France, 1899)

Philoctetes

Le Roi Candaule
  (La Revue Blanche, 1901)

King Candaules

Saül
  (Mercure de France, 1903)

Saul

Bethsabé
  (Bibliothèque de l'Occident, 1912)

Bathsheba

Œdipe
  (Gallimard, 1931)

Œdipus

Robert ou l'intérêt général
  (Alger, L'Arche, 1944–5)

Robert or The Common Weal

MISCELLANEOUS

*Souvenirs de la Cour d'Assises
  (Gallimard, 1914)

*Recollections of the Assize Court
  (Hutchinson & Co., 1941)

Corydon
  (ibid., 1924)

Corydon

*Si le grain ne meurt . . .
  (ibid., 1926)

*If It Die . . .
  (Random House, 1935)

Numquid et tu . . . ?
  (Éditions de la Pléiade, 1926)

Numquid et tu . . . ?

Un Esprit non prévenu
  (Éditions du Sagittaire, 1929)

An Unprejudiced Mind

L'Affaire Redureau
  (Gallimard, 1930)

The Redureau Case

La Sequestrée de Poitiers
  (ibid., 1930)

The Poitiers Incarceration Case

TRAVELS

*Voyage au Congo
  (Gallimard, 1927)

*Travels in the Congo
  (Alfred A. Knopf, 1929)

Dindiki
  (Liége, Éditions de la Lampe d'Aladdin, 1927)

Dindiki

*Le Retour du Tchad
  (Gallimard, 1928)

*in Travels in the Congo
  (Alfred A. Knopf, 1929)

*Retour de l'U.R.S.S.
  (ibid., 1936)

*Return from the U.S.S.R.
  (ibid., 1937)

*Retouches à mon Retour de
  l'U.R.S.S. (ibid., 1937)

*Afterthoughts on the U.S.S.R.
  (Dial Press, 1938)

JOURNALS

*Journal, 1889–1939
  (Gallimard, 1939)

*The Journals of André Gide,
  1889–
  (Alfred A. Knopf, 1947–   )

Pages de Journal, 1939–1942
  (ibid., 1946)

Extracts from the Journals, 1939–
1942

INDEX

A., 254
A., Dr., 412
A., S., 183, 229
Abed, 95
Abnormality and genius, 242
Abrami, M., 195–6
Acte gratuit, 398
Action Française, 192, 195, 196, 219, 226, 276, 324, 356
Adam, Mme Paul, 203
Adrianople (Turkey), 6
Æsthetics, 240–1
Africa, 15
Afyonkarahisar (Turkey), 14, 17, 19
Agrippa, 325
Air raids, 121
Ajaccio (Corsica), 335
Aksehir (Turkey), 14, 19
Alain, 321
Albéniz, Isaac, 21, 23, 45, 98, 100, 102, 123, 191, 204, 262, 263, 357, 389, 411
Alcoholism, 152
Alexander the Great, 292
Alibert, François-Paul, 210, 280, 306, 336, 418, 420
Allard, Roger, 280
Allégret, André, 54, 203, 223, 280, 334
Allégret, Élie, 21, 54, 59, 66, 69, 212, 255, 260, 280, 316, 318, 382
Allégret, Éric, 210, 218, 235
Allégret, Jean-Paul, 99, 222, 223
Allégret, Marc, 280, 318, 320, 355, 387, 398, 411
Allégret, Suzanne, 319, 322
Altkirch (Haut-Rhin), 57, 67
Ambition, 295
Amélie-les-Bains (Pyrénées-Orientales), 143
Amelioration of the race, 104
America, 280, 423
Amiel, Henri-Frédéric, 277, 285 n, 413
Amiens (Somme), 79

Amour-propre, 237–8, 271
Analysis and synthesis, 338
Anatolia (Turkey), 15
Andler, Charles, 263
Angelico, Fra, 5, 99
Ankara (Turkey), 15
Annecy (Haute-Savoie), 322
Annecy-Talloires (Haute-Savoie), 325
Anthropomorphism, 372
Ardor, 343
Ariadne, 403
Armenonville (Seine-et-Oise), 253
Arnauld, Antoine, 242
Arrogance, 404
Art and ethics, 358
Art and manner, 285
Art and religion, 399
Artist product of his epoch, 377
Artsybashev, Mikhail P., 261, 262 n
Attention, 263–4
Aubin, 197, 227
Aubrey, John, 233
Augustus, 292
Austria, 45
Auteuil (Paris, XVI), 3, 8, 54, 58
Auxerre (Yonne), 385, 387
Aveline, Claude, 388
Avignon (Vaucluse), 306

B., 423
B., H., 416
B., Mme, 118, 319
Bach, Johann Sebastian, 21, 81–2, 134, 191 n, 198, 203, 235, 276, 277, 284, 348, 355, 357, 389, 411 n, 413, 414
Bagdad (Iraq), 20
Bagnols (Gard), 143
Bagnols-de-Grenade, 202
Bakst, Léon, 218
Ballets russes, 261 n
Balzac, Honoré de, 70 n, 111, 112, 229, 238, 269 n, 284, 289, 312 n, 314 n, 365 n, 369 n, 370, 414 n

Banville, Théodore de, 284

Banyuls (Pyrénées-Orientales), 143

Barbey d'Aurevilly, Jules, 126, 214, 415

Barbusse, Henri, 199, 219

Barrès, Maurice, 47, 69, 195, 212, 238, 242–3, 250 n, 271, 290, 334, 353, 358, 394, 408, 409

Barthou, Louis, 349

Basel (Switzerland), 61, 402

Bassermann, Dieter, 21, 30, 44

Bassiano, Princesse de, 267

Bataille, Henry, 234

Baudelaire, Charles, 111, 166 n, 197, 199, 202, 215, 240, 250, 256, 265, 275, 285

Bayreuth (Germany), 65

Bazalgette, Léon, 101

Beardsley, Aubrey, 293

Beaulieu, Faure, 136 n

Beaune (Côte-d'Or), 387

Beaunier, André, 38, 110

Beauty and desire, 333

Beauvais (Oise), 81

Beddoes, Thomas Lovell, 310

Bees swarming, 324

Beethoven, Ludwig van, 21, 166, 203, 204, 216, 220, 222, 276, 414, 418

Belgium, 54, 55, 243

Bellone (dog), 384

Belot, Gustave, 66, 67

Bennett, Arnold, 100, 101, 256 n, 309, 394

Bénouville (Seine-Inférieure), 44

Béranger, Pierre Jean de, 362

Béraud, Henri, 324, 325, 326, 333, 350, 357, 358, 361, 387

Bergson, Henri, 348, 406 n

Berlin (Germany), 257

Berlioz, Hector, 267–8

Bernard, St., 215

Bernard, Tristan, 66

Berne (Switzerland), 157, 207

Bernstein, Henry, 47, 234, 397

Berthelot, Philippe, 47, 53, 73, 107

Bertin, 160, 161

Bertrand, Louis, 213

Besson, 410

Beuzeville (Eure), 130, 210

Bever, Adolphe van, 118, 202

Bey, Enver, 15, 16

Bible, 82

Bidou, Henry, 230

Binet-Sanglé, Charles, 241

Bing, Suzanne, 54

Biskra (Algeria), 16, 200

Blake, William, 70, 71, 297, 302, 307, 310, 311, 320, 361, 420

Blanche, Jacques-Émile, 33, 44, 45, 47, 69, 108, 116, 120, 123, 147, 148, 150, 151, 153, 165, 203, 211, 215, 320

Blanche, Mme Jacques-Émile, 46, 109, 123

Blei, Franz, 282

Blum, Léon, 3, 55

Blumenthal, Fondation, 257 n

Boccon-Gibauld, 116

Böcklin, Arnold, 402

Boileau, Nicolas, 111, 216 n

Bolshevism, 263

Bonheur, Raymond, 100

Bonnard, Pierre, 108, 233 n

Bonnet, Charles, 405

Bordeaux, Henry, 299

Boredom, 404

Borrow, George, 112

Bosphorus (Turkey), 7

Bossuet, Jacques Bénigne, 121, 122, 123, 125, 126, 143, 145, 214, 216, 272 n, 337, 348, 414 n

Botany, 11, 372–4

Botticelli, Sandro, 110, 311

Bougainville, Louis-Antoine de, 249

Bouhours, Father, 239

Bouilhet, Louis, 365

Boulenger, Jacques, 326

Bouni-Reclus, Mme, 110

Bourg-en-Bresse (Ain), 386

Bourget, Paul, 46 n, 110, 111, 285, 349

Bourget, Mme Paul, 110

Boylesve, René, 203, 284, 349, 368

Braffy (Calvados), 39, 70, 80, 84

Brahms, Johannes, 389

Braz, 141 n
Bréal, Auguste, 146
Brehm, Alfred-Edmond, 368
Breton, André, 367
Briand, Aristide, 73, 146, 149, 164, 196
Brignoles (Var), 307, 348, 385
Bronja, 316, 320
Brontë, Emily, 22 n, 38, 60, 392
Brou (Ain), 386
Brousson, Jean-Jacques, 360
Browning, Robert, 89, 117, 214, 234, 236, 263, 270 n, 274, 275 n, 280, 298, 306, 337, 349, 420
Brunetière, Ferdinand, 213
Brunot, Ferdinand, 239 n
Brunschvicg, Léon, 292 n
Brusa (Turkey), 6, 7, 10, 11
Brussels (Belgium), 65
Buffon, Georges Louis Leclerc, Comte de, 104
Buisson, Ferdinand, 66
Bumblebee and snapdragon, 216
Bunin, Ivan, 307, 309
Burckhardt, Jacob, 375
Busoni, Ferruccio, 191
Bussy, Simon, 391
Bussy, Mme Simon, 309, 328, 338
Butler, Samuel, 368 n

C., 116, 218
C., A., 104
C., Countess de, 46
C., H., 287
C., M. H., 290
Café de Flore, 54, 55, 58
Calmont, 148
Cambridge (England), 233
Cancelled trip to England, 100
Cannes (Alpes-Maritimes), 112 n
Capiello, Mme, 203
Capri (Italy), 301
Carantec, 228
Carcassonne (Aude), 202, 336, 418
Carnoules (Alpes-Maritimes), 335, 349
Carry-le-Rouet   (Bouches-du-Rhône), 306, 308

Casablanca (Morocco), 323
Castagno, Andrea del, 5
Catherine, 55
Catholicism, 199, 207, 250, 252, 293, 328, 330, 379, 381
Catholicism and Protestantism, 251
Catiline, 238
Cats, 26, 28, 35, 42
Cavalcanti, Alberto, 410
Céleste, 266
Céline, 423
Cézanne, Paul, 377
Chablis (Yonne), 387
Chabrier, Alexis, 265
Châlons (Marne), 52
Chamfort, Nicholas-Sébastien Roch, 291
Champion, Édouard, 331, 352
Chanivaz (Switzerland), 207
Chaplin, Charles Spencer, 280 n, 397
Characters, 75–6, 92
Chardin, Jean-Baptiste-Siméon, 419
Charleroi (Belgium), 74, 81
Chartier, Émile, 321
Chartres (Eure-et-Loire,), 354, 423
Chatalja (Turkey), 6
Chateaubriand, François-René de, 202, 215 n, 219
Chaumeix, Mme André, 203
Chausson, Mme, 100
Chauveau, Dr. Claude, 309
Chekhov, Anton, 262, 263, 346
Chénier, André, 416
Chesterton, G. K., 234
Chevalier, Ernest, 305
Chiron, Dr., 300
Chitré, 381
Chopin, Frédéric, 21, 25, 45, 98, 108, 133, 196, 265, 268, 357, 389, 414, 418, 421
Christ, 169, 170, 171, 172, 179, 180, 184, 200, 241, 244, 250–1, 322, 330, 340, 344, 379, 387, 414, 415
Christianismo contre le Christ, Le, 24
Christianity, 372, 380, 415
Chuquet, Arthur, 65, 68
Cicero, 242

Civic duties, 249

Claparède, Édouard, 405

Clarity and obscurity, 237

Classicism, 263

Claudel, Paul, 4, 5, 23, 39, 136, 250, 252, 274, 311, 336, 339, 361 n, 370, 380

Clemenceau, Georges, 45, 73

Cluny (Saône-et-Loire), 386

Coachman at Douarnenez, 364

Cocteau, Jean, 68, 92, 94, 228, 259, 261 n, 311, 321, 322, 325

Coleridge, Samuel Taylor, 274

Colmar (Haut-Rhin), 62, 67

Colonial administration, 426–7

Colpach (Luxemburg), 270, 283, 309

Combette, Bernard, 34, 36

Comédie-Française, La, 25

Commedia dell'arte revival, 118

Common sense, 415

Composition, 101

Composition, importance of, 286

Congo, 355, 370, 371, 380 n, 408, 411–12

Congreve, William, 377

Conjugal happiness, 412

Conrad, Joseph, 63 n, 103, 112, 141, 146, 166, 191 n, 192, 204, 211, 214 n, 219, 221, 233 n, 363, 368, 426

Constancy, 401

Constant, Benjamin, 335, 336 n, 349, 362

Constanta (Rumania), 162

Constantinople (Turkey), 7, 13

Contradictions, 313

Contradictions in the young, 367

Conversion to Catholicism, 117, 186, 199, 206 n, 225 n, 250, 262, 311, 381, 409

Coopération des idées, La, 241

Copeau, Agnès, 28, 33, 52, 84, 89, 318, 352

Copeau, Jacques, 3 n, 24, 25, 27, 29, 30, 32, 33, 34, 41, 43, 48, 52, 53, 54, 56, 57, 58, 63, 69, 71, 74, 77, 82, 89, 90, 91, 99, 116, 118, 140,

Copeau, Jacques (continued) 154, 157, 165, 194, 204, 270, 274, 279, 281, 301, 317, 318, 321, 353, 387

Copeau, Pascal, 387

Coppet, Marcel de, 257, 410

Coquelin, Constant, 385

Cordier, Yves, 141 n

Corneille, Pierre, 113, 239 n

Corsica, 335

Corte (Corsica), 335

Coulmann, M., 362

Courage, 78, 92

Courteline, Georges, 84, 332 n

Couve, M., 337

Crampon, Abbé, 179, 185, 379

Cranach, Lucas, 290

Crès, 411

Creusa, 403

Crime, 223

Criquetot (Seine-Inférieure), 50, 77, 80, 90, 136, 139, 193, 219

Crochemore, 217

Croué, Jean, 32

Curel, François de, 46 n

Curtius, Ernst-Robert, 307, 309, 403

Cuverville (Seine-Inférieure), 26, 33, 36, 44, 51, 56, 82, 83, 90, 91, 92, 99, 102, 130, 131, 140, 143, 155, 191, 197, 198, 210, 212, 224, 231, 261, 263, 268, 271, 312, 321, 336, 348, 368, 370, 379, 389, 391, 394, 404, 406, 412

Cycling, 223

D., 85, 116, 118, 159, 227, 259, 411

D., E., 99

Dadaism, 352

Daily Mail, 59, 68

Daily News, 79

Dante, 406

Darwin, Charles, 238

Daudet, Léon, 158, 226, 324, 325

Dearly, Max, 118 n

Debussy, Claude Achille, 228, 265

Decadence of France, 220

Defoe, Daniel, 310

Déhais, 139, 155, 160, 352

Deherme, Georges, 241
Delacre, Jules, 298
Delacre, Marianne, 100
Delacroix, Eugène, 294
Delcassé, 73, 74
Del Marmol, 116, 123, 126
Delna, 268
Delteil, Joseph, 362
Demon, the, *see* Devil
Dennery, Adolphe Philippe, 318 *n*
Dépêche de Rouen, 164, 191
Depopulation, 152
Descartes, René, 408, 415, 422
Desjardins, Anne, 355
Desjardins, Paul, 65, 309, 323
Desmarest, Albert, 415
Destain, 191
Determinism, 377
Devil, 84, 120, 127, 128, 146, 180,
    183, 187, 188–9, 296, 338, 363,
    420 *n*
Diaghilev, Serge de, 261 *n*
Dickens, Charles, 138, 362, 369
Diderot, Denis, 69, 271 *n*, 349 *n*,
    362, 363
Dieppe (Seine-Inférieure), 46, 212
Difficulty of access of great works,
    236
Dijon (Côte-d'Or), 61
Discipline, 341–2
Dishonesty, 205
Disque vert, Le, 351
Dissimulation, 409
Divan, Le, 301
Donne, John, 272, 324
Dostoyevsky, Feodor, 51 *n*, 138, 199,
    225, 227, 238, 242, 263, 274, 275,
    278, 279, 281, 298, 299, 300, 301,
    307, 332, 347, 392, 395, 420,
    422
Douarnenez (Finistère), 364
Douglas, Lord Alfred, 232
Drama, 27
Drésa, 255
Dreyfus affair, 271
Dreyfus, Alfred, 226
Drieu La Rochelle, Pierre, 313, 408
Drouin, Dominique, 228, 235

Drouin, Jacques, 87, 90
Drouin, Jeanne, 47, 77, 79, 82, 84,
    89, 105, 152, 161, 198, 206
Drouin, Marcel, 32, 33, 44, 53, 54,
    55, 57, 59, 66, 73, 84, 89, 90, 105,
    113, 119, 121, 124, 220, 246, 255,
    258, 295, 311, 318, 319, 339, 353,
    410
Druet, E., 119
Drunken dialogue, 329
Du B., P., 129
Du Bos, Charles, 99, 101, 104, 121,
    123, 161, 169, 257, 263, 277, 283,
    295, 297, 309, 319, 349, 355, 362,
    403
Ducoté, Édouard, 102, 122
Ducros, 157
Duhamel, Georges, 260, 358, 411
Dukas, Paul, 86
Dullin, Charles, 58, 61, 281, 321
Dumas, Alexandre, *fils,* 102 *n*, 285 *n*
Dumas, Georges, 53
Dumont, 22, 29, 37, 43, 85, 88
Duparc, Henri, 100
Dupouey, Pierre Dominique, 152,
    154, 157, 159, 219, 232, 376
Dupouey, Mme, 161
Duty, 205, 226, 341
Duvernois, Henri, 84

E., 254, 322
É., 411
E., M., 23
E., Mme, 228
Échanges, 304 *n*
Écho de Paris, 45, 59, 68
Eckermann, Johann, 382
Éclair, L', 38, 326
Écrits nouveaux, Les, 215
Edelstan, 352
Edinburgh Review, 124
Edmond, 50, 132, 163
Édouard, 81, 341
Education, 87; is liberation, 215
Edwards, Mme, 53, 55, 72, 91, 107,
    108
Effort, 209; and inclination, 195
El., 320

Elbeuf (Seine-Inférieure), 315, 355
El Kef (Tunisia), 141
Eliot, George, 225
Élise, 79
Em., 6, 33, 34, 36, 42, 43, 44, 49, 50, 51, 57, 60, 82, 85, 86, 89, 90, 99, 103, 105, 106, 110, 116, 123, 124, 131, 134, 139, 143, 146, 150, 152, 153, 154, 155, 159, 160, 167, 191, 193, 194, 195, 197, 198, 202, 206, 211, 215, 217, 219, 220, 224, 226, 227, 228, 230, 234, 253, 258, 269, 273, 274, 279, 280, 296, 311, 320, 381, 382, 393, 403, 411, 420–1
Emerson, Ralph Waldo, 343 n
End of a civilization, 94, 98
Engelberg (Switzerland), 207, 401
England, 48, 54, 55, 100
English and French poetry, 328
Ephesus (Greece), 19
Épinay, Mme d', 167
Equilibrium, 343
Ermitage, L', 262 n
Eskisehir (Turkey), 13
Espinas, Jeanne, 58
Espinas, Pierre, 52
Etchévère, Mme d', 21–2
Étretat (Seine-Inférieure), 25, 44, 77, 82, 84, 87, 152, 223, 360
Études, 424
Eucalyptus blossoms, 112
European culture, 154
Eurydice, 403
Evil, 187–8; does not compose, 274
Evolution, 294
Évreux (Eure), 52, 59, 91
Existence of God, 225
Exotic, charm of the, 21
Experience, 321; and compromise, 282
Exploitation of Africans, 407, 426
Eyoub (Turkey), 7

F., 42, 83, 107, 118
Fabre, Jean-Henri, 368
Fabrice, 207, 208, 209
Fabulet, Louis, 5, 29 n, 235 n

Faith: and reason, 121–2; and skepticism, 384
Falconet, Étienne-Maurice, 362
Families, 288
Fargue, Léon-Paul, 295
Farquhar, George, 377
Fauré, Gabriel, 21, 389
Faÿ, Bernard, 338, 351
Faÿ, Emmanuel, 255, 338, 422
Fécamp (Seine-Inférieure), 82
Fellow (dog), 88
Fénelon, François de Salignac de la Mothe, 129, 130, 142, 178, 183, 312
Feuillet, Octave, 259
Feydeau, Ernest, 418
Fielding, Henry, 230
Figaro, Le, 59, 68, 71, 110
First person singular, 265, 409
Fischer, Dr., 401
Flaubert, Gustave, 38, 210 n, 221, 285, 289, 291, 304, 312, 334, 365, 369 n, 370, 395, 418
Flé, Mme, 384
Florence (Italy), 5, 26, 47, 99
Foinet, 280
Fongueusemare (Seine-Inférieure), 84
Fontainas, André, 23
Fontaine, Arthur, 52, 56, 66, 74
Forman, M. B., 327 n, 366
Foyer Franco-Belge, 91, 92, 95, 99, 102, 103, 104, 105, 106, 116, 118, 119, 120, 121, 123, 126, 127, 161
France, Anatole, 20, 192, 337, 349, 356, 358, 360, 387
France and Germany, 103, 113, 162–3, 220, 230, 248–9, 283
Francis of Assisi, St., 285, 286
Franck, César, 98, 395 n
Franck, Henri, 4
Frankfurt (Germany), 61
Fratellini, Paul, 140
Free will, 367
Freger, Louis, 50, 163
Freger, Mme, 84, 136, 165
French character, 78–9
French equilibrium, 245

French failings, 224, 231, 232, 244, 249
French faults, 90, 105, 109, 113, 124–5, 155, 161, 162
French interest in Germany after the war, 214
French lack of adventure, 250
French language, 237
French literature abroad, 357–8
Freud, Sigmund, 298, 316, 347, 351
Fry, Roger, 270, 355
Future life and eternal life, 184

G., 108, 118, 121, 124, 385
G., Count, 105
G., E., 411
Galignani, 103
Galliéni, General Joseph-Simon, 79
Gallimard, Gaston, 21 n, 22, 33, 154, 257, 280, 411
Gallimard, Mme Gaston, 54
Galsworthy, John, 308
Gardening, 104, 132, 133, 136, 137, 139
Garnett, Constance, 138 n
Garrets, Mlle des, 319
Gaubert, Ernest, 102
Gautier, Théophile, 102, 202, 215, 284, 312
Gebhart, Émile, 308, 311
Geneva (Switzerland), 61, 207, 208, 401
Genoa (Italy), 321
Gérard, 43, 52, 54, 84, 124, 253
Germain, André, 215
German atrocities, 91, 114
German character, 90, 104, 131
German lack of tact, 282
Germany, 55, 60, 65, 205, 213, 283–4; and France, 80
Ghéon, Henri, 5, 15, 19, 21, 24, 25, 31, 33, 53, 54, 55, 57, 58, 60, 67, 90, 91, 92, 94, 105, 114, 117, 120, 136, 139, 140, 144, 105, 106, 202, 206, 207, 225, 251, 253, 256, 258, 259, 262, 276, 302, 311, 328, 329, 356, 363
Ghéon-Macquin, Marie, 300

Gibbon, Edward, 368
Gide, André: adventurer, 356; affinities, 307, 347; aging, 214, 270, 424; anxiety, 424; apathy, 114; attacks on, 275, 279, 296, 324, 337, 353, 361, 410, 424; attitude toward sin, 128–9; balance of sentences, 287; banishing metaphor, 287; becoming, 393, 413; bookishness, 320, 404; boredom, 389, 391, 400; casting off the past, 344; charity, 95; chasing after his youth, 281; complexity, 287; confidence in posterity, 269; constancy, 253, 262, 282; contemplation, 125; contraction of his works, 26; conversation, 408, 421; credo, 122; criticism of, 23, 38, 41; difficulty in recognizing people, 363; disequilibrium, 140; dislike of coquetry, 287; dizziness, 200, 204, 210, 264, 266, 299, 300, 301, 302, 331; dreams, 117; effect of Cuverville on his work, 102–3; exigency, 275; eyesight, 133, 167, 371; faith, 399, 415, 421, 425; fatigue, 98, 101, 105, 140, 167, 324, 349, 354, 382, 387; feeling of being dead, 106, 147; feeling of reality, 364–5; generosity, 227–8; going crazy, 91, 120; hatred of falsehood, 123, 339; hatred of virtuosity, 266; headaches, 89, 196; health, 21, 206, 217, 412; honors, 387; horror of rhetoric, 133; horticulturist, 297; idea of death, 195, 200, 201 n, 211, 217, 234, 254, 270, 298, 368, 395; idea of sin, 121; illness, 142; indecision, 243; indifference to faith, 179–80; influence of, 300; insomnia, 86, 90, 116, 137, 160, 167, 226, 227, 261, 279, 280, 334, 357, 360, 384, 412; jealousy, 218; joy in living, 154, 181, 217–18, 226–7, 231, 285, 350, 404; lack of confidence, 105, 264, 299; lack of popularity, 205; lack of success, 305; legend of,

Gide, André (*continued*)
361, 422; literary projects, 27;
melancholy, 156, 274; misquota-
tion of, 274; modesty, 39, 104;
moral continuity, 270; musician,
215; the naturalist, 112, 142, 287,
371, 405; notion of reality, 337;
novelty of his message, 287; observation of animals, 160; patience,
202; patriotism, 144; political
opinions, 243; postponement, 195;
prayer, 141, 156, 160, 179, 182;
preference for austerity, 274; profession of faith, 301; reading
aloud, 286, 319; reasons for writing, 306; receiving compliments,
46; relapses, 119, 128, 163, 227,
261, 299; respectful of others' sensitivity, 263; rhythm and sense,
323; self-analysis, 123; self-criti-
cism, 141; sense of justice, 352;
sensual curiosity, 117; smoking,
229, 233, 261, 266, 272, 382, 398;
state of dialogue, 343; study of
English, 350; study of German,
350; style, 258; success, 183; sympathy, 102, 423; theory of kathar-
sis, 306, 326, 392; tipping, 399;
torpor, 144, 150, 167, 199, 330,
380, 389, 396, 405; tranquillity,
120; travel, 103; way of writing,
347–8; writes for posterity, 312
Gide, Mme André, *see* Em.
Gide, Catherine, 383
Gide, Charles, 51, 54, 58, 66, 105,
151, 318, 407
Gide, Mme Charles, 145
Gide, Édouard, 57, 90
Gide, Paul, *see* Gérard
Gilbert, 59
Gilbert, Françoise, 85, 86, 87, 88, 90,
105, 121, 152
Gilbert, Nicole, 90, 280
Gilbert, Valentine, 48, 77, 79, 84, 85,
86, 89, 135, 139, 152, 156, 163,
164, 196, 215, 272, 280, 295,
319
Giraudoux, Jean, 194

Girl reading in métro station, 147
Gissing, George, 312–13
Gobillard, Paule, 300
Gobineau, Arthur de, 103, 351
God, 395; is becoming, 122, 294; son
of man, 122, 294
Godebski, Cipa, 148, 228, 298, 394
Godefrain, 101
Goderville (Seine-Inférieure), 273
Goethe, Johann Wolfgang von, 214,
285, 350, 382, 420
Gogol, Nikolay Vasilevich, 27, 311 n
Goldsmith, Oliver, 322
Goncourt brothers, 285, 372
Goncourt prize, 199 n
Gondolier at Venice, 364
Gospels, the, 117, 133, 169, 200,
250, 265, 281, 377, 379, 403
Gosse, Sir Edmund, 112, 123, 124,
132, 136, 146, 148, 149, 154, 356
Gouchtenaere, 232
Gourmont, Jean de, 361, 393
Gourmont, Remy de, 191, 405
Goya, Francisco, 101
Grammar, 144
Granados, Enrique, 135, 219, 222,
271, 348
Grandville, Jean-Ignace-Isidore, 372
Grantchester (England), 233
Gratuitousness of art, 276
Greco, El, 394
Greece, 19–20
Greek and Christian, 340
Greek literature, 420
Grenoble (Dauphiné), 385
Griffith, Mme, 60
Grimm, Melchior, 167, 271
Groethuysen, Bernard, 283
Gross, Hans, 357 n
Guérin, Maurice de, 126
Günsel, Herman de, 389
Gyp, 7

Haguenin, Émile, 296
Hammamet (Tunisia), 389
Hamp, Pierre, 168, 323
Handel, George Frideric, 88
Harcourt, Raoul d', 300

Hardy, Thomas, 71 *n*, 88 *n*, 146 *n*, 157, 164, 166, 306
Hare, the wild, 198
Hares to tame, 135–6
Harfleur (Seine-Inférieure), 168
Harmony, 404
Hastings (England), 46
Havre (Seine-Inférieure), 37, 39, 48, 76, 80, 83, 130, 135, 137, 161, 168
Havre-Éclair, 76
Hawthorne, Nathaniel, 337, 353
Haydn, Franz Josef, 121
Heidelberg (Germany), 403
Heligoland (Germany), 80
Hell within us, 251–2
Helleu (Pelletan), 166, 197
Heredia, José-Maria de, 107, 290
Hermant, Abel, 310, 326
Hérouard, André, 50, 89, 106, 135, 163, 217, 220
Hérouard, Mme, 106, 160, 198
Herrick, Robert, 233, 414
Herscher, J., 21
Hervieu, Paul, 105
Heywood, Thomas, 25 *n*
Hirsch, Baron, 6
Hirsch, Charles-Henry, 393
Hobbes, Thomas, 233
Homer, 292
Homme libre, L', 45, 73
Homosexuality, 110–11, 246, 265, 267, 276
Honfleur (Calvados), 80
Honegger, Arthur, 301
Honnête homme, 273
Horace, 60
Houssonloge, 93
Huber, François, 372
Hudson, W. H., 269
Huet, Pierre-Daniel, 327
Hugo, Victor, 236, 358, 395
Humanism, 380
Humières, Robert d', 116
Hummel, J.-H., 414
Hyères (Var), 112, 270, 302 *n*, 383
Hyères-Plage (Var), 333, 370
Hypocrisy, 203

Ibsen, Henrik, 220, 225, 259, 278 *n*, 308, 378
Iehl, Jules, 102
Iles de Lérins (Alpes-Maritimes), 112 *n*
Impossibility of a play's being a work of art, 255
Improvidence and improvisation, 105
Inclination, following or resisting, 288
Indirect presentation, 296
Individualism, 116, 249, 400
Influence, 420; of women, 256
Information, L', 59, 68
Ingres, Jean-Auguste-Dominique, 294
Intellectual wrinkles, 253
Interdependence of nations, 248
Inurement to misfortune, 106
Invention and criticism, 293
Invert, 246
Isaac, 172
Italy, 5, 20, **71**

J., 49, 246, 382, 408, 414
Jacob, Max, 331
Jalaguier, Albert, 201
Jaloux, Edmond, 203, 309
Jaloux, Mme Edmond, 203
James, Henry, 100, 102, 257, 409 *n*
James, William, 269, 337, 346
Jammes, Francis, 39, 122, 123, 199, 245, 290, 291, 292, 293, 294, 310, 311, 313, 320
Jansenism, 242, 312 *n*, 314 *n*
Japan, 65
Jarry, Alfred, 58 *n*, 304, 305, 370 *n*, 390 *n*
Jason, 208
Jaurès, Jean, 50
Jean, 144, 151
Jean-Aubry, G., 191 *n*
Jewish literature, 4–5
Jewish qualities, 283–4
Jews, 3–4, 47
Joanne, Adolphe, 14 *n*

Joffre, Joseph-Jacques-Césaire, 73, 76 n
Johannet, René, 279
John, St., 117, 141, 169, 170, 171, 173, 174, 175, 177, 178
Jonah, 176
Jonas, 176
Jouhandeau, Marcel, 418
Journal de Genève, 25, 129, 144, 191, 195, 251
Journal de la jeunesse, 160
Journalism, definition of, 289
Jouvet, Louis, 52, 321 n
Jouvet, Mme Louis, 70, 84
Joy and sorrow, 98
Juliette, 47

K., 41, 42, 44, 48, 49, 51, 82, 84
Kabir, 130, 138
Kaffirs, 212
Kairouan (Tunisia), 15
Kant, Immanuel, 243, 365
Keats, John, 214, 314, 322 n, 323, 326, 327 n, 365
Keller, Gottfried, 191 n, 399, 407
Keyserling, Hermann von, 301 n
Kipling, Rudyard, 102
Kippenberg, Anton, 30
Kl., 95
Know thyself, 299, 413
Konya (Turkey), 15, 18, 19

L., 50, 83, 130, 259, 393, 411
L., Mme, 393
Labasque, 101
La Bastide (Tarn), 270, 306, 307, 336
La Bruyère, Jean de, 272, 295, 297, 328, 389
Lacoste, 300
Lacretelle, Jacques de, 318 n
Lacroix, Mme, 100
Lafaurie, 84
La Fontaine, Jean de, 111 n, 250 n, 276, 291, 327, 414
Laforgue, Jules, 29 n, 235 n
La Harpe, Jean-François de, 215
Lalou, René, 411

La Mivoie (Seine-Inférieure), 415
La Motte, 160
Lancaster, G. B., 213
Langweil, Mlle, 104, 116
Langweil, Mme, 47
Lanux, Pierre de, 54, 57, 71
La Pérouse, 32, 63, 249, 350
Larbaud, Valery, 29 n, 46, 57, 207 n, 235, 311, 368
Larionov, M., 261 n
La Rochefoucauld, François de, 153, 237, 271 n, 368 n, 398
La Roque-Baignard (Seine-Inférieure), 30, 139
La Sablière, Mme de, 327
Lasserre, Pierre, 132, 294
Latin and Greek culture, 98
Laurencin, Marie, 327
Laurens, Paul-Albert, 3, 23, 54, 83, 91, 98, 200, 258, 280, 288, 301, 318
Lauris, 104, 105, 116, 123, 126, 146
Lausanne (Switzerland), 6, 397, 419
Léautaud, Paul, 40
Leaving Cuverville like dying, 273
Lebey, André, 388
Le Boréon (Alpes-Maritimes), 332
Lebrun, 141
Le Cardonnel, Louis, 41
Lechevalier, M., 151, 152, 161
Leconte de Lisle, Charles, 285 n
Le Dantec, Félix, 394
Lefèvre, Frédéric, 398
Le Grix, François, 338
Le Limon (Côte-d'Or), 48
Lemarié, Mme, 54
Léon, Xavier, 46
Le Pesquier (Var), 270, 303
Lépine, Louis, 48
Lerolle, Guillaume, 213–14
Lesage, Alain-René, 230 n
Les Ifs (Seine-Inférieure), 231
Les Sources, 202
Le Tertre, Bellême (Orne), 396
Letter to Maurras, 158
L'Hermite, Tristan, 224 n, 226
Lhote, André, 44
Liadov, Anatole, 261 n

Liberté, La, 59
Liberty, 245
Liége (Belgium), 57, 61, 93
Limoges (Haute-Vienne), 231
Lisieux (Calvados), 80
Liszt, Franz, 21, 166, 414, 421
Littré, Maximilien Paul Émile, 406
Llona, Victor, 357
Locke, William John, 211, 214
Logic, 403–4
Loisel, 165
London (England), 44
Longfellow, Henry Wadsworth, 292
Lorrain, Jean, 265
Loti, Pierre, 337, 387
Loucheur, Louis, 6
Louis, 331, 332
Louis XIV, 377
Louÿs, Pierre, 223, 365
Love and desire, 288
Lucerne (Switzerland), 208, 401
Luke, St., 174, 175, 178, 179, 200, 414 *n*
Lutétia, Hotel (Paris), 279
Luther, Martin, 242
Luxembourg, 65, 282
Lyautey, Marshal Louis-Hubert, 323

M., 3, 116, 207, 215, 216, 218, 219, 227, 228, 229, 230, 231, 235, 246, 247, 255, 256, 257, 279, 280, 296, 298, 309, 316, 318, 320, 325, 334, 336, 338, 341, 350, 355, 362, 363, 368, 387, 389, 391, 398, 406, 407, 410, 411, 422, 423
M., A., 255
M., W., 125
Macaulay, Thomas Babington, 117
MacCown, Eugène, 422
Macmillan, 30
Macquin, Marie, 195
Maeterlinck, Maurice, 371, 373
Maggiore, Lago (Italy), 21
Magny (Seine-et-Oise), 95, 100
Mahomet, 242
Maistre, Xavier de, 192
Mallarmé, Stéphane, 20 *n*, 290, 307 *n*, 405

Malvy, 234
Manning, Cardinal, 236
Marches de l'Est, Les, 157
Marges, Les, 26, 41
Margueritte brothers, 68
Marie, 112
Maritain, Jacques, 338, 339
Marivaux, Pierre Carlet de Chamblain de, 311
Mark, St., 174, 380
Marlowe, Christopher, 233
Marseille (Bouches-du-Rhône), 308, 336, 369
Martin du Gard, Hélène, 396
Martin du Gard, Roger, 44, 257, 258, 260, 261, 266, 267, 279, 280, 295, 296, 302, 309, 311, 316, 317, 320, 325, 355, 359, 363, 368, 394, 400, 415
Marvell, Andrew, 337
Massine, Leonide, 261 *n*
Massis, Henri, 38, 41, 274, 276, 277, 324, 337, 339, 347, 361, 387
Masson, Frédéric, 103
Matin, Le, 50, 59, 68, 74
Matthew, St., 174, 184
Maupassant, Guy de, 121
Maurois, André, 309 *n*, 315, 355, 409
Maurras, Charles, 157, 162, 191, 192, 219, 226, 251, 263, 321, 324 *n*, 358
Maury, Lucien, 31, 226
Maus, Octave, 130, 140
Mayol, 281
Mayrisch, Mme Émile, 5, 21, 30, 144, 253, 267, 279 *n*, 280, 282, 309
Meaning in music, 100
Mekedje (Turkey), 13
Melville, Herman, 250
Mendelssohn-Bartholdy, Felix, 100
Mendès, Catulle, 327
Méral, Paul, 232, 253
Mercure de France, 3 *n*, 55, 191, 361, 393, 411
Meredith, George, 223, 224, 229, 356 *n*, 360, 362

Merezhkovski, Dmitri, 263, 301 n
Mérimée, Prosper, 310, 311 n, 314 n
Mesnard, Paul, 420
Messimy, Adolphe, 73
Metaphors, 328
Metz (Moselle), 61
Michel, 208, 209, 213, 214
Michelangelo, 285
Michelet, Jules, 278
Michelet, René, 279, 389
Milan (Italy), 20
Milhaud, Darius, 99, 126, 196, 265
Military strategy, 162
Millerand, Alexandre, 73
Millet, 149
Milton, John, 84, 188, 252
Minerva, 374
Miquette, 28, 44, 88, 121, 134, 260
Mirbeau, Octave, 240
Misprints, 383
Mius, 33, 49, 51, 85, 137, 224
Modernism, 228
Modesty in writers, 289
Molière, 17 n, 25 n, 111, 213, 237,
    240, 250 n, 308 n
Monnier, Adrienne, 317, 390
Montaigne, Michel de, 238, 256, 320,
    323, 336, 352-3, 361, 388
Monte d'Oro (Corsica), 335
Montesquieu, Charles de Secondat,
    Baron de, 116, 250 n, 256, 294,
    338
Montessori method, 110
Montfort, Eugène, 26 n, 312
Montherlant, Henry de, 404, 418,
    419
Montigny-sur-Loing   (Seine-et-
    Marne), 301
Montivilliers (Seine-Inférieure), 257
Morand, Paul, 301
Moréas, Jean, 244, 303 n
Morocco, 323
Moune, La, 28
Mozart, Wolfgang Amadeus, 310,
    414
M' Reyer (Algeria), 14
Mühlfeld, Mme, 47, 203, 212, 259,
    267, 295

Mulhouse (Haut-Rhin), 57, 59, 67,
    69, 79
Murat, Princesse, 203
Murry, John Middleton, 301 n
Music, 18, 88, 100, 375–6
Musset, Alfred de, 298 n
Mussolini, Benito, 392
Mysticism, 421

National hypocrisy, 346
Nationalism, 244, 245, 248, 270,
    346, 353, 372
Naville, Arnold, 383
Neuchâtel (Switzerland), 397
Neuilly-sur-Seine (Seine), 32
Neuville, Father de, 315
New civilization, 98
New York, 338, 357
Newhaven (England), 46
News-dealer, 298
Newspapers, the, 164
Nicæa (Turkey), 10, 12
Nice (Alpes-Maritimes), 77, 333,
    335
Nicholas, 10–11, 14, 322
Nicodemus, 175, 177, 185
Nietzsche, Friedrich, 132, 213, 241,
    242, 263, 278, 285, 292, 298, 307,
    347, 420
Nihilism, 415
Niska (dog), 384
Noah, 172
Noailles, Anna de, 259, 349
Non-resistance, 113
Norton, Harry, 233
Notes for a study of Francis Jammes,
    290–4
Notes for Maeterlinck's books, 371
Nouvelle Revue Française, 3 n, 5 n,
    21, 23 n, 25, 26 n, 30, 33, 40, 52,
    54, 55, 101, 118, 121, 126, 140,
    154, 191 n, 256, 261 n, 262 n,
    272 n, 276, 277, 280, 321 n, 325,
    379, 381, 396, 404 n, 406, 410,
    411, 419, 424 n
Nouvion-en-Thiérache (Aisne), 58
Nouvelles littéraires, Les, 324, 326,
    334, 357, 398

Novels, diminutive, 40, 119, 153, 214, 219, 230, 289, 411–12

Objectivity, 306, 326, 348, 408; and subjectivity, 392
Oblique progeny of the great, 284
Observation and creation, 347
Obstinacy, 357
Odile, 87
Œdipus, 400
Offranville (Seine-Inférieure), 44, 48, 147, 164, 211
Olympus, 8, 11
Omniscient novelist, 359
Opera, 267
Orpheus, 216 n, 403
Orsay (Seine-et-Oise), 31
Orthez (Basses-Pyrénées), 293
Orvieto (Italy), 274
Osterwald, 178, 179, 185
Overbeck, Friedrich, 395
Oxford (England), 208

P., 410–11
P., M., 69
P., Mme, 5
Painting, 27, 402–3, 419; and music in literature, 215
Palace of faith, 400
Pallarès, M. V. de, 241
Parents, bad influence of, 288
Pareto, Vilfredo, 301 n
Paris-Midi, 59, 132
Pascal, Blaise, 111, 126, 128, 181, 215, 235, 250 n, 278, 292, 312 n, 314, 368, 422
Passy (Paris, XVI), 51
Pater, Walter, 210, 255, 306, 315
Patience, 104 n, 127, 129, 133, 144, 286, 295, 308
Patina, 322
Past, the, 124
Paul, St., 82, 171, 174, 179, 180, 242
Peacock, Thomas, 256
Pederast, 246–7
Péguy, Charles, 54, 83, 91, 154, 259
Peira-Cava (Alpes-Maritimes), 406
Pelletan, 202

Perfect art proof against time, 285
Perfection, need for, 210
Périer, W. B., 118 n
Pernand (Côte-d'Or), 387
Perpignan (Pyrénées-Orientales), 143
Perret, 411
Perspective toward oneself, 349
Petit Havrais, Le, 76
Petit Havre, Le, 79
Petit Journal illustré, 125
Petrarch, 210 n
Philippe, Charles-Louis, 111
Physical charm, 270
Physiological causes of intellectual impulses, 241
Piana (Corsica), 335
Piano, 21, 23, 24, 28, 36, 37, 42, 45, 82, 86, 98, 100, 102, 108, 116, 121, 123, 129, 134, 196, 203, 204, 210, 216, 219, 220, 222, 223, 235, 262, 263, 265, 267, 268, 271, 272, 274, 275, 276, 314, 348, 355, 356, 357, 368, 389, 410, 411, 413, 414, 421, 422, 423
Piano lessons, 105, 121, 144, 152, 215
Picasso, Pablo, 261
Pickford, Mary, 255
Pilon, Edmond, 294
Piot, René, 267
Pisa (Italy), 274
Plato, 210 n, 214, 246, 365
Pleasure of corrupting, 205
Plotinus, 360
Plutarch, 238
Poe, Edgar Allan, 20, 87 n, 281, 307 n
Poem by André Gide, 95–7
Poet versus artist, 290
Poetic prose, 371
Poincaré, Raymond, 47, 58, 61
Poland, 72
Pont l'Évêque (Calvados), 80, 90
Pontigny (Yonne), 309, 336, 387, 388
Porquerolles (Var), 302
Porto-Riche, Georges de, 5, 194

Postman and his sister, the, 273
Postponement of his message, 104
Poucel, Victor, 424
Pourtalès, Guy de, 349
Poussin, Nicolas, 237, 285
Poverty, 197; and frugality, 293; and luxury, 128
Prayer, 51, 340
Preciosity in literature, 386
Pressemane, Adrien, 196
Pressure of necessity, 98
Prévost, Jean, 422
Prévost, Marcel, 212
Prezzolini, Giuseppe, 309
Printing errors, 416, 419
Prodigal son, the, 344
Progrès civique, Le, 263, 380
Protestantism, 39, 337
Proteus, 209
Proust, Marcel, 68 n, 130, 222, 265, 266, 276, 279, 369 n, 406, 410
Prudence and cowardice, 314
Prunières, Henri, 280
Psichari, Ernest, 111
Public indifference to natural beauty, 119
Puritan upbringing, 208
Puritanism, 312–13, 342
Pushkin, Alexander, 27, 311, 314 n

Quinton, René, 238
Quotidien, Le, 349

R., J., 108
R., J. T., 45
R., Mme, 69
Racine, Jean, 111, 213, 239, 285, 309, 400 n, 420
Radiguet, Raymond, 351 n
Rameau, Jean-Philippe, 237
Rapallo (Italy), 322
Raphaël, Gaston, 282
Rasmussen, 411
Rathenau, Walter, 282, 283, 296
Raverat, Jacques, 5, 83, 84, 100, 188, 233, 257, 309
Readers and actors, 281
Récit, 39

Récits and novels, 260
Redon, Odilon, 101
Refugees, 93, 95, 102
Refusal to conclude, 225
Régis, Emmanuel, 111
Régnier, Henri de, 259, 290, 359
Régnier, Mathurin, 111
Reims (Marne), 85
Renan, Ernest, 107, 110, 236, 252, 285 n
Renard, Jules, 378, 382, 383, 384, 385, 396
Rennes (Ille-et-Vilaine), 305
Renunciation, 345
Resistance and stupidity, 205
Retinger, Joseph, 72, 74
Revolution, 226
Revue de Genève, 301, 311
Revue de Paris, 102, 212, 407, 411, 412
Revue des deux mondes, 38, 154
Revue française, 279
Revue française de musique, 100 n
Revue hebdomadaire, 103 n, 122
Revue musicale, 133 n
Revue universelle, 274, 337
Richepin, Jean, 91
Ricordi, 21
Rilke, Rainer Maria, 121, 125
Rimbaud, Arthur, 398 n
Rivière, Isabelle, 141, 191 n, 193, 379
Rivière, Jacques, 23, 24, 25, 33, 89 n, 191 n, 207, 229, 257, 267, 272, 299, 301, 309, 311, 314, 338, 361, 369, 379 n, 419
Roberty, Mathilde, 25, 193, 194, 195, 196, 222
Rolland, Romain, 91, 114, 131, 132, 138, 197 n, 237
Rollinat, Maurice, 285
Romains, Jules, 307
Rome (Italy), 274
Rondeaux, Georges, 48, 79, 82, 90, 106, 134, 154, 217, 224, 346, 381
Rondeaux, Grandmother, 415
Roquebrune (Alpes-Maritimes), 274, 321, 349, 369, 391

Rosenberg, Fedor, 410, 411
Rosny brothers, 313
Rossetti, Dante Gabriel, 376
Rostand, Edmond, 79, 385
Rothermere, Lady, 210, 212, 222, 253
Rothschild, Mme de, 65
Rouart, Eugène, 143, 151, 225, 253, 336, 392, 408
Rouen (Seine-Inférieure), 37, 137, 166, 273
Rousseau, Jean-Jacques, 169, 242, 271, 331, 397, 405 n, 414
Royal Academy, 356
Royal Society of Literature, 387
Rubinstein, Ida, 210, 218, 223, 255
Ruskin, John, 68 n, 368
Russia, 45
Russian Revolution, the, 205
Rutherford, Mark, 99, 100, 101, 117, 120, 121, 125, 132 n, 184
Ruyters, André, 22, 32, 54, 59, 60, 72, 82, 88, 227, 229, 253, 258, 259, 312
Ruyters, Luce, 90, 259
Rychner, 402

S., 85, 151
S., Mme M. de, 15
S., P., 251
S., S., 397
Sacrifice in art, 277
Sagone (Corsica), 335
Saint-Clair, 383, 391, 392
Sainte-Beuve, Augustin, 201, 202, 268, 287, 314, 315, 360, 362
Sainte-Maxime (Var), 391
Saint-Évremond, Charles de Saint-Denys de, 238, 328
Saint-Martin-Vésubie (Alpes-Maritimes), 330, 334
Sallust, 238
Salmon, André, 54
Samain, Albert, 388 n
Sandeau, Jules, 365
Sanders, General Liman von, 17
Sandré, Mme, 165
Santayana, George, 213, 214, 215

Satan, see Devil
Satie, Érik, 261
Satire of parties, 118
Satory (Seine-et-Oise), 100
Saucier, Roland, 411
Scève, Maurice, 210 n
Schlumberger, Jean, 21, 24, 25, 29, 33, 39, 44, 52, 54, 55, 57, 59, 60, 62, 68, 70, 71, 84, 90, 118, 166, 235, 253, 258, 267, 279, 280, 300, 309, 339
Schlumberger, Marc, 258
Schoen, Herr von, 53, 54
Schopenhauer, Arthur, 241, 365
Schubert, Franz, 421
Schumann, Robert, 21, 389
Schwob, Marcel, 4, 304, 305, 377
Scott-Moncrieff, C. K., 267 n
Scutari (Turkey), 7
Segond, 174, 175, 185
Selection, 104
Self-judgment, 207, 208–9
Self-satisfaction, 286
Selfishness, 303
Semur-en-Auxois (Yonne), 387
Serbia, 45
Serquigny (Eure), 131
Sert, José-Maria, 53, 107, 327, 394
Service and slavery, 245
Sévigné, Mme de, 199, 201, 406
Sex, 88
Shackleton, Anna, 211
Shakespeare, William, 25, 26, 27, 84, 111, 204, 214, 215, 216, 225, 256, 267, 270, 292, 301, 304, 310, 315, 322, 329, 333, 376, 383, 392
Shaw, George Bernard, 307
Shelley, Percy Bysshe, 315
Sichel, Pierre, 316, 319
Sickert, Walter, 45
Siena (Italy), 7, 274
Signoret, Emmanuel, 209
Simond, Daniel, 419
Simonsen, Raoul, 419
Simplicity and complexity, 238
Sin, 228
Sincerity, 276, 306, 342, 413, 418, 423

Sisyphus, 156, 416
Skeat, Walter William, 352
Smith, Logan Pearsall, 337
Smyrna (Turkey), 19, 144
Society, 108
Socrates, 242, 246
Sodomite, 246
Sophocles, 321
Souday, Paul, 31, 41, 103, 107, 110, 132, 144, 154, 192, 236, 251, 256, 312, 325, 338, 406
Soupault, Philippe, 313, 418
Spain, 58
Specifically French remarks, 250
Spontaneity, 6, 342; and inequality, 293
Stagnation, 277
Starling, 27, 28, 29, 30, 31, 33, 35, 37, 39, 41, 43
Steinheil, Mme Marguerite Japy, 234
Stendhal (pseud. of Henri Beyle), 33 n, 131, 167, 261 n, 267, 285, 317, 334, 369 n, 370, 386, 390, 408
Stern, 47
Sterne, Laurence, 192
Stevenson, R. L., 162, 346
Strachey, Lytton, 236, 309
Strachey, Miss, 309
Strauss, David Friedrich, 132
Stravinsky, Igor, 209, 322
Strohl, Jean, 399, 402, 405
Style and thought, 329
Suarès, André, 57, 58, 278, 279, 331, 353, 397
Suarès, Mme André, 52
Sue, Eugène, 314 n
Sunken submarine, 424–5
Surrealism, 352 n
Swift, Jonathan, 98
Switzerland, 62, 208
Sympathy, 310
Syntax, 416–17

T., 4, 43, 48, 49, 51, 75, 76, 144, 314, 343
T., Jean, 33, 34, 35, 36, 37, 382
T., S., 34

Tagore, Sir Rabindranath, 30 n, 34, 36, 99, 223
Tahiti, 382
Taine, Hippolyte, 234, 238, 285 n, 305, 376–7, 394
Tangier (Morocco), 323
Tannery, 74
Tarbes (Hautes-Pyrénées), 90
Teaching, 85, 86, 88
Temps, Le, 59, 73, 103, 110, 144, 162, 192, 195, 256, 312
Terence, 290
Terny, 118 n
Teugels, Jean, 109
Thackeray, William Makepeace, 138
Tharaud, Jean and Jérôme, 269
Théâtre, Mme, 114
Theophrastus, 389 n
Theories, 238
Théoule (Alpes-Maritimes), 407
Theseus, 403
Thibaudet, Albert, 304, 307, 348, 407
Thiébaud, Marcel, 411
Thousand and One Nights, 375
Tielrooy, Johannes Bernardus, 309
Timeliness, 240
Times, London, 73
Tissaudier, Bernard, 201 n
Toby (dog), 28, 43, 88, 160, 193, 194–5
Tolstoy, Leo, 209, 278, 378 n
Touggourt (Algeria), 12, 14
Toulon (Var), 302, 392
Toulouse (Haute-Garonne), 143, 202, 418
Touny-Lerys, 288 n
Tournier, 389
Toussenel, Alphonse, 162
Translating André Gide, 222
Translation, 5, 34, 191, 193
Transposition in Proust's work, 267
Traz, Robert de, 309, 311, 398
Trevelyan, Miss, 165, 256
Tronche, 33, 38, 52, 54
Trouville (Calvados), 39, 84
True and false greatness, 297
Tunis (Tunisia), 336, 389

Turenne, Vicomte de, 294
Turgenyev, Ivan, 84, 285 n
Tzara, Tristan, 352 n

Unamuno, Miguel de, 136, 301 n
United States of Europe, 56
Ushak (Turkey), 19

V., 77, 408, 411
Vagueness in Latin, 268
Valenciennes (Nord), 72
Valentine, see Gilbert, Valentine
Valéry, Jeannie, 88, 300
Valéry, Paul, 88, 244, 259, 267, 295,
   300, 301, 317, 318, 319, 327, 330,
   353, 370, 394, 401, 405
Vallette, Alfred, 393
Val-Richer, 62
Vanbrugh, Sir John, 377
Vandervelde, Émile, 168
Vanity, 306
Vannicola, Giuseppe, 301
Van Rysselberghe, Élisabeth, 68,
   117, 146, 270, 298, 299, 306, 309,
   310, 335, 406
Van Rysselberghe, Théo, 32, 33, 56,
   57, 59, 60, 62, 65, 68, 83, 90, 100,
   117, 130, 143, 150, 298
Van Rysselberghe, Mme Théo, 72,
   92, 106, 114, 116, 118, 123, 126,
   127, 140, 146, 161, 218, 253, 258,
   260, 267, 306, 309, 326, 334,
   383
Vase and the two friends, 289
Vaugelas, Claude Favre, Sieur de,
   239 n
Vauvenargues, Luc de Clapiers, Mar-
   quis de, 360
Vence (Alpes-Maritimes), 349
Venereal disease, 166
Venice (Italy), 7, 71
Verdun (Meuse), 75
Verhaeren, Émile, 166, 243, 245
Verlaine, Paul, 240, 246
Verne, Jules, 162
Verney, 118 n
Verona (Italy), 20

Versailles (Seine-et-Oise), 90, 147,
   267
Veules (Seine-Inférieure), 165
Vichy (Allier), 68
Vielé-Griffin, Francis, 29 n, 34,
   235 n, 245, 290
Vienna (Austria), 257
Vieux-Colombier, Théâtre du, 3 n,
   25, 30, 32, 69, 301 n, 316, 321
Vigny, Alfred de, 282
Vildrac, Charles, 316
Villa, the, 101, 106, 108, 123, 198,
   206, 212, 233, 253, 255, 256, 257,
   258, 295, 338, 362, 363, 368, 410
Villeroy, Auguste, 25
Virgil, 9 n, 324 n, 358 n, 412 n, 419 n
Virginie, 258
Virtue, 345
Virtuosity, 98
Viviani, René, 47, 53, 66, 73 n
Vizzavone (Corsica), 335
Vocabulary and syntax, 326
Vogüé, Eugène-Melchior de, 395 n
Voltaire, 250 n, 293, 307, 331

W., 120, 213
W., M. C. de, 107
Wagner, Richard, 241
Watteau, Antoine, 210
Weak and the strong, 302
Weiler, Lazare, 47
Weimar (Germany), 60
Wells, H. G., 201, 263
Werth, Léon, 54
Westphal, A., 175, 176, 177, 179,
   185 n
Wharton, Edith, 100, 110, 111, 116,
   132, 136
White, William Hale, 99 n, 132 n
Whitman, Walt, 5, 29, 30, 31, 101,
   216, 233 n, 235, 292
Widmer, Édouard, 105
Widmer, Isabelle, 142
Widmer, René, 119
Wilde, Oscar, 232, 376, 400, 409
Wordsworth, William, 291
Worral, 118 n
Worth, 255

X., 4, 76, 77, 80, 81, 82, 83, 91, 94,
    113, 119, 165, 200, 230, 270, 282,
    288, 375, 381
X., Doctor, 357
X., Mlle, 265
X., Mme, 95

Y., 49
Yeats, William Butler, 70
Yenisehir (Turkey), 12

Youth, 405; and age, 282
Yport, 83
Yung, Uncle, 76, 154
Yves, 410, 423

Z., 319
Zola, Émile, 6, 68, 111
Zollikon (Switzerland), 402
Zurich (Switzerland), 397, 398, 401,
    402

THE WORKS OF ANDRÉ GIDE

Referred to in *The Journals*

Amyntas, 411, 419

Aveugle, L', 224, 226, 231

Avenir de l'Europe, L', 301, 311

Cahiers d'André Walter, Les, 360, 385–6

Caractères, 273

Castor et Pollux, 222

Caves du Vatican, Les, 5, 30, 31, 38, 41, 46, 274, 305, 352, 356, 393, 398 n, 418 n

Conférences sur Dostoïevsky, 279

Conseils à un jeune écrivain, 123

Considérations sur la mythologie grecque, 24 n, 37, 223 n, 227, 395 n

Corydon, 5, 24, 220, 221, 222, 232, 245, 265, 266, 299, 308, 314, 324, 338, 353, 357, 405, 422

Dialogue avec Dieu, 396

Dostoïevsky, 278, 281, 299, 324, 339, 411

Ecole des femmes, L', 41 n, 391 n, 414

Entretien avec Nicodème, L', 140

Et Ego . . . , 192

Faux-Monnayeurs, Les, 24 n, 44 n, 84, 101, 113, 261, 267, 269, 271, 275, 280, 296, 301, 311, 314, 315, 319, 321 n, 327, 330, 348, 350 n, 353, 355, 356, 357, 359, 360, 362, 365, 368, 369, 370, 371, 390, 392, 393, 395, 397, 423

Foreword to *Numquid et tu . . . ?*, 186

Immoraliste, L', 38, 124, 211, 307, 392, 411, 420

Incidences, 166 n

Interviews imaginaires, 395 n

Journal, Le, 33, 36, 44, 48, 83, 106, 112, 126, 138, 142, 143, 210, 222, 258, 269, 347, 350, 356, 367, 371 n, 380, 394, 406, 410

Journal des Faux-Monnayeurs, Le, 254, 260, 264

Lettres à Angèle, 262

Marche turque, La, 6, 24–5, 27, 29, 33, 40

Morceaux choisis, 270, 274, 275, 277, 367 n

Notes sur Chopin, 24, 133 n

Nourritures terrestres, Les, 123, 211, 219, 232, 287, 300 n, 305, 356, 388, 391, 418

Nouvelles Nourritures, Les, 303

Numquid et tu . . . ?, 126, 136, 152, 183, 169–86, 186–7, 352 n, 403

Œdipe, 396, 400, 402

Œuvres complètes, 424 n

Paludes, 316

Philoctète, 356

Porte étroite, La, 31, 38, 46, 167, 211, 212, 246, 252

Préface à "Armance," 261, 264, 266, 267

Préface à Browning, 263

Préface à la "Dame de Pique," 311 n, 314

Préface aux Lettres de Dupouey, 219–20

Préface aux "Nourritures," 391

Preface to *Caves du Vatican*, 31, 38

Preface to *Fleurs du mal*, 166, 197, 202, 211, 212, 215

Prétextes, 222, 232

Prométhée mal enchaîné, Le, 210, 211, 212, 232, 398 n

Rapports intellectuels entre la France et l'Allemagne, Les, 272

Retour de l'enfant prodigue, Le, 126, 140, 416

Retour du Tchad, Le, 371 n, 391 n, 396 n, 406, 425 n

Roi Candaule, Le, 158, 393

Saül, 301, 305, 347, 393

Séquestrée de Poitiers, La, 385 n

Si le grain ne meurt . . . , 134, 135, 138, 142, 156, 157, 166, 167, 192,

Si le grain ne meurt (continued) 193, 194, 195, 197, 198, 199, 201, 211, 213, 214, 216, 217, 222, 236, 255, 257, 260, 261, 263, 267, 269, 314, 318, 321, 324, 337, 352, 392, 393

Sotie, 39

Souvenirs de la Cour d'Assises, 141

Symphonie pastorale, La, 224 n, 226, 231, 233, 234, 235, 392, 393

Thésée, 403

Traité des Dioscures, Le, 24, 35, 222, 395

Translation of *Antony and Cleopatra*, 204, 210, 211, 213, 215, 216, 217 n, 218, 223 n, 233, 255, 322, 383, 416

Translation of Blake, 302, 311

Translation of *Hamlet*, 302, 304, 308

Translation of *Typhoon*, 157, 166, 167, 192, 193, 198, 204, 212, 232

Translation of Whitman, 216, 235 n

Voyage au Congo, Le, 371 n, 380, 408 n, 425 n

A NOTE ON THE TYPE IN WHICH THIS BOOK IS SET

The text of this book is set in Caledonia, a Linotype face which belongs to the family of printing types called "modern face" by printers — a term used to mark the change in style of type-letters that occurred about 1800. Caledonia borders on the general design of Scotch Modern, but is more freely drawn than that letter.

The book was composed, printed, and bound by The Plimpton Press, Norwood, Massachusetts. The typography and binding design are by W. A. Dwiggins.